I'VE HEARD
THOSE SONGS BEFORE

BOOKS BY ELSTON BROOKS

I'VE HEARD THOSE SONGS BEFORE

DON'T DRY-CLEAN MY BLACKJACK

I'VE HEARD THOSE SONGS BEFORE

The Weekly Top Ten Tunes for the Past Fifty Years

By Elston Brooks

MORROW QUILL PAPERBACKS
New York   1981

Library of Congress Cataloging in Publication Data

Brooks, Elston.
    I've heard those songs before.

    "Morrow quill paperbacks."

    Includes index.
    1. Music, Popular (Songs, etc.)—United States—
Bibliography.   2. Music, Popular (Songs, etc.)—
United States—Discography.   I. Title.
ML128.V7B78   016.7845′00973   80-39725
ISBN 0-688-00379-6 (pbk.)

Printed in the United States of America

First Morrow Quill Paperback Edition

1   2   3   4   5   6   7   8   9   10

DEDICATED TO

*Frank Sinatra, the boy whose voice thrilled
millions; Joan Edwards, The Hit Paraders,
Mark Warnow and the Lucky Strike Orchestra,
Andre Baruch, Basil Ruysdael, Kenny Delmar,
F. E. Boone of Lexington, Kentucky, and L. A.
(Speed) Riggs of Goldsboro, North Carolina.*

*. . . and to Snooky, Dorothy, Gisele,
Russell, and all those Saturday nights
in front of radio and TV that will never return.*

Foreword

Nothing brings back a memory like a song.

I can't estimate how many times I've said that phrase on the radio down through the years and then gone on to prove the point by playing the record that was, oh say, Number One all over America on the night of March 27, 1943, or maybe the Number Ten song on July 20, 1940.

A quick check of the listings inside this book shows the Number One song that spring night of wartime 1943 was "I've Heard That Song Before," and in altered form it provided a title for this compilation. The Number Ten song that summer night in 1940 was "I'm Stepping Out With a Memory Tonight," a symbolic invitation to do the same with this book on every Saturday night from 1930 through the present.

Because while some people collect stamps and others have matchbook collections, I have the entire Top Ten song listings since 1930, the only such compilation in existence.

The temptation is to call it the weekly Hit Parade listings, and, indeed, that now-defunct radio-TV show "Your Hit Parade" does play a big part in twenty-four of the years of listings. But the show didn't appear on the air until April 20, 1935, and it disappeared from TV that very same week in 1959.

Basically, the sources for this compilation fall into three segments.

The listings from January 1930 through mid-April 1935 were obtained from the bound volumes of *Variety* in the New York Public Library, the histories of Broadway and motion picture musicals, and from information in Sigmund Spaeth's book *A History of Popular Music in America*.

From April 20, 1935, to its demise in that same April week in 1959, the source is "Your Hit Parade."

From April 1959 when "Your Hit Parade" finally surrendered to rock 'n' roll and left the airways, to the present, the Top Ten source has been the middle-of-the-road "Easy Listening" listings in *Billboard*.

How did it all get started for me?

As a youngster in 1942, I had started out jotting down the Hit Parade Saturday night radio listings whenever I could. Some years later I went to New York and persuaded an account executive at Batten, Barton, Durstine & Osborn, the agency for "Your Hit Parade," to allow me to look at their listings and fill in the gaps.

He brought out a common black loose-leaf notebook in which the week-by-week listings were typed. I had expected at least a leather-bound job, taken from a fireproof vault. This was trembling finger time for a Hit Parade buff as I opened the book and there they were! The very first "Your Hit Parade." The first song ever to be Number One. And even the listings from that Saturday night in 1944 when the program was preempted on radio for one of the national political conventions. I laboriously copied them down during a two-day session, and that Saturday night accepted a B.B.D.&O. ticket to witness the week's "Your Hit Parade" radio broadcast at NBC in Rockefeller Center.

In the years to come, there were inevitable gaps again, most notably during my two years of Army service. The source for filling these in was a volume titled *This Was Your Hit Parade* by John R. Williams, a Hit Parade buff from Camden, Maine, who obtained the listings the American Tobacco Company sent weekly to the New York Public Library, and who had them privately published in 1973. Mr. William's book is recommended for the "pure" Hit Parade listings, because I have taken three liberties with the actual listings.

For one thing, "Your Hit Parade" originally featured the Top Fifteen songs of the week, later went to ten, then to nine, and eventually to seven. (Gotta get in those Lucky Strike Extras.) I have kept the entire listings in this book at a consistent Top Ten, moving the logical songs in and out of the lower ranks during those periods.

Secondly, I have eliminated the occasional "Your Hit Parade" practice of introducing a newcomer one week, dropping it for a few weeks, and bringing it back later for a long run. In these few instances, I have made the song's tenure a steady one once it was on the Top Ten.

And thirdly, I have eliminated the program's rather irritating habit of bringing back "holiday" songs annually just because the season was upon us again. The feeling here was that songs like "Easter Parade," "White Christmas," and "Rudolph, the Red-Nosed Reindeer" should be listed only in their big origination years, indicative of the song hits from those particular years. (Another example of similar minor changes was the elimination of the old "Take Me Out to the Ballgame," which for unknown reasons suddenly appeared for one week in 1950, hardly indicative of the year's songs.)

Again, in the post-"Hit Parade" era, certain liberties have been taken with the Top Ten listings in *Billboard* magazine. The *Billboard* listings were dictated by the songs disc jockeys played for their biggest audience, the teen rock crowd. Incredibly such popular songs as "The Impossible Dream," "Moon River," songs from "The Sound of Music" and "Gypsy," Tony Bennett's "I Left My Heart in San Francisco," and many others didn't penetrate the Top Ten. These and others have been arbitrarily added with the sure knowledge that they were, indeed, among the weekly Top Ten of their respective origination years.

Included in each year's segment is a summation of news and anecdotal events. Newcomers to the Top Ten are indicated by an asterisk. In the back of the book is an alphabetical index for every song, indicating the year or years it was listed. The index also records how many weeks each song was on the listings (19), and how many weeks, if any, that it was Number One (19-2).

What has finally emerged here is intended as a permanent record, an instant bet settler, a true history of popular music from 1930, through the rock years, and up to the present. Or, as they used to say on "Your Hit Parade" each Saturday night, "the songs most requested of the nation's bandleaders, the best sellers in sheet music and phonograph records, the songs most heard on the air and most played on the automatic coin machines . . . an accurate, authentic tabulation of America's taste in popular music!"

What was the longest any song remained in the Top Ten? (See 1943.)

What was the first song ever to be Number One for ten weeks? (See 1941.)

What is the longest number of weeks a song was Number One? (See 1951.)

What was the first song ever to be Number One on radio's "Your Hit Parade"? (See 1935.)

What were the Top Ten tunes on Pearl Harbor Saturday night? (See 1941.)

What were the Top Ten tunes on that November weekend when President John F. Kennedy was assassinated? (See 1963.)

What songs were the only ones to appear in tandem as a single entry on the Top Ten? (See 1969.)

They're all inside.

But what's more important—what were the top tunes on your tenth birthday . . . or the day you were born . . . or met your wife or husband . . . or when you went into the service . . . or graduated from high school?

They're all inside, too.

Have fun.

I'VE HEARD
THOSE SONGS BEFORE

1930

It's fitting, if not somewhat symbolic, that the two top tunes of 1930 were "Happy Days Are Here Again" and "Little White Lies." Tin Pan Alley told us that happy days were here again, a little white lie that couldn't make the Depression go away. In any event, each was Number One on the Top Ten for six weeks apiece, tying for the honor of the year's most popular song.

Upbeat songs of cheer were the musical order of the day. Others were "Great Day," "On the Sunny Side of the Street," "Painting the Clouds With Sunshine," and "Sunny Side Up."

One might have called it Music to Stand in a Bread Line By, because the decade known as the Roaring Twenties had been swept out on a 1929 stock market collapse that ushered in what was to be known as the Tired Thirties.

America discovered miniature golf that year, and the indoor craze sweeping the nation was bridge. Boulder Dam was begun, the League of Nations was dying without knowing it, Prohibition was producing gangsterism and bathtub gin, and Admiral Byrd was given a ticker-tape welcome back from the Antarctic. It was the best use made that year of ticker tape. The Philadelphia Athletics took the St. Louis Cardinals in the World Series, and Knute Rockne had an undefeated football team at Notre Dame.

Radio, that upstart entertainment medium, was making static-marred stars of its own—Amos 'n' Andy, Walter Winchell, Will Rogers, and Rudy Vallee (whose "Betty Coed" and "The Stein Song" were two of the year's big hits). George Gershwin was supplying the tunes from Broadway with his *Strike Up the Band* and *Girl Crazy*. The new singing star at year's end was Ethel Zimmerman, who dropped the "Zim" off her name but left the "zing" in her songs.

For Hollywood it was the year of *All Quiet on the Western Front,* Garbo's *Anna Christie,* and the Marx Brothers in *Animal Crackers.* The movie industry was in the middle of the big changeover from silents to "talkies." No sweat for Tin Pan Alley. They merely turned out a tune called "If I Had a Talking Picture of You."

Remember . . . ?

Jan. 4, 1930

1:I'll See You Again
2:Why Was I Born?
3:Great Day
4:Without a Song
5:Sunny Side Up
6:Tiptoe Through the Tulips
7:You Do Something to Me
8:If I Had a Talking Picture of You
9:Painting the Clouds With Sunshine
10:More Than You Know

Jan. 11, 1930

1:I'll See You Again
2:Great Day
3:Without a Song
4:Tiptoe Through the Tulips
5:You Do Something to Me
6:Why Was I Born?
7:If I Had a Talking Picture of You
8:More Than You Know
9:Painting the Clouds With Sunshine
10:Sunny Side Up

Jan. 18, 1930

1:Great Day
2:I'll See You Again
3:Without a Song
4:You Do Something to Me
5:Painting the Clouds With Sunshine
6:Tiptoe Through the Tulips
7:Why Was I Born?
8:A Little Kiss Each Morning *
9:More Than You Know
10:If I Had a Talking Picture of You

Jan. 25, 1930

1:Great Day
2:Without a Song
3:I'll See You Again
4:Tiptoe Through the Tulips
5:You Do Something to Me
6:Painting the Clouds With Sunshine
7:More Than You Know
8:A Little Kiss Each Morning
9:Why Was I Born?
10:Strike Up the Band *

Feb. 1, 1930

1:Great Day
2:Without a Song
3:Tiptoe Through the Tulips
4:Painting the Clouds With Sunshine
5:More Than You Know
6:You Do Something to Me
7:I'll See You Again
8:Strike Up the Band
9:A Little Kiss Each Morning
10:Happy Days Are Here Again *

Feb. 8, 1930

1:Great Day
2:Tiptoe Through the Tulips
3:Without a Song
4:Painting the Clouds With Sunshine
5:Lady, Play Your Mandolin *
6:I'll See You Again
7:Happy Days Are Here Again
8:Strike Up the Band
9:A Little Kiss Each Morning
10:You Do Something to Me

Feb. 15, 1930

1:Tiptoe Through the Tulips
2:Painting the Clouds With Sunshine
3:Great Day
4:Without a Song
5:You Do Something to Me
6:Happy Days Are Here Again
7:Strike Up the Band
8:A Little Kiss Each Morning
9:Lady, Play Your Mandolin
10:I'll See You Again

Feb. 22, 1930

1:Tiptoe Through the Tulips
2:Happy Days Are Here Again
3:Painting the Clouds With Sunshine
4:Strike Up the Band
5:A Little Kiss Each Morning
6:Lady, Play Your Mandolin
7:Without a Song
8:Great Day
9:What Is This Thing Called Love? *
10:You Do Something to Me

* Newcomer

Mar. 1, 1930

1:Tiptoe Through the Tulips
2:Happy Days Are Here Again
3:Painting the Clouds With Sunshine
4:What Is This Thing Called Love?
5:Exactly Like You *
6:On the Sunny Side of the Street *
7:A Little Kiss Each Morning
8:Lady, Play Your Mandolin
9:I'm Alone Because I Love You *
10:Great Day

Mar. 8, 1930

1:Happy Days Are Here Again
2:Tiptoe Through the Tulips
3:What Is This Thing Called Love?
4:Exactly Like You
5:On the Sunny Side of the Street
6:Painting the Clouds With Sunshine
7:A Little Kiss Each Morning
8:Lady, Play Your Mandolin
9:The Waltz You Saved For Me *
10:I'm Alone Because I Love You

Mar. 15, 1930

1:Happy Days Are Here Again
2:What Is This Thing Called Love?
3:Exactly Like You
4:On the Sunny Side of the Street
5:Tiptoe Through the Tulips
6:The Waltz You Saved For Me
7:Painting the Clouds With Sunshine
8:I'm Alone Because I Love You
9:Lady, Play Your Mandolin
10:A Little Kiss Each Morning

Mar. 22, 1930

1:Happy Days Are Here Again
2:Exactly Like You
3:The Waltz You Saved For Me
4:What Is This Thing Called Love?
5:On the Sunny Side of the Street
6:It Happened in Monterey *
7:I'm Alone Because I Love You
8:Tiptoe Through the Tulips
9:A Little Kiss Each Morning
10:Painting the Clouds With Sunshine

Mar. 29, 1930

1:Happy Days Are Here Again
2:What Is This Thing Called Love?
3:On the Sunny Side of the Street
4:Exactly Like You
5:It Happened in Monterey
6:Should I? *
7:The Waltz You Saved For Me
8:Tiptoe Through the Tulips
9:Dancing On the Ceiling *
10:A Little Kiss Each Morning

Apr. 5, 1930

1:Happy Days Are Here Again
2:What Is This Thing Called Love?
3:Exactly Like You
4:It Happened in Monterey
5:Should I?
6:On the Sunny Side of the Street
7:The Waltz You Saved For Me
8:A Little Kiss Each Morning
9:Dancing On the Ceiling
10:Tiptoe Through the Tulips

Apr. 12, 1930

1:Happy Days Are Here Again
2:Exactly Like You
3:What Is This Thing Called Love?
4:It Happened in Monterey
5:Should I?
6:On the Sunny Side of the Street
7:Dancing On the Ceiling
8:You Brought a New Kind of Love to Me *
9:The Waltz You Saved For Me
10:A Little Kiss Each Morning

Apr. 19, 1930

1:What Is This Thing Called Love?
2:Exactly Like You
3:It Happened in Monterey
4:Happy Days Are Here Again
5:On the Sunny Side of the Street
6:The Waltz You Saved For Me
7:Should I?
8:You Brought a New Kind of Love to Me
9:Bye Bye Blues *
10:Dancing On the Ceiling

Apr. 26, 1930

1:Exactly Like You
2:What Is This Thing Called Love?
3:The Waltz You Saved For Me
4:Should I?
5:It Happened in Monterey
6:Bye Bye Blues
7:On the Sunny Side of the Street
8:You Brought a New Kind of Love to Me
9:When Your Hair Has Turned to Silver *
10:Happy Days Are Here Again

May 3, 1930

1:Exactly Like You
2:It Happened in Monterey
3:What Is This Thing Called Love?
4:You Brought a New Kind of Love to Me
5:On the Sunny Side of the Street
6:Bye Bye Blues
7:Should I?
8:The Waltz You Saved For Me
9:When Your Hair Has Turned to Silver
10:A Cottage For Sale *

May 10, 1930

1:Exactly Like You
2:When Your Hair Has Turned to Silver
3:Should I?
4:What Is This Thing Called Love?
5:A Cottage For Sale
6:Bye Bye Blues
7:It Happened in Monterey
8:You Brought a New Kind of Love to Me
9:On the Sunny Side of the Street
10:The Waltz You Saved For Me

May 17, 1930

1:Exactly Like You
2:When Your Hair Has Turned to Silver
3:A Cottage For Sale
4:Should I?
5:What Is This Thing Called Love?
6:My Baby Just Cares For Me *
7:It Happened in Monterey
8:Bye Bye Blues
9:You Brought a New Kind of Love to Me
10:On the Sunny Side of the Street

May 24, 1930

1:When Your Hair Has Turned to Silver
2:Exactly Like You
3:A Cottage For Sale
4:Bye Bye Blues
5:Should I?
6:My Baby Just Cares For Me
7:It Happened in Monterey
8:What Is This Thing Called Love?
9:You Brought a New Kind of Love to Me
10:Walkin' My Baby Back Home *

May 31, 1930

1:When Your Hair Has Turned to Silver
2:Bye Bye Blues
3:Exactly Like You
4:A Cottage For Sale
5:Should I?
6:Walkin' My Baby Back Home
7:So Beats My Heart For You *
8:You Brought a New Kind of Love to Me
9:It Happened in Monterey
10:What Is This Thing Called Love?

June 7, 1930

1:When Your Hair Has Turned to Silver
2:Bye Bye Blues
3:So Beats My Heart For You
4:Walkin' My Baby Back Home
5:Exactly Like You
6:A Cottage For Sale
7:My Future Just Passed *
8:Time On My Hands *
9:You Brought a New Kind of Love to Me
10:Should I?

June 14, 1930

1:Bye Bye Blues
2:When Your Hair Has Turned to Silver
3:So Beats My Heart For You
4:Walkin' My Baby Back Home
5:Time On My Hands
6:My Future Just Passed
7:You Brought a New Kind of Love to Me
8:A Cottage For Sale
9:Exactly Like You
10:Should I?

June 21, 1930

1:Bye Bye Blues
2:So Beats My Heart For You
3:When Your Hair Has Turned to Silver
4:Time On My Hands
5:Walkin' My Baby Back Home
6:Get Happy *
7:My Future Just Passed
8:A Cottage For Sale
9:You Brought a New Kind of Love to Me
10:Exactly Like You

June 28, 1930

1:So Beats My Heart For You
2:Bye Bye Blues
3:Time On My Hands
4:Get Happy
5:When Your Hair Has Turned to Silver
6:My Future Just Passed
7:Walkin' My Baby Back Home
8:Dancing With Tears In My Eyes *
9:You Brought a New Kind of Love to Me
10:A Cottage For Sale

July 5, 1930

1:So Beats My Heart For You
2:My Future Just Passed
3:Get Happy
4:Dancing With Tears In My Eyes
5:Time On My Hands
6:Bye Bye Blues
7:The Stein Song *
8:When Your Hair Has Turned to Silver
9:Walkin' My Baby Back Home
10:You Brought a New Kind of Love to Me

July 12, 1930

1:Time On My Hands
2:So Beats My Heart For You
3:Dancing With Tears In My Eyes
4:Bye Bye Blues
5:Walkin' My Baby Back Home
6:The Stein Song
7:Little White Lies *
8:My Future Just Passed
9:Get Happy
10:When Your Hair Has Turned to Silver

July 19, 1930

1:Time On My Hands
2:So Beats My Heart For You
3:Dancing With Tears In My Eyes
4:The Stein Song
5:Little White Lies
6:Get Happy
7:My Future Just Passed
8:Bye Bye Blues
9:Ten Cents a Dance *
10:Walkin' My Baby Back Home

July 26, 1930

1:Time On My Hands
2:Dancing With Tears In My Eyes
3:The Stein Song
4:So Beats My Heart For You
5:Little White Lies
6:Ten Cents a Dance
7:Get Happy
8:Cryin' For the Carolines *
9:My Future Just Passed
10:Bye Bye Blues

Aug. 2, 1930

1:Time On My Hands
2:Dancing With Tears In My Eyes
3:The Stein Song
4:Little White Lies
5:Ten Cents a Dance
6:Cryin' For the Carolines
7:Get Happy
8:So Beats My Heart For You
9:For You *
10:Bye Bye Blues

Aug. 9, 1930

1:Dancing With Tears In My Eyes
2:Time On My Hands
3:Little White Lies
4:Cryin' For the Carolines
5:The Stein Song
6:Ten Cents a Dance
7:Beyond the Blue Horizon *
8:So Beats My Heart For You
9:Betty Coed *
10:For You

Aug. 16, 1930

1:Dancing With Tears In My Eyes
2:Little White Lies
3:Ten Cents a Dance
4:Time On My Hands
5:For You
6:Betty Coed
7:Beyond the Blue Horizon
8:The Stein Song
9:So Beats My Heart For You
10:Cryin' For the Carolines

Aug. 23, 1930

1:Little White Lies
2:Dancing With Tears In My Eyes
3:The Stein Song
4:Beyond the Blue Horizon
5:Time On My Hands
6:Betty Coed
7:Cryin' For the Carolines
8:Ten Cents a Dance
9:So Beats My Heart For You
10:For You

Aug. 30, 1930

1:Little White Lies
2:Beyond the Blue Horizon
3:For You
4:Betty Coed
5:Dancing With Tears In My Eyes
6:The Stein Song
7:Cryin' For the Carolines
8:Sing Something Simple *
9:Time On My Hands
10:Ten Cents a Dance

Sept. 6, 1930

1:Little White Lies
2:For You
3:Betty Coed
4:Beyond the Blue Horizon
5:Sing Something Simple
6:Cryin' For the Carolines
7:Time On My Hands
8:I'm Confessin' *
9:Dancing With Tears In My Eyes
10:The Stein Song

Sept. 13, 1930

1:Little White Lies
2:For You
3:Beyond the Blue Horizon
4:Sing Something Simple
5:I'm Confessin'
6:Cryin' For the Carolines
7:Time On My Hands
8:Betty Coed
9:Dancing With Tears In My Eyes
10:Moonlight On the Colorado *

Sept. 20, 1930

1:Beyond the Blue Horizon
2:For You
3:Little White Lies
4:Moonlight On the Colorado
5:I'm Confessin'
6:Sing Something Simple
7:Dancing With Tears In My Eyes
8:Two Hearts in Three Quarter Time *
9:Time On My Hands
10:Cryin' For the Carolines

Sept. 27, 1930

1:Beyond the Blue Horizon
2:For You
3:Little White Lies
4:Moonlight On the Colorado
5:Two Hearts in Three Quarter Time
6:I'm Confessin'
7:Sing Something Simple
8:Cryin' For the Carolines
9:Time On My Hands
10:Fine and Dandy *

Oct. 4, 1930

1:For You
2:Beyond the Blue Horizon
3:Little White Lies
4:Two Hearts in Three Quarter Time
5:Fine and Dandy
6:Time On My Hands
7:I'm Confessin'
8:Sing Something Simple
9:Moonlight On the Colorado
10:Can This Be Love? *

Oct. 11, 1930

1:Beyond the Blue Horizon
2:Little White Lies
3:For You
4:Fine and Dandy
5:Two Hearts in Three Quarter Time
6:Can This Be Love?
7:Moonlight On the Colorado
8:Sing Something Simple
9:I'm Confessin'
10:I Still Get a Thrill *

Oct. 18, 1930

1:For You
2:Little White Lies
3:Beyond the Blue Horizon
4:Sing Something Simple
5:Moonlight On the Colorado
6:I Still Get a Thrill
7:Fine and Dandy
8:Can This Be Love?
9:Two Hearts in Three Quarter Time
10:I'm Confessin'

Oct. 25, 1930

1:Little White Lies
2:Beyond the Blue Horizon
3:For You
4:Three Little Words *
5:Moonlight On the Colorado
6:Sing Something Simple
7:I Still Get a Thrill
8:Can This Be Love?
9:Fine and Dandy
10:Two Hearts in Three Quarter Time

Nov. 1, 1930

1:Little White Lies
2:Sing Something Simple
3:Three Little Words
4:Two Hearts in Three Quarter Time
5:I Still Get a Thrill
6:For You
7:Fine and Dandy
8:Moonlight On the Colorado
9:Beyond the Blue Horizon
10:Can This Be Love?

Nov. 8, 1930

1:Three Little Words
2:I Still Get a Thrill
3:Sing Something Simple
4:Little White Lies
5:Cheerful Little Earful *
6:Beyond the Blue Horizon
7:For You
8:You're Driving Me Crazy *
9:Moonlight On the Colorado
10:Fine and Dandy

Nov. 15, 1930

1:Three Little Words
2:Cheerful Little Earful
3:I Still Get a Thrill
4:You're Driving Me Crazy
5:Embraceable You *
6:Little White Lies
7:Sing Something Simple
8:Beyond the Blue Horizon
9:For You
10:Body and Soul *

Nov. 22, 1930

1:Three Little Words
2:Cheerful Little Earful
3:You're Driving Me Crazy
4:Embraceable You
5:I Still Get a Thrill
6:Body and Soul
7:The Peanut Vendor *
8:Little White Lies
9:Beyond the Blue Horizon
10:Sing Something Simple

Nov. 29, 1930

1:Cheerful Little Earful
2:Three Little Words
3:Embraceable You
4:You're Driving Me Crazy
5:Body and Soul
6:The Peanut Vendor
7:I Still Get a Thrill
8:Little White Lies
9:I Got Rhythm *
10:My Ideal *

Dec. 6, 1930

1:Embraceable You
2:Cheerful Little Earful
3:Three Little Words
4:The Peanut Vendor
5:Body and Soul
6:You're Driving Me Crazy
7:I Got Rhythm
8:My Ideal
9:Something to Remember You By *
10:Bidin' My Time *

Dec. 13, 1930

1:Embraceable You
2:The Peanut Vendor
3:Body and Soul
4:I Got Rhythm
5:My Ideal
6:Something to Remember You By
7:You're Driving Me Crazy
8:Cheerful Little Earful
9:Three Little Words
10:Bidin' My Time

Dec. 20, 1930

1:Embraceable You
2:Body and Soul
3:My Ideal
4:Something to Remember You By
5:The Peanut Vendor
6:I Got Rhythm
7:Bidin' My Time
8:Would You Like to Take a Walk? *
9:Blue Again *
10:You're Driving Me Crazy

Dec. 27, 1930

1:Embraceable You
2:Body and Soul
3:Something to Remember You By
4:Blue Again
5:The Peanut Vendor
6:Bidin' My Time
7:My Ideal
8:Would You Like to Take a Walk?
9:I Got Rhythm
10:You're Driving Me Crazy

1931

It was the year that didn't mean you were hearing the last dance when the orchestra broke into the sweet strains of "Goodnight, Sweetheart." For 1931 was the origination year of that now traditional ballroom sign-off tune, and orchestras played it enough in the featured spot of the night to make it Number One for nine weeks and, hence, the top song of the year.

The musical year also gave birth to two songs that lived long after 1931 as signature radio themes—"When the Moon Comes Over the Mountain," for young songbird Kate Smith, and "Where the Blue of the Night Meets the Gold of the Day," for young crooner Bing Crosby.

Crooner Russ Columbo, at the height of his career, was contributing "Paradise," "Call Me Darling," and "You Try Somebody Else" to the Top Ten.

Jerome Kern's *The Cat and the Fiddle* was big on Broadway that year, giving us "She Didn't Say Yes" and "The Night Was Made for Love," and Cole Porter had *The New Yorkers,* which featured "Love For Sale." Radio, in its infancy, banned the lyrics as too risqué.

In the book field, Pearl Buck wrote *The Good Earth,* and Fannie Hurst depicted the woes of extramarital entanglements in *Back Street.*

The monarchy fell in Spain, Japan overran Manchuria, and the sports world was stunned by the death of Knute Rockne in an airplane crash. New York opened the world's tallest building, the Empire State, but in the Depression year of 1931 many of its 102 stories were unfilled.

On the screen Charlie Chaplin still had a hit with a "silent" in his *City Lights,* but the "talkies" being talked about were *Cimarron,* Karloff's *Frankenstein, The Front Page,* and a new Jimmy Cagney movie that caught the violent flavor of the times. It was called *Public Enemy.*

Soup kitchens were multiplying, and so was crime.

Jan. 3, 1931

1:Embraceable You
2:Body and Soul
3:Bidin' My Time
4:Something to Remember You By
5:The Peanut Vendor
6:Would You Like to Take a Walk?
7:Blue Again
8:I Got Rhythm
9:My Ideal
10:You're Driving Me Crazy

Jan. 10, 1931

1:Body and Soul
2:Embraceable You
3:Bidin' My Time
4:The Peanut Vendor
5:Something to Remember You By
6:Would You Like to Take a Walk?
7:Blue Again
8:Them There Eyes *
9:I Got Rhythm
10:My Ideal

Jan. 17, 1931

1:Body and Soul
2:Bidin' My Time
3:The Peanut Vendor
4:Something to Remember You By
5:Would You Like to Take a Walk?
6:Blue Again
7:Embraceable You
8:Them There Eyes
9:My Ideal
10:I Got Rhythm

Jan. 24, 1931

1:Body and Soul
2:Something to Remember You By
3:The Peanut Vendor
4:Them There Eyes
5:Would You Like to Take a Walk?
6:I Got Rhythm
7:My Ideal
8:Bidin' My Time
9:Embraceable You
10:Blue Again

Jan. 31, 1931

1:Something to Remember You By
2:Body and Soul
3:The Peanut Vendor
4:Would You Like to Take a Walk?
5:Love For Sale *
6:Them There Eyes
7:My Ideal
8:I Got Rhythm
9:Embraceable You
10:Bidin' My Time

Feb. 7, 1931

1:Something to Remember You By
2:Would You Like to Take a Walk?
3:The Peanut Vendor
4:Love For Sale
5:Them There Eyes
6:My Ideal
7:I Got Rhythm
8:Body and Soul
9:Bidin' My Time
10:Embraceable You

Feb. 14, 1931

1:Something to Remember You By
2:Love For Sale
3:Would You Like to Take a Walk?
4:The Peanut Vendor
5:My Ideal
6:Someday I'll Find You *
7:Them There Eyes
8:I Got Rhythm
9:Body and Soul
10:Embraceable You

Feb. 21, 1931

1:Something to Remember You By
2:Love For Sale
3:Would You Like to Take a Walk?
4:Someday I'll Find You
5:The Peanut Vendor
6:Them There Eyes
7:My Ideal
8:Mama Inez *
9:I Got Rhythm
10:Body and Soul

* Newcomer

Feb. 28, 1931

1:Something to Remember You By
2:Love For Sale
3:Someday I'll Find You
4:Would You Like to Take a Walk?
5:The Peanut Vendor
6:Body and Soul
7:Mama Inez
8:Them There Eyes
9:My Ideal
10:Smile, Darn Ya, Smile *

Mar. 7, 1931

1:Love For Sale
2:Someday I'll Find You
3:Something to Remember You By
4:Mama Inez
5:The Peanut Vendor
6:Would You Like to Take a Walk?
7:Smile, Darn Ya, Smile
8:Body and Soul
9:Them There Eyes
10:My Ideal

Mar. 14, 1931

1:Love For Sale
2:Someday I'll Find You
3:Smile, Darn Ya, Smile
4:Mama Inez
5:Something to Remember You By
6:I Surrender, Dear *
7:The Peanut Vendor
8:Would You Like to Take a Walk?
9:Them There Eyes
10:My Ideal

Mar. 21, 1931

1:Someday I'll Find You
2:Love For Sale
3:Smile, Darn Ya, Smile
4:I Surrender, Dear
5:Something to Remember You By
6:Mama Inez
7:Wabash Moon *
8:I Love a Parade *
9:The Peanut Vendor
10:Would You Like to Take a Walk?

Mar. 28, 1931

1:Someday I'll Find You
2:I Surrender, Dear
3:Love For Sale
4:Wabash Moon
5:I Love a Parade
6:Something to Remember You By
7:Smile, Darn Ya, Smile
8:Mama Inez
9:Would You Like to Take a Walk?
10:The Peanut Vendor

Apr. 4, 1931

1:Someday I'll Find You
2:Wabash Moon
3:I Surrender, Dear
4:Love For Sale
5:I Love a Parade
6:Out of Nowhere *
7:You Try Somebody Else *
8:Something to Remember You By
9:Smile, Darn Ya, Smile
10:Mama Inez

Apr. 11, 1931

1:Someday I'll Find You
2:I Surrender, Dear
3:Wabash Moon
4:I Love a Parade
5:Out of Nowhere
6:You Try Somebody Else
7:Love For Sale
8:Call Me Darling *
9:When Your Lover Has Gone *
10:Something to Remember You By

Apr. 18, 1931

1:I Surrender, Dear
2:Wabash Moon
3:Someday I'll Find You
4:You Try Somebody Else
5:Out of Nowhere
6:Call Me Darling
7:When Your Lover Has Gone
8:I Love a Parade
9:Love For Sale
10:Heartaches *

Apr. 25, 1931

1:I Surrender, Dear
2:Out of Nowhere
3:I Love a Parade
4:Love For Sale
5:Wabash Moon
6:Heartaches
7:When Your Lover Has Gone
8:Call Me Darling
9:You Try Somebody Else
10:Someday I'll Find You

May 2, 1931

1:I Surrender, Dear
2:Out of Nowhere
3:You Try Somebody Else
4:Heartaches
5:When Your Lover Has Gone
6:Call Me Darling
7:I Love a Parade
8:Love For Sale
9:Wabash Moon
10:Someday I'll Find You

May 9, 1931

1:Out of Nowhere
2:I Surrender, Dear
3:When Your Lover Has Gone
4:You Try Somebody Else
5:Heartaches
6:Call Me Darling
7:By the River Sainte Marie *
8:Please Don't Talk About Me *
9:Wabash Moon
10:I Love a Parade

May 16, 1931

1:Out of Nowhere
2:When Your Lover Has Gone
3:I Surrender, Dear
4:Heartaches
5:By the River Sainte Marie
6:Wabash Moon
7:You Try Somebody Else
8:Call Me Darling
9:Please Don't Talk About Me
10:Dream a Little Dream of Me *

May 23, 1931

1:Out of Nowhere
2:I Surrender, Dear
3:When Your Lover Has Gone
4:Heartaches
5:Please Don't Talk About Me
6:By the River Sainte Marie
7:Wabash Moon
8:Dream a Little Dream of Me
9:Call Me Darling
10:You Try Somebody Else

May 30, 1931

1:Out of Nowhere
2:Please Don't Talk About Me
3:Dream a Little Dream of Me
4:When Your Lover Has Gone
5:I Surrender, Dear
6:Wrap Your Troubles in Dreams *
7:Heartaches
8:By the River Sainte Marie
9:You Try Somebody Else
10:Call Me Darling

June 6, 1931

1:When Your Lover Has Gone
2:Please Don't Talk About Me
3:Out of Nowhere
4:Dream a Little Dream of Me
5:I Found a Million Dollar Baby *
6:Wrap Your Troubles in Dreams
7:I Surrender, Dear
8:Heartaches
9:By the River Sainte Marie
10:You Try Somebody Else

June 13, 1931

1:Dream a Little Dream of Me
2:When Your Lover Has Gone
3:I Found a Million Dollar Baby
4:Please Don't Talk About Me
5:Out of Nowhere
6:Wrap Your Troubles in Dreams
7:Just One More Chance *
8:Heartaches
9:I Surrender, Dear
10:You Try Somebody Else

June 20, 1931

1:Dream a Little Dream of Me
2:I Found a Million Dollar Baby
3:Please Don't Talk About Me
4:Just One More Chance
5:Dancing in the Dark *
6:When Your Lover Has Gone
7:Wrap Your Troubles in Dreams
8:Out of Nowhere
9:Heartaches
10:I Surrender, Dear

June 27, 1931

1:I Found a Million Dollar Baby
2:Dream a Little Dream of Me
3:Dancing in the Dark
4:Just One More Chance
5:Please Don't Talk About Me
6:New Sun in the Sky *
7:When Your Lover Has Gone
8:Wrap Your Troubles in Dreams
9:Out of Nowhere
10:Heartaches

July 4, 1931

1:I Found a Million Dollar Baby
2:Dancing in the Dark
3:Just One More Chance
4:New Sun in the Sky
5:Dream a Little Dream of Me
6:When the Moon Comes Over the Mountain *
7:I'm Through With Love *
8:Please Don't Talk About Me
9:Wrap Your Troubles in Dreams
10:Heartaches

July 11, 1931

1:I Found a Million Dollar Baby
2:Dancing in the Dark
3:When the Moon Comes Over the Mountain
4:New Sun in the Sky
5:Just One More Chance
6:I'm Through With Love
7:Dream a Little Dream of Me
8:I Love Louisa *
9:Sweet and Lovely *
10:Wrap Your Troubles in Dreams

July 18, 1931

1:Dancing in the Dark
2:I Found a Million Dollar Baby
3:When the Moon Comes Over the Mountain
4:I'm Through With Love
5:New Sun in the Sky
6:I Love Louisa
7:Sweet and Lovely
8:Just One More Chance
9:Dream a Little Dream of Me
10:Little Girl *

July 25, 1931

1:Dancing in the Dark
2:When the Moon Comes Over the Mountain
3:I'm Through With Love
4:New Sun in the Sky
5:Sweet and Lovely
6:I Love Louisa
7:I Found a Million Dollar Baby
8:Little Girl
9:Dream a Little Dream of Me
10:Just One More Chance

Aug. 1, 1931

1:Dancing in the Dark
2:When the Moon Comes Over the Mountain
3:Sweet and Lovely
4:I'm Through With Love
5:Just One More Chance
6:I Love Louisa
7:I Found a Million Dollar Baby
8:Little Girl
9:New Sun in the Sky
10:When Yuba Plays the Rumba On the Tuba *

Aug. 8, 1931

1:When the Moon Comes Over the Mountain
2:Dancing in the Dark
3:Sweet and Lovely
4:Little Girl
5:I Love Louisa
6:When Yuba Plays the Rumba On the Tuba
7:Just One More Chance
8:I'm Through With Love
9:I Found a Million Dollar Baby
10:Love Letters in the Sand *

Aug. 15, 1931

1:When the Moon Comes Over the Mountain
2:Sweet and Lovely
3:Dancing in the Dark
4:I'm Through With Love
5:Little Girl
6:Just One More Chance
7:I Found a Million Dollar Baby
8:When Yuba Plays the Rumba On the Tuba
9:I Love Louisa
10:Love Letters in the Sand

Aug. 22, 1931

1:When the Moon Comes Over the Mountain
2:Dancing in the Dark
3:Sweet and Lovely
4:Love Letters in the Sand
5:I'm Through With Love
6:Just One More Chance
7:I Love Louisa
8:Little Girl
9:Home *
10:Guilty *

Aug. 29, 1931

1:When the Moon Comes Over the Mountain
2:Sweet and Lovely
3:Dancing in the Dark
4:I'm Through With Love
5:Love Letters in the Sand
6:Just One More Chance
7:Home
8:Guilty
9:Little Girl
10:I Love Louisa

Sept. 5, 1931

1:When the Moon Comes Over the Mountain
2:Sweet and Lovely
3:Dancing in the Dark
4:Love Letters in the Sand
5:Goodnight, Sweetheart *
6:Home
7:I'm Through With Love
8:Just One More Chance
9:Guilty
10:Little Girl

Sept. 12, 1931

1:When the Moon Comes Over the Mountain
2:Sweet and Lovely
3:Dancing in the Dark
4:Goodnight, Sweetheart
5:Home
6:Love Letters in the Sand
7:Guilty
8:I Don't Know Why *
9:I'm Through With Love
10:Just One More Chance

Sept. 19, 1931

1:Sweet and Lovely
2:Dancing in the Dark
3:Goodnight, Sweetheart
4:When the Moon Comes Over the Mountain
5:Love Letters in the Sand
6:Home
7:Life Is Just a Bowl of Cherries *
8:Guilty
9:My Song *
10:I Don't Know Why

Sept. 26, 1931

1:Sweet and Lovely
2:Dancing in the Dark
3:Life Is Just a Bowl of Cherries
4:Love Letters in the Sand
5:Home
6:Goodnight, Sweetheart
7:My Song
8:That's Why Darkies Were Born *
9:When the Moon Comes Over the Mountain
10:I Don't Know Why

Oct. 3, 1931

1:Sweet and Lovely
2:Dancing in the Dark
3:Goodnight, Sweetheart
4:Life Is Just a Bowl of Cherries
5:Love Letters in the Sand
6:My Song
7:That's Why Darkies Were Born
8:When the Moon Comes Over the Mountain
9:Home
10:The Thrill Is Gone *

Oct. 10, 1931

1:Goodnight, Sweetheart
2:Sweet and Lovely
3:Life Is Just a Bowl of Cherries
4:Love Letters in the Sand
5:Home
6:My Song
7:The Thrill Is Gone
8:Dancing in the Dark
9:That's Why Darkies Were Born
10:River Stay 'Way From My Door *

Oct. 17, 1931

1:Goodnight, Sweetheart
2:Sweet and Lovely
3:Life Is Just a Bowl of Cherries
4:Home
5:Love Letters in the Sand
6:River Stay 'Way From My Door
7:My Song
8:Dancing in the Dark
9:The Thrill Is Gone
10:That's Why Darkies Were Born

Oct. 24, 1931

1:Goodnight, Sweetheart
2:Home
3:Sweet and Lovely
4:Life Is Just a Bowl of Cherries
5:Love Letters in the Sand
6:You Call It Madness *
7:My Song
8:The Thrill Is Gone
9:River Stay 'Way From My Door
10:A Faded Summer Love *

Oct. 31, 1931

1:Goodnight, Sweetheart
2:Sweet and Lovely
3:You Call It Madness
4:Life Is Just a Bowl of Cherries
5:A Faded Summer Love
6:Love Letters in the Sand
7:Home
8:My Song
9:She Didn't Say Yes *
10:The Night Was Made For Love *

Nov. 7, 1931

1:Goodnight, Sweetheart
2:You Call It Madness
3:A Faded Summer Love
4:Life Is Just a Bowl of Cherries
5:Love Letters in the Sand
6:Sweet and Lovely
7:She Didn't Say Yes
8:The Night Was Made For Love
9:Where the Blue of the Night Meets the
10:Home   Gold of the Day *

Nov. 14, 1931

1:Goodnight, Sweetheart
2:A Faded Summer Love
3:You Call It Madness
4:She Didn't Say Yes
5:Where the Blue of the Night Meets the
6:Paradise *   Gold of the Day
7:The Night Was Made For Love
8:Life Is Just a Bowl of Cherries
9:Love Letters in the Sand
10:Sweet and Lovely

Nov. 21, 1931

1:Goodnight, Sweetheart
2:You Call It Madness
3:A Faded Summer Love
4:Paradise
5:Where the Blue of the Night Meets the
6:All of Me *   Gold of the Day
7:The Night Was Made For Love
8:She Didn't Say Yes
9:You're My Everything *
10:Got a Date With an Angel *

Nov. 28, 1931

1:Goodnight, Sweetheart
2:You Call It Madness
3:All of Me
4:A Faded Summer Love
5:Paradise
6:Where the Blue of the Night Meets the
7:Stardust *   Gold of the Day
8:You're My Everything
9:Got a Date With an Angel
10:She Didn't Say Yes

Dec. 5, 1931

1:Goodnight, Sweetheart
2:She Didn't Say Yes
3:Where the Blue of the Night Meets the
4:Stardust   Gold of the Day
5:All of Me
6:You Call It Madness
7:Paradise
8:A Faded Summer Love
9:You're My Everything
10:Got a Date With an Angel

Dec. 12, 1931

1:All of Me
2:Goodnight, Sweetheart
3:Where the Blue of the Night Meets the
4:Paradise   Gold of the Day
5:Stardust
6:You're My Everything
7:Got a Date With an Angel
8:She Didn't Say Yes
9:Now's the Time to Fall in Love *
10:Was That the Human Thing to Do? *

Dec. 19, 1931

1:All of Me
2:You're My Everything
3:Paradise
4:Where the Blue of the Night Meets the
5:Stardust   Gold of the Day
6:Was That the Human Thing to Do?
7:Goodnight, Sweetheart
8:Now's the Time to Fall in Love
9:Cuban Love Song *
10:Got a Date With an Angel

Dec. 26, 1931

1:All of Me
2:Paradise
3:Where the Blue of the Night Meets the
4:Stardust   Gold of the Day
5:Cuban Love Song
6:You're My Everything
7:Was That the Human Thing to Do?
8:Now's the Time to Fall in Love
9:Got a Date With an Angel
10:Goodnight, Sweetheart

1932

If one song symbolized 1932 it was the mournful lament "Brother, Can You Spare a Dime?" That nearly said it all.

Dump-ground settlements made of corrugated iron and old packing crates mushroomed around the country, inevitably and unfairly being labeled "Hoovervilles." Ironically the top song of the year, seven weeks Number One, was titled "A Shanty in Old Shanty Town."

The shock of the year was the crime of the year when the nineteen-month-old son of world-famous hero Charles Lindbergh was kidnapped from his Hopewell, New Jersey, home and slain. It touched off a massive hunt for the killer.

Jimmy Walker, the song-writing playboy mayor of New York City, resigned under fire during a statewide investigation of corruption in his administration.

Japan attacked China, and the United States, blissfully oblivious, dedicated the Tomb of the Unknown Soldier in Arlington National Cemetery as "a monument to lasting peace."

Grand Hotel, I Am a Fugitive from a Chain Gang, and *Dr. Jekyll and Mr. Hyde* were the big movie attractions of the year.

Al Capone went to prison, not for the various crimes he was suspected of but for evading income-tax laws. In May the Bonus Army invaded Washington and vowed to camp there until Congress paid the veterans their bonuses in full. The Bonus Bill was defeated, and the "army" was dispersed by tear gas showered by the real Army.

That, and the stigma of the "Hoovervilles," proved the downfall of President Herbert Hoover in November. Franklin D. Roosevelt, riding the crest of a brilliant administration as governor of New York, was elected to the presidency with his running mate, John Nance Garner.

A nation which was hearing "Brother, Can You Spare a Dime?" settled back to wait for the Democratic inauguration next March.

Jan. 2, 1932

1:All of Me
2:Paradise
3:Stardust
4:Cuban Love Song
5:You're My Everything
6:Was That the Human Thing to Do?
7:Now's the Time to Fall in Love
8:Got a Date With an Angel
9:Love Is Sweeping the Country *
10:Where the Blue of the Night Meets the
      Gold of the Day

Jan. 9, 1932

1:Paradise
2:Stardust
3:All of Me
4:You're My Everything
5:Love Is Sweeping the Country
6:Of Thee I Sing *
7:Cuban Love Song
8:Was That the Human Thing to Do?
9:Now's the Time to Fall in Love
10:Got a Date With an Angel

Jan. 16, 1932

1:Paradise
2:Stardust
3:Of Thee I Sing
4:Love Is Sweeping the Country
5:All of Me
6:You're My Everything
7:Cuban Love Song
8:Who Cares? *
9:Now's the Time to Fall in Love
10:Was That the Human Thing to Do?

Jan. 23, 1932

1:Paradise
2:Of Thee I Sing
3:Love Is Sweeping the Country
4:All of Me
5:Stardust
6:Who Cares?
7:You're My Everything
8:Cuban Love Song
9:Was That the Human Thing to Do?
10:Now's the Time to Fall in Love

Jan. 30, 1932

1:Paradise
2:Love Is Sweeping the Country
3:Of Thee I Sing
4:Who Cares?
5:All of Me
6:Stardust
7:Cuban Love Song
8:My Silent Love *
9:You're My Everything
10:Now's the Time to Fall in Love

Feb. 6, 1932

1:Paradise
2:Of Thee I Sing
3:Who Cares?
4:My Silent Love
5:Love Is Sweeping the Country
6:All of Me
7:Stardust
8:You're My Everything
9:Now's the Time to Fall in Love
10:Cuban Love Song

Feb. 13, 1932

1:Paradise
2:Of Thee I Sing
3:My Silent Love
4:Who Cares?
5:Love Is Sweeping the Country
6:Drums In My Heart *
7:All of Me
8:Stardust
9:You're My Everything
10:Cuban Love Song

Feb. 20, 1932

1:Paradise
2:My Silent Love
3:Of Thee I Sing
4:All of Me
5:Stardust
6:Love Is Sweeping the Country
7:Drums In My Heart
8:Let's All Sing Like the Birdies Sing *
9:You're My Everything
10:Who Cares?

* Newcomer

Feb. 27, 1932

1:My Silent Love
2:Paradise
3:Of Thee I Sing
4:Love Is Sweeping the Country
5:Drums In My Heart
6:Let's All Sing Like the Birdies Sing
7:All of Me
8:Stardust
9:Just Friends *
10:You're My Everything

Mar. 5, 1932

1:My Silent Love
2:Of Thee I Sing
3:Paradise
4:Drums In My Heart
5:Just Friends
6:Love Is Sweeping the Country
7:Let's All Sing Like the Birdies Sing
8:All of Me
9:Soft Lights and Sweet Music *
10:Stardust

Mar. 12, 1932

1:My Silent Love
2:Just Friends
3:Drums In My Heart
4:Soft Lights and Sweet Music
5:Let's Have Another Cup of Coffee *
6:Paradise
7:Of Thee I Sing
8:Love Is Sweeping the Country
9:Let's All Sing Like the Birdies Sing
10:All of Me

Mar. 19, 1932

1:My Silent Love
2:Just Friends
3:Soft Lights and Sweet Music
4:Let's Have Another Cup of Coffee
5:Drums In My Heart
6:A Ghost of a Chance *
7:Paradise
8:Of Thee I Sing
9:Love Is Sweeping the Country
10:Let's All Sing Like the Birdies Sing

Mar. 26, 1932

1:Just Friends
2:Soft Lights and Sweet Music
3:My Silent Love
4:Let's Have Another Cup of Coffee
5:A Ghost of a Chance
6:Drums In My Heart
7:Love Is Sweeping the Country
8:Of Thee I Sing
9:Paradise
10:Lullaby of the Leaves *

Apr. 2, 1932

1:My Silent Love
2:Just Friends
3:Soft Lights and Sweet Music
4:A Ghost of a Chance
5:Let's Have Another Cup of Coffee
6:Lullaby of the Leaves
7:Drums In My Heart
8:Love Is Sweeping the Country
9:Of Thee I Sing
10:Paradise

Apr. 9, 1932

1:Just Friends
2:Soft Lights and Sweet Music
3:My Silent Love
4:A Ghost of a Chance
5:Lullaby of the Leaves
6:Let's Have Another Cup of Coffee
7:A Shanty in Old Shanty Town *
8:Drums In My Heart
9:Of Thee I Sing
10:Love Is Sweeping the Country

Apr. 16, 1932

1:Soft Lights and Sweet Music
2:Just Friends
3:A Ghost of a Chance
4:Lullaby of the Leaves
5:My Silent Love
6:A Shanty in Old Shanty Town
7:Let's Have Another Cup of Coffee
8:Speak To Me of Love *
9:Love Is Sweeping the Country
10:Of Thee I Sing

Apr. 23, 1932

1:Soft Lights and Sweet Music
2:Let's Have Another Cup of Coffee
3:A Ghost of a Chance
4:Just Friends
5:A Shanty in Old Shanty Town
6:Speak To Me of Love
7:My Silent Love
8:Lullaby of the Leaves
9:Of Thee I Sing
10:Love Is Sweeping the Country

Apr. 30, 1932

1:Let's Have Another Cup of Coffee
2:A Ghost of a Chance
3:Soft Lights and Sweet Music
4:Lullaby of the Leaves
5:Speak To Me of Love
6:A Shanty in Old Shanty Town
7:Just Friends
8:My Silent Love
9:Sweethearts Forever *
10:Three On a Match *

May 7, 1932

1:Let's Have Another Cup of Coffee
2:Soft Lights and Sweet Music
3:A Shanty in Old Shanty Town
4:Lullaby of the Leaves
5:Speak To Me of Love
6:A Ghost of a Chance
7:Sweethearts Forever
8:Three On a Match
9:Just Friends
10:My Silent Love

May 14, 1932

1:Soft Lights and Sweet Music
2:A Shanty in Old Shanty Town
3:Lullaby of the Leaves
4:Let's Have Another Cup of Coffee
5:Sweethearts Forever
6:Speak To Me of Love
7:Three On a Match
8:My Silent Love
9:A Ghost of a Chance
10:Just Friends

May 21, 1932

1:Soft Lights and Sweet Music
2:Lullaby of the Leaves
3:A Shanty in Old Shanty Town
4:Sweethearts Forever
5:Speak To Me of Love
6:Three On a Match
7:Let's Have Another Cup of Coffee
8:A Ghost of a Chance
9:Just Friends
10:Masquerade *

May 28, 1932

1:A Shanty in Old Shanty Town
2:Lullaby of the Leaves
3:Soft Lights and Sweet Music
4:Speak To Me of Love
5:Three On a Match
6:Sweethearts Forever
7:Masquerade
8:How Deep Is the Ocean? *
9:A Ghost of a Chance
10:Let's Have Another Cup of Coffee

June 4, 1932

1:A Shanty in Old Shanty Town
2:Lullaby of the Leaves
3:Masquerade
4:How Deep Is the Ocean?
5:Speak To Me of Love
6:Let's Have Another Cup of Coffee
7:Soft Lights and Sweet Music
8:A Ghost of a Chance
9:Three On a Match
10:Sweethearts Forever

June 11, 1932

1:A Shanty in Old Shanty Town
2:Masquerade
3:How Deep Is the Ocean?
4:Lullaby of the Leaves
5:A Ghost of a Chance
6:A Little Street Where Old Friends Meet *
7:Speak To Me of Love
8:Let's Have Another Cup of Coffee
9:Sweethearts Forever
10:Soft Lights and Sweet Music

June 18, 1932

1:A Shanty in Old Shanty Town
2:How Deep Is the Ocean?
3:Masquerade
4:A Little Street Where Old Friends Meet
5:Lullaby of the Leaves
6:A Ghost of a Chance
7:It Was So Beautiful *
8:Speak To Me of Love
9:Soft Lights and Sweet Music
10:Sweethearts Forever

June 25, 1932

1:A Shanty in Old Shanty Town
2:How Deep Is the Ocean?
3:A Little Street Where Old Friends Meet
4:Lullaby of the Leaves
5:It Was So Beautiful
6:Masquerade
7:Speak To Me of Love
8:Sweethearts Forever
9:A Ghost of a Chance
10:We Just Couldn't Say Goodbye *

July 2, 1932

1:A Shanty in Old Shanty Town
2:A Little Street Where Old Friends Meet
3:How Deep Is the Ocean?
4:It Was So Beautiful
5:Lullaby of the Leaves
6:We Just Couldn't Say Goodbye
7:Masquerade
8:A Ghost of a Chance
9:Sweethearts Forever
10:Speak To Me of Love

July 9, 1932

1:How Deep Is the Ocean?
2:A Shanty in Old Shanty Town
3:A Little Street Where Old Friends Meet
4:It Was So Beautiful
5:We Just Couldn't Say Goodbye
6:Lullaby of the Leaves
7:Just an Echo in the Valley *
8:Masquerade
9:A Ghost of a Chance
10:Sweethearts Forever

July 16, 1932

1:How Deep Is the Ocean?
2:A Little Street Where Old Friends Meet
3:A Shanty in Old Shanty Town
4:We Just Couldn't Say Goodbye
5:It Was So Beautiful
6:Just an Echo in the Valley
7:Lullaby of the Leaves
8:Masquerade
9:Strange Interlude *
10:A Ghost of a Chance

July 23, 1932

1:A Shanty in Old Shanty Town
2:How Deep Is the Ocean?
3:A Little Street Where Old Friends Meet
4:Just an Echo in the Valley
5:We Just Couldn't Say Goodbye
6:It Was So Beautiful
7:Masquerade
8:Strange Interlude
9:A Ghost of a Chance
10:Lullaby of the Leaves

July 30, 1932

1:A Little Street Where Old Friends Meet
2:How Deep Is the Ocean?
3:A Shanty in Old Shanty Town
4:Just an Echo in the Valley
5:It Was So Beautiful
6:We Just Couldn't Say Goodbye
7:Masquerade
8:Say It Isn't So *
9:Strange Interlude
10:Lullaby of the Leaves

Aug. 6, 1932

1:A Little Street Where Old Friends Meet
2:How Deep Is the Ocean?
3:Just an Echo in the Valley
4:Say It Isn't So
5:A Shanty in Old Shanty Town
6:We Just Couldn't Say Goodbye
7:It Was So Beautiful
8:Masquerade
9:Darkness On the Delta *
10:Lullaby of the Leaves

Aug. 13, 1932

1:A Little Street Where Old Friends Meet
2:Just an Echo in the Valley
3:Say It Isn't So
4:How Deep Is the Ocean?
5:It Was So Beautiful
6:We Just Couldn't Say Goodbye
7:A Shanty in Old Shanty Town
8:Darkness On the Delta
9:Masquerade
10:Let's Put Out the Lights *

Aug. 20, 1932

1:A Little Street Where Old Friends Meet
2:Say It Isn't So
3:Just an Echo in the Valley
4:It Was So Beautiful
5:Let's Put Out the Lights
6:Darkness On the Delta
7:How Deep Is the Ocean?
8:We Just Couldn't Say Goodbye
9:A Shanty in Old Shanty Town
10:Masquerade

Aug. 27, 1932

1:A Little Street Where Old Friends Meet
2:Just an Echo in the Valley
3:Say It Isn't So
4:Let's Put Out the Lights
5:Darkness On the Delta
6:It Was So Beautiful
7:Mimi *
8:How Deep Is the Ocean?
9:We Just Couldn't Say Goodbye
10:A Shanty in Old Shanty Town

Sept. 3, 1932

1:Just an Echo in the Valley
2:Say It Isn't So
3:Let's Put Out the Lights
4:A Little Street Where Old Friends Meet
5:Darkness On the Delta
6:Mimi
7:Three's a Crowd *
8:It Was So Beautiful
9:How Deep Is the Ocean?
10:We Just Couldn't Say Goodbye

Sept. 10, 1932

1:Say It Isn't So
2:Just an Echo in the Valley
3:Let's Put Out the Lights
4:Darkness On the Delta
5:Mimi
6:Three's a Crowd
7:A Little Street Where Old Friends Meet
8:We Just Couldn't Say Goodbye
9:How Deep Is the Ocean?
10:Here Lies Love *

Sept. 17, 1932

1:Say It Isn't So
2:Let's Put Out the Lights
3:Just an Echo in the Valley
4:Darkness On the Delta
5:Here Lies Love
6:Three's a Crowd
7:Mimi
8:A Little Street Where Old Friends Meet
9:Underneath the Harlem Moon *
10:We Just Couldn't Say Goodbye

Sept. 24, 1932

1:Just an Echo in the Valley
2:Say It Isn't So
3:Let's Put Out the Lights
4:Here Lies Love
5:Darkness On the Delta
6:Underneath the Harlem Moon
7:Mimi
8:Three's a Crowd
9:A Little Street Where Old Friends Meet
10:Play, Fiddle, Play *

Oct. 1, 1932

1:Just an Echo in the Valley
2:Here Lies Love
3:Say It Isn't So
4:Let's Put Out the Lights
5:Underneath the Harlem Moon
6:Darkness On the Delta
7:Play, Fiddle, Play
8:Mimi
9:Louisiana Hayride *
10:A Little Street Where Old Friends Meet

Oct. 8, 1932

1:Say It Isn't So
2:Just an Echo in the Valley
3:Let's Put Out the Lights
4:Here Lies Love
5:Please *
6:Underneath the Harlem Moon
7:Darkness On the Delta
8:Play, Fiddle, Play
9:Louisiana Hayride
10:Mimi

Oct. 15, 1932

1:Say It Isn't So
2:Please
3:Let's Put Out the Lights
4:Alone Together *
5:Here Lies Love
6:Underneath the Harlem Moon
7:Just an Echo in the Valley
8:Louisiana Hayride
9:Darkness On the Delta
10:Play, Fiddle, Play

Oct. 22, 1932

1:Say It Isn't So
2:Please
3:Alone Together
4:Here Lies Love
5:Let's Put Out the Lights
6:Underneath the Harlem Moon
7:Brother, Can You Spare a Dime? *
8:Play, Fiddle, Play
9:Louisiana Hayride
10:Just an Echo in the Valley

Oct. 29, 1932

1:Say It Isn't So
2:Alone Together
3:Please
4:Louisiana Hayride
5:Brother, Can You Spare a Dime?
6:Here Lies Love
7:Let's Put Out the Lights
8:Underneath the Harlem Moon
9:Just an Echo in the Valley
10:Play, Fiddle, Play

Nov. 5, 1932

1:Please
2:Say It Isn't So
3:Alone Together
4:Brother, Can You Spare a Dime?
5:Just an Echo in the Valley
6:Louisiana Hayride
7:Here Lies Love
8:Willow Weep For Me *
9:Let's Put Out the Lights
10:Underneath the Harlem Moon

Nov. 12, 1932

1:Please
2:Alone Together
3:Here Lies Love
4:Underneath the Harlem Moon
5:Brother, Can You Spare a Dime?
6:Say It Isn't So
7:Willow Weep For Me
8:Louisiana Hayride
9:Just an Echo in the Valley
10:Let's Put Out the Lights

Nov. 19, 1932

1:Please
2:Underneath the Harlem Moon
3:Here Lies Love
4:Alone Together
5:Willow Weep For Me
6:Brother, Can You Spare a Dime?
7:I've Told Every Little Star *
8:The Song Is You *
9:Louisiana Hayride
10:Say It Isn't So

Nov. 26, 1932

1:Please
2:Brother, Can You Spare a Dime?
3:Here Lies Love
4:Underneath the Harlem Moon
5:I've Told Every Little Star
6:The Song Is You
7:Willow Weep For Me
8:Alone Together
9:Louisiana Hayride
10:Say It Isn't So

Dec. 3, 1932

1:Please
2:I've Told Every Little Star
3:The Song Is You
4:Brother, Can You Spare a Dime?
5:Willow Weep For Me
6:You're an Old Smoothie *
7:Underneath the Harlem Moon
8:Rise 'n' Shine *
9:Here Lies Love
10:Alone Together

Dec. 10, 1932

1:I've Told Every Little Star
2:The Song Is You
3:Please
4:Brother, Can You Spare a Dime?
5:Night and Day *
6:You're an Old Smoothie
7:Rise 'n' Shine
8:Willow Weep For Me
9:Alone Together
10:Underneath the Harlem Moon

Dec. 17, 1932

1:I've Told Every Little Star
2:The Song Is You
3:Night and Day
4:You're an Old Smoothie
5:Brother, Can You Spare a Dime?
6:April in Paris *
7:Please
8:Willow Weep For Me
9:Rise 'n' Shine
10:Alone Together

Dec. 24, 1932

1:I've Told Every Little Star
2:Night and Day
3:The Song Is You
4:You're an Old Smoothie
5:April in Paris
6:Willow Weep For Me
7:Brother, Can You Spare a Dime?
8:Alone Together
9:Please
10:Rise 'n' Shine

Dec. 31, 1932

1:The Song Is You
2:I've Told Every Little Star
3:Night and Day
4:April in Paris
5:Brother, Can You Spare a Dime?
6:Rise 'n' Shine
7:Please
8:You're an Old Smoothie
9:Willow Weep For Me
10:Alone Together

1933

It was FDR's year, purely, simply, and flamboyantly.

He took office on March 4 with his famed "nothing to fear but fear itself" speech, and two days later proclaimed a bank holiday in an attempt to get the country on its financial feet again.

The people watched the celebrated First Hundred Days, and approved. The New Deal was here, and along with the familiar initials of FDR came a marching alphabet of governmental agencies ranging from the NRA to the CCC, the AAA, and the TVA.

Franklin D. Roosevelt was in the headlines even before he took office that year. In February, when he was President-elect, an assassination attempt was made on him in Miami by Giuseppe Zangara, who fired six shots. Although Roosevelt wasn't hit, Chicago mayor Anton Cermak was killed and four others were wounded. The assassin went to the electric chair a month later.

Halfway around the globe another man came to power that same year when Adolf Hitler became Chancellor of Germany, and the swastika flag came into being.

In America Prohibition was finally repealed, Chicago opened its World's Fair, and people were reading *Anthony Adverse, Lost Horizon,* and *God's Little Acre*—not necessarily in that order.

On Broadway it was Irving Berlin's *As Thousands Cheer* and Jerome Kern's *Roberta*. The top song of the year was "Stormy Weather," with six weeks as Number One.

At the movies top pictures were *Little Women* with Katharine Hepburn, and *The Private Life of Henry VIII* with Charles Laughton. But without a doubt the film sensation of the year was a color cartoon short by Walt Disney, *The Three Little Pigs*. It started the nation singing "Who's Afraid of the Big Bad Wolf?"; and those who can read something into anything swore it was a nervous public rebuttal to the Depression.

Jan. 7, 1933

1:The Song Is You
2:Night and Day
3:I've Told Every Little Star
4:April in Paris
5:Rise 'n' Shine
6:You're an Old Smoothie
7:Please
8:Alone Together
9:Willow Weep For Me
10:Brother, Can You Spare a Dime?

Jan. 14, 1933

1:Night and Day
2:I've Told Every Little Star
3:April in Paris
4:The Song Is You
5:You're an Old Smoothie
6:Try a Little Tenderness *
7:Please
8:Rise 'n' Shine
9:Brother, Can You Spare a Dime?
10:Alone Together

Jan. 21, 1933

1:Night and Day
2:The Song Is You
3:April in Paris
4:I've Told Every Little Star
5:Try a Little Tenderness
6:Street of Dreams *
7:You're an Old Smoothie
8:Please
9:Rise 'n' Shine
10:Ole Faithful *

Jan. 28, 1933

1:Night and Day
2:April in Paris
3:The Song Is You
4:Try a Little Tenderness
5:Street of Dreams
6:I've Told Every Little Star
7:Ole Faithful
8:You're an Old Smoothie
9:When It's Lamplighting Time in the Valley *
10:Rise 'n' Shine

Feb. 4, 1933

1:Night and Day
2:April in Paris
3:The Song Is You
4:Street of Dreams
5:Try a Little Tenderness
6:Ole Faithful
7:When It's Lamplighting Time in the Valley
8:I've Told Every Little Star
9:You're an Old Smoothie
10:My Moonlight Madonna *

Feb. 11, 1933

1:April in Paris
2:Night and Day
3:Try a Little Tenderness
4:Street of Dreams
5:The Song Is You
6:My Moonlight Madonna
7:When It's Lamplighting Time in the Valley
8:Ole Faithful
9:I've Told Every Little Star
10:You're an Old Smoothie

Feb. 18, 1933

1:Night and Day
2:April in Paris
3:Ole Faithful
4:When It's Lamplighting Time in the Valley
5:Street of Dreams
6:The Song Is You
7:I've Told Every Little Star
8:You're Getting to Be a Habit With Me *
9:My Moonlight Madonna
10:Try a Little Tenderness

Feb. 25, 1933

1:April in Paris
2:My Moonlight Madonna
3:Ole Faithful
4:Street of Dreams
5:When It's Lamplighting Time in the Valley
6:Night and Day
7:You're Getting to Be a Habit With Me
8:Try a Little Tenderness
9:The Song Is You
10:I've Told Every Little Star

* Newcomer

Mar. 4, 1933

1:April in Paris
2:My Moonlight Madonna
3:Street of Dreams
4:Ole Faithful
5:You're Getting to Be a Habit With Me
6:Shuffle Off to Buffalo *
7:When It's Lamplighting Time in the Valley
8:Night and Day
9:The Song Is You
10:Try a Little Tenderness

Mar. 11, 1933

1:Ole Faithful
2:April in Paris
3:Street of Dreams
4:Shuffle Off to Buffalo
5:My Moonlight Madonna
6:You're Getting to Be a Habit With Me
7:I Cover the Waterfront *
8:Night and Day
9:When It's Lamplighting Time in the Valley
10:Try a Little Tenderness

Mar. 18, 1933

1:April in Paris
2:Shuffle Off to Buffalo
3:Ole Faithful
4:You're Getting to Be a Habit With Me
5:I Cover the Waterfront
6:My Moonlight Madonna
7:Street of Dreams
8:Forty-Second Street *
9:Night and Day
10:When It's Lamplighting Time in the Valley

Mar. 25, 1933

1:Shuffle Off to Buffalo
2:My Moonlight Madonna
3:Forty-Second Street
4:Ole Faithful
5:I Cover the Waterfront
6:You're Getting to Be a Habit With Me
7:In the Valley of the Moon *
8:Street of Dreams
9:April in Paris
10:Night and Day

Apr. 1, 1933

1:Shuffle Off to Buffalo
2:Forty-Second Street
3:My Moonlight Madonna
4:April in Paris
5:Ole Faithful
6:Night and Day
7:I Cover the Waterfront
8:In the Valley of the Moon
9:You're Getting to Be a Habit With Me
10:Have You Ever Been Lonely? *

Apr. 8, 1933

1:Shuffle Off to Buffalo
2:Forty-Second Street
3:In the Valley of the Moon
4:My Moonlight Madonna
5:Lover *
6:Have You Ever Been Lonely?
7:You're Getting to Be a Habit With Me
8:Ole Faithful
9:I Cover the Waterfront
10:Night and Day

Apr. 15, 1933

1:Shuffle Off to Buffalo
2:In the Valley of the Moon
3:Lover
4:Forty-Second Street
5:Have You Ever Been Lonely?
6:My Moonlight Madonna
7:I'll Take an Option On You *
8:You're Getting to Be a Habit With Me
9:Ole Faithful
10:I Cover the Waterfront

Apr. 22, 1933

1:Lover
2:Shuffle Off to Buffalo
3:In the Valley of the Moon
4:I'll Take an Option On You
5:Have You Ever Been Lonely?
6:Forty-Second Street
7:My Moonlight Madonna
8:Hold Me *
9:You're Getting to Be a Habit With Me
10:Ole Faithful

Apr. 29, 1933

1:Lover
2:In the Valley of the Moon
3:I'll Take an Option On You
4:Hold Me
5:Shuffle Off to Buffalo
6:Stormy Weather *
7:Forty-Second Street
8:Have You Ever Been Lonely?
9:My Moonlight Madonna
10:You're Getting to Be a Habit With Me

May 6, 1933

1:In the Valley of the Moon
2:Lover
3:Hold Me
4:I'll Take an Option On You
5:Stormy Weather
6:Forty-Second Street
7:Have You Ever Been Lonely?
8:My Moonlight Madonna
9:Shuffle Off to Buffalo
10:Learn to Croon *

May 13, 1933

1:In the Valley of the Moon
2:Hold Me
3:Lover
4:Stormy Weather
5:I'll Take an Option On You
6:Learn to Croon
7:Have You Ever Been Lonely?
8:Forty-Second Street
9:My Moonlight Madonna
10:Shuffle Off to Buffalo

May 20, 1933

1:In the Valley of the Moon
2:Hold Me
3:Stormy Weather
4:Lover
5:I'll Take an Option On You
6:Learn to Croon
7:Under a Blanket of Blue *
8:Have You Ever Been Lonely?
9:Forty-Second Street
10:My Moonlight Madonna

May 27, 1933

1:Stormy Weather
2:Hold Me
3:In the Valley of the Moon
4:Under a Blanket of Blue
5:Lover
6:Learn to Croon
7:I'll Take an Option On You
8:Sophisticated Lady *
9:Have You Ever Been Lonely?
10:Forty-Second Street

June 3, 1933

1:Stormy Weather
2:Under a Blanket of Blue
3:Hold Me
4:In the Valley of the Moon
5:Learn to Croon
6:Lover
7:I'll Take an Option On You
8:Sophisticated Lady
9:Shadow Waltz *
10:Have You Ever Been Lonely?

June 10, 1933

1:Stormy Weather
2:Under a Blanket of Blue
3:Sophisticated Lady
4:Hold Me
5:Lover
6:Learn to Croon
7:Shadow Waltz
8:I'll Take an Option On You
9:In the Valley of the Moon
10:Don't Blame Me *

June 17, 1933

1:Stormy Weather
2:Under a Blanket of Blue
3:Sophisticated Lady
4:Shadow Waltz
5:Don't Blame Me
6:In the Valley of the Moon
7:Learn to Croon
8:Lover
9:Hold Me
10:I'll Take an Option On You

June 24, 1933

1:Stormy Weather
2:Under a Blanket of Blue
3:Shadow Waltz
4:Don't Blame Me
5:Sophisticated Lady
6:Hold Me
7:Learn to Croon
8:We're In the Money *
9:In the Valley of the Moon
10:Lover

July 1, 1933

1:Under a Blanket of Blue
2:Stormy Weather
3:Sophisticated Lady
4:Shadow Waltz
5:Don't Blame Me
6:Hold Me
7:We're In the Money
8:Lazy Bones *
9:Lover
10:Learn to Croon

July 8, 1933

1:Stormy Weather
2:Sophisticated Lady
3:Under a Blanket of Blue
4:Don't Blame Me
5:Shadow Waltz
6:We're In the Money
7:Hold Me
8:Lazy Bones
9:Lover
10:Blue Prelude *

July 15, 1933

1:Sophisticated Lady
2:Under a Blanket of Blue
3:Don't Blame Me
4:Shadow Waltz
5:Stormy Weather
6:Lazy Bones
7:We're In the Money
8:Blue Prelude
9:Hold Me
10:Lover

July 22, 1933

1:Under a Blanket of Blue
2:Sophisticated Lady
3:We're In the Money
4:Don't Blame Me
5:Blue Prelude
6:Lazy Bones
7:Marching Along Together *
8:Shadow Waltz
9:Stormy Weather
10:Hold Me

July 29, 1933

1:Sophisticated Lady
2:Under a Blanket of Blue
3:Lazy Bones
4:We're In the Money
5:Shadow Waltz
6:Don't Blame Me
7:Blue Prelude
8:Marching Along Together
9:Hold Me
10:It Isn't Fair *

Aug. 5, 1933

1:Lazy Bones
2:Under a Blanket of Blue
3:Sophisticated Lady
4:Blue Prelude
5:Don't Blame Me
6:Shadow Waltz
7:We're In the Money
8:Marching Along Together
9:It Isn't Fair
10:Who's Afraid of the Big Bad Wolf? *

Aug. 12, 1933

1:Lazy Bones
2:Blue Prelude
3:Under a Blanket of Blue
4:Shadow Waltz
5:Marching Along Together
6:Sophisticated Lady
7:Don't Blame Me
8:It Isn't Fair
9:Who's Afraid of the Big Bad Wolf?
10:We're In the Money

Aug. 19, 1933

1:Lazy Bones
2:Who's Afraid of the Big Bad Wolf?
3:Blue Prelude
4:It Isn't Fair
5:Marching Along Together
6:Don't Blame Me
7:Shadow Waltz
8:Under a Blanket of Blue
9:Sophisticated Lady
10:The Last Roundup *

Aug. 26, 1933

1:Lazy Bones
2:Who's Afraid of the Big Bad Wolf?
3:It Isn't Fair
4:Blue Prelude
5:The Last Roundup
6:Love Is the Sweetest Thing *
7:Don't Blame Me
8:Marching Along Together
9:Shadow Waltz
10:Under a Blanket of Blue

Sept. 2, 1933

1:Lazy Bones
2:It Isn't Fair
3:Love Is the Sweetest Thing
4:Who's Afraid of the Big Bad Wolf?
5:The Last Roundup
6:Blue Prelude
7:Don't Blame Me
8:Marching Along Together
9:It's the Talk of the Town *
10:Under a Blanket of Blue

Sept. 9, 1933

1:Who's Afraid of the Big Bad Wolf?
2:Love Is the Sweetest Thing
3:The Last Roundup
4:Lazy Bones
5:It Isn't Fair
6:It's the Talk of the Town
7:Blue Prelude
8:Don't Blame Me
9:It's Only a Paper Moon *
10:Marching Along Together

Sept. 16, 1933

1:Love Is the Sweetest Thing
2:The Last Roundup
3:Who's Afraid of the Big Bad Wolf?
4:Lazy Bones
5:It's the Talk of the Town
6:It's Only a Paper Moon
7:Don't Blame Me
8:It Isn't Fair
9:Blue Prelude
10:Marching Along Together

Sept. 23, 1933

1:Love Is the Sweetest Thing
2:The Last Roundup
3:It's the Talk of the Town
4:It's Only a Paper Moon
5:Who's Afraid of the Big Bad Wolf?
6:Annie Doesn't Live Here Anymore *
7:Don't Blame Me
8:It Isn't Fair
9:Lazy Bones
10:Blue Prelude

Sept. 30, 1933

1:Love Is the Sweetest Thing
2:The Last Roundup
3:It's the Talk of the Town
4:Annie Doesn't Live Here Anymore
5:It's Only a Paper Moon
6:Don't Blame Me
7:Blue Prelude
8:Lazy Bones
9:It Isn't Fair
10:Who's Afraid of the Big Bad Wolf?

Oct. 7, 1933

1:The Last Roundup
2:Love Is the Sweetest Thing
3:It's the Talk of the Town
4:By a Waterfall *
5:It's Only a Paper Moon
6:Annie Doesn't Live Here Anymore
7:Who's Afraid of the Big Bad Wolf?
8:It Isn't Fair
9:Don't Blame Me
10:Lazy Bones

Oct. 14, 1933

1:The Last Roundup
2:Love Is the Sweetest Thing
3:By a Waterfall
4:It's the Talk of the Town
5:Annie Doesn't Live Here Anymore
6:It's Only a Paper Moon
7:If I Love Again *
8:Who's Afraid of the Big Bad Wolf?
9:It Isn't Fair
10:Don't Blame Me

Oct. 21, 1933

1:The Last Roundup
2:By a Waterfall
3:It's the Talk of the Town
4:If I Love Again
5:Annie Doesn't Live Here Anymore
6:It's Only a Paper Moon
7:The Old Spinning Wheel *
8:Love Is the Sweetest Thing
9:It Isn't Fair
10:Who's Afraid of the Big Bad Wolf?

Oct. 28, 1933

1:By a Waterfall
2:It's the Talk of the Town
3:If I Love Again
4:The Last Roundup
5:The Old Spinning Wheel
6:It's Only a Paper Moon
7:Who's Afraid of the Big Bad Wolf?
8:Annie Doesn't Live Here Anymore
9:It Isn't Fair
10:Love Is the Sweetest Thing

Nov. 4, 1933

1:By a Waterfall
2:If I Love Again
3:It's the Talk of the Town
4:Annie Doesn't Live Here Anymore
5:The Old Spinning Wheel
6:The Last Roundup
7:It's Only a Paper Moon
8:Easter Parade *
9:Love Is the Sweetest Thing
10:Who's Afraid of the Big Bad Wolf?

Nov. 11, 1933

1:By a Waterfall
2:It's the Talk of the Town
3:If I Love Again
4:Easter Parade
5:Annie Doesn't Live Here Anymore
6:The Last Roundup
7:Who's Afraid of the Big Bad Wolf?
8:It's Only a Paper Moon
9:The Old Spinning Wheel
10:Love Is the Sweetest Thing

Nov. 18, 1933

1:It's the Talk of the Town
2:If I Love Again
3:By a Waterfall
4:Annie Doesn't Live Here Anymore
5:Easter Parade
6:Heatwave *
7:The Last Roundup
8:It's Only a Paper Moon
9:Love Is the Sweetest Thing
10:The Old Spinning Wheel

Nov. 25, 1933

1:If I Love Again
2:It's the Talk of the Town
3:Annie Doesn't Live Here Anymore
4:By a Waterfall
5:Smoke Gets In Your Eyes *
6:Easter Parade
7:Heatwave
8:The Last Roundup
9:It's Only a Paper Moon
10:Love Is the Sweetest Thing

Dec. 2, 1933

1:If I Love Again
2:It's the Talk of the Town
3:Smoke Gets In Your Eyes
4:Easter Parade
5:Heatwave
6:Did You Ever See a Dream Walking? *
7:Annie Doesn't Live Here Anymore
8:By a Waterfall
9:The Last Roundup
10:It's Only a Paper Moon

Dec. 9, 1933

1:If I Love Again
2:Smoke Gets In Your Eyes
3:Easter Parade
4:Did You Ever See a Dream Walking?
5:Heatwave
6:It's the Talk of the Town
7:Yesterdays *
8:Annie Doesn't Live Here Anymore
9:By a Waterfall
10:It's Only a Paper Moon

Dec. 16, 1933

1:Smoke Gets In Your Eyes
2:If I Love Again
3:Did You Ever See a Dream Walking?
4:Heatwave
5:Yesterdays
6:Easter Parade
7:Annie Doesn't Live Here Anymore
8:The Touch of Your Hand *
9:It's the Talk of the Town
10:By a Waterfall

Dec. 23, 1933

1:Smoke Gets In Your Eyes
2:Did You Ever See a Dream Walking?
3:Easter Parade
4:If I Love Again
5:Heatwave
6:Yesterdays
7:The Touch of Your Hand
8:Annie Doesn't Live Here Anymore
9:By a Waterfall
10:It's the Talk of the Town

Dec. 30, 1933

1:Smoke Gets In Your Eyes
2:Did You Ever See a Dream Walking?
3:The Touch of Your Hand
4:Yesterdays
5:If I Love Again
6:Heatwave
7:Easter Parade
8:By a Waterfall
9:It's the Talk of the Town
10:Annie Doesn't Live Here Anymore

1934

It was a year of violence. It was The G-Men versus The Bank Robbers and The Kidnappers. They got Pretty Boy Floyd, Baby Face Nelson, John Dillinger, and that couple who were to become so famous more than thirty years later that their first names required no last names for identification—Bonnie and Clyde.

Bruno Richard Hauptmann was arrested and charged with the kidnapping and murder of the Lindbergh baby.

Von Hindenburg died in Germany and Hitler combined the offices of president and chancellor to become Führer. Concentration camps appeared, and an alliance was made with Italian dictator Benito Mussolini. In America Russ Columbo died at twenty-six in a freak shooting accident.

Yet, with all this, one of the biggest news events of the year was a happy one in Ontario, Canada, where Mrs. Oliva Dionne gave birth to her famed quintuplets. And little Finland paid her World War I debt to the United States—the only nation to do so.

The St. Louis Cardinals won the World Series against the Detroit Tigers four games to three—with all four games being won by the pitching Dean brothers, Dizzy and Daffy.

Cole Porter's *Anything Goes,* with Ethel Merman, was the biggest thing on Broadway, and the biggest thing on the screen was *It Happened One Night,* which won Oscars for Best Picture, Best Director (Frank Capra), Best Actor (Clark Gable), and Best Actress (Claudette Colbert).

Best-selling books of the year were James Hilton's *Goodbye, Mr. Chips,* John O'Hara's *Appointment in Samarra,* and Walter Pitkin's book with the built-in reading audience, *Life Begins at 40.*

On the radio there were Eddie Cantor, Bing Crosby, and—still—Amos 'n' Andy. On the Top Ten, six weeks as Number One made "Lost in a Fog" the top song of 1934.

Jan. 6, 1934

1:Did You Ever See a Dream Walking?
2:Smoke Gets In Your Eyes
3:Yesterdays
4:The Touch of Your Hand
5:Heatwave
6:If I Love Again
7:Easter Parade
8:Everything I Have Is Yours *
9:By a Waterfall
10:Annie Doesn't Live Here Anymore

Jan. 13, 1934

1:Smoke Gets In Your Eyes
2:Did You Ever See a Dream Walking?
3:Yesterdays
4:The Touch of Your Hand
5:Everything I Have Is Yours
6:Temptation *
7:Heatwave
8:If I Love Again
9:Easter Parade
10:By a Waterfall

Jan. 20, 1934

1:Did You Ever See a Dream Walking?
2:Smoke Gets In Your Eyes
3:Everything I Have Is Yours
4:Temptation
5:Yesterdays
6:The Touch of Your Hand
7:If I Love Again
8:Easter Parade
9:Flying Down to Rio *
10:Heatwave

Jan. 27, 1934

1:Smoke Gets In Your Eyes
2:Did You Ever See a Dream Walking?
3:Temptation
4:Everything I Have Is Yours
5:Flying Down to Rio
6:Carioca *
7:Yesterdays
8:Heatwave
9:The Touch of Your Hand
10:Easter Parade

Feb. 3, 1934

1:Did You Ever See a Dream Walking?
2:Temptation
3:Smoke Gets In Your Eyes
4:Everything I Have Is Yours
5:Carioca
6:Flying Down to Rio
7:The Touch of Your Hand
8:Yesterdays
9:Easter Parade
10:Heatwave

Feb. 10, 1934

1:Did You Ever See a Dream Walking?
2:Temptation
3:Everything I Have Is Yours
4:Carioca
5:Flying Down to Rio
6:Smoke Gets In Your Eyes
7:Let's Fall in Love *
8:Yesterdays
9:Easter Parade
10:The Touch of Your Hand

Feb. 17, 1934

1:Did You Ever See a Dream Walking?
2:Temptation
3:Everything I Have Is Yours
4:Let's Fall in Love
5:Carioca
6:Flying Down to Rio
7:Smoke Gets In Your Eyes
8:Boulevard of Broken Dreams *
9:Yesterdays
10:The Touch of Your Hand

Feb. 24, 1934

1:Temptation
2:Did You Ever See a Dream Walking?
3:Let's Fall in Love
4:Carioca
5:Boulevard of Broken Dreams
6:Everything I Have Is Yours
7:Flying Down to Rio
8:Smoke Gets In Your Eyes
9:The Touch of Your Hand
10:Yesterdays

* Newcomer

Mar. 3, 1934

1:Temptation
2:Let's Fall in Love
3:Carioca
4:Boulevard of Broken Dreams
5:Flying Down to Rio
6:Orchids in the Moonlight *
7:Everything I Have Is Yours
8:Smoke Gets In Your Eyes
9:Did You Ever See a Dream Walking?
10:Yesterdays

Mar. 10, 1934

1:Temptation
2:Let's Fall in Love
3:Boulevard of Broken Dreams
4:Carioca
5:Orchids in the Moonlight
6:Did You Ever See a Dream Walking?
7:Wagon Wheels *
8:Flying Down to Rio
9:Everything I Have Is Yours
10:Smoke Gets In Your Eyes

Mar. 17, 1934

1:Let's Fall in Love
2:Temptation
3:Wagon Wheels
4:Carioca
5:Boulevard of Broken Dreams
6:Everything I Have Is Yours
7:You Oughta Be in Pictures *
8:Orchids in the Moonlight
9:Flying Down to Rio
10:Did You Ever See a Dream Walking?

Mar. 24, 1934

1:Let's Fall in Love
2:Wagon Wheels
3:Temptation
4:Boulevard of Broken Dreams
5:Carioca
6:You Oughta Be in Pictures
7:Everything I Have Is Yours
8:Flying Down to Rio
9:Orchids in the Moonlight
10:The Beat o' My Heart *

Mar. 31, 1934

1:Wagon Wheels
2:Let's Fall in Love
3:Temptation
4:Carioca
5:The Beat o' My Heart
6:Orchids in the Moonlight
7:Boulevard of Broken Dreams
8:Everything I Have Is Yours
9:You Oughta Be in Pictures
10:True *

Apr. 7, 1934

1:Wagon Wheels
2:You Oughta Be in Pictures
3:Temptation
4:The Beat o' My Heart
5:Carioca
6:Let's Fall in Love
7:Orchids in the Moonlight
8:True
9:Boulevard of Broken Dreams
10:I'll String Along With You *

Apr. 14, 1934

1:Wagon Wheels
2:The Beat o' My Heart
3:Temptation
4:You Oughta Be in Pictures
5:I'll String Along With You
6:Little Man, You've Had a Busy Day *
7:Carioca
8:Let's Fall in Love
9:Orchids in the Moonlight
10:Boulevard of Broken Dreams

Apr. 21, 1934

1:The Beat o' My Heart
2:Wagon Wheels
3:I'll String Along With You
4:Temptation
5:Little Man, You've Had a Busy Day
6:You Oughta Be in Pictures
7:The Champagne Waltz *
8:Thank You For a Lovely Evening *
9:Let's Fall in Love
10:Carioca

Apr. 28, 1934

1:The Beat o' My Heart
2:Wagon Wheels
3:The Champagne Waltz
4:I'll String Along With You
5:Temptation
6:Thank You For a Lovely Evening
7:Love Thy Neighbor *
8:Little Man, You've Had a Busy Day
9:You Oughta Be in Pictures
10:Let's Fall in Love

May 5, 1934

1:The Beat o' My Heart
2:The Champagne Waltz
3:Love Thy Neighbor
4:Thank You For a Lovely Evening
5:Little Man, You've Had a Busy Day
6:Temptation
7:I'll String Along With You
8:Wagon Wheels
9:Pardon My Southern Accent *
10:You Oughta Be in Pictures

May 12, 1934

1:Little Man, You've Had a Busy Day
2:Love Thy Neighbor
3:The Beat o' My Heart
4:The Champagne Waltz
5:Thank You For a Lovely Evening
6:I'll String Along With You
7:Pardon My Southern Accent
8:Temptation
9:No, No, a Thousand Times No *
10:Wagon Wheels

May 19, 1934

1:Love Thy Neighbor
2:Thank You For a Lovely Evening
3:The Champagne Waltz
4:Little Man, You've Had a Busy Day
5:The Beat o' My Heart
6:I'll String Along With You
7:No, No, a Thousand Times No
8:Temptation
9:Lost in a Fog *
10:Be Still, My Heart *

May 26, 1934

1:Love Thy Neighbor
2:Thank You For a Lovely Evening
3:The Beat o' My Heart
4:Lost in a Fog
5:Be Still, My Heart
6:The Champagne Waltz
7:Little Man, You've Had a Busy Day
8:I'll String Along With You
9:No, No, a Thousand Times No
10:All I Do Is Dream of You *

June 2, 1934

1:Love Thy Neighbor
2:Lost in a Fog
3:Thank You For a Lovely Evening
4:All I Do Is Dream of You
5:Cocktails For Two *
6:The Beat o' My Heart
7:The Champagne Waltz
8:Be Still, My Heart
9:The Very Thought of You *
10:Little Man, You've Had a Busy Day

June 9, 1934

1:Love Thy Neighbor
2:Lost in a Fog
3:All I Do Is Dream of You
4:Cocktails For Two
5:Be Still, My Heart
6:The Very Thought of You
7:What a Difference a Day Made *
8:Thank You For a Lovely Evening
9:The Beat o' My Heart
10:The Champagne Waltz

June 16, 1934

1:Lost in a Fog
2:Cocktails For Two
3:Be Still, My Heart
4:Love Thy Neighbor
5:The Very Thought of You
6:What a Difference a Day Made
7:All I Do Is Dream of You
8:Thank You For a Lovely Evening
9:The Champagne Waltz
10:The Beat o' My Heart

June 23, 1934

1:Lost in a Fog
2:Be Still, My Heart
3:Love Thy Neighbor
4:Cocktails For Two
5:What a Difference a Day Made
6:All I Do Is Dream of You
7:The Very Thought of You
8:Thank You For a Lovely Evening
9:Love Is Just Around the Corner *
10:The Beat o' My Heart

June 30, 1934

1:Lost in a Fog
2:Be Still, My Heart
3:What a Difference a Day Made
4:The Very Thought of You
5:Love Is Just Around the Corner
6:All I Do Is Dream of You
7:Cocktails For Two
8:Love Thy Neighbor
9:Thank You For a Lovely Evening
10:The Beat o' My Heart

July 7, 1934

1:Lost in a Fog
2:What a Difference a Day Made
3:Love Is Just Around the Corner
4:All I Do Is Dream of You
5:The Very Thought of You
6:Be Still, My Heart
7:The Moon Was Yellow *
8:I Saw Stars *
9:Love Thy Neighbor
10:Cocktails For Two

July 14, 1934

1:Lost in a Fog
2:What a Difference a Day Made
3:All I Do Is Dream of You
4:Love Is Just Around the Corner
5:The Very Thought of You
6:Be Still, My Heart
7:The Moon Was Yellow
8:Love Thy Neighbor
9:I Saw Stars
10:Cocktails For Two

July 21, 1934

1:Lost in a Fog
2:What a Difference a Day Made
3:Love Is Just Around the Corner
4:All I Do Is Dream of You
5:With My Eyes Wide Open I'm Dreaming *
6:One Night of Love *
7:The Very Thought of You
8:The Moon Was Yellow
9:I Saw Stars
10:Be Still, My Heart

July 28, 1934

1:What a Difference a Day Made
2:Lost in a Fog
3:With My Eyes Wide Open I'm Dreaming
4:The Very Thought of You
5:Love Is Just Around the Corner
6:One Night of Love
7:The Moon Was Yellow
8:All I Do Is Dream of You
9:I Saw Stars
10:I Only Have Eyes For You *

Aug. 4, 1934

1:What a Difference a Day Made
2:With My Eyes Wide Open I'm Dreaming
3:One Night of Love
4:The Very Thought of You
5:Love in Bloom *
6:Lost in a Fog
7:I Saw Stars
8:Love Is Just Around the Corner
9:I Only Have Eyes For You
10:The Moon Was Yellow

Aug. 11, 1934

1:With My Eyes Wide Open I'm Dreaming
2:One Night of Love
3:Love in Bloom
4:What a Difference a Day Made
5:Love Is Just Around the Corner
6:The Very Thought of You
7:I Saw Stars
8:I Only Have Eyes For You
9:Lost in a Fog
10:The Moon Was Yellow

Aug. 18, 1934

1:With My Eyes Wide Open I'm Dreaming
2:One Night of Love
3:Love in Bloom
4:I Only Have Eyes For You
5:What a Difference a Day Made
6:Two Cigarettes in the Dark *
7:The Very Thought of You
8:The Moon Was Yellow
9:Love Is Just Around the Corner
10:I Saw Stars

Aug. 25, 1934

1:One Night of Love
2:Love in Bloom
3:With My Eyes Wide Open I'm Dreaming
4:Two Cigarettes in the Dark
5:I Only Have Eyes For You
6:What a Difference a Day Made
7:The Very Thought of You
8:Love Is Just Around the Corner
9:Moonglow *
10:I Saw Stars

Sept. 1, 1934

1:One Night of Love
2:Love in Bloom
3:Two Cigarettes in the Dark
4:I Only Have Eyes For You
5:With My Eyes Wide Open I'm Dreaming
6:Moonglow
7:What a Difference a Day Made
8:My Old Flame *
9:The Very Thought of You
10:Love Is Just Around the Corner

Sept. 8, 1934

1:One Night of Love
2:Two Cigarettes in the Dark
3:Love in Bloom
4:I Only Have Eyes For You
5:Moonglow
6:My Old Flame
7:With My Eyes Wide Open I'm Dreaming
8:What a Difference a Day Made
9:You're a Builder-Upper *
10:The Very Thought of You

Sept. 15, 1934

1:Two Cigarettes in the Dark
2:One Night of Love
3:I Only Have Eyes For You
4:Moonglow
5:You're a Builder-Upper
6:Love in Bloom
7:My Old Flame
8:With My Eyes Wide Open I'm Dreaming
9:Out in the Cold Again *
10:What a Difference a Day Made

Sept. 22, 1934

1:Two Cigarettes in the Dark
2:I Only Have Eyes For You
3:One Night of Love
4:You're a Builder-Upper
5:Moonglow
6:Love in Bloom
7:Out in the Cold Again
8:My Old Flame
9:What a Difference a Day Made
10:With My Eyes Wide Open I'm Dreaming

Sept. 29, 1934

1:Two Cigarettes in the Dark
2:I Only Have Eyes For You
3:Moonglow
4:Love in Bloom
5:One Night of Love
6:Out in the Cold Again
7:You're a Builder-Upper
8:My Old Flame
9:With My Eyes Wide Open I'm Dreaming
10:Hands Across the Table *

Oct. 6, 1934

1:I Only Have Eyes For You
2:Two Cigarettes in the Dark
3:Out in the Cold Again
4:Hands Across the Table
5:Moonglow
6:Love in Bloom
7:Stars Fell On Alabama *
8:One Night of Love
9:You're a Builder-Upper
10:With My Eyes Wide Open I'm Dreaming

Oct. 13, 1934

1:I Only Have Eyes For You
2:Two Cigarettes in the Dark
3:Hands Across the Table
4:Stars Fell On Alabama
5:Out in the Cold Again
6:One Night of Love
7:Love in Bloom
8:Moonglow
9:You're a Builder-Upper
10:The Continental *

Oct. 20, 1934

1:I Only Have Eyes For You
2:Hands Across the Table
3:Stars Fell On Alabama
4:The Continental
5:Two Cigarettes in the Dark
6:Out in the Cold Again
7:Moonglow
8:One Night of Love
9:Love in Bloom
10:The Object of My Affection *

Oct. 27, 1934

1:I Only Have Eyes For You
2:The Continental
3:Hands Across the Table
4:Stars Fell On Alabama
5:Two Cigarettes in the Dark
6:The Object of My Affection
7:Out in the Cold Again
8:Moonglow
9:One Night of Love
10:Blue Moon *

Nov. 3, 1934

1:The Continental
2:Stars Fell On Alabama
3:I Only Have Eyes For You
4:Blue Moon
5:The Object of My Affection
6:Hands Across the Table
7:Two Cigarettes in the Dark
8:Out in the Cold Again
9:Moonglow
10:I'll Follow My Secret Heart *

Nov. 10, 1934

1:Stars Fell On Alabama
2:The Continental
3:Blue Moon
4:The Object of My Affection
5:I'll Follow My Secret Heart
6:Stay As Sweet As You Are *
7:I Only Have Eyes For You
8:Hands Across the Table
9:Moonglow
10:Out in the Cold Again

Nov. 17, 1934

1:Stars Fell On Alabama
2:I'll Follow My Secret Heart
3:The Object of My Affection
4:Stay As Sweet As You Are
5:The Continental
6:Blue Moon
7:I Only Have Eyes For You
8:Winter Wonderland *
9:Santa Claus Is Coming to Town *
10:Hands Across the Table

Nov. 24, 1934

1:Stars Fell On Alabama
2:The Object of My Affection
3:Stay As Sweet As You Are
4:I'll Follow My Secret Heart
5:Winter Wonderland
6:Blue Moon
7:Santa Claus Is Coming to Town
8:The Continental
9:I Only Have Eyes For You
10:Hands Across the Table

Dec. 1, 1934

1:Stay As Sweet As You Are
2:Stars Fell On Alabama
3:Winter Wonderland
4:I'll Follow My Secret Heart
5:Santa Claus Is Coming to Town
6:Anything Goes *
7:Blue Moon
8:I Get a Kick Out of You *
9:The Object of My Affection
10:The Continental

Dec. 8, 1934

1:Stay As Sweet As You Are
2:Stars Fell On Alabama
3:The Object of My Affection
4:Winter Wonderland
5:Anything Goes
6:I Get a Kick Out of You
7:Blue Moon
8:Santa Claus Is Coming to Town
9:I'll Follow My Secret Heart
10:The Continental

Dec. 15, 1934

1:Stay As Sweet As You Are
2:I Get a Kick Out of You
3:Santa Claus Is Coming to Town
4:Winter Wonderland
5:The Object of My Affection
6:Anything Goes
7:Blue Moon
8:You're the Top *
9:All Through the Night *
10:Stars Fell On Alabama

Dec. 22, 1934

1:Stay As Sweet As You Are
2:Santa Claus Is Coming to Town
3:I Get a Kick Out of You
4:Winter Wonderland
5:Blue Moon
6:The Object of My Affection
7:Anything Goes
8:All Through the Night
9:You're the Top
10:Blow, Gabriel, Blow *

Dec. 29, 1934

1:Santa Claus Is Coming to Town
2:The Object of My Affection
3:Blue Moon
4:I Get a Kick Out of You
5:Stay As Sweet As You Are
6:Winter Wonderland
7:Anything Goes
8:Blow, Gabriel, Blow
9:You're the Top
10:All Through the Night

1935

As far as this compilation is concerned, the most important musical event of 1935 occurred on the night of April 20 when radio recognized the top songs of the week with the first broadcast of a new weekly Saturday night network show, "Your Hit Parade."

The first song ever to be Number One on the show: "Soon." The top songs of the year: "Chasing Shadows" and "Cheek to Cheek," tied with five weeks apiece as Number One.

Shirley Temple reigned supreme in the movies, singing "On the Good Ship Lollipop" onto the Top Ten. Major films of the year were *Mutiny on the Bounty* and *The Informer*. On Broadway top shows were *Three Men on a Horse, Dead End, The Petrified Forest,* and George Gershwin's *Porgy and Bess*.

Civil war raged in Greece. Mussolini used dive bombers to attack spear-carrying Ethiopians. Mary Pickford divorced Douglas Fairbanks.

Will Rogers and Wiley Post died when Post's plane crashed near Point Barrow, Alaska. Huey Long, dictatorial leader of Louisiana, was assassinated in Baton Rouge. Gang leader Dutch Schultz was shot to death in a New Jersey saloon. The Supreme Court killed the Blue Eagle of the NRA, but the New Deal gave us the WPA in its place.

Bruno Richard Hauptmann was convicted in the Lindbergh case. Babe Ruth left the Yankees for the Boston Braves. James Braddock took the heavyweight boxing crown from Max Baer, but down in the ranks, coming up fast, was a young black boxer named J. L. Barrow of Detroit. He fought under the name of Joe Louis.

Americans were playing that new game, Monopoly, and engaging in a ten-cent chain-letter craze that was blanketing the country. What were they singing? These songs . . .

Jan. 5, 1935

1:The Object of My Affection
2:Winter Wonderland
3:I Get a Kick Out of You
4:Blue Moon
5:Anything Goes
6:Santa Claus Is Coming to Town
7:Blow, Gabriel, Blow
8:Stay As Sweet As You Are
9:All Through the Night
10:You're the Top

Jan. 12, 1935

1:The Object of My Affection
2:Blue Moon
3:I Get a Kick Out of You
4:Winter Wonderland
5:Anything Goes
6:June in January *
7:You and the Night and the Music *
8:Blow, Gabriel, Blow
9:You're the Top
10:All Through the Night

Jan. 19, 1935

1:The Object of My Affection
2:I Get a Kick Out of You
3:Blue Moon
4:June in January
5:You and the Night and the Music
6:Winter Wonderland
7:Anything Goes
8:Blow, Gabriel, Blow
9:All Through the Night
10:You're the Top

Jan. 26, 1935

1:Blue Moon
2:I Get a Kick Out of You
3:The Object of My Affection
4:June in January
5:You and the Night and the Music
6:If There Is Someone Lovelier Than You *
7:Winter Wonderland
8:Anything Goes
9:You're the Top
10:All Through the Night

Feb. 2, 1935

1:I Get a Kick Out of You
2:Blue Moon
3:June in January
4:You and the Night and the Music
5:If There Is Someone Lovelier Than You
6:On the Good Ship Lollipop *
7:The Object of My Affection
8:Winter Wonderland
9:You're the Top
10:Anything Goes

Feb. 9, 1935

1:I Get a Kick Out of You
2:June in January
3:You and the Night and the Music
4:On the Good Ship Lollipop
5:When I Grow Too Old to Dream *
6:Isle of Capri *
7:If There Is Someone Lovelier Than You
8:The Object of My Affection
9:Winter Wonderland
10:Blue Moon

Feb. 16, 1935

1:June in January
2:I Get a Kick Out of You
3:When I Grow Too Old to Dream
4:Isle of Capri
5:On the Good Ship Lollipop
6:Solitude *
7:Here Comes Cookie *
8:You and the Night and the Music
9:Blue Moon
10:If There Is Someone Lovelier Than You

Feb. 23, 1935

1:June in January
2:Isle of Capri
3:When I Grow Too Old to Dream
4:Solitude
5:Here Comes Cookie
6:On the Good Ship Lollipop
7:I Get a Kick Out of You
8:You and the Night and the Music
9:Blue Moon
10:Lovely to Look At *

* Newcomer

Mar. 2, 1935

1:Isle of Capri
2:Here Comes Cookie
3:When I Grow Too Old to Dream
4:Solitude
5:June in January
6:On the Good Ship Lollipop
7:Lovely to Look At
8:I Won't Dance *
9:Easy to Remember *
10:I Get a Kick Out of You

Mar. 9, 1935

1:Isle of Capri
2:Here Comes Cookie
3:When I Grow Too Old to Dream
4:Solitude
5:I Won't Dance
6:Easy to Remember
7:Lovely to Look At
8:Soon *
9:June in January
10:On the Good Ship Lollipop

Mar. 16, 1935

1:Isle of Capri
2:Solitude
3:Easy to Remember
4:When I Grow Too Old to Dream
5:Lovely to Look At
6:Soon
7:I Won't Dance
8:Here Comes Cookie
9:Lullaby of Broadway *
10:June in January

Mar. 23, 1935

1:Isle of Capri
2:Solitude
3:Here Comes Cookie
4:Easy to Remember
5:Soon
6:When I Grow Too Old to Dream
7:Lovely to Look At
8:I Won't Dance
9:Lullaby of Broadway
10:It's an Old Southern Custom *

Mar. 30, 1935

1:Here Comes Cookie
2:Isle of Capri
3:I Won't Dance
4:Soon
5:Lovely to Look At
6:Lullaby of Broadway
7:When I Grow Too Old to Dream
8:Easy to Remember
9:It's an Old Southern Custom
10:Solitude

Apr. 6, 1935

1:I Won't Dance
2:Soon
3:Isle of Capri
4:Lullaby of Broadway
5:Here Comes Cookie
6:Solitude
7:Easy to Remember
8:Lovely to Look At
9:When I Grow Too Old to Dream
10:If the Moon Turns Green *

Apr. 13, 1935

1:I Won't Dance
2:Soon
3:Lullaby of Broadway
4:Lovely to Look At
5:Isle of Capri
6:Every Day *
7:Easy to Remember
8:Here Comes Cookie
9:When I Grow Too Old to Dream
10:Solitude

Apr. 20, 1935

1:Soon
2:Lullaby of Broadway
3:Lovely to Look At
4:I Won't Dance
5:When I Grow Too Old to Dream
6:Isle of Capri
7:Every Day
8:I Was Lucky *
9:Everything's Been Done Before *
10:Easy to Remember

Apr. 27, 1935

1:Lovely to Look At
2:Lullaby of Broadway
3:When I Grow Too Old to Dream
4:Soon
5:Isle of Capri
6:I Was Lucky
7:I Won't Dance
8:Every Day
9:Whose Honey Are You? *
10:Once Upon a Midnight *

May 4, 1935

1:Lullaby of Broadway
2:Soon
3:Lovely to Look At
4:I Won't Dance
5:Life Is a Song *
6:Isle of Capri
7:When I Grow Too Old to Dream
8:I Was Lucky
9:Every Day
10:You're a Heavenly Thing *

May 11, 1935

1:Lullaby of Broadway
2:Soon
3:When I Grow Too Old to Dream
4:Life Is a Song
5:Lovely to Look At
6:About a Quarter to Nine *
7:I Won't Dance
8:She's a Latin From Manhattan *
9:Every Day
10:What's the Reason? *

May 18, 1935

1:What's the Reason?
2:I Won't Dance
3:When I Grow Too Old to Dream
4:Lullaby of Broadway
5:Lovely to Look At
6:She's a Latin From Manhattan
7:Life Is a Song
8:Tell Me That You Love Me *
9:About a Quarter to Nine
10:Love and a Dime *

May 25, 1935

1:What's the Reason?
2:When I Grow Too Old to Dream
3:She's a Latin From Manhattan
4:About a Quarter to Nine
5:Lullaby of Broadway
6:Life Is a Song
7:I Won't Dance
8:Tell Me That You Love Me
9:Way Back Home *
10:Lovely to Look At

June 1, 1935

1:Life Is a Song
2:Lullaby of Broadway
3:What's the Reason?
4:She's a Latin From Manhattan
5:About a Quarter to Nine
6:In the Middle of a Kiss *
7:In a Little Gypsy Tea Room *
8:Tell Me That You Love Me
9:Flowers For Madame *
10:Would There Be Love? *

June 8, 1935

1:Life Is a Song
2:What's the Reason?
3:Tell Me That You Love Me
4:Chasing Shadows *
5:About a Quarter to Nine
6:Lullaby of Broadway
7:In a Little Gypsy Tea Room
8:In the Middle of a Kiss
9:Seein' is Believin' *
10:She's a Latin From Manhattan

June 15, 1935

1:In a Little Gypsy Tea Room
2:Life Is a Song
3:What's the Reason?
4:In the Middle of a Kiss
5:About a Quarter to Nine
6:Lullaby of Broadway
7:Restless *
8:Chasing Shadows
9:She's a Latin From Manhattan
10:Tell Me That You Love Me

June 22, 1935

1:Chasing Shadows
2:In a Little Gypsy Tea Room
3:About a Quarter to Nine
4:In the Middle of a Kiss
5:What's the Reason?
6:The Lady in Red *
7:Life Is a Song
8:I'll Never Say "Never Again," Again *
9:Tell Me That You Love Me
10:Kiss Me Goodnight *

June 29, 1935

1:Chasing Shadows
2:In a Little Gypsy Tea Room
3:In the Middle of a Kiss
4:About a Quarter to Nine
5:Life Is a Song
6:What's the Reason?
7:The Lady in Red
8:Thrilled *
9:And Then Some *
10:I'll Never Say "Never Again," Again

July 6, 1935

1:Chasing Shadows
2:In a Little Gypsy Tea Room
3:The Lady in Red
4:I'll Never Say "Never Again," Again
5:What's the Reason?
6:Life Is a Song
7:Thrilled
8:In the Middle of a Kiss
9:And Then Some
10:Footloose and Fancy Free *

July 13, 1935

1:In a Little Gypsy Tea Room
2:Chasing Shadows
3:The Lady in Red
4:In the Middle of a Kiss
5:And Then Some
6:I'll Never Say "Never Again," Again
7:I'm Living in a Great Big Way *
8:Paris in the Spring *
9:Thrilled
10:Get Rhythm in Your Feet *

July 20, 1935

1:Chasing Shadows
2:In a Little Gypsy Tea Room
3:The Lady in Red
4:In the Middle of a Kiss
5:And Then Some
6:Let's Swing It *
7:Thrilled
8:I'll Never Say "Never Again," Again
9:Paris in the Spring
10:Star Gazing *

July 27, 1935

1:In the Middle of a Kiss
2:Chasing Shadows
3:And Then Some
4:In a Little Gypsy Tea Room
5:The Lady in Red
6:East of the Sun *
7:I'll Never Say "Never Again," Again
8:Paris in the Spring
9:Thrilled
10:Every Little Moment *

Aug. 3, 1935

1:Chasing Shadows
2:I'll Never Say "Never Again," Again
3:In a Little Gypsy Tea Room
4:You're All I Need
5:In the Middle of a Kiss
6:The Lady in Red
7:Love Me Forever *
8:East of the Sun
9:Paris in the Spring
10:And Then Some

Aug. 10, 1935

1:Paris in the Spring
2:And Then Some
3:East of the Sun
4:In a Little Gypsy Tea Room
5:You're All I Need
6:In the Middle of a Kiss
7:Love Me Forever
8:Chasing Shadows
9:The Lady in Red
10:I'll Never Say "Never Again," Again

Aug. 17, 1935

1:And Then Some
2:East of the Sun
3:In a Little Gypsy Tea Room
4:Paris in the Spring
5:I Couldn't Believe My Eyes *
6:I'm in the Mood For Love *
7:Love Me Forever
8:You're All I Need
9:In the Middle of a Kiss
10:Chasing Shadows

Aug. 24, 1935

1:East of the Sun
2:And Then Some
3:In a Little Gypsy Tea Room
4:Paris in the Spring
5:You're All I Need
6:Love Me Forever
7:I Couldn't Believe My Eyes
8:I'm in the Mood For Love
9:Every Single Little Tingle of My Heart *
10:The Rose in Her Hair *

Aug. 31, 1935

1:You're All I Need
2:In a Little Gypsy Tea Room
3:East of the Sun
4:I'm in the Mood For Love
5:Paris in the Spring
6:And Then Some
7:Love Me Forever
8:I Couldn't Believe My Eyes
9:Mad About the Boy *
10:Sweet and Slow *

Sept. 7, 1935

1:East of the Sun
2:You're All I Need
3:I'm in the Mood For Love
4:In a Little Gypsy Tea Room
5:Accent on Youth *
6:And Then Some
7:Cheek to Cheek *
8:Page Miss Glory *
9:Lulu's Back in Town *
10:Loafin' Time *

Sept. 14, 1935

1:I'm in the Mood For Love
2:East of the Sun
3:You're All I Need
4:Accent On Youth
5:Cheek to Cheek
6:Page Miss Glory
7:In a Little Gypsy Tea Room
8:Double Trouble *
9:Truckin' *
10:You're So Darn Charming *

Sept. 21, 1935

1:I'm in the Mood For Love
2:You're All I Need
3:Cheek to Cheek
4:East of the Sun
5:Without a Word of Warning *
6:Accent On Youth
7:No Strings *
8:Page Miss Glory
9:Rhythm and Romance *
10:Piccolino *

Sept. 28, 1935

1:Cheek to Cheek
2:I'm in the Mood For Love
3:Accent On Youth
4:Rhythm and Romance
5:You're All I Need
6:From the Top of Your Head *
7:Isn't This a Lovely Day? *
8:Page Miss Glory
9:Without a Word of Warning
10:I'm On a Seesaw *

Oct. 5, 1935

1:Cheek to Cheek
2:Top Hat, White Tie and Tails *
3:I'm in the Mood For Love
4:Isn't This a Lovely Day?
5:I'm On a Seesaw
6:That's What You Think *
7:I Wished On the Moon *
8:Without a Word of Warning
9:From the Top of Your Head
10:Every Now and Then *

Oct. 12, 1935

1:Cheek to Cheek
2:I'm in the Mood For Love
3:You Are My Lucky Star *
4:I'm On a Seesaw
5:Top Hat, White Tie and Tails
6:Isn't This a Lovely Day?
7:I Wished On the Moon
8:I Wish I Were Aladdin *
9:From the Top of Your Head
10:Without a Word of Warning

Oct. 19, 1935

1:Cheek to Cheek
2:I'm in the Mood For Love
3:You Are My Lucky Star
4:I'm On a Seesaw
5:Isn't This a Lovely Day?
6:The Gentleman Obviously Doesn't Believe *
7:On Treasure Island *
8:Without a Word of Warning
9:Top Hat, White Tie and Tails
10:Broadway Rhythm *

Oct. 26, 1935

1:Cheek to Cheek
2:You Are My Lucky Star
3:I've Got a Feeling You're Fooling *
4:I'm On a Seesaw
5:Isn't This a Lovely Day?
6:I'm in the Mood For Love
7:Without a Word of Warning
8:Top Hat, White Tie and Tails
9:On Treasure Island
10:Red Sails in the Sunset *

Nov. 2, 1935

1:You Are My Lucky Star
2:I'm in the Mood For Love
3:Cheek to Cheek
4:On Treasure Island
5:Here's to Romance *
6:I'm On a Seesaw
7:Red Sails in the Sunset
8:I've Got a Feeling You're Fooling
9:Top Hat, White Tie and Tails
10:Isn't This a Lovely Day?

Nov. 9, 1935

1:You Are My Lucky Star
2:Red Sails in the Sunset
3:On Treasure Island
4:Cheek to Cheek
5:Isn't This a Lovely Day?
6:I've Got a Feeling You're Fooling
7:I'm On a Seesaw
8:I Found a Dream *
9:It Never Dawned On Me *
10:Here's to Romance

Nov. 16, 1935

1:You Are My Lucky Star
2:Red Sails in the Sunset
3:I've Got a Feeling You're Fooling
4:On Treasure Island
5:Here's to Romance
6:Cheek to Cheek
7:Isn't This a Lovely Day?
8:I Found a Dream
9:I'm On a Seesaw
10:I'd Rather Listen to Your Eyes *

Nov. 23, 1935

1:Red Sails in the Sunset
2:On Treasure Island
3:You Are My Lucky Star
4:I've Got a Feeling You're Fooling
5:Twenty-Four Hours a Day *
6:No Other One *
7:I Found a Dream
8:Here's to Romance
9:Take Me Back to My Boots and Saddle *
10:I'm Sittin' High On a Hilltop *

Nov. 30, 1935

1:Red Sails in the Sunset
2:On Treasure Island
3:I Found a Dream
4:Take Me Back to My Boots and Saddle
5:You Are My Lucky Star
6:Don't Give Up the Ship *
7:No Other One
8:I've Got a Feeling You're Fooling
9:Thanks a Million *
10:I'm Sittin' High On a Hilltop

Dec. 7, 1935

1:Red Sails in the Sunset
2:On Treasure Island
3:A Little Bit Independent *
4:Roll Along Prairie Moon *
5:Don't Give Up the Ship
6:I Found a Dream
7:Take Me Back to My Boots and Saddle
8:I'm Sittin' High On a Hilltop
9:No Other One
10:Thanks a Million

Dec. 14, 1935

1:Red Sails in the Sunset
2:A Little Bit Independent
3:On Treasure Island
4:Thanks a Million
5:Take Me Back to My Boots and Saddle
6:Roll Along Prairie Moon
7:Eeny Meeny Miney Mo *
8:I'd Love to Take Orders From You *
9:I'm Sittin' High On a Hilltop
10:Where Am I? *

Dec. 21, 1935

1:On Treasure Island
2:Red Sails in the Sunset
3:A Little Bit Independent
4:Take Me Back to My Boots and Saddle
5:Where Am I?
6:Eeny Meeny Miney Mo
7:I'm Sittin' High On a Hilltop
8:One Night in Monte Carlo *
9:Thanks a Million
10:It's Dangerous to Love Like This *

Dec. 28, 1935

1:A Little Bit Independent
2:On Treasure Island
3:Red Sails in the Sunset
4:Where Am I?
5:Why Shouldn't I? *
6:I'm Sittin' High On a Hilltop
7:Take Me Back to My Boots and Saddle
8:Thanks a Million
9:Quicker Than You Can Say Jack Robinson *
10:Eeny Meeny Miney Mo

1936

It was the year of the ultimate love story, when a king gave up his throne to marry the woman he loved. The world listened in awe that December as England's Edward VIII made the historic and dramatic radio broadcast from Windsor Castle that he was abdicating to marry the Baltimore divorcée, Wallis Warfield Simpson.

In America the year's biggest craze was the "knock-knock" jokes (which even inspired a song onto the Top Ten one night), and the rage of the airwaves was Bob Burns with his bazooka. The novelty song of the year was the contagious "The Music Goes Round and Round," but the top songs of the year were "Did I Remember?" and "The Way You Look Tonight," each of which rode the Number One spot for six weeks apiece.

Little Orphan Annie was giving away Ovaltine Shake-Up Mugs on radio, *The Saturday Evening Post* was selling for a nickel, and a new magazine called *Life* made its debut and showed its class by charging a dime.

Now civil war flared in Spain. Germany announced all Jewish children from the ages of six to fourteen must leave public schools. Emperor Haile Selassie fled Ethiopia and Mussolini "annexed" it. The athlete of the year had to be Jesse Owens, the black American sprinter who gave the Nazis their only defeat that year in the Olympics at Berlin.

In this country, Route 66 was crowded with the mattress-covered cars of Oklahomans who had abandoned their Dust Bowl homes and were headed west for the promised land of California.

The state of New Jersey finally electrocuted Bruno Richard Hauptmann for the Lindbergh murder, and Franklin Roosevelt swept to a second term over GOP candidate Alf Landon by carrying every state but two.

Top favorites on Broadway were *You Can't Take It With You* and *The Women*. On screen we had *The Trail of the Lonesome Pine* and *San Francisco*. In the book field, there was only one: Margaret Mitchell's mammoth *Gone With the Wind*, which sold 50,000 copies its first day of publication.

Jan. 4, 1936

1:A Little Bit Independent
2:On Treasure Island
3:Red Sails in the Sunset
4:Moon Over Miami *
5:Thanks a Million
6:Eeny Meeny Miney Mo
7:The Music Goes Round and Round *
8:With All My Heart *
9:Take Me Back to My Boots and Saddle
10:I'm Sittin' High On a Hilltop

Jan. 11, 1936

1:The Music Goes Round and Round
2:A Little Bit Independent
3:Red Sails in the Sunset
4:With All My Heart
5:Take Me Back to My Boots and Saddle
6:Moon Over Miami
7:The Broken Record *
8:On Treasure Island
9:Alone *
10:If I Should Lose You *

Jan. 18, 1936

1:The Music Goes Round and Round
2:Moon Over Miami
3:Red Sails in the Sunset
4:With All My Heart
5:A Little Bit Independent
6:The Broken Record
7:Alone
8:I Feel Like a Feather in the Breeze *
9:Dinner For One, Please, James *
10:On Treasure Island

Jan. 25, 1936

1:The Music Goes Round and Round
2:Moon Over Miami
3:Alone
4:With All My Heart
5:I Feel Like a Feather in the Breeze
6:The Broken Record
7:Red Sails in the Sunset
8:Lights Out *
9:Rhythm in My Nursery Rhymes *
10:Dinner For One, Please, James

Feb. 1, 1936

1:Moon Over Miami
2:Alone
3:With All My Heart
4:The Music Goes Round and Round
5:Dinner For One, Please, James
6:The Broken Record
7:Red Sails in the Sunset
8:I Feel Like a Feather in the Breeze
9:Lights Out
10:Alone at a Table For Two *

Feb. 8, 1936

1:Alone
2:Moon Over Miami
3:I Feel Like a Feather in the Breeze
4:Lights Out
5:The Broken Record
6:The Music Goes Round and Round
7:You Hit the Spot *
8:Cling to Me *
9:Dinner For One, Please, James
10:With All My Heart

Feb. 15, 1936

1:Alone
2:Moon Over Miami
3:Lights Out
4:I Feel Like a Feather in the Breeze
5:Cling to Me
6:I'm Building Up to an Awful Letdown *
7:I'm Shooting High *
8:I'm Gonna Sit Right Down and Write Myself
9:You Hit the Spot   a Letter *
10:Dinner For One, Please, James

Feb. 22, 1936

1:Alone
2:Moon Over Miami
3:Lights Out
4:I'm Building Up to an Awful Letdown
5:I'm Shooting High
6:I Feel Like a Feather in the Breeze
7:Cling to Me
8:Dinner For One, Please, James
9:You Hit the Spot
10:I'm Gonna Sit Right Down and Write Myself
                                        a Letter

* Newcomer

Feb. 29, 1936

1:Alone
2:Lights Out
3:I'm Gonna Sit Right Down and Write Myself
4:Moon Over Miami   a Letter
5:You Hit the Spot
6:I'm Shooting High
7:Please Believe Me *
8:I'm Building Up to an Awful Letdown
9:Cling to Me
10:A Beautiful Lady in Blue *

Mar. 7, 1936

1:Lights Out
2:I'm Gonna Sit Right Down and Write Myself
3:Alone   a Letter
4:Please Believe Me
5:I'm Shooting High
6:It's Been So Long *
7:A Beautiful Lady in Blue
8:Cling to Me
9:Moon Over Miami
10:You Hit the Spot

Mar. 14, 1936

1:Alone
2:Lights Out
3:I'm Shooting High
4:Please Believe Me
5:Let's Face the Music and Dance *
6:I'm Gonna Sit Right Down and Write Myself
7:A Beautiful Lady in Blue   a Letter
8:Let Yourself Go *
9:I'm Putting All My Eggs in One Basket *
10:It's Been So Long

Mar. 21, 1936

1:Lights Out
2:Goody Goody *
3:Alone
4:It's Been So Long
5:Let Yourself Go
6:I'm Putting All My Eggs in One Basket
7:I'm Shooting High
8:Let's Face the Music and Dance
9:Please Believe Me
10:A Beautiful Lady in Blue

Mar. 28, 1936

1:Goody Goody
2:It's Been So Long
3:Let's Face the Music and Dance
4:I'm Putting All My Eggs in One Basket
5:Let Yourself Go
6:Lights Out
7:A Beautiful Lady in Blue
8:Alone
9:Wah Hoo *
10:What's the Name of That Song? *

Apr. 4, 1936

1:Goody Goody
2:I'm Putting All My Eggs in One Basket
3:Let Yourself Go
4:It's Been So Long
5:Let's Face the Music and Dance
6:A Beautiful Lady in Blue
7:Lost *
8:Lights Out
9:Alone
10:Little Rendezvous in Honolulu *

Apr. 11, 1936

1:Goody Goody
2:I'm Putting All My Eggs in One Basket
3:Let Yourself Go
4:Lost
5:A Beautiful Lady in Blue
6:Lights Out
7:Sing an Old-Fashioned Song to a Young
8:West Wind *   Sophisticated Lady *
9:It's Been So Long
10:Let's Face the Music and Dance

Apr. 18, 1936

1:Goody Goody
2:Lost
3:I'm Putting All My Eggs in One Basket
4:Let Yourself Go
5:It's Been So Long
6:A Melody From the Sky *
7:You Started Me Dreaming *
8:A Beautiful Lady in Blue
9:Lovely Lady *
10:Let's Face the Music and Dance

Apr. 25, 1936

1:Lost
2:I'm Putting All My Eggs in One Basket
3:Goody Goody
4:A Melody From the Sky
5:Let Yourself Go
6:The Touch of Your Lips *
7:You Started Me Dreaming
8:It's Been So Long
9:Let's Face the Music and Dance
10:A Beautiful Lady in Blue

May 2, 1936

1:Lost
2:Goody Goody
3:A Melody From the Sky
4:You Started Me Dreaming
5:It's Been So Long
6:Yours Truly Is Truly Yours *
7:All My Life *
8:You *
9:I'm Putting All My Eggs in One Basket
10:The Touch of Your Lips

May 9, 1936

1:Lost
2:You
3:A Melody From the Sky
4:Goody Goody
5:The Touch of Your Lips
6:I'm Putting All My Eggs in One Basket
7:All My Life
8:Love Is Like a Cigarette *
9:You Started Me Dreaming
10:It's Been So Long

May 16, 1936

1:A Melody From the Sky
2:Lost
3:Goody Goody
4:You
5:All My Life
6:You Started Me Dreaming
7:Tormented *
8:The Touch of Your Lips
9:Is It True What They Say About Dixie? *
10:I Don't Want to Make History *

May 23, 1936

1:You
2:A Melody From the Sky
3:Lost
4:The Touch of Your Lips
5:Is It True What They Say About Dixie?
6:You Started Me Dreaming
7:All My Life
8:Robins and Roses *
9:She Shall Have Music *
10:Wake Up and Sing *

May 30, 1936

1:Lost
2:A Melody From the Sky
3:You
4:All My Life
5:Robins and Roses
6:Is It True What They Say About Dixie?
7:She Shall Have Music
8:You Started Me Dreaming
9:The Touch of Your Lips
10:Christopher Columbus *

June 6, 1936

1:Is It True What They Say About Dixie?
2:All My Life
3:You
4:Robins and Roses
5:Lost
6:A Melody From the Sky
7:The Touch of Your Lips
8:She Shall Have Music
9:Would You? *
10:There's Always a Happy Ending *

June 13, 1936

1:Is It True What They Say About Dixie?
2:Robins and Roses
3:She Shall Have Music
4:All My Life
5:It's a Sin to Tell a Lie *
6:You
7:Would You?
8:A Melody From the Sky
9:Lost
10:The Glory of Love *

June 20, 1936

1:Is It True What They Say About Dixie?
2:Robins and Roses
3:All My Life
4:You
5:She Shall Have Music
6:It's a Sin to Tell a Lie
7:You Can't Pull the Wool Over My Eyes *
8:Take My Heart *
9:The Glory of Love
10:Would You?

June 27, 1936

1:Is It True What They Say About Dixie?
2:Robins and Roses
3:She Shall Have Music
4:All My Life
5:It's a Sin to Tell a Lie
6:Would You?
7:The Glory of Love
8:You Can't Pull the Wool Over My Eyes
9:These Foolish Things *
10:Take My Heart

July 4, 1936

1:The Glory of Love
2:Is It True What They Say About Dixie?
3:Robins and Roses
4:There's a Small Hotel *
5:Would You?
6:These Foolish Things
7:Take My Heart
8:It's a Sin to Tell a Lie
9:All My Life
10:You Can't Pull the Wool Over My Eyes

July 11, 1936

1:Is It True What They Say About Dixie?
2:Would You?
3:These Foolish Things
4:Take My Heart
5:There's a Small Hotel
6:Robins and Roses
7:The Glory of Love
8:It's a Sin to Tell a Lie
9:On the Beach at Bali Bali *
10:You Can't Pull the Wool Over My Eyes

July 18, 1936

1:Take My Heart
2:These Foolish Things
3:You Can't Pull the Wool Over My Eyes
4:Is It True What They Say About Dixie?
5:The Glory of Love
6:It's a Sin to Tell a Lie
7:Would You?
8:There's a Small Hotel
9:Robins and Roses
10:On the Beach at Bali Bali

July 25, 1936

1:Take My Heart
2:The Glory of Love
3:These Foolish Things
4:You Can't Pull the Wool Over My Eyes
5:Is It True What They Say About Dixie?
6:It's a Sin to Tell a Lie
7:There's a Small Hotel
8:On the Beach at Bali Bali
9:Would You?
10:Let's Sing Again *

Aug. 1, 1936

1:These Foolish Things
2:You Can't Pull the Wool Over My Eyes
3:Take My Heart
4:Would You?
5:The Glory of Love
6:Cross Patch *
7:Is It True What They Say About Dixie?
8:There's a Small Hotel
9:On the Beach at Bali Bali
10:It's a Sin to Tell a Lie

Aug. 8, 1936

1:These Foolish Things
2:Take My Heart
3:On the Beach at Bali Bali
4:The Glory of Love
5:When I'm With You *
6:You Can't Pull the Wool Over My Eyes
7:It's a Sin to Tell a Lie
8:Would You?
9:There's a Small Hotel
10:Did I Remember? *

Aug. 15, 1936

1:When I'm With You
2:These Foolish Things
3:Take My Heart
4:You Can't Pull the Wool Over My Eyes
5:On the Beach at Bali Bali
6:It's a Sin to Tell a Lie
7:Did I Remember?
8:The Glory of Love
9:Stompin' at the Savoy *
10:Afterglow *

Aug. 22, 1936

1:When I'm With You
2:These Foolish Things
3:Did I Remember?
4:On the Beach at Bali Bali
5:You Can't Pull the Wool Over My Eyes
6:Take My Heart
7:It's a Sin to Tell a Lie
8:Knock, Knock, Who's There? *
9:The Glory of Love
10:You're Not the Kind *

Aug. 29, 1936

1:Did I Remember?
2:When I'm With You
3:These Foolish Things
4:No Regrets *
5:A Rendezvous With a Dream *
6:A Star Fell Out of Heaven *
7:Until the Real Thing Comes Along *
8:On the Beach at Bali Bali
9:Take My Heart
10:It's a Sin to Tell a Lie

Sept. 5, 1936

1:Did I Remember?
2:When I'm With You
3:A Star Fell Out of Heaven
4:Until the Real Thing Comes Along
5:Take My Heart
6:These Foolish Things
7:No Regrets
8:On the Beach at Bali Bali
9:A Rendezvous With a Dream
10:I'm an Old Cowhand *

Sept. 12, 1936

1:Did I Remember?
2:Until the Real Thing Comes Along
3:When I'm With You
4:A Star Fell Out of Heaven
5:I'm an Old Cowhand
6:These Foolish Things
7:A Rendezvous With a Dream
8:Me and the Moon *
9:No Regrets
10:When Did You Leave Heaven? *

Sept. 19, 1936

1:Did I Remember?
2:Until the Real Thing Comes Along
3:A Star Fell Out of Heaven
4:When I'm With You
5:When Did You Leave Heaven?
6:No Regrets
7:I'm an Old Cowhand
8:Sing, Baby, Sing *
9:Me and the Moon
10:A Rendezvous With a Dream

Sept. 26, 1936

1:Did I Remember?
2:Until the Real Thing Comes Along
3:A Star Fell Out of Heaven
4:I'm an Old Cowhand
5:When Did You Leave Heaven?
6:When I'm With You
7:Sing, Baby, Sing
8:Empty Saddles *
9:Me and the Moon
10:I Can't Escape From You *

Oct. 3, 1936

1:Did I Remember?
2:Until the Real Thing Comes Along
3:When Did You Leave Heaven?
4:A Star Fell Out of Heaven
5:When I'm With You
6:Until Today *
7:Sing, Baby, Sing
8:Me and the Moon
9:The Way You Look Tonight *
10:I Can't Escape From You

Oct. 10, 1936

1:When Did You Leave Heaven?
2:Until the Real Thing Comes Along
3:A Star Fell Out of Heaven
4:The Way You Look Tonight
5:Did I Remember?
6:Sing, Baby, Sing
7:Me and the Moon
8:A Fine Romance *
9:When I'm With You
10:I Can't Escape From You

Oct. 17, 1936

1:When Did You Leave Heaven?
2:The Way You Look Tonight
3:Did I Remember?
4:Until the Real Thing Comes Along
5:Sing, Baby, Sing
6:I Can't Escape From You
7:A Fine Romance
8:A Star Fell Out of Heaven
9:Mickey Mouse's Birthday Party *
10:Me and the Moon

Oct. 24, 1936

1:The Way You Look Tonight
2:When Did You Leave Heaven?
3:Until the Real Thing Comes Along
4:Did I Remember?
5:Sing, Baby, Sing
6:Me and the Moon
7:A Fine Romance
8:A Star Fell Out of Heaven
9:I'll Sing You a Thousand Love Songs *
10:When a Lady Meets a Gentleman Down South *

Oct. 31, 1936

1:The Way You Look Tonight
2:When Did You Leave Heaven?
3:A Fine Romance
4:Sing, Baby, Sing
5:Until the Real Thing Comes Along
6:Did I Remember?
7:A Star Fell Out of Heaven
8:I'll Sing You a Thousand Love Songs
9:Me and the Moon
10:Who Loves You? *

Nov. 7, 1936

1:The Way You Look Tonight
2:When Did You Leave Heaven?
3:A Fine Romance
4:You Turned the Tables On Me *
5:I'll Sing You a Thousand Love Songs
6:Sing, Baby, Sing
7:Who Loves You?
8:Did You Mean It? *
9:Me and the Moon
10:South Sea Island Magic *

Nov. 14, 1936

1:The Way You Look Tonight
2:When Did You Leave Heaven?
3:I'll Sing You a Thousand Love Songs
4:A Fine Romance
5:Did You Mean It?
6:South Sea Island Magic
7:Who Loves You?
8:You Turned the Tables On Me
9:Close to Me *
10:Dream Awhile *

Nov. 21, 1936

1:The Way You Look Tonight
2:When Did You Leave Heaven?
3:You Turned the Tables On Me
4:Organ Grinder's Swing *
5:I'll Sing You a Thousand Love Songs
6:A Fine Romance
7:South Sea Island Magic
8:In the Chapel in the Moonlight *
9:Who Loves You?
10:Did You Mean It?

Nov. 28, 1936

1:The Way You Look Tonight
2:I'll Sing You a Thousand Love Songs
3:In the Chapel in the Moonlight
4:When Did You Leave Heaven?
5:You Turned the Tables On Me
6:Organ Grinder's Swing
7:It's De-Lovely *
8:South Sea Island Magic
9:Did You Mean It?
10:Who Loves You?

Dec. 5, 1936

1:I'll Sing You a Thousand Love Songs
2:In the Chapel in the Moonlight
3:You Turned the Tables On Me
4:The Way You Look Tonight
5:Did You Mean It?
6:It's De-Lovely
7:South Sea Island Magic
8:Organ Grinder's Swing
9:When Did You Leave Heaven?
10:To Mary, With Love *

Dec. 12, 1936

1:In the Chapel in the Moonlight
2:I'll Sing You a Thousand Love Songs
3:It's De-Lovely
4:I've Got You Under My Skin *
5:You Turned the Tables On Me
6:The Way You Look Tonight
7:Pennies From Heaven *
8:Organ Grinder's Swing
9:The Night Is Young and You're
      So Beautiful *
10:Here's Love in Your Eye *

Dec. 19, 1936

1:Pennies From Heaven
2:In the Chapel in the Moonlight
3:I'll Sing You a Thousand Love Songs
4:I've Got You Under My Skin
5:It's De-Lovely
6:The Way You Look Tonight
7:Organ Grinder's Swing
8:The Night Is Young and You're
      So Beautiful
9:I'm in a Dancing Mood *
10:When My Dream Boat Comes Home *

Dec. 26, 1936

1:In the Chapel in the Moonlight
2:It's De-Lovely
3:Pennies From Heaven
4:I've Got You Under My Skin
5:When My Dream Boat Comes Home
6:I'm in a Dancing Mood
7:I'll Sing You a Thousand Love Songs
8:The Night Is Young and You're
      So Beautiful
9:The Way You Look Tonight
10:Organ Grinder's Swing

1937

It was the year of The Big Bands, the dance called The Big Apple, and a new word in the vocabulary—jitterbug.

They called it swing, and the present masters of it were bandleaders Benny Goodman, Larry Clinton, and Artie Shaw.

But it wasn't a swing song that was 1937's top hit. Instead, it was the lilting "Once In Awhile," with seven weeks as Number One.

Elsewhere, 1937 was the year of the sit-down strike, radio Fireside Chats by FDR, the Jack Benny-Fred Allen "feud" on radio, and the undisputed favorites of the airwaves—Edgar Bergen and Charlie McCarthy.

The small town of New London, Texas, buried a whole generation after a gas-leak explosion in the school building killed 294 children and teachers.

The Japanese shelled and sank the U.S. gunboat *Panay*, with the loss of two lives. They apologized and paid.

Kids read Big Little Books and dreamed someday they would pilot the *China Clipper*. Adults read Dale Carnegie's new *How to Win Friends and Influence People*, and listened on the radio as Joe Louis, now known as the Brown Bomber, decked James J. Braddock to become the heavyweight boxing champ of the world.

Amelia Earhart Putnam vanished on a flight over the Pacific, never to be heard from again, and the German dirigible *Hindenburg*, making its first trans-Atlantic flight, burst into flames and killed thirty-six people as it came in for a landing at Lakehurst, New Jersey.

Broadway had Rodgers and Hart's *Babes in Arms*, and the movies had *Lost Horizon, The Good Earth, Captains Courageous*, and Dorothy Lamour in a sarong.

The movies also had Bank Night, Buck Night, and Dish Night. The Depression was still here.

Jan. 2, 1937

1:In the Chapel in the Moonlight
2:It's De-Lovely
3:I've Got You Under My Skin
4:Pennies From Heaven
5:I'll Sing You a Thousand Love Songs
6:I'm in a Dancing Mood
7:The Night Is Young and You're So Beautiful
8:When My Dream Boat Comes Home
9:Organ Grinder's Swing
10:The Way You Look Tonight

Jan. 9, 1937

1:Pennies From Heaven
2:It's De-Lovely
3:In the Chapel in the Moonlight
4:I've Got You Under My Skin
5:The Night Is Young and You're So Beautiful
6:I'm in a Dancing Mood
7:Easy to Love *
8:When My Dream Boat Comes Home
9:I'll Sing You a Thousand Love Songs
10:Organ Grinder's Swing

Jan. 16, 1937

1:It's De-Lovely
2:Pennies From Heaven
3:In the Chapel in the Moonlight
4:I've Got You Under My Skin
5:With Plenty of Money and You *
6:I'm in a Dancing Mood
7:The Night Is Young and You're So Beautiful
8:Easy to Love
9:When My Dream Boat Comes Home
10:I'll Sing You a Thousand Love Songs

Jan. 23, 1937

1:Pennies From Heaven
2:Goodnight, My Love *
3:When My Dream Boat Comes Home
4:It's De-Lovely
5:With Plenty of Money and You
6:In the Chapel in the Moonlight
7:I've Got You Under My Skin
8:The Night Is Young and You're So Beautiful
9:Easy to Love
10:I'm in a Dancing Mood

Jan. 30, 1937

1:Pennies From Heaven
2:It's De-Lovely
3:In the Chapel in the Moonlight
4:With Plenty of Money and You
5:When My Dream Boat Comes Home
6:Goodnight, My Love
7:I've Got You Under My Skin
8:The Night Is Young and You're So Beautiful
9:I'm in a Dancing Mood
10:Easy to Love

Feb. 6, 1937

1:Goodnight, My Love
2:Pennies From Heaven
3:With Plenty of Money and You
4:In the Chapel in the Moonlight
5:The Night Is Young and You're So Beautiful
6:When My Dream Boat Comes Home
7:There's Something in the Air *
8:I've Got You Under My Skin
9:It's De-Lovely
10:Easy to Love

Feb. 13, 1937

1:Goodnight, My Love
2:With Plenty of Money and You
3:Pennies From Heaven
4:The Night Is Young and You're So Beautiful
5:When My Dream Boat Comes Home
6:There's Something in the Air
7:Trust in Me *
8:In the Chapel in the Moonlight
9:I've Got You Under My Skin
10:It's De-Lovely

Feb. 20, 1937

1:With Plenty of Money and You
2:Goodnight, My Love
3:This Year's Kisses *
4:When My Dream Boat Comes Home
5:There's Something in the Air
6:In the Chapel in the Moonlight
7:Pennies From Heaven
8:Trust in Me
9:The Night Is Young and You're So Beautiful
10:I've Got You Under My Skin

* Newcomer

Feb. 27, 1937

1:Goodnight, My Love
2:Trust in Me
3:With Plenty of Money and You
4:The Night Is Young and You're So Beautiful
5:This Year's Kisses
6:When My Dream Boat Comes Home
7:Pennies From Heaven
8:There's Something in the Air
9:In the Chapel in the Moonlight
10:I've Got You Under My Skin

Mar. 6, 1937

1:Goodnight, My Love
2:This Year's Kisses
3:When My Dream Boat Comes Home
4:With Plenty of Money and You
5:Slumming On Park Avenue *
6:Moonlight and Shadows *
7:Love and Learn *
8:Trust in Me
9:Pennies From Heaven
10:The Night Is Young and You're So Beautiful

Mar. 13, 1937

1:This Year's Kisses
2:Goodnight, My Love
3:When My Dream Boat Comes Home
4:Trust in Me
5:I've Got My Love to Keep Me Warm *
6:You're Laughing At Me *
7:Serenade in the Night *
8:Moonlight and Shadows
9:With Plenty of Money and You
10:Pennies From Heaven

Mar. 20, 1937

1:This Year's Kisses
2:Moonlight and Shadows
3:When My Dream Boat Comes Home
4:Boo Hoo *
5:Little Old Lady *
6:Goodnight, My Love
7:What Will I Tell My Heart? *
8:I've Got My Love to Keep Me Warm
9:Trust in Me
10:With Plenty of Money and You

Mar. 27, 1937

1:This Year's Kisses
2:Boo Hoo
3:When My Dream Boat Comes Home
4:I've Got My Love to Keep Me Warm
5:What Will I Tell My Heart?
6:Goodnight, My Love
7:Moonlight and Shadows
8:Little Old Lady
9:With Plenty of Money and You
10:Trust in Me

Apr. 3, 1937

1:Boo Hoo
2:Little Old Lady
3:I've Got My Love to Keep Me Warm
4:What Will I Tell My Heart?
5:When the Poppies Bloom Again *
6:Moonlight and Shadows
7:Trust in Me
8:This Year's Kisses
9:When My Dream Boat Comes Home
10:Goodnight, My Love

Apr. 10, 1937

1:Boo Hoo
2:Little Old Lady
3:Moonlight and Shadows
4:Trust in Me
5:This Year's Kisses
6:I've Got My Love to Keep Me Warm
7:What Will I Tell My Heart?
8:When the Poppies Bloom Again
9:Goodnight, My Love
10:When My Dream Boat Comes Home

Apr. 17, 1937

1:Boo Hoo
2:Little Old Lady
3:Moonlight and Shadows
4:I've Got My Love to Keep Me Warm
5:What Will I Tell My Heart?
6:Too Marvelous For Words *
7:This Year's Kisses
8:Where Are You? *
9:Sweet Is the Word For You *
10:Trust in Me

Apr. 24, 1937

1:Boo Hoo
2:Little Old Lady
3:Too Marvelous For Words
4:Moonlight and Shadows
5:What Will I Tell My Heart?
6:September in the Rain *
7:I've Got My Love to Keep Me Warm
8:Where Are You?
9:Carelessly *
10:The Love Bug Will Bite You *

May 1, 1937

1:Boo Hoo
2:Little Old Lady
3:Too Marvelous For Words
4:Moonlight and Shadows
5:Carelessly
6:September in the Rain
7:Where Are You?
8:What Will I Tell My Heart?
9:The Love Bug Will Bite You
10:How Could You? *

May 8, 1937

1:Boo Hoo
2:The Love Bug Will Bite You
3:Too Marvelous For Words
4:September in the Rain
5:Moonlight and Shadows
6:Where Are You?
7:What Will I Tell My Heart?
8:Little Old Lady
9:Carelessly
10:Never in a Million Years *

May 15, 1937

1:September in the Rain
2:Boo Hoo
3:Never in a Million Years
4:Carelessly
5:There's a Lull in My Life *
6:Too Marvelous For Words
7:The Love Bug Will Bite You
8:Blue Hawaii *
9:Little Old Lady
10:Where Are You?

May 22, 1937

1:Carelessly
2:September in the Rain
3:There's a Lull in My Life
4:Boo Hoo
5:Where Are You?
6:Never in a Million Years
7:The Love Bug Will Bite You
8:Too Marvelous For Words
9:Little Old Lady
10:Blue Hawaii

May 29, 1937

1:Carelessly
2:Never in a Million Years
3:September in the Rain
4:The Love Bug Will Bite You
5:There's a Lull in My Life
6:Where Are You?
7:Little Old Lady
8:Sweet Leilani *
9:Blue Hawaii
10:Boo Hoo

June 5, 1937

1:September in the Rain
2:Carelessly
3:There's a Lull in My Life
4:Never in a Million Years
5:The Love Bug Will Bite You
6:Where Are You?
7:Let's Call the Whole Thing Off *
8:Blue Hawaii
9:They Can't Take That Away From Me *
10:Sweet Leilani

June 12, 1937

1:September in the Rain
2:Never in a Million Years
3:Carelessly
4:There's a Lull in My Life
5:Where Are You?
6:They Can't Take That Away From Me
7:It Looks Like Rain in Cherry Blossom Lane *
8:The Love Bug Will Bite You
9:Sweet Leilani
10:Blue Hawaii

June 19, 1937

1:September in the Rain
2:Carelessly
3:Never in a Million Years
4:It Looks Like Rain in Cherry Blossom Lane
5:There's a Lull in My Life
6:Sweet Leilani
7:They Can't Take That Away From Me
8:A Sailboat in the Moonlight *
9:The Love Bug Will Bite You
10:Blue Hawaii

June 26, 1937

1:September in the Rain
2:It Looks Like Rain in Cherry Blossom Lane
3:The Merry-Go-Round Broke Down *
4:Never in a Million Years
5:Sweet Leilani
6:Carelessly
7:Was It Rain? *
8:They Can't Take That Away From Me
9:A Sailboat in the Moonlight
10:There's a Lull in My Life

July 3, 1937

1:It Looks Like Rain in Cherry Blossom Lane
2:Sweet Leilani
3:The Merry-Go-Round Broke Down
4:September in the Rain
5:There's a Lull in My Life
6:Never in a Million Years
7:A Sailboat in the Moonlight
8:Carelessly
9:The You and Me That Used to Be *
10:They Can't Take That Away From Me

July 10, 1937

1:It Looks Like Rain in Cherry Blossom Lane
2:A Sailboat in the Moonlight
3:Sweet Leilani
4:The Merry-Go-Round Broke Down
5:Where Or When *
6:September in the Rain
7:Never in a Million Years
8:They Can't Take That Away From Me
9:The You and Me That Used to Be
10:Carelessly

July 17, 1937

1:It Looks Like Rain in Cherry Blossom Lane
2:The Merry-Go-Round Broke Down
3:A Sailboat in the Moonlight
4:Where Or When
5:September in the Rain
6:Sweet Leilani
7:The You and Me That Used to Be
8:Never in a Million Years
9:They Can't Take That Away From Me
10:Carelessly

July 24, 1937

1:It Looks Like Rain in Cherry Blossom Lane
2:The Merry-Go-Round Broke Down
3:A Sailboat in the Moonlight
4:Where Or When
5:Gone With the Wind *
6:The You and Me That Used to Be
7:Sweet Leilani
8:September in the Rain
9:Never in a Million Years
10:'Cause My Baby Says It's So *

July 31, 1937

1:It Looks Like Rain in Cherry Blossom Lane
2:The Merry-Go-Round Broke Down
3:A Sailboat in the Moonlight
4:Where Or When
5:Gone With the Wind
6:So Rare *
7:Sweet Leilani
8:Never in a Million Years
9:Tomorrow Is Another Day *
10:The You and Me That Used to Be

Aug. 7, 1937

1:A Sailboat in the Moonlight
2:It Looks Like Rain in Cherry Blossom Lane
3:Where Or When
4:The Merry-Go-Round Broke Down
5:The You and Me That Used to Be
6:So Rare
7:I Know Now *
8:Sweet Leilani
9:Gone With the Wind
10:Stop! You're Breaking My Heart *

Aug. 14, 1937

1:It Looks Like Rain in Cherry Blossom Lane
2:Where Or When
3:The Merry-Go-Round Broke Down
4:I Know Now
5:A Sailboat in the Moonlight
6:Satan Takes a Holiday *
7:Whispers in the Dark *
8:Sweet Leilani
9:My Cabin of Dreams *
10:So Rare

Aug. 21, 1937

1:A Sailboat in the Moonlight
2:I Know Now
3:Where Or When
4:It Looks Like Rain in Cherry Blossom Lane
5:So Rare
6:The Merry-Go-Round Broke Down
7:My Cabin of Dreams
8:The First Time I Saw You *
9:Stardust On the Moon *
10:Whispers in the Dark

Aug. 28, 1937

1:A Sailboat in the Moonlight
2:So Rare
3:Whispers in the Dark
4:It Looks Like Rain in Cherry Blossom Lane
5:My Cabin of Dreams
6:I Know Now
7:Where Or When
8:The First Time I Saw You
9:Stardust On the Moon
10:The Merry-Go-Round Broke Down

Sept. 4, 1937

1:Whispers in the Dark
2:I Know Now
3:My Cabin of Dreams
4:So Rare
5:The First Time I Saw You
6:Afraid to Dream *
7:A Sailboat in the Moonlight
8:It Looks Like Rain in Cherry Blossom Lane
9:Have You Got Any Castles, Baby? *
10:That Old Feeling *

Sept. 11, 1937

1:So Rare
2:My Cabin of Dreams
3:Whispers in the Dark
4:That Old Feeling
5:I Know Now
6:The First Time I Saw You
7:A Sailboat in the Moonlight
8:Afraid to Dream
9:Have You Got Any Castles, Baby?
10:Yours and Mine *

Sept. 18, 1937

1:Whispers in the Dark
2:So Rare
3:My Cabin of Dreams
4:I Know Now
5:That Old Feeling
6:Harbor Lights *
7:A Sailboat in the Moonlight
8:Afraid to Dream
9:Have You Got Any Castles, Baby?
10:Yours and Mine

Sept. 25, 1937

1:Whispers in the Dark
2:That Old Feeling
3:So Rare
4:My Cabin of Dreams
5:Have You Got Any Castles, Baby?
6:Afraid to Dream
7:Remember Me? *
8:I Know Now
9:The Moon Got in My Eyes *
10:Harbor Lights

Oct. 2, 1937

1:Whispers in the Dark
2:That Old Feeling
3:My Cabin of Dreams
4:Have You Got Any Castles, Baby?
5:The Moon Got in My Eyes
6:Harbor Lights
7:Afraid to Dream
8:So Rare
9:Roses in December *
10:Remember Me?

Oct. 9, 1937

1:That Old Feeling
2:Have You Got Any Castles, Baby?
3:Whispers in the Dark
4:Remember Me?
5:The Moon Got in My Eyes
6:So Rare
7:My Cabin of Dreams
8:Harbor Lights
9:Afraid to Dream
10:Roses in December

Oct. 16, 1937

1:That Old Feeling
2:Remember Me?
3:The Moon Got in My Eyes
4:My Cabin of Dreams
5:Whispers in the Dark
6:Harbor Lights
7:Have You Got Any Castles, Baby?
8:Afraid to Dream
9:Roses in December
10:You Can't Stop Me From Dreaming *

Oct. 23, 1937

1:That Old Feeling
2:Have You Got Any Castles, Baby?
3:Whispers in the Dark
4:The Moon Got in My Eyes
5:Remember Me?
6:Roses in December
7:So Many Memories *
8:Harbor Lights
9:You Can't Stop Me From Dreaming
10:My Cabin of Dreams

Oct. 30, 1937

1:That Old Feeling
2:Remember Me?
3:Roses in December
4:Vieni Vieni *
5:Have You Got Any Castles, Baby?
6:Harbor Lights
7:The Moon Got in My Eyes
8:You Can't Stop Me From Dreaming
9:Whispers in the Dark
10:Blossoms On Broadway *

Nov. 6, 1937

1:Remember Me?
2:That Old Feeling
3:Roses in December
4:You Can't Stop Me From Dreaming
5:Vieni Vieni
6:The Moon Got in My Eyes
7:The One Rose *
8:Harbor Lights
9:Have You Got Any Castles, Baby?
10:Blossoms On Broadway

Nov. 13, 1937

1:You Can't Stop Me From Dreaming
2:Remember Me?
3:Vieni Vieni
4:That Old Feeling
5:Blossoms On Broadway
6:The One Rose
7:Have You Got Any Castles, Baby?
8:Harbor Lights
9:Roses in December
10:You and I Know *

Nov. 20, 1937

1:Vieni Vieni
2:You Can't Stop Me From Dreaming
3:Once In Awhile *
4:Remember Me?
5:Blossoms On Broadway
6:The One Rose
7:That Old Feeling
8:If It's the Last Thing I Do *
9:Harbor Lights
10:Roses in December

Nov. 27, 1937

1:Once In Awhile
2:Vieni Vieni
3:You Can't Stop Me From Dreaming
4:Blossoms On Broadway
5:If It's the Last Thing I Do
6:Nice Work If You Can Get It *
7:The One Rose
8:Roses in December
9:Harbor Lights
10:Remember Me?

Dec. 4, 1937

1:Once In Awhile
2:You Can't Stop Me From Dreaming
3:Vieni Vieni
4:If It's the Last Thing I Do
5:Blossoms On Broadway
6:Remember Me?
7:Nice Work If You Can Get It
8:Roses in December
9:Farewell, My Love *
10:The One Rose

Dec. 11, 1937

1:Once In Awhile
2:You Can't Stop Me From Dreaming
3:Vieni Vieni
4:If It's the Last Thing I Do
5:Nice Work If You Can Get It
6:Farewell, My Love
7:There's a Gold Mine in the Sky *
8:I Still Love to Kiss You Goodnight *
9:Blossoms On Broadway
10:The One Rose

Dec. 18, 1937

1:Once In Awhile
2:Vieni Vieni
3:Blossoms On Broadway
4:Nice Work If You Can Get It
5:If It's the Last Thing I Do
6:Rosalie *
7:Farewell, My Love
8:There's a Gold Mine in the Sky
9:You Can't Stop Me From Dreaming
10:I Still Love to Kiss You Goodnight

Dec. 25, 1937

1:Once In Awhile
2:Rosalie
3:Nice Work If You Can Get It
4:You Can't Stop Me From Dreaming
5:I Still Love to Kiss You Goodnight
6:Vieni Vieni
7:There's a Gold Mine in the Sky
8:Blossoms On Broadway
9:True Confession *
10:If It's the Last Thing I Do

1938

One of the song hits of 1938 was called "The Dipsy Doodle"—and that pretty well said it for the year itself.

Orson Welles, the young major-domo of radio's "Mercury Theater," scared the Halloween nightlights out of the nation by broadcasting *The War of the Worlds*, complete with simulated newscasts of Martians landing in New Jersey, which sent people tumbling out of their homes in panic.

An aviator named Douglas Corrigan became known overnight as "Wrong Way Corrigan" when he flew the Atlantic and landed in Dublin after saying he had taken off from Brooklyn and was heading for Los Angeles in his light plane. "Stick with that story," a newspaperman told him, and a celebrity was born.

New cars were selling for $880, Jack Armstrong was giving away Hike-o-Meters for Wheaties box tops, the nation was playing Bingo, kids collected bubble gum cards of the China-Japan war, everyone was listening to "Information, Please" on the radio, and the big new dance (and song) was the "Lambeth Walk."

On a more somber note, Hitler invaded Austria, and British Prime Minister Neville Chamberlain went to Munich where he yielded to Nazi demands for the takeover of the Sudetenland in the interest of "peace in our time."

Screen newcomer Bob Hope made his debut in *The Big Broadcast of 1938*, singing "Thanks For the Memory" onto "Your Hit Parade." The old standard "Alexander's Ragtime Band" also made "Your Hit Parade" via the 1938 movie of the same name. Other big film hits were *Test Pilot, You Can't Take It With You,* and *Boys Town*. However, the undisputed movie sensation of the year was Walt Disney's *Snow White and the Seven Dwarfs,* the first feature-length cartoon, and it contributed two songs to the Top Ten, "Whistle While You Work" and "Heigh Ho." But the top song of the year, also undisputed, was "My Reverie," eight weeks Number One.

Jan. 1, 1938

1:Once In Awhile
2:Rosalie
3:Nice Work If You Can Get It
4:Bob White *
5:You're a Sweetheart *
6:There's a Gold Mine in the Sky
7:True Confession
8:Vieni Vieni
9:You Can't Stop Me From Dreaming
10:If It's the Last Thing I Do

Jan. 8, 1938

1:Once In Awhile
2:Rosalie
3:You're a Sweetheart
4:True Confession
5:There's a Gold Mine in the Sky
6:Bei Mir Bist Du Schon *
7:Vieni Vieni
8:Bob White
9:I Double Dare You *
10:Nice Work If You Can Get It

Jan. 15, 1938

1:Rosalie
2:Once In Awhile
3:Bei Mir Bist Du Schon
4:True Confession
5:You're a Sweetheart
6:There's a Gold Mine in the Sky
7:Nice Work If You Can Get It
8:Vieni Vieni
9:Bob White
10:I Double Dare You

Jan. 22, 1938

1:Bei Mir Bist Du Schon
2:Rosalie
3:True Confession
4:You're a Sweetheart
5:Once In Awhile
6:The Dipsy Doodle *
7:There's a Gold Mine in the Sky
8:I Double Dare You
9:Nice Work If You Can Get It
10:In the Still of the Night *

Jan. 29, 1938

1:You're a Sweetheart
2:Bei Mir Bist Du Schon
3:Rosalie
4:True Confession
5:Once In Awhile
6:I Double Dare You
7:The Dipsy Doodle
8:There's a Gold Mine in the Sky
9:Nice Work If You Can Get It
10:You Took the Words Right Out of My Heart *

Feb. 5, 1938

1:Rosalie
2:Bei Mir Bist Du Schon
3:You're a Sweetheart
4:The Dipsy Doodle
5:I Double Dare You
6:True Confession
7:There's a Gold Mine in the Sky
8:You Took the Words Right Out of My Heart
9:Mama, That Moon Is Here Again *
10:Whistle While You Work *

Feb. 12, 1938

1:Bei Mir Bist Du Schon
2:You're a Sweetheart
3:I Double Dare You
4:The Dipsy Doodle
5:Thanks For the Memory *
6:Rosalie
7:Whistle While You Work
8:Sweet Someone *
9:There's a Gold Mine in the Sky
10:True Confession

Feb. 19, 1938

1:You're a Sweetheart
2:Bei Mir Bist Du Schon
3:I Double Dare You
4:The Dipsy Doodle
5:True Confession
6:Thanks For the Memory
7:Rosalie
8:Sweet Someone
9:There's a Gold Mine in the Sky
10:Whistle While You Work

* Newcomer

Feb. 26, 1938

1:I Double Dare You
2:Thanks For the Memory
3:The Dipsy Doodle
4:You're a Sweetheart
5:Bei Mir Bist Du Schon
6:Rosalie
7:Goodnight, Angel *
8:There's a Gold Mine in the Sky
9:Whistle While You Work
10:I Can Dream, Can't I? *

Mar. 5, 1938

1:Thanks For the Memory
2:I Double Dare You
3:Whistle While You Work
4:You're a Sweetheart
5:Sweet As a Song *
6:There's a Gold Mine in the Sky
7:The Dipsy Doodle
8:Goodnight, Angel
9:I Can Dream, Can't I?
10:Rosalie

Mar. 12, 1938

1:Thanks For the Memory
2:Whistle While You Work
3:I Double Dare You
4:I Can Dream, Can't I?
5:The Dipsy Doodle
6:You're a Sweetheart
7:Sweet As a Song
8:There's a Gold Mine in the Sky
9:I See Your Face Before Me *
10:Goodnight, Angel

Mar. 19, 1938

1:Thanks For the Memory
2:Whistle While You Work
3:I Double Dare You
4:Sweet As a Song
5:The Dipsy Doodle
6:Please Be Kind *
7:Ti Pi Tin *
8:Heigh Ho *
9:Goodnight, Angel
10:Let's Sail to Dreamland *

Mar. 26, 1938

1:Ti Pi Tin
2:Thanks For the Memory
3:Whistle While You Work
4:Goodnight, Angel
5:It's Wonderful *
6:Heigh Ho
7:I Double Dare You
8:Sweet As a Song
9:Please Be Kind
10:The Dipsy Doodle

Apr. 2, 1938

1:Ti Pi Tin
2:Thanks For the Memory
3:Whistle While You Work
4:Goodnight, Angel
5:I Double Dare You
6:You're an Education *
7:Please Be Kind
8:It's Wonderful
9:Love Walked In *
10:Heigh Ho

Apr. 9, 1938

1:Ti Pi Tin
2:Thanks For the Memory
3:Please Be Kind
4:Heigh Ho
5:Whistle While You Work
6:You're an Education
7:Love Walked In
8:How'dja Like to Love Me? *
9:Goodnight, Angel
10:Always and Always *

Apr. 16, 1938

1:Ti Pi Tin
2:Please Be Kind
3:Love Walked In
4:Heigh Ho
5:Goodnight, Angel
6:You're an Education
7:Thanks For the Memory
8:I Fall in Love With You Every Day *
9:Whistle While You Work
10:How'dja Like to Love Me?

Apr. 23, 1938

1:Ti Pi Tin
2:Goodnight, Angel
3:Please Be Kind
4:Whistle While You Work
5:I Fall in Love With You Every Day
6:How'dja Like to Love Me?
7:Love Walked In
8:Heigh Ho
9:At a Perfume Counter *
10:You're an Education

Apr. 30, 1938

1:Ti Pi Tin
2:Please Be Kind
3:Love Walked In
4:How'dja Like to Love Me?
5:Don't Be That Way *
6:Cry, Baby, Cry *
7:Heigh Ho
8:I Fall in Love With You Every Day
9:Goodnight, Angel
10:You're an Education

May 7, 1938

1:Please Be Kind
2:Ti Pi Tin
3:Cry, Baby, Cry
4:How'dja Like to Love Me?
5:You're an Education
6:Heigh Ho
7:Love Walked In
8:Sunday in the Park *
9:On the Sentimental Side *
10:Don't Be That Way

May 14, 1938

1:Love Walked In
2:Please Be Kind
3:Cry, Baby, Cry
4:Don't Be That Way
5:Ti Pi Tin
6:How'dja Like to Love Me?
7:You're an Education
8:I Love to Whistle *
9:On the Sentimental Side
10:Heigh Ho

May 21, 1938

1:Love Walked In
2:Please Be Kind
3:Cry, Baby, Cry
4:Don't Be That Way
5:I Love to Whistle
6:Ti Pi Tin
7:On the Sentimental Side
8:You're an Education
9:You Couldn't Be Cuter *
10:Heigh Ho

May 28, 1938

1:Love Walked In
2:Please Be Kind
3:Don't Be That Way
4:Cry, Baby, Cry
5:Ti Pi Tin
6:Cathedral in the Pines *
7:You Couldn't Be Cuter
8:On the Sentimental Side
9:Heigh Ho
10:I Let a Song Go Out of My Heart *

June 4, 1938

1:Love Walked In
2:Don't Be That Way
3:Cry, Baby, Cry
4:Please Be Kind
5:On the Sentimental Side
6:Lovelight in the Starlight *
7:Cathedral in the Pines
8:Ti Pi Tin
9:Bewildered *
10:I Let a Song Go Out of My Heart

June 11, 1938

1:Cry, Baby, Cry
2:Says My Heart *
3:Lovelight in the Starlight
4:Love Walked In
5:You Leave Me Breathless *
6:Please Be Kind
7:Don't Be That Way
8:Let Me Whisper *
9:Cathedral in the Pines
10:I Let a Song Go Out of My Heart

June 18, 1938

1:Says My Heart
2:Cry, Baby, Cry
3:You Leave Me Breathless
4:Lovelight in the Starlight
5:Cathedral in the Pines
6:Don't Be That Way
7:Love Walked In
8:I Let a Song Go Out of My Heart
9:Let Me Whisper
10:Please Be Kind

June 25, 1938

1:Says My Heart
2:I Let a Song Go Out of My Heart
3:Music, Maestro, Please *
4:You Leave Me Breathless
5:Lovelight in the Starlight
6:Cry, Baby, Cry
7:Love Walked In
8:Oh, Ma, Ma *
9:Cathedral in the Pines
10:Don't Be That Way

July 2, 1938

1:Says My Heart
2:Music, Maestro, Please
3:I Let a Song Go Out of My Heart
4:You Leave Me Breathless
5:Lovelight in the Starlight
6:This Time It's Real *
7:Cathedral in the Pines
8:Oh, Ma, Ma
9:Love Walked In
10:My Margarita *

July 9, 1938

1:Says My Heart
2:I Let a Song Go Out of My Heart
3:Music, Maestro, Please
4:I Married an Angel *
5:You Leave Me Breathless
6:Flat Foot Floogey *
7:Lovelight in the Starlight
8:Oh, Ma, Ma
9:I Hadn't Anyone Till You *
10:Cathedral in the Pines

July 16, 1938

1:Music, Maestro, Please
2:Says My Heart
3:I Let a Song Go Out of My Heart
4:You Leave Me Breathless
5:I Hadn't Anyone Till You
6:I Married an Angel
7:Little Lady Make Believe *
8:Flat Foot Floogey
9:Cathedral in the Pines
10:Lovelight in the Starlight

July 23, 1938

1:Music, Maestro, Please
2:Says My Heart
3:I Let a Song Go Out of My Heart
4:I Hadn't Anyone Till You
5:Flat Foot Floogey
6:You Leave Me Breathless
7:Lovelight in the Starlight
8:I Married an Angel
9:Little Lady Make Believe
10:There's Honey On the Moon Tonight *

July 30, 1938

1:I Let a Song Go Out of My Heart
2:Says My Heart
3:Music, Maestro, Please
4:I Married an Angel
5:Flat Foot Floogey
6:When Mother Nature Sings Her Lullaby *
7:Where in the World? *
8:When They Played the Polka *
9:I Hadn't Anyone Till You
10:Little Lady Make Believe

Aug. 6, 1938

1:Music, Maestro, Please
2:I Let a Song Go Out of My Heart
3:Says My Heart
4:I Married an Angel
5:I Hadn't Anyone Till You
6:When Mother Nature Sings Her Lullaby
7:Flat Foot Floogey
8:Now It Can Be Told *
9:A-Tisket, A-Tasket *
10:Little Lady Make Believe

Aug. 13, 1938

1:Music, Maestro, Please
2:A-Tisket, A-Tasket
3:I Let a Song Go Out of My Heart
4:When Mother Nature Sings Her Lullaby
5:I Hadn't Anyone Till You
6:Says My Heart
7:I'm Gonna Lock My Heart *
8:Flat Foot Floogey
9:Now It Can Be Told
10:I Married an Angel

Aug. 20, 1938

1:A-Tisket, A-Tasket
2:Music, Maestro, Please
3:I'm Gonna Lock My Heart
4:I Let a Song Go Out of My Heart
5:I Hadn't Anyone Till You
6:Now It Can Be Told
7:Says My Heart
8:I Married an Angel
9:When Mother Nature Sings Her Lullaby
10:You Go to My Head *

Aug. 27, 1938

1:A-Tisket, A-Tasket
2:Music, Maestro, Please
3:I'm Gonna Lock My Heart
4:Now It Can Be Told
5:When Mother Nature Sings Her Lullaby
6:I Let a Song Go Out of My Heart
7:What Goes On Here in My Heart? *
8:You Go to My Head
9:Says My Heart
10:I Hadn't Anyone Till You

Sept. 3, 1938

1:A-Tisket, A-Tasket
2:Now It Can Be Told
3:You Go to My Head
4:I'm Gonna Lock My Heart
5:Music, Maestro, Please
6:When Mother Nature Sings Her Lullaby
7:I've Got a Pocketful of Dreams *
8:Stop Beating Round the Mulberry Bush *
9:What Goes On Here in My Heart?
10:So Help Me *

Sept. 10, 1938

1:A-Tisket, A-Tasket
2:I'm Gonna Lock My Heart
3:You Go to My Head
4:Now It Can Be Told
5:I've Got a Pocketful of Dreams
6:Music, Maestro, Please
7:Stop Beating Round the Mulberry Bush
8:What Goes On Here in My Heart?
9:So Help Me
10:Alexander's Ragtime Band *

Sept. 17, 1938

1:A-Tisket, A-Tasket
2:You Go to My Head
3:I've Got a Pocketful of Dreams
4:Now It Can Be Told
5:I'm Gonna Lock My Heart
6:Stop Beating Round the Mulberry Bush
7:I've Got a Date With a Dream *
8:So Help Me
9:Alexander's Ragtime Band
10:What Goes On Here in My Heart?

Sept. 24, 1938

1:A-Tisket, A-Tasket
2:I've Got a Pocketful of Dreams
3:You Go to My Head
4:Stop Beating Round the Mulberry Bush
5:So Help Me
6:What Goes On Here in My Heart?
7:Now It Can Be Told
8:Alexander's Ragtime Band
9:I'm Gonna Lock My Heart
10:I've Got a Date With a Dream

Oct. 1, 1938

1:I've Got a Pocketful of Dreams
2:A-Tisket, A-Tasket
3:Change Partners *
4:So Help Me
5:Now It Can Be Told
6:Stop Beating Round the Mulberry Bush
7:I've Got a Date With a Dream
8:What Goes On Here in My Heart?
9:You Go to My Head
10:Alexander's Ragtime Band

Oct. 8, 1938

1:I've Got a Pocketful of Dreams
2:Change Partners
3:Lambeth Walk *
4:Stop Beating Round the Mulberry Bush
5:So Help Me
6:A-Tisket, A-Tasket
7:What Goes On Here in My Heart?
8:At Long Last Love *
9:Alexander's Ragtime Band
10:Bambina *

Oct. 15, 1938

1:Change Partners
2:I've Got a Pocketful of Dreams
3:Stop Beating Round the Mulberry Bush
4:So Help Me
5:Lambeth Walk
6:Small Fry *
7:A-Tisket, A-Tasket
8:At Long Last Love
9:Alexander's Ragtime Band
10:Tu-Li-Tulip-Time *

Oct. 22, 1938

1:I've Got a Pocketful of Dreams
2:Stop Beating Round the Mulberry Bush
3:Alexander's Ragtime Band
4:Change Partners
5:So Help Me
6:At Long Last Love
7:While a Cigarette Was Burning *
8:Small Fry
9:Heart and Soul *
10:Lambeth Walk

Oct. 29, 1938

1:I've Got a Pocketful of Dreams
2:Change Partners
3:So Help Me
4:Stop Beating Round the Mulberry Bush
5:My Own *
6:Heart and Soul
7:While a Cigarette Was Burning
8:Lambeth Walk
9:At Long Last Love
10:Alexander's Ragtime Band

Nov. 5, 1938

1:Change Partners
2:I've Got a Pocketful of Dreams
3:Lambeth Walk
4:At Long Last Love
5:Heart and Soul
6:While a Cigarette Was Burning
7:So Help Me
8:My Own
9:My Reverie *
10:Stop Beating Round the Mulberry Bush

Nov. 12, 1938

1:My Reverie
2:Heart and Soul
3:I've Got a Pocketful of Dreams
4:Change Partners
5:My Own
6:While a Cigarette Was Burning
7:All Ashore *
8:At Long Last Love
9:Lambeth Walk
10:So Help Me

Nov. 19, 1938

1:My Reverie
2:Heart and Soul
3:Change Partners
4:Summer Souvenirs *
5:All Ashore
6:Who Blew Out the Flame? *
7:I've Got a Pocketful of Dreams
8:While a Cigarette Was Burning
9:Day After Day *
10:Lambeth Walk

Nov. 26, 1938

1:My Reverie
2:Heart and Soul
3:While a Cigarette Was Burning
4:I've Got a Pocketful of Dreams
5:All Ashore
6:Two Sleepy People *
7:Have You Forgotten So Soon? *
8:Lambeth Walk
9:Summer Souvenirs
10:Change Partners

Dec. 3, 1938

1:My Reverie
2:Heart and Soul
3:Two Sleepy People
4:While a Cigarette Was Burning
5:Have You Forgotten So Soon?
6:All Ashore
7:Deep in a Dream *
8:Sixty Seconds Got Together *
9:I've Got a Pocketful of Dreams
10:Lambeth Walk

Dec. 10, 1938

1:My Reverie
2:Two Sleepy People
3:While a Cigarette Was Burning
4:All Ashore
5:Deep in a Dream
6:Have You Forgotten So Soon?
7:Heart and Soul
8:Lambeth Walk
9:I've Got a Pocketful of Dreams
10:Sixty Seconds Got Together

Dec. 17, 1938

1:My Reverie
2:Two Sleepy People
3:You Must Have Been a Beautiful Baby *
4:All Ashore
5:Have You Forgotten So Soon?
6:While a Cigarette Was Burning
7:Deep in a Dream
8:Heart and Soul
9:Lambeth Walk
10:Sixty Seconds Got Together

Dec. 24, 1938

1:My Reverie
2:You Must Have Been a Beautiful Baby
3:Deep in a Dream
4:All Ashore
5:Two Sleepy People
6:This Can't Be Love *
7:Jeepers Creepers *
8:The Night Before Christmas *
9:What Have You Got That Gets Me? *
10:Heart and Soul

Dec. 31, 1938

1:You Must Have Been a Beautiful Baby
2:My Reverie
3:All Ashore
4:Two Sleepy People
5:Jeepers Creepers
6:I Won't Tell a Soul *
7:This Can't Be Love
8:Deep in a Dream
9:Ya Got Me *
10:What Have You Got That Gets Me?

1939

And then, suddenly, it was over. The uneasy peace was gone. The Great War, the War to End All Wars, now had to be relabeled World War I. For World War II was declared in Europe in September as Hitler disregarded the Munich agreement, overran Czechoslovakia, and then sent his tanks into Poland. The cry in this country was "This time we'll stay out."

We opened the New York World's Fair, with its Trylon and Perisphere trademark. The kids were reading about Superman and Batman in comic books, the adults were reading John Steinbeck's *The Grapes of Wrath,* and the college students were engaging in the new fad of swallowing goldfish.

Little Orphan Annie was giving away Decoder Badges on radio, a player with the New York Yankees named Joe DiMaggio was leading the American League in batting, and the newspapers were following the dramatic efforts of raising thirty-three men by diving bell from the submarine *Squalus* on the floor of the Atlantic.

Two of the all-time great motion pictures made it to the screen that year, both directed by Victor Fleming. *Gone With the Wind* swept the Oscars, and *The Wizard of Oz* began an endurance trek that was to continue through the far-in-the-future era of TV. The latter film produced one of the two top songs of the year, "Over the Rainbow." Its seven weeks as Number One tied it with "Deep Purple" for the 1939 honors.

In the Big Band field, the year belonged to Glenn Miller. His "Sunrise Serenade" was so popular, it was followed up on "Your Hit Parade" that same year with his "Moonlight Serenade." Elsewhere on "Your Hit Parade," Tin Pan Alley borrowed from the classics, with Tchaikovsky supplying the impetus for "Our Love" and "Moon Love," and "The Lamp Is Low" being drawn from Ravel.

On Broadway *Life With Father* began what was to be a record run for a play. The biggest show on radio was Kay Kyser's "Kollege of Musical Knowledge," and he supplied the year's biggest novelty tune, "Three Little Fishes." Vocalist of the year had to be wee Bonnie Baker, whose wee recording of "Oh, Johnny, Oh" became synonymous with 1939.

Jan. 7, 1939

1:My Reverie
2:Deep in a Dream
3:Two Sleepy People
4:You Must Have Been a Beautiful Baby
5:All Ashore
6:I Must See Annie Tonight *
7:Thanks For Everything *
8:F.D.R. Jones *
9:Jeepers Creepers
10:This Can't Be Love

Jan. 14, 1939

1:You Must Have Been a Beautiful Baby
2:Two Sleepy People
3:My Reverie
4:Jeepers Creepers
5:This Can't Be Love
6:Deep in a Dream
7:I Must See Annie Tonight
8:The Umbrella Man *
9:Thanks For Everything
10:F.D.R. Jones

Jan. 21, 1939

1:Jeepers Creepers
2:My Reverie
3:You Must Have Been a Beautiful Baby
4:I Must See Annie Tonight
5:This Can't Be Love
6:The Umbrella Man
7:Deep in a Dream
8:Two Sleepy People
9:F.D.R. Jones
10:Thanks For Everything

Jan. 28, 1939

1:You Must Have Been a Beautiful Baby
2:Jeepers Creepers
3:Deep in a Dream
4:This Can't Be Love
5:Two Sleepy People
6:The Umbrella Man
7:Thanks For Everything
8:My Reverie
9:Get Out of Town *
10:They Say *

Feb. 4, 1939

1:Jeepers Creepers
2:You Must Have Been a Beautiful Baby
3:Deep in a Dream
4:Thanks For Everything
5:This Can't Be Love
6:The Umbrella Man
7:Two Sleepy People
8:I Have Eyes *
9:They Say
10:Get Out of Town

Feb. 11, 1939

1:Jeepers Creepers
2:This Can't Be Love
3:Thanks For Everything
4:The Umbrella Man
5:They Say
6:Deep in a Dream
7:Two Sleepy People
8:You Must Have Been a Beautiful Baby
9:Get Out of Town
10:I Have Eyes

Feb. 18, 1939

1:Jeepers Creepers
2:This Can't Be Love
3:Deep in a Dream
4:I Have Eyes
5:Thanks For Everything
6:The Umbrella Man
7:Could Be *
8:They Say
9:Hurry Home *
10:Annabelle *

Feb. 25, 1939

1:Jeepers Creepers
2:Deep Purple *
3:Hurry Home
4:Could Be
5:The Umbrella Man
6:This Can't Be Love
7:I Promise You *
8:Penny Serenade *
9:Deep in a Dream
10:I Have Eyes

* Newcomer

Mar. 4, 1939

1:Deep Purple
2:The Umbrella Man
3:Penny Serenade
4:Jeepers Creepers
5:I Have Eyes
6:Could Be
7:You're a Sweet Little Headache *
8:I Get Along Without You Very Well *
9:Deep in a Dream
10:This Can't Be Love

Mar. 11, 1939

1:Deep Purple
2:Penny Serenade
3:You're a Sweet Little Headache
4:Could Be
5:The Umbrella Man
6:Jeepers Creepers
7:Gotta Get Some Shuteye *
8:I Have Eyes
9:I Get Along Without You Very Well
10:The Masquerade Is Over *

Mar. 18, 1939

1:Deep Purple
2:Penny Serenade
3:The Umbrella Man
4:I Have Eyes
5:Could Be
6:I Get Along Without You Very Well
7:Gotta Get Some Shuteye
8:You're a Sweet Little Headache
9:Heaven Can Wait *
10:The Masquerade Is Over

Mar. 25, 1939

1:Deep Purple
2:Penny Serenade
3:Could Be
4:Heaven Can Wait
5:The Umbrella Man
6:Gotta Get Some Shuteye
7:Good For Nothin' But Love *
8:I Get Along Without You Very Well
9:I Cried For You *
10:The Masquerade Is Over

Apr. 1, 1939

1:Deep Purple
2:Penny Serenade
3:Could Be
4:I Get Along Without You Very Well
5:Hold Tight *
6:The Masquerade Is Over
7:Gotta Get Some Shuteye
8:Little Sir Echo *
9:Heaven Can Wait
10:I Cried For You

Apr. 8, 1939

1:Deep Purple
2:Penny Serenade
3:I Get Along Without You Very Well
4:Heaven Can Wait
5:The Masquerade Is Over
6:Little Sir Echo
7:Hold Tight
8:Could Be
9:This Is It *
10:The Moon Is a Silver Dollar *

Apr. 15, 1939

1:Deep Purple
2:Heaven Can Wait
3:Penny Serenade
4:Hold Tight
5:I Get Along Without You Very Well
6:Little Sir Echo
7:The Masquerade Is Over
8:Little Skipper *
9:Our Love *
10:The Moon Is a Silver Dollar

Apr. 22, 1939

1:Heaven Can Wait
2:Little Sir Echo
3:Deep Purple
4:Our Love
5:Penny Serenade
6:Little Skipper
7:The Masquerade Is Over
8:I Get Along Without You Very Well
9:It's Never Too Late *
10:The Moon Is a Silver Dollar

Apr. 29, 1939

1:Heaven Can Wait
2:Deep Purple
3:Little Sir Echo
4:Our Love
5:Little Skipper
6:I Want My Share of Love *
7:The Masquerade Is Over
8:Penny Serenade
9:And the Angels Sing *
10:I'm Building a Sailboat of Dreams *

May 6, 1939

1:Our Love
2:Heaven Can Wait
3:Little Sir Echo
4:And the Angels Sing
5:Deep Purple
6:Little Skipper
7:Tears From My Inkwell *
8:Three Little Fishes *
9:I'm Building a Sailboat of Dreams
10:Don't Worry 'Bout Me *

May 13, 1939

1:Our Love
2:And the Angels Sing
3:Heaven Can Wait
4:Little Skipper
5:Three Little Fishes
6:Little Sir Echo
7:Deep Purple
8:I'm Building a Sailboat of Dreams
9:Don't Worry 'Bout Me
10:The Lady's in Love With You *

May 20, 1939

1:And the Angels Sing
2:Three Little Fishes
3:Our Love
4:Heaven Can Wait
5:Little Skipper
6:Little Sir Echo
7:Wishing *
8:Don't Worry 'Bout Me
9:The Lady's in Love With You
10:I Never Knew Heaven Could Speak *

May 27, 1939

1:And the Angels Sing
2:Three Little Fishes
3:Wishing
4:Our Love
5:Heaven Can Wait
6:Don't Worry 'Bout Me
7:A New Moon and An Old Serenade *
8:The Lady's in Love With You
9:I Never Knew Heaven Could Speak
10:Little Skipper

June 3, 1939

1:And the Angels Sing
2:Our Love
3:Three Little Fishes
4:Wishing
5:Don't Worry 'Bout Me
6:I Never Knew Heaven Could Speak
7:The Lady's in Love With You
8:A New Moon and An Old Serenade
9:If I Didn't Care *
10:Little Skipper

June 10, 1939

1:And the Angels Sing
2:Wishing
3:If I Didn't Care
4:The Lady's in Love With You
5:Three Little Fishes
6:Don't Worry 'Bout Me
7:Our Love
8:Little Skipper
9:I Never Knew Heaven Could Speak
10:A New Moon and An Old Serenade

June 17, 1939

1:Wishing
2:And the Angels Sing
3:The Lady's in Love With You
4:Three Little Fishes
5:Don't Worry 'Bout Me
6:I Never Knew Heaven Could Speak
7:If I Didn't Care
8:A New Moon and An Old Serenade
9:Our Love
10:Strange Enchantment *

June 24, 1939

1:Wishing
2:And the Angels Sing
3:Beer Barrel Polka *
4:Three Little Fishes
5:A New Moon and An Old Serenade
6:The Lady's in Love With You
7:Don't Worry 'Bout Me
8:If I Didn't Care
9:Strange Enchantment
10:Stairway to the Stars *

July 1, 1939

1:Wishing
2:The Lady's in Love With You
3:And the Angels Sing
4:If I Didn't Care
5:Stairway to the Stars
6:Beer Barrel Polka
7:Sunrise Serenade *
8:Don't Worry 'Bout Me
9:Strange Enchantment
10:Three Little Fishes

July 8, 1939

1:Wishing
2:Beer Barrel Polka
3:Stairway to the Stars
4:The Lady's in Love With You
5:And the Angels Sing
6:Sunrise Serenade
7:White Sails *
8:Strange Enchantment
9:If I Didn't Care
10:Don't Worry 'Bout Me

July 15, 1939

1:Stairway to the Stars
2:Beer Barrel Polka
3:Wishing
4:White Sails
5:Moon Love *
6:And the Angels Sing
7:Sunrise Serenade
8:Strange Enchantment
9:The Lady's in Love With You
10:If I Didn't Care

July 22, 1939

1:Stairway to the Stars
2:White Sails
3:Beer Barrel Polka
4:Wishing
5:Moon Love
6:Sunrise Serenade
7:In the Middle of a Dream *
8:The Lady's in Love With You
9:All I Remember Is You *
10:I Poured My Heart Into a Song *

July 29, 1939

1:Stairway to the Stars
2:White Sails
3:Moon Love
4:Sunrise Serenade
5:Wishing
6:Beer Barrel Polka
7:In the Middle of a Dream
8:I Poured My Heart Into a Song
9:This Is No Dream *
10:The Lady's in Love With You

Aug. 5, 1939

1:Stairway to the Stars
2:Sunrise Serenade
3:Beer Barrel Polka
4:Moon Love
5:White Sails
6:I Poured My Heart Into a Song
7:Wishing
8:The Lamp Is Low *
9:This Is No Dream
10:In the Middle of a Dream

Aug. 12, 1939

1:Moon Love
2:Stairway to the Stars
3:White Sails
4:I Poured My Heart Into a Song
5:Sunrise Serenade
6:The Lamp Is Low
7:Wishing
8:Beer Barrel Polka
9:Comes Love *
10:In the Middle of a Dream

Aug. 19, 1939

1:Moon Love
2:Stairway to the Stars
3:White Sails
4:I Poured My Heart Into a Song
5:Beer Barrel Polka
6:Sunrise Serenade
7:Comes Love
8:Blue Evening *
9:The Lamp Is Low
10:Over the Rainbow *

Aug. 26, 1939

1:Moon Love
2:Stairway to the Stars
3:Beer Barrel Polka
4:I Poured My Heart Into a Song
5:The Lamp Is Low
6:Comes Love
7:Over the Rainbow
8:Sunrise Serenade
9:White Sails
10:To You *

Sept. 2, 1939

1:Moon Love
2:Over the Rainbow
3:The Lamp Is Low
4:Comes Love
5:I Poured My Heart Into a Song
6:Stairway to the Stars
7:Sunrise Serenade
8:To You
9:Beer Barrel Polka
10:White Sails

Sept. 9, 1939

1:Over the Rainbow
2:Moon Love
3:To You
4:The Lamp Is Low
5:I Poured My Heart Into a Song
6:Stairway to the Stars
7:Oh, You Crazy Moon *
8:Beer Barrel Polka
9:Sunrise Serenade
10:Comes Love

Sept. 16, 1939

1:Over the Rainbow
2:Moon Love
3:Cinderella, Stay in My Arms *
4:Man With the Mandolin *
5:Comes Love
6:Sunrise Serenade
7:The Lamp Is Low
8:Oh, You Crazy Moon
9:Day In, Day Out *
10:To You

Sept. 23, 1939

1:Over the Rainbow
2:Oh, You Crazy Moon
3:Moon Love
4:A Man and His Dream *
5:Comes Love
6:Day In, Day Out
7:Sunrise Serenade
8:Cinderella, Stay in My Arms
9:Man With the Mandolin
10:To You

Sept. 30, 1939

1:Over the Rainbow
2:Oh, You Crazy Moon
3:Man With the Mandolin
4:Day In, Day Out
5:To You
6:Cinderella, Stay in My Arms
7:Sunrise Serenade
8:Moonlight Serenade *
9:A Man and His Dream
10:Moon Love

Oct. 7, 1939

1:Over the Rainbow
2:Oh, You Crazy Moon
3:Man With the Mandolin
4:Day In, Day Out
5:A Man and His Dream
6:Cinderella, Stay in My Arms
7:Melancholy Mood *
8:Sunrise Serenade
9:Moonlight Serenade
10:Go Fly a Kite *

Oct. 14, 1939

1:Over the Rainbow
2:Day In, Day Out
3:A Man and His Dream
4:Man With the Mandolin
5:Oh, You Crazy Moon
6:Moonlight Serenade
7:In An 18th Century Drawing Room *
8:What's New? *
9:Melancholy Mood
10:An Apple For the Teacher *

Oct. 21, 1939

1:Day In, Day Out
2:Man With the Mandolin
3:Over the Rainbow
4:Blue Orchids *
5:South of the Border *
6:What's New?
7:A Man and His Dream
8:It's a Hundred to One I'm in Love *
9:Oh, You Crazy Moon
10:Are You Having Any Fun? *

Oct. 28, 1939

1:Over the Rainbow
2:South of the Border
3:Day In, Day Out
4:Man With the Mandolin
5:Blue Orchids
6:My Prayer *
7:What's New?
8:Good Morning *
9:Are You Having Any Fun?
10:Oh, You Crazy Moon

Nov. 4, 1939

1:Blue Orchids
2:South of the Border
3:Over the Rainbow
4:What's New?
5:Man With the Mandolin
6:Are You Having Any Fun?
7:My Prayer
8:Lilacs in the Rain *
9:Day In, Day Out
10:Last Night *

Nov. 11, 1939

1:South of the Border
2:What's New?
3:Blue Orchids
4:My Prayer
5:Lilacs in the Rain
6:Scatterbrain *
7:Last Night
8:Day In, Day Out
9:Are You Having Any Fun?
10:Over the Rainbow

Nov. 18, 1939

1:South of the Border
2:Scatterbrain
3:My Prayer
4:What's New?
5:Blue Orchids
6:Day In, Day Out
7:Last Night
8:Are You Having Any Fun?
9:Over the Rainbow
10:Lilacs in the Rain

Nov. 25, 1939

1:South of the Border
2:Blue Orchids
3:My Prayer
4:Lilacs in the Rain
5:Scatterbrain
6:Last Night
7:What's New?
8:I Didn't Know What Time It Was *
9:Over the Rainbow
10:Are You Having Any Fun?

Dec. 2, 1939

1:Scatterbrain
2:South of the Border
3:Lilacs in the Rain
4:My Prayer
5:Last Night
6:I Didn't Know What Time It Was
7:Blue Orchids
8:Can I Help It? *
9:Are You Having Any Fun?
10:El Rancho Grande *

Dec. 9, 1939

1:South of the Border
2:Scatterbrain
3:My Prayer
4:Lilacs in the Rain
5:Blue Orchids
6:I Didn't Know What Time It Was
7:El Rancho Grande
8:Speaking of Heaven *
9:Oh, Johnny, Oh *
10:Last Night

Dec. 16, 1939

1:Scatterbrain
2:South of the Border
3:My Prayer
4:Lilacs in the Rain
5:Last Night
6:El Rancho Grande
7:Oh, Johnny, Oh
8:I Didn't Know What Time It Was
9:Speaking of Heaven
10:Blue Orchids

Dec. 23, 1939

1:South of the Border
2:Scatterbrain
3:Oh, Johnny, Oh
4:Lilacs in the Rain
5:All the Things You Are *
6:My Prayer
7:Last Night
8:I Didn't Know What Time It Was
9:Goody Goodbye *
10:Blue Orchids

Dec. 30, 1939

1:Scatterbrain
2:My Prayer
3:Lilacs in the Rain
4:Oh, Johnny, Oh
5:All the Things You Are
6:South of the Border
7:I Didn't Know What Time It Was
8:Blue Orchids
9:Stop! It's Wonderful *
10:Goody Goodbye

1940

With an almost audible sigh of relief, the decade known as the Tired Thirties gave way to the one that would be known as the Flaming Forties.

Hitler's blitzkreig remained unchecked as Norway, Denmark, Holland, Belgium, and, finally, France all fell. Winston Churchill became British Prime Minister. Britain, using a fleet of anything that could float, pulled off the greatest mass evacuation in history, removing its troops from Dunkirk. And that summer, with Britain standing alone between Hitler and world conquest, the Battle of Britain began in the skies over England.

Russia conquered Finland and sided with the Germans and Italians. The United States still vowed this time they'd stay out, but ominously the peacetime draft began in this country. The training weapons were often broomsticks utilized as rifles.

A group of political amateurs stampeded the Republican convention that year with gallery cries of "We Want Willkie." They got him, and Wendell Willkie rolled up the second biggest popular vote in history that November. The biggest, though, was polled by FDR, who won an unprecedented third term on the platform of "Don't change horses in midstream."

Wilbur Shaw won the Indianapolis 500 for the third time, Cornelius Warmardam became the first man to pole-vault fifteen feet, and the forty-hour work week went into effect. "I Love a Mystery" was a hot radio property. The joke craze was "Yehudi" jokes, supplied by Bob Hope's Jerry Colonna. Hollywood gave us *Rebecca* and Disney's second all-cartoon feature, *Pinocchio,* which contributed "When You Wish Upon a Star" to "Your Hit Parade." The year's novelty song followup to 1939's "Three Little Fishes" was "Playmates," with Kay Kyser again doing the honors. Tchaikovsky did his part again with "On the Isle of May."

But the biggest hits of 1940, each with seven weeks as Number One, were "The Woodpecker Song" (not to be confused with "Woody Woodpecker" of the Hit Parade eight years later) and the song that will always mean 1940 for the young romantics of that year, "I'll Never Smile Again."

Jan. 6, 1940

1:Scatterbrain
2:All the Things You Are
3:My Prayer
4:Faithful Forever *
5:South of the Border
6:Oh, Johnny, Oh
7:Stop! It's Wonderful
8:I Didn't Know What Time It Was
9:Lilacs in the Rain
10:Careless *

Jan. 13, 1940

1:Scatterbrain
2:Oh, Johnny, Oh
3:South of the Border
4:All the Things You Are
5:Faithful Forever
6:Careless
7:At the Balalaika *
8:My Prayer
9:Indian Summer *
10:Lilacs in the Rain

Jan. 20, 1940

1:Scatterbrain
2:All the Things You Are
3:Careless
4:Oh, Johnny, Oh
5:Faithful Forever
6:South of the Border
7:At the Balalaika
8:Indian Summer
9:My Prayer
10:Lilacs in the Rain

Jan. 27, 1940

1:All the Things You Are
2:Careless
3:Scatterbrain
4:Oh, Johnny, Oh
5:Indian Summer
6:Faithful Forever
7:South of the Border
8:At the Balalaika
9:My Prayer
10:This Changing World *

Feb. 3, 1940

1:Careless
2:All the Things You Are
3:Indian Summer
4:Faithful Forever
5:Oh, Johnny, Oh
6:Darn That Dream *
7:At the Balalaika
8:This Changing World
9:In the Mood *
10:Scatterbrain

Feb. 10, 1940

1:All the Things You Are
2:Careless
3:Indian Summer
4:Faithful Forever
5:The Little Red Fox *
6:Oh, Johnny, Oh
7:In An Old Dutch Garden *
8:Darn That Dream
9:At the Balalaika
10:To You, Sweetheart, Aloha *

Feb. 17, 1940

1:Careless
2:Indian Summer
3:At the Balalaika
4:All the Things You Are
5:Faithful Forever
6:In An Old Dutch Garden
7:Darn That Dream
8:It's a Blue World *
9:The Little Red Fox
10:Oh, Johnny, Oh

Feb. 24, 1940

1:Indian Summer
2:Careless
3:All the Things You Are
4:The Little Red Fox
5:Darn That Dream
6:At the Balalaika
7:In An Old Dutch Garden
8:Faithful Forever
9:Gaucho Serenade *
10:It's a Blue World

* Newcomer

Mar. 2, 1940

1:Careless
2:Indian Summer
3:Darn That Dream
4:At the Balalaika
5:It's a Blue World
6:All the Things You Are
7:Do I Love You? *
8:In An Old Dutch Garden
9:Faithful Forever
10:I've Got My Eyes On You *

Mar. 9, 1940

1:Careless
2:Indian Summer
3:In An Old Dutch Garden
4:Starlit Hour *
5:Darn That Dream
6:I've Got My Eyes On You
7:At the Balalaika
8:Do I Love You?
9:When You Wish Upon a Star *
10:It's a Blue World

Mar. 16, 1940

1:Darn That Dream
2:It's a Blue World
3:In An Old Dutch Garden
4:Indian Summer
5:On the Isle of May *
6:Starlit Hour
7:Careless
8:When You Wish Upon a Star
9:I've Got My Eyes On You
10:Do I Love You?

Mar. 23, 1940

1:Careless
2:It's a Blue World
3:Starlit Hour
4:On the Isle of May
5:Darn That Dream
6:In An Old Dutch Garden
7:When You Wish Upon a Star
8:Indian Summer
9:I've Got My Eyes On You
10:Do I Love You?

Mar. 30, 1940

1:When You Wish Upon a Star
2:It's a Blue World
3:Starlit Hour
4:Indian Summer
5:On the Isle of May
6:In An Old Dutch Garden
7:Leanin' On the Old Top Rail *
8:Careless
9:I've Got My Eyes On You
10:With the Wind and the Rain in Your Hair *

Apr. 6, 1940

1:When You Wish Upon a Star
2:Starlit Hour
3:The Woodpecker Song *
4:On the Isle of May
5:In An Old Dutch Garden
6:It's a Blue World
7:Leanin' On the Old Top Rail
8:With the Wind and the Rain in Your Hair
9:Indian Summer
10:Careless

Apr. 13, 1940

1:When You Wish Upon a Star
2:The Woodpecker Song
3:On the Isle of May
4:In An Old Dutch Garden
5:With the Wind and the Rain in Your Hair
6:Starlit Hour
7:The Singing Hills *
8:Let There Be Love *
9:Alice Blue Gown *
10:It's a Blue World

Apr. 20, 1940

1:When You Wish Upon a Star
2:With the Wind and the Rain in Your Hair
3:On the Isle of May
4:The Woodpecker Song
5:Let There Be Love
6:In An Old Dutch Garden
7:How High the Moon *
8:Starlit Hour
9:The Singing Hills
10:So Far, So Good *

Apr. 27, 1940

1:When You Wish Upon a Star
2:The Woodpecker Song
3:With the Wind and the Rain in Your Hair
4:The Singing Hills
5:Too Romantic *
6:On the Isle of May
7:How High the Moon
8:Starlit Hour
9:Let There Be Love
10:In An Old Dutch Garden

May 4, 1940

1:The Woodpecker Song
2:When You Wish Upon a Star
3:With the Wind and the Rain in Your Hair
4:The Singing Hills
5:On the Isle of May
6:How High the Moon
7:Too Romantic
8:Let There Be Love
9:Starlit Hour
10:You, You Darlin' *

May 11, 1940

1:The Woodpecker Song
2:With the Wind and the Rain in Your Hair
3:When You Wish Upon a Star
4:Let There Be Love
5:The Singing Hills
6:Say It *
7:On the Isle of May
8:Apple Blossoms and Chapel Bells *
9:Lovers' Lullaby *
10:Too Romantic

May 18, 1940

1:The Woodpecker Song
2:With the Wind and the Rain in Your Hair
3:The Singing Hills
4:Imagination *
5:When You Wish Upon a Star
6:Let There Be Love
7:Little Curly Hair in a Highchair *
8:Lovers' Lullaby
9:Say It
10:Too Romantic

May 25, 1940

1:The Woodpecker Song
2:Imagination
3:When You Wish Upon a Star
4:With the Wind and the Rain in Your Hair
5:Say It
6:Make Believe Island *
7:Little Curly Hair in a Highchair
8:The Singing Hills
9:Playmates *
10:Too Romantic

June 1, 1940

1:The Woodpecker Song
2:Say It
3:Too Romantic
4:Imagination
5:Playmates
6:Where Was I? *
7:The Singing Hills
8:When You Wish Upon a Star
9:With the Wind and the Rain in Your Hair
10:Make Believe Island

June 8, 1940

1:The Woodpecker Song
2:Say It
3:Where Was I?
4:Shake Down the Stars *
5:Imagination
6:With the Wind and the Rain in Your Hair
7:Playmates
8:It's a Wonderful World *
9:Too Romantic
10:Make Believe Island

June 15, 1940

1:The Woodpecker Song
2:Imagination
3:Say It
4:Make Believe Island
5:Shake Down the Stars
6:Devil May Care *
7:Blue Lovebird *
8:Where Was I?
9:Playmates
10:With the Wind and the Rain in Your Hair

June 22, 1940

1:Imagination
2:Make Believe Island
3:Where Was I?
4:Say It
5:The Woodpecker Song
6:Playmates
7:Shake Down the Stars
8:The Breeze and I *
9:Blue Lovebird
10:Devil May Care

June 29, 1940

1:Make Believe Island
2:Where Was I?
3:Imagination
4:The Woodpecker Song
5:Fools Rush In *
6:I Can't Love You Any More *
7:Playmates
8:The Breeze and I
9:Devil May Care
10:You're Lonely and I'm Lonely *

July 6, 1940

1:Imagination
2:The Woodpecker Song
3:Make Believe Island
4:Where Was I?
5:Playmates
6:I Can't Love You Any More
7:The Breeze and I
8:Fools Rush In
9:You're Lonely and I'm Lonely
10:Devil May Care

July 13, 1940

1:Imagination
2:Make Believe Island
3:The Woodpecker Song
4:Sierra Sue *
5:The Breeze and I
6:Fools Rush In
7:Where Was I?
8:Playmates
9:I Can't Love You Any More
10:Devil May Care

July 20, 1940

1:Fools Rush In
2:The Breeze and I
3:Make Believe Island
4:Playmates
5:Where Was I?
6:The Woodpecker Song
7:Sierra Sue
8:Imagination
9:I'll Never Smile Again *
10:I'm Stepping Out With a Memory Tonight *

July 27, 1940

1:Make Believe Island
2:I'll Never Smile Again
3:Sierra Sue
4:Fools Rush In
5:Imagination
6:The Breeze and I
7:I'm Stepping Out With a Memory Tonight
8:Playmates
9:Where Was I?
10:I'm Nobody's Baby *

Aug. 3, 1940

1:I'll Never Smile Again
2:The Breeze and I
3:Sierra Sue
4:Fools Rush In
5:Make Believe Island
6:Playmates
7:Imagination
8:Where Was I?
9:When the Swallows Come Back to Capistrano *
10:I'm Nobody's Baby

Aug. 10, 1940

1:I'll Never Smile Again
2:Fools Rush In
3:The Breeze and I
4:Sierra Sue
5:When the Swallows Come Back to Capistrano
6:Make Believe Island
7:I'm Nobody's Baby
8:Imagination
9:All This and Heaven Too *
10:You Think of Everything *

Aug. 17, 1940

1:Sierra Sue
2:I'll Never Smile Again
3:Fools Rush In
4:The Breeze and I
5:When the Swallows Come Back to Capistrano
6:Make Believe Island
7:Six Lessons From Madame LaZonga *
8:The Nearness of You *
9:I'm Nobody's Baby
10:All This and Heaven Too

Aug. 24, 1940

1:I'll Never Smile Again
2:When the Swallows Come Back to Capistrano
3:I'm Nobody's Baby
4:Fools Rush In
5:Sierra Sue
6:Blueberry Hill *
7:The Breeze and I
8:The Nearness of You
9:Practice Makes Perfect *
10:All This and Heaven Too

Aug. 31, 1940

1:I'll Never Smile Again
2:Sierra Sue
3:Fools Rush In
4:I'm Nobody's Baby
5:When the Swallows Come Back to Capistrano
6:All This and Heaven Too
7:Blueberry Hill
8:The Breeze and I
9:The Nearness of You
10:Practice Makes Perfect

Sept. 7, 1940

1:I'll Never Smile Again
2:When the Swallows Come Back to Capistrano
3:Sierra Sue
4:Blueberry Hill
5:Fools Rush In
6:I'm Nobody's Baby
7:All This and Heaven Too
8:The Nearness of You
9:Practice Makes Perfect
10:The Breeze and I

Sept. 14, 1940

1:I'll Never Smile Again
2:I'm Nobody's Baby
3:When the Swallows Come Back to Capistrano
4:All This and Heaven Too
5:Blueberry Hill
6:Sierra Sue
7:The Nearness of You
8:Practice Makes Perfect
9:Maybe *
10:The Breeze and I

Sept. 21, 1940

1:I'll Never Smile Again
2:Blueberry Hill
3:All This and Heaven Too
4:I'm Nobody's Baby
5:When the Swallows Come Back to Capistrano
6:Practice Makes Perfect
7:Sierra Sue
8:Trade Winds *
9:Maybe
10:The Same Old Story *

Sept. 28, 1940

1:Maybe
2:When the Swallows Come Back to Capistrano
3:I'll Never Smile Again
4:Blueberry Hill
5:Practice Makes Perfect
6:Trade Winds
7:I'm Nobody's Baby
8:Sierra Sue
9:Our Love Affair *
10:The Same Old Story

Oct. 5, 1940

1:Practice Makes Perfect
2:I'll Never Smile Again
3:Maybe
4:Blueberry Hill
5:I'm Nobody's Baby
6:When the Swallows Come Back to Capistrano
7:Only Forever *
8:Trade Winds
9:And So Do I *
10:Our Love Affair

Oct. 12, 1940

1:Maybe
2:Practice Makes Perfect
3:Blueberry Hill
4:I'll Never Smile Again
5:Trade Winds
6:Only Forever
7:The Call of the Canyon *
8:When the Swallows Come Back to Capistrano
9:A Million Dreams Ago *
10:Our Love Affair

Oct. 19, 1940

1:Maybe
2:Practice Makes Perfect
3:Trade Winds
4:Blueberry Hill
5:I'll Never Smile Again
6:Only Forever
7:When the Swallows Come Back to Capistrano
8:Our Love Affair
9:Ferryboat Serenade *
10:There I Go *

Oct. 26, 1940

1:Practice Makes Perfect
2:Trade Winds
3:Only Forever
4:Maybe
5:Our Love Affair
6:Ferryboat Serenade
7:Blueberry Hill
8:I'll Never Smile Again
9:There I Go
10:When the Swallows Come Back to Capistrano

Nov. 2, 1940

1:Only Forever
2:Practice Makes Perfect
3:Maybe
4:Ferryboat Serenade
5:Trade Winds
6:Blueberry Hill
7:Our Love Affair
8:I'll Never Smile Again
9:There I Go
10:Two Dreams Met *

Nov. 9, 1940

1:Only Forever
2:Ferryboat Serenade
3:Maybe
4:Practice Makes Perfect
5:Trade Winds
6:Blueberry Hill
7:There I Go
8:Our Love Affair
9:Looking For Yesterday *
10:Now I Lay Me Down to Dream *

Nov. 16, 1940

1:Only Forever
2:Ferryboat Serenade
3:Maybe
4:Practice Makes Perfect
5:Trade Winds
6:We Three *
7:There I Go
8:Our Love Affair
9:Blueberry Hill
10:Dream Valley *

Nov. 23, 1940

1:Ferryboat Serenade
2:Trade Winds
3:Only Forever
4:There I Go
5:Practice Makes Perfect
6:We Three
7:Maybe
8:Our Love Affair
9:Dream Valley
10:Blueberry Hill

Nov. 30, 1940

1:Trade Winds
2:Ferryboat Serenade
3:Only Forever
4:There I Go
5:We Three
6:Our Love Affair
7:Maybe
8:Practice Makes Perfect
9:So You're the One *
10:A Nightingale Sang in Berkeley Square *

Dec. 7, 1940

1:We Three
2:Ferryboat Serenade
3:There I Go
4:Only Forever
5:Down Argentina Way *
6:Trade Winds
7:A Nightingale Sang in Berkeley Square
8:Our Love Affair
9:Frenesi *
10:So You're the One

Dec. 14, 1940

1:There I Go
2:Ferryboat Serenade
3:We Three
'4:Only Forever
5:Trade Winds
6:A Nightingale Sang in Berkeley Square
7:Down Argentina Way
8:Frenesi
9:I Give You My Word *
10:So You're the One

Dec. 21, 1940

1:There I Go
2:Ferryboat Serenade
3:A Nightingale Sang in Berkeley Square
4:Down Argentina Way
5:We Three
6:Only Forever
7:Frenesi
8:Trade Winds
9:So You're the One
10:I Give You My Word

Dec. 28, 1940

1:There I Go
2:Frenesi
3:A Nightingale Sang in Berkeley Square
4:We Three
5:Down Argentina Way
6:Ferryboat Serenade
7:Only Forever
8:So You're the One
9:Trade Winds
10:I Give You My Word

1941

One rule remains constant. If you are old enough, you can unhesitatingly recall what you were doing December 7, 1941, on that Sunday when Japan bombed Pearl Harbor and this nation was plunged into World War II.

As such, the Saturday night "Your Hit Parade" of December 6, 1941, is the most requested memory-music date I hear. The Number One song that night was "Tonight We Love," popularized by the Freddy Martin recording; Tchaikovsky, dead since 1893, was still doing his bit for Tin Pan Alley. It was Glenn Miller's year, though. "Elmer's Tune" and "Chattanooga Choo Choo," hits because of his recordings, were right behind "Tonight We Love."

The war we found ourselves in by year's end had been responsible for many of 1941's hit tunes all year long—"My Sister and I" (Holland), "The White Cliffs of Dover" (Britain), and "Till Reveille" (the peacetime draft here).

The nonsense song of the year was undisputed—"The Hut Sut Song." Also undisputed was the top song of the year—"I Hear a Rhapsody." No song had ever been Number One more than eight weeks. "I Hear a Rhapsody" tied that, went on to nine weeks, and then set a new record of ten weeks in the top spot.

It was a good year for popular music in spite of an ASCAP ban on radio tunes that for a while threatened to make the public-domain "Jeanie With the Light Brown Hair" the most overworked girl on the airwaves. She didn't, however, make "Your Hit Parade."

President Roosevelt, prior to Pearl Harbor, signed the Lend-Lease Act to aid embattled Britain, proclaimed man's right to "The Four Freedoms," and met with Churchill in the North Atlantic to draft the Atlantic Charter.

It was the year of the Veronica Lake hairdo, and the baseball season in which Joe DiMaggio hit safely in a record fifty-six straight games. On the screen *Citizen Kane* was premiered on its way toward eventual milestone status. And *Lady in the Dark* was lighting up Broadway, although the Great White Way was to undergo a dimout in anticipation of possible air raids.

Jan. 4, 1941

1:There I Go
2:Frenesi
3:I Give You My Word
4:So You're the One
5:I Hear a Rhapsody *
6:Perfidia *
7:Down Argentina Way
8:You Walk By *
9:Keep An Eye on Your Heart *
10:A Nightingale Sang in Berkeley Square

Jan. 11, 1941

1:Frenesi
2:There I Go
3:I Give You My Word
4:So You're the One
5:I Hear a Rhapsody
6:You Walk By
7:Down Argentina Way
8:Perfidia
9:A Nightingale Sang in Berkeley Square
10:May I Never Love Again *

Jan. 18, 1941

1:Frenesi
2:There I Go
3:I Hear a Rhapsody
4:I Give You My Word
5:So You're the One
6:You Walk By
7:Down Argentina Way
8:May I Never Love Again
9:It All Comes Back to Me Now *
10:Perfidia

Jan. 25, 1941

1:Frenesi
2:I Hear a Rhapsody
3:There I Go
4:I Give You My Word
5:So You're the One
6:You Walk By
7:It All Comes Back to Me Now
8:There'll Be Some Changes Made *
9:May I Never Love Again
10:Perfidia

Feb. 1, 1941

1:I Hear a Rhapsody
2:Frenesi
3:I Give You My Word
4:There I Go
5:So You're the One
6:You Walk By
7:Perfidia
8:It All Comes Back to Me Now
9:There'll Be Some Changes Made
10:High On a Windy Hill *

Feb. 8, 1941

1:I Hear a Rhapsody
2:Frenesi
3:You Walk By
4:So You're the One
5:I Give You My Word
6:There I Go
7:Perfidia
8:High On a Windy Hill
9:It All Comes Back to Me Now
10:There'll Be Some Changes Made

Feb. 15, 1941

1:I Hear a Rhapsody
2:Frenesi
3:You Walk By
4:I Give You My Word
5:So You're the One
6:It All Comes Back to Me Now
7:High On a Windy Hill
8:Perfidia
9:There I Go
10:There'll Be Some Changes Made

Feb. 22, 1941

1:I Hear a Rhapsody
2:Frenesi
3:You Walk By
4:Perfidia
5:So You're the One
6:High On a Windy Hill
7:It All Comes Back to Me Now
8:I Give You My Word
9:There'll Be Some Changes Made
10:There I Go

* Newcomer

Mar. 1, 1941

1:I Hear a Rhapsody
2:You Walk By
3:Frenesi
4:It All Comes Back to Me Now
5:High On a Windy Hill
6:Perfidia
7:There'll Be Some Changes Made
8:So You're the One
9:I Give You My Word
10:It's So Peaceful in the Country *

Mar. 8, 1941

1:I Hear a Rhapsody
2:Frenesi
3:It All Comes Back to Me Now
4:You Walk By
5:High On a Windy Hill
6:Perfidia
7:There'll Be Some Changes Made
8:So You're the One
9:I Give You My Word
10:Let's Dream This One Out *

Mar. 15, 1941

1:I Hear a Rhapsody
2:It All Comes Back to Me Now
3:You Walk By
4:High On a Windy Hill
5:Perfidia
6:Frenesi
7:There'll Be Some Changes Made
8:So You're the One
9:Amapola *
10:Georgia On My Mind *

Mar. 22, 1941

1:I Hear a Rhapsody
2:It All Comes Back to Me Now
3:You Walk By
4:There'll Be Some Changes Made
5:High On a Windy Hill
6:Frenesi
7:Perfidia
8:Amapola
9:Georgia On My Mind
10:The Wise Old Owl *

Mar. 29, 1941

1:I Hear a Rhapsody
2:It All Comes Back to Me Now
3:Frenesi
4:High On a Windy Hill
5:Perfidia
6:You Walk By
7:There'll Be Some Changes Made
8:The Wise Old Owl
9:Oh, Look at Me Now *
10:Amapola

Apr. 5, 1941

1:Amapola
2:It All Comes Back to Me Now
3:There'll Be Some Changes Made
4:I Hear a Rhapsody
5:You Walk By
6:Perfidia
7:High On a Windy Hill
8:The Wise Old Owl
9:Oh, Look at Me Now
10:Frenesi

Apr. 12, 1941

1:I Hear a Rhapsody
2:There'll Be Some Changes Made
3:It All Comes Back to Me Now
4:Amapola
5:You Walk By
6:The Wise Old Owl
7:High On a Windy Hill
8:Frenesi
9:Perfidia
10:Oh, Look at Me Now

Apr. 19, 1941

1:The Wise Old Owl
2:Amapola
3:High On a Windy Hill
4:I Hear a Rhapsody
5:Perfidia
6:You Walk By
7:There'll Be Some Changes Made
8:Oh, Look at Me Now
9:Walking By the River *
10:It All Comes Back to Me Now

Apr. 26, 1941

1:Amapola
2:There'll Be Some Changes Made
3:Walking By the River
4:It All Comes Back to Me Now
5:The Wise Old Owl
6:Oh, Look at Me Now
7:High On a Windy Hill
8:Number 10 Lullaby Lane *
9:Do I Worry? *
10:Perfidia

May 3, 1941

1:Amapola
2:The Wise Old Owl
3:There'll Be Some Changes Made
4:Walking By the River
5:Do I Worry?
6:Oh, Look at Me Now
7:My Sister and I *
8:It All Comes Back to Me Now
9:Number 10 Lullaby Lane
10:Maria Elena *

May 10, 1941

1:Amapola
2:The Wise Old Owl
3:My Sister and I
4:Intermezzo *
5:Walking By the River
6:Do I Worry?
7:Oh, Look at Me Now
8:There'll Be Some Changes Made
9:Maria Elena
10:Number 10 Lullaby Lane

May 17, 1941

1:Amapola
2:My Sister and I
3:Do I Worry?
4:Intermezzo
5:The Wise Old Owl
6:Walking By the River
7:The Things I Love *
8:Maria Elena
9:Number 10 Lullaby Lane
10:Oh, Look at Me Now

May 24, 1941

1:Amapola
2:My Sister and I
3:Intermezzo
4:Maria Elena
5:Do I Worry?
6:Walking By the River
7:The Things I Love
8:Number 10 Lullaby Lane
9:Two Hearts That Pass in the Night *
10:G'Bye Now *

May 31, 1941

1:My Sister and I
2:Intermezzo
3:Amapola
4:Maria Elena
5:Do I Worry?
6:Number 10 Lullaby Lane
7:The Things I Love
8:G'Bye Now
9:Walking By the River
10:Two Hearts That Pass in the Night

June 7, 1941

1:My Sister and I
2:Intermezzo
3:Maria Elena
4:Amapola
5:Do I Worry?
6:The Things I Love
7:G'Bye Now
8:Walking By the River
9:Two Hearts That Pass in the Night
10:Number 10 Lullaby Lane

June 14, 1941

1:Intermezzo
2:Maria Elena
3:My Sister and I
4:The Things I Love
5:Do I Worry?
6:Amapola
7:The Hut Sut Song *
8:Just a Little Bit South of North Carolina *
9:Walking By the River
10:Two Hearts That Pass in the Night

June 21, 1941

1:Maria Elena
2:Intermezzo
3:My Sister and I
4:The Things I Love
5:The Hut Sut Song
6:Do I Worry?
7:Amapola
8:Just a Little Bit South of North Carolina
9:Two Hearts That Pass in the Night
10:Daddy *

June 28, 1941

1:Maria Elena
2:Intermezzo
3:The Hut Sut Song
4:The Things I Love
5:My Sister and I
6:Do I Worry?
7:Amapola
8:Daddy
9:Just a Little Bit South of North Carolina
10:Let's Get Away From It All *

July 5, 1941

1:The Hut Sut Song
2:Intermezzo
3:Maria Elena
4:The Things I Love
5:My Sister and I
6:Daddy
7:Just a Little Bit South of North Carolina
8:Let's Get Away From It All
9:Do I Worry?
10:Amapola

July 12, 1941

1:The Hut Sut Song
2:Maria Elena
3:Intermezzo
4:The Things I Love
5:Daddy
6:Just a Little Bit South of North Carolina
7:My Sister and I
8:Do I Worry?
9:Amapola
10:Green Eyes *

July 19, 1941

1:The Hut Sut Song
2:Intermezzo
3:Maria Elena
4:The Things I Love
5:Daddy
6:My Sister and I
7:Green Eyes
8:Just a Little Bit South of North Carolina
9:Do I Worry?
10:Amapola

July 26, 1941

1:Intermezzo
2:Daddy
3:The Hut Sut Song
4:Maria Elena
5:The Things I Love
6:Green Eyes
7:Just a Little Bit South of North Carolina
8:My Sister and I
9:Yours *
10:Do I Worry?

Aug. 2, 1941

1:Daddy
2:The Hut Sut Song
3:Maria Elena
4:Intermezzo
5:The Things I Love
6:Green Eyes
7:Yours
8:Just a Little Bit South of North Carolina
9:Till Reveille *
10:My Sister and I

Aug. 9, 1941

1:Daddy
2:Maria Elena
3:The Things I Love
4:Intermezzo
5:The Hut Sut Song
6:Green Eyes
7:Yours
8:Till Reveille
9:I Went Out of My Way *
10:Just a Little Bit South of North Carolina

Aug. 16, 1941

1:Daddy
2:Till Reveille
3:Green Eyes
4:The Things I Love
5:The Hut Sut Song
6:Maria Elena
7:Intermezzo
8:Yours
9:You and I *
10:Do You Care? *

Aug. 23, 1941

1:Daddy
2:Maria Elena
3:Green Eyes
4:The Things I Love
5:Intermezzo
6:Yours
7:You and I
8:The Hut Sut Song
9:Till Reveille
10:Do You Care?

Aug. 30, 1941

1:Daddy
2:Maria Elena
3:Till Reveille
4:Intermezzo
5:Green Eyes
6:The Things I Love
7:Yours
8:I Guess I'll Have to Dream the Rest *
9:You and I
10:Do You Care?

Sept. 6, 1941

1:Daddy
2:Yours
3:Till Reveille
4:Green Eyes
5:You and I
6:The Things I Love
7:Maria Elena
8:I Guess I'll Have to Dream the Rest
9:Intermezzo
10:Do You Care?

Sept. 13, 1941

1:You and I
2:Till Reveille
3:Green Eyes
4:Yours
5:Daddy
6:Do You Care?
7:Maria Elena
8:Intermezzo
9:The Things I Love
10:I Guess I'll Have to Dream the Rest

Sept. 20, 1941

1:You and I
2:Yours
3:Till Reveille
4:Green Eyes
5:I Guess I'll Have to Dream the Rest
6:Do You Care?
7:Daddy
8:Maria Elena
9:Time Was *
10:Jim *

Sept. 27, 1941

1:You and I
2:Yours
3:Till Reveille
4:I Guess I'll Have to Dream the Rest
5:I Don't Want to Set the World On Fire *
6:Do You Care?
7:Daddy
8:Time Was
9:Maria Elena
10:Jim

Oct. 4, 1941

1:You and I
2:Yours
3:I Don't Want to Set the World On Fire
4:Till Reveille
5:Do You Care?
6:Time Was
7:Jim
8:I Guess I'll Have to Dream the Rest
9:Intermezzo
10:Yes Indeed! *

Oct. 11, 1941

1:You and I
2:I Don't Want to Set the World On Fire
3:Till Reveille
4:Jim
5:I Guess I'll Have to Dream the Rest
6:Yours
7:Do You Care?
8:Time Was
9:Intermezzo
10:Tonight We Love *

Oct. 18, 1941

1:I Don't Want to Set the World On Fire
2:You and I
3:Jim
4:Yours
5:Till Reveille
6:Do You Care?
7:I Guess I'll Have to Dream the Rest
8:Time Was
9:Tonight We Love
10:Intermezzo

Oct. 25, 1941

1:I Don't Want to Set the World On Fire
2:You and I
3:Jim
4:Time Was
5:Do You Care?
6:Yours
7:I Guess I'll Have to Dream the Rest
8:Till Reveille
9:Tonight We Love
10:Hi, Neighbor *

Nov. 1, 1941

1:I Don't Want to Set the World On Fire
2:You and I
3:Jim
4:I Guess I'll Have to Dream the Rest
5:Do You Care?
6:Tonight We Love
7:Yours
8:Time Was
9:Till Reveille
10:I See a Million People *

Nov. 8, 1941

1:I Don't Want to Set the World On Fire
2:Tonight We Love
3:Jim
4:You and I
5:Do You Care?
6:I Guess I'll Have to Dream the Rest
7:Shepherd Serenade *
8:Time Was
9:Yours
10:Till Reveille

Nov. 15, 1941

1:Tonight We Love
2:I Don't Want to Set the World On Fire
3:You and I
4:Jim
5:Time Was
6:Shepherd Serenade
7:Do You Care?
8:Yours
9:I Guess I'll Have to Dream the Rest
10:Two in Love *

Nov. 22, 1941

1:Tonight We Love
2:I Don't Want to Set the World On Fire
3:Jim
4:Shepherd Serenade
5:Elmer's Tune *
6:Do You Care?
7:You and I
8:Chattanooga Choo Choo *
9:I Guess I'll Have to Dream the Rest
10:Two in Love

Nov. 29, 1941

1:Tonight We Love
2:Shepherd Serenade
3:Elmer's Tune
4:I Don't Want to Set the World On Fire
5:You and I
6:Jim
7:This Love of Mine *
8:Do You Care?
9:Two in Love
10:Chattanooga Choo Choo

Dec. 6, 1941

1:Tonight We Love
2:Elmer's Tune
3:Chattanooga Choo Choo
4:Shepherd Serenade
5:I Don't Want to Set the World On Fire
6:This Love of Mine
7:You and I
8:Jim
9:A Sinner Kissed An Angel *
10:Everything I Love *

Dec. 13, 1941

1:Elmer's Tune
2:Shepherd Serenade
3:Tonight We Love
4:Chattanooga Choo Choo
5:I Don't Want to Set the World On Fire
6:This Love of Mine
7:Orange Blossom Lane *
8:You and I
9:The White Cliffs of Dover *
10:Everything I Love

Dec. 20, 1941

1:Chattanooga Choo Choo
2:Elmer's Tune
3:Tonight We Love
4:Shepherd Serenade
5:This Love of Mine
6:I Don't Want to Set the World On Fire
7:Madelaine *
8:The White Cliffs of Dover
9:You and I
10:Everything I Love

Dec. 27, 1941

1:Elmer's Tune
2:Chattanooga Choo Choo
3:The White Cliffs of Dover
4:Tonight We Love
5:Shepherd Serenade
6:This Love of Mine
7:The Bells of San Raquel *
8:I Don't Want to Set the World On Fire
9:Madelaine
10:Everything I Love

1942

The war was going badly for the United States, operating with the skeletal remains of a fleet that had been all but destroyed at Pearl Harbor. Manila, Bataan, and Corregidor fell. Marines were fighting at Guadalcanal.

The only bright spots were the routing of the Japanese in the Battle of the Coral Sea, and the air raid on Tokyo led by Lieutenant Colonel Jimmy Doolittle. By November General Dwight D. Eisenhower invaded North Africa.

Back home the women were becoming WAACs, WAVEs, SPARs, and WASPs. Gasoline, tires, sugar, and coffee were obtained with ration stamps, and the lines stretched long. Even Lucky Strike Green went to war.

A tragic fire at the Cocoanut Grove nightclub in Boston killed 492 persons, including western star Buck Jones, and led to new building codes that required public doors to open out, not in.

The public was reading See Here, Private Hargrove, watching Mrs. Miniver on the screen, and hearing departing G.I.'s yell to one another "You'll be sor-r-r-y," a cry born earlier on the radio quiz show "Take It or Leave It" when the nervous contestant had to decide whether to take his $32 in winnings or gamble for the stupendous sum of $64.

Early in the year Tin Pan Alley turned out the quickie "Remember Pearl Harbor," but the war was reflected best in such upbeat numbers as "Don't Sit Under the Apple Tree," "This Is Worth Fighting For," and "Praise the Lord and Pass the Ammunition," and such sentimental ones as "I Don't Want to Walk Without You," "Miss You," "He Wears a Pair of Silver Wings," and "When the Lights Go On Again."

There was no doubt about the top song of 1942. Irving Berlin's "White Christmas," during the wartime Christmas season, became the second song in Hit Parade history to remain Number One for ten weeks.

Jan. 3, 1942

1:Chattanooga Choo Choo
2:The White Cliffs of Dover
3:Elmer's Tune
4:Tonight We Love
5:Shepherd Serenade
6:This Love of Mine
7:Everything I Love
8:The Bells of San Raquel
9:This Is No Laughing Matter *
10:Madelaine

Jan. 10, 1942

1:The White Cliffs of Dover
2:Elmer's Tune
3:Chattanooga Choo Choo
4:Shepherd Serenade
5:Tonight We Love
6:Madelaine
7:This Love of Mine
8:This Is No Laughing Matter
9:Everything I Love
10:The Bells of San Raquel

Jan. 17, 1942

1:Elmer's Tune
2:The White Cliffs of Dover
3:Chattanooga Choo Choo
4:The Bells of San Raquel
5:This Love of Mine
6:Tonight We Love
7:Shepherd Serenade
8:Madelaine
9:Everything I Love
10:This Is No Laughing Matter

Jan. 24, 1942

1:The White Cliffs of Dover
2:Elmer's Tune
3:Chattanooga Choo Choo
4:This Love of Mine
5:Rose O'Day *
6:Everything I Love
7:The Shrine of St. Cecilia *
8:Shepherd Serenade
9:I Got It Bad and That Ain't Good *
10:This Is No Laughing Matter

Jan. 31, 1942

1:The White Cliffs of Dover
2:Elmer's Tune
3:Rose O'Day
4:Chattanooga Choo Choo
5:Everything I Love
6:This Love of Mine
7:The Shrine of St. Cecilia
8:Blues in the Night *
9:Shepherd Serenade
10:Humpty Dumpty Heart *

Feb. 7, 1942

1:The White Cliffs of Dover
2:Rose O'Day
3:Blues in the Night
4:Elmer's Tune
5:Everything I Love
6:Chattanooga Choo Choo
7:The Shrine of St. Cecilia
8:We're the Couple in the Castle *
9:This Love of Mine
10:Deep in the Heart of Texas *

Feb. 14, 1942

1:The White Cliffs of Dover
2:Blues in the Night
3:Rose O'Day
4:Everything I Love
5:The Shrine of St. Cecilia
6:Elmer's Tune
7:Deep in the Heart of Texas
8:Remember Pearl Harbor *
9:Chattanooga Choo Choo
10:This Love of Mine

Feb. 21, 1942

1:Blues in the Night
2:The White Cliffs of Dover
3:Rose O'Day
4:Everything I Love
5:I Don't Want to Walk Without You *
6:The Shrine of St. Cecilia
7:Elmer's Tune
8:Chattanooga Choo Choo
9:Deep in the Heart of Texas
10:Remember Pearl Harbor

* Newcomer

Feb. 28, 1942

1:The White Cliffs of Dover
2:Blues in the Night
3:Deep in the Heart of Texas
4:Rose O'Day
5:The Shrine of St. Cecilia
6:How About You? *
7:Day Dreaming *
8:Remember Pearl Harbor
9:Everything I Love
10:I Don't Want to Walk Without You

Mar. 7, 1942

1:Blues in the Night
2:Deep in the Heart of Texas
3:I Don't Want to Walk Without You
4:The White Cliffs of Dover
5:Rose O'Day
6:How About You?
7:The Shrine of St. Cecilia
8:Everything I Love
9:Remember Pearl Harbor
10:Sometimes *

Mar. 14, 1942

1:Deep in the Heart of Texas
2:Blues in the Night
3:I Don't Want to Walk Without You
4:The White Cliffs of Dover
5:How About You?
6:Rose O'Day
7:The Shrine of St. Cecilia
8:Miss You *
9:Moonlight Cocktail *
10:How Do I Know It's Real? *

Mar. 21, 1942

1:Deep in the Heart of Texas
2:Blues in the Night
3:I Don't Want to Walk Without You
4:The White Cliffs of Dover
5:How About You?
6:Rose O'Day
7:Moonlight Cocktail
8:The Shrine of St. Cecilia
9:Somebody Else Is Taking My Place *
10:Miss You

Mar. 28, 1942

1:Deep in the Heart of Texas
2:I Don't Want to Walk Without You
3:Rose O'Day
4:Blues in the Night
5:Miss You
6:Somebody Else Is Taking My Place
7:The White Cliffs of Dover
8:Moonlight Cocktail
9:Tangerine *
10:How About You?

Apr. 4, 1942

1:Deep in the Heart of Texas
2:I Don't Want to Walk Without You
3:Somebody Else Is Taking My Place
4:Miss You
5:Blues in the Night
6:Moonlight Cocktail
7:The White Cliffs of Dover
8:She'll Always Remember *
9:Tangerine
10:I Remember You *

Apr. 11, 1942

1:Deep in the Heart of Texas
2:I Don't Want to Walk Without You
3:Somebody Else Is Taking My Place
4:Miss You
5:Moonlight Cocktail
6:Blues in the Night
7:Tangerine
8:She'll Always Remember
9:I Remember You
10:The White Cliffs of Dover

Apr. 18, 1942

1:I Don't Want to Walk Without You
2:Deep in the Heart of Texas
3:Somebody Else Is Taking My Place
4:Moonlight Cocktail
5:Tangerine
6:Skylark *
7:Blues in the Night
8:Miss You
9:I'll Pray for You *
10:I Remember You

Apr. 25, 1942

1:Somebody Else Is Taking My Place
2:Tangerine
3:I Don't Want to Walk Without You
4:Moonlight Cocktail
5:Skylark
6:Deep in the Heart of Texas
7:Don't Sit Under the Apple Tree *
8:Miss You
9:Blues in the Night
10:I Remember You

May 2, 1942

1:Somebody Else Is Taking My Place
2:Tangerine
3:Miss You
4:Moonlight Cocktail
5:I Don't Want to Walk Without You
6:Skylark
7:Deep in the Heart of Texas
8:Don't Sit Under the Apple Tree
9:Full Moon *
10:Happy in Love *

May 9, 1942

1:Somebody Else Is Taking My Place
2:Skylark
3:Tangerine
4:Don't Sit Under the Apple Tree
5:I Don't Want to Walk Without You
6:Moonlight Cocktail
7:Miss You
8:Jersey Bounce *
9:Happy in Love
10:Me and My Melinda *

May 16, 1942

1:Don't Sit Under the Apple Tree
2:Tangerine
3:Skylark
4:Somebody Else Is Taking My Place
5:I Don't Want to Walk Without You
6:Moonlight Cocktail
7:Jersey Bounce
8:Sleepy Lagoon *
9:Miss You
10:One Dozen Roses *

May 23, 1942

1:Don't Sit Under the Apple Tree
2:Somebody Else Is Taking My Place
3:Tangerine
4:Sleepy Lagoon
5:Skylark
6:Moonlight Cocktail
7:Johnny Doughboy *
8:Jersey Bounce
9:Miss You
10:One Dozen Roses

May 30, 1942

1:Don't Sit Under the Apple Tree
2:Tangerine
3:Somebody Else Is Taking My Place
4:Sleepy Lagoon
5:Skylark
6:One Dozen Roses
7:Jersey Bounce
8:Johnny Doughboy
9:Moonlight Cocktail
10:I'll Keep the Lovelight Burning *

June 6, 1942

1:Don't Sit Under the Apple Tree
2:Sleepy Lagoon
3:Johnny Doughboy
4:Skylark
5:Tangerine
6:Jersey Bounce
7:One Dozen Roses
8:Somebody Else Is Taking My Place
9:I'll Keep the Lovelight Burning
10:Moonlight Cocktail

June 13, 1942

1:Sleepy Lagoon
2:Don't Sit Under the Apple Tree
3:Johnny Doughboy
4:One Dozen Roses
5:Tangerine
6:Skylark
7:Jersey Bounce
8:Always in My Heart *
9:Three Little Sisters *
10:Who Wouldn't Love You? *

June 20, 1942

1:Don't Sit Under the Apple Tree
2:Johnny Doughboy
3:One Dozen Roses
4:Skylark
5:Jersey Bounce
6:Three Little Sisters
7:Sleepy Lagoon
8:Tangerine
9:Who Wouldn't Love You?
10:Always in My Heart

June 27, 1942

1:Sleepy Lagoon
2:One Dozen Roses
3:Johnny Doughboy
4:Jersey Bounce
5:Don't Sit Under the Apple Tree
6:Tangerine
7:Three Little Sisters
8:Who Wouldn't Love You?
9:Skylark
10:Always in My Heart

July 4, 1942

1:One Dozen Roses
2:Sleepy Lagoon
3:Johnny Doughboy
4:Jersey Bounce
5:Jingle, Jangle, Jingle *
6:Don't Sit Under the Apple Tree
7:Three Little Sisters
8:Always in My Heart
9:Who Wouldn't Love You?
10:Skylark

July 11, 1942

1:One Dozen Roses
2:Sleepy Lagoon
3:Johnny Doughboy
4:Jingle, Jangle, Jingle
5:Jersey Bounce
6:Don't Sit Under the Apple Tree
7:Three Little Sisters
8:Who Wouldn't Love You?
9:Here You Are *
10:This Is Worth Fighting For *

July 18, 1942

1:Sleepy Lagoon
2:One Dozen Roses
3:Jingle, Jangle, Jingle
4:Johnny Doughboy
5:Jersey Bounce
6:Who Wouldn't Love You?
7:Don't Sit Under the Apple Tree
8:Here You Are
9:Three Little Sisters
10:This Is Worth Fighting For

July 25, 1942

1:Jingle, Jangle, Jingle
2:Sleepy Lagoon
3:Who Wouldn't Love You?
4:One Dozen Roses
5:Johnny Doughboy
6:Jersey Bounce
7:He Wears a Pair of Silver Wings *
8:Three Little Sisters
9:Here You Are
10:Be Careful, It's My Heart *

Aug. 1, 1942

1:Jingle, Jangle, Jingle
2:One Dozen Roses
3:Who Wouldn't Love You?
4:He Wears a Pair of Silver Wings
5:Johnny Doughboy
6:Sleepy Lagoon
7:Idaho *
8:Jersey Bounce
9:Three Little Sisters
10:Be Careful, It's My Heart

Aug. 8, 1942

1:Jingle, Jangle, Jingle
2:Sleepy Lagoon
3:He Wears a Pair of Silver Wings
4:One Dozen Roses
5:Who Wouldn't Love You?
6:I Left My Heart at the Stage Door Canteen *
7:Johnny Doughboy
8:Jersey Bounce
9:Idaho
10:Be Careful, It's My Heart

Aug. 15, 1942

1:Jingle, Jangle, Jingle
2:He Wears a Pair of Silver Wings
3:One Dozen Roses
4:Who Wouldn't Love You?
5:I Left My Heart at the Stage Door Canteen
6:Idaho
7:Sleepy Lagoon
8:Take Me *
9:Be Careful, It's My Heart
10:Johnny Doughboy

Aug. 22, 1942

1:Jingle, Jangle, Jingle
2:He Wears a Pair of Silver Wings
3:Be Careful, It's My Heart
4:Idaho
5:Who Wouldn't Love You?
6:Sleepy Lagoon
7:I Left My Heart at the Stage Door Canteen
8:Johnny Doughboy
9:Take Me
10:One Dozen Roses

Aug. 29, 1942

1:He Wears a Pair of Silver Wings
2:Jingle, Jangle, Jingle
3:I Left My Heart at the Stage Door Canteen
4:Be Careful, It's My Heart
5:My Devotion *
6:Sleepy Lagoon
7:Who Wouldn't Love You?
8:Take Me
9:Idaho
10:At Last *

Sept. 5, 1942

1:He Wears a Pair of Silver Wings
2:I Left My Heart at the Stage Door Canteen
3:Jingle, Jangle, Jingle
4:My Devotion
5:Be Careful, It's My Heart
6:Idaho
7:I've Got a Gal in Kalamazoo *
8:Sleepy Lagoon
9:Take Me
10:At Last

Sept. 12, 1942

1:He Wears a Pair of Silver Wings
2:I Left My Heart at the Stage Door Canteen
3:Jingle, Jangle, Jingle
4:My Devotion
5:Be Careful, It's My Heart
6:I've Got a Gal in Kalamazoo
7:Idaho
8:At Last
9:Sleepy Lagoon
10:Take Me

Sept. 19, 1942

1:He Wears a Pair of Silver Wings
2:My Devotion
3:Be Careful, It's My Heart
4:I Left My Heart at the Stage Door Canteen
5:I've Got a Gal in Kalamazoo
6:Idaho
7:Jingle, Jangle, Jingle
8:Take Me
9:At Last
10:Wonder When My Baby's Coming Home? *

Sept. 26, 1942

1:My Devotion
2:I've Got a Gal in Kalamazoo
3:He Wears a Pair of Silver Wings
4:I Left My Heart at the Stage Door Canteen
5:Be Careful, It's My Heart
6:Serenade in Blue *
7:Jingle, Jangle, Jingle
8:At Last
9:Idaho
10:Wonder When My Baby's Coming Home?

Oct. 3, 1942

1:My Devotion
2:I've Got a Gal in Kalamazoo
3:Be Careful, It's My Heart
4:He Wears a Pair of Silver Wings
5:At Last
6:I Left My Heart at the Stage Door Canteen
7:Serenade in Blue
8:Jingle, Jangle, Jingle
9:Manhattan Serenade *
10:Idaho

Oct. 10, 1942

1:I've Got a Gal in Kalamazoo
2:Be Careful, It's My Heart
3:My Devotion
4:I Left My Heart at the Stage Door Canteen
5:Idaho
6:He Wears a Pair of Silver Wings
7:At Last
8:Serenade in Blue
9:Manhattan Serenade
10:He's My Guy *

Oct. 17, 1942

1:My Devotion
2:Be Careful, It's My Heart
3:I've Got a Gal in Kalamazoo
4:I Left My Heart at the Stage Door Canteen
5:Manhattan Serenade
6:Serenade in Blue
7:White Christmas *
8:He Wears a Pair of Silver Wings
9:He's My Guy
10:At Last

Oct. 24, 1942

1:My Devotion
2:White Christmas
3:I've Got a Gal in Kalamazoo
4:Serenade in Blue
5:Be Careful, It's My Heart
6:Dearly Beloved *
7:Manhattan Serenade
8:I Left My Heart at the Stage Door Canteen
9:Praise the Lord and Pass the Ammunition *
10:At Last

Oct. 31, 1942

1:White Christmas
2:Praise the Lord and Pass the Ammunition
3:My Devotion
4:I've Got a Gal in Kalamazoo
5:When the Lights Go On Again *
6:Be Careful, It's My Heart
7:Manhattan Serenade
8:Serenade in Blue
9:At Last
10:Dearly Beloved

Nov. 7, 1942

1:White Christmas
2:Praise the Lord and Pass the Ammunition
3:My Devotion
4:I've Got a Gal in Kalamazoo
5:Serenade in Blue
6:I Came Here to Talk For Joe *
7:Dearly Beloved
8:When the Lights Go On Again
9:Manhattan Serenade
10:Gobs of Love *

Nov. 14, 1942

1:White Christmas
2:Praise the Lord and Pass the Ammunition
3:My Devotion
4:When the Lights Go On Again
5:There Will Never Be Another You *
6:I've Got a Gal in Kalamazoo
7:Serenade in Blue
8:Manhattan Serenade
9:I Came Here to Talk For Joe
10:Dearly Beloved

Nov. 21, 1942

1:White Christmas
2:Praise the Lord and Pass the Ammunition
3:Manhattan Serenade
4:When the Lights Go On Again
5:Dearly Beloved
6:Mister Five by Five *
7:Serenade in Blue
8:My Devotion
9:Daybreak *
10:There Will Never Be Another You

Nov. 28, 1942

1:White Christmas
2:Praise the Lord and Pass the Ammunition
3:Dearly Beloved
4:Mister Five by Five
5:When the Lights Go On Again
6:Daybreak
7:My Devotion
8:Manhattan Serenade
9:There Will Never Be Another You
10:Serenade in Blue

Dec. 5, 1942

1:White Christmas
2:When the Lights Go On Again
3:Mister Five by Five
4:Dearly Beloved
5:Manhattan Serenade
6:Praise the Lord and Pass the Ammunition
7:Daybreak
8:I'm Getting Tired So I Can Sleep *
9:My Devotion
10:There Are Such Things *

Dec. 12, 1942

1:White Christmas
2:Mister Five by Five
3:When the Lights Go On Again
4:Dearly Beloved
5:Praise the Lord and Pass the Ammunition
6:Manhattan Serenade
7:Why Don't You Fall in Love With Me? *
8:I Had the Craziest Dream *
9:Daybreak
10:There Are Such Things

Dec. 19, 1942

1:White Christmas
2:Mister Five by Five
3:Praise the Lord and Pass the Ammunition
4:There Are Such Things
5:When the Lights Go On Again
6:Dearly Beloved
7:Why Don't You Fall in Love With Me?
8:I Had the Craziest Dream
9:Manhattan Serenade
10:Daybreak

Dec. 26, 1942

1:White Christmas
2:There Are Such Things
3:When the Lights Go On Again
4:Mister Five by Five
5:Praise the Lord and Pass the Ammunition
6:Why Don't You Fall in Love With Me?
7:Dearly Beloved
8:I Had the Craziest Dream
9:Manhattan Serenade
10:There's a Star-Spangled Banner Waving
                         Somewhere *

1943

The two biggest show-business smashes of 1943 were the first pairing of Richard Rodgers and Oscar Hammerstein II on Broadway for their *Oklahoma!,* and the incredible impact Swoon King Frank Sinatra made on the bobby-sox world.

The frail, bow-tied singer with the Tommy Dorsey orchestra had teenagers fainting in the aisles of New York's Paramount Theater in January, and on the night of February 6, 1943, he replaced Barry Wood as featured vocalist on "Your Hit Parade," and the girlish screams were heard nationwide each Saturday night. Soon he was singing his own hits onto the Top Ten—"That Old Black Magic," "It's Always You," "In the Blue of Evening," and "All or Nothing At All," a song he had recorded with Harry James in 1939 which had been brought off the shelf to cash in on his new popularity.

Oklahoma!, which revolutionized the musical-comedy stage away from operetta to the book format, gave the Hit Parade "Oh, What a Beautiful Mornin'" and "People Will Say We're in Love." The latter, although Number One only three times, set a longevity record in all positions—a staggering thirty weeks. But the top songs of the year, each with nine weeks as Number One, were "You'll Never Know" and "My Heart Tells Me."

At the movies we were seeing *Casablanca,* which furnished the Hit Parade with "As Time Goes By." It was the year of the zoot suit, the bloody race riot in Detroit, and FDR's signing of the first pay-as-you-go income tax bill. We were reading Wendell Willkie's *One World* and Betty Smith's *A Tree Grows in Brooklyn.* The war tide began to turn. North Africa was ours. Sicily was invaded. Mussolini resigned and Italy surrendered, although it still was held by the Germans. Meats, fats, cheese, and canned goods were added to the rationed list.

In the middle of the string of war-inspired tunes, ranging from "Don't Get Around Much Anymore" to "Comin' In On a Wing and a Prayer," hillbilly songwriter Al Dexter threatened court action unless the pop music Hit Parade recognized that everyone else was playing his honky-tonk tune, "Pistol-Packin' Mama." It appeared on "Your Hit Parade" shortly thereafter.

Jan. 2, 1943

1:White Christmas
2:I Had the Craziest Dream
3:There Are Such Things
4:Moonlight Becomes You *
5:When the Lights Go On Again
6:Praise the Lord and Pass the Ammunition
7:Dearly Beloved
8:Mister Five by Five
9:Why Don't You Fall in Love With Me?
10:You'd Be So Nice to Come Home To *

Jan. 9, 1943

1:There Are Such Things
2:White Christmas
3:Why Don't You Fall in Love With Me?
4:Moonlight Becomes You
5:When the Lights Go On Again
6:I Had the Craziest Dream
7:Mister Five by Five
8:Praise the Lord and Pass the Ammunition
9:Dearly Beloved
10:You'd Be So Nice to Come Home To

Jan. 16, 1943

1:There Are Such Things
2:I Had the Craziest Dream
3:Moonlight Becomes You
4:Mister Five by Five
5:When the Lights Go On Again
6:Why Don't You Fall in Love With Me?
7:White Christmas
8:Dearly Beloved
9:Brazil *
10:You'd Be So Nice to Come Home To

Jan. 23, 1943

1:Moonlight Becomes You
2:There Are Such Things
3:I Had the Craziest Dream
4:Why Don't You Fall in Love With Me?
5:When the Lights Go On Again
6:You'd Be So Nice to Come Home To
7:Mister Five by Five
8:White Christmas
9:Dearly Beloved
10:Brazil

Jan. 30, 1943

1:There Are Such Things
2:I Had the Craziest Dream
3:Why Don't You Fall in Love With Me?
4:When the Lights Go On Again
5:Moonlight Becomes You
6:Brazil
7:You'd Be So Nice to Come Home To
8:Moonlight Mood *
9:Dearly Beloved
10:Rose Ann of Charing Cross *

Feb. 6, 1943

1:Moonlight Becomes You
2:There Are Such Things
3:I Had the Craziest Dream
4:Why Don't You Fall in Love With Me?
5:When the Lights Go On Again
6:You'd Be So Nice to Come Home To
7:Brazil
8:Moonlight Mood
9:Dearly Beloved
10:Rose Ann of Charing Cross

Feb. 13, 1943

1:There Are Such Things
2:I Had the Craziest Dream
3:Moonlight Becomes You
4:You'd Be So Nice to Come Home To
5:Why Don't You Fall in Love With Me?
6:Rose Ann of Charing Cross
7:When the Lights Go On Again
8:Brazil
9:Moonlight Mood
10:Dearly Beloved

Feb. 20, 1943

1:There Are Such Things
2:Brazil
3:You'd Be So Nice to Come Home To
4:I've Heard That Song Before *
5:Why Don't You Fall in Love With Me?
6:Moonlight Becomes You
7:I Had the Craziest Dream
8:When the Lights Go On Again
9:Rose Ann of Charing Cross
10:Moonlight Mood

* Newcomer

Feb. 27, 1943

1:There Are Such Things
2:You'd Be So Nice to Come Home To
3:I've Heard That Song Before
4:Moonlight Becomes You
5:Brazil
6:Moonlight Mood
7:For Me and My Gal *
8:Why Don't You Fall in Love With Me?
9:I Had the Craziest Dream
10:That Old Black Magic *

Mar. 6, 1943

1:Brazil
2:I've Heard That Song Before
3:You'd Be So Nice to Come Home To
4:There Are Such Things
5:Moonlight Becomes You
6:I Had the Craziest Dream
7:That Old Black Magic
8:Moonlight Mood
9:Why Don't You Fall in Love With Me?
10:For Me and My Gal

Mar. 13, 1943

1:Brazil
2:I've Heard That Song Before
3:You'd Be So Nice to Come Home To
4:There Are Such Things
5:That Old Black Magic
6:Moonlight Becomes You
7:I Had the Craziest Dream
8:Taking a Chance On Love *
9:For Me and My Gal
10:Why Don't You Fall in Love With Me?

Mar. 20, 1943

1:I've Heard That Song Before
2:You'd Be So Nice to Come Home To
3:That Old Black Magic
4:Brazil
5:There Are Such Things
6:As Time Goes By *
7:Moonlight Becomes You
8:I Had the Craziest Dream
9:Taking a Chance On Love
10:For Me and My Gal

Mar. 27, 1943

1:I've Heard That Song Before
2:That Old Black Magic
3:As Time Goes By
4:You'd Be So Nice to Come Home To
5:Brazil
6:There Are Such Things
7:Don't Get Around Much Anymore *
8:Moonlight Becomes You
9:For Me and My Gal
10:Taking a Chance On Love

Apr. 3, 1943

1:I've Heard That Song Before
2:That Old Black Magic
3:As Time Goes By
4:You'd Be So Nice to Come Home To
5:Brazil
6:Taking a Chance On Love
7:There Are Such Things
8:Don't Get Around Much Anymore
9:Moonlight Becomes You
10:For Me and My Gal

Apr. 10, 1943

1:Brazil
2:I've Heard That Song Before
3:That Old Black Magic
4:As Time Goes By
5:You'd Be So Nice to Come Home To
6:Don't Get Around Much Anymore
7:Taking a Chance On Love
8:For Me and My Gal
9:It Can't Be Wrong *
10:There's a Harbor of Dreamboats *

Apr. 17, 1943

1:I've Heard That Song Before
2:As Time Goes By
3:That Old Black Magic
4:Don't Get Around Much Anymore
5:Brazil
6:You'd Be So Nice to Come Home To
7:It Can't Be Wrong
8:For Me and My Gal
9:There's a Harbor of Dreamboats
10:Taking a Chance On Love

Apr. 24, 1943

1:As Time Goes By
2:That Old Black Magic
3:Don't Get Around Much Anymore
4:I've Heard That Song Before
5:You'd Be So Nice to Come Home To
6:It Can't Be Wrong
7:Brazil
8:For Me and My Gal
9:Don't Cry *
10:Taking a Chance On Love

May 1, 1943

1:Don't Get Around Much Anymore
2:As Time Goes By
3:It Can't Be Wrong
4:Brazil
5:You'd Be So Nice to Come Home To
6:I've Heard That Song Before
7:That Old Black Magic
8:For Me and My Gal
9:Taking a Chance On Love
10:What's the Good Word, Mr. Bluebird? *

May 8, 1943

1:As Time Goes By
2:Don't Get Around Much Anymore
3:That Old Black Magic
4:I've Heard That Song Before
5:It Can't Be Wrong
6:Taking a Chance On Love
7:Brazil
8:What's the Good Word, Mr. Bluebird?
9:You'll Never Know *
10:Comin' In On a Wing and a Prayer *

May 15, 1943

1:As Time Goes By
2:That Old Black Magic
3:It Can't Be Wrong
4:Don't Get Around Much Anymore
5:Taking a Chance On Love
6:I've Heard That Song Before
7:Comin' In On a Wing and a Prayer
8:Brazil
9:You'll Never Know
10:In the Blue of Evening *

May 22, 1943

1:As Time Goes By
2:Don't Get Around Much Anymore
3:Comin' In On a Wing and a Prayer
4:It Can't Be Wrong
5:You'll Never Know
6:Let's Get Lost *
7:That Old Black Magic
8:I've Heard That Song Before
9:In the Blue of Evening
10:Taking a Chance On Love

May 29, 1943

1:Don't Get Around Much Anymore
2:As Time Goes By
3:Comin' In On a Wing and a Prayer
4:It Can't Be Wrong
5:You'll Never Know
6:That Old Black Magic
7:I've Heard That Song Before
8:Let's Get Lost
9:Taking a Chance On Love
10:In the Blue of Evening

June 5, 1943

1:Don't Get Around Much Anymore
2:You'll Never Know
3:Comin' In On a Wing and a Prayer
4:It Can't Be Wrong
5:Let's Get Lost
6:As Time Goes By
7:Taking a Chance On Love
8:That Old Black Magic
9:In the Blue of Evening
10:You Rhyme With Everything That's Beautiful *

June 12, 1943

1:Let's Get Lost
2:Comin' In On a Wing and a Prayer
3:You'll Never Know
4:Don't Get Around Much Anymore
5:As Time Goes By
6:It Can't Be Wrong
7:In the Blue of Evening
8:I Never Mention Your Name *
9:You Rhyme With Everything That's Beautiful
10:Taking a Chance On Love

June 19, 1943

1:Comin' In On a Wing and a Prayer
2:You'll Never Know
3:Let's Get Lost
4:As Time Goes By
5:In the Blue of Evening
6:Don't Get Around Much Anymore
7:It's Always You *
8:It Can't Be Wrong
9:Taking a Chance On Love
10:Johnny Zero *

June 26, 1943

1:Comin' In On a Wing and a Prayer
2:You'll Never Know
3:As Time Goes By
4:Let's Get Lost
5:In the Blue of Evening
6:Don't Get Around Much Anymore
7:Taking a Chance On Love
8:It's Always You
9:It Can't Be Wrong
10:Johnny Zero

July 3, 1943

1:You'll Never Know
2:Comin' In On a Wing and a Prayer
3:It Can't Be Wrong
4:In the Blue of Evening
5:Don't Get Around Much Anymore
6:As Time Goes By
7:Let's Get Lost
8:It's Always You
9:Johnny Zero
10:Taking a Chance On Love

July 10, 1943

1:You'll Never Know
2:Comin' In On a Wing and a Prayer
3:In the Blue of Evening
4:As Time Goes By
5:Don't Get Around Much Anymore
6:Let's Get Lost
7:People Will Say We're in Love *
8:It's Always You
9:Johnny Zero
10:It Can't Be Wrong

July 17, 1943

1:Comin' In On a Wing and a Prayer
2:You'll Never Know
3:In the Blue of Evening
4:It Can't Be Wrong
5:All or Nothing At All *
6:As Time Goes By
7:Let's Get Lost
8:It's Always You
9:Johnny Zero
10:People Will Say We're in Love

July 24, 1943

1:You'll Never Know
2:In the Blue of Evening
3:Comin' In On a Wing and a Prayer
4:It Can't Be Wrong
5:Let's Get Lost
6:People Will Say We're in Love
7:As Time Goes By
8:Johnny Zero
9:All or Nothing At All
10:It's Always You

July 31, 1943

1:You'll Never Know
2:Comin' In On a Wing and a Prayer
3:In the Blue of Evening
4:All or Nothing At All
5:Let's Get Lost
6:It's Always You
7:As Time Goes By
8:People Will Say We're in Love
9:It Can't Be Wrong
10:Johnny Zero

Aug. 7, 1943

1:You'll Never Know
2:In the Blue of Evening
3:All or Nothing At All
4:Comin' In On a Wing and a Prayer
5:People Will Say We're in Love
6:Let's Get Lost
7:It's Always You
8:It Can't Be Wrong
9:As Time Goes By
10:In My Arms *

Aug. 14, 1943

1:You'll Never Know
2:In the Blue of Evening
3:People Will Say We're in Love
4:Comin' In On a Wing and a Prayer
5:All or Nothing At All
6:It's Always You
7:Sunday, Monday or Always *
8:It Can't Be Wrong
9:I Heard You Cried Last Night *
10:In My Arms

Aug. 21, 1943

1:You'll Never Know
2:In the Blue of Evening
3:All or Nothing At All
4:People Will Say We're in Love
5:Comin' In On a Wing and a Prayer
6:In My Arms
7:It's Always You
8:Sunday, Monday or Always
9:Put Your Arms Around Me, Honey *
10:I Heard You Cried Last Night

Aug. 28, 1943

1:You'll Never Know
2:In the Blue of Evening
3:Sunday, Monday or Always
4:All or Nothing At All
5:In My Arms
6:People Will Say We're in Love
7:Put Your Arms Around Me, Honey
8:Comin' In On a Wing and a Prayer
9:I Heard You Cried Last Night
10:It's Always You

Sept. 4, 1943

1:You'll Never Know
2:Sunday, Monday or Always
3:In the Blue of Evening
4:People Will Say We're in Love
5:All or Nothing At All
6:I Heard You Cried Last Night
7:In My Arms
8:Comin' In On a Wing and a Prayer
9:Put Your Arms Around Me, Honey
10:It's Always You

Sept. 11, 1943

1:Sunday, Monday or Always
2:You'll Never Know
3:All or Nothing At All
4:In the Blue of Evening
5:People Will Say We're in Love
6:In My Arms
7:Paper Doll *
8:Put Your Arms Around Me, Honey
9:I Heard You Cried Last Night
10:Comin' In On a Wing and a Prayer

Sept. 18, 1943

1:Sunday, Monday or Always
2:People Will Say We're in Love
3:All or Nothing At All
4:I Heard You Cried Last Night
5:In the Blue of Evening
6:You'll Never Know
7:Put Your Arms Around Me, Honey
8:In My Arms
9:Paper Doll
10:Comin' In On a Wing and a Prayer

Sept. 25, 1943

1:All or Nothing At All
2:Paper Doll
3:People Will Say We're in Love
4:You'll Never Know
5:Sunday, Monday or Always
6:In the Blue of Evening
7:I Heard You Cried Last Night
8:Put Your Arms Around Me, Honey
9:In My Arms
10:Comin' In On a Wing and a Prayer

Oct. 2, 1943

1:Sunday, Monday or Always
2:People Will Say We're in Love
3:I Heard You Cried Last Night
4:Put Your Arms Around Me, Honey
5:You'll Never Know
6:All or Nothing At All
7:Paper Doll
8:In My Arms
9:Pistol-Packin' Mama *
10:In the Blue of Evening

Oct. 9, 1943

1:Sunday, Monday or Always
2:People Will Say We're in Love
3:I Heard You Cried Last Night
4:Paper Doll
5:Pistol-Packin' Mama
6:Put Your Arms Around Me, Honey
7:You'll Never Know
8:If You Please *
9:In My Arms
10:All or Nothing At All

Oct. 16, 1943

1:Sunday, Monday or Always
2:People Will Say We're in Love
3:Paper Doll
4:I Heard You Cried Last Night
5:Pistol-Packin' Mama
6:Put Your Arms Around Me, Honey
7:All or Nothing At All
8:You'll Never Know
9:They're Either Too Young Or Too Old *
10:If You Please

Oct. 23, 1943

1:Sunday, Monday or Always
2:People Will Say We're in Love
3:Paper Doll
4:Pistol-Packin' Mama
5:I Heard You Cried Last Night
6:If You Please
7:They're Either Too Young Or Too Old
8:All or Nothing At All
9:Put Your Arms Around Me, Honey
10:You'll Never Know

Oct. 30, 1943

1:People Will Say We're in Love
2:Pistol-Packin' Mama
3:Sunday, Monday or Always
4:Paper Doll
5:If You Please
6:Put Your Arms Around Me, Honey
7:They're Either Too Young Or Too Old
8:I Heard You Cried Last Night
9:For the First Time *
10:All or Nothing At All

Nov. 6, 1943

1:Paper Doll
2:People Will Say We're in Love
3:Pistol-Packin' Mama
4:Sunday, Monday or Always
5:They're Either Too Young Or Too Old
6:Put Your Arms Around Me, Honey
7:I Heard You Cried Last Night
8:For the First Time
9:If You Please
10:How Sweet You Are *

Nov. 13, 1943

1:Paper Doll
2:People Will Say We're in Love
3:Pistol-Packin' Mama
4:Put Your Arms Around Me, Honey
5:Sunday, Monday or Always
6:They're Either Too Young Or Too Old
7:My Heart Tells Me *
8:I Heard You Cried Last Night
9:How Sweet You Are
10:For the First Time

Nov. 20, 1943

1:People Will Say We're in Love
2:Paper Doll
3:They're Either Too Young Or Too Old
4:Sunday, Monday or Always
5:Pistol-Packin' Mama
6:How Sweet You Are
7:My Heart Tells Me
8:Put Your Arms Around Me, Honey
9:Oh, What a Beautiful Mornin' *
10:For the First Time

Nov. 27, 1943

1:Paper Doll
2:They're Either Too Young Or Too Old
3:Pistol-Packin' Mama
4:My Heart Tells Me
5:People Will Say We're in Love
6:Sunday, Monday or Always
7:Oh, What a Beautiful Mornin'
8:Little Did I Know *
9:Put Your Arms Around Me, Honey
10:For the First Time

Dec. 4, 1943

1:People Will Say We're in Love
2:Paper Doll
3:My Heart Tells Me
4:Pistol-Packin' Mama
5:They're Either Too Young Or Too Old
6:Oh, What a Beautiful Mornin'
7:Sunday, Monday or Always
8:Shoo Shoo Baby *
9:For the First Time
10:Speak Low *

Dec. 11, 1943

1:My Heart Tells Me
2:They're Either Too Young Or Too Old
3:People Will Say We're in Love
4:Paper Doll
5:Pistol-Packin' Mama
6:Oh, What a Beautiful Mornin'
7:Shoo Shoo Baby
8:Sunday, Monday or Always
9:For the First Time
10:Speak Low

Dec. 18, 1943

1:My Heart Tells Me
2:Oh, What a Beautiful Mornin'
3:Paper Doll
4:People Will Say We're in Love
5:Pistol-Packin' Mama
6:They're Either Too Young Or Too Old
7:For the First Time
8:Speak Low
9:Shoo Shoo Baby
10:I'll Be Home For Christmas *

Dec. 25, 1943

1:My Heart Tells Me
2:Paper Doll
3:I'll Be Home For Christmas
4:Oh, What a Beautiful Mornin'
5:People Will Say We're in Love
6:For the First Time
7:They're Either Too Young Or Too Old
8:Pistol-Packin' Mama
9:Shoo Shoo Baby
10:Speak Low

1944

The biggest event of 1944 was D-Day, the sixth of June, when Allied forces crossed the English Channel to invade Europe at Normandy. It was the beginning of an end that was still a year away. Paris was liberated, and the Battle of the Bulge began in December.

Back home, cars were either up on blocks or sporting windshield stickers that proclaimed A, B, or C gasoline priorities. There was a civilian cigarette shortage which inspired huge lines whenever they went on sale. Dick Tracy was chasing The Brow, and Skeezix was in the Army.

The tragedy of the year was the Ringling Brothers, Barnum and Bailey Circus fire that claimed 169 lives in Hartford, Connecticut.

Screen newcomer Jennifer Jones was capturing movie audiences in *The Song of Bernadette*, and Bing Crosby and Barry Fitzgerald turned their collars backward as priests in *Going My Way*. The latter film produced the song hit "Swinging On a Star," the movie *Cover Girl* gave us "Long Ago and Far Away," and Broadway's *Mexican Hayride* supplied "I Love You" to the Top Ten. The nonsense song of the year was "Mairzy Doats."

John Hersey's novel *A Bell for Adano* won the Pulitzer Prize, but the one everyone was reading behind the cover of another book, in that more naïve era, was Kathleen Winsor's racy *Forever Amber*.

If FDR's third term was unprecedented, his fourth term was earthshaking. He won it handily that November over Thomas Dewey.

Frank Sinatra made his first movie, *Higher and Higher*, and sang two songs from it onto "Your Hit Parade"—"A Lovely Way to Spend an Evening" and "I Couldn't Sleep a Wink Last Night." For some reason a rash of revivals broke into the Top Ten that year: "Always," "My Ideal," "I'm Confessin,'" "It Had to Be You," and "Together."

But it was the war-inspired tunes that dominated: "No Love, No Nothin'," "Goodnight Wherever You Are," "Milkman, Keep Those Bottles Quiet," "I'll Walk Alone," and "I'll Be Seeing You." The latter, written in 1938 but finding its own niche in 1944 by saying the right things in a wartime year, was the top song of the year, with ten weeks as Number One.

Jan. 1, 1944

1:My Heart Tells Me
2:They're Either Too Young Or Too Old
3:I'll Be Home For Christmas
4:Paper Doll
5:Shoo Shoo Baby
6:Oh, What a Beautiful Mornin'
7:People Will Say We're in Love
8:For the First Time
9:Pistol-Packin' Mama
10:No Love, No Nothin' *

Jan. 8, 1944

1:My Heart Tells Me
2:Paper Doll
3:People Will Say We're in Love
4:Shoo Shoo Baby
5:For the First Time
6:Oh, What a Beautiful Mornin'
7:I'll Be Home For Christmas
8:They're Either Too Young Or Too Old
9:No Love, No Nothin'
10:Pistol-Packin' Mama

Jan. 15, 1944

1:My Heart Tells Me
2:Shoo Shoo Baby
3:Paper Doll
4:People Will Say We're in Love
5:Oh, What a Beautiful Mornin'
6:For the First Time
7:My Ideal *
8:They're Either Too Young Or Too Old
9:Star Eyes *
10:No Love, No Nothin'

Jan. 22, 1944

1:My Heart Tells Me
2:Shoo Shoo Baby
3:My Ideal
4:Paper Doll
5:Oh, What a Beautiful Mornin'
6:No Love, No Nothin'
7:For the First Time
8:My Shining Hour *
9:People Will Say We're in Love
10:Star Eyes

Jan. 29, 1944

1:My Heart Tells Me
2:Shoo Shoo Baby
3:People Will Say We're in Love
4:No Love, No Nothin'
5:Oh, What a Beautiful Mornin'
6:Paper Doll
7:I Couldn't Sleep a Wink Last Night *
8:My Ideal
9:For the First Time
10:My Shining Hour

Feb. 5, 1944

1:My Heart Tells Me
2:Shoo Shoo Baby
3:No Love, No Nothin'
4:Besame Mucho *
5:My Ideal
6:Paper Doll
7:Mairzy Doats *
8:Oh, What a Beautiful Mornin'
9:When They Ask About You *
10:I Couldn't Sleep a Wink Last Night

Feb. 12, 1944

1:Shoo Shoo Baby
2:My Heart Tells Me
3:Mairzy Doats
4:Besame Mucho
5:No Love, No Nothin'
6:My Ideal
7:When They Ask About You
8:I Couldn't Sleep a Wink Last Night
9:Paper Doll
10:Oh, What a Beautiful Mornin'

Feb. 19, 1944

1:Shoo Shoo Baby
2:My Heart Tells Me
3:Besame Mucho
4:Mairzy Doats
5:No Love, No Nothin'
6:When They Ask About You
7:I Couldn't Sleep a Wink Last Night
8:A Lovely Way to Spend An Evening *
9:Oh, What a Beautiful Mornin'
10:My Ideal

* Newcomer

Feb. 26, 1944

1:Besame Mucho
2:My Heart Tells Me
3:Shoo Shoo Baby
4:Mairzy Doats
5:No Love, No Nothin'
6:A Lovely Way to Spend An Evening
7:I Couldn't Sleep a Wink Last Night
8:My Ideal
9:When They Ask About You
10:Oh, What a Beautiful Mornin'

Mar. 4, 1944

1:Besame Mucho
2:Mairzy Doats
3:I Couldn't Sleep a Wink Last Night
4:Shoo Shoo Baby
5:My Heart Tells Me
6:No Love, No Nothin'
7:When They Ask About You
8:Poinciana *
9:I Love You *
10:A Lovely Way to Spend An Evening

Mar. 11, 1944

1:Mairzy Doats
2:Besame Mucho
3:No Love, No Nothin'
4:My Heart Tells Me
5:I Couldn't Sleep a Wink Last Night
6:Shoo Shoo Baby
7:I Love You
8:When They Ask About You
9:A Lovely Way to Spend An Evening
10:Poinciana

Mar. 18, 1944

1:I Couldn't Sleep a Wink Last Night
2:Mairzy Doats
3:Besame Mucho
4:When They Ask About You
5:I Love You
6:A Lovely Way to Spend An Evening
7:Shoo Shoo Baby
8:No Love, No Nothin'
9:My Heart Tells Me
10:Poinciana

Mar. 25, 1944

1:Besame Mucho
2:Poinciana
3:Mairzy Doats
4:When They Ask About You
5:I Couldn't Sleep a Wink Last Night
6:I Love You
7:A Lovely Way to Spend An Evening
8:Don't Sweetheart Me *
9:Shoo Shoo Baby
10:It's Love, Love, Love *

Apr. 1, 1944

1:It's Love, Love, Love
2:I Couldn't Sleep a Wink Last Night
3:Besame Mucho
4:Poinciana
5:I Love You
6:Mairzy Doats
7:A Lovely Way to Spend An Evening
8:When They Ask About You
9:Shoo Shoo Baby
10:Don't Sweetheart Me

Apr. 8, 1944

1:It's Love, Love, Love
2:I Love You
3:Besame Mucho
4:Poinciana
5:When They Ask About You
6:Mairzy Doats
7:I'll Get By *
8:I Couldn't Sleep a Wink Last Night
9:Long Ago and Far Away *
10:A Lovely Way to Spend An Evening

Apr. 15, 1944

1:I Love You
2:It's Love, Love, Love
3:Besame Mucho
4:Mairzy Doats
5:Poinciana
6:Do Nothing Till You Hear From Me *
7:Long Ago and Far Away
8:I Couldn't Sleep a Wink Last Night
9:When They Ask About You
10:I'll Get By

Apr. 22, 1944

1:It's Love, Love, Love
2:I Love You
3:Poinciana
4:When They Ask About You
5:Besame Mucho
6:Mairzy Doats
7:I'll Get By
8:Long Ago and Far Away
9:San Fernando Valley *
10:I Couldn't Sleep a Wink Last Night

Apr. 29, 1944

1:I Love You
2:It's Love, Love, Love
3:Long Ago and Far Away
4:Poinciana
5:I'll Get By
6:When They Ask About You
7:San Fernando Valley
8:Goodnight Wherever You Are *
9:Besame Mucho
10:Mairzy Doats

May 6, 1944

1:I Love You
2:I'll Get By
3:Long Ago and Far Away
4:It's Love, Love, Love
5:I'll Be Seeing You *
6:When They Ask About You
7:Goodnight Wherever You Are
8:San Fernando Valley
9:Poinciana
10:Besame Mucho

May 13, 1944

1:Long Ago and Far Away
2:I Love You
3:It's Love, Love, Love
4:San Fernando Valley
5:I'll Get By
6:Poinciana
7:I'll Be Seeing You
8:Besame Mucho
9:Goodnight Wherever You Are
10:When They Ask About You

May 20, 1944

1:Long Ago and Far Away
2:San Fernando Valley
3:I'll Get By
4:It's Love, Love, Love
5:I Love You
6:Poinciana
7:I'll Be Seeing You
8:Goodnight Wherever You Are
9:Amor *
10:Besame Mucho

May 27, 1944

1:Long Ago and Far Away
2:I'll Get By
3:It's Love, Love, Love
4:San Fernando Valley
5:I'll Be Seeing You
6:Goodnight Wherever You Are
7:I Love You
8:Amor
9:Poinciana
10:Besame Mucho

June 3, 1944

1:Long Ago and Far Away
2:I'll Get By
3:I'll Be Seeing You
4:San Fernando Valley
5:It's Love, Love, Love
6:I Love You
7:Amor
8:Goodnight Wherever You Are
9:How Blue the Night *
10:Poinciana

June 10, 1944

1:Long Ago and Far Away
2:I'll Be Seeing You
3:I'll Get By
4:San Fernando Valley
5:Goodnight Wherever You Are
6:I Love You
7:Amor
8:It's Love, Love, Love
9:Swinging On a Star *
10:How Blue the Night

June 17, 1944

1:Long Ago and Far Away
2:I'll Be Seeing You
3:I'll Get By
4:San Fernando Valley
5:Amor
6:I Love You
7:It's Love, Love, Love
8:Goodnight Wherever You Are
9:Someday I'll Meet You Again *
10:Swinging On a Star

June 24, 1944

1:I'll Be Seeing You
2:I'll Get By
3:Long Ago and Far Away
4:Goodnight Wherever You Are
5:San Fernando Valley
6:Amor
7:Swinging On a Star
8:Time Waits For No One *
9:I Love You
10:Someday I'll Meet You Again

July 1, 1944

1:I'll Be Seeing You
2:Long Ago and Far Away
3:Amor
4:San Fernando Valley
5:Goodnight Wherever You Are
6:Swinging On a Star
7:I'll Get By
8:Time Waits For No One
9:I Love You
10:Someday I'll Meet You Again

July 8, 1944

1:I'll Be Seeing You
2:Amor
3:Long Ago and Far Away
4:I'll Get By
5:Milkman, Keep Those Bottles Quiet *
6:San Fernando Valley
7:Goodnight Wherever You Are
8:Time Waits For No One
9:Swinging On a Star
10:I Love You

July 15, 1944

1:I'll Be Seeing You
2:Long Ago and Far Away
3:Amor
4:I'll Get By
5:Swinging On a Star
6:Milkman, Keep Those Bottles Quiet
7:Time Waits For No One
8:San Fernando Valley
9:Goodnight Wherever You Are
10:I Love You

July 22, 1944

1:I'll Be Seeing You
2:Swinging On a Star
3:Long Ago and Far Away
4:Amor
5:I'll Get By
6:Goodnight Wherever You Are
7:Sweet Lorraine *
8:And Then You Kissed Me *
9:Milkman, Keep Those Bottles Quiet
10:Time Waits For No One

July 29, 1944

1:Amor
2:I'll Be Seeing You
3:Long Ago and Far Away
4:Swinging On a Star
5:I'll Get By
6:Time Waits For No One
7:Goodnight Wherever You Are
8:Milkman, Keep Those Bottles Quiet
9:It Could Happen to You *
10:Sweet Lorraine

Aug. 5, 1944

1:I'll Be Seeing You
2:Amor
3:Swinging On a Star
4:Time Waits For No One
5:Long Ago and Far Away
6:I'll Get By
7:Milkman, Keep Those Bottles Quiet
8:It Could Happen to You
9:Goodnight Wherever You Are
10:Sweet Lorraine

Aug. 12, 1944

1:I'll Be Seeing You
2:Amor
3:Swinging On a Star
4:I'll Get By
5:Long Ago and Far Away
6:I'll Walk Alone *
7:Milkman, Keep Those Bottles Quiet
8:Time Waits For No One
9:Is You Is Or Is You Ain't My Baby? *
10:It Could Happen to You

Aug. 19, 1944

1:Amor
2:Swinging On a Star
3:I'll Be Seeing You
4:Time Waits For No One
5:I'll Get By
6:Long Ago and Far Away
7:I'll Walk Alone
8:It Could Happen to You
9:Is You Is Or Is You Ain't My Baby?
10:Milkman, Keep Those Bottles Quiet

Aug. 26, 1944

1:I'll Be Seeing You
2:Time Waits For No One
3:Swinging On a Star
4:Amor
5:It Could Happen to You
6:It Had to Be You *
7:I'll Walk Alone
8:I'll Get By
9:Pretty Kitty Blue Eyes *
10:Is You Is Or Is You Ain't My Baby?

Sept. 2, 1944

1:I'll Be Seeing You
2:Swinging On a Star
3:Amor
4:Time Waits For No One
5:Is You Is Or Is You Ain't My Baby?
6:I'll Walk Alone
7:I'll Get By
8:It Could Happen to You
9:It Had to Be You
10:Pretty Kitty Blue Eyes

Sept. 9, 1944

1:I'll Be Seeing You
2:Swinging On a Star
3:Time Waits For No One
4:Is You Is Or Is You Ain't My Baby?
5:Amor
6:I'll Walk Alone
7:It Could Happen to You
8:A Fellow On a Furlough *
9:It Had to Be You
10:I'll Get By

Sept. 16, 1944

1:I'll Walk Alone
2:Swinging On a Star
3:Time Waits For No One
4:Is You Is Or Is You Ain't My Baby?
5:Amor
6:I'll Be Seeing You
7:It Could Happen to You
8:I'll Get By
9:It Had to Be You
10:A Fellow On a Furlough

Sept. 23, 1944

1:I'll Walk Alone
2:Is You Is Or Is You Ain't My Baby?
3:I'll Be Seeing You
4:Time Waits For No One
5:It Could Happen to You
6:Swinging On a Star
7:How Many Hearts Have You Broken? *
8:It Had to Be You
9:Amor
10:I'll Get By

Sept. 30, 1944

1:I'll Walk Alone
2:Is You Is Or Is You Ain't My Baby?
3:It Had to Be You
4:Time Waits For No One
5:Swinging On a Star
6:It Could Happen to You
7:How Many Hearts Have You Broken?
8:I'll Be Seeing You
9:Together *
10:Amor

Oct. 7, 1944

1:I'll Walk Alone
2:Is You Is Or Is You Ain't My Baby?
3:Together
4:How Many Hearts Have You Broken?
5:Time Waits For No One
6:Swinging On a Star
7:It Had to Be You
8:I'll Be Seeing You
9:It Could Happen to You
10:Amor

Oct. 14, 1944

1:I'll Walk Alone
2:Is You Is Or Is You Ain't My Baby?
3:It Had to Be You
4:Dance With a Dolly *
5:Time Waits For No One
6:It Could Happen to You
7:How Many Hearts Have You Broken?
8:Swinging On a Star
9:I'll Be Seeing You
10:Together

Oct. 21, 1944

1:I'll Walk Alone
2:Dance With a Dolly
3:How Many Hearts Have You Broken?
4:Is You Is Or Is You Ain't My Baby?
5:It Had to Be You
6:It Could Happen to You
7:Swinging On a Star
8:Always *
9:Let Me Love You Tonight *
10:Together

Oct. 28, 1944

1:I'll Walk Alone
2:Dance With a Dolly
3:The Trolley Song *
4:Is You Is Or Is You Ain't My Baby?
5:Together
6:How Many Hearts Have You Broken?
7:It Had to Be You
8:Always
9:Let Me Love You Tonight
10:I'm Making Believe *

Nov. 4, 1944

1:I'll Walk Alone
2:Dance With a Dolly
3:Is You Is Or Is You Ain't My Baby?
4:Together
5:How Many Hearts Have You Broken?
6:The Trolley Song
7:It Had to Be You
8:Always
9:Let Me Love You Tonight
10:I'm Making Believe

Nov. 11, 1944

1:Dance With a Dolly
2:I'll Walk Alone
3:The Trolley Song
4:Always
5:Together
6:How Many Hearts Have You Broken?
7:It Had to Be You
8:Strange Music *
9:I'm Making Believe
10:Let Me Love You Tonight

Nov. 18, 1944

1:The Trolley Song
2:I'll Walk Alone
3:Together
4:Dance With a Dolly
5:Always
6:Let Me Love You Tonight
7:I'm Making Believe
8:How Many Hearts Have You Broken?
9:Strange Music
10:It Had to Be You

Nov. 25, 1944

1:The Trolley Song
2:Dance With a Dolly
3:I'll Walk Alone
4:Together
5:Always
6:I'm Making Believe
7:Let Me Love You Tonight
8:How Many Hearts Have You Broken?
9:I Don't Want to Love You *
10:Strange Music

Dec. 2, 1944

1:The Trolley Song
2:Dance With a Dolly
3:I'm Making Believe
4:Together
5:Don't Fence Me In *
6:I'll Walk Alone
7:Always
8:I'm Confessin' *
9:There Goes That Song Again *
10:I Don't Want to Love You

Dec. 9, 1944

1:The Trolley Song
2:I'm Making Believe
3:Don't Fence Me In
4:I'll Walk Alone
5:Dance With a Dolly
6:Always
7:Together
8:I Dream of You *
9:I'm Confessin'
10:There Goes That Song Again

Dec. 16, 1944

1:The Trolley Song
2:Don't Fence Me In
3:I'm Confessin'
4:I'm Making Believe
5:Together
6:I Dream of You
7:There Goes That Song Again
8:Dance With a Dolly
9:I'll Walk Alone
10:Always

Dec. 23, 1944

1:Don't Fence Me In
2:The Trolley Song
3:I'm Making Believe
4:There Goes That Song Again
5:Dance With a Dolly
6:I'm Confessin'
7:I Dream of You
8:Together
9:I'll Walk Alone
10:Always

Dec. 30, 1944

1:Don't Fence Me In
2:The Trolley Song
3:There Goes That Song Again
4:I'm Confessin'
5:I'm Making Believe
6:I Dream of You
7:Dance With a Dolly
8:Always
9:Together
10:I'll Walk Alone

1945

Perhaps no other single year in contemporary times was so history-packed as 1945. It saw the deaths of Mussolini, Hitler, and Roosevelt. It saw the surrender of Germany. It saw the dropping of the world's first atomic bombs on Hiroshima and Nagasaki. It saw the unconditional surrender of Japan.

The war was over.

There was a new President, Harry Truman. There was the beginning formation of a new worldwide organization called the United Nations. There was a new boss in Japan—General Douglas MacArthur, who had fulfilled his promise to return.

Incredibly, one fog-shrouded morning in New York City, a B-25 crashed into the seventy-ninth floor of the Empire State Building, killing thirteen.

Suddenly there was a new word in the vocabulary: postwar. And the biggest pastime once again became the movies, with Ray Milland's *The Lost Weekend* and Joan Crawford's *Mildred Pierce* leading the way in 1945.

Frank Sinatra was gone from "Your Hit Parade," replaced by, of all people, the operatic Lawrence Tibbett. Glenn Miller was gone, a wartime casualty, and so was the Big Band era. The hit makers now weren't the bands, they were singers like Sinatra, Dinah Shore, Perry Como, and Dick Haymes. Both Como and Haymes had hit recordings of "Till the End of Time," taken from the classic "Polonaise," putting it in the Number One spot for seven weeks. However, the top song of 1945 had to be the eight-week Number One run of "Don't Fence Me In," even though it began its string in late 1944.

Rodgers and Hammerstein had a big year in 1945. Their second Broadway hit, *Carousel,* had produced "If I Loved You" for the Hit Parade, and their first and only movie, *State Fair,* had given the Top Ten listings "It Might As Well Be Spring" and "That's For Me."

But perhaps the best-remembered song of 1945 was one by Jule Styne and Sammy Cahn, made famous in the Harry James-Kitty Kallen recording, which seemed to say it all for the returning servicemen: "It's Been a Long, Long Time."

Jan. 6, 1945

1:Don't Fence Me In
2:There Goes That Song Again
3:I'm Making Believe
4:I Dream of You
5:The Trolley Song
6:Dance With a Dolly
7:Together
8:I'm Confessin'
9:Sweet Dreams, Sweetheart *
10:Always

Jan. 13, 1945

1:Don't Fence Me In
2:There Goes That Song Again
3:The Trolley Song
4:I Dream of You
5:I'm Making Believe
6:More and More *
7:Dance With a Dolly
8:I'm Confessin'
9:Together
10:Sweet Dreams, Sweetheart

Jan. 20, 1945

1:Don't Fence Me In
2:There Goes That Song Again
3:I'm Making Believe
4:I Dream of You
5:The Trolley Song
6:Accentuate the Positive *
7:I Didn't Know About You *
8:Dance With a Dolly
9:More and More
10:Sweet Dreams, Sweetheart

Jan. 27, 1945

1:Don't Fence Me In
2:There Goes That Song Again
3:I Dream of You
4:Accentuate the Positive
5:I'm Making Believe
6:Sweet Dreams, Sweetheart
7:The Trolley Song
8:Don't You Know I Care? *
9:Don't Ever Change *
10:More and More

* Newcomer

Feb. 3, 1945

1:Don't Fence Me In
2:There Goes That Song Again
3:Accentuate the Positive
4:I Dream of You
5:I'm Making Believe
6:Evelina *
7:Sweet Dreams, Sweetheart
8:Sleighride in July *
9:More and More
10:The Trolley Song

Feb. 10, 1945

1:Accentuate the Positive
2:Don't Fence Me In
3:There Goes That Song Again
4:I Dream of You
5:My Dreams Are Getting Better All the Time *
6:A Little On the Lonely Side *
7:I'm Making Believe
8:More and More
9:Sweet Dreams, Sweetheart
10:Sleighride in July

Feb. 17, 1945

1:Don't Fence Me In
2:Accentuate the Positive
3:More and More
4:There Goes That Song Again
5:Saturday Night *
6:I Dream of You
7:Rum and Coca-Cola *
8:A Little On the Lonely Side
9:Sweet Dreams, Sweetheart
10:My Dreams Are Getting Better All the Time

Feb. 24, 1945

1:Accentuate the Positive
2:I Dream of You
3:Don't Fence Me In
4:Saturday Night
5:A Little On the Lonely Side
6:Sweet Dreams, Sweetheart
7:Rum and Coca-Cola
8:There Goes That Song Again
9:More and More
10:My Dreams Are Getting Better All the Time

Mar. 3, 1945

1:Accentuate the Positive
2:I Dream of You
3:A Little On the Lonely Side
4:Saturday Night
5:My Dreams Are Getting Better All the Time
6:Don't Fence Me In
7:More and More
8:Sweet Dreams, Sweetheart
9:Rum and Coca-Cola
10:Everytime We Say Goodbye *

Mar. 10, 1945

1:Accentuate the Positive
2:Saturday Night
3:My Dreams Are Getting Better All the Time
4:Rum and Coca-Cola
5:Don't Fence Me In
6:More and More
7:Sweet Dreams, Sweetheart
8:A Little On the Lonely Side
9:I Dream of You
10:Everytime We Say Goodbye

Mar. 17, 1945

1:A Little On the Lonely Side
2:Saturday Night
3:Accentuate the Positive
4:My Dreams Are Getting Better All the Time
5:More and More
6:Rum and Coca-Cola
7:I'm Beginning to See the Light *
8:Sweet Dreams, Sweetheart
9:Don't Fence Me In
10:I Dream of You

Mar. 24, 1945

1:My Dreams Are Getting Better All the Time
2:A Little On the Lonely Side
3:Accentuate the Positive
4:Saturday Night
5:Rum and Coca-Cola
6:Sweet Dreams, Sweetheart
7:I'm Beginning to See the Light
8:Too-ra-loo-ra-loo-ral *
9:After Awhile *
10:More and More

Mar. 31, 1945

1:I'm Beginning to See the Light
2:A Little On the Lonely Side
3:My Dreams Are Getting Better All the Time
4:Saturday Night
5:Sweet Dreams, Sweetheart
6:Accentuate the Positive
7:Candy *
8:Rum and Coca-Cola
9:More and More
10:After Awhile

Apr. 7, 1945

1:My Dreams Are Getting Better All the Time
2:I'm Beginning to See the Light
3:A Little On the Lonely Side
4:Candy
5:Saturday Night
6:Rum and Coca-Cola
7:Sweet Dreams, Sweetheart
8:Let's Take the Long Way Home *
9:Accentuate the Positive
10:More and More

Apr. 14, 1945

1:My Dreams Are Getting Better All the Time
2:I'm Beginning to See the Light
3:Candy
4:A Little On the Lonely Side
5:Saturday Night
6:More and More
7:All of My Life *
8:Rum and Coca-Cola
9:Accentuate the Positive
10:Let's Take the Long Way Home

Apr. 21, 1945

1:Candy
2:I'm Beginning to See the Light
3:My Dreams Are Getting Better All the Time
4:Saturday Night
5:Just a Prayer Away *
6:Laura *
7:A Little On the Lonely Side
8:More and More
9:All of My Life
10:Rum and Coca-Cola

Apr. 28, 1945

1:Candy
2:I'm Beginning to See the Light
3:My Dreams Are Getting Better All the Time
4:All of My Life
5:Just a Prayer Away
6:A Little On the Lonely Side
7:The More I See You *
8:Laura
9:Rum and Coca-Cola
10:Saturday Night

May 5, 1945

1:Candy
2:I'm Beginning to See the Light
3:My Dreams Are Getting Better All the Time
4:Laura
5:All of My Life
6:Just a Prayer Away
7:Dream *
8:He's Home For a Little While *
9:A Little On the Lonely Side
10:The More I See You

May 12, 1945

1:Candy
2:Laura
3:Dream
4:My Dreams Are Getting Better All the Time
5:All of My Life
6:I'm Beginning to See the Light
7:I Should Care *
8:Just a Prayer Away
9:Sentimental Journey *
10:The More I See You

May 19, 1945

1:I'm Beginning to See the Light
2:Candy
3:Sentimental Journey
4:All of My Life
5:Just a Prayer Away
6:My Dreams Are Getting Better All the Time
7:Laura
8:Dream
9:I Should Care
10:The More I See You

May 26, 1945

1:Dream
2:Candy
3:I'm Beginning to See the Light
4:Sentimental Journey
5:Laura
6:All of My Life
7:Just a Prayer Away
8:I Should Care
9:My Dreams Are Getting Better All the Time
10:The More I See You

June 2, 1945

1:Laura
2:Dream
3:Sentimental Journey
4:All of My Life
5:Just a Prayer Away
6:Candy
7:I Should Care
8:My Dreams Are Getting Better All the Time
9:A Friend of Yours *
10:The More I See You

June 9, 1945

1:Sentimental Journey
2:Laura
3:Dream
4:I Should Care
5:Candy
6:All of My Life
7:There, I've Said It Again *
8:There Must Be a Way *
9:The More I See You
10:A Friend of Yours

June 16, 1945

1:Sentimental Journey
2:Dream
3:Laura
4:I Should Care
5:Candy
6:All of My Life
7:There, I've Said It Again
8:Bell Bottom Trousers *
9:The More I See You
10:There Must Be a Way

June 23, 1945

1:Sentimental Journey
2:Dream
3:Laura
4:There, I've Said It Again
5:Bell Bottom Trousers
6:There Must Be a Way
7:All of My Life
8:The More I See You
9:I Should Care
10:Candy

June 30, 1945

1:Sentimental Journey
2:Laura
3:Dream
4:All of My Life
5:There, I've Said It Again
6:Bell Bottom Trousers
7:The More I See You
8:You Belong to My Heart *
9:Ev'ry Time *
10:There Must Be a Way

July 7, 1945

1:Sentimental Journey
2:Laura
3:Dream
4:You Belong to My Heart
5:The More I See You
6:Bell Bottom Trousers
7:There, I've Said It Again
8:While You're Away *
9:Baia *
10:There Must Be a Way

July 14, 1945

1:Dream
2:Sentimental Journey
3:Bell Bottom Trousers
4:There, I've Said It Again
5:The More I See You
6:Laura
7:There Must Be a Way
8:Out of This World *
9:If I Loved You *
10:You Belong to My Heart

July 21, 1945

1:Dream
2:Sentimental Journey
3:The More I See You
4:Bell Bottom Trousers
5:Gotta Be This Or That *
6:You Belong to My Heart
7:Laura
8:If I Loved You
9:Can't You Read Between the Lines? *
10:There, I've Said It Again

July 28, 1945

1:The More I See You
2:Dream
3:Sentimental Journey
4:I Wish I Knew *
5:There, I've Said It Again
6:Bell Bottom Trousers
7:If I Loved You
8:The Wish That I Wish Tonight *
9:You Belong to My Heart
10:Gotta Be This Or That

Aug. 4, 1945

1:Dream
2:I Wish I Knew
3:If I Loved You
4:There, I've Said It Again
5:Sentimental Journey
6:I Don't Care Who Knows It *
7:The More I See You
8:Bell Bottom Trousers
9:Gotta Be This Or That
10:You Belong to My Heart

Aug. 11, 1945

1:Dream
2:There, I've Said It Again
3:If I Loved You
4:The More I See You
5:Sentimental Journey
6:I Don't Care Who Knows It
7:You Belong to My Heart
8:Bell Bottom Trousers
9:Gotta Be This Or That
10:I Wish I Knew

Aug. 18, 1945

1:If I Loved You
2:I Wish I Knew
3:Till the End of Time *
4:Gotta Be This Or That
5:On the Atchison, Topeka and Santa Fe *
6:Dream
7:There, I've Said It Again
8:The More I See You
9:Sentimental Journey
10:Bell Bottom Trousers

Aug. 25, 1945

1:If I Loved You
2:Till the End of Time
3:On the Atchison, Topeka and Santa Fe
4:Gotta Be This Or That
5:I Wish I Knew
6:Sentimental Journey
7:The More I See You
8:Dream
9:Bell Bottom Trousers
10:Remember When *

Sept. 1, 1945

1:Till the End of Time
2:On the Atchison, Topeka and Santa Fe
3:Gotta Be This Or That
4:The More I See You
5:If I Loved You
6:I Wish I Knew
7:Dream
8:There's No You *
9:Remember When
10:Bell Bottom Trousers

Sept. 8, 1945

1:Till the End of Time
2:If I Loved You
3:Gotta Be This Or That
4:On the Atchison, Topeka and Santa Fe
5:I Wish I Knew
6:Dream
7:I'm Gonna Love That Guy *
8:There's No You
9:The More I See You
10:Bell Bottom Trousers

Sept. 15, 1945

1:Till the End of Time
2:If I Loved You
3:On the Atchison, Topeka and Santa Fe
4:Gotta Be This Or That
5:I Wish I Knew
6:The More I See You
7:I'm Gonna Love That Guy
8:Bell Bottom Trousers
9:I'd Do It All Over Again *
10:There's No You

Sept. 22, 1945

1:If I Loved You
2:On the Atchison, Topeka and Santa Fe
3:Till the End of Time
4:Gotta Be This Or That
5:I'm Gonna Love That Guy
6:I Wish I Knew
7:I'll Buy That Dream *
8:Along the Navajo Trail *
9:Bell Bottom Trousers
10:The More I See You

Sept. 29, 1945

1:Till the End of Time
2:On the Atchison, Topeka and Santa Fe
3:If I Loved You
4:I'm Gonna Love That Guy
5:I'll Buy That Dream
6:Along the Navajo Trail
7:I Wish I Knew
8:Gotta Be This Or That
9:That's For Me *
10:The More I See You

Oct. 6, 1945

1:Till the End of Time
2:If I Loved You
3:I'm Gonna Love That Guy
4:Gotta Be This Or That
5:I'll Buy That Dream
6:On the Atchison, Topeka and Santa Fe
7:And There You Are *
8:That's For Me
9:I Wish I Knew
10:Along the Navajo Trail

Oct. 13, 1945

1:Till the End of Time
2:If I Loved You
3:Along the Navajo Trail
4:On the Atchison, Topeka and Santa Fe
5:Gotta Be This Or That
6:I'm Gonna Love That Guy
7:I'll Buy That Dream
8:Homesick, That's All *
9:That's For Me
10:I Wish I Knew

Oct. 20, 1945

1:I'll Buy That Dream
2:Till the End of Time
3:On the Atchison, Topeka and Santa Fe
4:If I Loved You
5:I'm Gonna Love That Guy
6:Along the Navajo Trail
7:That's For Me
8:Gotta Be This Or That
9:Autumn Serenade *
10:I Wish I Knew

Oct. 27, 1945

1:I'll Buy That Dream
2:That's For Me
3:Along the Navajo Trail
4:If I Loved You
5:Till the End of Time
6:On the Atchison, Topeka and Santa Fe
7:Gotta Be This Or That
8:It's Been a Long, Long Time *
9:I'm Gonna Love That Guy
10:I Wish I Knew

Nov. 3, 1945

1:Till the End of Time
2:I'll Buy That Dream
3:That's For Me
4:I'm Gonna Love That Guy
5:If I Loved You
6:On the Atchison, Topeka and Santa Fe
7:Along the Navajo Trail
8:It's Been a Long, Long Time
9:Love Letters *
10:Gotta Be This Or That

Nov. 10, 1945

1:It's Been a Long, Long Time
2:I'll Buy That Dream
3:On the Atchison, Topeka and Santa Fe
4:Till the End of Time
5:That's For Me
6:Along the Navajo Trail
7:Chickery Chick *
8:If I Loved You
9:Love Letters
10:I'm Gonna Love That Guy

Nov. 17, 1945

1:It's Been a Long, Long Time
2:Till the End of Time
3:I'll Buy That Dream
4:That's For Me
5:If I Loved You
6:Waiting For the Train to Come In *
7:No Can Do *
8:On the Atchison, Topeka and Santa Fe
9:Along the Navajo Trail
10:Chickery Chick

Nov. 24, 1945

1:It's Been a Long, Long Time
2:That's For Me
3:I'll Buy That Dream
4:It Might As Well Be Spring *
5:Till the End of Time
6:Along the Navajo Trail
7:A Stranger in Town *
8:Walking With My Honey *
9:Chickery Chick
10:Waiting For the Train to Come In

Dec. 1, 1945

1:It's Been a Long, Long Time
2:It Might As Well Be Spring
3:I'll Buy That Dream
4:Chickery Chick
5:Till the End of Time
6:That's For Me
7:I Can't Begin to Tell You *
8:Waiting For the Train to Come In
9:Did You Ever Get That Feeling in the

                              Moonlight? *

10:Along the Navajo Trail

Dec. 8, 1945

1:It's Been a Long, Long Time
2:That's For Me
3:It Might As Well Be Spring
4:Chickery Chick
5:I'll Buy That Dream
6:Waiting For the Train to Come In
7:Till the End of Time
8:Along the Navajo Trail
9:I Can't Begin to Tell You
10:Did You Ever Get That Feeling In

                    the Moonlight?

Dec. 15, 1945

1:It Might As Well Be Spring
2:It's Been a Long, Long Time
3:I Can't Begin to Tell You
4:Chickery Chick
5:Symphony *
6:That's For Me
7:I'll Buy That Dream
8:Till the End of Time
9:Just a Little Fond Affection *
10:Waiting For the Train to Come In

Dec. 22, 1945

1:It Might As Well Be Spring
2:I Can't Begin to Tell You
3:It's Been a Long, Long Time
4:Symphony
5:Chickery Chick
6:That's For Me
7:Waiting For the Train to Come In
8:Put That Ring On My Finger *
9:Till the End of Time
10:Just a Little Fond Affection

Dec. 29, 1945

1:It Might As Well Be Spring
2:I Can't Begin to Tell You
3:Symphony
4:It's Been a Long, Long Time
5:Chickery Chick
6:Put That Ring On My Finger
7:Just a Little Fond Affection
8:That's For Me
9:Waiting For the Train to Come In
10:Till the End of Time

1946

Peace, it was wonderful.

In 1946 there was a shortage of new cars, apartments, and white shirts. But, happily, there was no shortage of good music.

Three songs, "Oh! What It Seemed to Be," "The Gypsy," and "To Each His Own," tied for the top tune of the year, each with eight weeks as Number One.

On Broadway the story could be summed up in one musical, Irving Berlin's *Annie Get Your Gun.* The show had perhaps more individual song hits than any other in stage history, although only three, "They Say It's Wonderful," "I Got the Sun in the Morning," and "Doin' What Comes Naturally," made radio's "Your Hit Parade."

The intriguing thing to ponder about that musical is the little-known fact that Jerome Kern was set to write it but died in late 1945. Would he have written all those hits that Berlin did? Kern's last contributions to the Top Ten were "In Love in Vain" and "All Through the Day" from the 1946 movie *Centennial Summer.*

The revival mill supplied "I'm Always Chasing Rainbows" and an old Russ Columbo hit in a new Perry Como dressing, "Prisoner of Love." Broadway's *Call Me Mister,* which gave the Hit Parade "South America, Take It Away," was a musical tale of returning servicemen, so it was right at home in 1946. The same could be said for the top motion picture of 1946, the highly memorable *The Best Years of Our Lives.*

The United Nations opened that year, but there still were reminders of the war in the headlines. "Lord Haw Haw," who had broadcast for the Nazis, was hanged for treason in London. And at Nuremberg eleven top Nazis were sentenced to hang. Ten were executed, but Hermann Goering committed suicide by poison in his cell two hours before he was to go to the gallows.

Jan. 5, 1946

1:Symphony
2:I Can't Begin to Tell You
3:It Might As Well Be Spring
4:It's Been a Long, Long Time
5:Just a Little Fond Affection
6:That's For Me
7:Waiting For the Train to Come In
8:Chickery Chick
9:Let It Snow! Let It Snow! Let It Snow! *
10:Put That Ring On My Finger

Jan. 12, 1946

1:I Can't Begin to Tell You
2:Symphony
3:It Might As Well Be Spring
4:It's Been a Long, Long Time
5:Chickery Chick
6:That's For Me
7:Let It Snow! Let It Snow! Let It Snow!
8:Just a Little Fond Affection
9:Waiting For the Train to Come In
10:Put That Ring On My Finger

Jan. 19, 1946

1:Symphony
2:It Might As Well Be Spring
3:I Can't Begin to Tell You
4:Let It Snow! Let It Snow! Let It Snow!
5:Chickery Chick
6:It's Been a Long, Long Time
7:Come to Baby Do *
8:Wait and See *
9:Just a Little Fond Affection
10:Waiting For the Train to Come In

Jan. 26, 1946

1:Symphony
2:I Can't Begin to Tell You
3:Let It Snow! Let It Snow! Let It Snow!
4:It Might As Well Be Spring
5:Aren't You Glad You're You? *
6:I'm Always Chasing Rainbows *
7:It's Been a Long, Long Time
8:Just a Little Fond Affection
9:Chickery Chick
10:Wait and See

Feb. 2, 1946

1:Symphony
2:It Might As Well Be Spring
3:I Can't Begin to Tell You
4:Let It Snow! Let It Snow! Let It Snow!
5:Aren't You Glad You're You?
6:Just a Little Fond Affection
7:Chickery Chick
8:It's Been a Long, Long Time
9:I'm Always Chasing Rainbows
10:Wait and See

Feb. 9, 1946

1:Symphony
2:I Can't Begin to Tell You
3:Let It Snow! Let It Snow! Let It Snow!
4:It Might As Well Be Spring
5:Aren't You Glad You're You?
6:Day By Day *
7:Just a Little Fond Affection
8:Chickery Chick
9:I'm Always Chasing Rainbows
10:It's Been a Long, Long Time

Feb. 16, 1946

1:Symphony
2:I Can't Begin to Tell You
3:Aren't You Glad You're You?
4:I'm Always Chasing Rainbows
5:It Might As Well Be Spring
6:Let It Snow! Let It Snow! Let It Snow!
7:Day By Day
8:Oh! What It Seemed to Be *
9:Some Sunday Morning *
10:Just a Little Fond Affection

Feb. 23, 1946

1:Let It Snow! Let It Snow! Let It Snow!
2:I Can't Begin to Tell You
3:Symphony
4:I'm Always Chasing Rainbows
5:Doctor, Lawyer, Indian Chief *
6:Aren't You Glad You're You?
7:Oh! What It Seemed to Be
8:Day By Day
9:It Might As Well Be Spring
10:Just a Little Fond Affection

* Newcomer

Mar. 2, 1946

1:Let It Snow! Let It Snow! Let It Snow!
2:Symphony
3:I Can't Begin to Tell You
4:I'm Always Chasing Rainbows
5:Oh! What It Seemed to Be
6:Personality *
7:Day By Day
8:Doctor, Lawyer, Indian Chief
9:Aren't You Glad You're You?
10:It Might As Well Be Spring

Mar. 9, 1946

1:Symphony
2:Let It Snow! Let It Snow! Let It Snow!
3:Oh! What It Seemed to Be
4:Aren't You Glad You're You?
5:Day By Day
6:Personality
7:I Can't Begin to Tell You
8:Doctor, Lawyer, Indian Chief
9:I'm Always Chasing Rainbows
10:It Might As Well Be Spring

Mar. 16, 1946

1:Oh! What It Seemed to Be
2:Symphony
3:Let It Snow! Let It Snow! Let It Snow!
4:I'm Always Chasing Rainbows
5:Day By Day
6:Personality
7:Aren't You Glad You're You?
8:Doctor, Lawyer, Indian Chief
9:I Can't Begin to Tell You
10:It Might As Well Be Spring

Mar. 23, 1946

1:Oh! What It Seemed to Be
2:Personality
3:Day By Day
4:Let It Snow! Let It Snow! Let It Snow!
5:Symphony
6:I'm Always Chasing Rainbows
7:Doctor, Lawyer, Indian Chief
8:Aren't You Glad You're You?
9:You Won't Be Satisfied *
10:I Can't Begin to Tell You

Mar. 30, 1946

1:Oh! What It Seemed to Be
2:Day By Day
3:Personality
4:Doctor, Lawyer, Indian Chief
5:You Won't Be Satisfied
6:Symphony
7:I'm Always Chasing Rainbows
8:Aren't You Glad You're You?
9:Let It Snow! Let It Snow! Let It Snow!
10:I Can't Begin to Tell You

Apr. 6, 1946

1:Oh! What It Seemed to Be
2:Personality
3:You Won't Be Satisfied
4:Day By Day
5:Doctor, Lawyer, Indian Chief
6:Symphony
7:One-zy, Two-zy *
8:I'm Always Chasing Rainbows
9:All Through the Day *
10:Aren't You Glad You're You?

Apr. 13, 1946

1:Oh! What It Seemed to Be
2:You Won't Be Satisfied
3:Personality
4:Doctor, Lawyer, Indian Chief
5:Day By Day
6:I'm Always Chasing Rainbows
7:One-zy, Two-zy
8:Symphony
9:All Through the Day
10:Aren't You Glad You're You?

Apr. 20, 1946

1:Oh! What It Seemed to Be
2:Personality
3:Day By Day
4:You Won't Be Satisfied
5:Shoo Fly Pie *
6:Doctor, Lawyer, Indian Chief
7:One-zy, Two-zy
8:All Through the Day
9:Symphony
10:I'm Always Chasing Rainbows

Apr. 27, 1946

1:Oh! What It Seemed to Be
2:Day By Day
3:You Won't Be Satisfied
4:Shoo Fly Pie
5:All Through the Day
6:One-zy, Two-zy
7:Sioux City Sue *
8:Personality
9:Doctor, Lawyer, Indian Chief
10:Symphony

May 4, 1946

1:Oh! What It Seemed to Be
2:One-zy, Two-zy
3:Shoo Fly Pie
4:All Through the Day
5:Day By Day
6:Personality
7:You Won't Be Satisfied
8:Laughing On the Outside *
9:Sioux City Sue
10:Doctor, Lawyer, Indian Chief

May 11, 1946

1:All Through the Day
2:Laughing On the Outside
3:Oh! What It Seemed to Be
4:Shoo Fly Pie
5:You Won't Be Satisfied
6:Sioux City Sue
7:Prisoner of Love *
8:Seems Like Old Times *
9:The Gypsy *
10:One-zy, Two-zy

May 18, 1946

1:All Through the Day
2:The Gypsy
3:Shoo Fly Pie
4:Laughing On the Outside
5:Oh! What It Seemed to Be
6:Sioux City Sue
7:You Won't Be Satisfied
8:Prisoner of Love
9:Seems Like Old Times
10:One-zy, Two-zy

May 25, 1946

1:Laughing On the Outside
2:All Through the Day
3:The Gypsy
4:Oh! What It Seemed to Be
5:Prisoner of Love
6:Shoo Fly Pie
7:Sioux City Sue
8:Full Moon and Empty Arms *
9:They Say It's Wonderful *
10:You Won't Be Satisfied

June 1, 1946

1:The Gypsy
2:All Through the Day
3:Laughing On the Outside
4:Shoo Fly Pie
5:Prisoner of Love
6:Sioux City Sue
7:They Say It's Wonderful
8:Full Moon and Empty Arms
9:Oh! What It Seemed to Be
10:In Love in Vain *

June 8, 1946

1:The Gypsy
2:Laughing On the Outside
3:They Say It's Wonderful
4:Sioux City Sue
5:Prisoner of Love
6:All Through the Day
7:Oh! What It Seemed to Be
8:Full Moon and Empty Arms
9:Shoo Fly Pie
10:In Love in Vain

June 15, 1946

1:The Gypsy
2:All Through the Day
3:They Say It's Wonderful
4:Laughing On the Outside
5:Sioux City Sue
6:Prisoner of Love
7:In Love in Vain
8:Come Rain or Come Shine *
9:I Don't Know Enough About You *
10:Full Moon and Empty Arms

June 22, 1946

1:The Gypsy
2:They Say It's Wonderful
3:All Through the Day
4:Laughing On the Outside
5:Sioux City Sue
6:Prisoner of Love
7:I Don't Know Enough About You
8:Full Moon and Empty Arms
9:Come Rain or Come Shine
10:In Love in Vain

June 29, 1946

1:The Gypsy
2:They Say It's Wonderful
3:All Through the Day
4:Laughing On the Outside
5:Sioux City Sue
6:Full Moon and Empty Arms
7:In Love in Vain
8:I Don't Know Enough About You
9:Prisoner of Love
10:Come Rain or Come Shine

July 6, 1946

1:They Say It's Wonderful
2:The Gypsy
3:All Through the Day
4:Sioux City Sue
5:Prisoner of Love
6:Laughing On the Outside
7:I Don't Know Enough About You
8:In Love in Vain
9:I Got the Sun in the Morning *
10:Full Moon and Empty Arms

July 13, 1946

1:They Say It's Wonderful
2:The Gypsy
3:Prisoner of Love
4:All Through the Day
5:I Don't Know Enough About You
6:Laughing On the Outside
7:In Love in Vain
8:Sioux City Sue
9:Doin' What Comes Naturally *
10:I Got the Sun in the Morning

July 20, 1946

1:The Gypsy
2:They Say It's Wonderful
3:I Don't Know Enough About You
4:All Through the Day
5:Sioux City Sue
6:Doin' What Comes Naturally
7:In Love in Vain
8:I Got the Sun in the Morning
9:Laughing On the Outside
10:Prisoner of Love

July 27, 1946

1:They Say It's Wonderful
2:The Gypsy
3:Surrender *
4:I Don't Know Enough About You
5:Doin' What Comes Naturally
6:Prisoner of Love
7:All Through the Day
8:In Love in Vain
9:Sioux City Sue
10:I Got the Sun in the Morning

Aug. 3, 1946

1:The Gypsy
2:Doin' What Comes Naturally
3:They Say It's Wonderful
4:Surrender
5:I Don't Know Enough About You
6:All Through the Day
7:To Each His Own *
8:Prisoner of Love
9:I Got the Sun in the Morning
10:In Love in Vain

Aug. 10, 1946

1:They Say It's Wonderful
2:The Gypsy
3:Surrender
4:Doin' What Comes Naturally
5:To Each His Own
6:I Don't Know Enough About You
7:Prisoner of Love
8:I Got the Sun in the Morning
9:In Love in Vain
10:All Through the Day

Aug. 17, 1946

1:The Gypsy
2:They Say It's Wonderful
3:To Each His Own
4:I Don't Know Enough About You
5:Doin' What Comes Naturally
6:Surrender
7:Prisoner of Love
8:I Got the Sun in the Morning
9:In Love in Vain
10:All Through the Day

Aug. 24, 1946

1:To Each His Own
2:Surrender
3:They Say It's Wonderful
4:I Got the Sun in the Morning
5:The Gypsy
6:Doin' What Comes Naturally
7:In Love in Vain
8:Prisoner of Love
9:I Don't Know Enough About You
10:All Through the Day

Aug. 31, 1946

1:To Each His Own
2:Surrender
3:Doin' What Comes Naturally
4:They Say It's Wonderful
5:I Don't Know Enough About You
6:The Gypsy
7:I Got the Sun in the Morning
8:South America, Take It Away *
9:Five Minutes More *
10:Prisoner of Love

Sept. 7, 1946

1:To Each His Own
2:They Say It's Wonderful
3:Surrender
4:South America, Take It Away
5:Five Minutes More
6:I Got the Sun in the Morning
7:The Gypsy
8:Doin' What Comes Naturally
9:I Don't Know Enough About You
10:Prisoner of Love

Sept. 14, 1946

1:To Each His Own
2:Five Minutes More
3:Surrender
4:They Say It's Wonderful
5:South America, Take It Away
6:The Gypsy
7:I Got the Sun in the Morning
8:Doin' What Comes Naturally
9:I Don't Know Enough About You
10:Prisoner of Love

Sept. 21, 1946

1:To Each His Own
2:Five Minutes More
3:Surrender
4:They Say It's Wonderful
5:South America, Take It Away
6:Doin' What Comes Naturally
7:I Got the Sun in the Morning
8:The Gypsy
9:I Don't Know Enough About You
10:Prisoner of Love

Sept. 28, 1946

1:To Each His Own
2:Five Minutes More
3:South America, Take It Away
4:Surrender
5:They Say It's Wonderful
6:I Got the Sun in the Morning
7:Doin' What Comes Naturally
8:I Don't Know Enough About You
9:Linger In My Arms a Little Longer, Baby *
10:The Gypsy

Oct. 5, 1946

1:To Each His Own
2:Five Minutes More
3:South America, Take It Away
4:Surrender
5:They Say It's Wonderful
6:Doin' What Comes Naturally
7:I Got the Sun in the Morning
8:Rumors Are Flying *
9:Linger In My Arms a Little Longer, Baby
10:I Don't Know Enough About You

Oct. 12, 1946

1:To Each His Own
2:Five Minutes More
3:South America, Take It Away
4:Rumors Are Flying
5:Surrender
6:I Got the Sun in the Morning
7:You Keep Coming Back Like a Song *
8:Doin' What Comes Naturally
9:They Say It's Wonderful
10:Linger In My Arms a Little Longer, Baby

Oct. 19, 1946

1:Five Minutes More
2:To Each His Own
3:South America, Take It Away
4:They Say It's Wonderful
5:Doin' What Comes Naturally
6:Ole Buttermilk Sky *
7:Surrender
8:Rumors Are Flying
9:This Is Always *
10:You Keep Coming Back Like a Song

Oct. 26, 1946

1:Five Minutes More
2:South America, Take It Away
3:Rumors Are Flying
4:To Each His Own
5:This Is Always
6:Surrender
7:They Say It's Wonderful
8:Ole Buttermilk Sky
9:You Keep Coming Back Like a Song
10:Doin' What Comes Naturally

Nov. 2, 1946

1:Five Minutes More
2:South America, Take It Away
3:You Keep Coming Back Like a Song
4:Ole Buttermilk Sky
5:Rumors Are Flying
6:To Each His Own
7:This Is Always
8:They Say It's Wonderful
9:Surrender
10:Doin' What Comes Naturally

Nov. 9, 1946

1:Rumors Are Flying
2:Ole Buttermilk Sky
3:South America, Take It Away
4:This Is Always
5:You Keep Coming Back Like a Song
6:To Each His Own
7:Five Minutes More
8:The Whole World Is Singing My Song *
9:They Say It's Wonderful
10:Surrender

Nov. 16, 1946

1:Five Minutes More
2:Rumors Are Flying
3:You Keep Coming Back Like a Song
4:This Is Always
5:South America, Take It Away
6:Ole Buttermilk Sky
7:To Each His Own
8:Somewhere In the Night *
9:The Whole World Is Singing My Song
10:The Coffee Song *

Nov. 23, 1946

1:Rumors Are Flying
2:Ole Buttermilk Sky
3:The Whole World Is Singing My Song
4:Five Minutes More
5:You Keep Coming Back Like a Song
6:To Each His Own
7:South America, Take It Away
8:This Is Always
9:The Things We Did Last Summer *
10:Zip-A-Dee-Doo-Dah *

Nov. 30, 1946

1:Ole Buttermilk Sky
2:The Whole World Is Singing My Song
3:Five Minutes More
4:You Keep Coming Back Like a Song
5:Rumors Are Flying
6:The Old Lamplighter *
7:The Things We Did Last Summer
8:To Each His Own
9:Zip-A-Dee-Doo-Dah
10:This Is Always

Dec. 7, 1946

1:Ole Buttermilk Sky
2:Rumors Are Flying
3:The Old Lamplighter
4:The Whole World Is Singing My Song
5:You Keep Coming Back Like a Song
6:To Each His Own
7:Five Minutes More
8:The Things We Did Last Summer
9:Zip-A-Dee-Doo-Dah
10:This Is Always

Dec. 14, 1946

1:Ole Buttermilk Sky
2:Rumors Are Flying
3:The Things We Did Last Summer
4:The Old Lamplighter
5:The Whole World Is Singing My Song
6:For Sentimental Reasons *
7:Five Minutes More
8:For You, For Me, Forevermore *
9:Zip-A-Dee-Doo-Dah
10:You Keep Coming Back Like a Song

Dec. 21, 1946

1:Ole Buttermilk Sky
2:The Whole World Is Singing My Song
3:The Old Lamplighter
4:For Sentimental Reasons
5:Rumors Are Flying
6:You Keep Coming Back Like a Song
7:Zip-A-Dee-Doo-Dah
8:A Gal in Calico *
9:The Things We Did Last Summer
10:For You, For Me, Forevermore

Dec. 28, 1946

1:Ole Buttermilk Sky
2:The Old Lamplighter
3:For Sentimental Reasons
4:The Christmas Song *
5:The Things We Did Last Summer
6:The Whole World Is Singing My Song
7:A Gal in Calico
8:Rumors Are Flying
9:Zip-A-Dee-Doo-Dah
10:You Keep Coming Back Like a Song

1947

It was the year flying saucers were first spotted, surely an indication that the "future" was here. But conversely, it was also the year that music-dom dipped all the way back to 1913 for the top song of the year, "Peg O' My Heart," ten weeks Number One. Heartened by "Peg," Tin Pan Alley had 1909's "I Wonder Who's Kissing Her Now?" waiting in the wings to go on next. It did, to a lesser success.

Other revivals included 1931's "Guilty" and "Heartaches" (the latter a whistling hit recording by Ted Weems and Elmo Tanner). But there was no shortage of new tunes. Buddy Clark provided "Linda," as Frankie Laine revived "That's My Desire." Broadway's *Finian's Rainbow* and *Brigadoon* gave us "How Are Things in Glocca Morra?" and "Almost Like Being in Love," respectively. Rodgers and Hammerstein, now geared to turning out a Broadway musical every two years, gave us *Allegro* and its hit song, "So Far."

Al Jolson and Francis Craig had new careers in front of them. Everyone was doing Jolson impersonations after the immense popularity of the film *The Jolson Story,* released in late 1946, and the Jolson-sung sound track had delivered "The Anniversary Song" to the 1947 Hit Parade. Francis Craig was an obscure pianist who recorded "Red Rose" on the equally obscure Bullet label. "Red Rose" never made it, but disc jockeys flipped it over and played Craig's "Near You" to stardom. The year's most irritating song had to be "Civilization," a song a lot of people still think was titled "Bongo, Bongo, Bongo."

In April, 461 persons were killed in Texas City, Texas, when a ship blew up in the harbor and touched off a chain reaction of explosions and fires in the city. It was the year of "The New Look," with longer dresses for the fashion-conscious. Mickey Spillane introduced Mike Hammer in *I, the Jury.* And it was the year of the Truman Doctrine, the Taft-Hartley Act, and the Marshall Plan. On the nation's movie screens we had *Gentleman's Agreement, Miracle on 34th Street,* and *A Double Life.* In Congress, for the first time in fourteen years, we had a Republican majority and visions already of a Republican president in 1948. If one thing was certain, it was the conviction that Harry Truman couldn't win against anybody in '48.

Jan. 4, 1947

1:Ole Buttermilk Sky
2:The Old Lamplighter
3:For Sentimental Reasons
4:A Gal in Calico
5:Zip-A-Dee-Doo-Dah
6:The Whole World Is Singing My Song
7:The Things We Did Last Summer
8:You Keep Coming Back Like a Song
9:Rumors Are Flying
10:The Christmas Song

Jan. 11, 1947

1:For Sentimental Reasons
2:Ole Buttermilk Sky
3:The Old Lamplighter
4:Zip-A-Dee-Doo-Dah
5:A Gal in Calico
6:The Things We Did Last Summer
7:The Whole World Is Singing My Song
8:Rumors Are Flying
9:Sooner or Later *
10:You Keep Coming Back Like a Song

Jan. 18, 1947

1:For Sentimental Reasons
2:Ole Buttermilk Sky
3:A Gal in Calico
4:The Whole World Is Singing My Song
5:Zip-A-Dee-Doo-Dah
6:The Old Lamplighter
7:Sooner or Later
8:The Things We Did Last Summer
9:Oh, But I Do! *
10:I'll Close My Eyes *

Jan. 25, 1947

1:For Sentimental Reasons
2:A Gal in Calico
3:Ole Buttermilk Sky
4:Zip-A-Dee-Doo-Dah
5:The Old Lamplighter
6:Oh, But I Do!
7:Sooner or Later
8:The Whole World Is Singing My Song
9:I'll Close My Eyes
10:The Things We Did Last Summer

Feb. 1, 1947

1:For Sentimental Reasons
2:A Gal in Calico
3:Zip-A-Dee-Doo-Dah
4:The Old Lamplighter
5:Oh, But I Do!
6:Ole Buttermilk Sky
7:Sooner or Later
8:I'll Close My Eyes
9:The Whole World Is Singing My Song
10:Life Can Be Beautiful *

Feb. 8, 1947

1:For Sentimental Reasons
2:A Gal in Calico
3:Zip-A-Dee-Doo-Dah
4:Oh, But I Do!
5:The Old Lamplighter
6:Ole Buttermilk Sky
7:Sooner or Later
8:The Whole World Is Singing My Song
9:Guilty *
10:I'll Close My Eyes

Feb. 15, 1947

1:For Sentimental Reasons
2:A Gal in Calico
3:Oh, But I Do!
4:Zip-A-Dee-Doo-Dah
5:The Anniversary Song *
6:I'll Close My Eyes
7:The Old Lamplighter
8:Ole Buttermilk Sky
9:Managua, Nicaragua *
10:Guilty

Feb. 22, 1947

1:A Gal in Calico
2:The Anniversary Song
3:Oh, But I Do!
4:For Sentimental Reasons
5:I'll Close My Eyes
6:The Old Lamplighter
7:Zip-A-Dee-Doo-Dah
8:Ole Buttermilk Sky
9:Guilty
10:Managua, Nicaragua

* Newcomer

Mar. 1, 1947

1:For Sentimental Reasons
2:The Anniversary Song
3:Oh, But I Do!
4:Guilty
5:A Gal in Calico
6:Zip-A-Dee-Doo-Dah
7:Open the Door, Richard *
8:Managua, Nicaragua
9:I'll Close My Eyes
10:The Old Lamplighter

Mar. 8, 1947

1:The Anniversary Song
2:Managua, Nicaragua
3:Oh, But I Do!
4:A Gal in Calico
5:For Sentimental Reasons
6:I'll Close My Eyes
7:Guilty
8:Zip-A-Dee-Doo-Dah
9:How Are Things in Glocca Morra? *
10:You'll Always Be the One I Love *

Mar. 15, 1947

1:The Anniversary Song
2:Managua, Nicaragua
3:For Sentimental Reasons
4:Guilty
5:How Are Things in Glocca Morra?
6:I'll Close My Eyes
7:A Gal in Calico
8:Oh, But I Do!
9:It's a Good Day *
10:Zip-A-Dee-Doo-Dah

Mar. 22, 1947

1:The Anniversary Song
2:Managua, Nicaragua
3:How Are Things in Glocca Morra?
4:I'll Close My Eyes
5:Guilty
6:For Sentimental Reasons
7:A Gal in Calico
8:It's a Good Day
9:Zip-A-Dee-Doo-Dah
10:Oh, But I Do!

Mar. 29, 1947

1:The Anniversary Song
2:How Are Things in Glocca Morra?
3:Managua, Nicaragua
4:Heartaches *
5:For Sentimental Reasons
6:I'll Close My Eyes
7:Guilty
8:Linda *
9:It's a Good Day
10:Oh, But I Do!

Apr. 5, 1947

1:The Anniversary Song
2:How Are Things in Glocca Morra?
3:Managua, Nicaragua
4:Heartaches
5:I'll Close My Eyes
6:Linda
7:Guilty
8:For Sentimental Reasons
9:You Can't See the Sun When You're Crying *
10:It's a Good Day

Apr. 12, 1947

1:The Anniversary Song
2:Heartaches
3:How Are Things in Glocca Morra?
4:Linda
5:Managua, Nicaragua
6:I'll Close My Eyes
7:Guilty
8:You Can't See the Sun When You're Crying
9:For Sentimental Reasons
10:It's a Good Day

Apr. 19, 1947

1:Heartaches
2:Linda
3:The Anniversary Song
4:How Are Things in Glocca Morra?
5:Managua, Nicaragua
6:It's a Good Day
7:I'll Close My Eyes
8:Guilty
9:You Can't See the Sun When You're Crying
10:For Sentimental Reasons

Apr. 26, 1947

1:Heartaches
2:The Anniversary Song
3:Linda
4:Mam'selle *
5:How Are Things in Glocca Morra?
6:Managua, Nicaragua
7:It's a Good Day
8:I'll Close My Eyes
9:Guilty
10:For Sentimental Reasons

May 3, 1947

1:Linda
2:The Anniversary Song
3:Mam'selle
4:Managua, Nicaragua
5:Heartaches
6:How Are Things in Glocca Morra?
7:My Adobe Hacienda *
8:It's a Good Day
9:I'll Close My Eyes
10:Guilty

May 10, 1947

1:Linda
2:Heartaches
3:The Anniversary Song
4:Mam'selle
5:My Adobe Hacienda
6:Time After Time *
7:How Are Things in Glocca Morra?
8:Managua, Nicaragua
9:It's a Good Day
10:I'll Close My Eyes

May 17, 1947

1:Mam'selle
2:Linda
3:Heartaches
4:The Anniversary Song
5:My Adobe Hacienda
6:How Are Things in Glocca Morra?
7:Time After Time
8:Managua, Nicaragua
9:It's a Good Day
10:I'll Close My Eyes

May 24, 1947

1:Linda
2:My Adobe Hacienda
3:Heartaches
4:Mam'selle
5:How Are Things in Glocca Morra?
6:The Anniversary Song
7:Time After Time
8:Roses in the Rain *
9:It's the Same Old Dream *
10:It's a Good Day

May 31, 1947

1:Mam'selle
2:My Adobe Hacienda
3:Linda
4:Heartaches
5:The Anniversary Song
6:Time After Time
7:Peg O' My Heart *
8:How Are Things in Glocca Morra?
9:Roses in the Rain
10:It's the Same Old Dream

June 7, 1947

1:Mam'selle
2:Linda
3:My Adobe Hacienda
4:I Wonder, I Wonder, I Wonder *
5:Heartaches
6:The Anniversary Song
7:Time After Time
8:Peg O' My Heart
9:How Are Things in Glocca Morra?
10:It's the Same Old Dream

June 14, 1947

1:Linda
2:My Adobe Hacienda
3:Mam'selle
4:I Wonder, I Wonder, I Wonder
5:Heartaches
6:Midnight Masquerade *
7:Chi-Baba, Chi-Baba *
8:Peg O' My Heart
9:The Anniversary Song
10:Time After Time

June 21, 1947

1:Peg O' My Heart
2:Mam'selle
3:Linda
4:I Wonder, I Wonder, I Wonder
5:Chi-Baba, Chi-Baba
6:My Adobe Hacienda
7:Heartaches
8:Midnight Masquerade
9:The Anniversary Song
10:Time After Time

June 28, 1947

1:I Wonder, I Wonder, I Wonder
2:Peg O' My Heart
3:Mam'selle
4:My Adobe Hacienda
5:Chi-Baba, Chi-Baba
6:Linda
7:That's My Desire *
8:Heartaches
9:Midnight Masquerade
10:Time After Time

July 5, 1947

1:Peg O' My Heart
2:I Wonder, I Wonder, I Wonder
3:Mam'selle
4:Chi-Baba, Chi-Baba
5:My Adobe Hacienda
6:Linda
7:That's My Desire
8:Heartaches
9:Time After Time
10:Across the Alley From the Alamo *

July 12, 1947

1:Peg O' My Heart
2:I Wonder, I Wonder, I Wonder
3:Chi-Baba, Chi-Baba
4:That's My Desire
5:Mam'selle
6:Across the Alley From the Alamo
7:Linda
8:My Adobe Hacienda
9:Heartaches
10:Almost Like Being in Love *

July 19, 1947

1:Peg O' My Heart
2:I Wonder, I Wonder, I Wonder
3:Chi-Baba, Chi-Baba
4:Across the Alley From the Alamo
5:That's My Desire
6:Mam'selle
7:Linda
8:Almost Like Being in Love
9:My Adobe Hacienda
10:Heartaches

July 26, 1947

1:Peg O' My Heart
2:I Wonder, I Wonder, I Wonder
3:Chi-Baba, Chi-Baba
4:Across the Alley From the Alamo
5:Mam'selle
6:That's My Desire
7:Almost Like Being in Love
8:Linda
9:My Adobe Hacienda
10:Ivy *

Aug. 2, 1947

1:Peg O' My Heart
2:That's My Desire
3:I Wonder, I Wonder, I Wonder
4:Across the Alley From the Alamo
5:Chi-Baba, Chi-Baba
6:Ivy
7:Ask Anyone Who Knows *
8:Mam'selle
9:Almost Like Being in Love
10:Linda

Aug. 9, 1947

1:Peg O' My Heart
2:I Wonder, I Wonder, I Wonder
3:Chi-Baba, Chi-Baba
4:That's My Desire
5:Ask Anyone Who Knows
6:Across the Alley From the Alamo
7:I Wonder Who's Kissing Her Now? *
8:Ivy
9:Mam'selle
10:Almost Like Being in Love

Aug. 16, 1947

1:Peg O' My Heart
2:I Wonder, I Wonder, I Wonder
3:That's My Desire
4:Ask Anyone Who Knows
5:Chi-Baba, Chi-Baba
6:Across the Alley From the Alamo
7:I Wonder Who's Kissing Her Now?
8:Almost Like Being in Love
9:Mam'selle
10:Tallahassee *

Aug. 23, 1947

1:That's My Desire
2:Peg O' My Heart
3:I Wonder, I Wonder, I Wonder
4:Chi-Baba, Chi-Baba
5:Ask Anyone Who Knows
6:Tallahassee
7:I Wonder Who's Kissing Her Now?
8:Across the Alley From the Alamo
9:Almost Like Being in Love
10:Mam'selle

Aug. 30, 1947

1:Peg O' My Heart
2:That's My Desire
3:I Wonder Who's Kissing Her Now?
4:Ask Anyone Who Knows
5:Tallahassee
6:I Wonder, I Wonder, I Wonder
7:Almost Like Being in Love
8:Chi-Baba, Chi-Baba
9:Across the Alley From the Alamo
10:Mam'selle

Sept. 6, 1947

1:I Wonder Who's Kissing Her Now?
2:Peg O' My Heart
3:Ask Anyone Who Knows
4:Feudin' and Fightin' *
5:That's My Desire
6:I Wonder, I Wonder, I Wonder
7:An Apple Blossom Wedding *
8:Tallahassee
9:Almost Like Being in Love
10:Chi-Baba, Chi-Baba

Sept. 13, 1947

1:That's My Desire
2:Peg O' My Heart
3:I Wonder Who's Kissing Her Now?
4:I Wish I Didn't Love You So *
5:Feudin' and Fightin'
6:An Apple Blossom Wedding
7:Ask Anyone Who Knows
8:I Wonder, I Wonder, I Wonder
9:Tallahassee
10:Almost Like Being in Love

Sept. 20, 1947

1:Peg O' My Heart
2:That's My Desire
3:I Wonder Who's Kissing Her Now?
4:Feudin' and Fightin'
5:Ask Anyone Who Knows
6:I Wish I Didn't Love You So
7:Almost Like Being in Love
8:An Apple Blossom Wedding
9:I Wonder, I Wonder, I Wonder
10:Tallahassee

Sept. 27, 1947

1:Feudin' and Fightin'
2:I Wish I Didn't Love You So
3:I Wonder Who's Kissing Her Now?
4:Peg O' My Heart
5:That's My Desire
6:Ask Anyone Who Knows
7:An Apple Blossom Wedding
8:Almost Like Being in Love
9:Near You *
10:The Lady From 29 Palms *

Oct. 4, 1947

1:I Wish I Didn't Love You So
2:Near You
3:Feudin' and Fightin'
4:I Wonder Who's Kissing Her Now?
5:That's My Desire
6:The Lady From 29 Palms
7:Peg O' My Heart
8:Ask Anyone Who Knows
9:An Apple Blossom Wedding
10:Almost Like Being in Love

Oct. 11, 1947

1:I Wish I Didn't Love You So
2:Feudin' and Fightin'
3:Near You
4:Peg O' My Heart
5:You Do *
6:Almost Like Being in Love
7:I Wonder Who's Kissing Her Now?
8:The Lady From 29 Palms
9:An Apple Blossom Wedding
10:That's My Desire

Oct. 18, 1947

1:Near You
2:I Wish I Didn't Love You So
3:Feudin' and Fightin'
4:You Do
5:I Wonder Who's Kissing Her Now?
6:The Lady From 29 Palms
7:Peg O' My Heart
8:As Long As I'm Dreaming *
9:The Stars Will Remember *
10:An Apple Blossom Wedding

Oct. 25, 1947

1:Near You
2:I Wish I Didn't Love You So
3:I Wonder Who's Kissing Her Now?
4:You Do
5:Feudin' and Fightin'
6:The Lady From 29 Palms
7:Peg O' My Heart
8:The Stars Will Remember
9:An Apple Blossom Wedding
10:As Long As I'm Dreaming

Nov. 1, 1947

1:Near You
2:Feudin' and Fightin'
3:I Wish I Didn't Love You So
4:You Do
5:I Wonder Who's Kissing Her Now?
6:The Lady From 29 Palms
7:As Long As I'm Dreaming
8:An Apple Blossom Wedding
9:Peg O' My Heart
10:The Stars Will Remember

Nov. 8, 1947

1:Near You
2:You Do
3:Feudin' and Fightin'
4:I Wish I Didn't Love You So
5:The Lady From 29 Palms
6:And Mimi *
7:An Apple Blossom Wedding
8:I Wonder Who's Kissing Her Now?
9:The Stars Will Remember
10:As Long As I'm Dreaming

Nov. 15, 1947

1:I Wish I Didn't Love You So
2:Near You
3:You Do
4:Feudin' and Fightin'
5:And Mimi
6:An Apple Blossom Wedding
7:Civilization *
8:The Lady From 29 Palms
9:I Wonder Who's Kissing Her Now?
10:As Long As I'm Dreaming

Nov. 22, 1947

1:You Do
2:I Wish I Didn't Love You So
3:Near You
4:Feudin' and Fightin'
5:And Mimi
6:So Far *
7:Civilization
8:An Apple Blossom Wedding
9:As Long As I'm Dreaming
10:The Lady From 29 Palms

Nov. 29, 1947

1:Near You
2:You Do
3:I Wish I Didn't Love You So
4:And Mimi
5:How Soon? *
6:Civilization
7:So Far
8:Feudin' and Fightin'
9:The Lady From 29 Palms
10:Christmas Dreaming *

Dec. 6, 1947

1:Near You
2:You Do
3:And Mimi
4:Civilization
5:I Wish I Didn't Love You So
6:How Soon?
7:Ballerina *
8:So Far
9:Christmas Dreaming
10:Feudin' and Fightin'

Dec. 13, 1947

1:Civilization
2:How Soon?
3:You Do
4:And Mimi
5:Near You
6:Ballerina
7:I Wish I Didn't Love You So
8:Serenade of the Bells *
9:Christmas Dreaming
10:So Far

Dec. 20, 1947

1:How Soon?
2:Civilization
3:And Mimi
4:Ballerina
5:You Do
6:Serenade of the Bells
7:Near You
8:Christmas Dreaming
9:So Far
10:I Wish I Didn't Love You So

Dec. 27, 1947

1:Ballerina
2:How Soon?
3:Near You
4:You Do
5:And Mimi
6:Serenade of the Bells
7:Christmas Dreaming
8:Civilization
9:I Wish I Didn't Love You So
10:So Far

1948

Australia gave us "Now Is the Hour," England, "A Tree in the Meadow," and Hollywood, "Buttons and Bows." Between them they monopolized thirty weeks as the Number One song, because for the first time in the history of "Your Hit Parade," three songs were Number One ten weeks apiece in the same year and, of course, the top songs of 1948.

It was rough going for the rest down in the ranks, but Doris Day, a longtime band singer, discovered she was a movie star that year in her first film, *Romance on the High Seas,* and sang "It's Magic" onto the Top Ten. Nat "King" Cole sang about that hippie-before-his-time, "Nature Boy." Francis Craig followed up his "Near You" with "Beg Your Pardon." And the revival mill supplied "Baby Face," "I'm Looking Over a Four Leaf Clover," "The Best Things in Life Are Free," and "Little White Lies."

It was a banner year at the movies with Laurence Olivier's *Hamlet,* Jane Wyman's *Johnny Belinda,* and Humphrey Bogart's *The Treasure of the Sierra Madre.*

Mohandas K. Gandhi, Hindu spiritual leader of India, was assassinated by a fanatic in New Delhi.

Czechoslovakia joined the Communist bloc party, and the amazing Berlin Air Lift was begun by U. S. and British forces to get food and fuel to West Berlin past the Soviet land blockade. The Cold War was here.

It was the year the Jewish state of Israel was born as the British evacuated Palestine. Former Premier Tojo and six other Japanese war leaders were hanged in Tokyo as war criminals. Back in this country there was the drama of the showdown at the House Un-American Activities Committee between Whittaker Chambers, former *Time* magazine editor and admitted Communist, and the man Chambers testified he received secret documents from, Alger Hiss, former State Department official. Television was here now, and the face of America was being changed by sprouting rooftop antennas and darkened living rooms illuminated only by the glow from a seven-inch screen.

Oh, yes. Despite the odds, the pollsters, the Dixiecrats, the Henry Wallace third party, and the *Chicago Tribune,* which prematurely headlined that Thomas Dewey had won, Harry Truman was elected President of the United States.

Jan. 3, 1948

1:Ballerina
2:How Soon?
3:Near You
4:Serenade of the Bells
5:Civilization
6:Christmas Dreaming
7:And Mimi
8:You Do
9:So Far
10:Golden Earrings *

Jan. 10, 1948

1:Ballerina
2:How Soon?
3:Serenade of the Bells
4:Civilization
5:Near You
6:Golden Earrings
7:I'll Dance At Your Wedding *
8:And Mimi
9:You Do
10:So Far

Jan. 17, 1948

1:How Soon?
2:Ballerina
3:Serenade of the Bells
4:I'll Dance At Your Wedding
5:Golden Earrings
6:Civilization
7:So Far
8:Near You
9:Too Fat Polka *
10:And Mimi

Jan. 24, 1948

1:How Soon?
2:Ballerina
3:Serenade of the Bells
4:I'll Dance At Your Wedding
5:Golden Earrings
6:Civilization
7:Too Fat Polka
8:So Far
9:Near You
10:And Mimi

Jan. 31, 1948

1:Golden Earrings
2:Serenade of the Bells
3:Ballerina
4:How Soon?
5:I'll Dance At Your Wedding
6:Civilization
7:I'm Looking Over a Four Leaf Clover *
8:Too Fat Polka
9:So Far
10:Near You

Feb. 7, 1948

1:Ballerina
2:How Soon?
3:Golden Earrings
4:I'll Dance At Your Wedding
5:Now Is the Hour *
6:I'm Looking Over a Four Leaf Clover
7:Serenade of the Bells
8:Civilization
9:But Beautiful *
10:So Far

Feb. 14, 1948

1:Ballerina
2:I'll Dance At Your Wedding
3:Serenade of the Bells
4:Now Is the Hour
5:I'm Looking Over a Four Leaf Clover
6:But Beautiful
7:How Soon?
8:Golden Earrings
9:Civilization
10:The Best Things in Life Are Free *

Feb. 21, 1948

1:I'm Looking Over a Four Leaf Clover
2:Ballerina
3:Now Is the Hour
4:Golden Earrings
5:Serenade of the Bells
6:I'll Dance At Your Wedding
7:The Best Things in Life Are Free
8:But Beautiful
9:How Soon?
10:Civilization

* Newcomer

Feb. 28, 1948

1:Now Is the Hour
2:I'm Looking Over a Four Leaf Clover
3:Ballerina
4:Serenade of the Bells
5:Golden Earrings
6:Beg Your Pardon *
7:I'll Dance At Your Wedding
8:The Best Things in Life Are Free
9:But Beautiful
10:How Soon?

Mar. 6, 1948

1:Now Is the Hour
2:I'm Looking Over a Four Leaf Clover
3:Beg Your Pardon
4:Ballerina
5:Golden Earrings
6:Serenade of the Bells
7:Manana *
8:I'll Dance At Your Wedding
9:The Best Things in Life Are Free
10:But Beautiful

Mar. 13, 1948

1:Now Is the Hour
2:I'm Looking Over a Four Leaf Clover
3:Beg Your Pardon
4:Manana
5:Serenade of the Bells
6:Golden Earrings
7:Ballerina
8:But Beautiful
9:The Best Things in Life Are Free
10:I'll Dance At Your Wedding

Mar. 20, 1948

1:I'm Looking Over a Four Leaf Clover
2:Now Is the Hour
3:Manana
4:Serenade of the Bells
5:But Beautiful
6:Ballerina
7:Beg Your Pardon
8:Golden Earrings
9:The Best Things in Life Are Free
10:I'll Dance At Your Wedding

Mar. 27, 1948

1:Now Is the Hour
2:I'm Looking Over a Four Leaf Clover
3:Beg Your Pardon
4:Manana
5:But Beautiful
6:Serenade of the Bells
7:Ballerina
8:Fool That I Am *
9:Golden Earrings
10:The Best Things in Life Are Free

Apr. 3, 1948

1:Now Is the Hour
2:Manana
3:I'm Looking Over a Four Leaf Clover
4:Beg Your Pardon
5:But Beautiful
6:Serenade of the Bells
7:Fool That I Am
8:Ballerina
9:Golden Earrings
10:Sabre Dance *

Apr. 10, 1948

1:Manana
2:Now Is the Hour
3:I'm Looking Over a Four Leaf Clover
4:But Beautiful
5:Beg Your Pardon
6:Sabre Dance
7:Haunted Heart *
8:Fool That I Am
9:Serenade of the Bells
10:Ballerina

Apr. 17, 1948

1:Now Is the Hour
2:I'm Looking Over a Four Leaf Clover
3:Beg Your Pardon
4:But Beautiful
5:Manana
6:Baby Face *
7:The Dickey-Bird Song *
8:Sabre Dance
9:Haunted Heart
10:Fool That I Am

Apr. 24, 1948

1:Now Is the Hour
2:Manana
3:But Beautiful
4:Baby Face
5:I'm Looking Over a Four Leaf Clover
6:Beg Your Pardon
7:The Dickey-Bird Song
8:Sabre Dance
9:Haunted Heart
10:Laroo, Laroo, Lilli Bolero *

May 1, 1948

1:Now Is the Hour
2:The Dickey-Bird Song
3:Beg Your Pardon
4:I'm Looking Over a Four Leaf Clover
5:Manana
6:But Beautiful
7:Laroo, Laroo, Lilli Bolero
8:Baby Face
9:Haunted Heart
10:Sabre Dance

May 8, 1948

1:Now Is the Hour
2:Manana
3:The Dickey-Bird Song
4:Baby Face
5:But Beautiful
6:Laroo, Laroo, Lilli Bolero
7:Beg Your Pardon
8:Haunted Heart
9:Sabre Dance
10:I'm Looking Over a Four Leaf Clover

May 15, 1948

1:Now Is the Hour
2:Baby Face
3:The Dickey-Bird Song
4:Toolie, Oolie, Doolie *
5:Laroo, Laroo, Lilli Bolero
6:Sabre Dance
7:Haunted Heart
8:Manana
9:But Beautiful
10:Nature Boy *

May 22, 1948

1:Nature Boy
2:Now Is the Hour
3:The Dickey-Bird Song
4:Baby Face
5:Toolie, Oolie, Doolie
6:Laroo, Laroo, Lilli Bolero
7:Haunted Heart
8:Sabre Dance
9:Manana
10:But Beautiful

May 29, 1948

1:Nature Boy
2:Now Is the Hour
3:Baby Face
4:Toolie, Oolie, Doolie
5:You Can't Be True, Dear *
6:Haunted Heart
7:Laroo, Laroo, Lilli Bolero
8:The Dickie-Bird Song
9:Sabre Dance
10:Manana

June 5, 1948

1:Nature Boy
2:You Can't Be True, Dear
3:Now Is the Hour
4:Baby Face
5:Haunted Heart
6:Sabre Dance
7:Laroo, Laroo, Lilli Bolero
8:Toolie, Oolie, Doolie
9:The Dickie-Bird Song
10:Manana

June 12, 1948

1:Nature Boy
2:Toolie, Oolie, Doolie
3:Baby Face
4:You Can't Be True, Dear
5:Haunted Heart
6:Sabre Dance
7:Laroo, Laroo, Lilli Bolero
8:Now Is the Hour
9:The Dickie-Bird Song
10:Little White Lies *

June 19, 1948

1:Nature Boy
2:You Can't Be True, Dear
3:Baby Face
4:Toolie, Oolie, Doolie
5:The Dickie-Bird Song
6:Little White Lies
7:Haunted Heart
8:Laroo, Laroo, Lilli Bolero
9:Sabre Dance
10:Now Is the Hour

June 26, 1948

1:Nature Boy
2:Toolie, Oolie, Doolie
3:Woody Woodpecker *
4:You Can't Be True, Dear
5:My Happiness *
6:Little White Lies
7:Haunted Heart
8:Baby Face
9:Now Is the Hour
10:The Dickie-Bird Song

July 3, 1948

1:You Can't Be True, Dear
2:Nature Boy
3:Woody Woodpecker
4:Haunted Heart
5:Little White Lies
6:My Happiness
7:Now Is the Hour
8:Toolie, Oolie, Doolie
9:The Dickie-Bird Song
10:Baby Face

July 10, 1948

1:Woody Woodpecker
2:You Can't Be True, Dear
3:My Happiness
4:Little White Lies
5:Haunted Heart
6:Nature Boy
7:Toolie, Oolie, Doolie
8:Love of My Life *
9:Baby Face
10:The Dickey-Bird Song

July 17, 1948

1:You Can't Be True, Dear
2:Woody Woodpecker
3:Nature Boy
4:Little White Lies
5:Toolie, Oolie, Doolie
6:My Happiness
7:Haunted Heart
8:Love of My Life
9:The Dickey-Bird Song
10:Baby Face

July 24, 1948

1:Woody Woodpecker
2:You Can't Be True, Dear
3:My Happiness
4:It's Magic *
5:Toolie, Oolie, Doolie
6:A Tree in the Meadow *
7:Nature Boy
8:Little White Lies
9:Haunted Heart
10:Love of My Life

July 31, 1948

1:You Can't Be True, Dear
2:Woody Woodpecker
3:It's Magic
4:A Tree in the Meadow
5:My Happiness
6:Little White Lies
7:Love Somebody *
8:Toolie, Oolie, Doolie
9:Nature Boy
10:Love of My Life

Aug. 7, 1948

1:It's Magic
2:Woody Woodpecker
3:A Tree in the Meadow
4:My Happiness
5:Little White Lies
6:You Call Everybody Darling *
7:You Can't Be True, Dear
8:Love Somebody
9:Love of My Life
10:Nature Boy

Aug. 14, 1948

1:It's Magic
2:A Tree in the Meadow
3:You Can't Be True, Dear
4:My Happiness
5:Love Somebody
6:You Call Everybody Darling
7:Woody Woodpecker
8:Love of My Life
9:Little White Lies
10:Nature Boy

Aug. 21, 1948

1:A Tree in the Meadow
2:My Happiness
3:It's Magic
4:You Call Everybody Darling
5:Love Somebody
6:You Can't Be True, Dear
7:Woody Woodpecker
8:Maybe You'll Be There *
9:Love of My Life
10:Little White Lies

Aug. 28, 1948

1:A Tree in the Meadow
2:You Call Everybody Darling
3:It's Magic
4:My Happiness
5:Love Somebody
6:Maybe You'll Be There
7:You Can't Be True, Dear
8:Woody Woodpecker
9:Little White Lies
10:Love of My Life

Sept. 4, 1948

1:A Tree in the Meadow
2:It's Magic
3:You Call Everybody Darling
4:My Happiness
5:Love Somebody
6:Maybe You'll Be There
7:You Can't Be True, Dear
8:It Only Happens When I Dance With You *
9:Woody Woodpecker
10:Little White Lies

Sept. 11, 1948

1:A Tree in the Meadow
2:It's Magic
3:You Call Everybody Darling
4:My Happiness
5:Love Somebody
6:It Only Happens When I Dance With You
7:Hair of Gold, Eyes of Blue *
8:Maybe You'll Be There
9:You Can't Be True, Dear
10:Woody Woodpecker

Sept. 18, 1948

1:A Tree in the Meadow
2:It's Magic
3:You Call Everybody Darling
4:Bluebird of Happiness *
5:Hair of Gold, Eyes of Blue
6:Love Somebody
7:My Happiness
8:It Only Happens When I Dance With You
9:Maybe You'll Be There
10:You Can't Be True, Dear

Sept. 25, 1948

1:A Tree in the Meadow
2:It's Magic
3:You Call Everybody Darling
4:Maybe You'll Be There
5:Hair of Gold, Eyes of Blue
6:Love Somebody
7:My Happiness
8:Bluebird of Happiness
9:It Only Happens When I Dance With You
10:You Can't Be True, Dear

Oct. 2, 1948

1:A Tree in the Meadow
2:You Call Everybody Darling
3:It's Magic
4:Hair of Gold, Eyes of Blue
5:Maybe You'll Be There
6:Love Somebody
7:My Happiness
8:Every Day I Love You *
9:Underneath the Arches *
10:Bluebird of Happiness

Oct. 9, 1948

1:A Tree in the Meadow
2:You Call Everybody Darling
3:It's Magic
4:My Happiness
5:Maybe You'll Be There
6:Underneath the Arches
7:Hair of Gold, Eyes of Blue
8:Love Somebody
9:Every Day I Love You
10:Bluebird of Happiness

Oct. 16, 1948

1:A Tree in the Meadow
2:You Call Everybody Darling
3:Hair of Gold, Eyes of Blue
4:It's Magic
5:Bluebird of Happiness
6:My Happiness
7:Love Somebody
8:Underneath the Arches
9:Every Day I Love You
10:Maybe You'll Be There

Oct. 23, 1948

1:You Call Everybody Darling
2:A Tree in the Meadow
3:It's Magic
4:Hair of Gold, Eyes of Blue
5:Maybe You'll Be There
6:Buttons and Bows *
7:Every Day I Love You
8:My Happiness
9:Love Somebody
10:Underneath the Arches

Oct. 30, 1948

1:A Tree in the Meadow
2:Buttons and Bows
3:Hair of Gold, Eyes of Blue
4:Maybe You'll Be There
5:You Call Everybody Darling
6:Underneath the Arches
7:It's Magic
8:Every Day I Love You
9:My Happiness
10:Love Somebody

Nov. 6, 1948

1:Buttons and Bows
2:Hair of Gold, Eyes of Blue
3:A Tree in the Meadow
4:It's Magic
5:Maybe You'll Be There
6:You Were Only Fooling *
7:Every Day I Love You
8:You Call Everybody Darling
9:Underneath the Arches
10:My Happiness

Nov. 13, 1948

1:Buttons and Bows
2:On a Slow Boat to China *
3:You Call Everybody Darling
4:A Tree in the Meadow
5:You Were Only Fooling
6:Maybe You'll Be There
7:Hair of Gold, Eyes of Blue
8:Underneath the Arches
9:Every Day I Love You
10:It's Magic

Nov. 20, 1948

1:Buttons and Bows
2:On a Slow Boat to China
3:A Tree in the Meadow
4:You Were Only Fooling
5:Maybe You'll Be There
6:You Call Everybody Darling
7:Hair of Gold, Eyes of Blue
8:Underneath the Arches
9:Until *
10:Every Day I Love You

Nov. 27, 1948

1:Buttons and Bows
2:On a Slow Boat to China
3:You Were Only Fooling
4:Until
5:A Tree in the Meadow
6:Hair of Gold, Eyes of Blue
7:My Darling, My Darling *
8:Maybe You'll Be There
9:You Call Everybody Darling
10:Cuanto Le Gusta *

Dec. 4, 1948

1:Buttons and Bows
2:On a Slow Boat to China
3:My Darling, My Darling
4:You Were Only Fooling
5:Until
6:A Tree in the Meadow
7:Maybe You'll Be There
8:Cuanto Le Gusta
9:Hair of Gold, Eyes of Blue
10:You Call Everybody Darling

Dec. 11, 1948

1:Buttons and Bows
2:On a Slow Boat to China
3:My Darling, My Darling
4:You Were Only Fooling
5:Until
6:Hair of Gold, Eyes of Blue
7:Cuanto Le Gusta
8:A Little Bird Told Me *
9:A Tree in the Meadow
10:Maybe You'll Be There

Dec. 18, 1948

1:Buttons and Bows
2:My Darling, My Darling
3:On a Slow Boat to China
4:A Little Bird Told Me
5:You Were Only Fooling
6:Until
7:Cuanto Le Gusta
8:Maybe You'll Be There
9:Say Something Sweet to Your Sweetheart *
10:Hair of Gold, Eyes of Blue

Dec. 25, 1948

1:Buttons and Bows
2:On a Slow Boat to China
3:My Darling, My Darling
4:A Little Bird Told Me
5:Until
6:Lavender Blue *
7:You Were Only Fooling
8:All I Want For Christmas Is My Two Front
9:Cuanto Le Gusta   Teeth *
10:Maybe You'll Be There

1949

Rodgers and Hammerstein, following their every-two-years pattern of Broadway musicals, came back in stunning fashion in 1949, making Ezio Pinza and Mary Martin king and queen of Broadway in *South Pacific*. The R & H factor put four hits from the score on the Hit Parade—"Bali Hai," "A Wonderful Guy," "Younger Than Springtime," and the song that became the top tune of 1949 with ten weeks as Number One, "Some Enchanted Evening." The biggest legit hit on Broadway that year was Arthur Miller's *Death of a Salesman,* starring Lee J. Cobb.

The Hit Parade saw revivals of "I've Got My Love to Keep Me Warm" and "I Can Dream, Can't I?" The year's rouser was "Cruising Down the River." Top movie of the year was *All the King's Men*. Those who had television sets were mesmerized by Milton Berle, known alternately as "Uncle Miltie" and "Mr. Television."

In Camden, New Jersey, Howard Unruh, a twenty-eight-year-old World War II combat veteran, suddenly went berserk and started on a door-to-door killing spree that left twelve dead and four wounded. In San Marino, California, as the nation watched and waited, three-and-a-half-year-old Kathy Fiscus was removed dead from the abandoned well she had tumbled into fifty-two hours earlier. Singer Buddy Clark was killed in a plane crash, and Margaret Mitchell, author of *Gone With the Wind,* was killed when struck by a car in Atlanta. An era ended in this country when Joe Louis, heavyweight boxing champ since 1937, resigned the title.

Joseph Cardinal Mindszenty, Roman Catholic primate of Hungary, was given life imprisonment by the Communist government in Budapest on charges of treason. (He was freed in 1956.) After 328 days 2,343,315 tons of food and coal had been delivered, the Soviet blockade was lifted, and the Berlin Air Lift ended. Nationalist China's government fled to Formosa, giving the world two Chinese governments.

Memories of World War II were stirred as broadcasters Axis Sally and Tokyo Rose received prison sentences for treason. And shudders of possible wars to come were realized when Russia ended the U.S. monopoly on A-bombs by exploding their own in a first test.

Jan. 1, 1949

1:Buttons and Bows
2:My Darling, My Darling
3:On a Slow Boat to China
4:A Little Bird Told Me
5:Far Away Places *
6:You Were Only Fooling
7:Lavender Blue
8:Until
9:Cuanto Le Gusta
10:Maybe You'll Be There

Jan. 8, 1949

1:On a Slow Boat to China
2:Buttons and Bows
3:My Darling, My Darling
4:A Little Bird Told Me
5:You Were Only Fooling
6:Lavender Blue
7:Far Away Places
8:Cuanto Le Gusta
9:Until
10:Maybe You'll Be There

Jan. 15, 1949

1:On a Slow Boat to China
2:Buttons and Bows
3:My Darling, My Darling
4:A Little Bird Told Me
5:Far Away Places
6:Lavender Blue
7:Cuanto Le Gusta
8:You Were Only Fooling
9:Until
10:Here I'll Stay *

Jan. 22, 1949

1:Buttons and Bows
2:A Little Bird Told Me
3:On a Slow Boat to China
4:My Darling, My Darling
5:Lavender Blue
6:You Were Only Fooling
7:Far Away Places
8:Until
9:Cuanto Le Gusta
10:Here I'll Stay

Jan. 29, 1949

1:A Little Bird Told Me
2:My Darling, My Darling
3:Buttons and Bows
4:Far Away Places
5:On a Slow Boat to China
6:Galway Bay *
7:You Were Only Fooling
8:Lavender Blue
9:Powder Your Face With Sunshine *
10:Here I'll Stay

Feb. 5, 1949

1:A Little Bird Told Me
2:Far Away Places
3:Powder Your Face With Sunshine
4:On a Slow Boat to China
5:Buttons and Bows
6:My Darling, My Darling
7:Lavender Blue
8:Galway Bay
9:I've Got My Love to Keep Me Warm *
10:So In Love *

Feb. 12, 1949

1:A Little Bird Told Me
2:Powder Your Face With Sunshine
3:Far Away Places
4:Lavender Blue
5:My Darling, My Darling
6:Galway Bay
7:Buttons and Bows
8:I've Got My Love to Keep Me Warm
9:So In Love
10:On a Slow Boat to China

Feb. 19, 1949

1:Powder Your Face With Sunshine
2:Far Away Places
3:A Little Bird Told Me
4:Lavender Blue
5:My Darling, My Darling
6:I've Got My Love to Keep Me Warm
7:On a Slow Boat to China
8:Buttons and Bows
9:Galway Bay
10:So In Love

* Newcomer

Feb. 26, 1949

1:Far Away Places
2:Powder Your Face With Sunshine
3:A Little Bird Told Me
4:Lavender Blue
5:Galway Bay
6:I've Got My Love to Keep Me Warm
7:So In Love
8:Cruising Down the River *
9:On a Slow Boat to China
10:Sunflower *

Mar. 5, 1949

1:Far Away Places
2:Powder Your Face With Sunshine
3:Galway Bay
4:A Little Bird Told Me
5:I've Got My Love to Keep Me Warm
6:Cruising Down the River
7:Lavender Blue
8:So In Love
9:Sunflower
10:On a Slow Boat to China

Mar. 12, 1949

1:Far Away Places
2:Powder Your Face With Sunshine
3:I've Got My Love to Keep Me Warm
4:So In Love
5:Lavender Blue
6:Cruising Down the River
7:Red Roses For a Blue Lady *
8:Sunflower
9:Galway Bay
10:A Little Bird Told Me

Mar. 19, 1949

1:Powder Your Face With Sunshine
2:Cruising Down the River
3:So In Love
4:Far Away Places
5:A Little Bird Told Me
6:Red Roses For a Blue Lady
7:I've Got My Love to Keep Me Warm
8:Sunflower
9:Galway Bay
10:Lavender Blue

Mar. 26, 1949

1:Cruising Down the River
2:Galway Bay
3:Powder Your Face With Sunshine
4:Far Away Places
5:So In Love
6:Red Roses For a Blue Lady
7:Sunflower
8:I've Got My Love to Keep Me Warm
9:Lavender Blue
10:A Little Bird Told Me

Apr. 2, 1949

1:Cruising Down the River
2:Far Away Places
3:Red Roses For a Blue Lady
4:Sunflower
5:So In Love
6:Powder Your Face With Sunshine
7:I've Got My Love to Keep Me Warm
8:Galway Bay
9:Someone Like You *
10:Forever and Ever *

Apr. 9, 1949

1:Cruising Down the River
2:Sunflower
3:Powder Your Face With Sunshine
4:Far Away Places
5:So In Love
6:I've Got My Love to Keep Me Warm
7:Forever and Ever
8:Galway Bay
9:Red Roses For a Blue Lady
10:Someone Like You

Apr. 16, 1949

1:Cruising Down the River
2:Red Roses For a Blue Lady
3:Far Away Places
4:Sunflower
5:Powder Your Face With Sunshine
6:Forever and Ever
7:You Was *
8:Someone Like You
9:I've Got My Love to Keep Me Warm
10:So In Love

Apr. 23, 1949

1:Cruising Down the River
2:Sunflower
3:Forever and Ever
4:Red Roses For a Blue Lady
5:So In Love
6:Far Away Places
7:Powder Your Face With Sunshine
8:Careless Hands *
9:Someone Like You
10:"A" You're Adorable *

Apr. 30, 1949

1:Cruising Down the River
2:Forever and Ever
3:Red Roses For a Blue Lady
4:Sunflower
5:Again *
6:Powder Your Face With Sunshine
7:Careless Hands
8:Far Away Places
9:"A" You're Adorable
10:Someone Like You

May 7, 1949

1:Cruising Down the River
2:Red Roses For a Blue Lady
3:"A" You're Adorable
4:Again
5:Forever and Ever
6:Careless Hands
7:Powder Your Face With Sunshine
8:Someone Like You
9:Sunflower
10:Far Away Places

May 14, 1949

1:Cruising Down the River
2:Again
3:Forever and Ever
4:"A" You're Adorable
5:Careless Hands
6:Sunflower
7:Far Away Places
8:Red Roses For a Blue Lady
9:Riders in the Sky *
10:Someone Like You

May 21, 1949

1:Riders in the Sky
2:Again
3:Forever and Ever
4:Careless Hands
5:"A" You're Adorable
6:Some Enchanted Evening *
7:Cruising Down the River
8:Someone Like You
9:Sunflower
10:Red Roses For a Blue Lady

May 28, 1949

1:Again
2:Riders in the Sky
3:"A" You're Adorable
4:Cruising Down the River
5:Forever and Ever
6:Some Enchanted Evening
7:Careless Hands
8:Kiss Me Sweet *
9:Bali Hai *
10:Red Roses For a Blue Lady

June 4, 1949

1:Riders in the Sky
2:Again
3:Some Enchanted Evening
4:Careless Hands
5:"A" You're Adorable
6:Forever and Ever
7:Cruising Down the River
8:Bali Hai
9:I Don't See Me in Your Eyes Anymore *
10:Kiss Me Sweet

June 11, 1949

1:Riders in the Sky
2:Some Enchanted Evening
3:"A" You're Adorable
4:Again
5:Forever and Ever
6:Cruising Down the River
7:Bali Hai
8:A Wonderful Guy *
9:I Don't See Me in Your Eyes Anymore
10:Everywhere You Go *

June 18, 1949

1:Again
2:Riders in the Sky
3:Some Enchanted Evening
4:"A" You're Adorable
5:Forever and Ever
6:Bali Hai
7:A Wonderful Guy
8:I Don't See Me in Your Eyes Anymore
9:How It Lies, How It Lies, How It Lies *
10:Cruising Down the River

June 25, 1949

1:Some Enchanted Evening
2:Riders in the Sky
3:Bali Hai
4:Again
5:"A" You're Adorable
6:A Wonderful Guy
7:Forever and Ever
8:I Don't See Me in Your Eyes Anymore
9:Baby, It's Cold Outside *
10:Cruising Down the River

July 2, 1949

1:Some Enchanted Evening
2:Riders in the Sky
3:Bali Hai
4:Again
5:A Wonderful Guy
6:I Don't See Me in Your Eyes Anymore
7:Forever and Ever
8:"A" You're Adorable
9:Baby, It's Cold Outside
10:Cruising Down the River

July 9, 1949

1:Some Enchanted Evening
2:Again
3:Bali Hai
4:Riders in the Sky
5:A Wonderful Guy
6:Forever and Ever
7:Baby, It's Cold Outside
8:"A" You're Adorable
9:My One and Only Highland Fling *
10:I Don't See Me in Your Eyes Anymore

July 16, 1949

1:Some Enchanted Evening
2:Bali Hai
3:Again
4:Riders in the Sky
5:Forever and Ever
6:A Wonderful Guy
7:Baby, It's Cold Outside
8:"A" You're Adorable
9:I Don't See Me in Your Eyes Anymore
10:Just One Way to Say I Love You *

July 23, 1949

1:Some Enchanted Evening
2:Again
3:Bali Hai
4:A Wonderful Guy
5:There's Yes, Yes in Your Eyes *
6:Riders in the Sky
7:Baby, It's Cold Outside
8:Forever and Ever
9:I Don't See Me in Your Eyes Anymore
10:Just One Way to Say I Love You

July 30, 1949

1:Some Enchanted Evening
2:Bali Hai
3:Riders in the Sky
4:Again
5:A Wonderful Guy
6:Forever and Ever
7:Baby, It's Cold Outside
8:There's Yes, Yes in Your Eyes
9:I Don't See Me in Your Eyes Anymore
10:Just One Way to Say I Love You

Aug. 6, 1949

1:Some Enchanted Evening
2:Again
3:Riders in the Sky
4:Bali Hai
5:The Four Winds and the Seven Seas *
6:Baby, It's Cold Outside
7:There's Yes, Yes in Your Eyes
8:Forever and Ever
9:I Don't See Me in Your Eyes Anymore
10:Just One Way to Say I Love You

Aug. 13, 1949

1:Some Enchanted Evening
2:Bali Hai
3:Again
4:Baby, It's Cold Outside
5:Just One Way to Say I Love You
6:The Hucklebuck *
7:Forever and Ever
8:Room Full of Roses *
9:Riders in the Sky
10:There's Yes, Yes in Your Eyes

Aug. 20, 1949

1:Some Enchanted Evening
2:Room Full of Roses
3:Bali Hai
4:You're Breaking My Heart *
5:There's Yes, Yes in Your Eyes
6:Again
7:Just One Way to Say I Love You
8:Forever and Ever
9:Let's Take an Old-Fashioned Walk *
10:Lovers' Gold *

Aug. 27, 1949

1:You're Breaking My Heart
2:Room Full of Roses
3:Some Enchanted Evening
4:Let's Take an Old-Fashioned Walk
5:Bali Hai
6:Again
7:Just One Way to Say I Love You
8:There's Yes, Yes in Your Eyes
9:And It Still Goes *
10:It's a Great Feeling *

Sept. 3, 1949

1:Some Enchanted Evening
2:Room Full of Roses
3:You're Breaking My Heart
4:Just One Way to Say I Love You
5:Let's Take an Old-Fashioned Walk
6:Bali Hai
7:Again
8:Fiddle-Dee-Dee *
9:It's a Great Feeling
10:There's Yes, Yes in Your Eyes

Sept. 10, 1949

1:Room Full of Roses
2:You're Breaking My Heart
3:Maybe It's Because *
4:Some Enchanted Evening
5:Just One Way to Say I Love You
6:Let's Take an Old-Fashioned Walk
7:There's Yes, Yes in Your Eyes
8:Someday *
9:Bali Hai
10:Fiddle-Dee-Dee

Sept. 17, 1949

1:You're Breaking My Heart
2:Let's Take an Old-Fashioned Walk
3:Someday
4:Some Enchanted Evening
5:Room Full of Roses
6:Bali Hai
7:Maybe It's Because
8:Just One Way to Say I Love You
9:Fiddle-Dee-Dee
10:There's Yes, Yes in Your Eyes

Sept. 24, 1949

1:You're Breaking My Heart
2:Room Full of Roses
3:Someday
4:Some Enchanted Evening
5:Maybe It's Because
6:There's Yes, Yes in Your Eyes
7:Younger Than Springtime *
8:Just One Way to Say I Love You
9:Let's Take an Old-Fashioned Walk
10:Fiddle-Dee-Dee

Oct. 1, 1949

1:You're Breaking My Heart
2:Maybe It's Because
3:Some Enchanted Evening
4:Room Full of Roses
5:Someday
6:That Lucky Old Sun *
7:Let's Take an Old-Fashioned Walk
8:Fiddle-Dee-Dee
9:Jealous Heart *
10:There's Yes, Yes in Your Eyes

Oct. 8, 1949

1:Room Full of Roses
2:That Lucky Old Sun
3:Someday
4:Maybe It's Because
5:You're Breaking My Heart
6:Let's Take an Old-Fashioned Walk
7:Some Enchanted Evening
8:Twenty-Four Hours of Sunshine *
9:Jealous Heart
10:Fiddle-Dee-Dee

Oct. 15, 1949

1:You're Breaking My Heart
2:Someday
3:That Lucky Old Sun
4:Maybe It's Because
5:Room Full of Roses
6:Twenty-Four Hours of Sunshine
7:Jealous Heart
8:Some Enchanted Evening
9:Let's Take an Old-Fashioned Walk
10:Now That I Need You *

Oct. 22, 1949

1:You're Breaking My Heart
2:That Lucky Old Sun
3:Someday
4:Don't Cry, Joe *
5:Room Full of Roses
6:Maybe It's Because
7:Let's Take an Old-Fashioned Walk
8:Jealous Heart
9:The Last Mile Home *
10:Some Enchanted Evening

Oct. 29, 1949

1:That Lucky Old Sun
2:You're Breaking My Heart
3:Room Full of Roses
4:Don't Cry, Joe
5:Someday
6:I Can Dream, Can't I? *
7:Maybe It's Because
8:Jealous Heart
9:A Dreamer's Holiday *
10:Hop Scotch Polka *

Nov. 5, 1949

1:That Lucky Old Sun
2:You're Breaking My Heart
3:Don't Cry, Joe
4:I Can Dream, Can't I?
5:Room Full of Roses
6:Someday
7:Jealous Heart
8:A Dreamer's Holiday
9:Maybe It's Because
10:Hop Scotch Polka

Nov. 12, 1949

1:That Lucky Old Sun
2:Don't Cry, Joe
3:I Can Dream, Can't I?
4:You're Breaking My Heart
5:A Dreamer's Holiday
6:Slipping Around *
7:Room Full of Roses
8:Jealous Heart
9:Someday
10:Mule Train *

Nov. 19, 1949

1:Don't Cry, Joe
2:That Lucky Old Sun
3:I Can Dream, Can't I?
4:A Dreamer's Holiday
5:Mule Train
6:Slipping Around
7:Someday
8:You're Breaking My Heart
9:Jealous Heart
10:Room Full of Roses

Nov. 26, 1949

1:Don't Cry, Joe
2:I Can Dream, Can't I?
3:A Dreamer's Holiday
4:Mule Train
5:That Lucky Old Sun
6:Slipping Around
7:You're Breaking My Heart
8:Jealous Heart
9:Someday
10:Room Full of Roses

Dec. 3, 1949

1:Don't Cry, Joe
2:That Lucky Old Sun
3:I Can Dream, Can't I?
4:A Dreamer's Holiday
5:Mule Train
6:You're Breaking My Heart
7:Slipping Around
8:Dear Hearts and Gentle People *
9:Rudolph, the Red-Nosed Reindeer *
10:Jealous Heart

Dec. 10, 1949

1:Mule Train
2:I Can Dream, Can't I?
3:Don't Cry, Joe
4:A Dreamer's Holiday
5:That Lucky Old Sun
6:Slipping Around
7:Dear Hearts and Gentle People
8:You're Breaking My Heart
9:Rudolph, the Red-Nosed Reindeer
10:The Old Master Painter *

Dec. 17, 1949

1:I Can Dream, Can't I?
2:Don't Cry, Joe
3:A Dreamer's Holiday
4:Mule Train
5:Dear Hearts and Gentle People
6:That Lucky Old Sun
7:Slipping Around
8:Rudolph, the Red-Nosed Reindeer
9:You're Breaking My Heart
10:The Old Master Painter

Dec. 24, 1949

1:I Can Dream, Can't I?
2:A Dreamer's Holiday
3:Dear Hearts and Gentle People
4:Don't Cry, Joe
5:Mule Train
6:Rudolph, the Red-Nosed Reindeer
7:Slipping Around
8:The Old Master Painter
9:You're Breaking My Heart
10:That Lucky Old Sun

Dec. 31, 1949

1:A Dreamer's Holiday
2:Rudolph, the Red-Nosed Reindeer
3:Dear Hearts and Gentle People
4:Mule Train
5:I Can Dream, Can't I?
6:Don't Cry, Joe
7:Slipping Around
8:The Old Master Painter
9:That Lucky Old Sun
10:You're Breaking My Heart

1950

And so the decade known as the Flaming Forties, which actually had flared into global flames, gave way to the one that was going to be the Fabulous Fifties.

Six months deep into it, we were in another war.

The North Koreans crossed the thirty-eighth parallel in June, and President Harry Truman recalled later that the most difficult decision he ever made, including the one to drop the world's first atomic bomb, was to send American troops into Korea. By Christmas draft boards in average-sized big cities were calling up 200 men a day.

There was a rash of silly songs that year with titles like "Bibbidi Bobbidi Boo," "Rag Mop," "I Said My Pajamas," "I'd've Baked a Cake," "Tzena, Tzena, Tzena," and "The Thing." In the fall everyone was so tired of bidding "Goodnight, Irene" they were pleading for her to finally go on inside and hit the sack. Yet the top song of 1950 was a stirring love song, "My Foolish Heart," with nine weeks as Number One. The most intriguing tune of the year was the zither melody of "The Third Man Theme." Both came to "Your Hit Parade" from the movies of the same names.

Other fine films that year were *All About Eve, Born Yesterday, 12 O'Clock High, The Gunfighter,* and *Sunset Boulevard.* Broadway had *Guys and Dolls,* which furnished "A Bushel and a Peck," and the revival circuit had 1937's "Harbor Lights" back for another run.

It was the year of the Brink's robbery in Boston, where masked bandits got away with $2,775,-395.12. (The FBI got the culprits six years later.)

In an attempt to kill President Truman, two Puerto Rican fanatics tried to shoot their way into his Washington home. Guards killed one and wounded the other, at the cost of one guard's life and the wounding of two others.

And two new terms came into usage: "H-bomb" and "taking the Fifth." President Truman authorized the AEC to produce the new hydrogen bomb, and the Supreme Court ruled that under the Fifth Amendment no one could be forced to testify against himself.

Jan. 7, 1950

1:Dear Hearts and Gentle People
2:A Dreamer's Holiday
3:The Old Master Painter
4:I Can Dream, Can't I?
5:Don't Cry, Joe
6:Rudolph, the Red-Nosed Reindeer
7:I've Got a Lovely Bunch of Cocoanuts *
8:That Lucky Old Sun
9:Mule Train
10:Slipping Around

Jan. 14, 1950

1:Dear Hearts and Gentle People
2:A Dreamer's Holiday
3:I Can Dream, Can't I?
4:The Old Master Painter
5:I've Got a Lovely Bunch of Cocoanuts
6:Slipping Around
7:Don't Cry, Joe
8:Bye Bye, Baby *
9:Mule Train
10:Rudolph, the Red-Nosed Reindeer

Jan. 21, 1950

1:Dear Hearts and Gentle People
2:The Old Master Painter
3:I Can Dream, Can't I?
4:A Dreamer's Holiday
5:I've Got a Lovely Bunch of Cocoanuts
6:Bibbidi Bobbidi Boo *
7:Slipping Around
8:Don't Cry, Joe
9:The Johnson Rag *
10:Bye Bye, Baby

Jan. 28, 1950

1:Dear Hearts and Gentle People
2:The Old Master Painter
3:A Dreamer's Holiday
4:I Can Dream, Can't I?
5:There's No Tomorrow *
6:I've Got a Lovely Bunch of Cocoanuts
7:Bibbidi Bobbidi Boo
8:Bye Bye, Baby
9:The Johnson Rag
10:Slipping Around

Feb. 4, 1950

1:Dear Hearts and Gentle People
2:A Dreamer's Holiday
3:The Old Master Painter
4:I Can Dream, Can't I?
5:There's No Tomorrow
6:Bibbidi Bobbidi Boo
7:The Johnson Rag
8:I've Got a Lovely Bunch of Cocoanuts
9:A Dream Is a Wish Your Heart Makes *
10:Slipping Around

Feb. 11, 1950

1:Dear Hearts and Gentle People
2:The Old Master Painter
3:There's No Tomorrow
4:I Can Dream, Can't I?
5:Bibbidi Bobbidi Boo
6:Chattanoogie Shoe Shine Boy *
7:A Dreamer's Holiday
8:The Johnson Rag
9:I've Got a Lovely Bunch of Cocoanuts
10:A Dream Is a Wish Your Heart Makes

Feb. 18, 1950

1:Dear Hearts and Gentle People
2:There's No Tomorrow
3:The Old Master Painter
4:The Johnson Rag
5:A Dreamer's Holiday
6:I Can Dream, Can't I?
7:Chattanoogie Shoe Shine Boy
8:I Said My Pajamas *
9:Rag Mop *
10:Bibbidi Bobbidi Boo

Feb. 25, 1950

1:Chattanoogie Shoe Shine Boy
2:Dear Hearts and Gentle People
3:Bibbidi Bobbidi Boo
4:The Old Master Painter
5:I Said My Pajamas
6:Rag Mop
7:There's No Tomorrow
8:The Johnson Rag
9:Music, Music, Music *
10:A Dreamer's Holiday

* Newcomer

Mar. 4, 1950

1:Chattanoogie Shoe Shine Boy
2:Dear Hearts and Gentle People
3:Music, Music, Music
4:I Said My Pajamas
5:Bibbidi Bobbidi Boo
6:There's No Tomorrow
7:Rag Mop
8:The Old Master Painter
9:Have I Told You Lately That I Love You?
10: Sitting By the Window *

Mar. 11, 1950

1:Chattanoogie Shoe Shine Boy
2:Music, Music, Music
3:I Said My Pajamas
4:Rag Mop
5:There's No Tomorrow
6:Dear Hearts and Gentle People
7:Enjoy Yourself *
8:Sitting By the Window
9:Bibbidi Bobbidi Boo
10:The Old Master Painter

Mar. 18, 1950

1:Chattanoogie Shoe Shine Boy
2:I Said My Pajamas
3:Music, Music, Music
4:Dear Hearts and Gentle People
5:Daddy's Little Girl *
6:Rag Mop
7:There's No Tomorrow
8:Enjoy Yourself
9:My Foolish Heart *
10:Dearie *

Mar. 25, 1950

1:Chattanoogie Shoe Shine Boy
2:Music, Music, Music
3:There's No Tomorrow
4:I'd've Baked a Cake *
5:I Said My Pajamas
6:Rag Mop
7:Dearie
8:Enjoy Yourself
9:My Foolish Heart
10:Daddy's Little Girl

Apr. 1, 1950

1:Chattanoogie Shoe Shine Boy
2:I'd've Baked a Cake
3:Dearie
4:Music, Music, Music
5:It Isn't Fair *
6:My Foolish Heart
7:Enjoy Yourself
8:I Said My Pajamas
9:Daddy's Little Girl
10:There's No Tomorrow

Apr. 8, 1950

1:I'd've Baked a Cake
2:Music, Music, Music
3:Chattanoogie Shoe Shine Boy
4:My Foolish Heart
5:Dearie
6:It Isn't Fair
7:I Said My Pajamas
8:Peter Cottontail *
9:Daddy's Little Girl
10:Enjoy Yourself

Apr. 15, 1950

1:I'd've Baked a Cake
2:Peter Cottontail
3:Dearie
4:Music, Music, Music
5:My Foolish Heart
6:It Isn't Fair
7:Daddy's Little Girl
8:Chattanoogie Shoe Shine Boy
9:Enjoy Yourself
10:I Said My Pajamas

Apr. 22, 1950

1:I'd've Baked a Cake
2:My Foolish Heart
3:Dearie
4:It Isn't Fair
5:Daddy's Little Girl
6:Music, Music, Music
7:Candy and Cake *
8:Chattanoogie Shoe Shine Boy
9:Enjoy Yourself
10:The Third Man Theme *

Apr. 29, 1950

1:My Foolish Heart
2:The Third Man Theme
3:It Isn't Fair
4:Music, Music, Music
5:I'd've Baked a Cake
6:Dearie
7:Daddy's Little Girl
8:Candy and Cake
9:Chattanoogie Shoe Shine Boy
10:Sunshine Cake *

May 6, 1950

1:My Foolish Heart
2:I'd've Baked a Cake
3:The Third Man Theme
4:Dearie
5:It Isn't Fair
6:Music, Music, Music
7:Candy and Cake
8:Daddy's Little Girl
9:Sunshine Cake
10:Bewitched *

May 13, 1950

1:My Foolish Heart
2:It Isn't Fair
3:The Third Man Theme
4:I'd've Baked a Cake
5:Sentimental Me *
6:Dearie
7:Bewitched
8:Daddy's Little Girl
9:The Old Piano Roll Blues *
10:Music, Music, Music

May 20, 1950

1:My Foolish Heart
2:Bewitched
3:I'd've Baked a Cake
4:The Third Man Theme
5:Dearie
6:It Isn't Fair
7:Hoop-Dee-Doo *
8:Sentimental Me
9:Daddy's Little Girl
10:The Old Piano Roll Blues

May 27, 1950

1:My Foolish Heart
2:Bewitched
3:I'd've Baked a Cake
4:It Isn't Fair
5:Hoop-Dee-Doo
6:The Third Man Theme
7:The Old Piano Roll Blues
8:Sentimental Me
9:Dearie
10:Daddy's Little Girl

June 3, 1950

1:My Foolish Heart
2:Bewitched
3:The Third Man Theme
4:I'd've Baked a Cake
5:The Old Piano Roll Blues
6:Sentimental Me
7:It Isn't Fair
8:Hoop-Dee-Doo
9:Dearie
10:I Don't Care If the Sun Don't Shine *

June 10, 1950

1:My Foolish Heart
2:Bewitched
3:The Third Man Theme
4:The Old Piano Roll Blues
5:Hoop-Dee-Doo
6:Sentimental Me
7:It Isn't Fair
8:I'd've Baked a Cake
9:Dearie
10:I Don't Care If the Sun Don't Shine

June 17, 1950

1:My Foolish Heart
2:Bewitched
3:The Third Man Theme
4:Hoop-Dee-Doo
5:The Old Piano Roll Blues
6:Sentimental Me
7:It Isn't Fair
8:I Wanna Be Loved *
9:I'd've Baked a Cake
10:I Don't Care If the Sun Don't Shine

June 24, 1950

1:Bewitched
2:My Foolish Heart
3:Sentimental Me
4:Hoop-Dee-Doo
5:The Old Piano Roll Blues
6:The Third Man Theme
7:I Don't Care If the Sun Don't Shine
8:I Wanna Be Loved
9:It Isn't Fair
10:Count Every Star *

July 1, 1950

1:Bewitched
2:My Foolish Heart
3:Hoop-Dee-Doo
4:The Old Piano Roll Blues
5:Sentimental Me
6:The Third Man Theme
7:I Don't Care If the Sun Don't Shine
8:I Wanna Be Loved
9:Mona Lisa *
10:Count Every Star

July 8, 1950

1:My Foolish Heart
2:Bewitched
3:I Wanna Be Loved
4:The Third Man Theme
5:Hoop-Dee-Doo
6:I Don't Care If the Sun Don't Shine
7:Count Every Star
8:Mona Lisa
9:Sentimental Me
10:The Old Piano Roll Blues

July 15, 1950

1:Bewitched
2:I Wanna Be Loved
3:My Foolish Heart
4:Hoop-Dee-Doo
5:The Third Man Theme
6:Count Every Star
7:Mona Lisa
8:I Don't Care If the Sun Don't Shine
9:Sentimental Me
10:The Old Piano Roll Blues

July 22, 1950

1:Bewitched
2:Mona Lisa
3:I Wanna Be Loved
4:Hoop-Dee-Doo
5:The Third Man Theme
6:I Don't Care If the Sun Don't Shine
7:My Foolish Heart
8:The Old Piano Roll Blues
9:Count Every Star
10:Gone Fishin' *

July 29, 1950

1:Mona Lisa
2:Bewitched
3:My Foolish Heart
4:I Wanna Be Loved
5:The Third Man Theme
6:Count Every Star
7:I Don't Care If the Sun Don't Shine
8:Sometime *
9:I Didn't Slip, I Wasn't Pushed, I Fell *
10:Hoop-Dee-Doo

Aug. 5, 1950

1:Bewitched
2:Mona Lisa
3:Count Every Star
4:I Wanna Be Loved
5:Hoop-Dee-Doo
6:Sam's Song *
7:Tzena, Tzena, Tzena *
8:The Third Man Theme
9:My Foolish Heart
10:Sometime

Aug. 12, 1950

1:Mona Lisa
2:I Wanna Be Loved
3:Bewitched
4:Count Every Star
5:Sam's Song
6:The Third Man Theme
7:Hoop-Dee-Doo
8:Play a Simple Melody *
9:Goodnight, Irene *
10:Tzena, Tzena, Tzena

Aug. 19, 1950

1:Mona Lisa
2:Sam's Song
3:I Wanna Be Loved
4:Bewitched
5:Play a Simple Melody
6:Count Every Star
7:Goodnight, Irene
8:The Third Man Theme
9:Tzena, Tzena, Tzena
10:La Vie En Rose *

Aug. 26, 1950

1:Mona Lisa
2:Play a Simple Melody
3:Sam's Song
4:Goodnight, Irene
5:Count Every Star
6:Bewitched
7:I Wanna Be Loved
8:La Vie En Rose
9:Tzena, Tzena, Tzena
10:The Third Man Theme

Sept. 2, 1950

1:Mona Lisa
2:Play a Simple Melody
3:Goodnight, Irene
4:Sam's Song
5:Tzena, Tzena, Tzena
6:La Vie En Rose
7:I Wanna Be Loved
8:Bewitched
9:Count Every Star
10:The Third Man Theme

Sept. 9, 1950

1:Mona Lisa
2:Goodnight, Irene
3:Play a Simple Melody
4:La Vie En Rose
5:Sam's Song
6:All My Love *
7:Count Every Star
8:I Wanna Be Loved
9:Tzena, Tzena, Tzena
10:Bewitched

Sept. 16, 1950

1:Mona Lisa
2:Goodnight, Irene
3:Play a Simple Melody
4:Sam's Song
5:Tzena, Tzena, Tzena
6:All My Love
7:La Vie En Rose
8:Count Every Star
9:I Wanna Be Loved
10:Bewitched

Sept. 23, 1950

1:Mona Lisa
2:Goodnight, Irene
3:Play a Simple Melody
4:Sam's Song
5:All My Love
6:La Vie En Rose
7:I Wanna Be Loved
8:Tzena, Tzena, Tzena
9:Bonaparte's Retreat *
10:Bewitched

Sept. 30, 1950

1:Goodnight, Irene
2:La Vie En Rose
3:All My Love
4:Mona Lisa
5:Play a Simple Melody
6:Sam's Song
7:Can Anyone Explain? *
8:Bonaparte's Retreat
9:Tzena, Tzena, Tzena
10:I Wanna Be Loved

Oct. 7, 1950

1:La Vie En Rose
2:Goodnight, Irene
3:Mona Lisa
4:Sam's Song
5:All My Love
6:Play a Simple Melody
7:Bonaparte's Retreat
8:Can Anyone Explain?
9:Nevertheless *
10:I Love the Guy *

Oct. 14, 1950

1:Goodnight, Irene
2:All My Love
3:La Vie En Rose
4:Mona Lisa
5:Can Anyone Explain?
6:Play a Simple Melody
7:Sam's Song
8:Thinking of You *
9:Nevertheless
10:I Love the Guy

Oct. 21, 1950

1:Goodnight, Irene
2:Mona Lisa
3:All My Love
4:La Vie En Rose
5:Sam's Song
6:Harbor Lights *
7:Play a Simple Melody
8:Can Anyone Explain?
9:Thinking of You
10:Nevertheless

Oct. 28, 1950

1:All My Love
2:Harbor Lights
3:La Vie En Rose
4:Goodnight, Irene
5:Mona Lisa
6:Thinking of You
7:Play a Simple Melody
8:Can Anyone Explain?
9:Nevertheless
10:Sam's Song

Nov. 4, 1950

1:Goodnight, Irene
2:All My Love
3:Harbor Lights
4:La Vie En Rose
5:Thinking of You
6:Mona Lisa
7:Nevertheless
8:Orange-Colored Sky *
9:Can Anyone Explain?
10:Life Is So Peculiar *

Nov. 11, 1950

1:All My Love
2:Goodnight, Irene
3:Thinking of You
4:Harbor Lights
5:Nevertheless
6:La Vie En Rose
7:Orange-Colored Sky
8:Mona Lisa
9:A Marshmallow World *
10:A Bushel and a Peck *

Nov. 18, 1950

1:Harbor Lights
2:Goodnight, Irene
3:Thinking of You
4:All My Love
5:La Vie En Rose
6:A Bushel and a Peck
7:Nevertheless
8:Our Lady of Fatima *
9:A Marshmallow World
10:Orange-Colored Sky

Nov. 25, 1950

1:Harbor Lights
2:Nevertheless
3:All My Love
4:Thinking of You
5:A Bushel and a Peck
6:Goodnight, Irene
7:La Vie En Rose
8:A Marshmallow World
9:Orange-Colored Sky
10:Our Lady of Fatima

Dec. 2, 1950

1:All My Love
2:Thinking of You
3:A Bushel and a Peck
4:Nevertheless
5:Harbor Lights
6:La Vie En Rose
7:A Marshmallow World
8:Goodnight, Irene
9:Orange-Colored Sky
10:The Thing *

Dec. 9, 1950

1:Nevertheless
2:A Bushel and a Peck
3:All My Love
4:Harbor Lights
5:The Thing
6:Thinking of You
7:La Vie En Rose
8:Orange-Colored Sky
9:Tennessee Waltz *
10:A Marshmallow World

Dec. 16, 1950

1:A Bushel and a Peck
2:A Marshmallow World
3:Harbor Lights
4:All My Love
5:Nevertheless
6:The Thing
7:Tennessee Waltz
8:Thinking of You
9:Frosty the Snowman *
10:Orange-Colored Sky

Dec. 23, 1950

1:A Bushel and a Peck
2:Tennessee Waltz
3:The Thing
4:Harbor Lights
5:Nevertheless
6:A Marshmallow World
7:Thinking of You
8:Frosty the Snowman
9:All My Love
10:Orange-Colored Sky

Dec. 30, 1950

1:Frosty the Snowman
2:The Thing
3:Tennessee Waltz
4:A Bushel and a Peck
5:Harbor Lights
6:A Marshmallow World
7:Nevertheless
8:Thinking of You
9:All My Love
10:Orange-Colored Sky

1951

In a startling, dramatic announcement President Truman created the biggest news of 1951 by firing General Douglas MacArthur during the height of the Korean War that April. In an equally dramatic moment MacArthur came home for the first time since World War II began and made his emotional farewell to Congress, proclaiming that "old soldiers never die, they just fade away."

The most dramatic moment in sports came that fall with Bobby Thomson's incredible last-minute home run which won the pennant for the New York Giants in a last-day play-off with the Brooklyn Dodgers.

The Hit Parade had a dramatic moment of its own that year when Nat "King" Cole's recording of "Too Young" pushed that song into the Number One spot for twelve weeks, a new all-time record. No song could follow that act, but Tony Bennett's recording of "Because of You" tried mightily with eleven weeks as Number One, and Perry Como's "If" had ten weeks in the top spot.

It was the year of Mario Lanza, who supplied "Be My Love" and "The Loveliest Night of the Year" (which was "Over the Waves" with new lyrics), and the year of Les Paul and Mary Ford, who gave us electronic revivals of "How High the Moon" and "The World Is Waiting For the Sunrise." From Broadway Irving Berlin's *Call Me Madam* contributed "You're Just in Love," and Rodgers and Hammerstein's "The King and I" delivered "Hello, Young Lovers."

Devastating floods hit Kansas and Missouri, and the Army and Navy were given equal time in the year's two top books, James Jones's *From Here to Eternity* and Herman Wouk's Pulitzer Prize winner, *The Caine Mutiny*.

The biggest thing on TV that year, besides Dagmar on "Broadway Open House," was the televised hearings by Senator Estes Kefauver into organized crime. Millions of viewers saw the hands, but not the faces, of witnesses taking advantage of the new Fifth Amendment ruling.

Old movies dominated TV, but the new ones in the theaters that year were such winners as *An American in Paris, The African Queen, A Streetcar Named Desire,* and *A Place in the Sun.*

Jan. 6, 1951

1:Tennessee Waltz
2:A Bushel and a Peck
3:Nevertheless
4:The Thing
5:All My Love
6:A Marshmallow World
7:Harbor Lights
8:Frosty the Snowman
9:My Heart Cries For You *
10:Thinking of You

Jan. 13, 1951

1:Tennessee Waltz
2:The Thing
3:Harbor Lights
4:A Bushel and a Peck
5:Nevertheless
6:My Heart Cries For You
7:All My Love
8:A Marshmallow World
9:Thinking of You
10:You're Just in Love *

Jan. 20, 1951

1:Tennessee Waltz
2:The Thing
3:A Bushel and a Peck
4:Nevertheless
5:My Heart Cries For You
6:Harbor Lights
7:A Marshmallow World
8:You're Just in Love
9:Be My Love *
10:All My Love

Jan. 27, 1951

1:Tennessee Waltz
2:My Heart Cries For You
3:A Bushel and a Peck
4:Nevertheless
5:You're Just in Love
6:Be My Love
7:Harbor Lights
8:If *
9:The Thing
10:Use Your Imagination *

Feb. 3, 1951

1:Tennessee Waltz
2:My Heart Cries For You
3:If
4:Be My Love
5:A Bushel and a Peck
6:Harbor Lights
7:You're Just in Love
8:Nevertheless
9:The Thing
10:If I Were a Bell *

Feb. 10, 1951

1:My Heart Cries For You
2:Tennessee Waltz
3:If
4:You're Just in Love
5:Be My Love
6:Harbor Lights
7:A Bushel and a Peck
8:The Thing
9:Nevertheless
10:You and Your Beautiful Eyes *

Feb. 17, 1951

1:Tennessee Waltz
2:My Heart Cries For You
3:If
4:Be My Love
5:You're Just in Love
6:A Bushel and a Peck
7:Harbor Lights
8:Zing, Zing, Zoom, Zoom *
9:A Penny a Kiss *
10:Nevertheless

Feb. 24, 1951

1:If
2:My Heart Cries For You
3:Be My Love
4:Tennessee Waltz
5:You're Just in Love
6:A Bushel and a Peck
7:A Penny a Kiss
8:Harbor Lights
9:So Long *
10:Zing, Zing, Zoom, Zoom

* Newcomer

Mar. 3, 1951

1:If
2:My Heart Cries For You
3:Tennessee Waltz
4:Be My Love
5:You're Just in Love
6:A Penny a Kiss
7:Zing, Zing, Zoom, Zoom
8:So Long
9:Aba Daba Honeymoon *
10:The Roving Kind *

Mar. 10, 1951

1:If
2:Tennessee Waltz
3:Be My Love
4:You're Just in Love
5:My Heart Cries For You
6:Aba Daba Honeymoon
7:A Penny a Kiss
8:Zing, Zing, Zoom, Zoom
9:The Roving Kind
10:So Long

Mar. 17, 1951

1:If
2:Be My Love
3:You're Just in Love
4:My Heart Cries For You
5:Aba Daba Honeymoon
6:Tennessee Waltz
7:Would I Love You? *
8:A Penny a Kiss
9:Mockin'bird Hill *
10:Zing, Zing, Zoom, Zoom

Mar. 24, 1951

1:If
2:Be My Love
3:My Heart Cries For You
4:Mockin'bird Hill
5:You're Just in Love
6:Tennessee Waltz
7:Aba Daba Honeymoon
8:A Penny a Kiss
9:Would I Love You?
10:Zing, Zing, Zoom, Zoom

Mar. 31, 1951

1:If
2:Aba Daba Honeymoon
3:Mockin'bird Hill
4:Be My Love
5:Would I Love You?
6:My Heart Cries For You
7:You're Just in Love
8:Tennessee Waltz
9:A Penny a Kiss
10:It Is No Secret *

Apr. 7, 1951

1:If
2:Be My Love
3:Aba Daba Honeymoon
4:Mockin'bird Hill
5:Would I Love You?
6:You're Just in Love
7:My Heart Cries For You
8:Tennessee Waltz
9:Sparrow in the Treetop *
10:It Is No Secret

Apr. 14, 1951

1:Mockin'bird Hill
2:If
3:Would I Love You?
4:Aba Daba Honeymoon
5:Be My Love
6:Sparrow in the Treetop
7:You're Just in Love
8:My Heart Cries For You
9:It Is No Secret
10:Tennessee Waltz

Apr. 21, 1951

1:If
2:Mockin'bird Hill
3:Be My Love
4:Would I Love You?
5:Aba Daba Honeymoon
6:Sparrow in the Treetop
7:You're Just in Love
8:My Heart Cries For You
9:It Is No Secret
10:Tennessee Waltz

Apr. 28, 1951

1:Mockin'bird Hill
2:If
3:Be My Love
4:Aba Daba Honeymoon
5:Would I Love You?
6:Beautiful Brown Eyes *
7:Sparrow in the Treetop
8:It Is No Secret
9:I Apologize *
10:You're Just in Love

May 5, 1951

1:If
2:Mockin'bird Hill
3:Would I Love You?
4:Aba Daba Honeymoon
5:Be My Love
6:On Top of Old Smoky *
7:Sparrow in the Treetop
8:I Apologize
9:Too Young *
10:It Is No Secret

May 12, 1951

1:If
2:Mockin'bird Hill
3:On Top of Old Smoky
4:Sparrow in the Treetop
5:Would I Love You?
6:Be My Love
7:How High the Moon *
8:Too Young
9:Aba Daba Honeymoon
10:I Apologize

May 19, 1951

1:Mockin'bird Hill
2:Be My Love
3:Too Young
4:On Top of Old Smoky
5:Would I Love You?
6:If
7:How High the Moon
8:I Apologize
9:Sparrow in the Treetop
10:Aba Daba Honeymoon

May 26, 1951

1:On Top of Old Smoky
2:Too Young
3:Mockin'bird Hill
4:Would I Love You?
5:How High the Moon
6:Be My Love
7:If
8:The Loveliest Night of the Year *
9:Hot Canary *
10:I Apologize

June 2, 1951

1:Too Young
2:On Top of Old Smoky
3:Mockin'bird Hill
4:How High the Moon
5:Be My Love
6:If
7:I Apologize
8:Would I Love You?
9:The Loveliest Night of the Year
10:Mister and Mississippi *

June 9, 1951

1:On Top of Old Smoky
2:Too Young
3:Mockin'bird Hill
4:The Loveliest Night of the Year
5:How High the Moon
6:Would I Love You?
7:Mister and Mississippi
8:Be My Love
9:I Apologize
10:If

June 16, 1951

1:Too Young
2:On Top of Old Smoky
3:How High the Moon
4:Mockin'bird Hill
5:The Loveliest Night of the Year
6:Mister and Mississippi
7:Syncopated Clock *
8:I Apologize
9:Rose, Rose, I Love You *
10:Unless *

June 23, 1951

1:Too Young
2:On Top of Old Smoky
3:How High the Moon
4:Mister and Mississippi
5:The Loveliest Night of the Year
6:My Truly, Truly Fair *
7:Mockin'bird Hill
8:Rose, Rose, I Love You
9:I Apologize
10:Unless

June 30, 1951

1:Too Young
2:Mister and Mississipi
3:How High the Moon
4:The Loveliest Night of the Year
5:Mockin'bird Hill
6:On Top of Old Smoky
7:My Truly, Truly Fair
8:Unless
9:Jezebel *
10:I Apologize

July 7, 1951

1:Too Young
2:Mister and Mississippi
3:On Top of Old Smoky
4:How High the Moon
5:The Loveliest Night of the Year
6:My Truly, Truly Fair
7:Mockin'bird Hill
8:Jezebel
9:Hello, Young Lovers *
10:Unless

July 14, 1951

1:Too Young
2:Mister and Mississippi
3:The Loveliest Night of the Year
4:My Truly, Truly Fair
5:How High the Moon
6:On Top of Old Smoky
7:Mockin'bird Hill
8:Hello, Young Lovers
9:Jezebel
10:Unless

July 21, 1951

1:Too Young
2:Mister and Mississippi
3:The Loveliest Night of the Year
4:My Truly, Truly Fair
5:Because of You *
6:Mockin'bird Hill
7:On Top of Old Smoky
8:How High the Moon
9:Shanghai *
10:Jezebel

July 28, 1951

1:Too Young
2:My Truly, Truly Fair
3:Mister and Mississippi
4:The Loveliest Night of the Year
5:Shanghai
6:Because of You
7:On Top of Old Smoky
8:Come On-a My House *
9:Wonder Why *
10:In the Cool, Cool, Cool of the Evening *

Aug. 4, 1951

1:Too Young
2:Mister and Mississippi
3:Because of You
4:Shanghai
5:The Loveliest Night of the Year
6:Come On-a My House
7:My Truly, Truly Fair
8:In the Cool, Cool, Cool of the Evening
9:Sweet Violets *
10:Wonder Why

Aug. 11, 1951

1:Too Young
2:Come On-a My House
3:My Truly, Truly Fair
4:Shanghai
5:Because of You
6:Sweet Violets
7:The Loveliest Night of the Year
8:Wonder Why
9:In the Cool, Cool, Cool of the Evening
10:Mister and Mississippi

Aug. 18, 1951

1:Too Young
2:Because of You
3:My Truly, Truly Fair
4:Shanghai
5:Come On-a My House
6:Morning Side of the Mountain *
7:The Loveliest Night of the Year
8:Sweet Violets
9:In the Cool, Cool, Cool of the Evening
10:Mister and Mississippi

Aug. 25, 1951

1:Too Young
2:Because of You
3:Come On-a My House
4:Shanghai
5:The Loveliest Night of the Year
6:My Truly, Truly Fair
7:Sweet Violets
8:I Get Ideas *
9:Morning Side of the Mountain
10:In the Cool, Cool, Cool of the Evening

Sept. 1, 1951

1:Because of You
2:Come On-a My House
3:Shanghai
4:Too Young
5:The Loveliest Night of the Year
6:Morning Side of the Mountain
7:Sweet Violets
8:My Truly, Truly Fair
9:I Get Ideas
10:In the Cool, Cool, Cool of the Evening

Sept. 8, 1951

1:Because of You
2:Too Young
3:Come On-a My House
4:Shanghai
5:The Loveliest Night of the Year
6:I Get Ideas
7:Sweet Violets
8:My Truly, Truly Fair
9:In the Cool, Cool, Cool of the Evening
10:Morning Side of the Mountain

Sept. 15, 1951

1:Because of You
2:Too Young
3:The Loveliest Night of the Year
4:Shanghai
5:Come On-a My House
6:I Get Ideas
7:Sweet Violets
8:My Truly, Truly Fair
9:Morning Side of the Mountain
10:In the Cool, Cool, Cool of the Evening

Sept. 22, 1951

1:Because of You
2:Too Young
3:I Get Ideas
4:Come On-a My House
5:Shanghai
6:The Loveliest Night of the Year
7:Sweet Violets
8:Cold, Cold Heart *
9:My Truly, Truly Fair
10:In the Cool, Cool, Cool of the Evening

Sept. 29, 1951

1:Because of You
2:The Loveliest Night of the Year
3:Shanghai
4:Too Young
5:I Get Ideas
6:Cold, Cold Heart
7:In the Cool, Cool, Cool of the Evening
8:Come On-a My House
9:Sweet Violets
10:You'll Know *

Oct. 6, 1951

1:Because of You
2:I Get Ideas
3:Come On-a My House
4:Too Young
5:Shanghai
6:The Loveliest Night of the Year
7:Cold, Cold Heart
8:In the Cool, Cool, Cool of the Evening
9:Sweet Violets
10:The World Is Waiting For the Sunrise *

Oct. 13, 1951

1:Because of You
2:I Get Ideas
3:Cold, Cold Heart
4:Shanghai
5:Come On-a My House
6:The Loveliest Night of the Year
7:In the Cool, Cool, Cool of the Evening
8:Too Young
9:The World Is Waiting For the Sunrise
10:Sin *

Oct. 20, 1951

1:Because of You
2:I Get Ideas
3:Cold, Cold Heart
4:Shanghai
5:Too Young
6:The Loveliest Night of the Year
7:The World Is Waiting For the Sunrise
8:In the Cool, Cool, Cool of the Evening
9:Down Yonder *
10:Sin

Oct. 27, 1951

1:Because of You
2:Cold, Cold Heart
3:I Get Ideas
4:Sin
5:Shanghai
6:The Loveliest Night of the Year
7:The World Is Waiting For the Sunrise
8:Down Yonder
9:And So to Sleep Again *
10:In the Cool, Cool, Cool of the Evening

Nov. 3, 1951

1:Because of You
2:I Get Ideas
3:Down Yonder
4:Sin
5:Cold, Cold Heart
6:The Loveliest Night of the Year
7:In the Cool, Cool, Cool of the Evening
8:The World Is Waiting For the Sunrise
9:And So to Sleep Again
10:Shanghai

Nov. 10, 1951

1:Because of You
2:Sin
3:And So to Sleep Again
4:I Get Ideas
5:Cold, Cold Heart
6:Down Yonder
7:The Loveliest Night of the Year
8:The World Is Waiting For the Sunrise
9:Undecided *
10:Turn Back the Hands of Time *

Nov. 17, 1951

1:Sin
2:Cold, Cold Heart
3:Because of You
4:Down Yonder
5:I Get Ideas
6:And So to Sleep Again
7:Undecided
8:The Loveliest Night of the Year
9:The World Is Waiting For the Sunrise
10:Turn Back the Hands of Time

Nov. 24, 1951

1:Sin
2:Because of You
3:Down Yonder
4:Cold, Cold Heart
5:And So to Sleep Again
6:Undecided
7:I Get Ideas
8:Turn Back the Hands of Time
9:Domino *
10:The World Is Waiting For the Sunrise

Dec. 1, 1951

1:Sin
2:Because of You
3:Down Yonder
4:Cold, Cold Heart
5:I Get Ideas
6:Undecided
7:And So to Sleep Again
8:Domino
9:Turn Back the Hands of Time
10:Slow Poke *

Dec. 8, 1951

1:Sin
2:Because of You
3:Down Yonder
4:Undecided
5:And So to Sleep Again
6:Cold, Cold Heart
7:I Get Ideas
8:Domino
9:Slow Poke
10:Shrimp Boats *

Dec. 15, 1951

1:Sin
2:Because of You
3:Down Yonder
4:Undecided
5:And So to Sleep Again
6:I Get Ideas
7:Slow Poke
8:Shrimp Boats
9:Cold, Cold Heart
10:Domino

Dec. 22, 1951

1:Sin
2:Slow Poke
3:Down Yonder
4:Undecided
5:Domino
6:Shrimp Boats
7:Because of You
8:And So to Sleep Again
9:Cold, Cold Heart
10:Charmaine *

Dec. 29, 1951

1:Slow Poke
2:Undecided
3:Down Yonder
4:Charmaine
5:Domino
6:Sin
7:Cold, Cold Heart
8:Because of You
9:Shrimp Boats
10:And So to Sleep Again

1952

Dwight D. Eisenhower, war hero, college president, and idolized figure in history, reached the natural culmination of his career by being elected President of the United States in November, breaking the Democrats' monopoly on the White House that stretched back to 1933.

He vowed to go to Korea before he took office, which he did, but the conflict droned on with no victory in sight. By fall the first of 1950's draftees were returning to civilian life, their two years up with nothing settled at the thirty-eighth parallel.

One G.I. was busy in the music field. Virtually everything Private first class Eddie Fisher recorded made "Your Hit Parade" that year: "Tell Me Why," "I'm Yours," "Anytime," "Wish You Were Here" (from the Broadway musical of that year), "Outside of Heaven," and even that old chestnut "Lady of Spain." Other revivals of 1952 were Nat "King" Cole's "Walkin' My Baby Back Home" and the Mills Brothers' "Glow Worm." It was the year of Johnnie Ray, who tearfully gave us "Cry" and "Little White Cloud That Cried." But it was Jo Stafford who recorded the year's top tune, "You Belong to Me," nine weeks as Number One.

One of the top movies of the year was *High Noon*, and it supplied its title song to the Hit Parade. Other big films of 1952 were *The Greatest Show on Earth, Come Back, Little Sheba, Viva Zapata*, and *The Quiet Man*.

It was the year of college panty raids; of ship captain Kurt Carlsen, who refused to leave his sinking *Flying Enterprise;* of Arthur Godfrey, Bishop Sheen, and "I Love Lucy" on TV; and it was the time when an ex-G.I. named George Jorgensen went to Denmark for sex surgery and returned as Christine Jorgensen.

King George VI died and Elizabeth II became Queen of England. Rocky Marciano ko'd Jersey Joe Walcott for the heavyweight championship. Texans were cussing Edna Ferber's new novel, *Giant.*

And two dogs figured in the news. FDR's dog, Fala, died. Richard Nixon's dog, Checkers, was defended on network TV.

Jan. 5, 1952

1:Slow Poke
2:Sin
3:Down Yonder
4:Shrimp Boats
5:Undecided
6:And So to Sleep Again
7:Domino
8:Charmaine
9:Because of You
10:Cold, Cold Heart

Jan. 12, 1952

1:Sin
2:Slow Poke
3:Down Yonder
4:Undecided
5:Shrimp Boats
6:Charmaine
7:Domino
8:Cry *
9:Little White Cloud That Cried *
10:Because of You

Jan. 19, 1952

1:Slow Poke
2:Down Yonder
3:Sin
4:Undecided
5:Charmaine
6:Domino
7:Shrimp Boats
8:Cry
9:Little White Cloud That Cried
10:Because of You

Jan. 26, 1952

1:Slow Poke
2:Sin
3:Shrimp Boats
4:Down Yonder
5:Undecided
6:Anytime *
7:Cry
8:Domino
9:Little White Cloud That Cried
10:Charmaine

Feb. 2, 1952

1:Cry
2:Slow Poke
3:Down Yonder
4:Sin
5:Anytime
6:Shrimp Boats
7:Undecided
8:Little White Cloud That Cried
9:Tell Me Why *
10:Charmaine

Feb. 9, 1952

1:Slow Poke
2:Cry
3:Shrimp Boats
4:Sin
5:Little White Cloud That Cried
6:Undecided
7:Tell Me Why
8:Anytime
9:Down Yonder
10:Please, Mr. Sun *

Feb. 16, 1952

1:Slow Poke
2:Cry
3:Anytime
4:Shrimp Boats
5:Tell Me Why
6:Little White Cloud That Cried
7:Sin
8:Undecided
9:Down Yonder
10:Please, Mr. Sun

Feb. 23, 1952

1:Cry
2:Slow Poke
3:Anytime
4:Tell Me Why
5:Little White Cloud That Cried
6:Shrimp Boats
7:Please, Mr. Sun
8:Sin
9:Be My Life's Companion *
10:Undecided

* Newcomer

Mar. 1, 1952

1:Cry
2:Slow Poke
3:Anytime
4:Little White Cloud That Cried
5:Tell Me Why
6:Please, Mr. Sun
7:Shrimp Boats
8:Be My Life's Companion
9:Sin
10:Undecided

Mar. 8, 1952

1:Cry
2:Tell Me Why
3:Please, Mr. Sun
4:Slow Poke
5:Anytime
6:Little White Cloud That Cried
7:Shrimp Boats
8:Wheel of Fortune *
9:Be My Life's Companion
10:Sin

Mar. 15, 1952

1:Slow Poke
2:Tell Me Why
3:Please, Mr. Sun
4:Cry
5:Anytime
6:Wheel of Fortune
7:Little White Cloud That Cried
8:Be My Life's Companion
9:Sin
10:Shrimp Boats

Mar. 22, 1952

1:Cry
2:Wheel of Fortune
3:Anytime
4:Tell Me Why
5:Please, Mr. Sun
6:Slow Poke
7:Little White Cloud That Cried
8:Blue Tango *
9:Shrimp Boats
10:Be My Life's Companion

Mar. 29, 1952

1:Wheel of Fortune
2:Anytime
3:Please, Mr. Sun
4:Tell Me Why
5:Cry
6:Slow Poke
7:Be My Life's Companion
8:Little White Cloud That Cried
9:Blue Tango
10:Come What May *

Apr. 5, 1952

1:Wheel of Fortune
2:Anytime
3:Please, Mr. Sun
4:Cry
5:Tell Me Why
6:Be My Life's Companion
7:Blue Tango
8:Slow Poke
9:Little White Cloud That Cried
10:Blacksmith Blues *

Apr. 12, 1952

1:Wheel of Fortune
2:Please, Mr. Sun
3:Cry
4:Anytime
5:Blue Tango
6:Tell Me Why
7:Be My Life's Companion
8:Slow Poke
9:Blacksmith Blues
10:Little White Cloud That Cried

Apr. 19, 1952

1:Wheel of Fortune
2:Anytime
3:Please, Mr. Sun
4:Blue Tango
5:Blacksmith Blues
6:Cry
7:Be My Life's Companion
8:Tell Me Why
9:Little White Cloud That Cried
10:Slow Poke

Apr. 26, 1952

1:Wheel of Fortune
2:Anytime
3:Cry
4:Blacksmith Blues
5:Blue Tango
6:Please, Mr. Sun
7:Be My Life's Companion
8:A Guy Is a Guy *
9:Tell Me Why
10:Little White Cloud That Cried

May 3, 1952

1:Wheel of Fortune
2:Anytime
3:Blue Tango
4:A Guy Is a Guy
5:Please, Mr. Sun
6:Blacksmith Blues
7:Be Anything, But Be Mine *
8:Cry
9:Pittsburgh, Pennsylvania *
10:Be My Life's Companion

May 10, 1952

1:Blue Tango
2:Blacksmith Blues
3:Anytime
4:Wheel of Fortune
5:A Guy Is a Guy
6:Please, Mr. Sun
7:Be Anything, But Be Mine
8:Cry
9:Forgive Me *
10:Pittsburgh, Pennsylvania

May 17, 1952

1:Blue Tango
2:Anytime
3:Blacksmith Blues
4:A Guy Is a Guy
5:Kiss of Fire *
6:Be Anything, But Be Mine
7:Wheel of Fortune
8:Forgive Me
9:Pittsburgh, Pennsylvania
10:Cry

May 24, 1952

1:Kiss of Fire
2:Blue Tango
3:Be Anything, But Be Mine
4:Blacksmith Blues
5:A Guy Is a Guy
6:Anytime
7:Forgive Me
8:Pittsburgh, Pennsylvania
9:Wheel of Fortune
10:Cry

May 31, 1952

1:Kiss of Fire
2:A Guy Is a Guy
3:Be Anything, But Be Mine
4:Blue Tango
5:I'm Yours *
6:Blacksmith Blues
7:Forgive Me
8:Wheel of Fortune
9:Anytime
10:Pittsburgh, Pennsylvania

June 7, 1952

1:Kiss of Fire
2:Blue Tango
3:Be Anything, But Be Mine
4:A Guy Is a Guy
5:Blacksmith Blues
6:Anytime
7:I'm Yours
8:Wheel of Fortune
9:Forgive Me
10:Pittsburgh, Pennsylvania

June 14, 1952

1:Kiss of Fire
2:Blue Tango
3:Be Anything, But Be Mine
4:I'm Yours
5:A Guy Is a Guy
6:Forgive Me
7:Blacksmith Blues
8:Pittsburgh, Pennsylvania
9:Walkin' My Baby Back Home *
10:Wheel of Fortune

June 21, 1952

1:Kiss of Fire
2:I'm Yours
3:Be Anything, But Be Mine
4:Here In My Heart *
5:Blue Tango
6:A Guy Is a Guy
7:Pittsburgh, Pennsylvania
8:Forgive Me
9:Walkin' My Baby Back Home
10:Blacksmith Blues

June 28, 1952

1:Kiss of Fire
2:Be Anything, But Be Mine
3:I'm Yours
4:Blue Tango
5:Here In My Heart
6:Blacksmith Blues
7:Delicado *
8:A Guy Is a Guy
9:Walkin' My Baby Back Home
10:Forgive Me

July 5, 1952

1:I'm Yours
2:Kiss of Fire
3:Delicado
4:Be Anything, But Be Mine
5:Blue Tango
6:A Guy Is a Guy
7:Here In My Heart
8:Walkin' My Baby Back Home
9:Blacksmith Blues
10:Forgive Me

July 12, 1952

1:Kiss of Fire
2:Blue Tango
3:Delicado
4:I'm Yours
5:Walkin' My Baby Back Home
6:Here In My Heart
7:Be Anything, But Be Mine
8:Blacksmith Blues
9:Forgive Me
10:A Guy Is a Guy

July 19, 1952

1:I'm Yours
2:Here In My Heart
3:Delicado
4:Walkin' My Baby Back Home
5:Blue Tango
6:Kiss of Fire
7:Auf Wiederseh'n, Sweetheart *
8:Forgive Me
9:Half As Much *
10:Be Anything, But Be Mine

July 26, 1952

1:Walkin' My Baby Back Home
2:Auf Wiederseh'n, Sweetheart
3:Kiss of Fire
4:Blue Tango
5:Delicado
6:I'm Yours
7:Here In My Heart
8:Half As Much
9:Somewhere Along the Way *
10:So Madly in Love *

Aug. 2, 1952

1:I'm Yours
2:Delicado
3:Auf Wiederseh'n, Sweetheart
4:Walkin' My Baby Back Home
5:Blue Tango
6:Somewhere Along the Way
7:Kiss of Fire
8:Here In My Heart
9:Half As Much
10:So Madly in Love

Aug. 9, 1952

1:Walkin' My Baby Back Home
2:Auf Wiederseh'n, Sweetheart
3:I'm Yours
4:Delicado
5:Half As Much
6:Kiss of Fire
7:Blue Tango
8:Here In My Heart
9:Zing a Little Zong *
10:Somewhere Along the Way

Aug. 16, 1952

1:Walkin' My Baby Back Home
2:Auf Wiederseh'n, Sweetheart
3:Delicado
4:Blue Tango
5:Half As Much
6:I'm Yours
7:Somewhere Along the Way
8:Here In My Heart
9:Kiss of Fire
10:Zing a Little Zong

Aug. 23, 1952

1:Auf Wiederseh'n, Sweetheart
2:Walkin' My Baby Back Home
3:Kiss of Fire
4:Wish You Were Here *
5:Half As Much
6:I'm Yours
7:Delicado
8:Blue Tango
9:Somewhere Along the Way
10:Here In My Heart

Aug. 30, 1952

1:Auf Wiederseh'n, Sweetheart
2:Walkin' My Baby Back Home
3:Half As Much
4:Wish You Were Here
5:Blue Tango
6:Somewhere Along the Way
7:Here In My Heart
8:Delicado
9:Botch-A-Me *
10:I'm Yours

Sept. 6, 1952

1:Auf Wiederseh'n, Sweetheart
2:Walkin' My Baby Back Home
3:Half As Much
4:Wish You Were Here
5:Somewhere Along the Way
6:Blue Tango
7:Here In My Heart
8:You Belong to Me *
9:Botch-A-Me
10:I'm Yours

Sept. 13, 1952

1:Wish You Were Here
2:Auf Wiederseh'n, Sweetheart
3:Half As Much
4:Walkin' My Baby Back Home
5:You Belong to Me
6:Somewhere Along the Way
7:I'm Yours
8:Here In My Heart
9:Botch-A-Me
10:Blue Tango

Sept. 20, 1952

1:You Belong to Me
2:Wish You Were Here
3:Auf Wiederseh'n, Sweetheart
4:Half As Much
5:Walkin' My Baby Back Home
6:Somewhere Along the Way
7:I'm Yours
8:Blue Tango
9:Botch-A-Me
10:High Noon *

Sept. 27, 1952

1:You Belong to Me
2:Wish You Were Here
3:Half As Much
4:Auf Wiederseh'n, Sweetheart
5:Walkin' My Baby Back Home
6:Somewhere Along the Way
7:Jambalaya *
8:Botch-A-Me
9:I Went to Your Wedding *
10:High Noon

Oct. 4, 1952

1:You Belong to Me
2:Wish You Were Here
3:Auf Wiederseh'n, Sweetheart
4:I Went to Your Wedding
5:Half As Much
6:Somewhere Along the Way
7:Jambalaya
8:Walkin' My Baby Back Home
9:High Noon
10:Botch-A-Me

Oct. 11, 1952

1:You Belong to Me
2:Wish You Were Here
3:Jambalaya
4:I Went to Your Wedding
5:Half As Much
6:Auf Wiederseh'n, Sweetheart
7:Somewhere Along the Way
8:Because You're Mine *
9:Meet Mr. Callaghan *
10:Walkin' My Baby Back Home

Oct. 18, 1952

1:Wish You Were Here
2:You Belong to Me
3:I Went to Your Wedding
4:Jambalaya
5:Half As Much
6:Auf Wiederseh'n, Sweetheart
7:Somewhere Along the Way
8:Because You're Mine
9:Walkin' My Baby Back Home
10:Meet Mr. Callaghan

Oct. 25, 1952

1:You Belong to Me
2:Wish You Were Here
3:I Went to Your Wedding
4:Jambalaya
5:Half As Much
6:Somewhere Along the Way
7:Auf Wiederseh'n, Sweetheart
8:Because You're Mine
9:Meet Mr. Callaghan
10:Walkin' My Baby Back Home

Nov. 1, 1952

1:Wish You Were Here
2:You Belong to Me
3:Jambalaya
4:I Went to Your Wedding
5:Half As Much
6:Somewhere Along the Way
7:Auf Wiederseh'n, Sweetheart
8:Because You're Mine
9:Meet Mr. Callaghan
10:Glow Worm *

Nov. 8, 1952

1:You Belong to Me
2:Wish You Were Here
3:Jambalaya
4:Because You're Mine
5:I Went to Your Wedding
6:Somewhere Along the Way
7:Glow Worm
8:Half As Much
9:Trying *
10:Lady of Spain *

Nov. 15, 1952

1:You Belong to Me
2:Jambalaya
3:Wish You Were Here
4:I Went to Your Wedding
5:Glow Worm
6:Because You're Mine
7:Lady of Spain
8:Somewhere Along the Way
9:Half As Much
10:Trying

Nov. 22, 1952

1:You Belong to Me
2:Glow Worm
3:Because You're Mine
4:I Went to Your Wedding
5:Jambalaya
6:Wish You Were Here
7:Lady of Spain
8:Trying
9:Outside of Heaven *
10:Why Don't You Believe Me? *

Nov. 29, 1952

1:You Belong to Me
2:Jambalaya
3:Because You're Mine
4:Glow Worm
5:I Went to Your Wedding
6:Wish You Were Here
7:Lady of Spain
8:Outside of Heaven
9:Why Don't You Believe Me?
10:Trying

Dec. 6, 1952

1:Glow Worm
2:Because You're Mine
3:Jambalaya
4:You Belong to Me
5:I Went to Your Wedding
6:Wish You Were Here
7:Lady of Spain
8:Why Don't You Believe Me?
9:Outside of Heaven
10:Trying

Dec. 13, 1952

1:Glow Worm
2:You Belong to Me
3:Because You're Mine
4:Why Don't You Believe Me?
5:Jambalaya
6:I Went to Your Wedding
7:Outside of Heaven
8:Wish You Were Here
9:Lady of Spain
10:Takes Two to Tango *

Dec. 20, 1952

1:Why Don't You Believe Me?
2:Because You're Mine
3:Glow Worm
4:I Went to Your Wedding
5:You Belong to Me
6:Jambalaya
7:Don't Let the Stars Get in Your Eyes *
8:Outside of Heaven
9:Lady of Spain
10:I Saw Mommy Kissing Santa Claus *

Dec. 27, 1952

1:Why Don't You Believe Me?
2:Because You're Mine
3:Don't Let the Stars Get in Your Eyes
4:You Belong to Me
5:Glow Worm
6:Outside of Heaven
7:Jambalaya
8:I Saw Mommy Kissing Santa Claus
9:Lady of Spain
10:I Went to Your Wedding

1953

It was the year of the Kinsey report on sexual behavior, the year the Scrabble craze swept the nation, and the year man climbed higher, dived deeper, and flew faster than ever before.

Edmund Hillary scaled Mount Everest ("because it was there"), Auguste and Jacques Piccard descended 10,334 feet into the Mediterranean in a steel diving ball, and Air Force Major Charles Jeager streaked through the stratosphere at 1,650 mph, two and a half times the speed of sound.

The year saw the death of Joseph Stalin, and both the birth and death of the new movie process, 3-D films. The best movies of the year (none in 3-D) were *From Here to Eternity*, *Shane*, and *Stalag 17*.

Fighting stopped in Korea, but peace talks bogged down. The world watched the romance between Princess Margaret and Peter Townsend. Africa flinched under the bloody series of Mau Mau raids. Julius and Ethel Rosenberg, the convicted spies, went to the electric chair while pickets paraded. Carl Hall and Bonnie Heady went to the gas chamber after having three months earlier kidnapped and murdered six-year-old Bobby Greenlease, Jr., in Kansas City, Missouri, demanding and getting $600,000, the largest ransom in history.

TV was so big now it was the making of pro football, previously a castoff sport for forogotten college athletes. Red Grange was the knowledgeable but ungrammatical off-camera spokesman. (Fans loved him for saying, "Green Bay are a good team, but Detroit have the better line.") Jack Webb's "Dragnet" was so popular its dum-de-dum-dum theme could be heard from nearly any house on any block on summer nights when windows were open. "I Love Lucy" had the best rating system of all: Cities discovered the water intake mysteriously rose sharply all over America during "Lucy" commercials, leading to the "Tele-flush" theory that millions were going to the bathroom between acts. Lucille Ball herself carried off the year's best-planned publicity gimmick when TV's "Lucy" had a baby at the same time the real-life Lucy was delivering her new son.

Saturday night meant Jackie Gleason, Sid Caesar and Imogene Coca, and "Your Hit Parade" with Snooky Lanson, Dorothy Collins, Gisele MacKenzie, and Russell Arms. The top song they sang, with eight weeks as Number One in 1953, was "Song From Moulin Rouge."

Jan. 3, 1953

1:I Saw Mommy Kissing Santa Claus
2:Why Don't You Believe Me?
3:Don't Let the Stars Get in Your Eyes
4:Glow Worm
5:You Belong to Me
6:Because You're Mine
7:Outside of Heaven
8:Jambalaya
9:I Went to Your Wedding
10:Lady of Spain

Jan. 10, 1953

1:Why Don't You Believe Me?
2:Don't Let the Stars Get in Your Eyes
3:Glow Worm
4:Because You're Mine
5:Keep It a Secret *
6:You Belong to Me
7:Lady of Spain
8:Jambalaya
9:I Saw Mommy Kissing Santa Claus
10:I Went to Your Wedding

Jan. 17, 1953

1:Don't Let the Stars Get in Your Eyes
2:Why Don't You Believe Me?
3:Keep It a Secret
4:Glow Worm
5:Because You're Mine
6:Lady of Spain
7:I Went to Your Wedding
8:You Belong to Me
9:Jambalaya
10:Till I Waltz Again With You *

Jan. 24, 1953

1:Why Don't You Believe Me?
2:Don't Let the Stars Get in Your Eyes
3:Glow Worm
4:Keep It a Secret
5:Because You're Mine
6:Lady of Spain
7:Till I Waltz Again With You
8:You Belong to Me
9:I Went to Your Wedding
10:Oh Happy Day *

Jan. 31, 1953

1:Why Don't You Believe Me?
2:Don't Let the Stars Get in Your Eyes
3:Keep It a Secret
4:Because You're Mine
5:Till I Waltz Again With You
6:Lady of Spain
7:Glow Worm
8:I Went to Your Wedding
9:Oh Happy Day
10:You Belong to Me

Feb. 7, 1953

1:Don't Let the Stars Get in Your Eyes
2:Keep It a Secret
3:Why Don't You Believe Me?
4:Till I Waltz Again With You
5:Because You're Mine
6:Glow Worm
7:Lady of Spain
8:Oh Happy Day
9:Hold Me, Thrill Me, Kiss Me *
10:Tell Me You're Mine *

Feb. 14, 1953

1:Don't Let the Stars Get in Your Eyes
2:Till I Waltz Again With You
3:Keep It a Secret
4:Why Don't You Believe Me?
5:Because You're Mine
6:Glow Worm
7:Oh Happy Day
8:Lady of Spain
9:Tell Me You're Mine
10:Hold Me, Thrill Me, Kiss Me

Feb. 21, 1953

1:Don't Let the Stars Get in Your Eyes
2:Till I Waltz Again With You
3:Why Don't You Believe Me?
4:Keep It a Secret
5:Glow Worm
6:Oh Happy Day
7:Tell Me You're Mine
8:Hold Me, Thrill Me, Kiss Me
9:No Two People *
10:Because You're Mine

* Newcomer

Feb. 28, 1953

1:Till I Waltz Again With You
2:Don't Let the Stars Get in Your Eyes
3:Keep It a Secret
4:Why Don't You Believe Me?
5:Oh Happy Day
6:Tell Me You're Mine
7:Hold Me, Thrill Me, Kiss Me
8:Because You're Mine
9:Glow Worm
10:Have You Heard? *

Mar. 7, 1953

1:Don't Let the Stars Get in Your Eyes
2:Till I Waltz Again With You
3:Keep It a Secret
4:Why Don't You Believe Me?
5:Oh Happy Day
6:Hold Me, Thrill Me, Kiss Me
7:Tell Me You're Mine
8:Have You Heard?
9:Side by Side *
10:How Do You Speak to An Angel? *

Mar. 14, 1953

1:Till I Waltz Again With You
2:Don't Let the Stars Get in Your Eyes
3:Why Don't You Believe Me?
4:Keep It a Secret
5:Side by Side
6:Doggie in the Window *
7:Oh Happy Day
8:Have You Heard?
9:Hold Me, Thrill Me, Kiss Me
10:Pretend *

Mar. 21, 1953

1:Till I Waltz Again With You
2:Don't Let the Stars Get in Your Eyes
3:Doggie in the Window
4:Pretend
5:Side by Side
6:Hold Me, Thrill Me, Kiss Me
7:Keep It a Secret
8:Why Don't You Believe Me?
9:I Believe *
10:Have You Heard?

Mar. 28, 1953

1:Till I Waltz Again With You
2:Don't Let the Stars Get in Your Eyes
3:Pretend
4:Doggie in the Window
5:Keep It a Secret
6:Side by Side
7:Your Cheatin' Heart *
8:I Believe
9:Have You Heard?
10:Hold Me, Thrill Me, Kiss Me

Apr. 4, 1953

1:Pretend
2:Till I Waltz Again With You
3:Doggie in the Window
4:Don't Let the Stars Get in Your Eyes
5:Side by Side
6:Your Cheatin' Heart
7:I Believe
8:Have You Heard?
9:Keep It a Secret
10:Hold Me, Thrill Me, Kiss Me

Apr. 11, 1953

1:I Believe
2:Doggie in the Window
3:Till I Waltz Again With You
4:Pretend
5:Your Cheatin' Heart
6:Side by Side
7:Don't Let the Stars Get in Your Eyes
8:Have You Heard?
9:Hold Me, Thrill Me, Kiss Me
10:Keep It a Secret

Apr. 18, 1953

1:Doggie in the Window
2:Pretend
3:I Believe
4:Till I Waltz Again With You
5:Your Cheatin' Heart
6:Don't Let the Stars Get in Your Eyes
7:Side by Side
8:Wild Horses *
9:Song From Moulin Rouge *
10:Have You Heard?

Apr. 25, 1953

1:Pretend
2:Till I Waltz Again With You
3:I Believe
4:Doggie in the Window
5:Your Cheatin' Heart
6:Don't Let the Stars Get in Your Eyes
7:Side by Side
8:Song From Moulin Rouge
9:April in Portugal *
10:Wild Horses

May 2, 1953

1:I Believe
2:Pretend
3:Doggie in the Window
4:Till I Waltz Again With You
5:Your Cheatin' Heart
6:Song From Moulin Rouge
7:April in Portugal
8:Side by Side
9:Don't Let the Stars Get in Your Eyes
10:Wild Horses

May 9, 1953

1:Pretend
2:Song From Moulin Rouge
3:Doggie in the Window
4:Your Cheatin' Heart
5:I Believe
6:April in Portugal
7:Side by Side
8:Till I Waltz Again With You
9:Tell Me a Story *
10:Don't Let the Stars Get in Your Eyes

May 16, 1953

1:I Believe
2:April in Portugal
3:Song From Moulin Rouge
4:Pretend
5:Your Cheatin' Heart
6:Doggie in the Window
7:Ruby *
8:Side by Side
9:Till I Waltz Again With You
10:Tell Me a Story

May 23, 1953

1:Song From Moulin Rouge
2:I Believe
3:Pretend
4:Your Cheatin' Heart
5:April in Portugal
6:Doggie in the Window
7:Side by Side
8:Say You're Mine Again *
9:Ruby
10:I'm Walking Behind You *

May 30, 1953

1:Song From Moulin Rouge
2:I Believe
3:April in Portugal
4:Doggie in the Window
5:Ruby
6:Your Cheatin' Heart
7:Pretend
8:I'm Walking Behind You
9:Say You're Mine Again
10:Seven Lonely Days *

June 6, 1953

1:Song From Moulin Rouge
2:April in Portugal
3:Pretend
4:I Believe
5:Ruby
6:Your Cheatin' Heart
7:Say You're Mine Again
8:Doggie in the Window
9:Seven Lonely Days
10:I'm Walking Behind You

June 13, 1953

1:April in Portugal
2:Song From Moulin Rouge
3:I Believe
4:Ruby
5:I'm Walking Behind You
6:Say You're Mine Again
7:Pretend
8:Your Cheatin' Heart
9:Doggie in the Window
10:Seven Lonely Days

June 20, 1953

1: Song From Moulin Rouge
2: Ruby
3: I Believe
4: April in Portugal
5: I'm Walking Behind You
6: Pretend
7: Your Cheatin' Heart
8: Say You're Mine Again
9: Just Another Polka *
10: Seven Lonely Days

June 27, 1953

1: Song From Moulin Rouge
2: April in Portugal
3: I Believe
4: I'm Walking Behind You
5: Ruby
6: Say You're Mine Again
7: Your Cheatin' Heart
8: Pretend
9: Seven Lonely Days
10: Just Another Polka

July 4, 1953

1: Song From Moulin Rouge
2: Ruby
3: April in Portugal
4: I Believe
5: I'm Walking Behind You
6: Say You're Mine Again
7: No Other Love *
8: Your Cheatin' Heart
9: Pretend
10: Just Another Polka

July 11, 1953

1: Song From Moulin Rouge
2: Ruby
3: April in Portugal
4: I'm Walking Behind You
5: I Believe
6: No Other Love
7: Say You're Mine Again
8: Anna *
9: Vaya Con Dios *
10: Your Cheatin' Heart

July 18, 1953

1: April in Portugal
2: Song From Moulin Rouge
3: I'm Walking Behind You
4: I Believe
5: No Other Love
6: Ruby
7: Your Cheatin' Heart
8: Say You're Mine Again
9: Terry's Theme From Limelight *
10: Vaya Con Dios

July 25, 1953

1: Song From Moulin Rouge
2: April in Portugal
3: I'm Walking Behind You
4: No Other Love
5: Ruby
6: I Believe
7: Vaya Con Dios
8: P.S. I Love You *
9: Say You're Mine Again
10: Terry's Theme From Limelight

Aug. 1, 1953

1: I'm Walking Behind You
2: No Other Love
3: Ruby
4: Song From Moulin Rouge
5: Vaya Con Dios
6: April in Portugal
7: I Believe
8: P.S. I Love You
9: Terry's Theme From Limelight
10: Say You're Mine Again

Aug. 8, 1953

1: No Other Love
2: I'm Walking Behind You
3: I Believe
4: Vaya Con Dios
5: April in Portugal
6: P.S. I Love You
7: Song From Moulin Rouge
8: Ruby
9: Say You're Mine Again
10: Terry's Theme From Limelight

Aug. 15, 1953

1:No Other Love
2:Song From Moulin Rouge
3:I'm Walking Behind You
4:Vaya Con Dios
5:Ruby
6:April in Portugal
7:P.S. I Love You
8:I Believe
9:You, You, You *
10:Crying in the Chapel *

Aug. 22, 1953

1:I'm Walking Behind You
2:No Other Love
3:Song From Moulin Rouge
4:Vaya Con Dios
5:P.S. I Love You
6:You, You, You
7:I Believe
8:Crying in the Chapel
9:April in Portugal
10:Ruby

Aug. 29, 1953

1:I'm Walking Behind You
2:No Other Love
3:Vaya Con Dios
4:P.S. I Love You
5:Oh! *
6:Crying in the Chapel
7:You, You, You
8:Ruby
9:April in Portugal
10:Song From Moulin Rouge

Sept. 5, 1953

1:Vaya Con Dios
2:No Other Love
3:Song From Moulin Rouge
4:You, You, You
5:P.S. I Love You
6:Oh!
7:I'm Walking Behind You
8:Crying in the Chapel
9:With These Hands *
10:April in Portugal

Sept. 12, 1953

1:Vaya Con Dios
2:No Other Love
3:You, You, You
4:Oh!
5:Crying in the Chapel
6:Song From Moulin Rouge
7:P.S. I Love You
8:I'm Walking Behind You
9:I Love Paris *
10:With These Hands

Sept. 19, 1953

1:You, You, You
2:Vaya Con Dios
3:Crying in the Chapel
4:No Other Love
5:Oh!
6:P.S. I Love You
7:I'm Walking Behind You
8:With These Hands
9:I Love Paris
10:Song From Moulin Rouge

Sept. 26, 1953

1:No Other Love
2:Vaya Con Dios
3:Crying in the Chapel
4:You, You, You
5:I'm Walking Behind You
6:Oh!
7:P.S. I Love You
8:Song From Moulin Rouge
9:With These Hands
10:I Love Paris

Oct. 3, 1953

1:You, You, You
2:No Other Love
3:Vaya Con Dios
4:Oh!
5:Crying in the Chapel
6:P.S. I Love You
7:I'm Walking Behind You
8:Song From Moulin Rouge
9:I Love Paris
10:With These Hands

Oct. 10, 1953

1:Vaya Con Dios
2:You, You, You
3:No Other Love
4:Crying in the Chapel
5:Oh!
6:P.S. I Love You
7:Dragnet *
8:I'm Walking Behind You
9:I Love Paris
10:With These Hands

Oct. 17, 1953

1:Vaya Con Dios
2:You, You, You
3:Crying in the Chapel
4:Oh!
5:No Other Love
6:Ebb Tide *
7:I Love Paris
8:Dragnet
9:C'est Si Bon *
10:With These Hands

Oct. 24, 1953

1:You, You, You
2:No Other Love
3:Oh!
4:Vaya Con Dios
5:Crying in the Chapel
6:Ebb Tide
7:Dragnet
8:I Love Paris
9:Rags to Riches *
10:Many Times *

Oct. 31, 1953

1:Vaya Con Dios
2:You, You, You
3:Ebb Tide
4:Crying in the Chapel
5:Many Times
6:Oh!
7:Rags to Riches
8:Dragnet
9:No Other Love
10:I Love Paris

Nov. 7, 1953

1:Ebb Tide
2:You, You, You
3:Vaya Con Dios
4:Many Times
5:Crying in the Chapel
6:Oh!
7:I Love Paris
8:No Other Love
9:Rags to Riches
10:Dragnet

Nov. 14, 1953

1:Ebb Tide
2:Rags to Riches
3:Many Times
4:Vaya Con Dios
5:You, You, You
6:Crying in the Chapel
7:C'est Magnifique *
8:Oh!
9:No Other Love
10:Eh Cumpari *

Nov. 21, 1953

1:Ebb Tide
2:Vaya Con Dios
3:Many Times
4:You, You, You
5:No Other Love
6:Oh!
7:I See the Moon *
8:Rags to Riches
9:Crying in the Chapel
10:Eh Cumpari

Nov. 28, 1953

1:You, You, You
2:Ebb Tide
3:Vaya Con Dios
4:Many Times
5:Rags to Riches
6:Ricochet *
7:Oh!
8:I See the Moon
9:Crying in the Chapel
10:Eh Cumpari

Dec. 5, 1953

1:Rags to Riches
2:Ebb Tide
3:Many Times
4:You, You, You
5:Ricochet
6:Vaya Con Dios
7:Oh!
8:Crying in the Chapel
9:I See the Moon
10:Eh Cumpari

Dec. 12, 1953

1:Rags to Riches
2:You, You, You
3:Ebb Tide
4:Ricochet
5:Stranger in Paradise *
6:Vaya Con Dios
7:Many Times
8:Eh Cumpari
9:That's Amore *
10:Oh!

Dec. 19, 1953

1:Ebb Tide
2:Rags to Riches
3:That's Amore
4:Changing Partners *
5:Eh Cumpari
6:Many Times
7:Vaya Con Dios
8:Ricochet
9:You, You, You
10:Stranger in Paradise

Dec. 26, 1953

1:Ricochet
2:Ebb Tide
3:You, You, You
4:Rags to Riches
5:That's Amore
6:Stranger in Paradise
7:Vaya Con Dios
8:Changing Partners
9:Eh Cumpari
10:Many Times

1954

It was the year of two famous women. Marilyn Monroe, the product of an orphanage and a foster home, had become the most famous sex symbol in the world. And for fifty-six days the world watched as the French and a lone woman—a nurse named Geneviève de Galard-Terraube and dubbed The Angel of Dienbienphu—made a futile, losing last stand against the Reds in what was then called the Indochina War. Later it would become known as the Vietnam War.

In an astonishing event that year, five members of Congress were wounded in the House of Representatives when four Puerto Ricans, one a woman, fired shots at random from a spectators' gallery, demanding independence for Puerto Rico. The congressmen recovered; the attackers went to prison. The year had started off astonishingly, with millions of televiewers not believing their eyes on New Year's Day when they saw Tommy Lewis come off the Alabama bench at the Cotton Bowl and tackle Rice's Dicky Moegle as he headed for a TD.

The sensation of TV was new comic George Gobel, who had the country saying "I'll be a dirty bird." The darling of TV was dimpled pianist Liberace. But the show that left the housework undone around the nation was the televised Army-McCarthy hearings, easily the best and longest drama on the tube. When it was all over, Senator Joseph McCarthy was condemned by the Senate for his conduct at the hearings.

Roger Bannister banned forever the bugaboo of running a four-minute mile by turning the trick in 3:59.4. It was the year of the historic Supreme Court ruling that racial segregation in schools was unconstitutional. The new big dance of the year was the mambo. The murder trial of the year was in Cleveland, where Dr. Sam Sheppard was found guilty of slaying his wife, Marilyn. Color TV was futilely trying to make inroads on the market. The first atomic-powered submarine, the *Nautilus,* was launched. And then there were four: Emilie Dionne died at the age of twenty.

The top movie of the year was *On the Waterfront.* The top Broadway musical was *The Pajama Game,* and it supplied the top song of the year, "Hey, There," ten weeks as Number One.

204

Jan. 2, 1954

1:Ebb Tide
2:Stranger in Paradise
3:That's Amore
4:Ricochet
5:You, You, You
6:Off Shore *
7:Rags to Riches
8:Changing Partners
9:Eh Cumpari
10:Many Times

Jan. 9, 1954

1:Stranger in Paradise
2:That's Amore
3:Heart of My Heart *
4:Rags to Riches
5:Ricochet
6:Oh, My Papa *
7:You, You, You
8:Off Shore
9:Ebb Tide
10:Changing Partners

Jan. 16, 1954

1:Stranger in Paradise
2:That's Amore
3:Oh, My Papa
4:Changing Partners
5:Ricochet
6:Ebb Tide
7:Heart of My Heart
8:Rags to Riches
9:You, You, You
10:Off Shore

Jan. 23, 1954

1:Stranger in Paradise
2:That's Amore
3:Oh, My Papa
4:Changing Partners
5:Rags to Riches
6:Heart of My Heart
7:Secret Love *
8:Ricochet
9:Ebb Tide
10:You, You, You

Jan. 30, 1954

1:Stranger in Paradise
2:Oh, My Papa
3:That's Amore
4:Changing Partners
5:Secret Love
6:Rags to Riches
7:Ebb Tide
8:Heart of My Heart
9:Ricochet
10:You, You, You

Feb. 6, 1954

1:Stranger in Paradise
2:Oh, My Papa
3:Changing Partners
4:That's Amore
5:Secret Love
6:Heart of My Heart
7:Ricochet
8:You, You, You
9:Ebb Tide
10:Rags to Riches

Feb. 13, 1954

1:Secret Love
2:Stranger in Paradise
3:Oh, My Papa
4:That's Amore
5:Changing Partners
6:Heart of My Heart
7:Ricochet
8:Rags to Riches
9:Ebb Tide
10:You, You, You

Feb. 20, 1954

1:Stranger in Paradise
2:Secret Love
3:Oh, My Papa
4:That's Amore
5:Heart of My Heart
6:Changing Partners
7:Ricochet
8:Young at Heart *
9:Ebb Tide
10:Rags to Riches

* Newcomer

Feb. 27, 1954

1:Secret Love
2:Stranger in Paradise
3:That's Amore
4:Changing Partners
5:Oh, My Papa
6:Heart of My Heart
7:From the Vine Came the Grape *
8:Young at Heart
9:Rags to Riches
10:Ricochet

Mar. 6, 1954

1:Secret Love
2:Stranger in Paradise
3:Oh, My Papa
4:Make Love to Me *
5:Heart of My Heart
6:That's Amore
7:Young at Heart
8:Changing Partners
9:From the Vine Came the Grape
10:Ricochet

Mar. 13, 1954

1:Secret Love
2:Oh, My Papa
3:Stranger in Paradise
4:Make Love to Me
5:Young at Heart
6:Changing Partners
7:Heart of My Heart
8:That's Amore
9:Ricochet
10:From the Vine Came the Grape

Mar. 20, 1954

1:Secret Love
2:Make Love to Me
3:Young at Heart
4:Wanted *
5:Oh, My Papa
6:Stranger in Paradise
7:I Get So Lonely *
8:Changing Partners
9:Heart of My Heart
10:That's Amore

Mar. 27, 1954

1:Secret Love
2:Young at Heart
3:Make Love to Me
4:Wanted
5:I Get So Lonely
6:Stranger in Paradise
7:Oh, My Papa
8:Heart of My Heart
9:That's Amore
10:Changing Partners

Apr. 3, 1954

1:Secret Love
2:Wanted
3:Young at Heart
4:Cross Over the Bridge *
5:I Get So Lonely
6:Make Love to Me
7:Stranger in Paradise
8:Oh, My Papa
9:Heart of My Heart
10:Changing Partners

Apr. 10, 1954

1:Wanted
2:Secret Love
3:Make Love to Me
4:Young at Heart
5:I Get So Lonely
6:Cross Over the Bridge
7:Stranger in Paradise
8:Oh, My Papa
9:Changing Partners
10:Heart of My Heart

Apr. 17, 1954

1:Young at Heart
2:Make Love to Me
3:Wanted
4:Secret Love
5:I Get So Lonely
6:Cross Over the Bridge
7:Answer Me, My Love *
8:Stranger in Paradise
9:Oh, My Papa
10:Heart of My Heart

Apr. 24, 1954

1:Young at Heart
2:Wanted
3:Answer Me, My Love
4:Make Love to Me
5:Secret Love
6:Cross Over the Bridge
7:I Get So Lonely
8:A Girl, A Girl *
9:Man With the Banjo *
10:Oh, My Papa

May 1, 1954

1:Wanted
2:Young at Heart
3:Make Love to Me
4:Cross Over the Bridge
5:I Get So Lonely
6:Secret Love
7:Answer Me, My Love
8:Man With the Banjo
9:A Girl, A Girl
10:Oh, My Papa

May 8, 1954

1:Wanted
2:Young at Heart
3:Cross Over the Bridge
4:Make Love to Me
5:I Get So Lonely
6:Answer Me, My Love
7:Secret Love
8:A Girl, A Girl
9:Man With the Banjo
10:Here *

May 15, 1954

1:Wanted
2:Young at Heart
3:Make Love to Me
4:I Get So Lonely
5:Cross Over the Bridge
6:Answer Me, My Love
7:Here
8:Secret Love
9:A Girl, A Girl
10:Man With the Banjo

May 22, 1954

1:Wanted
2:Young at Heart
3:Make Love to Me
4:I Get So Lonely
5:Answer Me, My Love
6:Here
7:Cross Over the Bridge
8:Man With the Banjo
9:Secret Love
10:A Girl, A Girl

May 29, 1954

1:Wanted
2:Answer Me, My Love
3:Young at Heart
4:Little Things Mean a Lot *
5:Cross Over the Bridge
6:I Get So Lonely
7:Make Love to Me
8:Here
9:Man With the Banjo
10:Three Coins in the Fountain *

June 5, 1954

1:Wanted
2:Three Coins in the Fountain
3:Young at Heart
4:Little Things Mean a Lot
5:I Get So Lonely
6:The Happy Wanderer *
7:Answer Me, My Love
8:Cross Over the Bridge
9:Make Love to Me
10:Here

June 12, 1954

1:Little Things Mean a Lot
2:Three Coins in the Fountain
3:Wanted
4:The Happy Wanderer
5:I Get So Lonely
6:Hernando's Hideaway *
7:Young at Heart
8:Answer Me, My Love
9:Cross Over the Bridge
10:Make Love to Me

June 19, 1954

1:Three Coins in the Fountain
2:Little Things Mean a Lot
3:Wanted
4:Hernando's Hideaway
5:Young at Heart
6:Make Love to Me
7:Answer Me, My Love
8:The Happy Wanderer
9:I Get So Lonely
10:Cross Over the Bridge

June 26, 1954

1:Little Things Mean a Lot
2:Three Coins in the Fountain
3:Hernando's Hideaway
4:The Happy Wanderer
5:Wanted
6:Young at Heart
7:I Get So Lonely
8:Make Love to Me
9:Answer Me, My Love
10:If You Love Me, Really Love Me *

July 3, 1954

1:Three Coins in the Fountain
2:Little Things Mean a Lot
3:Hernando's Hideaway
4:The Happy Wanderer
5:Answer Me, My Love
6:Wanted
7:If You Love Me, Really Love Me
8:Young at Heart
9:I Get So Lonely
10:Make Love to Me

July 10, 1954

1:Little Things Mean a Lot
2:Hernando's Hideaway
3:Three Coins in the Fountain
4:The Happy Wanderer
5:If You Love Me, Really Love Me
6:Wanted
7:Young at Heart
8:Answer Me, My Love
9:I Get So Lonely
10:Make Love to Me

July 17, 1954

1:Three Coins in the Fountain
2:Little Things Mean a Lot
3:Hernando's Hideaway
4:The Happy Wanderer
5:If You Love Me, Really Love Me
6:The Little Shoemaker *
7:I Understand Just How You Feel *
8:Wanted
9:Young at Heart
10:Answer Me, My Love

July 24, 1954

1:Little Things Mean a Lot
2:Hernando's Hideaway
3:Three Coins in the Fountain
4:If You Love Me, Really Love Me
5:The Happy Wanderer
6:The Little Shoemaker
7:I Understand Just How You Feel
8:Young at Heart
9:Wanted
10:Answer Me, My Love

July 31, 1954

1:Little Things Mean a Lot
2:Hernando's Hideaway
3:Three Coins in the Fountain
4:The Little Shoemaker
5:The Happy Wanderer
6:Hey, There *
7:Sh-Boom *
8:I Understand Just How You Feel
9:If You Love Me, Really Love Me
10:Answer Me, My Love

Aug. 7, 1954

1:Three Coins in the Fountain
2:Hernando's Hideaway
3:Little Things Mean a Lot
4:The Little Shoemaker
5:Hey, There
6:Sh-Boom
7:I Understand Just How You Feel
8:The Happy Wanderer
9:If You Love Me, Really Love Me
10:Answer Me, My Love

Aug. 14, 1954

1:Hernando's Hideaway
2:Hey, There
3:The Little Shoemaker
4:Little Things Mean a Lot
5:Three Coins in the Fountain
6:The High and the Mighty *
7:Sh-Boom
8:I Understand Just How You Feel
9:The Happy Wanderer
10:If You Love Me, Really Love Me

Aug. 21, 1954

1:Little Things Mean a Lot
2:Hey, There
3:Sh-Boom
4:The Little Shoemaker
5:The High and the Mighty
6:Hernando's Hideaway
7:Three Coins in the Fountain
8:If You Love Me, Really Love Me
9:I Understand Just How You Feel
10:The Happy Wanderer

Aug. 28, 1954

1:Hey, There
2:The High and the Mighty
3:Sh-Boom
4:The Little Shoemaker
5:Hernando's Hideaway
6:Little Things Mean a Lot
7:Three Coins in the Fountain
8:If You Love Me, Really Love Me
9:I Understand Just How You Feel
10:Goodnight, Sweetheart, Goodnight *

Sept. 4, 1954

1:Hey, There
2:The High and the Mighty
3:The Little Shoemaker
4:Sh-Boom
5:In the Chapel in the Moonlight *
6:Little Things Mean a Lot
7:Hernando's Hideaway
8:Three Coins in the Fountain
9:If You Love Me, Really Love Me
10:Goodnight,Sweetheart, Goodnight

Sept. 11, 1954

1:Hey, There
2:The High and the Mighty
3:The Little Shoemaker
4:Sh-Boom
5:In the Chapel in the Moonlight
6:Little Things Mean a Lot
7:Hernando's Hideaway
8:Goodnight, Sweetheart, Goodnight
9:If You Love Me, Really Love Me
10:I'm a Fool to Care *

Sept. 18, 1954

1:Hey, There
2:The High and the Mighty
3:The Little Shoemaker
4:Sh-Boom
5:In the Chapel in the Moonlight
6:Little Things Mean a Lot
7:This Ole House *
8:Hernando's Hideaway
9:I'm a Fool to Care
10:Goodnight, Sweetheart, Goodnight

Sept. 25, 1954

1:Hey, There
2:The High and the Mighty
3:Sh-Boom
4:The Little Shoemaker
5:If I Give My Heart to You *
6:Skokiaan *
7:They Were Doin' the Mambo *
8:In the Chapel in the Moonlight
9:Little Things Mean a Lot
10:This Ole House

Oct. 2, 1954

1:Hey, There
2:The High and the Mighty
3:If I Give My Heart to You
4:The Little Shoemaker
5:Sh-Boom
6:Skokiaan
7:This Ole House
8:They Were Doin' the Mambo
9:In the Chapel in the Moonlight
10:Little Things Mean a Lot

Oct. 9, 1954

1:Hey, There
2:If I Give My Heart to You
3:The High and the Mighty
4:Skokiaan
5:This Ole House
6:Sh-Boom
7:I Need You Now *
8:The Little Shoemaker
9:They Were Doin' the Mambo
10:In the Chapel in the Moonlight

Oct. 16, 1954

1:Hey, There
2:If I Give My Heart to You
3:The High and the Mighty
4:I Need You Now
5:Skokiaan
6:This Ole House
7:Sh-Boom
8:In the Chapel in the Moonlight
9:They Were Doin' the Mambo
10:The Little Shoemaker

Oct. 23, 1954

1:Hey, There
2:This Ole House
3:I Need You Now
4:If I Give My Heart to You
5:Skokiaan
6:The High and the Mighty
7:Papa Loves Mambo *
8:Sh-Boom
9:In the Chapel in the Moonlight
10:They Were Doin' the Mambo

Oct. 30, 1954

1:I Need You Now
2:Hey, There
3:If I Give My Heart to You
4:Papa Loves Mambo
5:This Ole House
6:The High and the Mighty
7:Count Your Blessings *
8:Skokiaan
9:Sh-Boom
10:In the Chapel in the Moonlight

Nov. 6, 1954

1:If I Give My Heart to You
2:I Need You Now
3:This Ole House
4:Hold My Hand *
5:Hey, There
6:Papa Loves Mambo
7:Skokiaan
8:The High and the Mighty
9:Count Your Blessings
10:In the Chapel in the Moonlight

Nov. 13, 1954

1:Hey, There
2:I Need You Now
3:If I Give My Heart to You
4:Papa Loves Mambo
5:Count Your Blessings
6:This Ole House
7:Mister Sandman *
8:Hold My Hand
9:Skokiaan
10:The High and the Mighty

Nov. 20, 1954

1:If I Give My Heart to You
2:Hey, There
3:Papa Loves Mambo
4:This Ole House
5:Count Your Blessings
6:Mister Sandman
7:I Need You Now
8:Hold My Hand
9:The High and the Mighty
10:Skokiaan

Nov. 27, 1954

1:Mister Sandman
2:Papa Loves Mambo
3:I Need You Now
4:If I Give My Heart to You
5:Count Your Blessings
6:This Ole House
7:Teach Me Tonight *
8:Hey, There
9:Hold My Hand
10:The High and the Mighty

Dec. 4, 1954

1:Mister Sandman
2:Count Your Blessings
3:If I Give My Heart to You
4:This Ole House
5:Teach Me Tonight
6:Papa Loves Mambo
7:I Need You Now
8:Hold My Hand
9:The High and the Mighty
10:Hey, There

Dec. 11, 1954

1:Teach Me Tonight
2:Mister Sandman
3:Count Your Blessings
4:Papa Loves Mambo
5:If I Give My Heart to You
6:Let Me Go, Lover *
7:The Naughty Lady of Shady Lane *
8:This Ole House
9:I Need You Now
10:Hold My Hand

Dec. 18, 1954

1:Mister Sandman
2:Teach Me Tonight
3:Let Me Go, Lover
4:Count Your Blessings
5:Papa Loves Mambo
6:The Naughty Lady of Shady Lane
7:I Need You Now
8:If I Give My Heart to You
9:Hold My Hand
10:This Ole House

Dec. 25, 1954

1:Mister Sandman
2:Let Me Go, Lover
3:Count Your Blessings
4:The Naughty Lady of Shady Lane
5:I Need You Now
6:Teach Me Tonight
7:Papa Loves Mambo
8:Hold My Hand
9:This Ole House
10:If I Give My Heart to You

1955

It was just background music from one of the year's better movies, *The Blackboard Jungle*, but enough kids played it enough times to land it on the Hit Parade one July night—and it signaled the beginning of the end for an entire era of popular music. The song was the raucous "Rock Around the Clock." The Big Beat had a toehold.

Still, the top songs of the year, tied with nine weeks apiece as Number One, were "The Yellow Rose of Texas" and "The Ballad of Davy Crockett."

The latter had come from TV, where Fess Parker had created a national craze with coonskin caps. Television that year opened up a new career for bandleader Lawrence Welk, and it hooked the nation on the first of the big TV quiz shows, "The $64,000 Question," with Hal March supplying the questions to the contestants in the isolation booth.

On Broadway the show to see that year was *Damn Yankees*, which gave the Hit Parade "Whatever Lola Wants" and "Heart." In the movies it was the low-budget sleeper, *Marty*.

The front pages told of Ike's heart attack in Denver, which sent the stock market tumbling. Albert Einstein died, Winston Churchill retired, Juan Peron was overthrown in Argentina, and the AFL-CIO merged. After twenty years on the air, "Your Hit Parade" left radio, leaving everyone to watch the TV version.

It was a year of tragedy, when a disabled racing car hurtled into the crowd at Le Mans, France, killing eighty-two and injuring seventy-eight.

But it also was a year of hope—the year of the Summit Meeting at Geneva between the Big Four powers, and the year of the Salk polio vaccine.

Jan. 1, 1955

1:Mister Sandman
2:Let Me Go, Lover
3:Count Your Blessings
4:The Naughty Lady of Shady Lane
5:Papa Loves Mambo
6:Teach Me Tonight
7:I Need You Now
8:If I Give My Heart to You
9:Hold My Hand
10:This Ole House

Jan. 8, 1955

1:Let Me Go, Lover
2:Mister Sandman
3:Teach Me Tonight
4:Count Your Blessings
5:The Naughty Lady of Shady Lane
6:Papa Loves Mambo
7:I Need You Now
8:Melody of Love *
9:This Ole House
10:Hold My Hand

Jan. 15, 1955

1:Mister Sandman
2:The Naughty Lady of Shady Lane
3:Let Me Go, Lover
4:Teach Me Tonight
5:Count Your Blessings
6:Melody of Love
7:Make Yourself Comfortable *
8:Papa Loves Mambo
9:I Need You Now
10:Hold My Hand

Jan. 22, 1955

1:Mister Sandman
2:Let Me Go, Lover
3:Teach Me Tonight
4:The Naughty Lady of Shady Lane
5:Melody of Love
6:Hearts of Stone *
7:Count Your Blessings
8:Make Yourself Comfortable
9:Papa Loves Mambo
10:I Need You Now

Jan. 29, 1955

1:Let Me Go, Lover
2:Mister Sandman
3:Melody of Love
4:The Naughty Lady of Shady Lane
5:Hearts of Stone
6:Teach Me Tonight
7:Count Your Blessings
8:Make Yourself Comfortable
9:I Need You Now
10:Papa Loves Mambo

Feb. 5, 1955

1:Melody of Love
2:Let Me Go, Lover
3:Mister Sandman
4:The Naughty Lady of Shady Lane
5:Make Yourself Comfortable
6:Hearts of Stone
7:That's All I Want From You *
8:Teach Me Tonight
9:Count Your Blessings
10:I Need You Now

Feb. 12, 1955

1:Mister Sandman
2:Melody of Love
3:Let Me Go, Lover
4:Sincerely *
5:The Naughty Lady of Shady Lane
6:Hearts of Stone
7:That's All I Want From You
8:Make Yourself Comfortable
9:Teach Me Tonight
10:Count Your Blessings

Feb. 19, 1955

1:Melody of Love
2:Hearts of Stone
3:Mister Sandman
4:Let Me Go, Lover
5:Sincerely
6:Tweedle Dee *
7:That's All I Want From You
8:The Naughty Lady of Shady Lane
9:Make Yourself Comfortable
10:Teach Me Tonight

* Newcomer

Feb. 26, 1955

1:Melody of Love
2:Hearts of Stone
3:That's All I Want From You
4:Mister Sandman
5:Ko Ko Mo *
6:Sincerely
7:Tweedle Dee
8:Let Me Go, Lover
9:The Naughty Lady of Shady Lane
10:Make Yourself Comfortable

Mar. 5, 1955

1:Melody of Love
2:Sincerely
3:Tweedle Dee
4:Hearts of Stone
5:That's All I Want From You
6:Mister Sandman
7:Ko Ko Mo
8:Let Me Go, Lover
9:Make Yourself Comfortable
10:The Naughty Lady of Shady Lane

Mar. 12, 1955

1:Melody of Love
2:Ko Ko Mo
3:Sincerely
4:Tweedle Dee
5:Hearts of Stone
6:That's All I Want From You
7:Open Up Your Heart *
8:Mister Sandman
9:Let Me Go, Lover
10:The Naughty Lady of Shady Lane

Mar. 19, 1955

1:Tweedle Dee
2:Melody of Love
3:The Ballad of Davy Crockett *
4:Sincerely
5:Ko Ko Mo
6:That's All I Want From You
7:Mister Sandman
8:Hearts of Stone
9:Open Up Your Heart
10:Let Me Go, Lover

Mar. 26, 1955

1:Melody of Love
2:Sincerely
3:The Ballad of Davy Crockett
4:Tweedle Dee
5:How Important Can It Be? *
6:Ko Ko Mo
7:That's All I Want From You
8:Mister Sandman
9:Hearts of Stone
10:Open Up Your Heart

Apr. 2, 1955

1:The Ballad of Davy Crockett
2:Tweedle Dee
3:Melody of Love
4:How Important Can It Be?
5:Sincerely
6:Ko Ko Mo
7:That's All I Want From You
8:Mister Sandman
9:Hearts of Stone
10:Open Up Your Heart

Apr. 9, 1955

1:The Ballad of Davy Crockett
2:Tweedle Dee
3:Melody of Love
4:Sincerely
5:Ko Ko Mo
6:How Important Can It Be?
7:That's All I Want From You
8:Hearts of Stone
9:Mister Sandman
10:Cherry Pink and Apple Blossom White *

Apr. 16, 1955

1:The Ballad of Davy Crockett
2:Melody of Love
3:That's All I Want From You
4:Tweedle Dee
5:How Important Can It Be?
6:Sincerely
7:Cherry Pink and Apple Blossom White
8:Ko Ko Mo
9:Hearts of Stone
10:Mister Sandman

Apr. 23, 1955

1:The Ballad of Davy Crockett
2:Melody of Love
3:Cherry Pink and Apple Blossom White
4:Tweedle Dee
5:Sincerely
6:Dance With Me, Henry *
7:How Important Can It Be?
8:Ko Ko Mo
9:Hearts of Stone
10:That's All I Want From You

Apr. 30, 1955

1:The Ballad of Davy Crockett
2:Cherry Pink and Apple Blossom White
3:Melody of Love
4:Tweedle Dee
5:Unchained Melody *
6:How Important Can It Be?
7:Dance With Me, Henry
8:Sincerely
9:Ko Ko Mo
10:Hearts of Stone

May 7, 1955

1:The Ballad of Davy Crockett
2:Unchained Melody
3:Cherry Pink and Apple Blossom White
4:Dance With Me, Henry
5:Tweedle Dee
6:Melody of Love
7:How Important Can It Be?
8:Sincerely
9:Hearts of Stone
10:Ko Ko Mo

May 14, 1955

1:The Ballad of Davy Crockett
2:Cherry Pink and Apple Blossom White
3:Unchained Melody
4:Tweedle Dee
5:Melody of Love
6:Dance With Me, Henry
7:Whatever Lola Wants *
8:How Important Can It Be?
9:Sincerely
10:Ko Ko Mo

May 21, 1955

1:The Ballad of Davy Crockett
2:Unchained Melody
3:Cherry Pink and Apple Blossom White
4:Dance With Me, Henry
5:Melody of Love
6:Tweedle Dee
7:Whatever Lola Wants
8:Sincerely
9:How Important Can It Be?
10:Ko Ko Mo

May 28, 1955

1:The Ballad of Davy Crockett
2:Cherry Pink and Apple Blossom White
3:Unchained Melody
4:Dance With Me, Henry
5:Whatever Lola Wants
6:Tweedle Dee
7:Melody of Love
8:Heart *
9:Sincerely
10:How Important Can It Be?

June 4, 1955

1:Unchained Melody
2:The Ballad of Davy Crockett
3:Cherry Pink and Apple Blossom White
4:Whatever Lola Wants
5:Dance With Me, Henry
6:Heart
7:Honey-Babe *
8:Tweedle Dee
9:Melody of Love
10:How Important Can It Be?

June 11, 1955

1:Unchained Melody
2:Cherry Pink and Apple Blossom White
3:The Ballad of Davy Crockett
4:Dance With Me, Henry
5:Whatever Lola Wants
6:Heart
7:Learnin' the Blues *
8:Honey-Babe
9:Tweedle Dee
10:Melody of Love

June 18, 1955

1:Unchained Melody
2:Cherry Pink and Apple Blossom White
3:The Ballad of Davy Crockett
4:Something's Gotta Give *
5:Whatever Lola Wants
6:Honey-Babe
7:Heart
8:Learnin' the Blues
9:Dance With Me, Henry
10:Tweedle Dee

June 25, 1955

1:Cherry Pink and Apple Blossom White
2:Unchained Melody
3:Heart
4:Learnin' the Blues
5:Something's Gotta Give
6:Whatever Lola Wants
7:Dance With Me, Henry
8:The Ballad of Davy Crockett
9:Honey-Babe
10:Tweedle Dee

July 2, 1955

1:Unchained Melody
2:Cherry Pink and Apple Blossom White
3:The Ballad of Davy Crockett
4:Learnin' the Blues
5:Something's Gotta Give
6:Heart
7:Honey-Babe
8:Whatever Lola Wants
9:Dance With Me, Henry
10:Tweedle Dee

July 9, 1955

1:Unchained Melody
2:Cherry Pink and Apple Blossom White
3:Learnin' the Blues
4:Something's Gotta Give
5:Rock Around the Clock *
6:Heart
7:A Blossom Fell *
8:The Ballad of Davy Crockett
9:Honey-Babe
10:Whatever Lola Wants

July 16, 1955

1:Unchained Melody
2:Cherry Pink and Apple Blossom White
3:Something's Gotta Give
4:Learnin' the Blues
5:A Blossom Fell
6:Rock Around the Clock
7:Honey-Babe
8:Heart
9:The Ballad of Davy Crockett
10:Whatever Lola Wants

July 23, 1955

1:Something's Gotta Give
2:Unchained Melody
3:Cherry Pink and Apple Blossom White
4:Rock Around the Clock
5:Learnin' the Blues
6:A Blossom Fell
7:Heart
8:Honey-Babe
9:The Ballad of Davy Crockett
10:Whatever Lola Wants

July 30, 1955

1:Unchained Melody
2:Rock Around the Clock
3:Learnin' the Blues
4:Something's Gotta Give
5:Hard to Get *
6:Cherry Pink and Apple Blossom White
7:Sweet and Gentle *
8:A Blossom Fell
9:Heart
10:Honey-Babe

Aug. 6, 1955

1:Learnin' the Blues
2:Rock Around the Clock
3:Hard to Get
4:Unchained Melody
5:Sweet and Gentle
6:Something's Gotta Give
7:Cherry Pink and Apple Blossom White
8:A Blossom Fell
9:Heart
10:Honey-Babe

Aug. 13, 1955

1:Rock Around the Clock
2:Learnin' the Blues
3:Unchained Melody
4:Hard to Get
5:Something's Gotta Give
6:The Yellow Rose of Texas *
7:Sweet and Gentle
8:Cherry Pink and Apple Blossom White
9:A Blossom Fell
10:Heart

Aug. 20, 1955

1:Rock Around the Clock
2:Learnin' the Blues
3:The Yellow Rose of Texas
4:Hard to Get
5:Something's Gotta Give
6:Unchained Melody
7:A Blossom Fell
8:Sweet and Gentle
9:Cherry Pink and Apple Blossom White
10:Heart

Aug. 27, 1955

1:The Yellow Rose of Texas
2:Rock Around the Clock
3:Ain't That a Shame? *
4:A Blossom Fell
5:Hard to Get
6:Hummingbird *
7:Wake the Town and Tell the People *
8:Learnin' the Blues
9:Something's Gotta Give
10:Unchained Melody

Sept. 3, 1955

1:The Yellow Rose of Texas
2:Rock Around the Clock
3:Ain't That a Shame?
4:Hard to Get
5:Love Is a Many-Splendored Thing *
6:Learnin' the Blues
7:Seventeen *
8:Hummingbird
9:Wake the Town and Tell the People
10:A Blossom Fell

Sept. 10, 1955

1:The Yellow Rose of Texas
2:Hard to Get
3:Seventeen
4:Ain't That a Shame?
5:Learnin' the Blues
6:Love Is a Many-Splendored Thing
7:Rock Around the Clock
8:Wake the Town and Tell the People
9:Hummingbird
10:A Blossom Fell

Sept. 17, 1955

1:The Yellow Rose of Texas
2:Love Is a Many-Splendored Thing
3:Wake the Town and Tell the People
4:Ain't That a Shame?
5:Autumn Leaves *
6:Seventeen
7:Rock Around the Clock
8:Hard to Get
9:Learnin' the Blues
10:Hummingbird

Sept. 24, 1955

1:The Yellow Rose of Texas
2:Ain't That a Shame?
3:Love Is a Many-Splendored Thing
4:Autumn Leaves
5:Wake the Town and Tell the People
6:Hard to Get
7:Seventeen
8:Rock Around the Clock
9:Hummingbird
10:Learnin' the Blues

Oct. 1, 1955

1:The Yellow Rose of Texas
2:Autumn Leaves
3:Love Is a Many-Splendored Thing
4:Wake the Town and Tell the People
5:Seventeen
6:The Longest Walk *
7:Rock Around the Clock
8:Hard to Get
9:Ain't That a Shame?
10:Hummingbird

Oct. 8, 1955

1:The Yellow Rose of Texas
2:Love Is a Many-Splendored Thing
3:Autumn Leaves
4:Seventeen
5:Wake the Town and Tell the People
6:The Bible Tells Me So *
7:Ain't That a Shame?
8:The Longest Walk
9:Rock Around the Clock
10:Hard to Get

Oct. 15, 1955

1:The Yellow Rose of Texas
2:Love Is a Many-Splendored Thing
3:Autumn Leaves
4:The Longest Walk
5:Tina Marie *
6:Wake the Town and Tell the People
7:Seventeen
8:The Bible Tells Me So
9:Ain't That a Shame?
10:Rock Around the Clock

Oct. 22, 1955

1:The Yellow Rose of Texas
2:Love Is a Many-Splendored Thing
3:Autumn Leaves
4:Wake the Town and Tell the People
5:The Bible Tells Me So
6:The Longest Walk
7:Seventeen
8:Tina Marie
9:Ain't That a Shame?
10:Rock Around the Clock

Oct. 29, 1955

1:Autumn Leaves
2:Love Is a Many-Splendored Thing
3:The Yellow Rose of Texas
4:Suddenly There's a Valley *
5:Seventeen
6:The Bible Tells Me So
7:Moments to Remember *
8:Wake the Town and Tell the People
9:The Longest Walk
10:Tina Marie

Nov. 5, 1955

1:Love Is a Many-Splendored Thing
2:Autumn Leaves
3:The Yellow Rose of Texas
4:Moments to Remember
5:Suddenly There's a Valley
6:Seventeen
7:He *
8:Wake the Town and Tell the People
9:Tina Marie
10:The Longest Walk

Nov. 12, 1955

1:Autumn Leaves
2:Love Is a Many-Splendored Thing
3:The Yellow Rose of Texas
4:Suddenly There's a Valley
5:Moments to Remember
6:Love and Marriage *
7:Shifting, Whispering Sands *
8:He
9:Seventeen
10:Wake the Town and Tell the People

Nov. 19, 1955

1:Love Is a Many-Splendored Thing
2:Autumn Leaves
3:He
4:Suddenly There's a Valley
5:Moments to Remember
6:Sixteen Tons *
7:Love and Marriage
8:The Yellow Rose of Texas
9:Shifting, Whispering Sands
10:Seventeen

Nov. 26, 1955

1:Autumn Leaves
2:Love Is a Many-Splendored Thing
3:Love and Marriage
4:Sixteen Tons
5:Moments to Remember
6:Suddenly There's a Valley
7:He
8:Shifting, Whispering Sands
9:Seventeen
10:The Yellow Rose of Texas

Dec. 3, 1955

1:Sixteen Tons
2:Autumn Leaves
3:Love Is a Many-Splendored Thing
4:Moments to Remember
5:He
6:Love and Marriage
7:Only You *
8:Suddenly There's a Valley
9:Shifting, Whispering Sands
10:Seventeen

Dec. 10, 1955

1:Sixteen Tons
2:Autumn Leaves
3:Love Is a Many-Splendored Thing
4:Love and Marriage
5:I Hear You Knocking *
6:He
7:Moments to Remember
8:Only You
9:Suddenly There's a Valley
10:Memories Are Made of This *

Dec. 17, 1955

1:Sixteen Tons
2:Autumn Leaves
3:Love and Marriage
4:Moments to Remember
5:Love Is a Many-Splendored Thing
6:He
7:Only You
8:Memories Are Made of This
9:I Hear You Knocking
10:Suddenly There's a Valley

Dec. 24, 1955

1:Sixteen Tons
2:Autumn Leaves
3:Memories Are Made of This
4:Love and Marriage
5:Love Is a Many-Splendored Thing
6:He
7:Moments to Remember
8:Only You
9:I Hear You Knocking
10:Suddenly There's a Valley

Dec. 31, 1955

1:Sixteen Tons
2:Memories Are Made of This
3:Autumn Leaves
4:He
5:Moments to Remember
6:Love Is a Many-Splendored Thing
7:Love and Marriage
8:I Hear You Knocking
9:Suddenly There's a Valley
10:Only You

1956

Just as the two biggest show-business impacts of 1943 had been a singer (Frank Sinatra) and a Broadway musical *(Oklahoma!)*, the same two categories marked 1956 with a similar impact. This time it was Elvis Presley and *My Fair Lady*.

The young Memphis truck driver with sideburns, guitar, and fluid drive in his pelvis revolutionized the music world in 1956, pushed "Your Hit Parade" closer to its eventual extinction, and touched off the most fanatical, screaming, fainting cult of feminine followers since Sinatra's bobby-soxers. Virtually everything he recorded landed on the Hit Parade, turning the Saturday night songfest into a procession of titles like "Heartbreak Hotel," "Blue Suede Shoes," "Hound Dog," and, on a quieter note, "Love Me Tender."

Yet, if it was the year of rock 'n' roll, it also was the year of Lerner 'n' Loewe. Their *My Fair Lady*, later destined to break the Broadway long-run record for a musical set by *Oklahoma!*, gave the Hit Parade "On the Street Where You Live" and "I Could Have Danced All Night."

For all that, the top song of the year was "Canadian Sunset," with seven weeks as Number One. ("Singing the Blues" also tied that figure, but the majority of its run carried over into 1957.)

Revivals for the year included 1934's "Moonglow," 1939's "My Prayer," and 1940's "Blueberry Hill."

Egypt seized the Suez Canal, Grace Metalious was seizing royalties with her novel, *Peyton Place,* and Ike was seizing the White House for a second term by nine million votes. It was the year two airliners collided and crashed into the Grand Canyon, and the ocean liner *Andrea Doria* went to the bottom forty-five miles south of Nantucket Island, Massachusetts, after a collision with the *Stockholm*.

The Hungarian revolt was crushed by Soviet tanks, a Marine drill instructor was convicted of negligent homicide after six recruits drowned in an enforced march through a stream at Parris Island, South Carolina, and Grace Kelly of Hollywood became Princess Grace of Monaco.

In such a year there was nothing left except for someone to pitch the first perfect game in the history of the World Series. Don Larsen of the Yankees did it against Brooklyn.

Jan. 7, 1956

1:Sixteen Tons
2:Memories Are Made of This
3:Love and Marriage
4:Autumn Leaves
5:Moments to Remember
6:He
7:It's Almost Tomorrow *
8:Love Is a Many-Splendored Thing
9:Only You
10:Suddenly There's a Valley

Jan. 14, 1956

1:Sixteen Tons
2:Memories Are Made of This
3:Moments to Remember
4:Love and Marriage
5:A Woman in Love *
6:It's Almost Tomorrow
7:Autumn Leaves
8:He
9:Love Is a Many-Splendored Thing
10:Only You

Jan. 21, 1956

1:Memories Are Made of This
2:Sixteen Tons
3:He
4:Autumn Leaves
5:Love and Marriage
6:Lisbon Antigua *
7:Moments to Remember
8:A Woman in Love
9:It's Almost Tomorrow
10:Only You

Jan. 28, 1956

1:Memories Are Made of This
2:Sixteen Tons
3:It's Almost Tomorrow
4:Rock and Roll Waltz *
5:The Great Pretender *
6:Lisbon Antigua
7:Autumn Leaves
8:He
9:Love and Marriage
10:Moments to Remember

Feb. 4, 1956

1:Memories Are Made of This
2:Sixteen Tons
3:Lisbon Antigua
4:Rock and Roll Waltz
5:The Great Pretender
6:Love and Marriage
7:Band of Gold *
8:Autumn Leaves
9:He
10:It's Almost Tomorrow

Feb. 11, 1956

1:Memories Are Made of This
2:Rock and Roll Waltz
3:Sixteen Tons
4:Lisbon Antigua
5:The Great Pretender
6:Band of Gold
7:He
8:It's Almost Tomorrow
9:Love and Marriage
10:Autumn Leaves

Feb. 18, 1956

1:Rock and Roll Waltz
2:Lisbon Antigua
3:The Great Pretender
4:Memories Are Made of This
5:Sixteen Tons
6:It's Almost Tomorrow
7:Dungaree Doll *
8:Band of Gold
9:He
10:Love and Marriage

Feb. 25, 1956

1:Lisbon Antigua
2:Rock and Roll Waltz
3:Memories Are Made of This
4:The Great Pretender
5:Band of Gold
6:Moritat *
7:Sixteen Tons
8:Dungaree Doll
9:It's Almost Tomorrow
10:He

* Newcomer

Mar. 3, 1956

1:Rock and Roll Waltz
2:Lisbon Antigua
3:The Great Pretender
4:No, Not Much *
5:Memories Are Made of This
6:Moritat
7:Band of Gold
8:Sixteen Tons
9:Dungaree Doll
10:It's Almost Tomorrow

Mar. 10, 1956

1:Lisbon Antigua
2:Rock and Roll Waltz
3:No, Not Much
4:Poor People of Paris *
5:Moritat
6:Memories Are Made of This
7:The Great Pretender
8:Band of Gold
9:Sixteen Tons
10:Dungaree Doll

Mar. 17, 1956

1:Lisbon Antigua
2:Rock and Roll Waltz
3:No, Not Much
4:The Great Pretender
5:Poor People of Paris
6:Moritat
7:Band of Gold
8:Memories Are Made of This
9:Dungaree Doll
10:Sixteen Tons

Mar. 24, 1956

1:Rock and Roll Waltz
2:Poor People of Paris
3:Lisbon Antigua
4:Moritat
5:No, Not Much
6:The Great Pretender
7:Memories Are Made of This
8:Band of Gold
9:Sixteen Tons
10:Dungaree Doll

Mar. 31, 1956

1:Lisbon Antigua
2:Rock and Roll Waltz
3:No, Not Much
4:Poor People of Paris
5:Moritat
6:Hot Diggity *
7:The Great Pretender
8:Memories Are Made of This
9:Band of Gold
10:Dungaree Doll

Apr. 7, 1956

1:Poor People of Paris
2:No, Not Much
3:Hot Diggity
4:Lisbon Antigua
5:Moritat
6:Rock and Roll Waltz
7:The Great Pretender
8:Dungaree Doll
9:Band of Gold
10:Memories Are Made of This

Apr. 14, 1956

1:Poor People of Paris
2:Lisbon Antigua
3:Moritat
4:Hot Diggity
5:No, Not Much
6:Rock and Roll Waltz
7:Blue Suede Shoes *
8:The Great Pretender
9:Memories Are Made of This
10:Band of Gold

Apr. 21, 1956

1:Poor People of Paris
2:Lisbon Antigua
3:No, Not Much
4:Hot Diggity
5:Why Do Fools Fall in Love? *
6:Rock and Roll Waltz
7:Blue Suede Shoes
8:Moritat
9:The Great Pretender
10:Band of Gold

Apr. 28, 1956

1:Poor People of Paris
2:Hot Diggity
3:Blue Suede Shoes
4:Mister Wonderful *
5:Heartbreak Hotel *
6:Lisbon Antigua
7:Rock and Roll Waltz
8:No, Not Much
9:Why Do Fools Fall in Love?
10:Moritat

May 5, 1956

1:Poor People of Paris
2:Blue Suede Shoes
3:Hot Diggity
4:Moonglow *
5:Lisbon Antigua
6:Heartbreak Hotel
7:Moritat
8:Mister Wonderful
9:Why Do Fools Fall in Love?
10:Picnic *

May 12, 1956

1:Poor People of Paris
2:Blue Suede Shoes
3:Hot Diggity
4:Heartbreak Hotel
5:Moonglow
6:Picnic
7:Ivory Tower *
8:Mister Wonderful
9:Lisbon Antigua
10:Why Do Fools Fall in Love?

May 19, 1956

1:Heartbreak Hotel
2:Moonglow
3:Hot Diggity
4:Poor People of Paris
5:Blue Suede Shoes
6:Picnic
7:Ivory Tower
8:Lisbon Antigua
9:Mister Wonderful
10:Why Do Fools Fall in Love?

May 26, 1956

1:Heartbreak Hotel
2:Moonglow
3:Hot Diggity
4:Poor People of Paris
5:Ivory Tower
6:Picnic
7:Blue Suede Shoes
8:Mister Wonderful
9:Why Do Fools Fall in Love?
10:Lisbon Antigua

June 2, 1956

1:Moonglow
2:Picnic
3:Hot Diggity
4:Standing On the Corner *
5:Heartbreak Hotel
6:On the Street Where You Live *
7:Ivory Tower
8:Poor People of Paris
9:Blue Suede Shoes
10:Mister Wonderful

June 9, 1956

1:Picnic
2:Standing On the Corner
3:Moonglow
4:Ivory Tower
5:The Wayward Wind *
6:Hot Diggity
7:Heartbreak Hotel
8:On the Street Where You Live
9:Poor People of Paris
10:Blue Suede Shoes

June 16, 1956

1:Moonglow
2:Picnic
3:The Wayward Wind
4:Standing On the Corner
5:Ivory Tower
6:On the Street Where You Live
7:Heartbreak Hotel
8:Hot Diggity
9:Blue Suede Shoes
10:Poor People of Paris

June 23, 1956

1:Picnic
2:Moonglow
3:The Wayward Wind
4:Standing On the Corner
5:On the Street Where You Live
6:Ivory Tower
7:I Could Have Danced All Night *
8:Heartbreak Hotel
9:Hot Diggity
10:Blue Suede Shoes

June 30, 1956

1:Moonglow
2:Picnic
3:The Wayward Wind
4:On the Street Where You Live
5:Standing On the Corner
6:Ivory Tower
7:I Could Have Danced All Night
8:Heartbreak Hotel
9:Hot Diggity
10:I Almost Lost My Mind *

July 7, 1956

1:Picnic
2:Moonglow
3:Standing On the Corner
4:On the Street Where You Live
5:The Wayward Wind
6:I Almost Lost My Mind
7:Ivory Tower
8:I Could Have Danced All Night
9:Heartbreak Hotel
10:Hot Diggity

July 14, 1956

1:The Wayward Wind
2:Picnic
3:Moonglow
4:On the Street Where You Live
5:Standing On the Corner
6:I Could Have Danced All Night
7:I Almost Lost My Mind
8:Ivory Tower
9:Walk Hand in Hand *
10:I Want You, I Need You, I Love You *

July 21, 1956

1:The Wayward Wind
2:On the Street Where You Live
3:Picnic
4:Moonglow
5:Allegheny Moon *
6:Standing On the Corner
7:I Could Have Danced All Night
8:I Almost Lost My Mind
9:I Want You, I Need You, I Love You
10:Walk Hand in Hand

July 28, 1956

1:The Wayward Wind
2:On the Street Where You Live
3:Allegheny Moon
4:Moonglow
5:I Almost Lost My Mind
6:Picnic
7:Standing On the Corner
8:I Could Have Danced All Night
9:Walk Hand in Hand
10:I Want You, I Need You, I Love You

Aug. 4, 1956

1:On the Street Where You Live
2:The Wayward Wind
3:Moonglow
4:Whatever Will Be, Will Be *
5:Allegheny Moon
6:My Prayer *
7:Picnic
8:I Almost Lost My Mind
9:Standing On the Corner
10:I Could Have Danced All Night

Aug. 11, 1956

1:Whatever Will Be, Will Be
2:Allegheny Moon
3:The Wayward Wind
4:On the Street Where You Live
5:My Prayer
6:I Amost Lost My Mind
7:Canadian Sunset *
8:Moonglow
9:Picnic
10:I Could Have Danced All Night

Aug. 18, 1956

1:My Prayer
2:Whatever Will Be, Will Be
3:The Wayward Wind
4:Allegheny Moon
5:On the Street Where You Live
6:Canadian Sunset
7:I Almost Lost My Mind
8:I Could Have Danced All Night
9:Picnic
10:Moonglow

Aug. 25, 1956

1:Whatever Will Be, Will Be
2:Allegheny Moon
3:My Prayer
4:The Wayward Wind
5:I Almost Lost My Mind
6:Canadian Sunset
7:On the Street Where You Live
8:I Could Have Danced All Night
9:Hound Dog *
10:Don't Be Cruel *

Sept. 1, 1956

1:Canadian Sunset
2:Allegheny Moon
3:My Prayer
4:Whatever Will Be, Will Be
5:On the Street Where You Live
6:Hound Dog
7:The Wayward Wind
8:I Almost Lost My Mind
9:Don't Be Cruel
10:I Could Have Danced All Night

Sept. 8, 1956

1:Whatever Will Be, Will Be
2:My Prayer
3:Canadian Sunset
4:Allegheny Moon
5:Hound Dog
6:On the Street Where You Live
7:Don't Be Cruel
8:The Wayward Wind
9:I Could Have Danced All Night
10:I Almost Lost My Mind

Sept. 15, 1956

1:Canadian Sunset
2:My Prayer
3:Whatever Will Be, Will Be
4:Hound Dog
5:Don't Be Cruel
6:Allegheny Moon
7:On the Street Where You Live
8:I Could Have Danced All Night
9:The Wayward Wind
10:I Almost Lost My Mind

Sept. 22, 1956

1:Whatever Will Be, Will Be
2:Canadian Sunset
3:My Prayer
4:Allegheny Moon
5:Tonight You Belong to Me *
6:Don't Be Cruel
7:Hound Dog
8:On the Street Where You Live
9:I Could Have Danced All Night
10:I Almost Lost My Mind

Sept. 29, 1956

1:Canadian Sunset
2:Whatever Will Be, Will Be
3:Allegheny Moon
4:My Prayer
5:Hound Dog
6:Don't Be Cruel
7:Tonight You Belong to Me
8:I Could Have Danced All Night
9:On the Street Where You Live
10:Just Walking in the Rain *

Oct. 6, 1956

1:Canadian Sunset
2:Don't Be Cruel
3:Whatever Will Be, Will Be
4:Allegheny Moon
5:My Prayer
6:Hound Dog
7:Tonight You Belong to Me
8:Just Walking in the Rain
9:On the Street Where You Live
10:I Could Have Danced All Night

Oct. 13, 1956

1:Canadian Sunset
2:Don't Be Cruel
3:Tonight You Belong to Me
4:Allegheny Moon
5:Whatever Will Be, Will Be
6:Just Walking in the Rain
7:True Love *
8:My Prayer
9:Hound Dog
10:On the Street Where You Live

Oct. 20, 1956

1:Canadian Sunset
2:Tonight You Belong to Me
3:My Prayer
4:Don't Be Cruel
5:Just Walking in the Rain
6:Allegheny Moon
7:Whatever Will Be, Will Be
8:True Love
9:On the Street Where You Live
10:Hound Dog

Oct. 27, 1956

1:Canadian Sunset
2:Tonight You Belong to Me
3:True Love
4:Don't Be Cruel
5:Love Me Tender *
6:Whatever Will Be, Will Be
7:Just Walking in the Rain
8:My Prayer
9:Allegheny Moon
10:On the Street Where You Live

Nov. 3, 1956

1:Love Me Tender
2:Canadian Sunset
3:True Love
4:Green Door *
5:Friendly Persuasion *
6:Don't Be Cruel
7:Just Walking in the Rain
8:Tonight You Belong to Me
9:Whatever Will Be, Will Be
10:My Prayer

Nov. 10, 1956

1:Just Walking in the Rain
2:Canadian Sunset
3:True Love
4:Love Me Tender
5:Friendly Persuasion
6:Green Door
7:Blueberry Hill *
8:Don't Be Cruel
9:Tonight You Belong to Me
10:Whatever Will Be, Will Be

Nov. 17, 1956

1:Love Me Tender
2:True Love
3:Just Walking in the Rain
4:Canadian Sunset
5:Blueberry Hill
6:Green Door
7:Friendly Persuasion
8:Don't Be Cruel
9:Tonight You Belong to Me
10:Whatever Will Be, Will Be

Nov. 24, 1956

1:Love Me Tender
2:True Love
3:Singing the Blues *
4:Blueberry Hill
5:Cindy, Oh Cindy *
6:Green Door
7:Just Walking in the Rain
8:Canadian Sunset
9:Friendly Persuasion
10:Tonight You Belong to Me

Dec. 1, 1956

1:Love Me Tender
2:True Love
3:Green Door
4:Just Walking in the Rain
5:Singing the Blues
6:Friendly Persuasion
7:Blueberry Hill
8:Cindy, Oh Cindy
9:Canadian Sunset
10:Tonight You Belong to Me

Dec. 8, 1956

1:Love Me Tender
2:Singing the Blues
3:Green Door
4:True Love
5:Just Walking in the Rain
6:Cindy, Oh Cindy
7:Friendly Persuasion
8:Just in Time *
9:The Party's Over *
10:Blueberry Hill

Dec. 15, 1956

1:Singing the Blues
2:Love Me Tender
3:True Love
4:Just Walking in the Rain
5:Green Door
6:Blueberry Hill
7:Hey, Jealous Lover *
8:Cindy, Oh Cindy
9:Just in Time
10:The Party's Over

Dec. 22, 1956

1:Singing the Blues
2:Love Me Tender
3:Green Door
4:True Love
5:Blueberry Hill
6:Cindy, Oh Cindy
7:Just Walking in the Rain
8:Hey, Jealous Lover
9:The Party's Over
10:Just in Time

Dec. 29, 1956

1:Singing the Blues
2:Love Me Tender
3:Green Door
4:Blueberry Hill
5:True Love
6:Just Walking in the Rain
7:Cindy, Oh Cindy
8:Just in Time
9:Hey, Jealous Lover
10:The Party's Over

1957

Two new terms, neither a favorite of the American people, came into use that year—sputnik and recession. The Russians had the first, winning the race to launch the first orbiting satellite, and Americans had the latter.

Britain tested its first H-bomb, President Eisenhower sent federal troops to Little Rock, Arkansas, to enforce the Supreme Court's school integration edict, and the talk of the baseball world that year was the Milwaukee Braves, who beat the Yankees to win their very first World Series.

The talk of the United States Senate was about—and came from—Senator Strom Thurmond of South Carolina, who filibustered for twenty-four hours and eighteen minutes, eclipsing Wayne Morse's 1953 record of twenty-two hours and twenty-six minutes.

The Bridge on the River Kwai was the top Hollywood product, and late in the year Meredith Willson's *The Music Man* opened on Broadway to critical acclaim. Earlier, *West Side Story* had supplied "Tonight" to the Top Ten.

The Hit Parade didn't quite know what to do as rock 'n' roll boiled and crashed around the Top Ten charts. The adult cry began to be heard: "What will they have to look back on as romantic music of the times?" As if in answer, the teen cry was heard: "Listen, dear, they're playing our songs—'Teddy Bear,' 'All Shook Up,' and 'Raunchy.'"

Amid all the strange and new, three oldies came back to live again on the Top Ten: 1937's "So Rare," 1936's "I'm Gonna Sit Right Down and Write Myself a Letter," and 1931's "Love Letters in the Sand."

Oddly enough, considering the trend, it was the latter, popularized by Pat Boone, that tied with Debbie Reynolds's "Tammy" as the top song of 1957. Each was Number One for ten weeks.

Jan. 5, 1957

1:Singing the Blues
2:Love Me Tender
3:True Love
4:Green Door
5:Just Walking in the Rain
6:Blueberry Hill
7:Cindy, Oh Cindy
8:Hey, Jealous Lover
9:The Party's Over
10:Just in Time

Jan. 12, 1957

1:Singing the Blues
2:Love Me Tender
3:Green Door
4:True Love
5:Just Walking in the Rain
6:Blueberry Hill
7:Hey, Jealous Lover
8:Just in Time
9:The Party's Over
10:Cindy, Oh Cindy

Jan. 19, 1957

1:Singing the Blues
2:The Banana Boat Song *
3:Love Me Tender
4:Green Door
5:Blueberry Hill
6:Young Love *
7:True Love
8:Just Walking in the Rain
9:Hey, Jealous Lover
10:Just in Time

Jan. 26, 1957

1:Singing the Blues
2:The Banana Boat Song
3:Young Love
4:Don't Forbid Me *
5:True Love
6:Just Walking in the Rain
7:Love Me Tender
8:Green Door
9:Blueberry Hill
10:Hey, Jealous Lover

Feb. 2, 1957

1:The Banana Boat Song
2:Singing the Blues
3:Young Love
4:True Love
5:Don't Forbid Me
6:Blueberry Hill
7:Love Me Tender
8:Just Walking in the Rain
9:Green Door
10:Hey, Jealous Lover

Feb. 9, 1957

1:Young Love
2:The Banana Boat Song
3:Singing the Blues
4:Don't Forbid Me
5:Moonlight Gambler *
6:Blueberry Hill
7:True Love
8:Love Me Tender
9:Just Walking in the Rain
10:Green Door

Feb. 16, 1957

1:Young Love
2:Don't Forbid Me
3:The Banana Boat Song
4:Singing the Blues
5:Moonlight Gambler
6:Marianne *
7:Too Much *
8:Blueberry Hill
9:True Love
10:Love Me Tender

Feb. 23, 1957

1:Young Love
2:Don't Forbid Me
3:The Banana Boat Song
4:Marianne
5:Moonlight Gambler
6:Too Much
7:Singing the Blues
8:True Love
9:Love Me Tender
10:Blueberry Hill

* Newcomer

Mar. 2, 1957

1:Young Love
2:Marianne
3:Don't Forbid Me
4:Too Much
5:The Banana Boat Song
6:Singing the Blues
7:Moonlight Gambler
8:Blueberry Hill
9:True Love
10:Love Me Tender

Mar. 9, 1957

1:Young Love
2:Marianne
3:Don't Forbid Me
4:The Banana Boat Song
5:Too Much
6:Moonlight Gambler
7:Butterfly *
8:Singing the Blues
9:Blueberry Hill
10:True Love

Mar. 16, 1957

1:Marianne
2:Young Love
3:Butterfly
4:Don't Forbid Me
5:The Banana Boat Song
6:Round and Round *
7:Too Much
8:Moonlight Gambler
9:Singing the Blues
10:Blueberry Hill

Mar. 23, 1957

1:Marianne
2:Young Love
3:Butterfly
4:Round and Round
5:Party Doll *
6:Don't Forbid Me
7:The Banana Boat Song
8:Too Much
9:Moonlight Gambler
10:Singing the Blues

Mar. 30, 1957

1:Marianne
2:Butterfly
3:Young Love
4:Round and Round
5:Party Doll
6:The Banana Boat Song
7:Teen-Age Crush *
8:Don't Forbid Me
9:Too Much
10:Moonlight Gambler

Apr. 6, 1957

1:Round and Round
2:Butterfly
3:Marianne
4:Party Doll
5:Young Love
6:I'm Walkin' *
7:Little Darlin' *
8:Teen-Age Crush
9:The Banana Boat Song
10:Don't Forbid Me

Apr. 13, 1957

1:Round and Round
2:Butterfly
3:Marianne
4:Party Doll
5:Young Love
6:All Shook Up *
7:Little Darlin'
8:I'm Walkin'
9:Teen-Age Crush
10:The Banana Boat Song

Apr. 20, 1957

1:Round and Round
2:Butterfly
3:All Shook Up
4:Little Darlin'
5:Party Doll
6:Marianne
7:I'm Walkin'
8:Young Love
9:Teen-Age Crush
10:The Banana Boat Song

Apr. 27, 1957

1:Round and Round
2:All Shook Up
3:Marianne
4:Butterfly
5:Little Darlin'
6:Party Doll
7:I'm Walkin'
8:Young Love
9:The Banana Boat Song
10:Teen-Age Crush

May 4, 1957

1:Round and Round
2:All Shook Up
3:Little Darlin'
4:Butterfly
5:Party Doll
6:Why, Baby, Why? *
7:Gone *
8:Marianne
9:I'm Walkin'
10:Young Love

May 11, 1957

1:All Shook Up
2:Round and Round
3:Little Darlin'
4:I'm Walkin'
5:Party Doll
6:Gone
7:Butterfly
8:Why, Baby, Why?
9:Marianne
10:Young Love

May 18, 1957

1:All Shook Up
2:Round and Round
3:Little Darlin'
4:Dark Moon *
5:Party Doll
6:Gone
7:I'm Walkin'
8:Butterfly
9:Why, Baby, Why?
10:Marianne

May 25, 1957

1:Little Darlin'
2:All Shook Up
3:Round and Round
4:Dark Moon
5:Gone
6:So Rare *
7:I'm Walkin'
8:Party Doll
9:Butterfly
10:Why, Baby, Why?

June 1, 1957

1:All Shook Up
2:Dark Moon
3:Little Darlin'
4:So Rare
5:Love Letters in the Sand *
6:Round and Round
7:A White Sport Coat *
8:Gone
9:I'm Walkin'
10:Party Doll

June 8, 1957

1:Love Letters in the Sand
2:Dark Moon
3:All Shook Up
4:Little Darlin'
5:So Rare
6:School Day *
7:A White Sport Coat
8:Round and Round
9:Gone
10:I'm Walkin'

June 15, 1957

1:Love Letters in the Sand
2:So Rare
3:Dark Moon
4:All Shook Up
5:A White Sport Coat
6:Little Darlin'
7:School Day
8:Gone
9:I'm Walkin'
10:Round and Round

June 22, 1957

1:Love Letters in the Sand
2:So Rare
3:All Shook Up
4:Dark Moon
5:A White Sport Coat
6:Little Darlin'
7:Four Walls *
8:School Day
9:Round and Round
10:Gone

June 29, 1957

1:Love Letters in the Sand
2:So Rare
3:Bye Bye Love *
4:Dark Moon
5:A White Sport Coat
6:Around the World *
7:Old Cape Cod *
8:All Shook Up
9:Little Darlin'
10:Four Walls

July 6, 1957

1:Love Letters in the Sand
2:So Rare
3:Bye Bye Love
4:Dark Moon
5:Around the World
6:A White Sport Coat
7:Old Cape Cod
8:Four Walls
9:All Shook Up
10:Little Darlin'

July 13, 1957

1:Love Letters in the Sand
2:So Rare
3:Bye Bye Love
4:Around the World
5:Old Cape Cod
6:Dark Moon
7:I'm Gonna Sit Right Down and Write
8:Four Walls   Myself a Letter *
9:All Shook Up
10:A White Sport Coat

July 20, 1957

1:Love Letters in the Sand
2:So Rare
3:Bye Bye Love
4:Around the World
5:I'm Gonna Sit Right Down and Write
6:Old Cape Cod   Myself a Letter
7:It's Not For Me to Say *
8:Dark Moon
9:A White Sport Coat
10:Four Walls

July 27, 1957

1:Love Letters in the Sand
2:Around the World
3:I'm Gonna Sit Right Down and Write
4:So Rare   Myself a Letter
5:Old Cape Cod
6:Bye Bye Love
7:Teddy Bear *
8:It's Not For Me to Say
9:A White Sport Coat
10:Four Walls

Aug. 3, 1957

1:Love Letters in the Sand
2:Around the World
3:I'm Gonna Sit Right Down and Write
4:Teddy Bear   Myself a Letter
5:Old Cape Cod
6:So Rare
7:Bye Bye Love
8:It's Not For Me to Say
9:Four Walls
10:A White Sport Coat

Aug. 10, 1957

1:Love Letters in the Sand
2:Around the World
3:I'm Gonna Sit Right Down and Write
4:Bye Bye Love   Myself a Letter
5:Old Cape Cod
6:White Silver Sands *
7:Tammy *
8:Teddy Bear
9:So Rare
10:It's Not For Me to Say

Aug. 17, 1957

1:Around the World
2:Tammy
3:Love Letters in the Sand
4:I'm Gonna Sit Right Down and Write Myself
5:It's Not For Me to Say   a Letter
6:Teddy Bear
7:Bye Bye Love
8:Old Cape Cod
9:White Silver Sands
10:So Rare

Aug. 24, 1957

1:Tammy
2:Around the World
3:I'm Gonna Sit Right Down and Write Myself
4:White Silver Sands   a Letter
5:Love Letters in the Sand
6:It's Not For Me to Say
7:Bye Bye Love
8:Teddy Bear
9:Old Cape Cod
10:So Rare

Aug. 31, 1957

1:Tammy
2:Around the World
3:I'm Gonna Sit Right Down and Write Myself
4:Fascination*   a Letter
5:Teddy Bear
6:Love Letters in the Sand
7:It's Not For Me to Say
8:White Silver Sands
9:Bye Bye Love
10:Old Cape Cod

Sept. 7, 1957

1:Tammy
2:Around the World
3:I'm Gonna Sit Right Down and Write Myself
4:Fascination   a Letter
5:Diana *
6:Rainbow *
7:In the Middle of An Island *
8:Teddy Bear
9:Love Letters in the Sand
10:It's Not For Me to Say

Sept. 14, 1957

1:Tammy
2:Around the World
3:Diana
4:Fascination
5:Honeycomb *
6:I'm Gonna Sit Right Down and Write Myself
7:In the Middle of An Island   a Letter
8:Rainbow
9:Teddy Bear
10:It's Not For Me to Say

Sept. 21, 1957

1:Tammy
2:Fascination
3:Diana
4:Around the World
5:Honeycomb
6:In the Middle of An Island
7:That'll Be the Day *
8:Rainbow
9:It's Not For Me to Say
10:Teddy Bear

Sept. 28, 1957

1:Tammy
2:Fascination
3:Diana
4:That'll Be the Day
5:Around the World
6:Honeycomb
7:In the Middle of An Island
8:It's Not For Me to Say
9:Rainbow
10:Teddy Bear

Oct. 5, 1957

1:Tammy
2:Fascination
3:Honeycomb
4:Diana
5:That'll Be the Day
6:Around the World
7:In the Middle of An Island
8:Tonight *
9:It's Not For Me to Say
10:Rainbow

Oct. 12, 1957

1:Tammy
2:Fascination
3:Chances Are *
4:Honeycomb
5:Wake Up, Little Susie *
6:Diana
7:Around the World
8:Tonight
9:That'll Be the Day
10:In the Middle of An Island

Oct. 19, 1957

1:Tammy
2:Honeycomb
3:Fascination
4:Chances Are
5:Wake Up, Little Susie
6:In the Middle of An Island
7:Diana
8:Around the World
9:Tonight
10:That'll Be the Day

Oct. 26, 1957

1:Tammy
2:Fascination
3:Honeycomb
4:Chances Are
5:Wake Up, Little Susie
6:Around the World
7:Jailhouse Rock *
8:In the Middle of An Island
9:Diana
10:Tonight

Nov. 2, 1957

1:Fascination
2:Chances Are
3:Wake Up, Little Susie
4:Tammy
5:Jailhouse Rock
6:Melodie D'Amour *
7:Honeycomb
8:Around the World
9:Tonight
10:Till *

Nov. 9, 1957

1:Chances Are
2:Honeycomb
3:Fascination
4:Wake Up, Little Susie
5:Jailhouse Rock
6:Tammy
7:Silhouettes *
8:Melodie D'Amour
9:Till
10:Tonight

Nov. 16, 1957

1:Chances Are
2:Wake Up, Little Susie
3:Jailhouse Rock
4:Fascination
5:Melodie D'Amour
6:Honeycomb
7:Silhouettes
8:Tonight
9:Till
10:Tammy

Nov. 23, 1957

1:Chances Are
2:April Love *
3:Melodie D'Amour
4:You Send Me *
5:Fascination
6:Wake Up, Little Susie
7:Jailhouse Rock
8:Till
9:Tonight
10:Silhouettes

Nov. 30, 1957

1:April Love
2:Fascination
3:Jailhouse Rock
4:All the Way *
5:Silhouettes
6:You Send Me
7:Chances Are
8:Melodie D'Amour
9:Till
10:My Special Angel *

Dec. 7, 1957

1:April Love
2:You Send Me
3:Chances Are
4:All the Way
5:Silhouettes
6:Jailhouse Rock
7:Melodie D'Amour
8:My Special Angel
9:Fascination
10:Till

Dec. 21, 1957

1:April Love
2:All the Way
3:You Send Me
4:Raunchy
5:Silhouettes
6:Jailhouse Rock
7:Chances Are
8:My Special Angel
9:Peggy Sue *
10:Kisses Sweeter Than Wine

Dec. 14, 1957

1:All the Way
2:April Love
3:You Send Me
4:Raunchy *
5:Chances Are
6:Kisses Sweeter Than Wine *
7:Silhouettes
8:Jailhouse Rock
9:My Special Angel
10:Till

Dec. 28, 1957

1:April Love
2:All the Way
3:Raunchy
4:You Send Me
5:Kisses Sweeter Than Wine
6:Peggy Sue
7:Silhouettes
8:Chances Are
9:Jailhouse Rock
10:My Special Angel

1958

It was the year Khrushchev came to power in Russia, and a young Texan named Van Cliburn unlocked the Iron Curtain with eighty-eight keys.

Charles de Gaulle came back to power in France, Fidel Castro drove Batista from Cuba, and the new ruler of American homes each night was Jack Paar on the "Tonight" show. The Giants and the Dodgers went to the West Coast, and Sherman Adams, Ike's chief aide, went back to private life after a congressional subcommittee investigation was held on influence and gift-giving in governmental agencies.

The United States put up its first satellite, Explorer I. The recession deepened and then slackened. Little Rock closed its schools rather than integrate. And Russian poet Boris Pasternak was forced to decline the Nobel Prize for his *Doctor Zhivago*.

There was revolt in Iraq, and U.S. troops were sent to Lebanon. At home, we dedicated two more Tombs of Unknown Soldiers for World War II and Korea. Pope Pius XII died, and the Vatican election produced Pope John XXIII.

We were in the midst of what became known as the Golden Age of TV drama, with "Playhouse 90" leading the field. But the best drama on the tube that year was the very first overtime game in the history of National Football League championship games. The Baltimore Colts scored first in the overtime, beating the New York Giants 23–17.

Flower Drum Song was the new Rodgers and Hammerstein musical on Broadway, and Lerner and Loewe's *Gigi* was the top movie of the year. The top song of 1958 was Tommy Edwards's recording of "It's All in the Game," with eight weeks as Number One.

The novelty songs of the year were "The Chipmunk Song" and "The Purple People Eater." A couple of revivals had the kids thinking they had discovered new songs in Connie Francis's recording of "Who's Sorry Now?" and The Platters' rendition of "Smoke Gets in Your Eyes." In the latter, that was almost the case. Chances are, Jerome Kern, had he been alive, wouldn't have recognized his own tune from 1933's *Roberta* in its wailing 1958 rock dressing.

Jan. 4, 1958

1:April Love
2:All the Way
3:Raunchy
4:At the Hop *
5:Peggy Sue
6:You Send Me
7:Kisses Sweeter Than Wine
8:Silhouettes
9:My Special Angel
10:Chances Are

Jan. 11, 1958

1:April Love
2:All the Way
3:At the Hop
4:Raunchy
5:You Send Me
6:Peggy Sue
7:Kisses Sweeter Than Wine
8:My Special Angel
9:Chances Are
10:Silhouettes

Jan. 18, 1958

1:April Love
2:All the Way
3:At the Hop
4:Raunchy
5:Peggy Sue
6:Kisses Sweeter Than Wine
7:Liechtensteiner Polka *
8:You Send Me
9:Chances Are
10:Till There Was You *

Jan. 25, 1958

1:At the Hop
2:All the Way
3:April Love
4:Peggy Sue
5:Sugartime *
6:Raunchy
7:Get a Job *
8:Till There Was You
9:Kisses Sweeter Than Wine
10:You Send Me

Feb. 1, 1958

1:At the Hop
2:All the Way
3:April Love
4:Peggy Sue
5:Raunchy
6:Get a Job
7:Sail Along Silvery Moon *
8:Sugartime
9:Till There Was You
10:Kisses Sweeter Than Wine

Feb. 8, 1958

1:At the Hop
2:Sugartime
3:Sail Along Silvery Moon
4:Get a Job
5:The Stroll *
6:April Love
7:All the Way
8:Raunchy
9:Catch a Falling Star *
10:Till There Was You

Feb. 15, 1958

1:Catch a Falling Star
2:Sail Along Silvery Moon
3:Sugartime
4:At the Hop
5:Get a Job
6:Witchcraft *
7:The Stroll
8:April Love
9:Till There Was You
10:All the Way

Feb. 22, 1958

1:Sugartime
2:At the Hop
3:Sail Along Silvery Moon
4:Catch a Falling Star
5:Get a Job
6:The Stroll
7:Short Shorts *
8:Witchcraft
9:Till There Was You
10:All the Way

* Newcomer

Mar. 1, 1958

1:Catch a Falling Star
2:Sugartime
3:Sail Along Silvery Moon
4:Witchcraft
5:Get a Job
6:At the Hop
7:The Stroll
8:Till There Was You
9:All the Way
10:Short Shorts

Mar. 8, 1958

1:Catch a Falling Star
2:Get a Job
3:Sail Along Silvery Moon
4:Sugartime
5:Tequila *
6:Don't *
7:At the Hop
8:Witchcraft
9:The Stroll
10:Till There Was You

Mar. 15, 1958

1:Sugartime
2:Catch a Falling Star
3:Sail Along Silvery Moon
4:Tequila
5:Who's Sorry Now? *
6:Twenty-Six Miles *
7:Get a Job
8:Don't
9:At the Hop
10:Witchcraft

Mar. 22, 1958

1:Catch a Falling Star
2:Tequila
3:Sugartime
4:Sail Along Silvery Moon
5:It's Too Soon to Know *
6:Who's Sorry Now?
7:Sweet Little Sixteen *
8:Twenty-Six Miles
9:Get a Job
10:Don't

Mar. 29, 1958

1:Tequila
2:Catch a Falling Star
3:Who's Sorry Now?
4:Sugartime
5:Twenty-Six Miles
6:Lollipop *
7:Sail Along Silvery Moon
8:It's Too Soon to Know
9:Sweet Little Sixteen
10:Don't

Apr. 5, 1958

1:Tequila
2:Catch a Falling Star
3:Lollipop
4:Are You Sincere? *
5:Who's Sorry Now?
6:Sail Along Silvery Moon
7:Sugartime
8:Twenty-Six Miles
9:It's Too Soon to Know
10:Sweet Little Sixteen

Apr. 12, 1958

1:Tequila
2:Sail Along Silvery Moon
3:Who's Sorry Now?
4:Lollipop
5:He's Got the Whole World in His Hands *
6:Catch a Falling Star
7:Are You Sincere?
8:Sugartime
9:Twenty-Six Miles
10:It's Too Soon to Know

Apr. 19, 1958

1:He's Got the Whole World in His Hands
2:Tequila
3:Who's Sorry Now?
4:Lollipop
5:Catch a Falling Star
6:Twilight Time *
7:Witch Doctor *
8:Sail Along Silvery Moon
9:Are You Sincere?
10:Sugartime

Apr. 26, 1958

1:He's Got the Whole World in His Hands
2:Tequila
3:Witch Doctor
4:Twilight Time
5:Who's Sorry Now?
6:Return to Me *
7:Lollipop
8:Catch a Falling Star
9:Sail Along Silvery Moon
10:Are You Sincere?

May 3, 1958

1:He's Got the Whole World in His Hands
2:Witch Doctor
3:Twilight Time
4:Chanson D'Amour *
5:All I Have to Do Is Dream *
6:Return to Me
7:Tequila
8:Who's Sorry Now?
9:Lollipop
10:Catch a Falling Star

May 10, 1958

1:Twilight Time
2:He's Got the Whole World in His Hands
3:Witch Doctor
4:All I Have to Do Is Dream
5:Return to Me
6:Chanson D'Amour
7:Tequila
8:Lollipop
9:Who's Sorry Now?
10:Catch a Falling Star

May 17, 1958

1:Chanson D'Amour
2:Twilight Time
3:All I Have to Do Is Dream
4:Witch Doctor
5:He's Got the Whole World in His Hands
6:Return to Me
7:Wear My Ring Around Your Neck *
8:Tequila
9:Lollipop
10:Who's Sorry Now?

May 24, 1958

1:All I Have to Do Is Dream
2:Chanson D'Amour
3:Witch Doctor
4:Return to Me
5:Twilight Time
6:He's Got the Whole World in His Hands
7:Kewpie Doll *
8:Wear My Ring Around Your Neck
9:Tequila
10:Lollipop

May 31, 1958

1:All I Have to Do Is Dream
2:Twilight Time
3:Return to Me
4:Witch Doctor
5:Chanson D'Amour
6:Kewpie Doll
7:He's Got the Whole World in His Hands
8:Wear My Ring Around Your Neck
9:Lollipop
10:Tequila

June 7, 1958

1:All I Have to Do Is Dream
2:Return to Me
3:Witch Doctor
4:The Purple People Eater *
5:Chanson D'Amour
6:Twilight Time
7:Secretly *
8:Kewpie Doll
9:He's Got the Whole World in His Hands
10:Wear My Ring Around Your Neck

June 14, 1958

1:The Purple People Eater
2:All I Have to Do Is Dream
3:Return to Me
4:Witch Doctor
5:Chanson D'Amour
6:Secretly
7:Twilight Time
8:Wear My Ring Around Your Neck
9:Kewpie Doll
10:He's Got the Whole World in His Hands

June 21, 1958

1:The Purple People Eater
2:All I Have to Do Is Dream
3:Chanson D'Amour
4:Secretly
5:Kewpie Doll
6:Gigi *
7:Twilight Time
8:Return to Me
9:Wear My Ring Around Your Neck
10:Witch Doctor

June 28, 1958

1:The Purple People Eater
2:All I Have to Do Is Dream
3:Secretly
4:Kewpie Doll
5:Twilight Time
6:Gigi
7:Patricia *
8:Chanson D'Amour
9:Return to Me
10:Wear My Ring Around Your Neck

July 5, 1958

1:The Purple People Eater
2:Secretly
3:Gigi
4:Kewpie Doll
5:Patricia
6:Twilight Time
7:Yakety Yak *
8:Return to Me
9:All I Have to Do Is Dream
10:Chanson D'Amour

July 12, 1958

1:The Purple People Eater
2:Secretly
3:Patricia
4:Gigi
5:Yakety Yak
6:Twilight Time
7:Return to Me
8:Kewpie Doll
9:All I Have to Do Is Dream
10:Chanson D'Amour

July 19, 1958

1:The Purple People Eater
2:Patricia
3:Yakety Yak
4:Gigi
5:Secretly
6:Return to Me
7:Volare *
8:Twilight Time
9:Kewpie Doll
10:All I Have to Do Is Dream

July 26, 1958

1:Patricia
2:Yakety Yak
3:The Purple People Eater
4:Volare
5:Gigi
6:Fever *
7:Secretly
8:Return to Me
9:Twilight Time
10:Kewpie Doll

Aug. 2, 1958

1:Yakety Yak
2:Patricia
3:Volare
4:Gigi
5:Fever
6:Poor Little Fool *
7:The Purple People Eater
8:Twilight Time
9:Return to Me
10:Secretly

Aug. 9, 1958

1:Patricia
2:Poor Little Fool
3:Volare
4:Fever
5:Yakety Yak
6:Gigi
7:Little Star *
8:The Purple People Eater
9:Secretly
10:Return to Me

Aug. 16, 1958

1:Poor Little Fool
2:Volare
3:Patricia
4:Fever
5:Little Star
6:Yakety Yak
7:Gigi
8:Return to Me
9:Secretly
10:The Purple People Eater

Aug. 23, 1958

1:Volare
2:Poor Little Fool
3:Patricia
4:Fever
5:It's All in the Game *
6:Little Star
7:Yakety Yak
8:Gigi
9:Return to Me
10:Secretly

Aug. 30, 1958

1:Volare
2:Poor Little Fool
3:Little Star
4:It's All in the Game
5:Fever
6:Patricia
7:Yakety Yak
8:Tea For Two Cha-Cha *
9:Gigi
10:Secretly

Sept. 6, 1958

1:Volare
2:Little Star
3:It's All in the Game
4:Poor Little Fool
5:Tea For Two Cha-Cha
6:Fever
7:Patricia
8:Gigi
9:Yakety Yak
10:Secretly

Sept. 13, 1958

1:Volare
2:It's All in the Game
3:Tea For Two Cha-Cha
4:Little Star
5:Fever
6:Tom Dooley *
7:Poor Little Fool
8:Firefly *
9:Patricia
10:Gigi

Sept. 20, 1958

1:Volare
2:It's All in the Game
3:Tea For Two Cha-Cha
4:Tom Dooley
5:Little Star
6:Patricia
7:Firefly
8:Fever
9:Gigi
10:Poor Little Fool

Sept. 27, 1958

1:It's All in the Game
2:Volare
3:Tom Dooley
4:Tea For Two Cha-Cha
5:Little Star
6:Patricia
7:Chantilly Lace *
8:Firefly
9:Fever
10:Poor Little Fool

Oct. 4, 1958

1:It's All in the Game
2:Volare
3:Little Star
4:Tom Dooley
5:Chantilly Lace
6:Patricia
7:Bird Dog *
8:Tea For Two Cha-Cha
9:Firefly
10:Rockin' Robin *

Oct. 11, 1958

1:It's All in the Game
2:Volare
3:Bird Dog
4:Rockin' Robin
5:Little Star
6:Tears On My Pillow *
7:Susie Darlin' *
8:Tom Dooley
9:Chantilly Lace
10:Tea For Two Cha-Cha

Oct. 18, 1958

1:It's All in the Game
2:Volare
3:Bird Dog
4:Rockin' Robin
5:Tears On My Pillow
6:Susie Darlin'
7:Little Star
8:Tom Dooley
9:Tea For Two Cha-Cha
10:Chantilly Lace

Oct. 25, 1958

1:It's All in the Game
2:Rockin' Robin
3:Volare
4:Bird Dog
5:Topsy II *
6:It's Only Make Believe *
7:Tears On My Pillow
8:Tom Dooley
9:Tea For Two Cha-Cha
10:Chantilly Lace

Nov. 1, 1958

1:It's All in the Game
2:It's Only Make Believe
3:Topsy II
4:Tom Dooley
5:Rockin' Robin
6:Tea For Two Cha-Cha
7:Bird Dog
8:Tears On My Pillow
9:Volare
10:Chantilly Lace

Nov. 8, 1958

1:It's All in the Game
2:It's Only Make Believe
3:Tom Dooley
4:Topsy II
5:Rockin' Robin
6:Tea For Two Cha-Cha
7:Chantilly Lace
8:The End *
9:Tears On My Pillow
10:Bird Dog

Nov. 15, 1958

1:It's All in the Game
2:It's Only Make Believe
3:Tom Dooley
4:Topsy II
5:To Know Him Is to Love Him *
6:The End
7:Tea For Two Cha-Cha
8:Chantilly Lace
9:Rockin' Robin
10:Tears On My Pillow

Nov. 22, 1958

1:Tom Dooley
2:It's Only Make Believe
3:It's All in the Game
4:Topsy II
5:To Know Him Is to Love Him
6:The End
7:Chantilly Lace
8:Lonesome Town *
9:Beep Beep *
10:Tea For Two Cha-Cha

Nov. 29, 1958

1:Tom Dooley
2:To Know Him Is to Love Him
3:It's Only Make Believe
4:Topsy II
5:It's All in the Game
6:Beep Beep
7:Lonesome Town
8:I Got Stung *
9:One Night *
10:The End

Dec. 6, 1958

1:Tom Dooley
2:To Know Him Is to Love Him
3:It's Only Make Believe
4:Topsy II
5:Lonesome Town
6:Beep Beep
7:It's All in the Game
8:One Night
9:I Got Stung
10:Problems *

Dec. 13, 1958

1:Tom Dooley
2:To Know Him Is to Love Him
3:It's Only Make Believe
4:Lonesome Town
5:One Night
6:Beep Beep
7:Problems
8:I Got Stung
9:Topsy II
10:It's All in the Game

Dec. 20, 1958

1:Tom Dooley
2:To Know Him Is to Love Him
3:One Night
4:It's Only Make Believe
5:Lonesome Town
6:Problems
7:Beep Beep
8:I Got Stung
9:Smoke Gets In Your Eyes *
10:The Chipmunk Song *

Dec. 27, 1958

1:To Know Him Is to Love Him
2:The Chipmunk Song
3:Tom Dooley
4:Lonesome Town
5:Problems
6:Smoke Gets In Your Eyes
7:One Night
8:It's Only Make Believe
9:Beep Beep
10:I Got Stung

1959

It could be called the year of The Big Fix. A fixed chariot race on the movie screen reaped a record eleven Oscars for *Ben-Hur*. And the news of a rigged quiz show on television reaped doom for the popular "Twenty-One" and other TV shows like it.

The nation's top hero had been Columbia University teacher Charles Van Doren, continually winning contestant on "Twenty-One," until it was revealed he had been coached in advance on the questions. The show disappeared from the tube after that.

"Your Hit Parade" also vanished from television that year, surrendering to the new world of overnight rock 'n' roll hits that were considered "Golden Oldies" six weeks later.

The top song of the year was Bobby Darin's "Mack the Knife," a lyric version of 1956's "Moritat," which was Number One for nine weeks. *Gypsy* and *The Sound of Music* were the big musicals on Broadway, both supplying tunes to the Top Ten. And "My Happiness" came back from the 1948 Hit Parade to live again.

The jet age arrived with the 707, bringing with it the term The Jet Set, as commercial passenger flights became globe-shrinking jaunts of 660 mph at a 39,000-foot altitude.

The book everyone was reading was Allen Drury's saga of Washington, *Advise and Consent*. The world needed new maps with the emergence of new African nations, and the United States needed a new flag as Alaska and Hawaii became states.

Russia hit the moon with a rocket, Ingemar Johansson of Sweden hit Floyd Patterson's jaw for the heavyweight boxing title, and Khrushchev hit the ceiling when he visited this country and was denied a trip to Disneyland for security reasons.

Jan. 3, 1959

1:The Chipmunk Song
2:Smoke Gets In Your Eyes
3:To Know Him Is to Love Him
4:Tom Dooley
5:One Night
6:Lonesome Town
7:Problems
8:Beep Beep
9:It's Only Make Believe
10:Whole Lotta Loving *

Jan. 10, 1959

1:The Chipmunk Song
2:Smoke Gets In Your Eyes
3:To Know Him Is to Love Him
4:Tom Dooley
5:One Night
6:Lonesome Town
7:Problems
8:My Happiness *
9:Beep Beep
10:Whole Lotta Loving

Jan. 17, 1959

1:The Chipmunk Song
2:Smoke Gets In Your Eyes
3:My Happiness
4:To Know Him Is to Love Him
5:Tom Dooley
6:Lonesome Town
7:One Night
8:Gotta Travel On *
9:Whole Lotta Loving
10:Problems

Jan. 24, 1959

1:Smoke Gets In Your Eyes
2:The Chipmunk Song
3:My Happiness
4:Sixteen Candles *
5:Donna *
6:To Know Him Is to Love Him
7:Gotta Travel On
8:A Lover's Question *
9:Tom Dooley
10:Whole Lotta Loving

Jan. 31, 1959

1:Smoke Gets In Your Eyes
2:Donna
3:My Happiness
4:Sixteen Candles
5:Stagger Lee *
6:The Chipmunk Song
7:Gotta Travel On
8:A Lover's Question
9:Lonely Teardrops *
10:To Know Him Is to Love Him

Feb. 7, 1959

1:Smoke Gets In Your Eyes
2:Donna
3:Sixteen Candles
4:My Happiness
5:Stagger Lee
6:The All-American Boy *
7:Gotta Travel On
8:Lonely Teardrops
9:The Children's Marching Song *
10:A Lover's Question

Feb. 14, 1959

1:Smoke Gets In Your Eyes
2:Sixteen Candles
3:Stagger Lee
4:Donna
5:My Happiness
6:The All-American Boy
7:Gotta Travel On
8:The Children's Marching Song
9:Lonely Teardrops
10:Goodbye, Baby *

Feb. 21, 1959

1:Stagger Lee
2:Smoke Gets In Your Eyes
3:Sixteen Candles
4:Donna
5:The Children's Marching Song
6:My Happiness
7:The All-American Boy
8:Hawaiian Wedding Song *
9:Gotta Travel On
10:Lonely Teardrops

* Newcomer

Feb. 28, 1959

1:Stagger Lee
2:Donna
3:Sixteen Candles
4:The Children's Marching Song
5:Smoke Gets In Your Eyes
6:My Happiness
7:The All-American Boy
8:Petite Fleur *
9:Hawaiian Wedding Song
10:Charlie Brown *

Mar. 7, 1959

1:Stagger Lee
2:Donna
3:The Children's Marching Song
4:Venus *
5:Charlie Brown
6:Sixteen Candles
7:Smoke Gets In Your Eyes
8:Petite Fleur
9:Hawaiian Wedding Song
10:My Happiness

Mar. 14, 1959

1:Venus
2:Stagger Lee
3:Donna
4:Charlie Brown
5:Alvin's Harmonica *
6:Petite Fleur
7:The Children's Marching Song
8:Hawaiian Wedding Song
9:I've Had It *
10:Sixteen Candles

Mar. 21, 1959

1:Venus
2:Charlie Brown
3:Alvin's Harmonica
4:Stagger Lee
5:Donna
6:It's Just a Matter of Time *
7:I've Had It
8:Hawaiian Wedding Song
9:The Children's Marching Song
10:Petite Fleur

Mar. 28, 1959

1:Venus
2:Charlie Brown
3:Alvin's Harmonica
4:It's Just a Matter of Time
5:Tragedy *
6:Come Softly to Me *
7:Stagger Lee
8:Donna
9:I've Had It
10:Hawaiian Wedding Song

Apr. 4, 1959

1:Venus
2:Charlie Brown
3:Come Softly to Me
4:It's Just a Matter of Time
5:Alvin's Harmonica
6:Tragedy
7:Never Be Anyone Else But You *
8:Pink Shoelaces *
9:I've Had It
10:Hawaiian Wedding Song

Apr. 11, 1959

1:Venus
2:Come Softly to Me
3:Charlie Brown
4:It's Just a Matter of Time
5:Pink Shoelaces
6:Never Be Anyone Else But You
7:Tragedy
8:Alvin's Harmonica
9:It's Late *
10:Hawaiian Wedding Song

Apr. 18, 1959

1:Come Softly to Me
2:Venus
3:Pink Shoelaces
4:Never Be Anyone Else But You
5:It's Just a Matter of Time
6:Charlie Brown
7:Tragedy
8:I Need Your Love Tonight *
9:Guitar Boogie Shuffle *
10:A Fool Such As I *

Apr. 25, 1959

1:Come Softly to Me
2:Pink Shoelaces
3:Never Be Anyone Else But You
4:It's Just a Matter of Time
5:I Need Your Love Tonight
6:A Fool Such As I
7:Guitar Boogie Shuffle
8:It Doesn't Matter Anymore *
9:Venus
10:Tragedy

May 2, 1959

1:Come Softly to Me
2:Pink Shoelaces
3:A Fool Such As I
4:I Need Your Love Tonight
5:It Doesn't Matter Anymore
6:Guitar Boogie Shuffle
7:Raining in My Heart *
8:Never Be Anyone Else But You
9:Venus
10:It's Just a Matter of Time

May 9, 1959

1:Come Softly to Me
2:A Fool Such As I
3:I Need Your Love Tonight
4:Pink Shoelaces
5:It Doesn't Matter Anymore
6:Raining in My Heart
7:Guitar Boogie Shuffle
8:The Happy Organ *
9:Never Be Anyone Else But You
10:Venus

May 16, 1959

1:Come Softly to Me
2:The Happy Organ
3:A Fool Such As I
4:It Doesn't Matter Anymore
5:Kansas City *
6:Raining in My Heart
7:I Need Your Love Tonight
8:Pink Shoelaces
9:Guitar Boogie Shuffle
10:Never Be Anyone Else But You

May 23, 1959

1:The Happy Organ
2:Kansas City
3:Come Softly to Me
4:It Doesn't Matter Anymore
5:Raining in My Heart
6:A Fool Such As I
7:Pink Shoelaces
8:I Need Your Love Tonight
9:My Heart Is An Open Book *
10:Never Be Anyone Else But You

May 30, 1959

1:Kansas City
2:The Happy Organ
3:The Battle of New Orleans *
4:My Heart Is An Open Book
5:Come Softly to Me
6:It Doesn't Matter Anymore
7:A Fool Such As I
8:Pink Shoelaces
9:Raining in My Heart
10:I Need Your Love Tonight

June 6, 1959

1:The Battle of New Orleans
2:Kansas City
3:The Happy Organ
4:My Heart Is An Open Book
5:Come Softly to Me
6:A Fool Such As I
7:Pink Shoelaces
8:It Doesn't Matter Anymore
9:I Need Your Love Tonight
10:Raining in My Heart

June 13, 1959

1:The Battle of New Orleans
2:Kansas City
3:My Heart Is An Open Book
4:The Happy Organ
5:Dream Lover *
6:It Doesn't Matter Anymore
7:Quiet Village *
8:A Fool Such As I
9:Come Softly to Me
10:Pink Shoelaces

June 20, 1959

1:The Battle of New Orleans
2:Kansas City
3:The Happy Organ
4:Dream Lover
5:Quiet Village
6:My Heart Is An Open Book
7:A Fool Such As I
8:It Doesn't Matter Anymore
9:Pink Shoelaces
10:Come Softly to Me

June 27, 1959

1:The Battle of New Orleans
2:Dream Lover
3:Quiet Village
4:Kansas City
5:The Happy Organ
6:Small World *
7:A Fool Such As I
8:Everything's Coming Up Roses *
9:My Heart Is An Open Book
10:It Doesn't Matter Anymore

July 4, 1959

1:The Battle of New Orleans
2:Quiet Village
3:Dream Lover
4:Small World
5:Kansas City
6:The Happy Organ
7:Lonely Boy *
8:Everything's Coming Up Roses
9:A Fool Such As I
10:My Heart Is An Open Book

July 11, 1959

1:The Battle of New Orleans
2:Quiet Village
3:Lonely Boy
4:Dream Lover
5:The Happy Organ
6:High Hopes *
7:Small World
8:Everything's Coming Up Roses
9:Kansas City
10:A Fool Such As I

July 18, 1959

1:Lonely Boy
2:The Battle of New Orleans
3:Quiet Village
4:High Hopes
5:Small World
6:Dream Lover
7:The Happy Organ
8:Kansas City
9:A Fool Such As I
10:Everything's Coming Up Roses

July 25, 1959

1:Lonely Boy
2:Quiet Village
3:High Hopes
4:Small World
5:The Battle of New Orleans
6:Dream Lover
7:A Big Hunk O' Love *
8:The Happy Organ
9:Everything's Coming Up Roses
10:Kansas City

Aug. 1, 1959

1:Lonely Boy
2:High Hopes
3:Small World
4:Quiet Village
5:Sea of Love *
6:The Battle of New Orleans
7:A Big Hunk O' Love
8:Everything's Coming Up Roses
9:Dream Lover
10:The Happy Organ

Aug. 8, 1959

1:Lonely Boy
2:A Big Hunk O' Love
3:Sea of Love
4:High Hopes
5:Small World
6:The Three Bells *
7:Everything's Coming Up Roses
8:The Battle of New Orleans
9:Quiet Village
10:Dream Lover

Aug. 15, 1959

1:A Big Hunk O' Love
2:Sea of Love
3:The Three Bells
4:Lonely Boy
5:High Hopes
6:Small World
7:Everything's Coming Up Roses
8:Dream Lover
9:The Battle of New Orleans
10:Quiet Village

Aug. 22, 1959

1:A Big Hunk O' Love
2:The Three Bells
3:Sea of Love
4:High Hopes
5:Small World
6:Lonely Boy
7:Everything's Coming Up Roses
8:Sleep Walk *
9:The Battle of New Orleans
10:Dream Lover

Aug. 29, 1959

1:The Three Bells
2:Sea of Love
3:A Big Hunk O' Love
4:High Hopes
5:Sleep Walk
6:Small World
7:Lonely Boy
8:Everything's Coming Up Roses
9:Dream Lover
10:The Battle of New Orleans

Sept. 5, 1959

1:The Three Bells
2:Sea of Love
3:Sleep Walk
4:High Hopes
5:A Big Hunk O' Love
6:Small World
7:Mack the Knife *
8:Lonely Boy
9:The Battle of New Orleans
10:Everything's Coming Up Roses

Sept. 12, 1959

1:The Three Bells
2:Sleep Walk
3:Sea of Love
4:Mack the Knife
5:High Hopes
6:A Big Hunk O' Love
7:Small World
8:Everything's Coming Up Roses
9:Lonely Boy
10:The Battle of New Orleans

Sept. 19, 1959

1:The Three Bells
2:Sleep Walk
3:Mack the Knife
4:Sea of Love
5:High Hopes
6:A Big Hunk O' Love
7:Together Wherever We Go *
8:Lonely Boy
9:Small World
10:Everything's Coming Up Roses

Sept. 26, 1959

1:Sleep Walk
2:Mack the Knife
3:The Three Bells
4:Sea of Love
5:High Hopes
6:Together Wherever We Go
7:A Big Hunk O' Love
8:Small World
9:Everything's Coming Up Roses
10:Lonely Boy

Oct. 3, 1959

1:Sleep Walk
2:Mack the Knife
3:Sea of Love
4:Together Wherever We Go
5:The Three Bells
6:High Hopes
7:A Big Hunk O' Love
8:Mister Blue *
9:Lonely Boy
10:Small World

Oct. 10, 1959

1:Mack the Knife
2:Sleep Walk
3:The Three Bells
4:Together Wherever We Go
5:Sea of Love
6:Mister Blue
7:High Hopes
8:Misty *
9:A Big Hunk O' Love
10:Lonely Boy

Oct. 17, 1959

1:Mack the Knife
2:Sleep Walk
3:Mister Blue
4:Misty
5:The Three Bells
6:Sea of Love
7:Together Wherever We Go
8:High Hopes
9:Lonely Boy
10:A Big Hunk O' Love

Oct. 24, 1959

1:Mack the Knife
2:Sleep Walk
3:Mister Blue
4:Misty
5:Heartaches By the Number *
6:The Three Bells
7:Together Wherever We Go
8:Sea of Love
9:A Big Hunk O' Love
10:High Hopes

Oct. 31, 1959

1:Mack the Knife
2:Misty
3:Mister Blue
4:Heartaches By the Number
5:High Hopes
6:Sleep Walk
7:The Three Bells
8:Together Wherever We Go
9:Sea of Love
10:A Big Hunk O' Love

Nov. 7, 1959

1:Mack the Knife
2:Mister Blue
3:Misty
4:Heartaches By the Number
5:Together Wherever We Go
6:Sleep Walk
7:High Hopes
8:The Three Bells
9:Sea of Love
10:A Big Hunk O' Love

Nov. 14, 1959

1:Mack the Knife
2:Misty
3:Mister Blue
4:Heartaches By the Number
5:El Paso *
6:Sleep Walk
7:Together Wherever We Go
8:The Three Bells
9:A Big Hunk O' Love
10:Sea of Love

Nov. 21, 1959

1:Mack the Knife
2:Mister Blue
3:Heartaches By the Number
4:Misty
5:El Paso
6:Together Wherever We Go
7:The Best of Everything *
8:Sleep Walk
9:Sea of Love
10:The Three Bells

Nov. 28, 1959

1:Mack the Knife
2:Misty
3:Mister Blue
4:El Paso
5:Heartaches By the Number
6:The Best of Everything
7:Together Wherever We Go
8:Sleep Walk
9:The Three Bells
10:Sea of Love

Dec. 5, 1959

1:Mack the Knife
2:Mister Blue
3:Heartaches By the Number
4:Misty
5:El Paso
6:The Best of Everything
7:Why *
8:Together Wherever We Go
9:Sleep Walk
10:The Three Bells

Dec. 12, 1959

1:Mister Blue
2:Heartaches By the Number
3:Misty
4:Mack the Knife
5:El Paso
6:Why
7:The Best of Everything
8:Climb Every Mountain *
9:The Sound of Music *
10:Together Wherever We Go

Dec. 19, 1959

1:Heartaches By the Number
2:Why
3:Misty
4:El Paso
5:Mister Blue
6:The Best of Everything
7:The Sound of Music
8:My Favorite Things *
9:Mack the Knife
10:Climb Every Mountain

Dec. 26, 1959

1:Heartaches By the Number
2:Why
3:El Paso
4:Misty
5:The Sound of Music
6:My Favorite Things
7:The Best of Everything
8:Climb Every Mountain
9:Mister Blue
10:Mack the Knife

1960

The Soaring Sixties soared into sight with a paradox. They said John F. Kennedy was too young to run at forty-three, and Stan Musial was too old to run at thirty-eight.

But Kennedy ran all the way to the White House that November, winded after winning the closest election in United States history over Richard Nixon.

It was the year of the beatniks, the bearded poets of the new coffeehouses, and the year of the on-camera walkout by Jack Paar on his NBC-TV "Tonight" show.

Seventeen African nations changed their names, Khrushchev took off his shoe and banged it on a desk during a United Nations session, and Princess Margaret became Mrs. Antony Armstrong-Jones.

The best seller of the year was Harper Lee's *To Kill a Mockingbird*. The tragedy of the year was the midair collision of two airliners over New York, killing 137.

The Apartment was the Oscar-winning picture of 1960, and Casey Stengel, the pennant-winning manager, was released from the Yankees after winning his latest one.

It was the year of lunch-counter sit-ins by blacks throughout the South, and the year of Gary Powers, whose U-2 reconnaissance plane was shot down over Soviet Russia.

Caryl Chessman, who had won eight stays of execution since his 1948 conviction on robbery and kidnapping charges as California's Red Light Bandit, kept his ninth date and walked to his death in the San Quentin gas chamber.

Musically, it was an uninspired year, with only thirty-eight newcomers appearing on the Top Ten. "Theme From A Summer Place" was the year's top tune, with nine weeks as Number One.

Jan. 2, 1960
_____

1:Why
2:El Paso
3:Heartaches By the Number
4:The Sound of Music
5:Misty
6:Running Bear *
7:My Favorite Things
8:The Best of Everything
9:Climb Every Mountain
10:Mister Blue

Jan. 9, 1960
_____

1:El Paso
2:Why
3:Running Bear
4:Heartaches By the Number
5:Misty
6:My Favorite Things
7:The Sound of Music
8:The Best of Everything
9:He'll Have to Go *
10:Climb Every Mountain

Jan. 16, 1960
_____

1:El Paso
2:Running Bear
3:Heartaches By the Number
4:Misty
5:Why
6:The Sound of Music
7:He'll Have to Go
8:My Favorite Things
9:Climb Every Mountain
10:The Best of Everything

Jan. 23, 1960
_____

1:Running Bear
2:El Paso
3:Misty
4:Why
5:He'll Have to Go
6:Heartaches By the Number
7:Handy Man *
8:Teen Angel *
9:The Sound of Music
10:My Favorite Things

Jan. 30, 1960
_____

1:Running Bear
2:El Paso
3:Teen Angel
4:He'll Have to Go
5:Handy Man
6:Misty
7:Why
8:Heartaches By the Number
9:The Sound of Music
10:My Favorite Things

Feb. 6, 1960
_____

1:Running Bear
2:Teen Angel
3:He'll Have to Go
4:El Paso
5:Theme From A Summer Place *
6:Handy Man
7:Why
8:Misty
9:My Favorite Things
10:The Sound of Music

Feb. 13, 1960
_____

1:Teen Angel
2:He'll Have to Go
3:Theme From A Summer Place
4:Running Bear
5:The Sound of Music
6:Misty
7:My Favorite Things
8:El Paso
9:Handy Man
10:Why

Feb. 20, 1960
_____

1:Teen Angel
2:Theme From A Summer Place
3:The Sound of Music
4:My Favorite Things
5:Misty
6:He'll Have to Go
7:Running Bear
8:El Paso
9:Why
10:Handy Man

* Newcomer

Feb. 27, 1960

1:Theme From A Summer Place
2:The Sound of Music
3:My Favorite Things
4:Teen Angel
5:Misty
6:El Paso
7:He'll Have to Go
8:Greenfields *
9:Running Bear
10:Handy Man

Mar. 5, 1960

1:Theme From A Summer Place
2:The Sound of Music
3:Teen Angel
4:My Favorite Things
5:Greenfields
6:He'll Have to Go
7:El Paso
8:Misty
9:Handy Man
10:Running Bear

Mar. 12, 1960

1:Theme From A Summer Place
2:Greenfields
3:Teen Angel
4:The Sound of Music
5:Sink the Bismarck *
6:My Favorite Things
7:He'll Have to Go
8:El Paso
9:Running Bear
10:Misty

Mar. 19, 1960

1:Theme From A Summer Place
2:Greenfields
3:Sink the Bismarck
4:The Sound of Music
5:Teen Angel
6:My Favorite Things
7:El Paso
8:He'll Have to Go
9:Misty
10:Running Bear

Mar. 26, 1960

1:Theme From A Summer Place
2:Sink the Bismarck
3:Greenfields
4:The Sound of Music
5:He'll Have to Go
6:El Paso
7:My Favorite Things
8:Running Bear
9:Misty
10:Teen Angel

Apr. 2, 1960

1:Theme From A Summer Place
2:The Sound of Music
3:Sink the Bismarck
4:Greenfields
5:He'll Have to Go
6:Teen Angel
7:My Favorite Things
8:Running Bear
9:El Paso
10:Misty

Apr. 9, 1960

1:Theme From A Summer Place
2:Sink the Bismarck
3:Greenfields
4:The Sound of Music
5:Stuck On You *
6:He'll Have to Go
7:Running Bear
8:My Favorite Things
9:Teen Angel
10:El Paso

Apr. 16, 1960

1:Theme From A Summer Place
2:He'll Have to Go
3:Greenfields
4:Stuck On You
5:Sink the Bismarck
6:Running Bear
7:The Sound of Music
8:My Favorite Things
9:Teen Angel
10:El Paso

Apr. 23, 1960

1:Theme From A Summer Place
2:Stuck On You
3:Greenfields
4:Sink the Bismarck
5:Cathy's Clown *
6:Good Timin' *
7:He'll Have to Go
8:Running Bear
9:Teen Angel
10:The Sound of Music

Apr. 30, 1960

1:Stuck On You
2:Cathy's Clown
3:Theme From A Summer Place
4:Good Timin'
5:Greenfields
6:Sink the Bismarck
7:Put On a Happy Face *
8:Teen Angel
9:He'll Have to Go
10:Running Bear

May 7, 1960

1:Stuck On You
2:Cathy's Clown
3:Good Timin'
4:Theme From A Summer Place
5:Put On a Happy Face
6:A Lot of Livin' to Do *
7:Greenfields
8:Sink the Bismarck
9:Teen Angel
10:He'll Have to Go

May 14, 1960

1:Stuck On You
2:Cathy's Clown
3:Put On a Happy Face
4:Good Timin'
5:A Lot of Livin' to Do
6:Theme From A Summer Place
7:Wonderful World *
8:Greenfields
9:Sink the Bismarck
10:Teen Angel

May 21, 1960

1:Stuck On You
2:Good Timin'
3:Cathy's Clown
4:Put On a Happy Face
5:A Lot of Livin' to Do
6:Wonderful World
7:Theme From A Summer Place
8:Everybody's Somebody's Fool *
9:Greenfields
10:Sink the Bismarck

May 28, 1960

1:Cathy's Clown
2:Stuck On You
3:Put On a Happy Face
4:Wonderful World
5:Everybody's Somebody's Fool
6:Good Timin'
7:A Lot of Livin' to Do
8:Sink the Bismarck
9:Theme From a Summer Place
10:Greenfields

June 4, 1960

1:Cathy's Clown
2:Stuck On You
3:Wonderful World
4:Everybody's Somebody's Fool
5:Good Timin'
6:I'm Sorry *
7:Alley Oop *
8:Put On a Happy Face
9:A Lot of Livin' to Do
10:Theme From A Summer Place

June 11, 1960

1:Cathy's Clown
2:Wonderful World
3:Everybody's Somebody's Fool
4:I'm Sorry
5:Stuck On You
6:Alley Oop
7:Good Timin'
8:Put On a Happy Face
9:Theme From a Summer Place
10:A Lot of Livin' to Do

June 18, 1960

1:Cathy's Clown
2:Everybody's Somebody's Fool
3:I'm Sorry
4:Wonderful World
5:Alley Oop
6:Good Timin'
7:Stuck On You
8:Tell Laura I Love Her *
9:Put On a Happy Face
10:A Lot of Livin' to Do

June 25, 1960

1:Cathy's Clown
2:Everybody's Somebody's Fool
3:Alley Oop
4:I'm Sorry
5:Wonderful World
6:Good Timin'
7:Tell Laura I Love Her
8:Put On a Happy Face
9:Stuck On You
10:A Lot of Livin' to Do

July 2, 1960

1:Everybody's Somebody's Fool
2:Cathy's Clown
3:I'm Sorry
4:Alley Oop
5:Wonderful World
6:Theme From The Apartment *
7:Good Timin'
8:Tell Laura I Love Her
9:Put On a Happy Face
10:Stuck On You

July 9, 1960

1:Everybody's Somebody's Fool
2:Alley Oop
3:I'm Sorry
4:Theme From The Apartment
5:Cathy's Clown
6:Wonderful World
7:Tell Laura I Love Her
8:Put On a Happy Face
9:Itsy Bitsy Bikini *
10:Good Timin'

July 16, 1960

1:Alley Oop
2:I'm Sorry
3:Everybody's Somebody's Fool
4:Theme From The Apartment
5:Itsy Bitsy Bikini
6:Cathy's Clown
7:Wonderful World
8:Tell Laura I Love Her
9:Good Timin'
10:Put On a Happy Face

July 23, 1960

1:I'm Sorry
2:Itsy Bitsy Bikini
3:Alley Oop
4:Everybody's Somebody's Fool
5:Theme From The Apartment
6:It's Now or Never *
7:Cathy's Clown
8:Wonderful World
9:Tell Laura I Love Her
10:Put On a Happy Face

July 30, 1960

1:I'm Sorry
2:Theme From The Apartment
3:Itsy Bitsy Bikini
4:It's Now or Never
5:Alley Oop
6:Everybody's Somebody's Fool
7:Cathy's Clown
8:Tell Laura I Love Her
9:Put On a Happy Face
10:Wonderful World

Aug. 6, 1960

1:I'm Sorry
2:Itsy Bitsy Bikini
3:Theme From The Apartment
4:It's Now or Never
5:Everybody's Somebody's Fool
6:Cathy's Clown
7:Wonderful World
8:Put On a Happy Face
9:Alley Oop
10:Tell Laura I Love Her

256

Aug. 13, 1960

1:Itsy Bitsy Bikini
2:It's Now or Never
3:I'm Sorry
4:Theme From The Apartment
5:Everybody's Somebody's Fool
6:Cathy's Clown
7:Try to Remember *
8:Put On a Happy Face
9:Alley Oop
10:Wonderful World

Aug. 20, 1960

1:It's Now or Never
2:Itsy Bitsy Bikini
3:Theme From The Apartment
4:I'm Sorry
5:Everybody's Somebody's Fool
6:Try to Remember
7:My Heart Has a Mind of Its Own *
8:Wonderful World
9:Put On a Happy Face
10:Alley Oop

Aug. 27, 1960

1:It's Now or Never
2:Itsy Bitsy Bikini
3:Try to Remember
4:My Heart Has a Mind of Its Own
5:Theme From The Apartment
6:I'm Sorry
7:Everybody's Somebody's Fool
8:Put On a Happy Face
9:Alley Oop
10:Wonderful World

Sept. 3, 1960

1:It's Now or Never
2:My Heart Has a Mind of Its Own
3:Itsy Bitsy Bikini
4:Try to Remember
5:I'm Sorry
6:Theme From The Apartment
7:Nice 'n' Easy *
8:Everybody's Somebody's Fool
9:Wonderful World
10:Alley Oop

Sept. 10, 1960

1:It's Now or Never
2:My Heart Has a Mind of Its Own
3:Try to Remember
4:Itsy Bitsy Bikini
5:I'm Sorry
6:The Second Time Around *
7:Theme From The Apartment
8:Nice 'n' Easy
9:Everybody's Somebody's Fool
10:Alley Oop

Sept. 17, 1960

1:It's Now or Never
2:My Heart Has a Mind of Its Own
3:The Second Time Around
4:Never On Sunday *
5:Itsy Bitsy Bikini
6:Try to Remember
7:Nice 'n' Easy
8:I'm Sorry
9:Theme From The Apartment
10:Everybody's Somebody's Fool

Sept. 24, 1960

1:My Heart Has a Mind of Its Own
2:It's Now or Never
3:The Second Time Around
4:Never On Sunday
5:Nice 'n' Easy
6:Try to Remember
7:Itsy Bitsy Bikini
8:Theme From The Apartment
9:I'm Sorry
10:Everybody's Somebody's Fool

Oct. 1, 1960

1:My Heart Has a Mind of Its Own
2:The Second Time Around
3:Never On Sunday
4:Nice 'n' Easy
5:It's Now or Never
6:North to Alaska *
7:Mister Custer *
8:Try to Remember
9:Itsy Bitsy Bikini
10:Theme From The Apartment

Oct. 8, 1960

1:My Heart Has a Mind of Its Own
2:Never On Sunday
3:Mister Custer
4:The Second Time Around
5:Save the Last Dance For Me *
6:North to Alaska
7:Nice 'n' Easy
8:Try to Remember
9:It's Now or Never
10:Itsy Bitsy Bikini

Oct. 15, 1960

1:Mister Custer
2:Never On Sunday
3:The Second Time Around
4:My Heart Has a Mind of Its Own
5:North to Alaska
6:Save the Last Dance For Me
7:Nice 'n' Easy
8:I Want to Be Wanted *
9:Try to Remember
10:It's Now or Never

Oct. 22, 1960

1:Save the Last Dance For Me
2:Never On Sunday
3:Mister Custer
4:The Second Time Around
5:North to Alaska
6:Stay *
7:I Want to Be Wanted
8:Nice 'n' Easy
9:My Heart Has a Mind of Its Own
10:Try to Remember

Oct. 29, 1960

1:Save the Last Dance For Me
2:Never On Sunday
3:I Want to Be Wanted
4:North to Alaska
5:Stay
6:The Second Time Around
7:Mister Custer
8:A Thousand Stars *
9:Nice 'n' Easy
10:My Heart Has a Mind of Its Own

Nov. 5, 1960

1:Save the Last Dance For Me
2:I Want to Be Wanted
3:Never On Sunday
4:Stay
5:North to Alaska
6:Last Date *
7:A Thousand Stars
8:The Second Time Around
9:Mister Custer
10:Nice 'n' Easy

Nov. 12, 1960

1:I Want to Be Wanted
2:Save the Last Dance For Me
3:Stay
4:Last Date
5:Never On Sunday
6:North to Alaska
7:A Thousand Stars
8:The Green Leaves of Summer *
9:The Second Time Around
10:Nice 'n' Easy

Nov. 19, 1960

1:I Want to Be Wanted
2:Stay
3:Last Date
4:Save the Last Dance For Me
5:A Thousand Stars
6:Never On Sunday
7:Are You Lonesome Tonight? *
8:The Green Leaves of Summer
9:North to Alaska
10:The Second Time Around

Nov. 26, 1960

1:Stay
2:I Want to Be Wanted
3:Are You Lonesome Tonight?
4:Last Date
5:A Thousand Stars
6:The Green Leaves of Summer
7:Never On Sunday
8:Save the Last Dance For Me
9:The Second Time Around
10:North to Alaska

Dec. 3, 1960

1:Are You Lonesome Tonight?
2:Stay
3:Last Date
4:A Thousand Stars
5:The Green Leaves of Summer
6:Wonderland By Night *
7:I Want to Be Wanted
8:Never On Sunday
9:The Second Time Around
10:Save the Last Dance For Me

Dec. 10, 1960

1:Are You Lonesome Tonight?
2:Last Date
3:A Thousand Stars
4:Wonderland By Night
5:Stay
6:The Green Leaves of Summer
7:Exodus *
8:Never On Sunday
9:Save the Last Dance For Me
10:I Want to Be Wanted

Dec. 17, 1960

1:Are You Lonesome Tonight?
2:Last Date
3:Wonderland By Night
4:Exodus
5:The Green Leaves of Summer
6:A Thousand Stars
7:Stay
8:Never On Sunday
9:I Want to Be Wanted
10:Save the Last Dance For Me

Dec. 24, 1960

1:Are You Lonesome Tonight?
2:Wonderland By Night
3:Exodus
4:Last Date
5:The Green Leaves of Summer
6:Will You Love Me Tomorrow? *
7:A Thousand Stars
8:Stay
9:You're Sixteen *
10:I Want to Be Wanted

Dec. 31, 1960

1:Are You Lonesome Tonight?
2:Exodus
3:Wonderland By Night
4:The Green Leaves of Summer
5:Will You Love Me Tomorrow?
6:Last Date
7:A Thousand Stars
8:You're Sixteen
9:I Want to Be Wanted
10:Stay

1961

The first tip-off to the kind of year it was going to be should have come when you realized it read the same way if you turned 1961 upside down.

It was the year of The Wall (in Berlin) and The Twist (in the Peppermint Lounge in New York City).

Bad girl of the year was Carla, the destructive hurricane. Gagarin and Titov orbited into space, giving Russia another first. Shepard and Grissom made this country's first downrange suborbital space ride.

JFK gave us the Peace Corps, and started thousands reading the James Bond books. But the book millions were reading was Harold Robbins's *The Carpetbaggers.*

There were busloads of Freedom Riders in the Deep South, and hijackings of airliners to Cuba.

The ill-planned counterrevolutionary invasion of Cuba collapsed into what would be called the Bay of Pigs Fiasco.

Ex-Congo premier Patrice Lumumba was murdered in Katanga, United Nations secretary-general Dag Hammarskjold was killed in a plane crash, and ex-Gestapo chief Adolf Eichmann received the death sentence at his trial in Israel.

Again it was an uninspired and disappointing musical year. A recording by Bobby Lewis produced the top song, "Tossin' and Turnin'," which was Number One for seven weeks. The two biggest musicals on Broadway were *Camelot* and *How to Succeed in Business Without Really Trying,* and they each contributed to the Top Ten songs of the year. A recording of "Blue Moon" by The Marcels brought that song, hardly recognizable, back from 1934.

But the biggest record of 1961 was one that was broken. Roger Maris of the New York Yankees finally smashed his sixty-first home run, breaking Babe Ruth's single-season record set in 1927. It's true that the season was longer now, giving Maris more games in which to accomplish the feat, but at least the year had seen a new champ.

Jan. 7, 1961

1:Are You Lonesome Tonight?
2:Wonderland By Night
3:Exodus
4:Will You Love Me Tomorrow?
5:The Green Leaves of Summer
6:Last Date
7:Calcutta *
8:A Thousand Stars
9:You're Sixteen
10:Stay

Jan. 14, 1961

1:Wonderland By Night
2:Are You Lonesome Tonight?
3:Exodus
4:Calcutta
5:Will You Love Me Tomorrow?
6:Last Date
7:The Green Leaves of Summer
8:Make Someone Happy *
9:A Thousand Stars
10:You're Sixteen

Jan. 21, 1961

1:Wonderland By Night
2:Exodus
3:Will You Love Me Tomorrow?
4:Are You Lonesome Tonight?
5:Calcutta
6:Make Someone Happy
7:Last Date
8:The Green Leaves of Summer
9:You're Sixteen
10:A Thousand Stars

Jan. 28, 1961

1:Wonderland By Night
2:Will You Love Me Tomorrow?
3:Exodus
4:Calcutta
5:Make Someone Happy
6:Are You Lonesome Tonight?
7:Hey, Look Me Over *
8:Last Date
9:The Green Leaves of Summer
10:You're Sixteen

Feb. 4, 1961

1:Will You Love Me Tomorrow?
2:Wonderland By Night
3:Calcutta
4:Exodus
5:Make Someone Happy
6:Hey, Look Me Over
7:If Ever I Would Leave You *
8:Are You Lonesome Tonight?
9:Last Date
10:The Green Leaves of Summer

Feb. 11, 1961

1:Will You Love Me Tomorrow?
2:Calcutta
3:Exodus
4:Make Someone Happy
5:Hey, Look Me Over
6:Wonderland By Night
7:If Ever I Would Leave You
8:Camelot *
9:Are You Lonesome Tonight?
10:Last Date

Feb. 18, 1961

1:Calcutta
2:Exodus
3:Make Someone Happy
4:Hey, Look Me Over
5:Will You Love Me Tomorrow?
6:If Ever I Would Leave You
7:Camelot
8:Wonderland By Night
9:Last Date
10:Are You Lonesome Tonight?

Feb. 25, 1961

1:Calcutta
2:Make Someone Happy
3:Exodus
4:Hey, Look Me Over
5:If Ever I Would Leave You
6:Camelot
7:Will You Love Me Tomorrow?
8:Wonderland By Night
9:Are You Lonesome Tonight?
10:Pony Time *

* Newcomer

Mar. 4, 1961

1:Calcutta
2:If Ever I Would Leave You
3:Camelot
4:Make Someone Happy
5:Hey, Look Me Over
6:Exodus
7:Pony Time
8:Will You Love Me Tomorrow?
9:Wonderland By Night
10:Are You Lonesome Tonight?

Mar. 11, 1961

1:Calcutta
2:Camelot
3:Make Someone Happy
4:If Ever I Would Leave You
5:Where the Boys Are *
6:Hey, Look Me Over
7:Pony Time
8:Wonderland By Night
9:Are You Lonesome Tonight
10:Exodus

Mar. 18, 1961

1:Calcutta
2:Camelot
3:Where the Boys Are
4:Blue Moon *
5:Make Someone Happy
6:Pony Time
7:If Ever I Would Leave You
8:Hey, Look Me Over
9:Exodus
10:Wonderland By Night

Mar. 25, 1961

1:Calcutta
2:Where the Boys Are
3:Blue Moon
4:Pony Time
5:Camelot
6:Make Someone Happy
7:Dedicated to the One I Love *
8:If Ever I Would Leave You
9:Hey, Look Me Over
10:Exodus

Apr. 1, 1961

1:Blue Moon
2:Where the Boys Are
3:Calcutta
4:Pony Time
5:Dedicated to the One I Love
6:Make Someone Happy
7:Camelot
8:If Ever I Would Leave You
9:Hey, Look Me Over
10:One Mint Julep *

Apr. 8, 1961

1:Blue Moon
2:Where the Boys Are
3:Dedicated to the One I Love
4:Pony Time
5:One Mint Julep
6:Runaway *
7:Calcutta
8:Make Someone Happy
9:If Ever I Would Leave You
10:Hey, Look Me Over

Apr. 15, 1961

1:Blue Moon
2:Dedicated to the One I Love
3:Where the Boys Are
4:Runaway
5:One Mint Julep
6:Pony Time
7:If Ever I Would Leave You
8:Make Someone Happy
9:Hey, Look Me Over
10:Calcutta

Apr. 22, 1961

1:Blue Moon
2:Runaway
3:Dedicated to the One I Love
4:One Mint Julep
5:Where the Boys Are
6:Calcutta
7:If Ever I Would Leave You
8:Hey, Look Me Over
9:Make Someone Happy
10:A Hundred Pounds of Clay *

Apr. 29, 1961

1:Runaway
2:Blue Moon
3:One Mint Julep
4:Dedicated to the One I Love
5:Where the Boys Are
6:A Hundred Pounds of Clay
7:Calcutta
8:If Ever I Would Leave You
9:Make Someone Happy
10:Hey, Look Me Over

May 6, 1961

1:Runaway
2:One Mint Julep
3:Blue Moon
4:A Hundred Pounds of Clay
5:Dedicated to the One I Love
6:Where the Boys Are
7:Moody River *
8:Calcutta
9:Hey, Look Me Over
10:If Ever I Would Leave You

May 13, 1961

1:Runaway
2:Blue Moon
3:A Hundred Pounds of Clay
4:Moody River
5:One Mint Julep
6:Where the Boys Are
7:Dedicated to the One I Love
8:If Ever I Would Leave You
9:Calcutta
10:Hey, Look Me Over

May 20, 1961

1:Runaway
2:A Hundred Pounds of Clay
3:Moody River
4:One Mint Julep
5:Blue Moon
6:Where the Boys Are
7:Mother-in-Law *
8:Dedicated to the One I Love
9:Calcutta
10:If Ever I Would Leave You

May 27, 1961

1:Runaway
2:Moody River
3:Mother-in-Law
4:A Hundred Pounds of Clay
5:Travelin' Man *
6:One Mint Julep
7:Blue Moon
8:Where the Boys Are
9:Dedicated to the One I Love
10:Calcutta

June 3, 1961

1:Moody River
2:Runaway
3:Travelin' Man
4:A Hundred Pounds of Clay
5:Mother-in-Law
6:Where the Boys Are
7:The Boll Weevil Song *
8:Dedicated to the One I Love
9:Blue Moon
10:One Mint Julep

June 10, 1961

1:Travelin' Man
2:Moody River
3:Runaway
4:A Hundred Pounds of Clay
5:The Boll Weevil Song
6:Mother-in-Law
7:Yellow Bird *
8:Where the Boys Are
9:Dedicated to the One I Love
10:Blue Moon

June 17, 1961

1:Travelin' Man
2:Moody River
3:Yellow Bird
4:The Boll Weevil Song
5:Runaway
6:A Hundred Pounds of Clay
7:Mother-in-Law
8:Running Scared *
9:Where the Boys Are
10:Dedicated to the One I Love

June 24, 1961

1:Moody River
2:Travelin' Man
3:Yellow Bird
4:Running Scared
5:The Boll Weevil Song
6:Runaway
7:A Hundred Pounds of Clay
8:Quarter to Three *
9:Where the Boys Are
10:Mother-in-Law

July 1, 1961

1:Moody River
2:Yellow Bird
3:Quarter to Three
4:Travelin' Man
5:Running Scared
6:Tossin' and Turnin' *
7:The Boll Weevil Song
8:Runaway
9:A Hundred Pounds of Clay
10:Where the Boys Are

July 8, 1961

1:Moody River
2:Quarter to Three
3:Yellow Bird
4:Tossin' and Turnin'
5:Running Scared
6:Travelin' Man
7:Where the Boys Are
8:A Hundred Pounds of Clay
9:Runaway
10:The Boll Weevil Song

July 15, 1961

1:Tossin' and Turnin'
2:Moody River
3:Quarter to Three
4:Yellow Bird
5:Running Scared
6:Travelin' Man
7:A Hundred Pounds of Clay
8:Where the Boys Are
9:The Boll Weevil Song
10:Runaway

July 22, 1961

1:Tossin' and Turnin'
2:Moody River
3:Yellow Bird
4:Quarter to Three
5:Wooden Heart *
6:Running Scared
7:Travelin' Man
8:A Hundred Pounds of Clay
9:Runaway
10:Where the Boys Are

July 29, 1961

1:Tossin' and Turnin'
2:Yellow Bird
3:Wooden Heart
4:Moody River
5:Quarter to Three
6:A Hundred Pounds of Clay
7:Travelin' Man
8:Running Scared
9:Where the Boys Are
10:Runaway

Aug. 5, 1961

1:Tossin' and Turnin'
2:Wooden Heart
3:Yellow Bird
4:Moody River
5:The Mountain's High *
6:Quarter to Three
7:A Hundred Pounds of Clay
8:Travelin' Man
9:Running Scared
10:Runaway

Aug. 12, 1961

1:Tossin' and Turnin'
2:Wooden Heart
3:The Mountain's High
4:Quarter to Three
5:Michael *
6:Yellow Bird
7:Who Put the Bomp? *
8:Moody River
9:Travelin' Man
10:A Hundred Pounds of Clay

Aug. 19, 1961

1:Tossin' and Turnin'
2:The Mountain's High
3:Michael
4:Wooden Heart
5:Who Put the Bomp?
6:Quarter to Three
7:Crying *
8:Mexico *
9:A Hundred Pounds of Clay
10:Yellow Bird

Aug. 26, 1961

1:Tossin' and Turnin'
2:Michael
3:The Mountain's High
4:Who Put the Bomp?
5:Wooden Heart
6:Crying
7:Quarter to Three
8:Mexico
9:Yellow Bird
10:A Hundred Pounds of Clay

Sept. 2, 1961

1:Michael
2:The Mountain's High
3:Tossin' and Turnin'
4:Crying
5:Wooden Heart
6:Who Put the Bomp?
7:Take Good Care of My Baby *
8:Quarter to Three
9:Mexico
10:Yellow Bird

Sept. 9, 1961

1:Michael
2:The Mountain's High
3:Take Good Care of My Baby
4:Crying
5:Who Put the Bomp?
6:Sad Movies *
7:Tossin' and Turnin'
8:Wooden Heart
9:Quarter to Three
10:Mexico

Sept. 16, 1961

1:Take Good Care of My Baby
2:Michael
3:The Mountain's High
4:Crying
5:Sad Movies
6:Bristol Stomp *
7:Who Put the Bomp?
8:Tossin' and Turnin'
9:Mexico
10:Wooden Heart

Sept. 23, 1961

1:Take Good Care of My Baby
2:Crying
3:Sad Movies
4:Michael
5:Bristol Stomp
6:The Mountain's High
7:Who Put the Bomp?
8:Hit the Road, Jack *
9:Tossin' and Turnin'
10:Wooden Heart

Sept. 30, 1961

1:Take Good Care of My Baby
2:Sad Movies
3:Bristol Stomp
4:Hit the Road, Jack
5:Michael
6:Crying
7:Who Put the Bomp?
8:The Mountain's High
9:Runaround Sue *
10:Tossin' and Turnin'

Oct. 7, 1961

1:Take Good Care of My Baby
2:Hit the Road, Jack
3:Sad Movies
4:Runaround Sue
5:Bristol Stomp
6:Crying
7:Michael
8:Who Put the Bomp?
9:The Mountain's High
10:Big Bad John *

Oct. 14, 1961

1:Hit the Road, Jack
2:Take Good Care of My Baby
3:Runaround Sue
4:Sad Movies
5:Big Bad John
6:Crying
7:Michael
8:Moon River *
9:Bristol Stomp
10:Who Put the Bomp?

Oct. 21, 1961

1:Hit the Road, Jack
2:Runaround Sue
3:Take Good Care of My Baby
4:Big Bad John
5:Sad Movies
6:Moon River
7:Crying
8:Michael
9:Please, Mr. Postman *
10:Bristol Stomp

Oct. 28, 1961

1:Runaround Sue
2:Hit the Road, Jack
3:Big Bad John
4:Moon River
5:Sad Movies
6:Take Good Care of My Baby
7:Please, Mr. Postman
8:Bristol Stomp
9:Michael
10:Crying

Nov. 4, 1961

1:Runaround Sue
2:Big Bad John
3:Moon River
4:Hit the Road, Jack
5:Please, Mr. Postman
6:Sad Movies
7:Take Good Care of My Baby
8:Crying
9:Michael
10:Bristol Stomp

Nov. 11, 1961

1:Big Bad John
2:Moon River
3:Runaround Sue
4:Please, Mr. Postman
5:Hit the Road, Jack
6:Sad Movies
7:Bristol Stomp
8:Michael
9:Take Good Care of My Baby
10:Crying

Nov. 18, 1961

1:Big Bad John
2:Moon River
3:Please, Mr. Postman
4:Runaround Sue
5:Hit the Road, Jack
6:The Lion Sleeps Tonight *
7:Sad Movies
8:The Twist *
9:Take Good Care of My Baby
10:Bristol Stomp

Nov. 25, 1961

1:Big Bad John
2:Moon River
3:Please, Mr. Postman
4:The Lion Sleeps Tonight
5:Run to Him *
6:The Twist
7:Runaround Sue
8:Hit the Road, Jack
9:Sad Movies
10:Take Good Care of My Baby

Dec. 2, 1961

1:Big Bad John
2:Moon River
3:The Lion Sleeps Tonight
4:Please, Mr. Postman
5:Run to Him
6:Peppermint Twist *
7:The Twist
8:Sad Movies
9:Hit the Road, Jack
10:Runaround Sue

Dec. 9, 1961

1:Big Bad John
2:Moon River
3:The Lion Sleeps Tonight
4:Peppermint Twist
5:Run to Him
6:Please, Mr. Postman
7:The Twist
8:Walk On By *
9:Can't Help Falling in Love *
10:Runaround Sue

Dec. 16, 1961

1:Moon River
2:Please, Mr. Postman
3:Big Bad John
4:The Lion Sleeps Tonight
5:The Twist
6:Walk On By
7:Peppermint Twist
8:Can't Help Falling in Love
9:Runaround Sue
10:Run to Him

Dec. 23, 1961

1:Moon River
2:The Lion Sleeps Tonight
3:Please, Mr. Postman
4:Run to Him
5:The Twist
6:I Believe in You *
7:Can't Help Falling in Love
8:Peppermint Twist
9:Big Bad John
10:Walk On By

Dec. 30, 1961

1:Moon River
2:The Lion Sleeps Tonight
3:Run to Him
4:Walk On By
5:The Twist
6:I Believe in You
7:Peppermint Twist
8:Can't Help Falling in Love
9:Please, Mr. Postman
10:Big Bad John

1962

The first U.S. Marine to go into orbit in 1962 was that track-star military athlete John Uelses, with the new controversial Fiberglas pole. The second was Lieutenant Colonel John H. Glenn, Jr., who orbited the earth three times in Friendship 7, and could have been elected President of the United States if the elections had been held that next week.

The actual President of the United States was being likened unto Superman as JFK bent the steel industry to his way of thinking about proposed price increases.

It was also the year that President Kennedy federalized the Mississippi National Guard, calling for the state to admit a black man, James Meredith, to the state university. Two died in the riots as he was admitted.

And it was the year of the Cuban missile crisis, when Kennedy went on TV to announce his successful ultimatum to Russia.

A 114-day newspaper strike closed down seven dailies in New York City, the Seattle World's Fair was opened, Telstar was sent into orbit to permit transoceanic TV, and in New Orleans a group of white people financed a busload of black Freedom Riders to New York City.

A chartered 707 jet crashed on takeoff at the Paris airport, killing 130 Atlanta citizens in what was then history's worst single plane disaster.

In the entertainment world, Lawrence of Arabia and To Kill a Mockingbird made it to the screen. Vaughn Meader had the hottest comedy album in the country, impersonating JFK on "The First Family." And in Rome, Elizabeth Taylor and Richard Burton were filming the costly Cleopatra, a movie with pyramids in the background and a triangle on the side.

Richard Rodgers, writing his first musical alone after the death of Oscar Hammerstein II, had No Strings on Broadway. It gave the Top Ten "The Sweetest Sounds." However, the sweetest sounds were the strains of "Moon River," whose nine weeks as Number One made it the top song of 1962, even though it began its string in the final three weeks of 1961.

Jan. 6, 1962

1:Moon River
2:Run to Him
3:The Lion Sleeps Tonight
4:Walk On By
5:I Believe in You
6:Can't Help Falling in Love
7:Peppermint Twist
8:The Twist
9:A Little Bitty Tear *
10:Please, Mr. Postman

Jan. 13, 1962

1:Moon River
2:Walk On By
3:Run to Him
4:I Believe in You
5:The Lion Sleeps Tonight
6:A Little Bitty Tear
7:Can't Help Falling in Love
8:Peppermint Twist
9:Please, Mr. Postman
10:The Twist

Jan. 20, 1962

1:Moon River
2:I Believe in You
3:Can't Help Falling in Love
4:Peppermint Twist
5:A Little Bitty Tear
6:The Wanderer *
7:Walk On By
8:The Lion Sleeps Tonight
9:Run to Him
10:The Twist

Jan. 27, 1962

1:Moon River
2:Can't Help Falling in Love
3:Peppermint Twist
4:A Little Bitty Tear
5:The Wanderer
6:I Believe in You
7:The Lion Sleeps Tonight
8:Walk On By
9:The Twist
10:Run to Him

Feb. 3, 1962

1:Peppermint Twist
2:Moon River
3:Can't Help Falling in Love
4:The Wanderer
5:A Little Bitty Tear
6:I Believe in You
7:Duke of Earl *
8:Midnight in Moscow *
9:The Lion Sleeps Tonight
10:Walk On By

Feb. 10, 1962

1:Moon River
2:Can't Help Falling in Love
3:The Wanderer
4:A Little Bitty Tear
5:Peppermint Twist
6:Duke of Earl
7:Midnight in Moscow
8:I Believe in You
9:Walk On By
10:The Lion Sleeps Tonight

Feb. 17, 1962

1:Moon River
2:The Wanderer
3:A Little Bitty Tear
4:Duke of Earl
5:Can't Help Falling in Love
6:Midnight in Moscow
7:Hey! Baby *
8:I Believe in You
9:Peppermint Twist
10:The Lion Sleeps Tonight

Feb. 24, 1962

1:The Wanderer
2:A Little Bitty Tear
3:Moon River
4:Hey! Baby
5:Duke of Earl
6:Midnight in Moscow
7:Tender Is the Night *
8:Can't Help Falling in Love
9:Peppermint Twist
10:I Believe in You

* Newcomer

Mar. 3, 1962

1:The Wanderer
2:Hey! Baby
3:A Little Bitty Tear
4:Moon River
5:Tender Is the Night
6:Duke of Earl
7:Don't Break the Heart That Loves You *
8:Midnight in Moscow
9:Can't Help Falling in Love
10:Peppermint Twist

Mar. 10, 1962

1:Hey! Baby
2:The Wanderer
3:Tender Is the Night
4:Don't Break the Heart That Loves You
5:A Little Bitty Tear
6:Moon River
7:Duke of Earl
8:Lollipops and Roses *
9:Can't Help Falling in Love
10:Midnight in Moscow

Mar. 17, 1962

1:Hey! Baby
2:Don't Break the Heart That Loves You
3:Tender Is the Night
4:The Wanderer
5:Lollipops and Roses
6:A Little Bitty Tear
7:Moon River
8:Johnny Angel *
9:Duke of Earl
10:Can't Help Falling in Love

Mar. 24, 1962

1:Hey! Baby
2:Don't Break the Heart That Loves You
3:Johnny Angel
4:Tender Is the Night
5:Lollipops and Roses
6:The Wanderer
7:A Little Bitty Tear
8:Moon River
9:Good Luck Charm *
10:Duke of Earl

Mar. 31, 1962

1:Don't Break the Heart That Loves You
2:Johnny Angel
3:Hey! Baby
4:Lollipops and Roses
5:Tender Is the Night
6:The Sweetest Sounds *
7:Good Luck Charm
8:Once Upon a Time *
9:The Wanderer
10:A Little Bitty Tear

Apr. 7, 1962

1:Johnny Angel
2:Don't Break the Heart That Loves You
3:Lollipops and Roses
4:Tender Is the Night
5:Once Upon a Time
6:The Sweetest Sounds
7:Good Luck Charm
8:Hey! Baby
9:Soldier Boy *
10:The Wanderer

Apr. 14, 1962

1:Johnny Angel
2:Good Luck Charm
3:Once Upon a Time
4:The Sweetest Sounds
5:Don't Break the Heart That Loves You
6:Soldier Boy
7:Stranger On the Shore *
8:Hey! Baby
9:Lollipops and Roses
10:Tender Is the Night

Apr. 21, 1962

1:Good Luck Charm
2:Johnny Angel
3:Once Upon a Time
4:Soldier Boy
5:Stranger On the Shore
6:The Sweetest Sounds
7:Don't Break the Heart That Loves You
8:P.T. 109 *
9:Hey! Baby
10:Lollipops and Roses

Apr. 28, 1962

1:Good Luck Charm
2:Soldier Boy
3:The Sweetest Sounds
4:Once Upon a Time
5:Stranger On the Shore
6:P.T. 109
7:Johnny Angel
8:Don't Break the Heart That Loves You
9:Lollipops and Roses
10:Hey! Baby

May 5, 1962

1:Soldier Boy
2:Good Luck Charm
3:Stranger On the Shore
4:P.T. 109
5:Once Upon a Time
6:The Sweetest Sounds
7:Don't Break the Heart That Loves You
8:I Can't Stop Loving You *
9:Johnny Angel
10:Lollipops and Roses

May 12, 1962

1:Soldier Boy
2:Stranger On the Shore
3:P.T. 109
4:The Sweetest Sounds
5:Good Luck Charm
6:Once Upon a Time
7:I Can't Stop Loving You
8:Don't Break the Heart That Loves You
9:Lollipops and Roses
10:Johnny Angel

May 19, 1962

1:Stranger On the Shore
2:Soldier Boy
3:I Can't Stop Loving You
4:Once Upon a Time
5:The Sweetest Sounds
6:P.T. 109
7:Good Luck Charm
8:The Man Who Shot Liberty Valance *
9:Johnny Angel
10:Don't Break the Heart That Loves You

May 26, 1962

1:Stranger On the Shore
2:I Can't Stop Loving You
3:Soldier Boy
4:P.T. 109
5:The Sweetest Sounds
6:Once Upon a Time
7:The Man Who Shot Liberty Valance
8:Good Luck Charm
9:The Stripper *
10:Johnny Angel

June 2, 1962

1:I Can't Stop Loving You
2:Stranger On the Shore
3:P.T. 109
4:The Sweetest Sounds
5:The Stripper
6:Soldier Boy
7:Once Upon a Time
8:Al Di La *
9:The Man Who Shot Liberty Valance
10:Good Luck Charm

June 9, 1962

1:I Can't Stop Loving You
2:P.T. 109
3:Stranger On the Shore
4:The Stripper
5:Once Upon a Time
6:Al Di La
7:The Sweetest Sounds
8:Soldier Boy
9:Good Luck Charm
10:The Man Who Shot Liberty Valance

June 16, 1962

1:I Can't Stop Loving You
2:The Stripper
3:P.T. 109
4:The Man Who Shot Liberty Valance
5:Al Di La
6:Stranger On the Shore
7:Roses Are Red *
8:Once Upon a Time
9:The Sweetest Sounds
10:Soldier Boy

June 23, 1962

1:I Can't Stop Loving You
2:The Stripper
3:Al Di La
4:Roses Are Red
5:Once Upon a Time
6:The Man Who Shot Liberty Valance
7:P.T. 109
8:The Sweetest Sounds
9:Stranger On the Shore
10:Wolverton Mountain *

June 30, 1962

1:I Can't Stop Loving You
2:The Stripper
3:Roses Are Red
4:Al Di La
5:Wolverton Mountain
6:Once Upon a Time
7:The Sweetest Sounds
8:The Man Who Shot Liberty Valance
9:P.T. 109
10:Stranger On the Shore

July 7, 1962

1:The Stripper
2:Roses Are Red
3:I Can't Stop Loving You
4:Al Di La
5:Wolverton Mountain
6:The Sweetest Sounds
7:Breaking Up Is Hard to Do *
8:Once Upon a Time
9:Stranger On the Shore
10:The Man Who Shot Liberty Valance

July 14, 1962

1:Roses Are Red
2:The Stripper
3:I Can't Stop Loving You
4:Al Di La
5:Breaking Up Is Hard to Do
6:Wolverton Mountain
7:The Sweetest Sounds
8:Once Upon a Time
9:Stranger On the Shore
10:The Loco-Motion *

July 21, 1962

1:Roses Are Red
2:The Stripper
3:Breaking Up Is Hard to Do
4:Al Di La
5:I Can't Stop Loving You
6:The Sweetest Sounds
7:The Loco-Motion
8:Wolverton Mountain
9:Once Upon a Time
10:Stranger On the Shore

July 28, 1962

1:Roses Are Red
2:Breaking Up Is Hard to Do
3:The Stripper
4:The Loco-Motion
5:Al Di La
6:Alley Cat *
7:I Can't Stop Loving You
8:The Sweetest Sounds
9:Wolverton Mountain
10:Stranger On the Shore

Aug. 4, 1962

1:Roses Are Red
2:Breaking Up Is Hard to Do
3:The Loco-Motion
4:The Stripper
5:Alley Cat
6:Al Di La
7:Ramblin' Rose *
8:I Can't Stop Loving You
9:The Sweetest Sounds
10:Wolverton Mountain

Aug. 11, 1962

1:Breaking Up Is Hard to Do
2:Roses Are Red
3:The Loco-Motion
4:Alley Cat
5:The Stripper
6:Ramblin' Rose
7:Al Di La
8:I Can't Stop Loving You
9:I Left My Heart in San Francisco *
10:Wolverton Mountain

Aug. 18, 1962

1:Breaking Up Is Hard to Do
2:Roses Are Red
3:Alley Cat
4:The Loco-Motion
5:Ramblin' Rose
6:I Left My Heart in San Francisco
7:Al Di La
8:The Stripper
9:Wolverton Mountain
10:I Can't Stop Loving You

Aug. 25, 1962

1:Breaking Up Is Hard to Do
2:The Loco-Motion
3:Alley Cat
4:Ramblin' Rose
5:I Left My Heart in San Francisco
6:Roses Are Red
7:Sheila *
8:Al Di La
9:The Stripper
10:I Can't Stop Loving You

Sept. 1, 1962

1:I Left My Heart in San Francisco
2:Alley Cat
3:Breaking Up Is Hard to Do
4:Ramblin' Rose
5:The Loco-Motion
6:Sheila
7:Roses Are Red
8:Sherry *
9:The Stripper
10:Al Di La

Sept. 8, 1962

1:I Left My Heart in San Francisco
2:Ramblin' Rose
3:Alley Cat
4:Sheila
5:Sherry
6:Breaking Up Is Hard to Do
7:The Loco-Motion
8:Roses Are Red
9:Al Di La
10:The Stripper

Sept. 15, 1962

1:I Left My Heart in San Francisco
2:Ramblin' Rose
3:Sheila
4:Alley Cat
5:Sherry
6:Breaking Up Is Hard to Do
7:What Kind of Fool Am I? *
8:Roses Are Red
9:The Stripper
10:The Loco-Motion

Sept. 22, 1962

1:Ramblin' Rose
2:I Left My Heart in San Francisco
3:Sheila
4:Sherry
5:What Kind of Fool Am I?
6:Alley Cat
7:Breaking Up Is Hard to Do
8:Once in a Lifetime *
9:Roses Are Red
10:The Stripper

Sept. 29, 1962

1:I Left My Heart in San Francisco
2:Ramblin' Rose
3:Sherry
4:What Kind of Fool Am I?
5:Sheila
6:Once in a Lifetime
7:He's a Rebel *
8:Alley Cat
9:Breaking Up Is Hard to Do
10:Roses Are Red

Oct. 6, 1962

1:Ramblin' Rose
2:I Left My Heart in San Francisco
3:Sherry
4:What Kind of Fool Am I?
5:He's a Rebel
6:Sheila
7:Once in a Lifetime
8:Monster Mash *
9:Alley Cat
10:Breaking Up Is Hard to Do

Oct. 13, 1962

1:I Left My Heart in San Francisco
2:Sherry
3:Ramblin' Rose
4:What Kind of Fool Am I?
5:Sheila
6:He's a Rebel
7:Monster Mash
8:Once in a Lifetime
9:Breaking Up Is Hard to Do
10:Alley Cat

Oct. 20, 1962

1:Sherry
2:I Left My Heart in San Francisco
3:He's a Rebel
4:What Kind of Fool Am I?
5:Ramblin' Rose
6:Sheila
7:Return to Sender *
8:Monster Mash
9:Once in a Lifetime
10:Bobby's Girl *

Oct. 27, 1962

1:Sherry
2:He's a Rebel
3:What Kind of Fool Am I?
4:I Left My Heart in San Francisco
5:Ramblin' Rose
6:Return to Sender
7:Bobby's Girl
8:Sheila
9:Monster Mash
10:Once in a Lifetime

Nov. 3, 1962

1:Sherry
2:What Kind of Fool Am I?
3:He's a Rebel
4:Return to Sender
5:Bobby's Girl
6:Big Girls Don't Cry *
7:I Left My Heart in San Francisco
8:Ramblin' Rose
9:Sheila
10:Monster Mash

Nov. 10, 1962

1:Sherry
2:What Kind of Fool Am I?
3:Big Girls Don't Cry
4:Return to Sender
5:He's a Rebel
6:Bobby's Girl
7:Ramblin' Rose
8:Sheila
9:I Left My Heart in San Francisco
10:Monster Mash

Nov. 17, 1962

1:Sherry
2:Big Girls Don't Cry
3:Return to Sender
4:Bobby's Girl
5:He's a Rebel
6:What Kind of Fool Am I?
7:Sheila
8:I Left My Heart in San Francisco
9:Monster Mash
10:Ramblin' Rose

Nov. 24, 1962

1:Big Girls Don't Cry
2:Sherry
3:Return to Sender
4:Bobby's Girl
5:What Kind of Fool Am I?
6:He's a Rebel
7:Ramblin' Rose
8:I Left My Heart in San Francisco
9:Gonna Build a Mountain *
10:Sheila

Dec. 1, 1962

1:Big Girls Don't Cry
2:Return to Sender
3:Bobby's Girl
4:Sherry
5:What Kind of Fool Am I?
6:Gonna Build a Mountain
7:He's a Rebel
8:I Left My Heart in San Francisco
9:Sheila
10:Ramblin' Rose

Dec. 8, 1962

1:Big Girls Don't Cry
2:Bobby's Girl
3:Return to Sender
4:Sherry
5:Go Away, Little Girl *
6:Gonna Build a Mountain
7:What Kind of Fool Am I?
8:He's a Rebel
9:Sheila
10:I Left My Heart in San Francisco

Dec. 15, 1962

1:Big Girls Don't Cry
2:Bobby's Girl
3:Go Away, Little Girl
4:Return to Sender
5:Sherry
6:He's a Rebel
7:Sheila
8:What Kind of Fool Am I?
9:I Left My Heart in San Francisco
10:Gonna Build a Mountain

Dec. 22, 1962

1:Big Girls Don't Cry
2:Go Away, Little Girl
3:Return to Sender
4:Bobby's Girl
5:He's a Rebel
6:What Kind of Fool Am I?
7:Telstar *
8:Gonna Build a Mountain
9:Sherry
10:Sheila

Dec. 29, 1962

1:Go Away, Little Girl
2:Return to Sender
3:Big Girls Don't Cry
4:Bobby's Girl
5:Telstar
6:Sherry
7:Gonna Build a Mountain
8:He's a Rebel
9:Sheila
10:What Kind of Fool Am I?

1963

What were you doing November 22, 1963? Just as it was remembered later that "Tonight We Love" was the Number One song on Pearl Harbor Saturday, 1941, now it was noted that a song called "I'm Leaving It Up to You" was Number One on that black weekend of 1963.

It had been a good year for ten months and twenty-one days up until that incredible, history-packed weekend which introduced the names Oswald and Ruby into history. Suddenly we had a new President. The headline initials were now LBJ, not JFK.

JFK had said he was going to get the country back on its feet—and he did in 1963 by starting off the year with his walking fad, which spread nationwide.

Later were to come a different kind—the Freedom Walks in the South. Racial unrest was stirring. There were troops sent to Birmingham, the National Guard was mobilized to enforce integration at the University of Alabama, and blacks marched on Washington for full civil rights immediately.

The year saw the conviction of Texas wheeler-dealer Billy Sol Estes, the Supreme Court ruling that Bible reading couldn't be required in schools, and The Great Train Robbery, when a masked gang got away with millions in England.

Christine Keeler was tried and found wanton in the Profumo sex scandal that rocked the British government, Russia shot the first woman into space, Pope John XXIII died and was replaced by Pope Paul VI. It was the year Johnny Carson replaced Jack Paar on the "Tonight" show, and the year Buddhist priests began setting fire to themselves in Vietnam.

Quintuplets, four girls and a boy, were born to Mr. and Mrs. Andrew Fischer of Aberdeen, South Dakota. Two guys named *Tom Jones* and *Hud* were big at the movies.

It was the year of the bossa nova, and the time when three revivals were all on the Top Ten at the same time. Somehow, dressed up in 1963's Big Beat, "Deep Purple," "Maria Elena," and "There, I've Said It Again" didn't sound like they did in 1939, 1941, and 1945. Undoubtedly the finest song of 1963 was "More," and it proved it by being Number One more times than any other song that year—eight weeks.

Jan. 5, 1963

1:Go Away, Little Girl
2:Big Girls Don't Cry
3:Return to Sender
4:Bobby's Girl
5:Telstar
6:Days of Wine and Roses *
7:Walk Right In *
8:Gonna Build a Mountain
9:Hey! Paula *
10:What Kind of Fool Am I?

Jan. 12, 1963

1:Go Away, Little Girl
2:Big Girls Don't Cry
3:Telstar
4:Walk Right In
5:Days of Wine and Roses
6:Hey! Paula
7:Return to Sender
8:Bobby's Girl
9:Gonna Build a Mountain
10:I Wanna Be Around *

Jan. 19, 1963

1:Go Away, Little Girl
2:Walk Right In
3:Hey! Paula
4:Days of Wine and Roses
5:I Wanna Be Around
6:Telstar
7:Big Girls Don't Cry
8:Gonna Build a Mountain
9:Return to Sender
10:Bobby's Girl

Jan. 26, 1963

1:Walk Right In
2:Go Away, Little Girl
3:Hey! Paula
4:Days of Wine and Roses
5:I Wanna Be Around
6:Rhythm of the Rain *
7:As Long As He Needs Me *
8:Big Girls Don't Cry
9:Telstar
10:Gonna Build a Mountain

Feb. 2, 1963

1:Walk Right In
2:Hey! Paula
3:Days of Wine and Roses
4:Rhythm of the Rain
5:I Wanna Be Around
6:As Long As He Needs Me
7:Go Away, Little Girl
8:Walk Like a Man *
9:Big Girls Don't Cry
10:Telstar

Feb. 9, 1963

1:Hey! Paula
2:Days of Wine and Roses
3:Walk Right In
4:As Long As He Needs Me
5:Rhythm of the Rain
6:I Wanna Be Around
7:Walk Like a Man
8:Go Away, Little Girl
9:Our Day Will Come *
10:Big Girls Don't Cry

Feb. 16, 1963

1:Hey! Paula
2:Days of Wine and Roses
3:Rhythm of the Rain
4:I Wanna Be Around
5:As Long As He Needs Me
6:Walk Like a Man
7:Walk Right In
8:Our Day Will Come
9:Go Away, Little Girl
10:Blame It On the Bossa Nova *

Feb. 23, 1963

1:Hey! Paula
2:Days of Wine and Roses
3:Rhythm of the Rain
4:Walk Like a Man
5:Our Day Will Come
6:Blame It On the Bossa Nova
7:I Wanna Be Around
8:As Long As He Needs Me
9:Walk Right In
10:Go Away, Little Girl

* Newcomer

Mar. 2, 1963

1:Days of Wine and Roses
2:Rhythm of the Rain
3:Walk Like a Man
4:Hey! Paula
5:Our Day Will Come
6:I Wanna Be Around
7:Blame It On the Bossa Nova
8:As Long As He Needs Me
9:He's So Fine *
10:Walk Right In

Mar. 9, 1963

1:Days of Wine and Roses
2:Walk Like a Man
3:Our Day Will Come
4:He's So Fine
5:The End of the World *
6:Rhythm of the Rain
7:Hey! Paula
8:I Wanna Be Around
9:Blame It On the Bossa Nova
10:As Long As He Needs Me

Mar. 16, 1963

1:Days of Wine and Roses
2:Our Day Will Come
3:Walk Like a Man
4:He's So Fine
5:The End of the World
6:I Wanna Be Around
7:Blame It On the Bossa Nova
8:Rhythm of the Rain
9:As Long As He Needs Me
10:Hey! Paula

Mar. 23, 1963

1:Our Day Will Come
2:Days of Wine and Roses
3:The End of the World
4:He's So Fine
5:Rhythm of the Rain
6:I Wanna Be Around
7:Puff, the Magic Dragon *
8:Blame It On the Bossa Nova
9:Walk Like a Man
10:As Long As He Needs Me

Mar. 30, 1963

1:Our Day Will Come
2:He's So Fine
3:The End of the World
4:Days of Wine and Roses
5:Puff, the Magic Dragon
6:Rhythm of the Rain
7:I Wanna Be Around
8:Blame It On the Bossa Nova
9:As Long As He Needs Me
10:Walk Like a Man

Apr. 6, 1963

1:He's So Fine
2:The End of the World
3:Our Day Will Come
4:Puff, the Magic Dragon
5:Days of Wine and Roses
6:I Will Follow Him *
7:I Wanna Be Around
8:Rhythm of the Rain
9:Blame It On the Bossa Nova
10:Walk Like a Man

Apr. 13, 1963

1:He's So Fine
2:Our Day Will Come
3:Puff, the Magic Dragon
4:The End of the World
5:I Will Follow Him
6:Days of Wine and Roses
7:Blame It On the Bossa Nova
8:If You Wanna Be Happy *
9:Rhythm of the Rain
10:I Wanna Be Around

Apr. 20, 1963

1:He's So Fine
2:Puff, the Magic Dragon
3:I Will Follow Him
4:Our Day Will Come
5:If You Wanna Be Happy
6:The End of the World
7:Days of Wine and Roses
8:Blame It On the Bossa Nova
9:Call Me Irresponsible *
10:Rhythm of the Rain

Apr. 27, 1963

1:He's So Fine
2:I Will Follow Him
3:Puff, the Magic Dragon
4:If You Wanna Be Happy
5:Our Day Will Come
6:Call Me Irresponsible
7:Can't Get Used to Losing You *
8:The End of the World
9:Blame It On the Bossa Nova
10:Days of Wine and Roses

May 4, 1963

1:I Will Follow Him
2:Puff, the Magic Dragon
3:He's So Fine
4:If You Wanna Be Happy
5:Can't Get Used to Losing You
6:Call Me Irresponsible
7:Our Day Will Come
8:It's My Party *
9:The End of the World
10:Blame It On the Bossa Nova

May 11, 1963

1:I Will Follow Him
2:If You Wanna Be Happy
3:Puff, the Magic Dragon
4:It's My Party
5:Call Me Irresponsible
6:Can't Get Used to Losing You
7:He's So Fine
8:Sukiyaki *
9:Our Day Will Come
10:The End of the World

May 18, 1963

1:If You Wanna Be Happy
2:Can't Get Used to Losing You
3:I Will Follow Him
4:It's My Party
5:Call Me Irresponsible
6:Puff, the Magic Dragon
7:Sukiyaki
8:He's So Fine
9:The End of the World
10:Our Day Will Come

May 25, 1963

1:If You Wanna Be Happy
2:It's My Party
3:Call Me Irresponsible
4:Sukiyaki
5:I Will Follow Him
6:Can't Get Used to Losing You
7:Blue on Blue *
8:Puff, the Magic Dragon
9:He's So Fine
10:The End of the World

June 1, 1963

1:Call Me Irresponsible
2:If You Wanna Be Happy
3:It's My Party
4:Sukiyaki
5:Blue on Blue
6:I Will Follow Him
7:Can't Get Used to Losing You
8:Puff, the Magic Dragon
9:Those Lazy-Hazy-Crazy Days of Summer *
10:The Good Life *

June 8, 1963

1:Call Me Irresponsible
2:It's My Party
3:Sukiyaki
4:Blue on Blue
5:Those Lazy-Hazy-Crazy Days of Summer
6:Can't Get Used to Losing You
7:The Good Life
8:If You Wanna Be Happy
9:I Will Follow Him
10:Puff, the Magic Dragon

June 15, 1963

1:Call Me Irresponsible
2:Sukiyaki
3:Blue on Blue
4:Those Lazy-Hazy-Crazy Days of Summer
5:The Good Life
6:Can't Get Used to Losing You
7:It's My Party
8:Puff, the Magic Dragon
9:If You Wanna Be Happy
10:I Will Follow Him

June 22, 1963

1:Sukiyaki
2:Call Me Irresponsible
3:Those Lazy-Hazy-Crazy Days of Summer
4:The Good Life
5:Blue on Blue
6:Easier Said Than Done *
7:Can't Get Used to Losing You
8:It's My Party
9:Puff, the Magic Dragon
10:If You Wanna Be Happy

June 28, 1963

1:Sukiyaki
2:Those Lazy-Hazy-Crazy Days of Summer
3:The Good Life
4:Blue on Blue
5:Easier Said Than Done
6:Call Me Irresponsible
7:Tie Me Kangaroo Down, Sport *
8:Can't Get Used to Losing You
9:Puff, the Magic Dragon
10:It's My Party

July 6, 1963

1:Sukiyaki
2:Those Lazy-Hazy-Crazy Days of Summer
3:Blue on Blue
4:Easier Said Than Done
5:The Good Life
6:Tie Me Kangaroo Down, Sport
7:Blowin' in the Wind *
8:Call Me Irresponsible
9:Can't Get Used to Losing You
10:Puff, the Magic Dragon

July 13, 1963

1:Easier Said Than Done
2:Sukiyaki
3:Those Lazy-Hazy-Crazy Days of Summer
4:Blue on Blue
5:Tie Me Kangaroo Down, Sport
6:Blowin' in the Wind
7:The Good Life
8:More *
9:Call Me Irresponsible
10:Can't Get Used to Losing You

July 20, 1963

1:Easier Said Than Done
2:Those Lazy-Hazy-Crazy Days of Summer
3:More
4:Blue on Blue
5:Tie Me Kangaroo Down, Sport
6:Blowin' in the Wind
7:Sukiyaki
8:The Good Life
9:Surf City *
10:Call Me Irresponsible

July 27, 1963

1:More
2:Tie Me Kangaroo Down, Sport
3:Blowin' in the Wind
4:Easier Said Than Done
5:Blue on Blue
6:Those Lazy-Hazy-Crazy Days of Summer
7:Surf City
8:Sukiyaki
9:The Good Life
10:So Much in Love *

Aug. 3, 1963

1:More
2:Blowin' in the Wind
3:Tie Me Kangaroo Down, Sport
4:Surf City
5:So Much in Love
6:Blue on Blue
7:Those Lazy-Hazy-Crazy Days of Summer
8:Easier Said Than Done
9:Sukiyaki
10:Mockingbird *

Aug. 10, 1963

1:More
2:Blowin' in the Wind
3:Surf City
4:So Much in Love
5:Tie Me Kangaroo Down, Sport
6:Mockingbird
7:Blue on Blue
8:Those Lazy-Hazy-Crazy Days of Summer
9:Easier Said Than Done
10:Hello Mudduh, Hello Fadduh *

Aug. 17, 1963

1:More
2:Blowin' in the Wind
3:So Much in Love
4:Surf City
5:Mockingbird
6:Tie Me Kangaroo Down, Sport
7:Hello Mudduh, Hello Fadduh
8:Those Lazy-Hazy-Crazy Days of Summer
9:My Boyfriend's Back *
10:Blue on Blue

Aug. 24, 1963

1:More
2:So Much in Love
3:Blowin' in the Wind
4:Surf City
5:My Boyfriend's Back
6:Mockingbird
7:Tie Me Kangaroo Down, Sport
8:Hello Mudduh, Hello Fadduh
9:Blue on Blue
10:Those Lazy-Hazy-Crazy Days of Summer

Aug. 31, 1963

1:More
2:Hello Mudduh, Hello Fadduh
3:So Much in Love
4:My Boyfriend's Back
5:Blowin' in the Wind
6:Surf City
7:Mockingbird
8:That Sunday, That Summer *
9:Tie Me Kangaroo Down, Sport
10:Those Lazy-Hazy-Crazy Days of Summer

Sept. 7, 1963

1:More
2:My Boyfriend's Back
3:So Much in Love
4:Hello Mudduh, Hello Fadduh
5:Surf City
6:That Sunday, That Summer
7:Blue Velvet *
8:Mockingbird
9:Blowin' in the Wind
10:Tie Me Kangaroo Down, Sport

Sept. 14, 1963

1:More
2:My Boyfriend's Back
3:Blue Velvet
4:That Sunday, That Summer
5:So Much in Love
6:Surf City
7:Mockingbird
8:Hello Mudduh, Hello Fadduh
9:Tie Me Kangaroo Down, Sport
10:Blowin' in the Wind

Sept. 21, 1963

1:Blue Velvet
2:More
3:That Sunday, That Summer
4:My Boyfriend's Back
5:So Much in Love
6:Surf City
7:Mockingbird
8:Blowin' in the Wind
9:Hello Mudduh, Hello Fadduh
10:Tie Me Kangaroo Down, Sport

Sept. 28, 1963

1:Blue Velvet
2:That Sunday, That Summer
3:More
4:Mockingbird
5:Blowin' in the Wind
6:Sugar Shack *
7:My Boyfriend's Back
8:So Much in Love
9:Surf City
10:Hello Mudduh, Hello Fadduh

Oct. 5, 1963

1:Blue Velvet
2:That Sunday, That Summer
3:More
4:Sugar Shack
5:Mockingbird
6:Blowin' in the Wind
7:Deep Purple *
8:My Boyfriend's Back
9:So Much in Love
10:Surf City

Oct. 12, 1963

1:Blue Velvet
2:Sugar Shack
3:That Sunday, That Summer
4:More
5:Blowin' in the Wind
6:Deep Purple
7:Mockingbird
8:So Much in Love
9:My Boyfriend's Back
10:Surf City

Oct. 19, 1963

1:Sugar Shack
2:Blue Velvet
3:More
4:That Sunday, That Summer
5:Deep Purple
6:Blowin' in the Wind
7:Maria Elena *
8:Mockingbird
9:So Much in Love
10:My Boyfriend's Back

Oct. 26, 1963

1:Sugar Shack
2:Blue Velvet
3:Deep Purple
4:More
5:That Sunday, That Summer
6:Maria Elena
7:Blowin' in the Wind
8:Mockingbird
9:My Boyfriend's Back
10:So Much in Love

Nov. 2, 1963

1:Sugar Shack
2:Deep Purple
3:Maria Elena
4:Blue Velvet
5:More
6:I'm Leaving It Up to You *
7:Blowin' in the Wind
8:That Sunday, That Summer
9:Mockingbird
10:My Boyfriend's Back

Nov. 9, 1963

1:Sugar Shack
2:Deep Purple
3:Maria Elena
4:I'm Leaving It Up to You
5:Blue Velvet
6:More
7:Dominique *
8:Blowin' in the Wind
9:Mockingbird
10:That Sunday, That Summer

Nov. 16, 1963

1:Sugar Shack
2:I'm Leaving It Up to You
3:Deep Purple
4:Maria Elena
5:Dominique
6:Blue Velvet
7:More
8:That Sunday, That Summer
9:Mockingbird
10:Blowin' in the Wind

Nov. 23, 1963

1:I'm Leaving It Up to You
2:Deep Purple
3:Sugar Shack
4:Dominique
5:Maria Elena
6:More
7:Wives and Lovers *
8:Blue Velvet
9:Blowin' in the Wind
10:Mockingbird

Nov. 30, 1963

1:I'm Leaving It Up to You
2:Dominique
3:Deep Purple
4:Maria Elena
5:Wives and Lovers
6:More
7:Blue Velvet
8:Sugar Shack
9:Louie, Louie *
10:Blowin' in the Wind

Dec. 7, 1963

1:Dominique
2:I'm Leaving It Up to You
3:Deep Purple
4:Wives and Lovers
5:Louie, Louie
6:There, I've Said It Again *
7:Maria Elena
8:More
9:Blue Velvet
10:Sugar Shack

Dec. 14, 1963

1:Dominique
2:Wives and Lovers
3:Louie, Louie
4:I'm Leaving It Up to You
5:There, I've Said It Again
6:Deep Purple
7:More
8:Maria Elena
9:Sugar Shack
10:Blue Velvet

Dec. 21, 1963

1:Dominique
2:Wives and Lovers
3:There, I've Said It Again
4:Louie, Louie
5:I'm Leaving It Up to You
6:Charade *
7:Deep Purple
8:Maria Elena
9:Blue Velvet
10:More

Dec. 28, 1963

1:Dominique
2:Louie, Louie
3:There, I've Said It Again
4:Charade
5:Wives and Lovers
6:Deep Purple
7:More
8:I'm Leaving It Up to You
9:Maria Elena
10:Blue Velvet

1964

For the third time, a single year played host to the double show-business impact of a sensational singing artist and a milestone Broadway musical. In 1943 it had been Sinatra and *Oklahoma!* In 1956 it was Presley and *My Fair Lady.* And in 1964 it was The Beatles and *Hello, Dolly.*

The mop-topped quartet from England took the nation and the music world by storm with shrill electronic renditions of "Can't Buy Me Love," "A Hard Day's Night," "She Loves You," "Please Please Me," "Love Me Do," "I Feel Fine," and "I Want to Hold Your Hand," which became the year's top song, with seven weeks as Number One.

Carol Channing's *Hello, Dolly,* which eventually would break the long-run record for a musical set by *My Fair Lady,* gave the Top Ten its title song, although that was largely through Louis Armstrong's recording.

It was a banner year for Broadway in that 1964 also saw the debut of Barbra Streisand's *Funny Girl* and Zero Mostel's *Fiddler on the Roof,* both of which supplied songs to the Top Ten.

Khrushchev was out, and LBJ stayed in—by 61 percent of the vote in the November landslide over the Republicans' Barry Goldwater.

Herbert Hoover, Douglas MacArthur, and the poll tax all died that year. New York opened its World's Fair with black protest sit-ins. LBJ presented his Civil Rights Act, and the FBI made mass arrests for the murders of three civil-rights workers slain and buried in a recently built Mississippi earth dam.

It was the year of topless bathing suits for women, discotheques, and the Tonkin Bay incident that stepped up our involvement in Vietnam.

Moon pictures were flashed back to earth, *Goldfinger* began reaping movie box-office gold at Christmas, a poet named Cassius Clay became the heavyweight boxing champ, and the best seller was the Warren Report, which stated there was no conspiracy in the assassination of John F. Kennedy.

Jan. 4, 1964

1:Dominique
2:There, I've Said It Again
3:Charade
4:Louie, Louie
5:Wives and Lovers
6:Java *
7:Deep Purple
8:I'm Leaving It Up to You
9:Blue Velvet
10:Maria Elena

Jan. 11, 1964

1:There, I've Said It Again
2:Dominique
3:Charade
4:Java
5:Wives and Lovers
6:Louie, Louie
7:I'm Leaving It Up to You
8:Maria Elena
9:Deep Purple
10:Blue Velvet

Jan. 18, 1964

1:There, I've Said It Again
2:Charade
3:Java
4:I Want to Hold Your Hand *
5:Dominique
6:Wives and Lovers
7:Louie, Louie
8:I'm Leaving It Up to You
9:Maria Elena
10:Deep Purple

Jan. 25, 1964

1:There, I've Said It Again
2:Louie, Louie
3:I Want to Hold Your Hand
4:Java
5:Charade
6:Forget Him *
7:Dominique
8:I'm Leaving It Up to You
9:Wives and Lovers
10:Maria Elena

Feb. 1, 1964

1:I Want to Hold Your Hand
2:Louie, Louie
3:There, I've Said It Again
4:Java
5:Forget Him
6:Charade
7:Anyone Who Had a Heart *
8:Dominique
9:I'm Leaving It Up to You
10:Wives and Lovers

Feb. 8, 1964

1:I Want to Hold Your Hand
2:Java
3:There, I've Said It Again
4:Anyone Who Had a Heart
5:She Loves You *
6:Forget Him
7:Louie, Louie
8:Charade
9:Dominique
10:Wives and Lovers

Feb. 15, 1964

1:I Want to Hold Your Hand
2:Java
3:She Loves You
4:Anyone Who Had a Heart
5:Forget Him
6:There, I've Said It Again
7:Hello, Dolly *
8:Louie, Louie
9:Charade
10:Wives and Lovers

Feb. 22, 1964

1:I Want to Hold Your Hand
2:She Loves You
3:There, I've Said It Again
4:Anyone Who Had a Heart
5:Hello, Dolly
6:Forget Him
7:Wives and Lovers
8:Charade
9:Java
10:Louie, Louie

* Newcomer

Feb. 29, 1964

1:I Want to Hold Your Hand
2:She Loves You
3:Hello, Dolly
4:There, I've Said It Again
5:Forget Him
6:Anyone Who Had a Heart
7:Java
8:Charade
9:Louie, Louie
10:Wives and Lovers

Mar. 7, 1964

1:I Want to Hold Your Hand
2:Hello, Dolly
3:She Loves You
4:Java
5:Charade
6:Please Please Me *
7:There, I've Said It Again
8:Anyone Who Had a Heart
9:Forget Him
10:Louie, Louie

Mar. 14, 1964

1:I Want to Hold Your Hand
2:She Loves You
3:Hello, Dolly
4:Please Please Me
5:Java
6:Charade
7:Dawn *
8:There, I've Said It Again
9:Anyone Who Had a Heart
10:Forget Him

Mar. 21, 1964

1:She Loves You
2:Hello, Dolly
3:I Want to Hold Your Hand
4:Please Please Me
5:Dawn
6:Java
7:There, I've Said It Again
8:Anyone Who Had a Heart
9:Forget Him
10:Charade

Mar. 28, 1964

1:She Loves You
2:I Want to Hold Your Hand
3:Please Please Me
4:Dawn
5:Hello, Dolly
6:My Heart Belongs to Only You *
7:Can't Buy Me Love *
8:Java
9:There, I've Said It Again
10:Anyone Who Had a Heart

Apr. 4, 1964

1:Hello, Dolly
2:Can't Buy Me Love
3:She Loves You
4:I Want to Hold Your Hand
5:Please Please Me
6:Dawn
7:My Heart Belongs to Only You
8:People *
9:There, I've Said It Again
10:Java

Apr. 11, 1964

1:Can't Buy Me Love
2:Hello, Dolly
3:Please Please Me
4:Dawn
5:People
6:She Loves You
7:I Want to Hold Your Hand
8:My Guy *
9:My Heart Belongs to Only You
10:There, I've Said It Again

Apr. 18, 1964

1:Can't Buy Me Love
2:Hello, Dolly
3:Dawn
4:People
5:My Guy
6:Glad All Over *
7:Please Please Me
8:She Loves You
9:I Want to Hold Your Hand
10:My Heart Belongs to Only You

Apr. 25, 1964

1:Hello, Dolly
2:Can't Buy Me Love
3:People
4:My Guy
5:Glad All Over
6:Dawn
7:Please Please Me
8:She Loves You
9:My Heart Belongs to Only You
10:I Want to Hold Your Hand

May 2, 1964

1:Hello, Dolly
2:Can't Buy Me Love
3:My Guy
4:People
5:Glad All Over
6:She Loves You
7:Dawn
8:Please Please Me
9:Love Me Do *
10:My Heart Belongs to Only You

May 9, 1964

1:Can't Buy Me Love
2:Hello, Dolly
3:People
4:My Guy
5:Love Me Do
6:Chapel of Love *
7:Glad All Over
8:Dawn
9:She Loves You
10:Please Please Me

May 16, 1964

1:Hello, Dolly
2:Can't Buy Me Love
3:People
4:Love Me Do
5:Chapel of Love
6:My Guy
7:Glad All Over
8:Dawn
9:It's Over *
10:She Loves You

May 23, 1964

1:Can't Buy Me Love
2:Hello, Dolly
3:People
4:Chapel of Love
5:Love Me Do
6:My Guy
7:It's Over
8:Glad All Over
9:A World Without Love *
10:Dawn

May 30, 1964

1:Can't Buy Me Love
2:People
3:Hello, Dolly
4:Chapel of Love
5:Love Me Do
6:A World Without Love
7:It's Over
8:My Guy
9:Dawn
10:Love Me With All Your Heart *

June 6, 1964

1:Hello, Dolly
2:People
3:Chapel of Love
4:Can't Buy Me Love
5:A World Without Love
6:Love Me Do
7:Love Me With All Your Heart
8:It's Over
9:Don't Let the Sun Catch You Crying *
10:My Guy

June 13, 1964

1:Hello, Dolly
2:People
3:Chapel of Love
4:A World Without Love
5:Love Me With All Your Heart
6:Don't Let the Sun Catch You Crying
7:Love Me Do
8:It's Over
9:Can't Buy Me Love
10:My Guy

June 20, 1964

1:People
2:Hello, Dolly
3:A World Without Love
4:Love Me With All Your Heart
5:Don't Let the Sun Catch You Crying
6:Chapel of Love
7:Love Me Do
8:The Girl From Ipanema *
9:It's Over
10:Can't Buy Me Love

June 27, 1964

1:People
2:A World Without Love
3:Hello, Dolly
4:Don't Let the Sun Catch You Crying
5:Love Me With All Your Heart
6:The Girl From Ipanema
7:Chapel of Love
8:Love Me Do
9:I Get Around *
10:It's Over

July 4, 1964

1:A World Without Love
2:People
3:Hello, Dolly
4:The Girl From Ipanema
5:Love Me With All Your Heart
6:I Get Around
7:Don't Let the Sun Catch You Crying
8:Chapel of Love
9:Rag Doll *
10:Love Me Do

July 11, 1964

1:People
2:A World Without Love
3:The Girl From Ipanema
4:Hello, Dolly
5:Rag Doll
6:Love Me With All Your Heart
7:I Get Around
8:The Little Old Lady From Pasadena *
9:Don't Let the Sun Catch You Crying
10:Chapel of Love

July 18, 1964

1:People
2:The Girl From Ipanema
3:A World Without Love
4:Rag Doll
5:I Get Around
6:The Little Old Lady From Pasadena
7:Hello, Dolly
8:Love Me With All Your Heart
9:A Hard Day's Night *
10:Don't Let the Sun Catch You Crying

July 25, 1964

1:People
2:I Get Around
3:Rag Doll
4:A Hard Day's Night
5:The Girl From Ipanema
6:The Little Old Lady From Pasadena
7:A World Without Love
8:Love Me With All Your Heart
9:Don't Let the Sun Catch You Crying
10:Everybody Loves Somebody *

Aug. 1, 1964

1:A Hard Day's Night
2:People
3:Rag Doll
4:Everybody Loves Somebody
5:I Get Around
6:The Girl From Ipanema
7:Love Me With All Your Heart
8:The Little Old Lady From Pasadena
9:A World Without Love
10:Don't Let the Sun Catch You Crying

Aug. 8, 1964

1:A Hard Day's Night
2:Everybody Loves Somebody
3:People
4:The Girl From Ipanema
5:Rag Doll
6:I Get Around
7:The Little Old Lady From Pasadena
8:A World Without Love
9:Where Did Our Love Go? *
10:Love Me With All Your Heart

Aug. 15, 1964

1:Everybody Loves Somebody
2:A Hard Day's Night
3:The Girl From Ipanema
4:People
5:Where Did Our Love Go?
6:I Get Around
7:Rag Doll
8:The Little Old Lady From Pasadena
9:A World Without Love
10:The House of the Rising Sun *

Aug. 22, 1964

1:Everybody Loves Somebody
2:Where Did Our Love Go?
3:A Hard Day's Night
4:The House of the Rising Sun
5:Dang Me *
6:People
7:The Girl From Ipanema
8:A World Without Love
9:The Little Old Lady From Pasadena
10:Rag Doll

Aug. 29, 1964

1:Everybody Loves Somebody
2:Where Did Our Love Go?
3:The House of the Rising Sun
4:Dang Me
5:A Hard Day's Night
6:People
7:A World Without Love
8:The Little Old Lady From Pasadena
9:Rag Doll
10:The Girl From Ipanema

Sept. 5, 1964

1:Everybody Loves Somebody
2:The House of the Rising Sun
3:Dang Me
4:Where Did Our Love Go?
5:A World Without Love
6:Oh, Pretty Woman *
7:A Hard Day's Night
8:People
9:The Girl From Ipanema
10:The Little Old Lady From Pasadena

Sept. 12, 1964

1:Everybody Loves Somebody
2:Where Did Our Love Go?
3:The House of the Rising Sun
4:Oh, Pretty Woman
5:Dang Me
6:We'll Sing in the Sunshine *
7:A World Without Love
8:A Hard Day's Night
9:The Girl From Ipanema
10:The Little Old Lady From Pasadena

Sept. 19, 1964

1:Everybody Loves Somebody
2:Oh, Pretty Woman
3:Dang Me
4:Where Did Our Love Go?
5:We'll Sing in the Sunshine
6:The House of the Rising Sun
7:Last Kiss *
8:A World Without Love
9:A Hard Day's Night
10:The Girl From Ipanema

Sept. 26, 1964

1:Oh, Pretty Woman
2:We'll Sing in the Sunshine
3:Everybody Loves Somebody
4:Last Kiss
5:Dang Me
6:Where Did Our Love Go?
7:Do Wah Diddy Diddy *
8:The House of the Rising Sun
9:A World Without Love
10:A Hard Day's Night

Oct. 3, 1964

1:Oh, Pretty Woman
2:We'll Sing in the Sunshine
3:Last Kiss
4:Do Wah Diddy Diddy
5:Dang Me
6:Everybody Loves Somebody
7:Where Did Our Love Go?
8:The House of the Rising Sun
9:A Hard Day's Night
10:A World Without Love

Oct. 10, 1964

1:Oh, Pretty Woman
2:Last Kiss
3:Do Wah Diddy Diddy
4:We'll Sing in the Sunshine
5:Dang Me
6:Baby Love *
7:Everybody Loves Somebody
8:Where Did Our Love Go?
9:The House of the Rising Sun
10:A Hard Day's Night

Oct. 17, 1964

1:Oh, Pretty Woman
2:We'll Sing in the Sunshine
3:Last Kiss
4:Do Wah Diddy Diddy
5:Baby Love
6:Dang Me
7:Everybody Loves Somebody
8:A Hard Day's Night
9:The House of the Rising Sun
10:Where Did Our Love Go?

Oct. 24, 1964

1:We'll Sing in the Sunshine
2:Oh, Pretty Woman
3:Last Kiss
4:Baby Love
5:Do Wah Diddy Diddy
6:Leader of the Pack *
7:Dang Me
8:Everybody Loves Somebody
9:Where Did Our Love Go?
10:The House of the Rising Sun

Oct. 31, 1964

1:We'll Sing in the Sunshine
2:Oh, Pretty Woman
3:Baby Love
4:Do Wah Diddy Diddy
5:Leader of the Pack
6:Last Kiss
7:Ringo *
8:Dang Me
9:Everybody Loves Somebody
10:The House of the Rising Sun

Nov. 7, 1964

1:We'll Sing in the Sunshine
2:Leader of the Pack
3:Ringo
4:Baby Love
5:Do Wah Diddy Diddy
6:Where Love Has Gone *
7:Last Kiss
8:Oh, Pretty Woman
9:The House of the Rising Sun
10:Dang Me

Nov. 14, 1964

1:Ringo
2:We'll Sing in the Sunshine
3:Baby Love
4:Leader of the Pack
5:Where Love Has Gone
6:Goin' Out of My Head *
7:Do Wah Diddy Diddy
8:Last Kiss
9:Oh, Pretty Woman
10:The House of the Rising Sun

Nov. 21, 1964

1:Ringo
2:Leader of the Pack
3:Baby Love
4:Goin' Out of My Head
5:We'll Sing in the Sunshine
6:Sunrise, Sunset *
7:Where Love Has Gone
8:Do Wah Diddy Diddy
9:Last Kiss
10:Oh, Pretty Woman

Nov. 28, 1964

1:Ringo
2:Leader of the Pack
3:Goin' Out of My Head
4:We'll Sing in the Sunshine
5:Sunrise, Sunset
6:Where Love Has Gone
7:Mister Lonely *
8:Baby Love
9:Do Wah Diddy Diddy
10:Last Kiss

Dec. 5, 1964

1:Ringo
2:Leader of the Pack
3:Goin' Out of My Head
4:Mister Lonely
5:Come See About Me *
6:We'll Sing in the Sunshine
7:Where Love Has Gone
8:Sunrise, Sunset
9:Matchmaker, Matchmaker *
10:Baby Love

Dec. 12, 1964

1:Mister Lonely
2:Ringo
3:Come See About Me
4:Goin' Out of My Head
5:We'll Sing in the Sunshine
6:Matchmaker, Matchmaker
7:Leader of the Pack
8:Sunrise, Sunset
9:Baby Love
10:Where Love Has Gone

Dec. 19, 1964

1:Mister Lonely
2:Come See About Me
3:Goin' Out of My Head
4:Ringo
5:I Feel Fine *
6:Sunrise, Sunset
7:We'll Sing in the Sunshine
8:Matchmaker, Matchmaker
9:Where Love Has Gone
10:Leader of the Pack

Dec. 26, 1964

1:Mister Lonely
2:Come See About Me
3:I Feel Fine
4:Goin' Out of My Head
5:Ringo
6:Where Love Has Gone
7:Sunrise, Sunset
8:Leader of the Pack
9:We'll Sing in the Sunshine
10:Matchmaker, Matchmaker

1965

It was a year of draft card burnings, peace demonstrations, and marches on Washington. As our involvement in Vietnam grew, so did the picket lines.

There were civil rights marches from Selma to Montgomery in Alabama, and there was the disastrous five-day Watts riot in Los Angeles that left 33 dead, 800 injured, 3,000 arrested, and $200,000,000 in damages.

Man walked in space for the first time (a Russian first, then the United States' Edward White), looked at his first photographs of Mars sent back from that planet quicker than the drugstore used to do it, and saw Europe and North America linked for live TV via the Early Bird satellite.

They pulled the plug on New York City and the northeastern United States during the Big Blackout of 1965, leaving 30,000,000 people in the dark for twelve hours.

LBJ was unveiling both his Great Society and the scar from his gall bladder operation for photographers that year, earning him the title of The Abdominal Showman.

Winston Churchill died, the last of the major World War II leaders. Pope Paul visited New York. Truman Capote was publishing his best seller, *In Cold Blood.*

Bad girl of the year was Hurricane Betsy. Favorite girl of the screen was Julie Andrews, a hit in both *Mary Poppins* and *The Sound of Music,* the latter film eventually outgrossing *Gone With the Wind.*

The year's songs ranged from revivals (1953's "Crying in the Chapel") to protest songs ("Eve of Destruction"). Some were surprised that two of the raucous Beatles wrote one of the year's better, more melodic songs, "Yesterday," not to be confused with Jerome Kern's "Yesterdays." The new singers putting hits on the Top Ten were Roger Miller, Petula Clark, and Tom Jones. Good music seemed to be coming back, a fact verified by the year's top song, with six weeks as Number One, "The Shadow of Your Smile."

Jan. 2, 1965

1:I Feel Fine
2:Mister Lonely
3:Come See About Me
4:Goin' Out of My Head
5:Downtown *
6:Sunrise, Sunset
7:Ringo
8:Matchmaker, Matchmaker
9:Leader of the Pack
10:Where Love Has Gone

Jan. 9, 1965

1:I Feel Fine
2:Mister Lonely
3:Downtown
4:Goin' Out of My Head
5:Come See About Me
6:You've Lost That Lovin' Feelin' *
7:Sunrise, Sunset
8:Ringo
9:Where Love Has Gone
10:Matchmaker, Matchmaker

Jan. 16, 1965

1:I Feel Fine
2:Downtown
3:Goin' Out of My Head
4:You've Lost That Lovin' Feelin'
5:Come See About Me
6:Mister Lonely
7:This Diamond Ring *
8:Ringo
9:Sunrise, Sunset
10:Matchmaker, Matchmaker

Jan. 23, 1965

1:Downtown
2:I Feel Fine
3:You've Lost That Lovin' Feelin'
4:This Diamond Ring
5:Goin' Out of My Head
6:My Girl *
7:Come See About Me
8:Mister Lonely
9:Ringo
10:Sunrise, Sunset

Jan. 30, 1965

1:Downtown
2:You've Lost That Lovin' Feelin'
3:This Diamond Ring
4:My Girl
5:Goldfinger *
6:King of the Road *
7:I Feel Fine
8:Goin' Out of My Head
9:Come See About Me
10:Mister Lonely

Feb. 6, 1965

1:You've Lost That Lovin' Feelin'
2:Downtown
3:Goldfinger
4:King of the Road
5:This Diamond Ring
6:My Girl
7:I Feel Fine
8:Goin' Out of My Head
9:Ferry Cross the Mersey *
10:Come See About Me

Feb. 13, 1965

1:You've Lost That Lovin' Feelin'
2:Goldfinger
3:Downtown
4:King of the Road
5:This Diamond Ring
6:My Girl
7:Ferry Cross the Mersey
8:I Feel Fine
9:Come See About Me
10:Goin' Out of My Head

Feb. 20, 1965

1:Downtown
2:Goldfinger
3:You've Lost That Lovin' Feelin'
4:King of the Road
5:This Diamond Ring
6:Ferry Cross the Mersey
7:My Girl
8:Stop! In the Name of Love *
9:I Feel Fine
10:Goin' Out of My Head

* Newcomer

Feb. 27, 1965

1:Downtown
2:Goldfinger
3:King of the Road
4:You've Lost That Lovin' Feelin'
5:Ferry Cross the Mersey
6:Stop! In the Name of Love
7:This Diamond Ring
8:Pass Me By *
9:My Girl
10:I Feel Fine

Mar. 6, 1965

1:Goldfinger
2:Downtown
3:King of the Road
4:Stop! In the Name of Love
5:You've Lost That Lovin' Feelin'
6:Ferry Cross the Mersey
7:Pass Me By
8:This Diamond Ring
9:I Feel Fine
10:My Girl

Mar. 13, 1965

1:Goldfinger
2:King of the Road
3:Downtown
4:Stop! In the Name of Love
5:Ferry Cross the Mersey
6:Pass Me By
7:I'm Telling You Now *
8:You've Lost That Lovin' Feelin'
9:My Girl
10:This Diamond Ring

Mar. 20, 1965

1:Goldfinger
2:King of the Road
3:Stop! In the Name of Love
4:Downtown
5:I'm Telling You Now
6:Ferry Cross the Mersey
7:Pass Me By
8:Dear Heart *
9:You've Lost That Lovin' Feelin'
10:My Girl

Mar. 27, 1965

1:King of the Road
2:Goldfinger
3:Stop! In the Name of Love
4:I'm Telling You Now
5:Downtown
6:Pass Me By
7:Dear Heart
8:Ferry Cross the Mersey
9:You've Lost That Lovin' Feelin'
10:My Girl

Apr. 3, 1965

1:King of the Road
2:Goldfinger
3:I'm Telling You Now
4:Stop! In the Name of Love
5:Dear Heart
6:Pass Me By
7:Ferry Cross the Mersey
8:Downtown
9:My Girl
10:You've Lost That Lovin' Feelin'

Apr. 10, 1965

1:King of the Road
2:I'm Telling You Now
3:Goldfinger
4:Dear Heart
5:Stop! In the Name of Love
6:Pass Me By
7:A Spoonful of Sugar *
8:Ferry Cross the Mersey
9:You've Lost That Lovin' Feelin'
10:Downtown

Apr. 17, 1965

1:I'm Telling You Now
2:King of the Road
3:Dear Heart
4:Goldfinger
5:Stop! In the Name of Love
6:A Spoonful of Sugar
7:Pass Me By
8:Downtown
9:You've Lost That Lovin' Feelin'
10:Ferry Cross the Mersey

Apr. 24, 1965

1:I'm Telling You Now
2:Dear Heart
3:King of the Road
4:Stop! In the Name of Love
5:A Spoonful of Sugar
6:Chim Chim Cheree *
7:Goldfinger
8:Pass Me By
9:Downtown
10:You've Lost That Lovin' Feelin'

May 1, 1965

1:I'm Telling You Now
2:Dear Heart
3:Stop! In the Name of Love
4:Chim Chim Cheree
5:A Spoonful of Sugar
6:Mrs. Brown, You've Got a Lovely Daughter *
7:King of the Road
8:Goldfinger
9:Downtown
10:Pass Me By

May 8, 1965

1:Stop! In the Name of Love
2:I'm Telling You Now
3:Dear Heart
4:Chim Chim Cheree
5:Mrs. Brown, You've Got a Lovely Daughter
6:A Spoonful of Sugar
7:Ticket to Ride *
8:Crying in the Chapel *
9:King of the Road
10:Goldfinger

May 15, 1965

1:Stop! In the Name of Love
2:Dear Heart
3:Chim Chim Cheree
4:Mrs. Brown, You've Got a Lovely Daughter
5:Ticket to Ride
6:Crying in the Chapel
7:I'm Telling You Now
8:A Spoonful of Sugar
9:Goldfinger
10:King of the Road

May 22, 1965

1:Ticket to Ride
2:Mrs. Brown, You've Got a Lovely Daughter
3:Stop! In the Name of Love
4:Dear Heart
5:Crying in the Chapel
6:Chim Chim Cheree
7:Help Me, Rhonda *
8:I'm Telling You Now
9:A Spoonful of Sugar
10:Goldfinger

May 29, 1965

1:Mrs. Brown, You've Got a Lovely Daughter
2:Ticket to Ride
3:Dear Heart
4:Help Me, Rhonda
5:Hush, Hush, Sweet Charlotte *
6:Crying in the Chapel
7:Chim Chim Cheree
8:Stop! In the Name of Love
9:I'm Telling You Now
10:Baby, the Rain Must Fall *

June 5, 1965

1:Ticket to Ride
2:Help Me, Rhonda
3:Hush, Hush, Sweet Charlotte
4:Mrs. Brown, You've Got a Lovely Daughter
5:Crying in the Chapel
6:Dear Heart
7:Baby, the Rain Must Fall
8:Chim Chim Cheree
9:Stop! In the Name of Love
10:Mister Tambourine Man *

June 12, 1965

1:Dear Heart
2:Crying in the Chapel
3:Ticket to Ride
4:Help Me, Rhonda
5:Hush, Hush, Sweet Charlotte
6:Baby, the Rain Must Fall
7:Engine, Engine Number Nine *
8:Mister Tambourine Man
9:Mrs. Brown, You've Got a Lovely Daughter
10:Chim Chim Cheree

June 19, 1965

1:Crying in the Chapel
2:Dear Heart
3:Hush, Hush, Sweet Charlotte
4:Engine, Engine Number Nine
5:Ticket to Ride
6:Help Me, Rhonda
7:Baby, the Rain Must Fall
8:Mister Tambourine Man
9:A Walk in the Black Forest *
10:Mrs. Brown, You've Got a Lovely Daughter

June 26, 1965

1:Crying in the Chapel
2:Hush, Hush, Sweet Charlotte
3:Engine, Engine Number Nine
4:Baby, the Rain Must Fall
5:A Walk in the Black Forest
6:Mister Tambourine Man
7:Dear Heart
8:Ticket to Ride
9:Help Me, Rhonda
10:Satisfaction *

July 3, 1965

1:Crying in the Chapel
2:Baby, the Rain Must Fall
3:Hush, Hush, Sweet Charlotte
4:Engine, Engine Number Nine
5:Mister Tambourine Man
6:A Walk in the Black Forest
7:Satisfaction
8:Dear Heart
9:What the World Needs Now Is Love *
10:Ticket to Ride

July 10, 1965

1:Hush, Hush, Sweet Charlotte
2:A Walk in the Black Forest
3:Baby, the Rain Must Fall
4:Crying in the Chapel
5:Mister Tambourine Man
6:Engine, Engine Number Nine
7:What the World Needs Now Is Love
8:A World of Our Own *
9:Satisfaction
10:Dear Heart

July 17, 1965

1:Hush, Hush, Sweet Charlotte
2:Baby, the Rain Must Fall
3:A Walk in the Black Forest
4:Satisfaction
5:Mister Tambourine Man
6:Engine, Engine Number Nine
7:What the World Needs Now Is Love
8:A World of Our Own
9:Dear Heart
10:Crying in the Chapel

July 24, 1965

1:A Walk in the Black Forest
2:Hush, Hush, Sweet Charlotte
3:Satisfaction
4:Mister Tambourine Man
5:Baby, the Rain Must Fall
6:What the World Needs Now Is Love
7:Engine, Engine Number Nine
8:The Sweetheart Tree *
9:A World of Our Own
10:Crying in the Chapel

July 31, 1965

1:A Walk in the Black Forest
2:What the World Needs Now Is Love
3:Mister Tambourine Man
4:Satisfaction
5:Baby, the Rain Must Fall
6:Hush, Hush, Sweet Charlotte
7:The Sweetheart Tree
8:Engine, Engine Number Nine
9:I'm Henry VIII, I Am *
10:A World of Our Own

Aug. 7, 1965

1:A Walk in the Black Forest
2:What the World Needs Now Is Love
3:Satisfaction
4:Baby, the Rain Must Fall
5:Mister Tambourine Man
6:I'm Henry VIII, I Am
7:What's New, Pussycat? *
8:Hush, Hush, Sweet Charlotte
9:The Sweetheart Tree
10:Engine, Engine Number Nine

Aug. 14, 1965

1:A Walk in the Black Forest
2:What the World Needs Now Is Love
3:Baby, the Rain Must Fall
4:I'm Henry VIII, I Am
5:What's New, Pussycat?
6:I Got You, Babe *
7:Satisfaction
8:Mister Tambourine Man
9:Hush, Hush, Sweet Charlotte
10:The Sweetheart Tree

Aug. 21, 1965

1:What the World Needs Now Is Love
2:A Walk in the Black Forest
3:What's New, Pussycat?
4:I Got You, Babe
5:Baby, the Rain Must Fall
6:Help! *
7:Houston *
8:I'm Henry VIII, I Am
9:Satisfaction
10:Mister Tambourine Man

Aug. 28, 1965

1:What the World Needs Now Is Love
2:What's New, Pussycat?
3:Help!
4:I Got You, Babe
5:Houston
6:A Walk in the Black Forest
7:Baby, the Rain Must Fall
8:Eve of Destruction *
9:Mister Tambourine Man
10:Satisfaction

Sept. 4, 1965

1:I Got You, Babe
2:What the World Needs Now Is Love
3:Help!
4:Houston
5:What's New, Pussycat?
6:Eve of Destruction
7:A Walk in the Black Forest
8:Baby, the Rain Must Fall
9:Summer Wind *
10:Satisfaction

Sept. 11, 1965

1:Help!
2:I Got You, Babe
3:Houston
4:Eve of Destruction
5:What's New, Pussycat?
6:What the World Needs Now Is Love
7:Summer Wind
8:A Walk in the Black Forest
9:Satisfaction
10:Baby, the Rain Must Fall

Sept. 18, 1965

1:I Got You, Babe
2:Help!
3:Houston
4:Eve of Destruction
5:Summer Wind
6:What's New, Pussycat?
7:What the World Needs Now Is Love
8:Kansas City Star *
9:Baby, the Rain Must Fall
10:Satisfaction

Sept. 25, 1965

1:I Got You, Babe
2:Help!
3:Eve of Destruction
4:Houston
5:Summer Wind
6:Kansas City Star
7:Yesterday *
8:What's New, Pussycat?
9:What the World Needs Now Is Love
10:Satisfaction

Oct. 2, 1965

1:Help!
2:I Got You, Babe
3:Houston
4:Yesterday
5:Summer Wind
6:Eve of Destruction
7:A Taste of Honey *
8:Kansas City Star
9:What's New, Pussycat?
10:What the World Needs Now Is Love

Oct. 9, 1965

1:Yesterday
2:Summer Wind
3:Help!
4:I Got You, Babe
5:Houston
6:A Taste of Honey
7:One-Two-Three *
8:Eve of Destruction
9:Kansas City Star
10:What's New, Pussycat?

Oct. 16, 1965

1:Yesterday
2:Summer Wind
3:A Taste of Honey
4:One-Two-Three
5:I Got You, Babe
6:Help!
7:Houston
8:Get Off Of My Cloud *
9:Kansas City Star
10:Eve of Destruction

Oct. 23, 1965

1:Yesterday
2:A Taste of Honey
3:One-Two-Three
4:Summer Wind
5:Get Off Of My Cloud
6:I Got You, Babe
7:Help!
8:I Will Wait For You *
9:Houston
10:Kansas City Star

Oct. 30, 1965

1:Yesterday
2:One-Two-Three
3:A Taste of Honey
4:Get Off Of My Cloud
5:I Will Wait For You
6:Summer Wind
7:I Got You, Babe
8:Help!
9:Kansas City Star
10:Houston

Nov. 6, 1965

1:Yesterday
2:Get Off Of My Cloud
3:One-Two-Three
4:I Will Wait For You
5:Summer Wind
6:A Taste of Honey
7:Houston
8:Help!
9:I Got You, Babe
10:Kansas City Star

Nov. 13, 1965

1:A Taste of Honey
2:Yesterday
3:One-Two-Three
4:I Will Wait For You
5:The Shadow of Your Smile *
6:Get Off Of My Cloud
7:Summer Wind
8:I Got You, Babe
9:Help!
10:Houston

Nov. 20, 1965

1:A Taste of Honey
2:I Will Wait For You
3:The Shadow of Your Smile
4:One-Two-Three
5:Yesterday
6:Make the World Go Away *
7:Get Off Of My Cloud
8:Summer Wind
9:Houston
10:Help!

Nov. 27, 1965

1:The Shadow of Your Smile
2:A Taste of Honey
3:I Will Wait For You
4:One-Two-Three
5:Make the World Go Away
6:Yesterday
7:Turn! Turn! Turn! *
8:Get Off Of My Cloud
9:Summer Wind
10:Houston

Dec. 4, 1965

1:The Shadow of Your Smile
2:I Will Wait For You
3:Make the World Go Away
4:Turn! Turn! Turn!
5:One-Two-Three
6:On a Clear Day You Can See Forever *
7:A Taste of Honey
8:Yesterday
9:The Sounds of Silence *
10:Get Off Of My Cloud

Dec. 11, 1965

1:The Shadow of Your Smile
2:Make the World Go Away
3:Turn! Turn! Turn!
4:I Will Wait For You
5:On a Clear Day You Can See Forever
6:The Sounds of Silence
7:One-Two-Three
8:Yesterday
9:Come Back to Me *
10:A Taste of Honey

Dec. 18, 1965

1:The Shadow of Your Smile
2:Turn! Turn! Turn!
3:On a Clear Day You Can See Forever
4:I Will Wait For You
5:Make the World Go Away
6:Come Back to Me
7:The Sounds of Silence
8:One-Two-Three
9:A Taste of Honey
10:Yesterday

Dec. 25, 1965

1:The Shadow of Your Smile
2:On a Clear Day You Can See Forever
3:Make the World Go Away
4:The Sounds of Silence
5:Turn! Turn! Turn!
6:I Will Wait For You
7:Come Back to Me
8:One-Two-Three
9:Yesterday
10:Everybody Has the Right to Be Wrong *

1966

It was a year of rioting in the streets and of mass murder in the headlines.

Stokely Carmichael gave birth to the cry of "Black Power," and blacks in Chicago and Cleveland took the cue from Watts the summer before when 1966's long, hot summer rolled around.

But nothing shocked the nation like the brutal slayings of eight nurses in Chicago by Richard Speck, and the University of Texas tower snipings by Charles Whitman, who was killed by police bullets after he had killed his wife and mother and then slain twelve strangers from his tower perch while wounding forty-five.

Musically the year was summed up in a Frank Sinatra song that made the Top Ten: "It Was a Very Good Year." Good music definitely was back, and 1966 will always be the year of glorious records. Jim Ryun broke one in the mile run, and musicdom gave us two in "Somewhere My Love" ("Lara's Theme" from *Doctor Zhivago)* and "Strangers in the Night," which became the year's top song, with seven weeks as Number One.

We had *Doctor Zhivago* and *Who's Afraid of Virginia Woolf?* at the movies, *Mame* and *Cabaret* on Broadway, and the new tongue-in-cheek "Batman" on TV.

Medicare went into effect, the airlines went on strike, the President gave away his daughter Luci to Pat Nugent, and Jacqueline Susann had the year's best seller in *Valley of the Dolls.* However, the U.S. government played a scene straight out of James Bond's *Thunderball,* when it finally recovered intact an H-bomb that had been lost in the sea near Spain.

The Supreme Court imposed sweeping curbs on the power of police to interrogate subjects, and we looked up one election day to realize a movie actor who had once starred in *Bedtime for Bonzo* was now California Governor Ronald Reagan.

It was a Mod, Mod, Mod, Mod World. Miniskirts were here, and men's hair was getting longer. Notre Dame went for the tie instead of the win in its dream football game with Michigan State, and it appeared the United States was going for the same in Vietnam.

Jan. 1, 1966

1:The Shadow of Your Smile
2:On a Clear Day You Can See Forever
3:I Will Wait For You
4:Come Back to Me
5:Turn! Turn! Turn!
6:Make the World Go Away
7:Spanish Eyes *
8:England Swings *
9:The Sounds of Silence
10:One-Two-Three

Jan. 8, 1966

1:On a Clear Day You Can See Forever
2:The Shadow of Your Smile
3:Come Back to Me
4:Spanish Eyes
5:I Will Wait For You
6:Make the World Go Away
7:England Swings
8:Turn! Turn! Turn!
9:One-Two-Three
10:Flowers On the Wall *

Jan. 15, 1966

1:On a Clear Day You Can See Forever
2:The Shadow of Your Smile
3:Spanish Eyes
4:England Swings
5:Flowers On the Wall
6:Come Back to Me
7:Make the World Go Away
8:I Will Wait For You
9:The Men in My Little Girl's Life *
10:Turn! Turn! Turn!

Jan. 22, 1966

1:On a Clear Day You Can See Forever
2:Spanish Eyes
3:Flowers On the Wall
4:The Shadow of Your Smile
5:The Men in My Little Girl's Life
6:England Swings
7:Come Back to Me
8:Make the World Go Away
9:Turn! Turn! Turn!
10:I Will Wait For You

Jan. 29, 1966

1:On a Clear Day You Can See Forever
2:Spanish Eyes
3:Flowers On the Wall
4:The Men in My Little Girl's Life
5:England Swings
6:It Was a Very Good Year *
7:These Boots Are Made For Walkin' *
8:The Shadow of Your Smile
9:Make the World Go Away
10:Come Back to Me

Feb. 5, 1966

1:On a Clear Day You Can See Forever
2:Flowers On the Wall
3:The Men in My Little Girl's Life
4:Spanish Eyes
5:These Boots Are Made For Walkin'
6:It Was a Very Good Year
7:The Ballad of the Green Berets *
8:England Swings
9:The Shadow of Your Smile
10:Make the World Go Away

Feb. 12, 1966

1:The Men in My Little Girl's Life
2:Flowers On the Wall
3:These Boots Are Made For Walkin'
4:On a Clear Day You Can See Forever
5:Spanish Eyes
6:The Ballad of the Green Berets
7:It Was a Very Good Year
8:The Shadow of Your Smile
9:Make the World Go Away
10:England Swings

Feb. 19, 1966

1: The Men in My Little Girl's Life
2:These Boots Are Made For Walkin'
3:Flowers On the Wall
4:The Ballad of the Green Berets
5:Spanish Eyes
6:It Was a Very Good Year
7:On a Clear Day You Can See Forever
8:Soul and Inspiration *
9:The Shadow of Your Smile
10:Make the World Go Away

* Newcomer

Feb. 26, 1966

1:These Boots Are Made For Walkin'
2:Soul and Inspiration
3:The Ballad of the Green Berets
4:Flowers On the Wall
5:The Men in My Little Girl's Life
6:Spanish Eyes
7:It Was a Very Good Year
8:On a Clear Day You Can See Forever
9:Make the World Go Away
10:The Shadow of Your Smile

Mar. 5, 1966

1:These Boots Are Made For Walkin'
2:The Ballad of the Green Berets
3:Flowers On the Wall
4:The Men in My Little Girl's Life
5:Spanish Eyes
6:Soul and Inspiration
7:Thunderball *
8:It Was a Very Good Year
9:On a Clear Day You Can See Forever
10:The Shadow of Your Smile

Mar. 12, 1966

1:The Ballad of the Green Berets
2:These Boots Are Made For Walkin'
3:The Men in My Little Girl's Life
4:Flowers On the Wall
5:Thunderball
6:Spanish Eyes
7:Second-Hand Rose *
8:Soul and Inspiration
9:It Was a Very Good Year
10:On a Clear Day You Can See Forever

Mar. 19, 1966

1:The Ballad of the Green Berets
2:Flowers On the Wall
3:These Boots Are Made For Walkin'
4:Thunderball
5:The Men in My Little Girl's Life
6:Second-Hand Rose
7:Spanish Eyes
8:Call Me *
9:Moment to Moment *
10:Soul and Inspiration

Mar. 26, 1966

1:The Ballad of the Green Berets
2:Flowers On the Wall
3:Thunderball
4:The Men in My Little Girl's Life
5:These Boots Are Made For Walkin'
6:Second-Hand Rose
7:Call Me
8:Moment to Moment
9:Soul and Inspiration
10:Spanish Eyes

Apr. 2, 1966

1:The Ballad of the Green Berets
2:Thunderball
3:Call Me
4:Second-Hand Rose
5:Flowers On the Wall
6:Soul and Inspiration
7:Moment to Moment
8:The Men in My Little Girl's Life
9:These Boots Are Made For Walkin'
10:Michelle *

Apr. 9, 1966

1:The Ballad of the Green Berets
2:Soul and Inspiration
3:Call Me
4:Moment to Moment
5:Michelle
6:The Men in My Little Girl's Life
7:Second-Hand Rose
8:Thunderball
9:Flowers On the Wall
10:These Boots Are Made For Walkin'

Apr. 16, 1966

1:Soul and Inspiration
2:Call Me
3:The Ballad of the Green Berets
4:Michelle
5:Moment to Moment
6:Monday, Monday *
7:What Now, My Love? *
8:The Men in My Little Girl's Life
9:Thunderball
10:Second-Hand Rose

Apr. 23, 1966

1:Soul and Inspiration
2:Michelle
3:Monday, Monday
4:Call Me
5:The Ballad of the Green Berets
6:What Now, My Love?
7:Moment to Moment
8:Second-Hand Rose
9:The Men in My Little Girl's Life
10:Thunderball

Apr. 30, 1966

1:Soul and Inspiration
2:Monday, Monday
3:Michelle
4:What Now, My Love?
5:Call Me
6:Spanish Flea *
7:The Ballad of the Green Berets
8:Moment to Moment
9:You're Gonna Hear From Me *
10:The Men in My Little Girl's Life

May 7, 1966

1:Monday, Monday
2:Soul and Inspiration
3:What Now, My Love?
4:Michelle
5:Call Me
6:Strangers in the Night *
7:Spanish Flea
8:You're Gonna Hear From Me
9:Moment to Moment
10:The Men in My Little Girl's Life

May 14, 1966

1:Monday, Monday
2:Soul and Inspiration
3:Strangers in the Night
4:What Now, My Love?
5:Michelle
6:Spanish Flea
7:You're Gonna Hear From Me
8:Call Me
9:The Men in My Little Girl's Life
10:Moment to Moment

May 21, 1966

1:Monday, Monday
2:Strangers in the Night
3:What Now, My Love?
4:Michelle
5:Soul and Inspiration
6:You're Gonna Hear From Me
7:Spanish Flea
8:Mame *
9:Moment to Moment
10:Call Me

May 28, 1966

1:Strangers in the Night
2:Monday, Monday
3:What Now, My Love?
4:Michelle
5:You're Gonna Hear From Me
6:Mame
7:Soul and Inspiration
8:Moment to Moment
9:Call Me
10:Spanish Flea

June 4, 1966

1:Strangers in the Night
2:What Now, My Love?
3:Michelle
4:Mame
5:Call Me
6:The Impossible Dream *
7:You're Gonna Hear From Me
8:Monday, Monday
9:Soul and Inspiration
10:Moment to Moment

June 11, 1966

1:Strangers in the Night
2:What Now, My Love?
3:Michelle
4:Mame
5:The Impossible Dream
6:Call Me
7:The Last Word in Lonesome Is Me *
8:You're Gonna Hear From Me
9:Monday, Monday
10:Soul and Inspiration

June 18, 1966

1:Strangers in the Night
2:What Now, My Love?
3:The Impossible Dream
4:Mame
5:Michelle
6:The Last Word in Lonesome Is Me
7:If He Walked Into My Life *
8:Call Me
9:You're Gonna Hear From Me
10:Monday, Monday

June 25, 1966

1:Strangers in the Night
2:The Impossible Dream
3:Mame
4:What Now, My Love?
5:If He Walked Into My Life
6:Michelle
7:Somewhere My Love *
8:The Last Word in Lonesome Is Me
9:Call Me
10:You're Gonna Hear From Me

July 2, 1966

1:Strangers in the Night
2:The Impossible Dream
3:Mame
4:If He Walked Into My Life
5:Somewhere My Love
6:What Now, My Love?
7:The Last Word in Lonesome Is Me
8:Call Me
9:You're Gonna Hear From Me
10:Michelle

July 9, 1966

1:Strangers in the Night
2:The Impossible Dream
3:Somewhere My Love
4:If He Walked Into My Life
5:Mame
6:You Don't Have to Say You Love Me *
7:What Now, My Love?
8:Michelle
9:Call Me
10:The Last Word in Lonesome Is Me

July 16, 1966

1:The Impossible Dream
2:Strangers in the Night
3:Somewhere My Love
4:If He Walked Into My Life
5:You Don't Have to Say You Love Me
6:Mame
7:What Now, My Love?
8:The Last Word in Lonesome Is Me
9:Elusive Butterfly *
10:Michelle

July 23, 1966

1:The Impossible Dream
2:Somewhere My Love
3:If He Walked Into My Life
4:You Don't Have to Say You Love Me
5:Strangers in the Night
6:Mame
7:Elusive Butterfly
8:What Now, My Love?
9:The Last Word in Lonesome Is Me
10:Sunny *

July 30, 1966

1:Somewhere My Love
2:The Impossible Dream
3:If He Walked Into My Life
4:You Don't Have to Say You Love Me
5:Elusive Butterfly
6:Mame
7:Strangers in the Night
8:Sunny
9:What Now, My Love?
10:Almost Persuaded *

Aug. 6, 1966

1:Somewhere My Love
2:The Impossible Dream
3:You Don't Have to Say You Love Me
4:If He Walked Into My Life
5:Mame
6:Elusive Butterfly
7:Sunny
8:Strangers in the Night
9:Almost Persuaded
10:What Now, My Love?

Aug. 13, 1966

1:Somewhere My Love
2:If He Walked Into My Life
3:The Impossible Dream
4:You Don't Have to Say You Love Me
5:Elusive Butterfly
6:Sunny
7:Mame
8:Almost Persuaded
9:Strangers in the Night
10:Guantanamera *

Aug. 20, 1966

1:Somewhere My Love
2:If He Walked Into My Life
3:You Don't Have to Say You Love Me
4:Sunny
5:Elusive Butterfly
6:The Impossible Dream
7:Guantanamera
8:Mame
9:Strangers in the Night
10:Almost Persuaded

Aug. 27, 1966

1:Somewhere My Love
2:Sunny
3:If He Walked Into My Life
4:You Don't Have to Say You Love Me
5:Elusive Butterfly
6:Born Free *
7:The Impossible Dream
8:Guantanamera
9:Mame
10:Strangers in the Night

Sept. 3, 1966

1:Somewhere My Love
2:Sunny
3:Born Free
4:If He Walked Into My Life
5:You Don't Have to Say You Love Me
6:Elusive Butterfly
7:Guantanamera
8:The Impossible Dream
9:In the Arms of Love *
10:Mame

Sept. 10, 1966

1:Born Free
2:Sunny
3:Somewhere My Love
4:If He Walked Into My Life
5:In the Arms of Love
6:Alfie *
7:Guantanamera
8:You Don't Have to Say You Love Me
9:Elusive Butterfly
10:The Impossible Dream

Sept. 17, 1966

1:Born Free
2:Sunny
3:In the Arms of Love
4:Alfie
5:Somewhere My Love
6:Guantanamera
7:If He Walked Into My Life
8:Cherish *
9:You Don't Have to Say You Love Me
10:Elusive Butterfly

Sept. 24, 1966

1:Born Free
2:In the Arms of Love
3:Sunny
4:Alfie
5:Cherish
6:Reach Out, I'll Be There *
7:Somewhere My Love
8:Guantanamera
9:If He Walked Into My Life
10:You Don't Have to Say You Love Me

Oct. 1, 1966

1:Born Free
2:In the Arms of Love
3:Alfie
4:Sunny
5:Reach Out, I'll Be There
6:Cherish
7:If He Walked Into My Life
8:Somewhere My Love
9:You Don't Have to Say You Love Me
10:Guantanamera

Oct. 8, 1966

1:Born Free
2:Alfie
3:In the Arms of Love
4:Cherish
5:Reach Out, I'll Be There
6:Sunny
7:The Wheel of Hurt *
8:Dommage, Dommage *
9:Somewhere My Love
10:You Don't Have to Say You Love Me

Oct. 15, 1966

1:In the Arms of Love
2:Alfie
3:Born Free
4:Cherish
5:Reach Out, I'll Be There
6:The Wheel of Hurt
7:Dommage, Dommage
8:Sunny
9:Ninety-Six Tears *
10:Somewhere My Love

Oct. 22, 1966

1:In the Arms of Love
2:Alfie
3:Reach Out, I'll Be There
4:Cherish
5:The Wheel of Hurt
6:Born Free
7:Dommage, Dommage
8:Ninety-Six Tears
9:Sunny
10:And We Were Lovers *

Oct. 29, 1966

1:In the Arms of Love
2:Reach Out, I'll Be There
3:The Wheel of Hurt
4:Born Free
5:And We Were Lovers
6:Cherish
7:Winchester Cathedral *
8:Dommage, Dommage
9:Alfie
10:Ninety-Six Tears

Nov. 5, 1966

1:In the Arms of Love
2:Reach Out, I'll Be There
3:And We Were Lovers
4:Winchester Cathedral
5:The Wheel of Hurt
6:Cherish
7:A Time For Love *
8:Born Free
9:Ninety-Six Tears
10:Dommage, Dommage

Nov. 12, 1966

1:In the Arms of Love
2:Winchester Cathedral
3:And We Were Lovers
4:The Wheel of Hurt
5:Cherish
6:Reach Out, I'll Be There
7:Dommage, Dommage
8:Free Again *
9:A Time For Love
10:Born Free

Nov. 19, 1966

1:And We Were Lovers
2:Winchester Cathedral
3:In the Arms of Love
4:The Wheel of Hurt
5:Reach Out, I'll Be There
6:A Day in the Life of a Fool *
7:Free Again
8:A Time For Love
9:Cherish
10:Dommage, Dommage

Nov. 26, 1966

1:Winchester Cathedral
2:And We Were Lovers
3:The Wheel of Hurt
4:In the Arms of Love
5:A Day in the Life of a Fool
6:Reach Out, I'll Be There
7:Cherish
8:Games That Lovers Play *
9:Free Again
10:A Time For Love

Dec. 3, 1966
_____

1:Winchester Cathedral
2:And We Were Lovers
3:A Day in the Life of a Fool
4:The Wheel of Hurt
5:Games That Lovers Play
6:In the Arms of Love
7:Good Vibrations *
8:Reach Out, I'll Be There
9:Cherish
10:Free Again

Dec. 10, 1966
_____

1:Winchester Cathedral
2:And We Were Lovers
3:Good Vibrations
4:Free Again
5:A Day in the Life of a Fool
6:Cabaret *
7:Games That Lovers Play
8:In the Arms of Love
9:The Wheel of Hurt
10:Reach Out, I'll Be There

Dec. 17, 1966
_____

1:Winchester Cathedral
2:Good Vibrations
3:And We Were Lovers
4:A Day in the Life of a Fool
5:That's Life *
6:Cabaret
7:Free Again
8:Games That Lovers Play
9:The Wheel of Hurt
10:In the Arms of Love

Dec. 24, 1966
_____

1:Winchester Cathedral
2:Good Vibrations
3:A Day in the Life of a Fool
4:That's Life
5:Cabaret
6:And We Were Lovers
7:Games That Lovers Play
8:Free Again
9:In the Arms of Love
10:The Wheel of Hurt

Dec. 31, 1966
_____

1:Winchester Cathedral
2:That's Life
3:Good Vibrations
4:Cabaret
5:A Day in the Life of a Fool
6:And We Were Lovers
7:Free Again
8:Games That Lovers Play
9:The Wheel of Hurt
10:In the Arms of Love

1967

It was the year you began to feel your age. Elvis got married at thirty-two, Shirley Temple ran for Congress, and "What's My Line?" died of hardening of the ratings.

Britain devalued the pound—and to prove it, sent us Twiggy. It was the year of the new Soul Music. And the year the kids went to pot, they said. There were hippies, flower children, LSD trippers. San Francisco's Haight-Ashbury became the most well-known intersection in the country.

Israel won the Six-Day War with the Arabs, and back in this country discontent grew as casualties mounted in Vietnam. Cassius Clay, now known as Muhammad Ali, had refused to be drafted and had his heavyweight boxing crown removed as he was sentenced to five years in prison. Dr. Spock, the baby doctor, went from pacifiers to pacifism. When the long, hot summer arrived, it was Newark and Detroit blacks who rioted in those cities at the cost of sixty-five lives.

Jack Ruby died in Parkland Hospital, the same site where John F. Kennedy and Lee Harvey Oswald had died. Lynda Bird Johnson got married in the White House. Medical history was made with the first human heart transplant. The year started with the first Super Bowl, pro football championship game. It ended with *Bonnie and Clyde* as the big movie and the big dress fad. But Bonnie wasn't the bad girl of the year; it was Hurricane Beulah.

The tragedy of the year occurred when astronauts Edward White, first American to walk in space, Virgil Grissom, and Roger Chaffee burned to death on the pad at Cape Kennedy during a training exercise. LBJ met with Russia's Kosygin at Glassboro, New Jersey, Congress voted not to seat New York Representative Adam Clayton Powell, and Svetlana Alliluyeva, Stalin's daughter, defected to this country and published her memoirs. The big publishing news, though, was William Manchester's mammoth *The Death of a President,* which irked the Kennedys and Johnsons but fascinated the reading public.

The year's most contagious tune was "Ode to Billy Joe." The year's brightest new singing star was Vikki Carr, whose "It Must Be Him" tied "Gentle On My Mind" as the year's top tune, each being Number One for six weeks.

Jan. 7, 1967

1:That's Life
2:Winchester Cathedral
3:Games That Lovers Play
4:Free Again
5:And We Were Lovers
6:Cabaret
7:Good Vibrations
8:Sugar Town *
9:Wish Me a Rainbow *
10:A Day in the Life of a Fool

Jan. 14, 1967

1:That's Life
2:Winchester Cathedral
3:Sugar Town
4:Free Again
5:Games That Lovers Play
6:A Man and A Woman *
7:If You Go Away *
8:And We Were Lovers
9:Cabaret
10:Wish Me a Rainbow

Jan. 21, 1967

1:That's Life
2:Sugar Town
3:Whichester Cathedral
4:Games That Lovers Play
5:A Man and A Woman
6:My Cup Runneth Over *
7:If You Go Away
8:And We Were Lovers
9:Free Again
10:Cabaret

Jan. 28, 1967

1:That's Life
2:Sugar Town
3:A Man and A Woman
4:My Cup Runneth Over
5:Games That Lovers Play
6:If You Go Away
7:Winchester Cathedral
8:All *
9:Cabaret
10:Free Again

Feb. 4, 1967

1:Sugar Town
2:That's Life
3:A Man and A Woman
4:My Cup Runneth Over
5:If You Go Away
6:All
7:Games That Lovers Play
8:Winchester Cathedral
9:Cabaret
10:Georgy Girl *

Feb. 11, 1967

1:Sugar Town
2:My Cup Runneth Over
3:That's Life
4:A Man and A Woman
5:If You Go Away
6:Georgy Girl
7:Games That Lovers Play
8:All
9:Winchester Cathedral
10:Cabaret

Feb. 18, 1967

1:My Cup Runneth Over
2:Sugar Town
3:That's Life
4:If You Go Away
5:A Man and A Woman
6:Games That Lovers Play
7:All
8:Georgy Girl
9:Lady *
10:Winchester Cathedral

Feb. 25, 1967

1:My Cup Runneth Over
2:Sugar Town
3:Georgy Girl
4:If You Go Away
5:That's Life
6:A Man and A Woman
7:Lady
8:Games That Lovers Play
9:Tiny Bubbles *
10:All

* Newcomer

Mar. 4, 1967

1:My Cup Runneth Over
2:If You Go Away
3:Georgy Girl
4:Lady
5:Sugar Town
6:That's Life
7:A Man and A Woman
8:Tiny Bubbles
9:All
10:Games That Lovers Play

Mar. 11, 1967

1:My Cup Runneth Over
2:A Man and A Woman
3:Lady
4:Georgy Girl
5:If You Go Away
6:Sugar Town
7:That's Life
8:Sweet Maria *
9:Tiny Bubbles
10:All

Mar. 18, 1967

1:A Man and A Woman
2:Lady
3:My Cup Runneth Over
4:Georgy Girl
5:Sweet Maria
6:Somethin' Stupid *
7:If You Go Away
8:Sugar Town
9:That's Life
10:Tiny Bubbles

Mar. 25, 1967

1:A Man and A Woman
2:Lady
3:Georgy Girl
4:My Cup Runneth Over
5:Somethin' Stupid
6:Music to Watch Girls By *
7:If You Go Away
8:Sweet Maria
9:Sugar Town
10:That's Life

Apr. 1, 1967

1:Lady
2:Georgy Girl
3:A Man and A Woman
4:Somethin' Stupid
5:Music to Watch Girls By
6:My Cup Runneth Over
7:Sweet Maria
8:If You Go Away
9:There's a Kind of Hush *
10:Sugar Town

Apr. 8, 1967

1:Lady
2:Somethin' Stupid
3:Music to Watch Girls By
4:Georgy Girl
5:My Cup Runneth Over
6:There's a Kind of Hush
7:A Man and A Woman
8:This Is My Song *
9:If You Go Away
10:Sugar Town

Apr. 15, 1967

1:Somethin' Stupid
2:Lady
3:There's a Kind of Hush
4:Georgy Girl
5:This Is My Song
6:Music to Watch Girls By
7:My Cup Runneth Over
8:Thoroughly Modern Millie *
9:A Man and A Woman
10:If You Go Away

Apr. 22, 1967

1:Somethin' Stupid
2:There's a Kind of Hush
3:Music to Watch Girls By
4:This Is My Song
5:Thoroughly Modern Millie
6:Georgy Girl
7:Lady
8:My Cup Runneth Over
9:If You Go Away
10:A Man and A Woman

Apr. 29, 1967

1:Somethin' Stupid
2:There's a Kind of Hush
3:This Is My Song
4:Thoroughly Modern Millie
5:Lady
6:Music to Watch Girls By
7:The Happening *
8:My Cup Runneth Over
9:Georgy Girl
10:If You Go Away

May 6, 1967

1:Somethin' Stupid
2:This Is My Song
3:Thoroughly Modern Millie
4:There's a Kind of Hush
5:Music to Watch Girls By
6:Lady
7:The Happening
8:Georgy Girl
9:My Cup Runneth Over
10:If You Go Away

May 13, 1967

1:Somethin' Stupid
2:This Is My Song
3:Thoroughly Modern Millie
4:The Happening
5:There's a Kind of Hush
6:Music to Watch Girls By
7:Lady
8:Release Me *
9:Georgy Girl
10:My Cup Runneth Over

May 20, 1967

1:This Is My Song
2:Somethin' Stupid
3:There's a Kind of Hush
4:Thoroughly Modern Millie
5:Release Me
6:The Happening
7:Lady
8:Music to Watch Girls By
9:Time, Time *
10:Georgy Girl

May 27, 1967

1:This Is My Song
2:Thoroughly Modern Millie
3:Somethin' Stupid
4:The Happening
5:Music to Watch Girls By
6:Time, Time
7:Release Me
8:There's a Kind of Hush
9:Yellow Days *
10:Lady

June 3, 1967

1:This Is My Song
2:Thoroughly Modern Millie
3:The Happening
4:Time, Time
5:Release Me
6:Yellow Days
7:Music to Watch Girls By
8:Somethin' Stupid
9:There's a Kind of Hush
10:Light My Fire *

June 10, 1967

1:This Is My Song
2:Yellow Days
3:Time, Time
4:Thoroughly Modern Millie
5:Light My Fire
6:Release Me
7:The Happening
8:There's a Kind of Hush
9:Music to Watch Girls By
10:Lay Some Happiness On Me *

June 17, 1967

1:This Is My Song
2:Yellow Days
3:Time, Time
4:Light My Fire
5:Release Me
6:Thoroughly Modern Millie
7:Lay Some Happiness On Me
8:There's a Kind of Hush
9:Music to Watch Girls By
10:The Happening

June 24, 1967

1:Yellow Days
2:Time, Time
3:Release Me
4:This Is My Song
5:Windy *
6:Thoroughly Modern Millie
7:Light My Fire
8:Lay Some Happiness On Me
9:There's a Kind of Hush
10:Music to Watch Girls By

July 1, 1967

1:Yellow Days
2:Time, Time
3:Windy
4:This Is My Song
5:Light My Fire
6:Release Me
7:Don't Sleep in the Subway *
8:Thoroughly Modern Millie
9:Lay Some Happiness On Me
10:There's a Kind of Hush

July 8, 1967

1:Windy
2:Yellow Days
3:Don't Sleep in the Subway
4:Time, Time
5:This Is My Song
6:Release Me
7:Thoroughly Modern Millie
8:Can't Take My Eyes Off You *
9:Light My Fire
10:Lay Some Happiness On Me

July 15, 1967

1:Windy
2:Don't Sleep in the Subway
3:Yellow Days
4:This Is My Song
5:Release Me
6:Time, Time
7:Can't Take My Eyes Off You
8:Thoroughly Modern Millie
9:Light My Fire
10:You Only Live Twice *

July 22, 1967

1:Windy
2:Don't Sleep in the Subway
3:Yellow Days
4:Can't Take My Eyes Off You
5:This Is My Song
6:Release Me
7:You Only Live Twice
8:The Look of Love *
9:Time, Time
10:Light My Fire

July 29, 1967

1:Windy
2:Don't Sleep in the Subway
3:Can't Take My Eyes Off You
4:This Is My Song
5:Yellow Days
6:The Look of Love
7:You Only Live Twice
8:Release Me
9:Time, Time
10:Up, Up and Away *

Aug. 5, 1967

1:Don't Sleep in the Subway
2:Windy
3:Can't Take My Eyes Off You
4:Up, Up and Away
5:The Look of Love
6:Yellow Days
7:This Is My Song
8:You Only Live Twice
9:Release Me
10:Time, Time

Aug. 12, 1967

1:Don't Sleep in the Subway
2:Can't Take My Eyes Off You
3:Up, Up and Away
4:The Look of Love
5:Ode to Billy Joe *
6:Windy
7:Yellow Days
8:You Only Live Twice
9:This Is My Song
10:Lover's Roulette *

Aug. 19, 1967

1:Don't Sleep in the Subway
2:Can't Take My Eyes Off You
3:Ode to Billy Joe
4:Up, Up and Away
5:The Look of Love
6:You Only Live Twice
7:Windy
8:Yellow Days
9:Lover's Roulette
10:This Is My Song

Aug. 26, 1967

1:Ode to Billy Joe
2:Can't Take My Eyes Off You
3:Up, Up and Away
4:Don't Sleep in the Subway
5:The Look of Love
6:Windy
7:Lover's Roulette
8:You Only Live Twice
9:The World We Knew *
10:Yellow Days

Sept. 2, 1967

1:Can't Take My Eyes Off You
2:Ode to Billy Joe
3:Up, Up and Away
4:The Look of Love
5:Don't Sleep in the Subway
6:Lover's Roulette
7:The World We Knew
8:Windy
9:It Must Be Him *
10:You Only Live Twice

Sept. 9, 1967

1:Ode to Billy Joe
2:Can't Take My Eyes Off You
3:Up, Up and Away
4:The Look of Love
5:The World We Knew
6:It Must Be Him
7:Don't Sleep in the Subway
8:Lover's Roulette
9:You Only Live Twice
10:Windy

Sept. 16, 1967

1:Ode to Billy Joe
2:The World We Knew
3:Can't Take My Eyes Off You
4:It Must Be Him
5:Up, Up and Away
6:The Look of Love
7:Never My Love *
8:Don't Sleep in the Subway
9:Lover's Roulette
10:Windy

Sept. 23, 1967

1:Ode to Billy Joe
2:Can't Take My Eyes Off You
3:The World We Knew
4:It Must Be Him
5:Never My Love
6:The Look of Love
7:Up, Up and Away
8:Lover's Roulette
9:Windy
10:Don't Sleep in the Subway

Sept. 30, 1967

1:Can't Take My Eyes Off You
2:The World We Knew
3:Ode to Billy Joe
4:Never My Love
5:It Must Be Him
6:Up, Up and Away
7:The Look of Love
8:The Letter *
9:Lover's Roulette
10:Windy

Oct. 7, 1967

1:The World We Knew
2:It Must Be Him
3:Can't Take My Eyes Off You
4:Never My Love
5:Ode to Billy Joe
6:The Letter
7:Up, Up and Away
8:The Look of Love
9:Windy
10:Lover's Roulette

Oct. 14, 1967

1:The World We Knew
2:It Must Be Him
3:Ode to Billy Joe
4:Never My Love
5:The Letter
6:Up, Up and Away
7:Can't Take My Eyes Off You
8:To Sir, With Love *
9:The Look of Love
10:Lover's Roulette

Oct. 21, 1967

1:It Must Be Him
2:The World We Knew
3:Never My Love
4:The Letter
5:Up, Up and Away
6:To Sir, With Love
7:Ode to Billy Joe
8:Can't Take My Eyes Off You
9:The Look of Love
10:Talk to the Animals *

Oct. 28, 1967

1:It Must Be Him
2:Never My Love
3:The World We Knew
4:The Letter
5:To Sir, With Love
6:Talk to the Animals
7:Ode to Billy Joe
8:Up, Up and Away
9:Can't Take My Eyes Off You
10:For Once in My Life *

Nov. 4, 1967

1:It Must Be Him
2:Never My Love
3:The World We Knew
4:To Sir, With Love
5:Talk to the Animals
6:For Once in My Life
7:The Letter
8:Ode to Billy Joe
9:Up, Up and Away
10:Can't Take My Eyes Off You

Nov. 11, 1967

1:To Sir, With Love
2:It Must Be Him
3:Never My Love
4:For Once in My Life
5:The World We Knew
6:Talk to the Animals
7:Up, Up and Away
8:Gentle On My Mind *
9:Can't Take My Eyes Off You
10:Ode to Billy Joe

Nov. 18, 1967

1:It Must Be Him
2:To Sir, With Love
3:For Once in My Life
4:Never My Love
5:Talk to the Animals
6:Gentle On My Mind
7:The World We Knew
8:I Say a Little Prayer *
9:Ode to Billy Joe
10:Can't Take My Eyes Off You

Nov. 25, 1967

1:It Must Be Him
2:To Sir, With Love
3:Never My Love
4:Talk to the Animals
5:For Once in My Life
6:Gentle On My Mind
7:I Say a Little Prayer
8:The World We Knew
9:Can't Take My Eyes Off You
10:Ode to Billy Joe

Dec. 2, 1967

1:It Must Be Him
2:Gentle On My Mind
3:To Sir, With Love
4:For Once in My Life
5:I Say a Little Prayer
6:Never My Love
7:Talk to the Animals
8:By the Time I Get to Phoenix *
9:The World We Knew
10:Ode to Billy Joe

Dec. 9, 1967

1:Gentle On My Mind
2:It Must Be Him
3:To Sir, With Love
4:For Once in My Life
5:I Say a Little Prayer
6:By the Time I Get to Phoenix
7:Talk to the Animals
8:I Almost Called Your Name *
9:Never My Love
10:The World We Knew

Dec. 16, 1967

1:Gentle On My Mind
2:For Once in My Life
3:I Say a Little Prayer
4:It Must Be Him
5:By the Time I Get to Phoenix
6:To Sir, With Love
7:Talk to the Animals
8:I Almost Called Your Name
9:The Last Waltz *
10:Never My Love

Dec. 23, 1967

1:Gentle On My Mind
2:For Once in My Life
3:I Say a Little Prayer
4:By the Time I Get to Phoenix
5:Talk to the Animals
6:I Almost Called Your Name
7:The Last Waltz
8:It Must Be Him
9:Never My Love
10:To Sir, With Love

Dec. 30, 1967

1:Gentle On My Mind
2:I Say a Little Prayer
3:By the Time I Get to Phoenix
4:For Once in My Life
5:The Last Waltz
6:I Almost Called Your Name
7:Never My Love
8:Talk to the Animals
9:To Sir, With Love
10:It Must Be Him

1968

It was the most history-packed year since 1945. Incredibly, 1968 saw the capture of the U.S. intelligence ship *Pueblo* by North Korea, LBJ saying no to another term in a stunning TV throwaway sentence, the assassinations of Martin Luther King and Senator Robert Kennedy, the slow beginnings of Vietnam peace talks in Paris, the muddy spectacle of Resurrection City tents in Washington, the Chicago youth riots at the Democratic Convention, the election of Richard Nixon as President in a comeback squeaker over Hubert Humphrey, the startling marriage of Jackie Kennedy to Aristotle Onassis, the Christmastime release of the *Pueblo* crew, and the Christmastime orbiting of the moon by American astronauts Frank Borman, James Lovell, and William Anders.

It was the year of Tiny Tim, Nehru suits, Black Power gloves at the Olympics, and a gold rush that didn't refer to an old Charlie Chaplin movie. Elvis became a father, Jerry Lewis became a grandfather, and Nixon and Eisenhower got married. That's what the headlines said when daughter Julie was wed to grandson David.

Everyone wanted to be under thirty, except Denny McLain of the Detroit Tigers, who finally went over the number one memorable day on the pitcher's mound. Roberto DeVicenzo gave the sports autograph of the year by signing his incorrect score card at the Masters, and Dancer's Image stood in a stall singing "What Kind of Foal Am I?," after being the first Kentucky Derby winner to be disqualified.

Singer Glen Campbell and songwriter Jim Webb had Number One tunes with "By the Time I Get to Phoenix," from late 1967, and "Wichita Lineman." Jeannie C. Riley had the big novelty tune, "Harper Valley P.T.A." Bobby Goldsboro had the most memorable, "Honey." But Herb Alpert had the year's top one, "This Guy's in Love With You," nine weeks as Number One.

There was a revival of airliner hijackings to Cuba, fashion ushered in the see-through blouse, and Rowan and Martin's "Laugh-In" established itself as the top new TV show of the year, giving the language "Sock it to me" and "Here come de judge." Top movies were *The Graduate, The Odd Couple, Rosemary's Baby,* and *2001: A Space Odyssey.* The top foreign film import was *Closely Watched Trains,* but the most closely watched train was on TV one painful June day making Robert Kennedy's New York-to-Washington funeral trek.

316

Jan. 6, 1968

1:Gentle On My Mind
2:By the Time I Get to Phoenix
3:I Say a Little Prayer
4:The Last Waltz
5:For Once in My Life
6:Step to the Rear *
7:Woman, Woman *
8:I Almost Called Your Name
9:Talk to the Animals
10:To Sir, With Love

Jan. 13, 1968

1:Gentle On My Mind
2:By the Time I Get to Phoenix
3:I Say a Little Prayer
4:The Last Waltz
5:Step to the Rear
6:For Once in My Life
7:Talk to Animals
8:Woman, Woman
9:To Sir, With Love
10:What a Wonderful World *

Jan. 20, 1968

1:By the Time I Get to Phoenix
2:Gentle On My Mind
3:The Last Waltz
4:I Say a Little Prayer
5:Step to the Rear
6:For Once in My Life
7:Woman, Woman
8:What a Wonderful World
9:Talk to the Animals
10:To Sir, With Love

Jan. 27, 1968

1:By the Time I Get to Phoenix
2:The Last Waltz
3:Gentle On My Mind
4:Step to the Rear
5:I Say a Little Prayer
6:Woman, Woman
7:For Once in My Life
8:What a Wonderful World
9:In the Misty Moonlight *
10:Sittin' On the Dock of the Bay *

Feb. 3, 1968

1:By the Time I Get to Phoenix
2:The Last Waltz
3:Step to the Rear
4:Gentle On My Mind
5:What a Wonderful World
6:In the Misty Moonlight
7:Sittin' On the Dock of the Bay
8:I Say a Little Prayer
9:Woman, Woman
10:For Once in My Life

Feb. 10, 1968

1:By the Time I Get to Phoenix
2:The Last Waltz
3:Sittin' On the Dock of the Bay
4:In the Misty Moonlight
5:Step to the Rear
6:Gentle On My Mind
7:What a Wonderful World
8:Live For Life *
9:I Say a Little Prayer
10:Woman, Woman

Feb. 17, 1968

1:By the Time I Get to Phoenix
2:Sittin' On the Dock of the Bay
3:In the Misty Moonlight
4:The Last Waltz
5:Step to the Rear
6:Gentle On My Mind
7:Live For Life
8:What a Wonderful World
9:I Say a Little Prayer
10:Love Is Blue *

Feb. 24, 1968

1:By the Time I Get to Phoenix
2:Sittin' On the Dock of the Bay
3:Love Is Blue
4:In the Misty Moonlight
5:The Last Waltz
6:Live For Life
7:Step to the Rear
8:Gentle On My Mind
9:Theme From Valley of the Dolls *
10:What a Wonderful World

* Newcomer

Mar. 2, 1968

1:Love Is Blue
2:By the Time I Get to Phoenix
3:In the Misty Moonlight
4:Sittin' On the Dock of the Bay
5:The Last Waltz
6:Live For Life
7:Step to the Rear
8:Theme From Valley of the Dolls
9:Gentle On My Mind
10:What a Wonderful World

Mar. 9, 1968

1:Love Is Blue
2:By the Time I Get to Phoenix
3:The Last Waltz
4:Live For Life
5:In the Misty Moonlight
6:Theme From Valley of the Dolls
7:Sittin' On the Dock of the Bay
8:Step to the Rear
9:The Other Man's Grass Is Always Greener *
10:The Lesson *

Mar. 16, 1968

1:Sittin' On the Dock of the Bay
2:Theme From Valley of the Dolls
3:Love Is Blue
4:By the Time I Get to Phoenix
5:The Last Waltz
6:Live For Life
7:In the Misty Moonlight
8:The Other Man's Grass Is Always Greener
9:The Lesson
10:Step to the Rear

Mar. 23, 1968

1:Sittin' On the Dock of the Bay
2:Love Is Blue
3:Theme From Valley of the Dolls
4:The Lesson
5:Live For Life
6:The Last Waltz
7:In the Misty Moonlight
8:By the Time I Get to Phoenix
9:Who Will Answer? *
10:I've Gotta Be Me *

Mar. 30, 1968

1:Love Is Blue
2:Theme From Valley of the Dolls
3:The Lesson
4:The Last Waltz
5:In the Misty Moonlight
6:Sittin' On the Dock of the Bay
7:I've Gotta Be Me
8:By the Time I Get to Phoenix
9:Who Will Answer?
10:Live For Life

Apr. 6, 1968

1:Love Is Blue
2:Theme From Valley of the Dolls
3:The Lesson
4:In the Misty Moonlight
5:Live For Life
6:I've Gotta Be Me
7:Sittin' On the Dock of the Bay
8:Cab Driver *
9:By the Time I Get to Phoenix
10:The Last Waltz

Apr. 13, 1968

1:Love Is Blue
2:Theme From Valley of the Dolls
3:Cab Driver
4:The Lesson
5:Honey *
6:I've Gotta Be Me
7:Kiss Me Goodbye *
8:Sittin' On the Dock of the Bay
9:In the Misty Moonlight
10:Live For Life

Apr. 20, 1968

1:Love Is Blue
2:Cab Driver
3:Honey
4:Theme From Valley of the Dolls
5:I've Gotta Be Me
6:Kiss Me Goodbye
7:The Lesson
8:The Father of Girls *
9:Little Green Apples *
10:Sittin' On the Dock of the Bay

Apr. 27, 1968

1:Honey
2:Love Is Blue
3:Kiss Me Goodbye
4:Cab Driver
5:The Father of Girls
6:Little Green Apples
7:Scarborough Fair *
8:Theme From Valley of the Dolls
9:I've Gotta Be Me
10:The Lesson

May 4, 1968

1:Honey
2:Love Is Blue
3:Scarborough Fair
4:Kiss Me Goodbye
5:Cab Driver
6:Little Green Apples
7:The Father of Girls
8:The Good, the Bad and the Ugly *
9:Theme From Valley of the Dolls
10:I've Gotta Be Me

May 11, 1968

1:Honey
2:The Good, the Bad and the Ugly
3:Love Is Blue
4:Scarborough Fair
5:Kiss Me Goodbye
6:I Can't Believe I'm Losing You *
7:Cab Driver
8:Theme From Valley of the Dolls
9:Little Green Apples
10:The Father of Girls

May 18, 1968

1:Honey
2:The Good, the Bad and the Ugly
3:I Can't Believe I'm Losing You
4:Love Is Blue
5:Scarborough Fair
6:Theme From Valley of the Dolls
7:Delilah *
8:Kiss Me Goodbye
9:Cab Driver
10:Little Green Apples

May 25, 1968

1:Honey
2:The Good, the Bad and the Ugly
3:I Can't Believe I'm Losing You
4:Delilah
5:Do You Know the Way to San Jose? *
6:Love Is Blue
7:Scarborough Fair
8:Little Green Apples
9:This Guy's in Love With You *
10:Kiss Me Goodbye

June 1, 1968

1:Honey
2:The Good, the Bad and the Ugly
3:This Guy's in Love With You
4:Delilah
5:Do You Know the Way to San Jose?
6:I Can't Believe I'm Losing You
7:Love Is Blue
8:Scarborough Fair
9:Kiss Me Goodbye
10:Mrs. Robinson *

June 8, 1968

1:Honey
2:This Guy's in Love With You
3:The Good, the Bad and the Ugly
4:Do You Know the Way to San Jose?
5:Mrs. Robinson
6:A Man Without Love *
7:Delilah
8:I Can't Believe I'm Losing You
9:Love Is Blue
10:Kiss Me Goodbye

June 15, 1968

1:This Guy's in Love With You
2:Honey
3:The Good, the Bad and the Ugly
4:Mrs. Robinson
5:A Man Without Love
6:Do You Know the Way to San Jose?
7:Lonely Is the Name *
8:Delilah
9:I Can't Believe I'm Losing You
10:Sweet Memories *

June 22, 1968

1:This Guy's in Love With You
2:A Man Without Love
3:Mrs. Robinson
4:The Good, the Bad and the Ugly
5:Do You Know the Way to San Jose?
6:Lonely Is the Name
7:Sweet Memories
8:Honey
9:Delilah
10:I Can't Believe I'm Losing You

June 29, 1968

1:This Guy's in Love With You
2:A Man Without Love
3:Sweet Memories
4:Mrs. Robinson
5:Lonely Is the Name
6:The Good, the Bad and the Ugly
7:My Shy Violet *
8:Do You Know the Way to San Jose?
9:Honey
10:I Can't Believe I'm Losing You

July 6, 1968

1:This Guy's in Love With You
2:A Man Without Love
3:My Shy Violet
4:Sweet Memories
5:The Good, the Bad and the Ugly
6:Don't Break My Pretty Balloon *
7:Mrs. Robinson
8:Honey
9:Lonely Is the Name
10:Do You Know the Way to San Jose?

July 13, 1968

1:This Guy's in Love With You
2:A Man Without Love
3:Sweet Memories
4:My Shy Violet
5:Don't Break My Pretty Balloon
6:Autumn of My Life *
7:Honey
8:The Good, the Bad and the Ugly
9:Lonely Is the Name
10:Mrs. Robinson

July 20, 1968

1:This Guy's in Love With You
2:A Man Without Love
3:Autumn of My Life
4:Sweet Memories
5:My Shy Violet
6:Don't Break My Pretty Balloon
7:MacArthur Park *
8:Mrs. Robinson
9:Honey
10:Dreams of the Everyday Housewife *

July 27, 1968

1:This Guy's in Love With You
2:Autumn of My Life
3:Sweet Memories
4:A Man Without Love
5:Don't Break My Pretty Balloon
6:MacArthur Park
7:Dreams of the Everyday Housewife
8:Honey
9:My Shy Violet
10:Classical Gas *

Aug. 3, 1968

1:This Guy's in Love With You
2:Autumn of My Life
3:Classical Gas
4:Dreams of the Everyday Housewife
5:Sweet Memories
6:A Man Without Love
7:Honey
8:MacArthur Park
9:Don't Break My Pretty Balloon
10:My Shy Violet

Aug. 10, 1968

1:This Guy's in Love With You
2:Autumn of My Life
3:Dreams of the Everyday Housewife
4:Classical Gas
5:Sweet Memories
6:A Man Without Love
7:MacArthur Park
8:Honey
9:With Pen in Hand *
10:Don't Break My Pretty Balloon

Aug. 17, 1968

1:Classical Gas
2:Autumn of My Life
3:This Guy's in Love With You
4:Dreams of the Everyday Housewife
5:With Pen in Hand
6:MacArthur Park
7:A Man Without Love
8:Sweet Memories
9:Don't Break My Pretty Balloon
10:Honey

Aug. 24, 1968

1:Classical Gas
2:Autumn of My Life
3:With Pen in Hand
4:Dreams of the Everyday Housewife
5:Fool On the Hill *
6:This Guy's in Love With You
7:MacArthur Park
8:A Man Without Love
9:Honey
10:Sweet Memories

Aug. 31, 1968

1:Classical Gas
2:Fool On the Hill
3:Autumn of My Life
4:With Pen in Hand
5:My Way of Life *
6:Dreams of the Everyday Housewife
7:This Guy's in Love With You
8:MacArthur Park
9:A Man Without Love
10:Sweet Memories

Sept. 7, 1968

1:Fool On the Hill
2:Classical Gas
3:My Way of Life
4:With Pen in Hand
5:Autumn of My Life
6:To Wait For Love *
7:Dreams of the Everyday Housewife
8:This Guy's in Love With You
9:MacArthur Park
10:A Man Without Love

Sept. 14, 1968

1:Fool On the Hill
2:Classical Gas
3:My Way of Life
4:To Wait For Love
5:Hey, Jude *
6:Harper Valley P.T.A. *
7:With Pen in Hand
8:Autumn of My Life
9:Dreams of the Everyday Housewife
10:This Guy's in Love With You

Sept. 21, 1968

1:Fool On the Hill
2:To Wait For Love
3:Hey, Jude
4:My Way of Life
5:Harper Valley P.T.A.
6:Classical Gas
7:My Special Angel *
8:With Pen in Hand
9:Autumn of My Life
10:Dreams of the Everyday Housewife

Sept. 28, 1968

1:Harper Valley P.T.A.
2:Fool On the Hill
3:Hey, Jude
4:My Way of Life
5:To Wait For Love
6:My Special Angel
7:Classical Gas
8:Help Yourself *
9:With Pen in Hand
10:Autumn of My Life

Oct. 5, 1968

1:Harper Valley P.T.A.
2:Hey, Jude
3:My Way of Life
4:Fool On the Hill
5:My Special Angel
6:To Wait For Love
7:Help Yourself
8:Then You Can Tell Me Goodbye *
9:With Pen in Hand
10:Classical Gas

Oct. 12, 1968

1:Hey, Jude
2:Harper Valley P.T.A.
3:My Special Angel
4:Help Yourself
5:Fool On the Hill
6:Then You Can Tell Me Goodbye
7:My Way of Life
8:To Wait For Love
9:Those Were the Days *
10:With Pen in Hand

Oct. 19, 1968

1:Hey, Jude
2:My Special Angel
3:Those Were the Days
4:Help Yourself
5:Fool On the Hill
6:Then You Can Tell Me Goodbye
7:Harper Valley P.T.A.
8:My Way of Life
9:To Wait For Love
10:Les Bicyclettes De Belsize *

Oct. 26, 1968

1:Hey, Jude
2:Those Were the Days
3:My Special Angel
4:Fool On the Hill
5:Then You Can Tell Me Goodbye
6:Les Bicyclettes De Belsize
7:Help Yourself
8:Harper Valley P.T.A.
9:Cycles *
10:My Way of Life

Nov. 2, 1968

1:Hey, Jude
2:Those Were the Days
3:Les Bicyclettes De Belsize
4:Cycles
5:My Special Angel
6:Fool On the Hill
7:Then You Can Tell Me Goodbye
8:Help Yourself
9:The Straight Life *
10:Harper Valley P.T.A.

Nov. 9, 1968

1:Hey, Jude
2:Those Were the Days
3:My Special Angel
4:Cycles
5:Les Bicyclettes De Belsize
6:The Straight Life
7:Fool On the Hill
8:Harper Valley P.T.A.
9:Help Yourself
10:Then You Can Tell Me Goodbye

Nov. 16, 1968

1:Hey, Jude
2:Those Were the Days
3:Cycles
4:Les Bicyclettes De Belsize
5:My Special Angel
6:The Straight Life
7:Wichita Lineman *
8:Fool On the Hill
9:Then You Can Tell Me Goodbye
10:Help Yourself

Nov. 23, 1968

1:Those Were the Days
2:Cycles
3:Hey, Jude
4:Wichita Lineman
5:Les Bicyclettes De Belsize
6:The Straight Life
7:Promises, Promises *
8:My Special Angel
9:Fool On the Hill
10:Then You Can Tell Me Goodbye

Nov. 30, 1968

1:Those Were the Days
2:Cycles
3:Wichita Lineman
4:Les Bicyclettes De Belsize
5:The Straight Life
6:Promises, Promises
7:My Special Angel
8:Hey, Jude
9:Fool On the Hill
10:Then You Can Tell Me Goodbye

Dec. 7, 1968

1:Those Were the Days
2:Wichita Lineman
3:Les Bicyclettes De Belsize
4:Cycles
5:The Straight Life
6:Promises, Promises
7:Saturday Night at the World *
8:My Special Angel
9:Hey, Jude
10:Fool On the Hill

Dec. 14, 1968

1:Those Were the Days
2:Wichita Lineman
3:Cycles
4:Promises, Promises
5:The Straight Life
6:Saturday Night at the World
7:Hey, Jude
8:L.A., Break Down *
9:Les Bicyclettes De Belsize
10:My Special Angel

Dec. 21, 1968

1:Wichita Lineman
2:Cycles
3:Promises, Promises
4:Those Were the Days
5:L.A., Break Down
6:Saturday Night at the World
7:The Straight Life
8:My Special Angel
9:Hey, Jude
10:Les Bicyclettes De Belsize

Dec. 28, 1968

1:Wichita Lineman
2:Promises, Promises
3:Cycles
4:L.A., Break Down
5:Saturday Night at the World
6:The Straight Life
7:Those Were the Days
8:Les Bicyclettes De Belsize
9:My Special Angel
10:Hey, Jude

1969

It will forever and always be the year that man first walked on the moon. A world that couldn't believe its eyes, much less that Americans had beaten the Russians there, watched TV in awe that night of July 20, 1969, as Neil Armstrong became the first man to leave his footprints on the moon. His first words, "That's one small step for man, one giant leap for mankind," became a quote for the ages. Minutes later he was joined by astronaut Edwin Aldrin, Jr., as Michael Collins orbited above them in Apollo 11. And four months later, while Richard F. Gordon, Jr., did the orbiting, Apollo 12 astronauts Charles Conrad, Jr., and Alan Bean accomplished the feat for America for the second time in the same year.

Aside from the moon, the second most famous location in the 1969 headlines was Chappaquiddick, where the tragedy of the Kennedys loomed again as Senator Edward Kennedy's car went off the bridge, and he waited all night before notifying authorities that a young secretary had drowned in the mishap.

In such a year it seemed nothing could further surprise or stun the nation. But the New York Jets, of the underdog American Football League, had beaten the NFL champs for the first time in the Super Bowl, and the lowly, laughable New York Mets won not only the pennant but also the World Series.

It was the year of rock festivals in open fields, Hurricane Camille, female racetrack jockeys, and a new wave of youth-oriented movies led by *Midnight Cowboy* and *Easy Rider.* Campus rebellions by college students were on the front pages, and long hair and sideburns were "in" for men. The year ushered in a sexual permissiveness not seen since the days of the Roman Empire. It was anything-goes in the movies and on the newsstands. There were nudes and sexual acts on the Broadway stage in *Oh! Calcutta!* and *Hair,* the latter being a rock musical that gave the Top Ten its first tandem song as one entry, "Aquarius/Let the Sunshine In." Six weeks as Number One, it tied with "A Time For Us," from the film *Romeo and Juliet,* as 1969's top song.

Dwight D. Eisenhower, Ho Chi Minh, and *The Saturday Evening Post* all died; the best seller of the year was *Portnoy's Complaint;* and the exposure of the year was the My Lai Massacre, which intensified dissatisfaction with the United States' part in the Vietnam war.

Jan. 4, 1969

1:Wichita Lineman
2:L.A., Break Down
3:Cycles
4:Promises, Promises
5:Saturday Night at the World
6:Both Sides Now *
7:Rain in My Heart *
8:The Straight Life
9:Those Were the Days
10:Les Bicyclettes De Belsize

Jan. 11, 1969

1:Wichita Lineman
2:L.A., Break Down
3:Both Sides Now
4:Promises, Promises
5:Cycles
6:Rain in My Heart
7:Stand By Your Man *
8:Saturday Night at the World
9:Les Bicyclettes De Belsize
10:The Straight Life

Jan. 18, 1969

1:Wichita Lineman
2:Both Sides Now
3:L.A., Break Down
4:Rain in My Heart
5:Promises, Promises
6:Cycles
7:Saturday Night at the World
8:Stand By Your Man
9:The Straight Life
10:Feelin' *

Jan. 25, 1969

1:Wichita Lineman
2:Rain in My Heart
3:Both Sides Now
4:L.A., Break Down
5:Stand By Your Man
6:Feelin'
7:Saturday Night at the World
8:Cycles
9:Promises, Promises
10:Talk Until Daylight *

Feb. 1, 1969

1:Wichita Lineman
2:Rain in My Heart
3:Stand By Your Man
4:Saturday Night at the World
5:Both Sides Now
6:Feelin'
7:L.A., Break Down
8:Talk Until Daylight
9:Cycles
10:Promises, Promises

Feb. 8, 1969

1:Rain in My Heart
2:Stand By Your Man
3:Wichita Lineman
4:Feelin'
5:You Gave Me a Mountain *
6:Saturday Night at the World
7:Talk Until Daylight
8:L.A., Break Down
9:Both Sides Now
10:Promises, Promises

Feb. 15, 1969

1:Rain in My Heart
2:You Gave Me a Mountain
3:Wichita Lineman
4:Stand By Your Man
5:Johnny One Time *
6:Feelin'
7:Saturday Night at the World
8:Talk Until Daylight
9:L.A., Break Down
10:Both Sides Now

Feb. 22, 1969

1:Rain in My Heart
2:You Gave Me a Mountain
3:Johnny One Time
4:Stand By Your Man
5:Traces *
6:Proud Mary *
7:Feelin'
8:Talk Until Daylight
9:Wichita Lineman
10:Both Sides Now

* Newcomer

Mar. 1, 1969

1:You Gave Me a Mountain
2:Johnny One Time
3:Rain in My Heart
4:Traces
5:Proud Mary
6:The Wedding Cake *
7:Stand By Your Man
8:Feelin'
9:Talk Until Daylight
10:Both Sides Now

Mar. 8, 1969

1:You Gave Me a Mountain
2:Traces
3:Johnny One Time
4:Proud Mary
5:The Wedding Cake
6:Feelin'
7:Galveston *
8:Stand By Your Man
9:Rain in My Heart
10:Both Sides Now

Mar. 15, 1969

1:Traces
2:Proud Mary
3:You Gave Me a Mountain
4:The Wedding Cake
5:Johnny One Time
6:Galveston
7:Stand By Your Man
8:Rain in My Heart
9:Both Sides Now
10:Aquarius/Let the Sunshine In *

Mar. 22, 1969

1:Traces
2:Proud Mary
3:Johnny One Time
4:Galveston
5:Aquarius/Let the Sunshine In
6:You Gave Me a Mountain
7:The Wedding Cake
8:Stand By Your Man
9:Rain in My Heart
10:Both Sides Now

Mar. 29, 1969

1:Traces
2:Aquarius/Let the Sunshine In
3:Proud Mary
4:Galveston
5:You Gave Me a Mountain
6:Johnny One Time
7:The Wedding Cake
8:My Way *
9:Stand By Your Man
10:Rain in My Heart

Apr. 5, 1969

1:Traces
2:Aquarius/Let the Sunshine In
3:Galveston
4:My Way
5:Proud Mary
6:You Gave Me a Mountain
7:Johnny One Time
8:The Wedding Cake
9:Rain in My Heart
10:I'll Catch the Sun *

Apr. 12, 1969

1:Aquarius/Let the Sunshine In
2:Traces
3:Galveston
4:My Way
5:Proud Mary
6:I'll Catch the Sun
7:You Gave Me a Mountain
8:Johnny One Time
9:The Wedding Cake
10:Memories *

Apr. 19, 1969

1:Aquarius/Let the Sunshine In
2:Galveston
3:My Way
4:Traces
5:I'll Catch the Sun
6:Memories
7:Proud Mary
8:You Gave Me a Mountain
9:Happy Heart *
10:The Wedding Cake

Apr. 26, 1969

1:Galveston
2:Aquarius/Let the Sunshine In
3:My Way
4:Happy Heart
5:I'll Catch the Sun
6:Traces
7:Seattle *
8:Memories
9:You Gave Me a Mountain
10:Proud Mary

May 3, 1969

1:Aquarius/Let the Sunshine In
2:Galveston
3:My Way
4:Happy Heart
5:Seattle
6:I'll Catch the Sun
7:Traces
8:Love Can Make You Happy *
9:Memories
10:You Gave Me a Mountain

May 10, 1969

1:Galveston
2:Aquarius/Let the Sunshine In
3:Happy Heart
4:My Way
5:Seattle
6:Love Can Make You Happy
7:Goodbye *
8:Traces
9:I'll Catch the Sun
10:Memories

May 17, 1969

1:Aquarius/Let the Sunshine In
2:Galveston
3:My Way
4:Happy Heart
5:Love Can Make You Happy
6:Goodbye
7:Seattle
8:Traces
9:A Time For Us *
10:I'll Catch the Sun

May 24, 1969

1:Aquarius/Let the Sunshine In
2:My Way
3:Happy Heart
4:Galveston
5:Seattle
6:Love Can Make You Happy
7:A Time For Us
8:Goodbye
9:I'll Catch the Sun
10:Traces

May 31, 1969

1:Aquarius/Let the Sunshine In
2:Happy Heart
3:Love Can Make You Happy
4:A Time For Us
5:Goodbye
6:My Way
7:Seattle
8:Hold Me Tight *
9:Galveston
10:I'll Catch the Sun

June 7, 1969

1:Happy Heart
2:Aquarius/Let the Sunshine In
3:A Time For Us
4:Love Can Make You Happy
5:Goodbye
6:Love Me Tonight *
7:Seattle
8:Hold Me Tight
9:My Way
10:Galveston

June 14, 1969

1:Happy Heart
2:A Time For Us
3:Aquarius/Let the Sunshine In
4:Love Can Make You Happy
5:Love Me Tonight
6:Goodbye
7:Hold Me Tight
8:Seattle
9:The April Fools *
10:My Way

June 21, 1969

1:A Time For Us
2:Love Me Tonight
3:Love Can Make You Happy
4:Happy Heart
5:Aquarius/Let the Sunshine In
6:Goodbye
7:The April Fools
8:Seattle
9:Hold Me Tight
10:My Way

June 28, 1969

1:A Time For Us
2:Love Me Tonight
3:Love Can Make You Happy
4:The April Fools
5:Happy Heart
6:Yesterday When I Was Young *
7:Aquarius/Let the Sunshine In
8:Hold Me Tight
9:Goodbye
10:Seattle

July 5, 1969

1:A Time For Us
2:Love Me Tonight
3:Yesterday When I Was Young
4:The April Fools
5:Spinning Wheel *
6:Quentin's Theme *
7:Love Can Make You Happy
8:Happy Heart
9:Hold Me Tight
10:Didn't We? *

July 12, 1969

1:A Time For Us
2:Love Me Tonight
3:Spinning Wheel
4:Quentin's Theme
5:Yesterday When I Was Young
6:Didn't We?
7:The April Fools
8:The Days of Sand and Shovels *
9:Love Can Make You Happy
10:Happy Heart

July 19, 1969

1:A Time For Us
2:Spinning Wheel
3:Love Me Tonight
4:Quentin's Theme
5:Yesterday When I Was Young
6:Didn't We?
7:The Days of Sand and Shovels
8:In the Year 2525 *
9:The April Fools
10:But For Love *

July 26, 1969

1:A Time For Us
2:Spinning Wheel
3:In the Year 2525
4:Quentin's Theme
5:Yesterday When I Was Young
6:The Days of Sand and Shovels
7:Love Me Tonight
8:Didn't We?
9:But For Love
10:The April Fools

Aug. 2, 1969

1:Spinning Wheel
2:In the Year 2525
3:A Time For Us
4:Yesterday When I Was Young
5:Quentin's Theme
6:Sweet Caroline *
7:The Days of Sand and Shovels
8:Love Me Tonight
9:Didn't We?
10:But For Love

Aug. 9, 1969

1:Spinning Wheel
2:A Time For Us
3:In the Year 2525
4:Sweet Caroline
5:Quentin's Theme
6:Yesterday When I Was Young
7:True Grit *
8:The Days of Sand and Shovels
9:Love Me Tonight
10:But For Love

328

Aug. 16, 1969

1:In the Year 2525
2:Sweet Caroline
3:A Time For Us
4:Yesterday When I Was Young
5:Spinning Wheel
6:Quentin's Theme
7:True Grit
8:A Boy Named Sue *
9:The Days of Sand and Shovels
10:Love Me Tonight

Aug. 23, 1969

1:In the Year 2525
2:Sweet Caroline
3:A Boy Named Sue
4:A Time For Us
5:Quentin's Theme
6:True Grit
7:Yesterday When I Was Young
8:Spinning Wheel
9:Jean *
10:The Days of Sand and Shovels

Aug. 30, 1969

1:A Boy Named Sue
2:Sweet Caroline
3:In the Year 2525
4:True Grit
5:A Time For Us
6:Jean
7:Quentin's Theme
8:The Days of Sand and Shovels
9:Yesterday When I Was Young
10:Spinning Wheel

Sept. 6, 1969

1:A Boy Named Sue
2:Sweet Caroline
3:Jean
4:True Grit
5:In the Year 2525
6:A Time For Us
7:Everybody's Talkin' *
8:Quentin's Theme
9:Yesterday When I Was Young
10:The Days of Sand and Shovels

Sept. 13, 1969

1:Jean
2:A Boy Named Sue
3:Sweet Caroline
4:True Grit
5:Everybody's Talkin'
6:In the Year 2525
7:A Time For Us
8:We *
9:Quentin's Theme
10:Yesterday When I Was Young

Sept. 20, 1969

1:Jean
2:A Boy Named Sue
3:Sweet Caroline
4:Everybody's Talkin'
5:True Grit
6:Is That All There Is? *
7:A Time For Us
8:Eternity *
9:We
10:In the Year 2525

Sept. 27, 1969

1:Jean
2:A Boy Named Sue
3:Everybody's Talkin'
4:Sweet Caroline
5:Is That All There Is?
6:We
7:True Grit
8:Eternity
9:A Time For Us
10:In the Year 2525

Oct. 4, 1969

1:Jean
2:Everybody's Talkin'
3:Is That All There Is?
4:We
5:Love's Been Good to Me *
6:A Boy Named Sue
7:Eternity
8:Sweet Caroline
9:True Grit
10:A Time For Us

Oct. 11, 1969

1:Jean
2:Everybody's Talkin'
3:Is That All There Is?
4:Eternity
5:Love's Been Good to Me
6:We
7:Sweet Caroline
8:From Atlanta to Goodbye *
9:True Grit
10:A Boy Named Sue

Oct. 18, 1969

1:Is That All There Is?
2:Jean
3:Everybody's Talkin'
4:Eternity
5:Love's Been Good to Me
6:From Atlanta to Goodbye
7:We
8:True Grit
9:A Boy Named Sue
10:Sweet Caroline

Oct. 25, 1969

1:Is That All There Is?
2:Jean
3:Everybody's Talkin'
4:Eternity
5:Love's Been Good to Me
6:Wedding Bell Blues *
7:From Atlanta to Goodbye
8:True Grit
9:We
10:A Boy Named Sue

Nov. 1, 1969

1:Is That All There Is?
2:Jean
3:Everybody's Talkin'
4:Wedding Bell Blues
5:Eternity
6:Try a Little Kindness *
7:Love's Been Good to Me
8:True Grit
9:From Atlanta to Goodbye
10:We

Nov. 8, 1969

1:Wedding Bell Blues
2:Is That All There Is?
3:Eternity
4:Jean
5:Try a Little Kindness
6:Everybody's Talkin'
7:Leaving On a Jet Plane *
8:Midnight Cowboy *
9:Love's Been Good to Me
10:True Grit

Nov. 15, 1969

1:Wedding Bell Blues
2:Try a Little Kindness
3:Is That All There Is?
4:Leaving On a Jet Plane
5:Jean
6:Midnight Cowboy
7:Eternity
8:Everybody's Talkin'
9:True Grit
10:Love's Been Good to Me

Nov. 22, 1969

1:Wedding Bell Blues
2:Leaving On a Jet Plane
3:Midnight Cowboy
4:Try a Little Kindness
5:I Guess the Lord Must Be in New York City *
6:Raindrops Keep Fallin' On My Head *
7:Is That All There Is?
8:Jean
9:Everybody's Talkin'
10:Love's Been Good to Me

Nov. 29, 1969

1:Leaving On a Jet Plane
2:Midnight Cowboy
3:Raindrops Keep Fallin' On My Head
4:Try a Little Kindness
5:Wedding Bell Blues
6:I Guess the Lord Must Be in New York City
7:Take a Letter, Maria *
8:Is That All There Is?
9:Jean
10:Everybody's Talkin'

Dec. 6, 1969

1:Leaving On a Jet Plane
2:Raindrops Keep Fallin' On My Head
3:Midnight Cowboy
4:Try a Little Kindness
5:Wedding Bell Blues
6:Take a Letter, Maria
7:And When I Die *
8:I Guess the Lord Must Be in New York City
9:Everybody's Talkin'
10:Jean

Dec. 13, 1969

1:Leaving On a Jet Plane
2:Raindrops Keep Fallin' On My Head
3:And When I Die
4:Midnight Cowboy
5:Take a Letter, Maria
6:Try a Little Kindness
7:Wedding Bell Blues
8:A Woman's Way *
9:Jean
10:Everybody's Talkin'

Dec. 20, 1969

1:Leaving On a Jet Plane
2:Raindrops Keep Fallin' On My Head
3:And When I Die
4:Midnight Cowboy
5:Everybody's Talkin'
6:A Woman's Way
7:Take a Letter, Maria
8:Jean
9:Wedding Bell Blues
10:Try a Little Kindness

Dec. 27, 1969

1:Raindrops Keep Fallin' On My Head
2:Midnight Cowboy
3:Leaving On a Jet Plane
4:Try a Little Kindness
5:Take a Letter, Maria
6:And When I Die
7:A Woman's Way
8:Everybody's Talkin'
9:Jean
10:Wedding Bell Blues

1970

The Spectacular Seventies came in with a bang. There was the roar of National Guard gunfire on the campus of Ohio's Kent State University that left four student demonstrators dead. There was the sound of four hijacked jets being blown up in the desert by Arabs. The world's worst natural disaster occurred in Pakistan when huge tidal waves left hundreds of thousands dead, and in this country there was the disastrous Hurricane Celia.

Dramas of the year were (books) *The Godfather,* (movies) *Patton* and *Love Story,* and (real life) Apollo 13 astronauts James Lovell, Fred Haise, and John Swigert limping back from outer space to a successful splashdown after a malfunction scrubbed their proposed moon landing and threatened for a while to leave them stranded like the astronauts in the 1970 fictionalized movie, *Marooned.*

The unpopular Vietnam war droned on as President Nixon sent troops in—and out—of Cambodia. An unknown millionaire named Michael Brody began giving away his money to anyone who phoned him for a donation. Johnny Cash had a boy and named him Johnny instead of Sue.

Broadway finally said "Good-bye, Dolly" after she set a new longevity record for a musical—2,844 performances. Newest college fad was the longest kiss—twenty-seven hours and fourteen minutes—set by an Omaha couple. (Sure, he kissed you once, but will he kiss you again?)

It was the year of the Women's Liberation movement, of the hardhat workers who came out backing President Nixon, and of the nation's first postal strike. In sports UCLA won an unprecedented fourth straight national basketball title, and Tom Dempsey of the New Orleans Saints kicked a record-shattering sixty-three-yard field goal. The bizarre Charles Manson trial for the Sharon Tate murders held the headlines. Tragic airplane crashes wiped out the football teams of Wichita State and Marshall University. Pro coach Vince Lombardi died, and the epitaph for Marie Dionne could have read: And then there were three.

The hottest new recording group was The Carpenters, whose "Close to You" and "We've Only Just Begun," each with seven weeks as Number One, were the top songs of 1970.

332

Jan. 3, 1970

1:Raindrops Keep Fallin' On My Head
2:Leaving On a Jet Plane
3:And When I Die
4:Try a Little Kindness
5:Take a Letter, Maria
6:Early in the Morning *
7:Wedding Bell Blues
8:Midnight Cowboy
9:A Woman's Way
10:Everybody's Talkin'

Jan. 10, 1970

1:Raindrops Keep Fallin' On My Head
2:Leaving On a Jet Plane
3:Early in the Morning
4:Take a Letter, Maria
5:And When I Die
6:Midnight Cowboy
7:Without Love *
8:Try a Little Kindness
9:Wedding Bell Blues
10:A Woman's Way

Jan. 17, 1970

1:Raindrops Keep Fallin' On My Head
2:Early in the Morning
3:Without Love
4:Leaving On a Jet Plane
5:Midnight Cowboy
6:Take a Letter, Maria
7:And When I Die
8:Try a Little Kindness
9:A Woman's Way
10:Wedding Bell Blues

Jan. 24, 1970

1:Raindrops Keep Fallin' On My Head
2:Without Love
3:Early in the Morning
4:Leaving On a Jet Plane
5:Honey, Come Back *
6:Take a Letter, Maria
7:Midnight Cowboy
8:Try a Little Kindness
9:And When I Die
10:Wedding Bell Blues

Jan. 31, 1970

1:Without Love
2:Raindrops Keep Fallin' On My Head
3:Honey, Come Back
4:Early in the Morning
5:Rainy Night in Georgia *
6:Leaving On a Jet Plane
7:Try a Little Kindness
8:Take a Letter, Maria
9:And When I Die
10:Midnight Cowboy

Feb. 7, 1970

1:Without Love
2:Honey, Come Back
3:Rainy Night in Georgia
4:Raindrops Keep Fallin' On My Head
5:Winter World of Love *
6:Early in the Morning
7:Leaving On a Jet Plane
8:Try a Little Kindness
9:Take a Letter, Maria
10:And When I Die

Feb. 14, 1970

1:Without Love
2:Honey, Come Back
3:Winter World of Love
4:Rainy Night in Georgia
5:Raindrops Keep Fallin' On My Head
6:Bridge Over Troubled Water *
7:New World Coming *
8:Early in the Morning
9:Take a Letter, Maria
10:And When I Die

Feb. 21, 1970

1:Without Love
2:Honey, Come Back
3:Bridge Over Troubled Water
4:Rainy Night in Georgia
5:New World Coming
6:Winter World of Love
7:Raindrops Keep Fallin' On My Head
8:Early in the Morning
9:Easy Come, Easy Go *
10:Hey There, Lonely Girl *

* Newcomer

Feb. 28, 1970

1:Bridge Over Troubled Water
2:New World Coming
3:Rainy Night in Georgia
4:Without Love
5:Honey, Come Back
6:Winter World of Love
7:Hey There, Lonely Girl
8:Easy Come, Easy Go
9:Early in the Morning
10:Raindrops Keep Fallin' On My Head

Mar. 7, 1970

1:Bridge Over Troubled Water
2:Rainy Night in Georgia
3:New World Coming
4:Honey, Come Back
5:Without Love
6:Easy Come, Easy Go
7:Kentucky Rain *
8:Winter World of Love
9:Hey There, Lonely Girl
10:Early in the Morning

Mar. 14, 1970

1:Bridge Over Troubled Water
2:Rainy Night in Georgia
3:Kentucky Rain
4:Easy Come, Easy Go
5:New World Coming
6:Honey, Come Back
7:Without Love
8:Hey There, Lonely Girl
9:Winter World of Love
10:Early in the Morning

Mar. 21, 1970

1:Bridge Over Troubled Water
2:Rainy Night in Georgia
3:Easy Come, Easy Go
4:Hey There, Lonely Girl
5:Kentucky Rain
6:Honey, Come Back
7:New World Coming
8:My Elusive Dreams *
9:Winter World of Love
10:Without Love

Mar. 28, 1970

1:Bridge Over Troubled Water
2:Easy Come, Easy Go
3:Kentucky Rain
4:Rainy Night in Georgia
5:My Elusive Dreams
6:Let It Be *
7:New World Coming
8:Hey There, Lonely Girl
9:Honey, Come Back
10:Winter World of Love

Apr. 4, 1970

1:Bridge Over Troubled Water
2:Easy Come, Easy Go
3:Kentucky Rain
4:Let It Be
5:My Elusive Dreams
6:I Would Be in Love (Anyway) *
7:Rainy Night in Georgia
8:Hey There, Lonely Girl
9:Honey, Come Back
10:New World Coming

Apr. 11, 1970

1:Let It Be
2:Easy Come, Easy Go
3:Bridge Over Troubled Water
4:I Would Be in Love (Anyway)
5:For the Love of Him *
6:Kentucky Rain
7:My Elusive Dreams
8:Rainy Night in Georgia
9:Hey There, Lonely Girl
10:Honey, Come Back

Apr. 18, 1970

1:Let It Be
2:Easy Come, Easy Go
3:For the Love of Him
4:I Would Be in Love (Anyway)
5:Everybody's Out of Town *
6:Love or Let Me Be Lonely *
7:Bridge Over Troubled Water
8:Kentucky Rain
9:My Elusive Dreams
10:Rainy Night in Georgia

Apr. 25, 1970

1:Let It Be
2:For the Love of Him
3:Everybody's Out of Town
4:I Would Be in Love (Anyway)
5:Easy Come, Easy Go
6:Everything Is Beautiful *
7:Love or Let Me Be Lonely
8:Tennessee Birdwalk *
9:Bridge Over Troubled Water
10:Kentucky Rain

May 2, 1970

1:Let It Be
2:For the Love of Him
3:Everybody's Out of Town
4:Everything Is Beautiful
5:Tennessee Birdwalk
6:Let Me Go to Him *
7:I Would Be in Love (Anyway)
8:Easy Come, Easy Go
9:Love or Let Me Be Lonely
10:Kentucky Rain

May 9, 1970

1:For the Love of Him
2:Everything Is Beautiful
3:Let Me Go to Him
4:Let It Be
5:Everybody's Out of Town
6:Love or Let Me Be Lonely
7:Tennessee Birdwalk
8:I Would Be in Love (Anyway)
9:Kentucky Rain
10:Easy Come, Easy Go

May 16, 1970

1:For the Love of Him
2:Everything Is Beautiful
3:Let Me Go to Him
4:Everybody's Out of Town
5:Tennessee Birdwalk
6:Love or Let Me Be Lonely
7:Let It Be
8:United We Stand *
9:Easy Come, Easy Go
10:I Would Be in Love (Anyway)

May 23, 1970

1:Everything Is Beautiful
2:For the Love of Him
3:Let Me Go to Him
4:Everybody's Out of Town
5:Tennessee Birdwalk
6:United We Stand
7:Let It Be
8:Love or Let Me Be Lonely
9:Easy Come, Easy Go
10:The Wonder of You *

May 30, 1970

1:Everything Is Beautiful
2:For the Love of Him
3:The Wonder of You
4:United We Stand
5:Let Me Go to Him
6:Tennessee Birdwalk
7:Everybody's Out of Town
8:Love or Let Me Be Lonely
9:Easy Come, Easy Go
10:Let It Be

June 6, 1970

1:Everything Is Beautiful
2:The Wonder of You
3:United We Stand
4:For the Love of Him
5:Tennessee Birdwalk
6:The Long and Winding Road *
7:Let Me Go to Him
8:Everybody's Out of Town
9:Love or Let Me Be Lonely
10:Easy Come, Easy Go

June 13, 1970

1:Everything Is Beautiful
2:United We Stand
3:The Wonder of You
4:For the Love of Him
5:The Long and Winding Road
6:Tennessee Birdwalk
7:Come Saturday Morning *
8:Let Me Go to Him
9:Everybody's Out of Town
10:Love or Let Me Be Lonely

June 20, 1970

1:The Long and Winding Road
2:The Wonder of You
3:Everything Is Beautiful
4:Come Saturday Morning
5:United We Stand
6:One Day of Your Life *
7:For the Love of Him
8:Tennessee Birdwalk
9:Let Me Go to Him
10:Everybody's Out of Town

June 27, 1970

1:The Long and Winding Road
2:The Wonder of You
3:One Day of Your Life
4:Everything Is Beautiful
5:United We Stand
6:Come Saturday Morning
7:Close to You *
8:For the Love of Him
9:Let Me Go to Him
10:Everybody's Out of Town

July 4, 1970

1:The Long and Winding Road
2:The Wonder of You
3:Close to You
4:United We Stand
5:Everything Is Beautiful
6:One Day of Your Life
7:I Just Can't Help Believing *
8:Make It With You *
9:Come Saturday Morning
10:For the Love of Him

July 11, 1970

1:Close to You
2:One Day of Your Life
3:I Just Can't Help Believing
4:The Long and Winding Road
5:Make It With You
6:The Wonder of You
7:United We Stand
8:Paper Mache *
9:Everything Is Beautiful
10:For the Love of Him

July 18, 1970

1:Close to You
2:I Just Can't Help Believing
3:One Day of Your Life
4:Make It With You
5:Paper Mache
6:Everything a Man Could Ever Need *
7:United We Stand
8:The Wonder of You
9:Everything Is Beautiful
10:The Long and Winding Road

July 25, 1970

1:Close to You
2:I Just Can't Help Believing
3:Everything a Man Could Ever Need
4:One Day of Your Life
5:Make It With You
6:Paper Mache
7:United We Stand
8:The Long and Winding Road
9:The Wonder of You
10:Everything Is Beautiful

Aug. 1, 1970

1:Close to You
2:I Just Can't Help Believing
3:Everything a Man Could Ever Need
4:Make It With You
5:Paper Mache
6:One Day of Your Life
7:Snowbird *
8:United We Stand
9:Everything Is Beautiful
10:The Wonder of You

Aug. 8, 1970

1:Close to You
2:I Just Can't Help Believing
3:Make It With You
4:Paper Mache
5:Snowbird
6:Everything a Man Could Ever Need
7:One Day of Your Life
8:United We Stand
9:The Wonder of You
10:Everything Is Beautiful

Aug. 15, 1970

1:Close to You
2:Make It With You
3:Paper Mache
4:I Just Can't Help Believing
5:Snowbird
6:Everything a Man Could Ever Need
7:In the Summertime *
8:United We Stand
9:One Day of Your Life
10:The Wonder of You

Aug. 22, 1970

1:Make It With You
2:Close to You
3:I Just Can't Help Believing
4:Snowbird
5:Paper Mache
6:In the Summertime
7:Everything a Man Could Ever Need
8:Ain't No Mountain High Enough *
9:United We Stand
10:One Day of Your Life

Aug. 29, 1970

1:Close to You
2:Snowbird
3:Make It With You
4:I Just Can't Help Believing
5:In the Summertime
6:Paper Mache
7:Ain't No Mountain High Enough
8:Everything a Man Could Ever Need
9:One Day of Your Life
10:United We Stand

Sept. 5, 1970

1:Snowbird
2:Close to You
3:Make It With You
4:I Just Can't Help Believing
5:Paper Mache
6:Julie, Do Ya Love Me? *
7:Cracklin' Rosie *
8:Ain't No Mountain High Enough
9:In the Summertime
10:Everything a Man Could Ever Need

Sept. 12, 1970

1:Snowbird
2:Ain't No Mountain High Enough
3:Julie, Do Ya Love Me?
4:Cracklin' Rosie
5:Look What They've Done to My Song, Ma *
6:Close to You
7:I Just Can't Help Believing
8:Make It With You
9:In the Summertime
10:Paper Mache

Sept. 19, 1970

1:Snowbird
2:Julie, Do Ya Love Me?
3:Cracklin' Rosie
4:Look What They've Done to My Song, Ma
5:Ain't No Mountain High Enough
6:Close to You
7:I Just Can't Help Believing
8:Make It With You
9:We've Only Just Begun *
10:In the Summertime

Sept. 26, 1970

1:Snowbird
2:Julie, Do Ya Love Me?
3:Look What They've Done to My Song, Ma
4:Cracklin' Rosie
5:Close to You
6:We've Only Just Begun
7:Something *
8:Ain't No Mountain High Enough
9:I Just Can't Help Believing
10:Make It With You

Oct. 3, 1970

1:Snowbird
2:Julie, Do Ya Love Me?
3:Cracklin' Rosie
4:Look What They've Done to My Song, Ma
5:We've Only Just Begun
6:Ain't No Mountain High Enough
7:Something
8:Close to You
9:Make It With You
10:I Just Can't Help Believing

Oct. 10, 1970

1:We've Only Just Begun
2:Cracklin' Rosie
3:Snowbird
4:Look What They've Done to My Song, Ma
5:Julie, Do Ya Love Me?
6:Ain't No Mountain High Enough
7:Something
8:Fire and Rain *
9:Close to You
10:I Just Can't Help Believing

Oct. 17, 1970

1:We've Only Just Begun
2:Cracklin' Rosie
3:Look What They've Done to My Song, Ma
4:Something
5:Snowbird
6:And the Grass Won't Pay No Mind *
7:Fire and Rain
8:Close to You
9:Ain't No Mountain High Enough
10:Julie, Do Ya Love Me?

Oct. 24, 1970

1:We've Only Just Begun
2:Cracklin' Rosie
3:Something
4:Look What They've Done to My Song, Ma
5:And the Grass Won't Pay No Mind
6:Fire and Rain
7:Snowbird
8:Ain't No Mountain High Enough
9:Close to You
10:Julie, Do Ya Love Me?

Oct. 31, 1970

1:We've Only Just Begun
2:Something
3:Fire and Rain
4:Look What They've Done to My Song, Ma
5:Cracklin' Rosie
6:And the Grass Won't Pay No Mind
7:I Think I Love You *
8:One Less Bell to Answer *
9:Snowbird
10:Close to You

Nov. 7, 1970

1:We've Only Just Begun
2:Fire and Rain
3:Look What They've Done to My Song, Ma
4:I Think I Love You
5:One Less Bell to Answer
6:Stoney End *
7:And the Grass Won't Pay No Mind
8:Something
9:Cracklin' Rosie
10:Snowbird

Nov. 14, 1970

1:We've Only Just Begun
2:Stoney End
3:Fire and Rain
4:One Less Bell to Answer
5:It Don't Matter to Me *
6:It's Impossible *
7:I Think I Love You
8:And the Grass Won't Pay No Mind
9:Look What They've Done to My Song, Ma
10:Something

Nov. 21, 1970

1:We've Only Just Begun
2:Stoney End
3:It Don't Matter to Me
4:It's Impossible
5:Fire and Rain
6:I Think I Love You
7:And the Grass Won't Pay No Mind
8:One Less Bell to Answer
9:Something
10:Look What They've Done to My Song, Ma

Nov. 28, 1970

1:It's Impossible
2:We've Only Just Begun
3:Stoney End
4:One Less Bell to Answer
5:Fire and Rain
6:I Think I Love You
7:It Don't Matter to Me
8:Something
9:And the Grass Won't Pay No Mind
10:Look What They've Done to My Song, Ma

338

Dec. 5, 1970

1:It's Impossible
2:Stoney End
3:We've Only Just Begun
4:One Less Bell to Answer
5:I Think I Love You
6:Fire and Rain
7:And the Grass Won't Pay No Mind
8:It Don't Matter to Me
9:Something
10:He Ain't Heavy, He's My Brother *

Dec. 12, 1970

1:It's Impossible
2:Stoney End
3:One Less Bell to Answer
4:He Ain't Heavy, He's My Brother
5:Most of All *
6:We've Only Just Begun
7:Something
8:I Think I Love You
9:Fire and Rain
10:It Don't Matter to Me

Dec. 19, 1970

1:It's Impossible
2:One Less Bell to Answer
3:Stoney End
4:Most of All
5:He Ain't Heavy, He's My Brother
6:Knock Three Times *
7:We've Only Just Begun
8:I Think I Love You
9:Fire and Rain
10:It Don't Matter to Me

Dec. 26, 1970

1:It's Impossible
2:One Less Bell to Answer
3:Most of All
4:Stoney End
5:He Ain't Heavy, He's My Brother
6:Knock Three Times
7:I Think I Love You
8:We've Only Just Begun
9:It Don't Matter to Me
10:Fire and Rain

1971

It was the year of the Smile button, hot pants, water beds, and a religious movement among youth that spawned the term "Jesus freaks." Broadway had *Jesus Christ Superstar* and, for another generation, tap-dancing Ruby Keeler in a revival of *No, No, Nanette.* The biggest thing on television was Archie Bunker in "All in the Family." At the movies it was *The French Connection.* And the year's winner on the Top Ten was "Where Do I Begin?" with nine weeks as Number One, from the late 1970 movie *Love Story,* still generating long box-office lines in 1971.

At year's end there was something new in the air. Hijackers were demanding ransom and parachutes for bail-out escapes. *Look* magazine died, and Lieutenant William Calley got life for his part in the My Lai Massacre. Charles Manson and his demoniacal followers got death sentences in their trial for the Sharon Tate massacre. President Nixon devalued the dollar. Red China was in at the UN, Nationalist China was out. The new term in the news was the Pentagon Papers, and the government took *The New York Times* to court over their publication. The eighteen-year-olds got the vote, and George C. Scott got the Oscar for *Patton* but refused it. An earthquake hit Los Angeles and, unbelievably, the militants got around to bombing the U.S. Capitol in Washington over the prolonged Vietnam War.

The year brought death to forty-two in the Attica Prison riot, to 162 in Japan in history's worst airplane crash, and to three Russian cosmonauts who were found dead in their capsule when it was brought back to earth. And in Yuba City, California, Juan Corona was accused of history's greatest mass killing when searchers found the bodies of twenty-five transient workers buried on his property.

UCLA won an unprecedented fifth national basketball championship. Joe Frazier won the heavyweight boxing crown by beating Muhammad Ali in the "Fight of the Century." Lee Trevino, in a four-week period, won the U.S., Canadian, and British Opens, but the golfer of the year had to be Alan Shepard, who hit a shot on the moon. Twice in 1971 Americans walked on the moon again, but the Apollo 14 and 15 lunar landings were almost too commonplace now for viewers to watch on TV.

Jan. 2, 1971

1:One Less Bell to Answer
2:It's Impossible
3:Most of All
4:He Ain't Heavy, He's My Brother
5:Watching Scotty Grow *
6:Stoney End
7:Knock Three Times
8:We've Only Just Begun
9:Fire and Rain
10:I Think I Love You

Jan. 9, 1971

1:One Less Bell to Answer
2:Most of All
3:Watching Scotty Grow
4:It's Impossible
5:Knock Three Times
6:He Ain't Heavy, He's My Brother
7:Stoney End
8:I Think I Love You
9:We've Only Just Begun
10:Fire and Rain

Jan. 16, 1971

1:Watching Scotty Grow
2:Most of All
3:It's Impossible
4:One Less Bell to Answer
5:Knock Three Times
6:Where Do I Begin? *
7:Stoney End
8:He Ain't Heavy, He's My Brother
9:Fire and Rain
10:I Think I Love You

Jan. 23, 1971

1:Watching Scotty Grow
2:Where Do I Begin?
3:It's Impossible
4:Knock Three Times
5:One Less Bell to Answer
6:Most of All
7:Beautiful People *
8:Stoney End
9:He Ain't Heavy, He's My Brother
10:I Think I Love You

Jan. 30, 1971

1:Watching Scotty Grow
2:Where Do I Begin?
3:Knock Three Times
4:It's Impossible
5:One Less Bell to Answer
6:If You Could Read My Mind *
7:The Green Grass Starts to Grow *
8:Most of All
9:Beautiful People
10:Stoney End

Feb. 6, 1971

1:Watching Scotty Grow
2:Knock Three Times
3:Where Do I Begin?
4:If You Could Read My Mind
5:Beautiful People
6:It's Impossible
7:The Green Grass Starts to Grow
8:Stoney End
9:Most of All
10:One Less Bell to Answer

Feb. 13, 1971

1:Watching Scotty Grow
2:If You Could Read My Mind
3:Where Do I Begin?
4:Beautiful People
5:Knock Three Times
6:It's Impossible
7:Most of All
8:The Green Grass Starts to Grow
9:Does Anybody Really Know What Time It Is? *
10:Stoney End

Feb. 20, 1971

1:If You Could Read My Mind
2:Where Do I Begin?
3:Watching Scotty Grow
4:Beautiful People
5:Knock Three Times
6:For All We Know *
7:Does Anybody Really Know What Time It Is?
8:It's Impossible
9:The Green Grass Starts to Grow
10:Most of All

* Newcomer

Feb. 27, 1971

1:Where Do I Begin?
2:If You Could Read My Mind
3:For All We Know
4:Watching Scotty Grow
5:Beautiful People
6:She's a Lady *
7:It's Impossible
8:Knock Three Times
9:Does Anybody Really Know What Time It Is?
10:The Green Grass Starts to Grow

Mar. 6, 1971

1:For All We Know
2:Where Do I Begin?
3:She's a Lady
4:If You Could Read My Mind
5:Watching Scotty Grow
6:Beautiful People
7:It's Impossible
8:Does Anybody Really Know What Time It Is?
9:The Green Grass Starts to Grow
10:Knock Three Times

Mar. 13, 1971

1:For All We Know
2:Where Do I Begin?
3:She's a Lady
4:Does Anybody Really Know What Time It Is?
5:If You Could Read My Mind
6:Love's Lines, Angles and Rhymes *
7:Watching Scotty Grow
8:Beautiful People
9:It's Impossible
10:The Green Grass Starts to Grow

Mar. 20, 1971

1:Where Do I Begin?
2:For All We Know
3:Love's Lines, Angles and Rhymes
4:She's a Lady
5:If You Could Read My Mind
6:Watching Scotty Grow
7:No Love At All *
8:Beautiful People
9:It's Impossible
10:Does Anybody Really Know What Time It Is?

Mar. 27, 1971

1:Where Do I Begin?
2:For All We Know
3:No Love At All
4:Love's Lines, Angles and Rhymes
5:She's a Lady
6:I Think of You *
7:If You Could Read My Mind
8:Watching Scotty Grow
9:Beautiful People
10:It's Impossible

Apr. 3, 1971

1:Where Do I Begin?
2:For All We Know
3:I Think of You
4:Love's Lines, Angles and Rhymes
5:No Love At All
6:Dream Baby *
7:Me and My Arrow *
8:She's a Lady
9:If You Could Read My Mind
10:Watching Scotty Grow

Apr. 10, 1971

1:Where Do I Begin?
2:Dream Baby
3:No Love At All
4:Love's Lines, Angles and Rhymes
5:I Won't Mention It Again *
6:Me and My Arrow
7:I Think of You
8:For All We Know
9:She's a Lady
10:If You Could Read My Mind

Apr. 17, 1971

1:Where Do I Begin?
2:Dream Baby
3:No Love At All
4:I Won't Mention It Again
5:Me and My Arrow
6:Love's Lines, Angles and Rhymes
7:I Think of You
8:For All We Know
9:Me and You and a Dog Named Boo *
10:She's a Lady

Apr. 24, 1971

1:Where Do I Begin?
2:Dream Baby
3:Me and My Arrow
4:I Won't Mention It Again
5:I Am...I Said *
6:Me and You and a Dog Named Boo
7:Love's Lines, Angles and Rhymes
8:No Love At All
9:I Think of You
10:For All We Know

May 1, 1971

1:Where Do I Begin?
2:Me and My Arrow
3:I Am...I Said
4:Me and You and a Dog Named Boo
5:I Won't Mention It Again
6:Dream Baby
7:Stay Awhile *
8:Love's Lines, Angles and Rhymes
9:No Love At All
10:I Think of You

May 8, 1971

1:Where Do I Begin?
2:I Am...I Said
3:Me and You and a Dog Named Boo
4:Me and My Arrow
5:I Won't Mention It Again
6:Stay Awhile
7:Dream Baby
8:Love's Lines, Angles and Rhymes
9:I Think of You
10:No Love At All

May 15, 1971

1:I Am...I Said
2:Me and You and a Dog Named Boo
3:Me and My Arrow
4:Stay Awhile
5:Where Do I Begin?
6:The Drum *
7:I Won't Mention It Again
8:Dream Baby
9:I Think of You
10:Love's Lines, Angles and Rhymes

May 22, 1971

1:I Am...I Said
2:Me and You and a Dog Named Boo
3:The Drum
4:Me and My Arrow
5:Rainy Days and Mondays *
6:Stay Awhile
7:Where Do I Begin?
8:I Won't Mention It Again
9:I Think of You
10:Dream Baby

May 29, 1971

1:I Am...I Said
2:Rainy Days and Mondays
3:The Drum
4:Me and My Arrow
5:Me and You and a Dog Named Boo
6:That's the Way I've Always Heard It Should Be
7:Stay Awhile
8:I Won't Mention It Again
9:I Think of You
10:Where Do I Begin?

June 5, 1971

1:Rainy Days and Mondays
2:The Drum
3:I Am...I Said
4:That's the Way I've Always Heard It Should Be
5:Stay Awhile
6:I Don't Know How to Love Him *
7:Me and My Arrow
8:When You're Hot, You're Hot *
9:Me and You and a Dog Named Boo
10:I Won't Mention It Again

June 12, 1971

1:Rainy Days and Mondays
2:The Drum
3:When You're Hot, You're Hot
4:Me and You and a Dog Named Boo
5:I Don't Know How to Love Him
6:That's the Way I've Always Heard It Should Be
7:Don't Pull Your Love *
8:I Am...I Said
9:Stay Awhile
10:Me and My Arrow

June 19, 1971

1:Rainy Days and Mondays
2:The Drum
3:When You're Hot, You're Hot
4:Don't Pull Your Love
5:That's the Way I've Always Heard It Should Be
6:I Don't Know How to Love Him
7:Here Comes That Rainy Day Feeling Again *
8:Me and You and a Dog Named Boo
9:I Am...I Said
10:Stay Awhile

June 26, 1971

1:Rainy Days and Mondays
2:Don't Pull Your Love
3:When You're Hot, You're Hot
4:That's the Way I've Always Heard It Should Be
5:Here Comes That Rainy Day Feeling Again
6:Take Me Home, Country Roads *
7:The Drum
8:I Don't Know How to Love Him
9:Stay Awhile
10:Me and You and a Dog Named Boo

July 3, 1971

1:Rainy Days and Mondays
2:Don't Pull Your Love
3:That's the Way I've Always Heard It Should Be
4:Here Comes That Rainy Day Feeling Again
5:It's Too Late *
6:When You're Hot, You're Hot
7:Take Me Home, Country Roads
8:I Don't Know How to Love Him
9:The Drum
10:Stay Awhile

July 10, 1971

1:Rainy Days and Mondays
2:That's the Way I've Always Heard It Should Be
3:It's Too Late
4:Don't Pull Your Love
5:How Can You Mend a Broken Heart? *
6:Take Me Home, Country Roads
7:Never Ending Song of Love *
8:When You're Hot, You're Hot
9:Here Comes That Rainy Day Feeling Again
10:I Don't Know How to Love Him

July 17, 1971

1:It's Too Late
2:Take Me Home, Country Roads
3:Rainy Days and Mondays
4:How Can You Mend a Broken Heart?
5:Don't Pull Your Love
6:If Not For You *
7:That's the Way I've Always Heard It Should Be
8:Never Ending Song of Love
9:I Don't Know How to Love Him
10:Here Comes That Rainy Day Feeling Again

July 24, 1971

1:It's Too Late
2:Take Me Home, Country Roads
3:How Can You Mend a Broken Heart?
4:If Not For You
5:Don't Pull Your Love
6:Never Ending Song of Love
7:Rainy Days and Mondays
8:That's the Way I've Always Heard It Should Be
9:Here Comes That Rainy Day Feeling Again
10:I Don't Know How to Love Him

July 31, 1971

1:How Can You Mend a Broken Heart?
2:If Not For You
3:It's Too Late
4:Take Me Home, Country Roads
5:Don't Pull Your Love
6:Never Ending Song of Love
7:That's the Way I've Always Heard It Should Be
8:Here Comes That Rainy Day Feeling Again
9:Rainy Days and Mondays
10:I Don't Know How to Love Him

Aug. 7, 1971

1:How Can You Mend a Broken Heart?
2:If Not For You
3:It's Too Late
4:Don't Pull Your Love
5:Take Me Home, Country Roads
6:Never Ending Song of Love
7:That's the Way I've Always Heard It Should Be
8:The Last Time I Saw Her *
9:Here Comes That Rainy Day Feeling Again
10:Rainy Days and Mondays

Aug. 14, 1971

1:How Can You Mend a Broken Heart?
2:It's Too Late
3:If Not For You
4:Don't Pull Your Love
5:The Last Time I Saw Her
6:Take Me Home, Country Roads
7:The Night They Drove Old Dixie Down *
8:Never Ending Song of Love
9:That's the Way I've Always Heard It Should Be
10:Here Comes That Rainy Day Feeling Again

Aug. 21, 1971

1:How Can You Mend a Broken Heart?
2:If Not For You
3:Take Me Home, Country Roads
4:The Night They Drove Old Dixie Down
5:Never Ending Song of Love
6:The Last Time I Saw Her
7:It's Too Late
8:Don't Pull Your Love
9:Here Comes That Rainy Day Feeling Again
10:That's the Way I've Always Heard It Should Be

Aug. 28, 1971

1:If Not For You
2:How Can You Mend a Broken Heart?
3:The Night They Drove Old Dixie Down
4:Take Me Home, Country Roads
5:Losing My Mind *
6:Never Ending Song of Love
7:That's the Way I Always Heard It Should Be
8:Don't Pull Your Love
9:It's Too Late
10:The Last Time I Saw Her

Sept. 4, 1971

1:The Night They Drove Old Dixie Down
2:How Can You Mend a Broken Heart?
3:If Not For You
4:Take Me Home, Country Roads
5:Superstar *
6:Losing My Mind
7:The Last Time I Saw Her
8:It's Too Late
9:Never Ending Song of Love
10:Don't Pull Your Love

Sept. 11, 1971

1:The Night They Drove Old Dixie Down
2:Superstar
3:How Can You Mend a Broken Heart?
4:Losing My Mind
5:If Not For You
6:Take Me Home, Country Roads
7:Never Ending Song of Love
8:Don't Pull Your Love
9:It's Too Late
10:The Last Time I Saw Her

Sept. 18, 1971

1:The Night They Drove Old Dixie Down
2:Superstar
3:Losing My Mind
4:How Can You Mend a Broken Heart?
5:If Not For You
6:Take Me Home, Country Roads
7:Gypsies, Tramps and Thieves *
8:The Last Time I Saw Her
9:Never Ending Song of Love
10:It's Too Late

Sept. 25, 1971

1:The Night They Drove Old Dixie Down
2:Superstar
3:How Can You Mend a Broken Heart?
4:Losing My Mind
5:If Not For You
6:Gypsies, Tramps and Thieves
7:Take Me Home, Country Roads
8:Never Ending Song of Love
9:It's Too Late
10:The Last Time I Saw Her

Oct. 2, 1971

1:The Night They Drove Old Dixie Down
2:Superstar
3:Gypsies, Tramps and Thieves
4:Losing My Mind
5:If Not For You
6:How Can You Mend a Broken Heart?
7:Never Ending Song of Love
8:Talk It Over in the Morning *
9:The Last Time I Saw Her
10:Take Me Home, Country Roads

Oct. 9, 1971

1:Superstar
2:The Night They Drove Old Dixie Down
3:Talk It Over in the Morning
4:Losing My Mind
5:Gypsies, Tramps and Thieves
6:If Not For You
7:How Can You Mend a Broken Heart?
8:Never Ending Song of Love
9:The Last Time I Saw Her
10:Take Me Home, Country Roads

Oct. 16, 1971

1:Superstar
2:The Night They Drove Old Dixie Down
3:Losing My Mind
4:Talk It Over in the Morning
5:Gypsies, Tramps and Thieves
6:The Last Time I Saw Her
7:Never Ending Song of Love
8:If Not For You
9:Loving Her Was Easier *
10:How Can You Mend a Broken Heart?

Oct. 23, 1971

1:Superstar
2:Gypsies, Tramps and Thieves
3:Loving Her Was Easier
4:Losing My Mind
5:Talk It Over in the Morning
6:The Night They Drove Old Dixie Down
7:Baby, I'm-a Want You *
8:Never Ending Song of Love
9:If Not For You
10:The Last Time I Saw Her

Oct. 30, 1971

1:Superstar
2:Loving Her Was Easier
3:Gypsies, Tramps and Thieves
4:Baby, I'm-a Want You
5:The Night They Drove Old Dixie Down
6:Talk It Over in the Morning
7:Losing My Mind
8:Theme From Summer of '42 *
9:The Last Time I Saw Her
10:If Not For You

Nov. 6, 1971

1:Superstar
2:Baby, I'm-a Want You
3:Gypsies, Tramps and Thieves
4:Loving Her Was Easier
5:Theme From Summer of '42
6:The Night They Drove Old Dixie Down
7:Talk It Over in the Morning
8:Losing My Mind
9:If Not For You
10:The Last Time I Saw Her

Nov. 13, 1971

1:Baby, I'm-a Want You
2:Gypsies, Tramps and Thieves
3:Superstar
4:Theme From Summer of '42
5:Loving Her Was Easier
6:Losing My Mind
7:Talk It Over in the Morning
8:Stones *
9:The Night They Drove Old Dixie Down
10:The Last Time I Saw Her

Nov. 20, 1971

1:Baby, I'm-a Want You
2:Theme From Summer of '42
3:Stones
4:Gypsies, Tramps and Thieves
5:All I Ever Need Is You *
6:Losing My Mind
7:Superstar
8:Loving Her Was Easier
9:The Night They Drove Old Dixie Down
10:Talk It Over in the Morning

Nov. 27, 1971

1:Baby, I'm-a Want You
2:Stones
3:All I Ever Need Is You
4:Theme From Summer of '42
5:Gypsies, Tramps and Thieves
6:An Old-Fashioned Love Song *
7:Superstar
8:Losing My Mind
9:The Night They Drove Old Dixie Down
10:Loving Her Was Easier

Dec. 4, 1971

1:All I Ever Need Is You
2:Stones
3:Baby, I'm-a Want You
4:Theme From Summer of '42
5:An Old-Fashioned Love Song
6:Gypsies, Tramps and Thieves
7:I'd Like to Teach the World to Sing *
8:Superstar
9:The Night They Drove Old Dixie Down
10:Losing My Mind

Dec. 11, 1971

1:All I Ever Need Is You
2:Stones
3:An Old-Fashioned Love Song
4:Baby, I'm-a Want You
5:Theme From Summer of '42
6:I'd Like to Teach the World to Sing
7:Brand New Key *
8:Superstar
9:Gypsies, Tramps and Thieves
10:Losing My Mind

Dec. 18, 1971

1:All I Ever Need Is You
2:Stones
3:An Old-Fashioned Love Song
4:Theme From Summer of '42
5:Brand New Key
6:Baby, I'm-a Want You
7:I'd Like to Teach the World to Sing
8:Turn Your Radio On *
9:Superstar
10:Bless the Beasts and Children *

Dec. 25, 1971

1:All I Ever Need Is You
2:An Old-Fashioned Love Song
3:Baby, I'm-a Want You
4:Stones
5:I'd Like to Teach the World to Sing
6:Brand New Key
7:Theme From Summer of '42
8:Bless the Beasts and Children
9:Turn Your Radio On
10:Superstar

1972

The year was Richard Nixon's. In a succession of headlines he went to Red China, he went to Russia, and in November he went to town with the second biggest landslide victory in presidential election history. His opponent, Senator George McGovern, came from far back in the pack to Democratic nomination glory only to lose ground nationally over the dumping of Thomas Eagleton as his running mate after the disclosure of Eagleton's past mental health treatment. The campaign year had started as if the nation were watching a painful rerun on TV as Alabama Governor George Wallace lay on a shopping center lot, shot down by a would-be assassin. He lived but was left paralyzed from the waist down.

The sportsman of the year was Mark Spitz, who swam his way to an unprecedented seven Gold Medals in the Olympics. But the world's violence even carried over to the Olympics in Munich, where Palestinian terrorists engaged in a grim kidnapping bloodbath that left seventeen dead. Elsewhere, Japanese terrorists, hired by the Arabs, used machine guns and grenades to massacre twenty-five persons and injure seventy as hapless airline passengers waited for their luggage in Tel Aviv.

Disasters of the year: A Soviet jet crashed in Russia, killing 172 on a Friday the thirteenth . . . Hurricane Agnes killed ninety-six in floods . . . A flood in Rapid City, South Dakota, claimed 235 lives . . . Managua, Nicaragua, became the burial site for 10,000 earthquake victims.

Records of the year: *The Godfather* became moviedom's all-time grosser its first year out . . . *Fiddler on the Roof* closed after 3,242 performances, becoming Broadway's longest-running show, play or musical . . . Texas State Senator Mike McKool set the world filibuster record, talking in Austin for forty-two hours, thirty-three minutes . . . Bob Seagren set a new pole-vault record at 18 feet, 5¾ inches . . . UCLA won its sixth straight national basketball crown . . . "Alone Again (Naturally)" was the year's top song, with seven weeks as Number One.

Two more moon walks were hardly watched by jaded TV viewers. Harry Truman, J. Edgar Hoover, and *Life* magazine all died. American prima donna Bobby Fischer beat Russia's Boris Spassky in the Super Bowl of chess, and Clifford Irving was Ghost Writer of the Year, pocketing $650,000 for a hoax Howard Hughes biography that went unprinted.

Jan. 1, 1972

1:An Old-Fashioned Love Song
2:All I Ever Need Is You
3:Brand New Key
4:Stones
5:I'd Like to Teach the World to Sing
6:American Pie *
7:Theme From Summer of '42
8:Baby, I'm-a Want You
9:It's One of Those Nights *
10:Superstar

Jan. 8, 1972

1:An Old-Fashioned Love Song
2:Brand New Key
3:American Pie
4:I'd Like to Teach the World to Sing
5:All I Ever Need Is You
6:It's One of Those Nights
7:Stones
8:Theme From Summer of '42
9:Baby, I'm-a Want You
10:Music From Across the Way *

Jan. 15, 1972

1:American Pie
2:It's One of Those Nights
3:I'd Like to Teach the World to Sing
4:An Old-Fashioned Love Song
5:All I Ever Need Is You
6:Brand New Key
7:Stones
8:Theme From Summer of '42
9:Music From Across the Way
10:Baby, I'm-a Want You

Jan. 22, 1972

1:American Pie
2:It's One of Those Nights
3:I'd Like to Teach the World to Sing
4:Music From Across the Way
5:An Old-Fashioned Love Song
6:Brand New Key
7:Stones
8:Diamonds Are Forever *
9:Theme From Summer of '42
10:All I Ever Need Is You

Jan. 29, 1972

1:American Pie
2:It's One of Those Nights
3:I'd Like to Teach the World to Sing
4:Diamonds Are Forever
5:Music From Across the Way
6:An Old-Fashioned Love Song
7:Brand New Key
8:Stones
9:Without You *
10:Theme From Summer of '42

Feb. 5, 1972

1:American Pie
2:It's One of Those Nights
3:Diamonds Are Forever
4:Without You
5:I'd Like to Teach the World to Sing
6:Music From Across the Way
7:Theme From Summer of '42
8:Every Day of My Life *
9:Brand New Key
10:An Old-Fashioned Love Song

Feb. 12, 1972

1:It's One of Those Nights
2:Without You
3:American Pie
4:Diamonds Are Forever
5:Every Day of My Life
6:Music From Across the Way
7:I'd Like to Teach the World to Sing
8:Brand New Key
9:An Old-Fashioned Love Song
10:Theme From Summer of '42

Feb. 19, 1972

1:Without You
2:Diamonds Are Forever
3:American Pie
4:Every Day of My Life
5:It's One of Those Nights
6:Music From Across the Way
7:I'd Like to Teach the World to Sing
8:Brand New Key
9:The Nickel Song *
10:Theme From Summer of '42

* Newcomer

Feb. 26, 1972

1:Without You
2:Every Day of My Life
3:Diamonds Are Forever
4:It's One of Those Nights
5:The Nickel Song
6:American Pie
7:Brand New Key
8:Music From Across the Way
9:The Way of Love *
10:I'd Like to Teach the World to Sing

Mar. 4, 1972

1:Without You
2:Every Day of My Life
3:The Nickel Song
4:The Way of Love
5:Diamonds Are Forever
6:Hurting Each Other *
7:American Pie
8:Music From Across the Way
9:Brand New Key
10:It's One of Those Nights

Mar. 11, 1972

1:Without You
2:The Way of Love
3:Every Day of My Life
4:Hurting Each Other
5:Diamonds Are Forever
6:American Pie
7:The Candy Man *
8:It's One of Those Nights
9:The Nickel Song
10:Music From Across the Way

Mar. 18, 1972

1:Without You
2:The Way of Love
3:Every Day of My Life
4:Diamonds Are Forever
5:The Candy Man
6:Hurting Each Other
7:It's One of Those Nights
8:American Pie
9:Music From Across the Way
10:A Cowboy's Work Is Never Done *

Mar. 25, 1972

1:Every Day of My Life
2:The Way of Love
3:A Cowboy's Work Is Never Done
4:Without You
5:The Candy Man
6:The First Time Ever I Saw Your Face *
7:Hurting Each Other
8:Diamonds Are Forever
9:It's One of Those Nights
10:American Pie

Apr. 1, 1972

1:Every Day of My Life
2:A Cowboy's Work Is Never Done
3:The First Time Ever I Saw Your Face
4:The Way of Love
5:Hurting Each Other
6:Without You
7:The Candy Man
8:It's One of Those Nights
9:Diamonds Are Forever
10:American Pie

Apr. 8, 1972

1:The First Time Ever I Saw Your Face
2:Every Day of My Life
3:A Cowboy's Work Is Never Done
4:The Candy Man
5:The Way of Love
6:I Didn't Get to Sleep At All *
7:Hurting Each Other
8:Without You
9:It's One of Those Nights
10:Diamonds Are Forever

Apr. 15, 1972

1:The First Time Ever I Saw Your Face
2:Every Day of My Life
3:A Cowboy's Work Is Never Done
4:The Candy Man
5:I Didn't Get to Sleep At All
6:The Way of Love
7:Vincent *
8:It's One of Those Nights
9:A Horse With No Name *
10:Without You

Apr. 22, 1972

1:The First Time Ever I Saw Your Face
2:I Didn't Get to Sleep At All
3:A Cowboy's Work Is Never Done
4:Vincent
5:A Horse With No Name
6:The Candy Man
7:Every Day of My Life
8:The Way of Love
9:Without You
10:It's One of Those Nights

Apr. 29, 1972

1:The First Time Ever I Saw Your Face
2:Vincent
3:I Didn't Get to Sleep At All
4:The Candy Man
5:Me and Julio Down By the Schoolyard *
6:A Horse With No Name
7:A Cowboy's Work Is Never Done
8:Every Day of My Life
9:The Way of Love
10:Without You

May 6, 1972

1:The First Time Ever I Saw Your Face
2:I Didn't Get to Sleep At All
3:Vincent
4:The Candy Man
5:Me and Julio Down By the Schoolyard
6:Morning Has Broken *
7:A Cowboy's Work Is Never Done
8:A Horse With No Name
9:Every Day of My Life
10:The Way of Love

May 13, 1972

1:I Didn't Get to Sleep At All
2:The Candy Man
3:Morning Has Broken
4:The First Time Ever I Saw Your Face
5:Vincent
6:Me and Julio Down By the Schoolyard
7:Song Sung Blue *
8:A Cowboy's Work Is Never Done
9:A Horse With No Name
10:Every Day of My Life

May 20, 1972

1:The Candy Man
2:Morning Has Broken
3:I Didn't Get to Sleep At All
4:Song Sung Blue
5:It's Going to Take Some Time *
6:Vincent
7:The First Time Ever I Saw Your Face
8:Me and Julio Down By the Schoolyard
9:A Horse With No Name
10:A Cowboy's Work Is Never Done

May 27, 1972

1:The Candy Man
2:Song Sung Blue
3:It's Going to Take Some Time
4:I Didn't Get to Sleep At All
5:Morning Has Broken
6:Vincent
7:The First Time Ever I Saw Your Face
8:Me and Julio Down By the Schoolyard
9:Living In a House Divided *
10:A Cowboy's Work Is Never Done

June 3, 1972

1:The Candy Man
2:Song Sung Blue
3:It's Going to Take Some Time
4:I Didn't Get to Sleep At All
5:Living In a House Divided
6:How Can I Be Sure? *
7:Morning Has Broken
8:Me and Julio Down By the Schoolyard
9:The First Time Ever I Saw Your Face
10:Vincent

June 10, 1972

1:Song Sung Blue
2:It's Going to Take Some Time
3:I Didn't Get to Sleep At All
4:The Candy Man
5:Living In a House Divided
6:Love Theme From The Godfather *
7:How Can I Be Sure?
8:Morning Has Broken
9:Me and Julio Down By the Schoolyard
10:The First Time Ever I Saw Your Face

June 17, 1972

1:Song Sung Blue
2:It's Going to Take Some Time
3:Living In a House Divided
4:The Candy Man
5:I Didn't Get to Sleep At All
6:How Can I Be Sure?
7:Morning Has Broken
8:Love Theme From The Godfather
9:The First Time Ever I Saw Your Face
10:Me and Julio Down By the Schoolyard

June 24, 1972

1:Song Sung Blue
2:It's Going to Take Some Time
3:The Candy Man
4:Living In a House Divided
5:How Can I Be Sure?
6:I Didn't Get to Sleep At All
7:Love Theme From The Godfather
8:Morning Has Broken
9:Me and Julio Down By the Schoolyard
10:The First Time Ever I Saw Your Face

July 1, 1972

1:Song Sung Blue
2:Living In a House Divided
3:How Can I Be Sure?
4:It's Going to Take Some Time
5:The Candy Man
6:Where Is the Love? *
7:I Didn't Get to Sleep At All
8:Love Theme From The Godfather
9:Morning Has Broken
10:The First Time Ever I Saw Your Face

July 8, 1972

1:Song Sung Blue
2:How Can I Be Sure?
3:Where Is the Love?
4:Living In a House Divided
5:It's Going to Take Some Time
6:Alone Again (Naturally) *
7:The Candy Man
8:Love Theme From The Godfather
9:I Didn't Get to Sleep At All
10:Morning Has Broken

July 15, 1972

1:Song Sung Blue
2:Where Is the Love?
3:Alone Again (Naturally)
4:How Can I Be Sure?
5:Too Late to Turn Back Now *
6:Living In a House Divided
7:It's Going to Take Some Time
8:The Candy Man
9:Love Theme From The Godfather
10:I Didn't Get to Sleep At All

July 22, 1972

1:Where Is the Love?
2:Alone Again (Naturally)
3:Too Late to Turn Back Now
4:Song Sung Blue
5:Brandy *
6:Living In a House Divided
7:How Can I Be Sure?
8:It's Going to Take Some Time
9:Love Theme From The Godfather
10:The Candy Man

July 29, 1972

1:Alone Again (Naturally)
2:Where Is the Love?
3:Too Late to Turn Back Now
4:Brandy
5:Song Sung Blue
6:When You Say Love *
7:Living In a House Divided
8:How Can I Be Sure?
9:It's Going to Take Some Time
10:Love Theme From The Godfather

Aug. 5, 1972

1:Alone Again (Naturally)
2:Where Is the Love?
3:When You Say Love
4:Brandy
5:Too Late to Turn Back Now
6:Goodbye to Love *
7:Daddy, Don't You Walk So Fast *
8:Song Sung Blue
9:Living In a House Divided
10:Love Theme From The Godfather

Aug. 12, 1972

1:Alone Again (Naturally)
2:When You Say Love
3:Goodbye to Love
4:Brandy
5:Where Is the Love?
6:Too Late to Turn Back Now
7:Daddy, Don't You Walk So Fast
8:Love Theme From The Godfather
9:Song Sung Blue
10:Living In a House Divided

Aug. 19, 1972

1:Alone Again (Naturally)
2:When You Say Love
3:Goodbye to Love
4:Brandy
5:Baby, Don't Get Hooked On Me *
6:Where Is the Love?
7:Too Late to Turn Back Now
8:Daddy, Don't You Walk So Fast
9:Song Sung Blue
10:Living In a House Divided

Aug. 26, 1972

1:Alone Again (Naturally)
2:When You Say Love
3:Goodbye to Love
4:Baby, Don't Get Hooked On Me
5:Brandy
6:Where Is the Love?
7:Daddy, Don't You Walk So Fast
8:Too Late to Turn Back Now
9:Living In a House Divided
10:Song Sung Blue

Sept. 2, 1972

1:Alone Again (Naturally)
2:Goodbye to Love
3:Baby, Don't Get Hooked On Me
4:When You Say Love
5:Run to Me *
6:Brandy
7:Too Late to Turn Back Now
8:Daddy, Don't You Walk So Fast
9:Song Sung Blue
10:Where Is the Love?

Sept. 9, 1972

1:Alone Again (Naturally)
2:Goodbye to Love
3:Baby, Don't Get Hooked On Me
4:Run to Me
5:When You Say Love
6:Brandy
7:Too Late to Turn Back Now
8:Black and White *
9:Daddy, Don't You Walk So Fast
10:Song Sung Blue

Sept. 16, 1972

1:Baby, Don't Get Hooked On Me
2:Goodbye to Love
3:Run to Me
4:Black and White
5:Alone Again (Naturally)
6:When You Say Love
7:If I Could Reach You *
8:Brandy
9:Too Late to Turn Back Now
10:Daddy, Don't You Walk So Fast

Sept. 23, 1972

1:Baby, Don't Get Hooked On Me
2:Black and White
3:If I Could Reach You
4:Run to Me
5:Goodbye to Love
6:Alone Again (Naturally)
7:When You Say Love
8:Brandy
9:Daddy, Don't You Walk So Fast
10:Too Late to Turn Back Now

Sept. 30, 1972

1:Baby, Don't Get Hooked On Me
2:Black and White
3:If I Could Reach You
4:Goodbye to Love
5:I Am Woman *
6:Run to Me
7:Alone Again (Naturally)
8:When You Say Love
9:Brandy
10:Daddy, Don't You Walk So Fast

Oct. 7, 1972

1:Black and White
2:Baby, Don't Get Hooked On Me
3:If I Could Reach You
4:I Am Woman
5:Goodbye to Love
6:Alone Again (Naturally)
7:Brandy
8:Run to Me
9:Daddy, Don't You Walk So Fast
10:When You Say Love

Oct. 14, 1972

1:Black and White
2:If I Could Reach You
3:Baby, Don't Get Hooked On Me
4:I Am Woman
5:We Can Make It Together *
6:Goodbye to Love
7:Alone Again (Naturally)
8:Brandy
9:Run to Me
10:When You Say Love

Oct. 21, 1972

1:If I Could Reach You
2:Black and White
3:We Can Make It Together
4:I Am Woman
5:Baby, Don't Get Hooked On Me
6:Alone Again (Naturally)
7:Goodbye to Love
8:Run to Me
9:When You Say Love
10:Brandy

Oct. 28, 1972

1:If I Could Reach You
2:We Can Make It Together
3:Black and White
4:I Am Woman
5:Baby, Don't Get Hooked On Me
6:Alone Again (Naturally)
7:Clair *
8:Brandy
9:Goodbye to Love
10:Run to Me

Nov. 4, 1972

1:If I Could Reach You
2:We Can Make It Together
3:I Am Woman
4:Clair
5:I Can See Clearly Now *
6:I'd Love You to Want Me *
7:Black and White
8:Baby, Don't Get Hooked On Me
9:Alone Again (Naturally)
10:Brandy

Nov. 11, 1972

1:If I Could Reach You
2:I Can See Clearly Now
3:I'd Love You to Want Me
4:I Am Woman
5:We Can Make It Together
6:It Never Rains in Southern California *
7:Clair
8:Black and White
9:Alone Again (Naturally)
10:Baby, Don't Get Hooked On Me

Nov. 18, 1972

1:I Can See Clearly Now
2:I'd Love You to Want Me
3:I Am Woman
4:If I Could Reach You
5:It Never Rains in Southern California
6:Clair
7:We Can Make It Together
8:Alone Again (Naturally)
9:Black and White
10:Baby, Don't Get Hooked On Me

Nov. 25, 1972

1:I Can See Clearly Now
2:I'd Love You to Want Me
3:I Am Woman
4:Clair
5:It Never Rains in Southern California
6:If I Could Reach You
7:We Can Make It Together
8:Summer Breeze *
9:Funny Face *
10:Alone Again (Naturally)

Dec. 2, 1972

1:I Am Woman
2:I Can See Clearly Now
3:Clair
4:I'd Love You to Want Me
5:It Never Rains in Southern California
6:Summer Breeze
7:Funny Face
8:If I Could Reach You
9:Alone Again (Naturally)
10:We Can Make It Together

Dec. 9, 1972

1:Clair
2:I Am Woman
3:It Never Rains in Southern California
4:Summer Breeze
5:I'd Love You to Want Me
6:Funny Face
7:Sweet Surrender *
8:Walk On Water *
9:I Can See Clearly Now
10:If I Could Reach You

Dec. 16, 1972

1:Clair
2:It Never Rains in Southern California
3:Sweet Surrender
4:Walk On Water
5:Funny Face
6:I Am Woman
7:Summer Breeze
8:I'd Love You to Want Me
9:Been to Canaan *
10:I Can See Clearly Now

Dec. 23, 1972

1:Clair
2:Sweet Surrender
3:Walk On Water
4:Funny Face
5:It Never Rains in Southern California
6:Been to Canaan
7:I Am Woman
8:Summer Breeze
9:I'd Love You to Want Me
10:I Can See Clearly Now

Dec. 30, 1972

1:Sweet Surrender
2:Walk On Water
3:Clair
4:Been to Canaan
5:It Never Rains in Southern California
6:Funny Face
7:I Am Woman
8:I Can See Clearly Now
9:Summer Breeze
10:I'd Love You to Want Me

1973

It started out, jubilantly enough, as the year the Vietnam War ended, and the POWs came home. It ended as the year when Vice-President Spiro Agnew resigned because of alleged bribery payoffs when he was Governor of Maryland, and the Congress was crying for the impeachment of President Richard Nixon over the cover-up of the Watergate scandal.

Gerald Ford was appointed Vice-President. Richard Nixon refused to resign as the televised Watergate hearings droned on, uncovering more damning evidence of White House knowledge about the 1972 burglary of Democratic headquarters in Washington's Watergate complex. There were the missing White House tapes, the infamous eighteen-minute erasure in one of them, the firings and indictments of high officials. And out of Senator Sam Ervin's televised hearings, the year's most overworked phrase: "At this point in time . . ."

The year first saw a meat shortage and sky-high prices for it. Then came the Energy Crisis, with its dimouts of city lights and a gasoline shortage that found motorists lining up for sixty-cent gas when they could find service stations open. Inflation, long talked about, became a reality.

The year's blackest headlines: A New Orleans sniper left six dead and seventeen wounded before he was slain atop a French Quarter hotel . . . Israeli fighter planes shot down a civilian Libyan jetliner, killing 106 aboard . . . Dean Arnold Corll, David Owen Brooks, and Elmer Wayne Henley operated a homosexual slaying factory in Houston that turned up the bodies of twenty-seven missing teenage boys . . . Arab hijackers mowed down a Rome airport with bullets and fire bombs, taking thirty-two lives . . . Israel went to war again against Egypt and Syria.

In January, Lyndon Johnson died. The year saw militant Indians taking over Wounded Knee, South Dakota, for seventy days. Marlon Brando won the Oscar for *The Godfather* but refused it. UCLA won its seventh straight national basketball championship. Secretariat became the first horse since 1948 to win racing's Triple Crown. O. J. Simpson set a new pro football rushing record, 2,003 yards in a season. Tennis hustler Bobby Riggs lost to Billie Jean King in the Ms. match of the year. Bette Midler's record impersonation of the Andrews Sisters put "Boogie Woogie Bugle Boy" on the Top Ten, which the original didn't do in 1941. But the top song was "And I Love You So," with five weeks as Number One.

Jan. 6, 1973

1:Sweet Surrender
2:Walk On Water
3:Been to Canaan
4:Clair
5:Oh, Babe, What Would You Say? *
6:Me and Mrs. Jones *
7:You're So Vain *
8:Funny Face
9:It Never Rains in Southern California
10:I Am Woman

Jan. 13, 1973

1:Been to Canaan
2:Me and Mrs. Jones
3:You're So Vain
4:Oh, Babe, What Would You Say?
5:Sweet Surrender
6:Clair
7:Walk On Water
8:Rocky Mountain High *
9:Funny Face
10:It Never Rains in Southern California

Jan. 20, 1973

1:Me and Mrs. Jones
2:You're So Vain
3:Been to Canaan
4:Oh, Babe, What Would You Say?
5:Separate Ways *
6:Rocky Mountain High
7:Sweet Surrender
8:Pieces of April *
9:Clair
10:Walk On Water

Jan. 27, 1973

1:Me and Mrs. Jones
2:You're So Vain
3:Oh, Babe, What Would You Say?
4:Separate Ways
5:Rocky Mountain High
6:Don't Expect Me to Be Your Friend *
7:Pieces of April
8:Been to Canaan
9:Clair
10:Walk On Water

Feb. 3, 1973

1:You're So Vain
2:Me and Mrs. Jones
3:Don't Expect Me to Be Your Friend
4:Rocky Mountain High
5:Separate Ways
6:Dueling Banjos *
7:Oh, Babe, What Would You Say?
8:Pieces of April
9:Clair
10:Been to Canaan

Feb. 10, 1973

1:Don't Expect Me to Be Your Friend
2:Dueling Banjos
3:Rocky Mountain High
4:You're So Vain
5:Me and Mrs. Jones
6:Living Together, Growing Together *
7:Killing Me Softly With His Song *
8:Separate Ways
9:Oh, Babe, What Would You Say?
10:Pieces of April

Feb. 17, 1973

1:Dueling Banjos
2:Don't Expect Me to Be Your Friend
3:Rocky Mountain High
4:Killing Me Softly With His Song
5:Living Together, Growing Together
6:Me and Mrs. Jones
7:Oh, Babe, What Would You Say?
8:You're So Vain
9:Pieces of April
10:Separate Ways

Feb. 24, 1973

1:Dueling Banjos
2:Killing Me Softly With His Song
3:Don't Expect Me to Be Your Friend
4:Rocky Mountain High
5:Living Together, Growing Together
6:Last Song *
7:You're So Vain
8:Danny's Song *
9:Me and Mrs. Jones
10:Pieces of April

* Newcomer

Mar. 3, 1973

1:Killing Me Softly With His Song
2:Last Song
3:Danny's Song
4:Dueling Banjos
5:Rocky Mountain High
6:Don't Expect Me to Be Your Friend
7:Living Together, Growing Together
8:Me and Mrs. Jones
9:Pieces of April
10:You're So Vain

Mar. 10, 1973

1:Last Song
2:Danny's Song
3:Killing Me Softly With His Song
4:Dueling Banjos
5:Living Together, Growing Together
6:Rocky Mountain High
7:Don't Expect Me to Be Your Friend
8:Tie a Yellow Ribbon Round the Ole Oak Tree *
9:Me and Mrs. Jones
10:Pieces of April

Mar. 17, 1973

1:Danny's Song
2:Killing Me Softly With His Song
3:Last Song
4:Dueling Banjos
5:Tie a Yellow Ribbon Round the Ole Oak Tree
6:Sing *
7:Daisy a Day *
8:Don't Expect Me to Be Your Friend
9:Rocky Mountain High
10:Me and Mrs. Jones

Mar. 24, 1973

1:Danny's Song
2:Sing
3:Killing Me Softly With His Song
4:Tie a Yellow Ribbon Round the Ole Oak Tree
5:Last Song
6:Daisy a Day
7:The Night the Lights Went Out in Georgia *
8:Dueling Banjos
9:Don't Expect Me to Be Your Friend
10:Rocky Mountain High

Mar. 31, 1973

1:Sing
2:Tie a Yellow Ribbon Round the Ole Oak Tree
3:Danny's Song
4:Killing Me Softly With His Song
5:Daisy a Day
6:The Night the Lights Went Out in Georgia
7:Last Song
8:Dueling Banjos
9:Out of the Question *
10:Don't Expect Me to Be Your Friend

Apr. 7, 1973

1:Sing
2:Tie a Yellow Ribbon Round the Ole Oak Tree
3:Daisy a Day
4:The Night the Lights Went Out in Georgia
5:Danny's Song
6:Out of the Question
7:Killing Me Softly With His Song
8:Last Song
9:Don't Expect Me to Be Your Friend
10:Dueling Banjos

Apr. 14, 1973

1:Tie a Yellow Ribbon Round the Ole Oak Tree
2:Sing
3:Daisy a Day
4:Out of the Question
5:You Are the Sunshine of My Life *
6:The Night the Lights Went Out in Georgia
7:And I Love You So *
8:Danny's Song
9:Killing Me Softly With His Song
10:Last Song

Apr. 21, 1973

1:Tie a Yellow Ribbon Round the Ole Oak Tree
2:Sing
3:Out of the Question
4:You Are the Sunshine of My Life
5:Daisy a Day
6:The Night the Lights Went Out in Georgia
7:And I Love You So
8:Neither One of Us *
9:Ain't No Woman *
10:Killing Me Softly With His Song

358

Apr. 28, 1973

1:Tie a Yellow Ribbon Round the Ole Oak Tree
2:You Are the Sunshine of My Life
3:Out of the Question
4:Sing
5:And I Love You So
6:Daniel *
7:Daisy a Day
8:The Night the Lights Went Out in Georgia
9:Neither One of Us
10:Ain't No Woman

May 5, 1973

1:You Are the Sunshine of My Life
2:Tie a Yellow Ribbon Round the Ole Oak Tree
3:Out of the Question
4:Daniel
5:Neither One of Us
6:Ain't No Woman
7:And I Love You So
8:Sing
9:The Night the Lights Went Out in Georgia
10:Daisy a Day

May 12, 1973

1:You Are the Sunshine of My Life
2:Daniel
3:Out of the Question
4:And I Love You So
5:Tie a Yellow Ribbon Round the Ole Oak Tree
6:Ain't No Woman
7:Neither One of Us
8:Sing
9:My Love *
10:The Night the Lights Went Out in Georgia

May 19, 1973

1:And I Love You So
2:Daniel
3:You Are the Sunshine of My Life
4:My Love
5:Out of the Question
6:Tie a Yellow Ribbon Round the Ole Oak Tree
7:Neither One of Us
8:Ain't No Woman
9:The Night the Lights Went Out in Georgia
10:Sing

May 26, 1973

1:And I Love You So
2:Daniel
3:My Love
4:You Are the Sunshine of My Life
5:Out of the Question
6:Neither One of Us
7:Tie a Yellow Ribbon Round the Ole Oak Tree
8:Ain't No Woman
9:Sing
10:The Night the Lights Went Out in Georgia

June 2, 1973

1:And I Love You So
2:My Love
3:Daniel
4:You Are the Sunshine of My Life
5:Playground in My Mind *
6:Boogie Woogie Bugle Boy *
7:Tie a Yellow Ribbon Round the Ole Oak Tree
8:Neither One of Us
9:Out of the Question
10:Ain't No Woman

June 9, 1973

1:And I Love You So
2:My Love
3:Boogie Woogie Bugle Boy
4:Daniel
5:Give Me Love *
6:Playground in My Mind
7:You Are the Sunshine of My Life
8:Behind Closed Doors *
9:Tie a Yellow Ribbon Round the Ole Oak Tree
10:Neither One of Us

June 16, 1973

1:And I Love You So
2:Boogie Woogie Bugle Boy
3:My Love
4:Give Me Love
5:Daniel
6:Behind Closed Doors
7:Playground in My Mind
8:You Are the Sunshine of My Life
9:Yesterday Once More *
10:Tie a Yellow Ribbon Round the Ole Oak Tree

June 23, 1973

1:Boogie Woogie Bugle Boy
2:My Love
3:Give Me Love
4:And I Love You So
5:Daniel
6:Yesterday Once More
7:Behind Closed Doors
8:Stuck in the Middle With You *
9:Playground in My Mind
10:You Are the Sunshine of My Life

June 30, 1973

1:Boogie Woogie Bugle Boy
2:Give Me Love
3:Yesterday Once More
4:My Love
5:And I Love You So
6:Behind Closed Doors
7:Bad, Bad Leroy Brown *
8:Playground in My Mind
9:Stuck in the Middle With You
10:Daniel

July 7, 1973

1:Yesterday Once More
2:Boogie Woogie Bugle Boy
3:Give Me Love
4:My Love
5:Bad, Bad Leroy Brown
6:And I Love You So
7:Get Down *
8:Behind Closed Doors
9:Playground in My Mind
10:Stuck in the Middle With You

July 14, 1973

1:Yesterday Once More
2:Boogie Woogie Bugle Boy
3:Give Me Love
4:Get Down
5:Bad, Bad Leroy Brown
6:Touch Me in the Morning *
7:My Love
8:And I Love You So
9:Behind Closed Doors
10:Stuck in the Middle With You

July 21, 1973

1:Yesterday Once More
2:Touch Me in the Morning
3:Boogie Woogie Bugle Boy
4:Get Down
5:Delta Dawn *
6:Bad, Bad Leroy Brown
7:Give Me Love
8:My Love
9:Behind Closed Doors
10:And I Love You So

July 28, 1973

1:Yesterday Once More
2:Touch Me in the Morning
3:Delta Dawn
4:Get Down
5:Say, Has Anybody Seen My Sweet Gypsy Rose? *
6:Boogie Woogie Bugle Boy
7:Bad, Bad Leroy Brown
8:Behind Closed Doors
9:Give Me Love
10:And I Love You So

Aug. 4, 1973

1:Delta Dawn
2:Touch Me in the Morning
3:Say, Has Anybody Seen My Sweet Gypsy Rose?
4:Get Down
5:Yesterday Once More
6:Boogie Woogie Bugle Boy
7:Live and Let Die *
8:Behind Closed Doors
9:Bad, Bad Leroy Brown
10:Give Me Love

Aug. 11, 1973

1:Delta Dawn
2:Say, Has Anybody Seen My Sweet Gypsy Rose?
3:Get Down
4:Touch Me in the Morning
5:Live and Let Die
6:Yesterday Once More
7:Send a Little Love My Way *
8:Boogie Woogie Bugle Boy
9:Behind Closed Doors
10:Bad, Bad Leroy Brown

Aug. 18, 1973

1:Say, Has Anybody Seen My Sweet Gypsy Rose?
2:Delta Dawn
3:Get Down
4:Touch Me in the Morning
5:Live and Let Die
6:Send a Little Love My Way
7:Yesterday Once More
8:Bad, Bad Leroy Brown
9:Behind Closed Doors
10:Boogie Woogie Bugle Boy

Aug. 25, 1973

1:Say, Has Anybody Seen My Sweet Gypsy Rose?
2:Delta Dawn
3:Get Down
4:Live and Let Die
5:Send a Little Love My Way
6:Loves Me Like a Rock *
7:Touch Me in the Morning
8:Yesterday Once More
9:Behind Closed Doors
10:Bad, Bad Leroy Brown

Sept. 1, 1973

1:Say, Has Anybody Seen My Sweet Gypsy Rose?
2:Delta Dawn
3:Loves Me Like a Rock
4:Get Down
5:My Maria *
6:Live and Let Die
7:Send a Little Love My Way
8:Touch Me in the Morning
9:Yesterday Once More
10:Behind Closed Doors

Sept. 8, 1973

1:Say, Has Anybody Seen My Sweet Gypsy Rose?
2:Loves Me Like a Rock
3:My Maria
4:Delta Dawn
5:Get Down
6:Send a Little Love My Way
7:Live and Let Die
8:Touch Me in the Morning
9:Behind Closed Doors
10:Yesterday Once More

Sept. 15, 1973

1:Loves Me Like a Rock
2:My Maria
3:Say, Has Anybody Seen My Sweet Gypsy Rose?
4:Delta Dawn
5:Get Down
6:Send a Little Love My Way
7:Live and Let Die
8:Touch Me in the Morning
9:Yesterday Once More
10:Behind Closed Doors

Sept. 22, 1973

1:Loves Me Like a Rock
2:My Maria
3:Say, Has Anybody Seen My Sweet Gypsy Rose?
4:Delta Dawn
5:Knockin' On Heaven's Door *
6:Send a Little Love My Way
7:Live and Let Die
8:Get Down
9:Touch Me in the Morning
10:Yesterday Once More

Sept. 29, 1973

1:My Maria
2:Loves Me Like a Rock
3:Knockin' On Heaven's Door
4:All I Know *
5:Say, Has Anybody Seen My Sweet Gypsy Rose?
6:Delta Dawn
7:Live and Let Die
8:Send a Little Love My Way
9:Get Down
10:Touch Me in the Morning

Oct. 6, 1973

1:My Maria
2:All I Know
3:Loves Me Like a Rock
4:Knockin' On Heaven's Door
5:Say, Has Anybody Seen My Sweet Gypsy Rose?
6:Delta Dawn
7:Send a Little Love My Way
8:Live and Let Die
9:Touch Me in the Morning
10:Get Down

Oct. 13, 1973

1:All I Know
2:Loves Me Like a Rock
3:Knockin' On Heaven's Door
4:My Maria
5:We May Never Pass This Way *
6:Say, Has Anybody Seen My Sweet Gypsy Rose?
7:Delta Dawn
8:Send a Little Love My Way
9:Live and Let Die
10:Touch Me in the Morning

Oct. 20, 1973

1:All I Know
2:Knockin' On Heaven's Door
3:Loves Me Like a Rock
4:Jesse *
5:Half-Breed *
6:My Maria
7:We May Never Pass This Way
8:Say, Has Anybody Seen My Sweet Gypsy Rose?
9:Delta Dawn
10:Send a Little Love My Way

Oct. 27, 1973

1:All I Know
2:We May Never Pass This Way
3:Knockin' On Heaven's Door
4:Jesse
5:The Most Beautiful Girl *
6:Top of the World *
7:Half-Breed
8:Loves Me Like a Rock
9:My Maria
10:Say, Has Anybody Seen My Sweet Gypsy Rose?

Nov. 3, 1973

1:All I Know
2:We May Never Pass This Way
3:The Most Beautiful Girl
4:Knockin' On Heaven's Door
5:Jesse
6:Top of the World
7:Half-Breed
8:Loves Me Like a Rock
9:Say, Has Anybody Seen My Sweet Gypsy Rose?
10:My Maria

Nov. 10, 1973

1:The Most Beautiful Girl
2:We May Never Pass This Way
3:All I Know
4:Top of the World
5:Knockin' On Heaven's Door
6:Jesse
7:I Got a Name *
8:Half-Breed
9:My Maria
10:Loves Me Like a Rock

Nov. 17, 1973

1:The Most Beautiful Girl
2:Top of the World
3:We May Never Pass This Way
4:I Got a Name
5:All I Know
6:Photograph *
7:Knockin' On Heaven's Door
8:Jesse
9:Half-Breed
10:My Maria

Nov. 24, 1973

1:The Most Beautiful Girl
2:Top of the World
3:We May Never Pass This Way
4:I Got a Name
5:Photograph
6:Leave Me Alone *
7:All I Know
8:Knockin' On Heaven's Door
9:Jesse
10:Half-Breed

Dec. 1, 1973

1:Top of the World
2:The Most Beautiful Girl
3:Leave Me Alone
4:Photograph
5:I Got a Name
6:We May Never Pass This Way
7:All I Know
8:Knockin' On Heaven's Door
9:Half-Breed
10:Jesse

Dec. 8, 1973

1:Leave Me Alone
2:The Most Beautiful Girl
3:Photograph
4:Top of the World
5:Who's in the Strawberry Patch
    With Sally? *
6:I Got a Name
7:Let Me Be There *
8:All I Know
9:We May Never Pass This Way
10:Knockin' On Heaven's Door

Dec. 15, 1973

1:Leave Me Alone
2:The Most Beautiful Girl
3:Who's in the Strawberry Patch
    With Sally?
4:Photograph
5:Let Me Be There
6:Top of the World
7:Time in a Bottle *
8:The Way We Were *
9:I Got a Name
10:We May Never Pass This Way

Dec. 22, 1973

1:Leave Me Alone
2:The Most Beautiful Girl
3:Who's in the Strawberry Patch
    With Sally?
4:Let Me Be There
5:Time in a Bottle
6:Photograph
7:The Way We Were
8:Top of the World
9:We May Never Pass This Way
10:I Got a Name

Dec. 29, 1973

1:Time in a Bottle
2:Leave Me Alone
3:Let Me Be There
4:Who's in the Strawberry Patch
    With Sally?
5:The Way We Were
6:The Most Beautiful Girl
7:Top of the World
8:Photograph
9:I Got a Name
10:We May Never Pass This Way

1974

As the world settled down to watch one hot and frantic night in August, Richard Nixon forever stamped himself and 1974 into history by delivering a television address in which he became the first President of the United States to resign his office.

Faced with a Supreme Court edict that he must surrender incriminating tapes about the Watergate scandal, he chose resignation rather than impending impeachment. Gerald Ford, himself an appointed Vice-President following Spiro Agnew's 1973 resignation, became President of the United States and a month later granted Nixon a presidential pardon. When Ford appointed Nelson Rockefeller as Vice-President, the nation for the first time had two men not elected to the two highest offices.

It was also the year of the bizarre Patricia Hearst kidnapping, her equally bizarre defection to her Symbionese Liberation Army abductors, and the later Los Angeles shoot-out that wiped out the gang but failed to turn up the heiress.

It was the year of nude streakers, a dubious fad that began on campuses and spread to unexpected appearances on network TV. At the movies we had *The Godfather, Part II, The Exorcist,* and *The Towering Inferno.* In the Top Ten "I Honestly Love You" was the year's top song, with five weeks as Number One. In sports Hank Aaron hit number 715 one memorable night in Atlanta to break Babe Ruth's home-run record. At season's end he had made it 733 homers. But the most startling record of the year was set by an American Lockheed SR-71 that zipped from New York to London in one hour and fifty-five minutes. Flop of the year: Daredevil Evel Knievel, who went into the drink while trying to rocket over Snake River Canyon.

Muhammad Ali regained his heavyweight crown by knocking out George Foreman in Africa. Rioting over school busing came to Boston. Congressman Wilbur Mills of Arkansas made headlines with stripper Fanne Fox. Semi-Depression gripped the nation with the combination of inflation and unemployment. The starkest headlines told of political kidnappings, a black gunman assassinating Martin Luther King's mother at church services in Atlanta, and of history's worst aviation disaster when 346 persons were killed in the crash of a Turkish jumbo jet in Paris.

Jan. 5, 1974

1:Time in a Bottle
2:The Way We Were
3:Leave Me Alone
4:Let Me Be There
5:The Most Beautiful Girl
6:Who's in the Strawberry Patch With Sally?
7:Eres Tu *
8:Love's Theme *
9:Photograph
10:Top of the World

Jan. 12, 1974

1:The Way We Were
2:Time in a Bottle
3:Leave Me Alone
4:Love's Theme
5:The Most Beautiful Girl
6:Eres Tu
7:Who's in the Strawberry Patch With Sally?
8:Photograph
9:Let Me Be There
10:Top of the World

Jan. 19, 1974

1:The Way We Were
2:Love's Theme
3:Time in a Bottle
4:Leave Me Alone
5:Let Me Be There
6:The Most Beautiful Girl
7:You're Sixteen *
8:Who's in the Strawberry Patch With Sally?
9:Eres Tu
10:Love Song *

Jan. 26, 1974

1:Love's Theme
2:The Way We Were
3:You're Sixteen
4:Time in a Bottle
5:Leave Me Alone
6:Love Song
7:Let Me Be There
8:The Most Beautiful Girl
9:Who's in the Strawberry Patch With Sally?
10:Eres Tu

Feb. 2, 1974

1:Love's Theme
2:You're Sixteen
3:The Way We Were
4:Love Song
5:Last Time I Saw Him *
6:Eres Tu
7:Time in a Bottle
8:Leave Me Alone
9:Let Me Be There
10:The Most Beautiful Girl

Feb. 9, 1974

1:Love Song
2:Love's Theme
3:The Way We Were
4:Last Time I Saw Him
5:You're Sixteen
6:Time in a Bottle
7:Eres Tu
8:Let Me Be There
9:Leave Me Alone
10:I Shall Sing *

Feb. 16, 1974

1:Last Time I Saw Him
2:Love's Theme
3:Love Song
4:The Way We Were
5:I Shall Sing
6:I Love *
7:You're Sixteen
8:Time in a Bottle
9:Eres Tu
10:Let Me Be There

Feb. 23, 1974

1:Last Time I Saw Him
2:Love's Theme
3:Love Song
4:I Shall Sing
5:The Way We Were
6:I Love
7:You're Sixteen
8:Sunshine On My Shoulders *
9:Eres Tu
10:Time in a Bottle

* Newcomer

Mar. 2, 1974

1:Last Time I Saw Him
2:I Love
3:Love's Theme
4:Love Song
5:The Way We Were
6:Seasons in the Sun *
7:Eres Tu
8:I Shall Sing
9:Sunshine On My Shoulders
10:You're Sixteen

Mar. 9, 1974

1:Last Time I Saw Him
2:Sunshine On My Shoulders
3:Seasons in the Sun
4:I Love
5:Love's Theme
6:Love Song
7:Eres Tu
8:The Way We Were
9:I Shall Sing
10:You're Sixteen

Mar. 16, 1974

1:Sunshine On My Shoulders
2:Seasons in the Sun
3:Last Time I Saw Him
4:I Love
5:A Very Special Love Song *
6:Love's Theme
7:Eres Tu
8:Love Song
9:The Way We Were
10:I Shall Sing

Mar. 23, 1974

1:Sunshine On My Shoulders
2:Seasons in the Sun
3:A Very Special Love Song
4:Last Time I Saw Him
5:I Love
6:Eres Tu
7:Love's Theme
8:The Entertainer *
9:The Way We Were
10:I'll Have to Say I Love You in a Song *

Mar. 30, 1974

1:A Very Special Love Song
2:Seasons in the Sun
3:Sunshine On My Shoulders
4:Last Time I Saw Him
5:The Entertainer
6:Midnight At the Oasis *
7:I'll Have to Say I Love You in a Song
8:I Love
9:Eres Tu
10:Love's Theme

Apr. 6, 1974

1:A Very Special Love Song
2:Seasons in the Sun
3:I'll Have to Say I Love You in a Song
4:The Entertainer
5:Midnight At the Oasis
6:Sunshine On My Shoulders
7:Keep On Singing *
8:Last Time I Saw Him
9:Eres Tu
10:I Love

Apr. 13, 1974

1:A Very Special Love Song
2:I'll Have to Say I Love You in a Song
3:Keep On Singing
4:The Entertainer
5:Midnight At the Oasis
6:Seasons in the Sun
7:Sunshine On My Shoulders
8:Last Time I Saw Him
9:You're the Best Thing That Ever Happened
10:Eres Tu   to Me *

Apr. 20, 1974

1:Keep On Singing
2:I'll Have to Say I Love You in a Song
3:The Entertainer
4:A Very Special Love Song
5:You're the Best Thing That Ever Happened
6:Midnight At the Oasis   to Me
7:Help Me *
8:Last Time I Saw Him
9:Sunshine On My Shoulders
10:Seasons in the Sun

Apr. 27, 1974

1:I'll Have to Say I Love You in a Song
2:Keep On Singing
3:Help Me
4:The Entertainer
5:A Very Special Love Song
6:You're the Best Thing That Ever Happened
7:Midnight At the Oasis   to Me
8:Happiness Is Me and You *
9:Seasons in the Sun
10:Sunshine On My Shoulders

May 4, 1974

1:Keep On Singing
2:I'll Have to Say I Love You in a Song
3:Help Me
4:The Entertainer
5:You're the Best Thing That Ever Happened
6:A Very Special Love Song   to Me
7:I Won't Last a Day Without You *
8:Happiness Is Me and You
9:Midnight At the Oasis
10:Sunshine On My Shoulders

May 11, 1974

1:The Entertainer
2:Keep On Singing
3:Help Me
4:I Won't Last a Day Without You
5:I'll Have to Say I Love You in a Song
6:Midnight At the Oasis
7:A Very Special Love Song
8:You're the Best Thing That Ever Happened
9:Sunshine On My Shoulders   to Me
10:Happiness Is Me and You

May 18, 1974

1:The Entertainer
2:Help Me
3:I Won't Last a Day Without You
4:Keep On Singing
5:You Won't See Me *
6:I'll Have to Say I Love You in a Song
7:If You Love Me *
8:Midnight At the Oasis
9:A Very Special Love Song
10:You're the Best Thing That Ever Happened
                                      to Me

May 25, 1974

1:Help Me
2:I Won't Last a Day Without You
3:The Entertainer
4:You Won't See Me
5:If You Love Me
6:Keep On Singing
7:I'll Have to Say I Love You in a
8:Midnight At the Oasis   Song
9:My Girl Bill *
10:A Very Special Love Song

June 1, 1974

1:I Won't Last a Day Without You
2:You Won't See Me
3:Help Me
4:If You Love Me
5:Sundown *
6:The Entertainer
7:My Girl Bill
8:Keep On Singing
9:Midnight At the Oasis
10:I'll Have to Say I Love You in a
                                  Song

June 8, 1974

1:I Won't Last a Day Without You
2:Sundown
3:You Won't See Me
4:If You Love Me
5:Help Me
6:The Entertainer
7:My Girl Bill
8:Midnight At the Oasis
9:You Make Me Feel Brand New *
10:Keep On Singing

June 15, 1974

1:Sundown
2:You Won't See Me
3:If You Love Me
4:I Won't Last a Day Without You
5:Help Me
6:You Make Me Feel Brand New
7:My Girl Bill
8:The Entertainer
9:Annie's Song *
10:I Don't Know What He Told You *

June 22, 1974

1:You Won't See Me
2:Sundown
3:If You Love Me
4:You Make Me Feel Brand New
5:Annie's Song
6:I Won't Last a Day Without You
7:Help Me
8:My Girl Bill
9:I Don't Know What He Told You
10:The Entertainer

June 29, 1974

1:You Won't See Me
2:If You Love Me
3:Sundown
4:Annie's Song
5:You Make Me Feel Brand New
6:I Don't Know What He Told You
7:I Won't Last a Day Without You
8:Come Monday *
9:Help Me
10:My Girl Bill

July 6, 1974

1:Annie's Song
2:If You Love Me
3:You Won't See Me
4:I Don't Know What He Told You
5:Come Monday
6:Sundown
7:You and Me Against the World *
8:The Air That I Breathe *
9:You Make Me Feel Brand New
10:I Won't Last a Day Without You

July 13, 1974

1:Annie's Song
2:You Make Me Feel Brand New
3:You and Me Against the World
4:Come Monday
5:I Don't Know What He Told You
6:If You Love Me
7:The Air That I Breathe
8:You Won't See Me
9:Sundown
10:I Won't Last a Day Without You

July 20, 1974

1:Annie's Song
2:You and Me Against the World
3:Come Monday
4:You Make Me Feel Brand New
5:The Air That I Breathe
6:I Don't Know What He Told You
7:If You Love Me
8:You Won't See Me
9:Sundown
10:I Won't Last a Day Without You

July 27, 1974

1:You and Me Against the World
2:Annie's Song
3:The Air That I Breathe
4:Come Monday
5:Feel Like Makin' Love *
6:I Don't Know What He Told You
7:Weave Me the Sunshine *
8:If You Love Me
9:Sundown
10:You Make Me Feel Brand New

Aug. 3, 1974

1:You and Me Against the World
2:Annie's Song
3:Feel Like Makin' Love
4:The Air That I Breathe
5:Come Monday
6:Weave Me the Sunshine
7:I Don't Know What He Told You
8:You Make Me Feel Brand New
9:If You Love Me
10:Sundown

Aug. 10, 1974

1:Feel Like Makin' Love
2:You and Me Against the World
3:Annie's Song
4:The Air That I Breathe
5:Come Monday
6:Don't Let the Sun Go Down On Me *
7:I'm Leaving It Up to You *
8:Weave Me the Sunshine
9:I Don't Know What He Told You
10:You Make Me Feel Brand New

Aug. 17, 1974

1:Feel Like Makin' Love
2:Don't Let the Sun Go Down On Me
3:I'm Leaving It Up to You
4:Annie's Song
5:You and Me Against the World
6:Having My Baby *
7:The Air That I Breathe
8:Come Monday
9:You Turned My World Around *
10:Weave Me the Sunshine

Aug. 24, 1974

1:Feel Like Makin' Love
2:I'm Leaving It Up to You
3:Don't Let the Sun Go Down On Me
4:Having My Baby
5:Annie's Song
6:You and Me Against the World
7:You Turned My World Around
8:The Air That I Breathe
9:Come Monday
10:Weave Me the Sunshine

Aug. 31, 1974

1:I'm Leaving It Up to You
2:Feel Like Makin' Love
3:Don't Let the Sun Go Down On Me
4:Having My Baby
5:You Turned My World Around
6:I Love My Friend *
7:Annie's Song
8:You and Me Against the World
9:The Air That I Breathe
10:I Honestly Love You *

Sept. 7, 1974

1:I'm Leaving It Up to You
2:I Love My Friend
3:Feel Like Makin' Love
4:I Honestly Love You
5:Having My Baby
6:Don't Let the Sun Go Down On Me
7:You Turned My World Around
8:You and Me Against the World
9:Annie's Song
10:The Air That I Breathe

Sept. 14, 1974

1:I Honestly Love You
2:I Love My Friend
3:Feel Like Makin' Love
4:I'm Leaving It Up to You
5:Free Man in Paris *
6:Don't Let the Sun Go Down On Me
7:You and Me Against the World
8:Then Came You *
9:Having My Baby
10:You Turned My World Around

Sept. 21, 1974

1:I Honestly Love You
2:Free Man in Paris
3:I Love My Friend
4:Feel Like Makin' Love
5:I'm Leaving It Up to You
6:Then Came You
7:Stop and Smell the Roses *
8:You and Me Against the World
9:Don't Let the Sun Go Down On Me
10:Having My Baby

Sept. 28, 1974

1:I Honestly Love You
2:Free Man in Paris
3:I Love My Friend
4:Then Came You
5:Stop and Smell the Roses
6:Carefree Highway *
7:Love Me For a Reason *
8:Feel Like Makin' Love
9:I'm Leaving It Up to You
10:You and Me Against the World

Oct. 5, 1974

1:I Honestly Love You
2:Stop and Smell the Roses
3:Carefree Highway
4:Love Me For a Reason
5:Free Man in Paris
6:Then Came You
7:Steppin' Out *
8:Feel Like Makin' Love
9:I Love My Friend
10:I'm Leaving It Up to You

Oct. 12, 1974

1:I Honestly Love You
2:Carefree Highway
3:Steppin' Out
4:Love Me For a Reason
5:Stop and Smell the Roses
6:Second Avenue *
7:Then Came You
8:Back Home Again *
9:Free Man in Paris
10:Feel Like Makin' Love

Oct. 19, 1974

1:Stop and Smell the Roses
2:Carefree Highway
3:Back Home Again
4:Love Me For a Reason
5:Second Avenue
6:I Honestly Love You
7:Steppin' Out
8:Then Came You
9:My Melody of Love *
10:Free Man in Paris

Oct. 26, 1974

1:Back Home Again
2:Carefree Highway
3:Love Me For a Reason
4:Stop and Smell the Roses
5:My Melody of Love
6:Second Avenue
7:I Honestly Love You
8:Steppin' Out
9:Then Came You
10:Laughter in the Rain *

Nov. 2, 1974

1:Back Home Again
2:Love Me For a Reason
3:Carefree Highway
4:My Melody of Love
5:Stop and Smell the Roses
6:Laughter in the Rain
7:Second Avenue
8:Steppin' Out
9:I Honestly Love You
10:I Can Help *

Nov. 9, 1974

1:My Melody of Love
2:Back Home Again
3:Carefree Highway
4:Laughter in the Rain
5:Love Me For a Reason
6:Longfellow Serenade *
7:Stop and Smell the Roses
8:I Can Help
9:Steppin' Out
10:Second Avenue

Nov. 16, 1974

1:My Melody of Love
2:Laughter in the Rain
3:Back Home Again
4:Longfellow Serenade
5:I Can Help
6:Carefree Highway
7:Angie Baby *
8:Love Me For a Reason
9:Stop and Smell the Roses
10:Steppin' Out

Nov. 23, 1974

1:Laughter in the Rain
2:Longfellow Serenade
3:Angie Baby
4:My Melody of Love
5:I Can Help
6:Back Home Again
7:Carefree Highway
8:Love Me For a Reason
9:Steppin' Out
10:Stop and Smell the Roses

Nov. 30, 1974

1:Laughter in the Rain
2:Angie Baby
3:Longfellow Serenade
4:I Can Help
5:My Melody of Love
6:Back Home Again
7:Carefree Highway
8:Mandy *
9:Love Me For a Reason
10:Steppin' Out

Dec. 7, 1974

1:Laughter in the Rain
2:Angie Baby
3:Longfellow Serenade
4:I Can Help
5:Mandy
6:When Will I See You Again? *
7:Wishing You Were Here *
8:My Melody of Love
9:Back Home Again
10:Carefree Highway

Dec. 14, 1974

1:Angie Baby
2:Laughter in the Rain
3:When Will I See You Again?
4:Wishing You Were Here
5:Mandy
6:Longfellow Serenade
7:My Eyes Adored You *
8:I Can Help
9:Back Home Again
10:My Melody of Love

Dec. 21, 1974

1:Angie Baby
2:When Will I See You Again?
3:Wishing You Were Here
4:Laughter in the Rain
5:My Eyes Adored You
6:Mandy
7:Back Home Again
8:I Can Help
9:My Melody of Love
10:Longfellow Serenade

Dec. 28, 1974

1:Angie Baby
2:Mandy
3:My Eyes Adored You
4:Wishing You Were Here
5:When Will I See You Again?
6:Laughter in the Rain
7:I Can Help
8:Longfellow Serenade
9:My Melody of Love
10:Back Home Again

1975

It was the year the Viet Cong suddenly marched on South Vietnam and Cambodia, quickly crushed both into unconditional surrender, and finally ended thirty years of warfare.

Tragically, the initial U.S. evacuation flight of Vietnamese orphans, carrying 243 children, crashed on takeoff in Saigon, killing 155 aboard. Later, more than 150,000 Vietnamese refugees flooded into the United States looking for homes and jobs. Another *Pueblo*-type incident ended on a triumphant note for the U.S. when President Ford sent Marines to the rescue to retrieve the American freighter *Mayaguez* and its crew after Cambodia captured the ship.

Incredibly, in this country two women, one of them the notorious Lynette "Squeaky" Fromme of the Charles Manson "family," tried unsuccessfully to shoot President Ford within a seventeen-day period in California. That state made headlines again when Patty Hearst was finally captured, surrendering at gunpoint.

Fighting flared in Beirut and Angola. Jimmy Hoffa disappeared, supposedly a murder victim, and the World Football League died, apparently of apathy and underfinancing. New York City was going broke, and the rest of the country was reeling under inflation. The only thing going higher than prices was Dave Roberts, who pole-vaulted to a new record of eighteen feet, 6½ inches. New Zealand's John Walker set a new record in the mile run, 3:49.4.

King Faisal of Saudia Arabia was assassinated by a nephew who shot him within the walls of the royal palace, and in this country Japanese Emperor Hirohito—thirty years late—finally got to the White House.

The most overworked words of the year were Bicentennial and détente. In a feat of celestial détente, U.S. and Soviet astronauts linked up and went capsule-visiting in space. President Ford also went visiting, and critics said he took a show boat to China.

There was never any question about the top movie of the year as *Jaws* grossed more than $100,000,000 in six months to set a new all-time box-office record. The year's top song, with a more modest five weeks as Number One, was "Please, Mister, Please."

Jan. 4, 1975

1:Mandy
2:My Eyes Adored You
3:Angie Baby
4:Wishing You Were Here
5:Please, Mr. Postman *
6:When Will I See You Again?
7:Laughter in the Rain
8:I Can Help
9:Longfellow Serenade
10:My Melody of Love

Jan. 11, 1975

1:Mandy
2:My Eyes Adored You
3:Please, Mr. Postman
4:Angie Baby
5:The Best of My Love *
6:Wishing You Were Here
7:Laughter in the Rain
8:I Can Help
9:When Will I See You Again?
10:Longfellow Serenade

Jan. 18, 1975

1:Please, Mr. Postman
2:Mandy
3:The Best of My Love
4:My Eyes Adored You
5:Look in My Eyes, Pretty Woman *
6:Angie Baby
7:Wishing You Were Here
8:Laughter in the Rain
9:I Can Help
10:When Will I See You Again?

Jan. 25, 1975

1:Please, Mr. Postman
2:The Best of My Love
3:Look in My Eyes, Pretty Woman
4:Mandy
5:My Eyes Adored You
6:Angie Baby
7:Laughter in the Rain
8:When Will I See You Again?
9:I Can Help
10:Wishing You Were Here

Feb. 1, 1975

1:The Best of My Love
2:Please, Mr. Postman
3:Look in My Eyes, Pretty Woman
4:Mandy
5:Lonely People *
6:My Eyes Adored You
7:Nightingale *
8:Angie Baby
9:Laughter in the Rain
10:I Can Help

Feb. 8, 1975

1:The Best of My Love
2:Lonely People
3:Nightingale
4:Look in My Eyes, Pretty Woman
5:Mandy
6:Please, Mr. Postman
7:My Eyes Adored You
8:Angie Baby
9:To the Door of the Sun *
10:Laughter in the Rain

Feb. 15, 1975

1:Lonely People
2:Nightingale
3:The Best of My Love
4:To the Door of the Sun
5:Poetry Man *
6:Have You Never Been Mellow? *
7:Look in My Eyes, Pretty Woman
8:Mandy
9:Please, Mr. Postman
10:My Eyes Adored You

Feb. 22, 1975

1:Nightingale
2:Lonely People
3:Poetry Man
4:Have You Never Been Mellow?
5:The Best of My Love
6:To the Door of the Sun
7:Look in My Eyes, Pretty Woman
8:Please, Mr. Postman
9:My Eyes Adored You
10:Mandy

* Newcomer

Mar. 1, 1975

1:Nightingale
2:Poetry Man
3:Have You Never Been Mellow?
4:Lonely People
5:I've Been This Way Before *
6:To the Door of the Sun
7:The Best of My Love
8:Look in My Eyes, Pretty Woman
9:Please, Mr. Postman
10:My Eyes Adored You

Mar. 8, 1975

1:Have You Never Been Mellow?
2:I've Been This Way Before
3:Poetry Man
4:Lonely People
5:Nightingale
6:To the Door of the Sun
7:Another Somebody Done Somebody Wrong Song *
8:Emotion *
9:The Best of My Love
10:Look in My Eyes, Pretty Woman

Mar. 15, 1975

1:Have You Never Been Mellow?
2:I've Been This Way Before
3:Another Somebody Done Somebody Wrong Song
4:Emotion
5:Poetry Man
6:Lonely People
7:Nightingale
8:The Best of My Love
9:Look in My Eyes, Pretty Woman
10:To the Door of the Sun

Mar. 22, 1975

1:Another Somebody Done Somebody Wrong Song
2:Emotion
3:Have You Never Been Mellow?
4:I've Been This Way Before
5:Poetry Man
6:Lonely People
7:Nightingale
8:The Best of My Love
9:To the Door of the Sun
10:Look in My Eyes, Pretty Woman

Mar. 29, 1975

1:Another Somebody Done Somebody Wrong Song
2:Emotion
3:Have You Never Been Mellow?
4:Poetry Man
5:I've Been This Way Before
6:He Don't Love You *
7:The Best of My Love
8:Nightingale
9:Lonely People
10:To the Door of the Sun

Apr. 5, 1975

1:Another Somebody Done Somebody Wrong Song
2:Emotion
3:He Don't Love You
4:Have You Never Been Mellow?
5:Poetry Man
6:My Boy *
7:I've Been This Way Before
8:Lonely People
9:The Best of My Love
10:Nightingale

Apr. 12, 1975

1:Another Somebody Done Somebody Wrong Song
2:He Don't Love You
3:My Boy
4:Emotion
5:Have You Never Been Mellow?
6:Poetry Man
7:I've Been This Way Before
8:The Last Farewell *
9:Nightingale
10:Lonely People

Apr. 19, 1975

1:He Don't Love You
2:Another Somebody Done Somebody Wrong Song
3:The Last Farewell
4:My Boy
5:Only Yesterday *
6:The Immigrant *
7:Emotion
8:Have You Never Been Mellow?
9:Poetry Man
10:I've Been This Way Before

Apr. 26, 1975

1:He Don't Love You
2:The Last Farewell
3:Only Yesterday
4:The Immigrant
5:Rainy Day People *
6:Another Somebody Done Somebody Wrong Song
7:My Boy
8:Emotion
9:Have You Never Been Mellow?
10:Poetry Man

May 3, 1975

1:Only Yesterday
2:The Immigrant
3:Rainy Day People
4:The Last Farewell
5:He Don't Love You
6:Ninety-Nine Miles From L.A. *
7:Another Somebody Done Somebody Wrong Song
8:Emotion
9:My Boy
10:Have You Never Been Mellow?

May 10, 1975

1:Only Yesterday
2:The Immigrant
3:Rainy Day People
4:Ninety-Nine Miles From L.A.
5:The Last Farewell
6:He Don't Love You
7:Another Somebody Done Somebody Wrong Song
8:My Boy
9:Have You Never Been Mellow?
10:Emotion

May 17, 1975

1:Rainy Day People
2:Ninety-Nine Miles From L.A.
3:Only Yesterday
4:The Immigrant
5:The Last Farewell
6:Love Will Keep Us Together *
7:He Don't Love You
8:Another Somebody Done Somebody Wrong Song
9:My Boy
10:Wildfire *

May 24, 1975

1:Ninety-Nine Miles From L.A.
2:Love Will Keep Us Together
3:Rainy Day People
4:Only Yesterday
5:Wildfire
6:I'll Play For You *
7:The Immigrant
8:The Last Farewell
9:He Don't Love You
10:Another Somebody Done Somebody Wrong Song

May 31, 1975

1:Love Will Keep Us Together
2:Wildfire
3:Ninety-Nine Miles From L.A.
4:I'll Play For You
5:Rainy Day People
6:Only Yesterday
7:Midnight Blue *
8:The Last Farewell
9:Wonderful Baby *
10:He Don't Love You

June 7, 1975

1:Love Will Keep Us Together
2:Wildfire
3:Wonderful Baby
4:I'll Play For You
5:Midnight Blue
6:Rainy Day People
7:Only Yesterday
8:When Will I Be Loved? *
9:Ninety-Nine Miles From L.A.
10:The Last Farewell

June 14, 1975

1:Wildfire
2:Midnight Blue
3:Love Will Keep Us Together
4:Wonderful Baby
5:When Will I Be Loved?
6:I'll Play For You
7:Only Yesterday
8:Rainy Day People
9:Ninety-Nine Miles From L.A.
10:The Last Farewell

June 21, 1975

1:Midnight Blue
2:Wildfire
3:When Will I Be Loved?
4:Love Will Keep Us Together
5:Everytime You Touch Me *
6:Wonderful Baby
7:I'll Play For You
8:Only Yesterday
9:Rainy Day People
10:Ninety-Nine Miles From L.A.

June 28, 1975

1:Midnight Blue
2:Everytime You Touch Me
3:When Will I Be Loved?
4:Wildfire
5:Love Will Keep Us Together
6:Wonderful Baby
7:I'll Play For You
8:Ninety-Nine Miles From L.A.
9:Rainy Day People
10:Only Yesterday

July 5, 1975

1:Midnight Blue
2:Everytime You Touch Me
3:Please, Mister, Please *
4:Feelings *
5:When Will I Be Loved?
6:Wildfire
7:Love Will Keep Us Together
8:Wonderful Baby
9:I'll Play For You
10:Ninety-Nine Miles From L.A.

July 12, 1975

1:Please, Mister, Please
2:Midnight Blue
3:Everytime You Touch Me
4:Rhinestone Cowboy *
5:Feelings
6:Wildfire
7:Love Will Keep Us Together
8:When Will I Be Loved?
9:Wonderful Baby
10:I'll Play For You

July 19, 1975

1:Please, Mister, Please
2:Rhinestone Cowboy
3:Feelings
4:Everytime You Touch Me
5:At Seventeen *
6:Midnight Blue
7:When Will I Be Loved?
8:Wildfire
9:Love Will Keep Us Together
10:Wonderful Baby

July 26, 1975

1:Please, Mister, Please
2:Rhinestone Cowboy
3:Feelings
4:At Seventeen
5:Everytime You Touch Me
6:Midnight Blue
7:Wildfire
8:When Will I Be Loved?
9:Wonderful Baby
10:Love Will Keep Us Together

Aug. 2, 1975

1:Please, Mister, Please
2:Rhinestone Cowboy
3:Feelings
4:At Seventeen
5:Mornin', Beautiful *
6:Everytime You Touch Me
7:How Sweet It Is *
8:Midnight Blue
9:Wildfire
10:When Will I Be Loved?

Aug. 9, 1975

1:Please, Mister, Please
2:At Seventeen
3:Rhinestone Cowboy
4:Feelings
5:Mornin', Beautiful
6:How Sweet It Is
7:Bluebird *
8:Everytime You Touch Me
9:Midnight Blue
10:Wildfire

Aug. 16, 1975

1:At Seventeen
2:Rhinestone Cowboy
3:Please, Mister, Please
4:Mornin', Beautiful
5:How Sweet It Is
6:Bluebird
7:Fallin' In Love *
8:Could It Be Magic? *
9:Feelings
10:Everytime You Touch Me

Aug. 23, 1975

1:At Seventeen
2:How Sweet It Is
3:Fallin' In Love
4:Could It Be Magic?
5:Mornin', Beautiful
6:Rhinestone Cowboy
7:Feelings
8:Bluebird
9:Please, Mister, Please
10:Everytime You Touch Me

Aug. 30, 1975

1:At Seventeen
2:Fallin' In Love
3:How Sweet It Is
4:I Believe There's Nothing Stronger
5:Solitaire *   Than Our Love *
6:Could It Be Magic?
7:Mornin', Beautiful
8:Rhinestone Cowboy
9:Feelings
10:Please, Mister, Please

Sept. 6, 1975

1:At Seventeen
2:Solitaire
3:I Believe There's Nothing Stronger
4:How Sweet It Is   Than Our Love
5:Fallin' In Love
6:Rhinestone Cowboy
7:Could It Be Magic?
8:Mornin', Beautiful
9:Please, Mister, Please
10:Feelings

Sept. 13, 1975

1:Solitaire
2:I Believe There's Nothing Stronger
3:At Seventeen   Than Our Love
4:Fallin' In Love
5:How Sweet It Is
6:The Proud One *
7:I Believe I'm Gonna Love You *
8:Rhinestone Cowboy
9:Could It Be Magic?
10:Please, Mister, Please

Sept. 20, 1975

1:Solitaire
2:The Proud One
3:I Believe I'm Gonna Love You
4:Ain't No Way to Treat a Lady *
5:I Believe There's Nothing Stronger
6:Fallin' In Love   Than Our Love
7:How Sweet It Is
8:At Seventeen
9:Rhinestone Cowboy
10:Could It Be Magic?

Sept. 27, 1975

1:Solitaire
2:I Believe I'm Gonna Love You
3:Ain't No Way to Treat a Lady
4:The Proud One
5:I Believe There's Nothing Stronger
6:Fallin' In Love   Than Our Love
7:How Sweet It Is
8:At Seventeen
9:Could It Be Magic?
10:Rhinestone Cowboy

Oct. 4, 1975

1:Ain't No Way to Treat a Lady
2:I Believe I'm Gonna Love You
3:Solitaire
4:The Proud One
5:I Believe There's Nothing Stronger
6:At Seventeen   Than Our Love.
7:Rhinestone Cowboy
8:Fallin' In Love
9:How Sweet It Is
10:Could It Be Magic?

Oct. 11, 1975

1:Ain't No Way to Treat a Lady
2:I Believe I'm Gonna Love You
3:The Proud One
4:Solitaire
5:Carolina In the Pines *
6:Something Better to Do *
7:I Believe There's Nothing Stronger
8:At Seventeen   Than Our Love
9:Rhinestone Cowboy
10:Fallin' In Love

Oct. 18, 1975

1:Ain't No Way to Treat a Lady
2:Something Better to Do
3:Carolina In the Pines
4:The Way I Want to Touch You *
5:I Believe I'm Gonna Love You
6:Solitaire
7:The Proud One
8:I Believe There's Nothing Stronger
9:At Seventeen   Than Our Love
10:Rhinestone Cowboy

Oct. 25, 1975

1:Something Better to Do
2:Carolina In the Pines
3:The Way I Want to Touch You
4:Ain't No Way to Treat a Lady
5:Solitaire
6:I Believe There's Nothing Stronger Than
7:I Believe I'm Gonna Love You   Our Love
8:At Seventeen
9:Rhinestone Cowboy
10:The Proud One

Nov. 1, 1975

1:Something Better to Do
2:The Way I Want to Touch You
3:Carolina In the Pines
4:Ain't No Way to Treat a Lady
5:Lyin' Eyes *
6:Just Too Many People *
7:Solitaire
8:I Believe There's Nothing Stronger
9:At Seventeen   Than Our Love
10:I Believe I'm Gonna Love You

Nov. 8, 1975

1:Something Better to Do
2:The Way I Want to Touch You
3:Lyin' Eyes
4:My Little Town *
5:Just Too Many People
6:Carolina In the Pines
7:Ain't No Way to Treat a Lady
8:Solitaire
9:I Believe I'm Gonna Love You
10:At Seventeen

Nov. 15, 1975

1:The Way I Want to Touch You
2:My Little Town
3:Lyin' Eyes
4:Just Too Many People
5:Something Better to Do
6:Carolina In the Pines
7:Ain't No Way to Treat a Lady
8:Solitaire
9:Theme From Mahogany *
10:I Believe I'm Gonna Love You

Nov. 22, 1975

1:The Way I Want to Touch You
2:My Little Town
3:Just Too Many People
4:Theme From Mahogany
5:Something Better to Do
6:Lyin' Eyes
7:I Write the Songs *
8:Carolina In the Pines
9:Ain't No Way to Treat a Lady
10:Solitaire

Nov. 29, 1975

1:My Little Town
2:Theme From Mahogany
3:I Write the Songs
4:Just Too Many People
5:The Way I Want to Touch You
6:Something Better to Do
7:Lyin' Eyes
8:Carolina In the Pines
9:Solitaire
10:Ain't No Way to Treat a Lady

Dec. 6, 1975

1:Theme From Mahogany
2:My Little Town
3:I Write the Songs
4:Just Too Many People
5:Sky High *
6:Country Boy *
7:Skybird *
8:Lyin' Eyes
9:The Way I Want to Touch You
10:Something Better to Do

Dec. 13, 1975

1:Theme From Mahogany
2:I Write the Songs
3:My Little Town
4:Country Boy
5:Skybird
6:Sky High
7:Times of Your Life *
8:Just Too Many People
9:The Way I Want to Touch You
10:Lyin' Eyes

Dec. 20, 1975

1:I Write the Songs
2:Theme From Mahogany
3:Country Boy
4:Times of Your Life
5:My Little Town
6:Skybird
7:Sky High
8:Fly Away *
9:Just Too Many People
10:The Way I Want to Touch You

Dec. 27, 1975

1:I Write the Songs
2:Country Boy
3:Times of Your Life
4:Theme From Mahogany
5:Fly Away
6:My Little Town
7:Sky High
8:Skybird
9:The Way I Want to Touch You
10:Just Too Many People

1976

It was, quite simply, the year of Jimmy Carter, the man who came out of nowhere, made a no-suspense show out of the Democratic National Convention, and in November was elected President of the United States. Gerald Ford, the nation's first nonelected President, lost narrowly, becoming the first incumbent since Herbert Hoover to be turned out of the White House.

It was also, of course, the year of the peanut joke, the *Playboy* magazine "lust" jokes inspired by Carter's ill-advised interview, and the Washington "Can she type?" jokes, inspired by secretary Elizabeth Ray, a nontypist who charged she was on Congressman Wayne Hays's payroll for sexual favors.

It was a year of records. Seven Americans won the Nobel Prize, giving the United States an unprecedented sweep of the 1976 awards. Abilene Christian College's Ove Johansson kicked a sixty-nine-yard field goal against East Texas State, breaking Tom Dempsey's pro football record. Dave Roberts pole-vaulted 18 feet, 8½ inches, Dwight Stones high-jumped a record 7 feet, 7¼ inches, and Hank Aaron finally retired from baseball, leaving the home-run record at 755. But the best record of 1976 was Barry Manilow's "Tryin' to Get the Feeling Again," the top song with six weeks as Number One.

On the Fourth of July, America's Bicentennial exploded in a cascade of fireworks and tall ships sailing majestically into New York's Hudson River. Amazingly, America's Viking I spacecraft landed on Mars, sending back razor-sharp photos of the planet's surface. Down on this planet, death claimed the world's two top billionaires, J. Paul Getty and recluse Howard Hughes, the latter, ironically, being a man who had to die to prove he was alive.

It was the End of the Sixth Happiness for Zsa Zsa Gabor and Elizabeth Taylor, both shedding husband number six and promptly marrying husband number seven. Agriculture Secretary Earl Butz, a man of the soil, told an earthy joke about blacks and had to go back to the farm. Flop of the year: swine-flu shots. Mysterious killer of the year: the Philadelphia legionnaires' disease, which claimed the lives of twenty-five conventioneers in that city. Headlines of the year: Three masked men kidnapped twenty-six children and the driver from a school bus in Chowchilla, California, burying them in an underground prison from which they escaped before ransom demands could be made . . . Israeli commandos flew 2,620 miles for a lightning strike on Uganda's Entebbe Airport to kill pro-Palestinian skyjackers and rescue 104 hostages.

Jan. 3, 1976

1:I Write the Songs
2:Times of Your Life
3:Fly Away
4:Country Boy
5:Theme From Mahogany
6:Paloma Blanca *
7:My Little Town
8:Sky High
9:Skybird
10:Fifty Ways to Leave Your Lover *

Jan. 10, 1976

1:Fly Away
2:Times of Your Life
3:Paloma Blanca
4:I Write the Songs
5:Country Boy
6:Fifty Ways to Leave Your Lover
7:My Little Town
8:Theme From Mahogany
9:Skybird
10:Tracks of My Tears *

Jan. 17, 1976

1:Fly Away
2:Times of Your Life
3:I Write the Songs
4:Fifty Ways to Leave Your Lover
5:Country Boy
6:Tracks of My Tears
7:Paloma Blanca
8:Skybird
9:Theme From Mahogany
10:Break Away *

Jan. 24, 1976

1:Fly Away
2:Times of Your Life
3:Fifty Ways to Leave Your Lover
4:Tracks of My Tears
5:Paloma Blanca
6:I Write the Songs
7:Country Boy
8:Theme From Mahogany
9:Break Away
10:Skybird

Jan. 31, 1976

1:Fly Away
2:Paloma Blanca
3:Fifty Ways to Leave Your Lover
4:Tracks of My Tears
5:Break Away
6:Times of Your Life
7:Take It to the Limit *
8:I Write the Songs
9:Country Boy
10:Theme From Mahogany

Feb. 7, 1976

1:Paloma Blanca
2:Fly Away
3:Break Away
4:Tracks of My Tears
5:Fifty Ways to Leave Your Lover
6:Take It to the Limit
7:All By Myself *
8:Times of Your Life
9:I Write the Songs
10:Lonely Night *

Feb. 14, 1976

1:Paloma Blanca
2:Break Away
3:Fifty Ways to Leave Your Lover
4:Tracks of My Tears
5:All By Myself
6:Take It to the Limit
7:Fly Away
8:Lonely Night
9:Times of Your Life
10:Only Love Is Real *

Feb. 21, 1976

1:Break Away
2:Fifty Ways to Leave Your Lover
3:Lonely Night
4:Tracks of My Tears
5:Take It to the Limit
6:All By Myself
7:Paloma Blanca
8:Fly Away
9:Only Love Is Real
10:The Call *

* Newcomer

Feb. 28, 1976

1:Fifty Ways to Leave Your Lover
2:Lonely Night
3:Break Away
4:Take It to the Limit
5:Tracks of My Tears
6:All By Myself
7:Paloma Blanca
8:Fly Away
9:Only Love Is Real
10:The Call

Mar. 6, 1976

1:Fifty Ways to Leave Your Lover
2:Lonely Night
3:Take It to the Limit
4:Break Away
5:Tracks of My Tears
6:All By Myself
7:Only Love Is Real
8:The Call
9:Paloma Blanca
10:Fly Away

Mar. 13, 1976

1:Lonely Night
2:Fifty Ways to Leave Your Lover
3:Take It to the Limit
4:Break Away
5:Tracks of My Tears
6:Only Love Is Real
7:The Call
8:Let Your Love Flow *
9:All By Myself
10:Paloma Blanca

Mar. 20, 1976

1:Lonely Night
2:Only Love Is Real
3:The Call
4:Break Away
5:Fifty Ways to Leave Your Lover
6:Paloma Blanca
7:Tracks of My Tears
8:Take It to the Limit
9:Let Your Love Flow
10:All By Myself

Mar. 27, 1976

1:Lonely Night
2:Only Love Is Real
3:The Call
4:Let Your Love Flow
5:Come On Over *
6:Looking For Space *
7:Break Away
8:Fifty Ways to Leave Your Lover
9:All By Myself
10:Take It to the Limit

Apr. 3, 1976

1:Lonely Night
2:Let Your Love Flow
3:Looking For Space
4:Come On Over
5:The Call
6:Only Love Is Real
7:All By Myself
8:Take It to the Limit
9:Break Away
10:Fifty Ways to Leave Your Lover

Apr. 10, 1976

1:Lonely Night
2:Come On Over
3:Looking For Space
4:Let Your Love Flow
5:Fifty Ways to Leave Your Lover
6:Tryin' to Get the Feeling Again *
7:Only Love Is Real
8:The Call
9:All By Myself
10:Take It to the Limit

Apr. 17, 1976

1:Come On Over
2:Lonely Night
3:Tryin' to Get the Feeling Again
4:Looking For Space
5:Let Your Love Flow
6:Only Love Is Real
7:The Call
8:Fifty Ways to Leave Your Lover
9:Welcome Back *
10:All By Myself

Apr. 24, 1976

1:Come On Over
2:Tryin' to Get the Feeling Again
3:Looking For Space
4:Let Your Love Flow
5:Only Love Is Real
6:Welcome Back
7:The Call
8:Lonely Night
9:All By Myself
10:Silly Love Songs *

May 1, 1976

1:Tryin' to Get the Feeling Again
2:Come On Over
3:Welcome Back
4:Looking For Space
5:Silly Love Songs
6:Let Your Love Flow
7:I Do, I Do, I Do, I Do, I Do *
8:Only Love Is Real
9:Lonely Night
10:The Call

May 8, 1976

1:Tryin' to Get the Feeling Again
2:Welcome Back
3:Come On Over
4:Silly Love Songs
5:I Do, I Do, I Do, I Do, I Do
6:Let Your Love Flow
7:Looking For Space
8:Only Love Is Real
9:Shop Around *
10:Lonely Night

May 15, 1976

1:Tryin' to Get the Feeling Again
2:Welcome Back
3:Silly Love Songs
4:Shop Around
5:Come On Over
6:Let Your Love Flow
7:I Do, I Do, I Do, I Do, I Do
8:Looking For Space
9:Lonely Night
10:Only Love Is Real

May 22, 1976

1:Tryin' to Get the Feeling Again
2:Silly Love Songs
3:Welcome Back
4:Shop Around
5:Never Gonna Fall in Love Again *
6:Come On Over
7:Let Your Love Flow
8:I Do, I Do, I Do, I Do, I Do
9:Only Love Is Real
10:Lonely Night

May 29, 1976

1:Tryin' to Get the Feeling Again
2:Silly Love Songs
3:Welcome Back
4:Never Gonna Fall in Love Again
5:Shop Around
6:Save Your Kisses For Me *
7:Come On Over
8:I Do, I Do, I Do, I Do, I Do
9:Let Your Love Flow
10:Lonely Night

June 5, 1976

1:Tryin' to Get the Feeling Again
2:Shop Around
3:Silly Love Songs
4:Save Your Kisses For Me
5:Never Gonna Fall in Love Again
6:Welcome Back
7:Come On Over
8:I Do, I Do, I Do, I Do, I Do
9:Moonlight Feels Right *
10:Let Your Love Flow

June 12, 1976

1:Never Gonna Fall in Love Again
2:Save Your Kisses For Me
3:Silly Love Songs
4:Shop Around
5:Tryin' to Get the Feeling Again
6:Moonlight Feels Right
7:Afternoon Delight *
8:Welcome Back
9:Come On Over
10:I Do, I Do, I Do, I Do, I Do

June 19, 1976

1:Never Gonna Fall in Love Again
2:Moonlight Feels Right
3:Save Your Kisses For Me
4:Today's the Day *
5:Shop Around
6:Silly Love Songs
7:Afternoon Delight
8:Tryin' to Get the Feeling Again
9:Get Up and Boogie *
10:Welcome Back

June 26, 1976

1:Never Gonna Fall in Love Again
2:Today's the Day
3:Moonlight Feels Right
4:Save Your Kisses For Me
5:I Need to Be in Love *
6:Afternoon Delight
7:Shop Around
8:Get Up and Boogie
9:Tryin' to Get the Feeling Again
10:Silly Love Songs

July 3, 1976

1:Never Gonna Fall in Love Again
2:Today's the Day
3:Moonlight Feels Right
4:I Need to Be in Love
5:Afternoon Delight
6:I'm Easy *
7:Save Your Kisses For Me
8:Tryin' to Get the Feeling Again
9:More, More, More *
10:Get Up and Boogie

July 10, 1976

1:I Need to Be in Love
2:Today's the Day
3:I'm Easy
4:Moonlight Feels Right
5:Afternoon Delight
6:Never Gonna Fall in Love Again
7:If You Know What I Mean *
8:You'll Never Find Another Love Like Mine *
9:More, More, More
10:Tryin' to Get the Feeling Again

July 17, 1976

1:I Need to Be in Love
2:If You Know What I Mean
3:You'll Never Find Another Love Like Mine
4:Today's the Day
5:I'm Easy
6:Afternoon Delight
7:Moonlight Feels Right
8:Never Gonna Fall in Love Again
9:I'd Really Love to See You Tonight *
10:More, More, More

July 24, 1976

1:I'm Easy
2:If You Know What I Mean
3:You'll Never Find Another Love Like Mine
4:I'd Really Love to See You Tonight
5:I Need to Be in Love
6:Moonlight Feels Right
7:Today's the Day
8:Afternoon Delight
9:Never Gonna Fall in Love Again
10:More, More, More

July 31, 1976

1:I'm Easy
2:You'll Never Find Another Love Like Mine
3:I'd Really Love to See You Tonight
4:If You Know What I Mean
5:Moonlight Feels Right
6:I Need to Be in Love
7:Afternoon Delight
8:Never Gonna Fall in Love Again
9:Today's the Day
10:Let 'Em In *

Aug. 7, 1976

1:You'll Never Find Another Love Like Mine
2:I'm Easy
3:I'd Really Love to See You Tonight
4:Let 'Em In
5:If You Know What I Mean
6:Moonlight Feels Right
7:I Need to Be in Love
8:Don't Go Breaking My Heart *
9:Never Gonna Fall in Love Again
10:Afternoon Delight

Aug. 14, 1976

1:You'll Never Find Another Love Like Mine
2:If You Know What I Mean
3:Let 'Em In
4:I'd Really Love to See You Tonight
5:I'm Easy
6:Don't Go Breaking My Heart
7:Moonlight Feels Right
8:I Need to Be in Love
9:Afternoon Delight
10:Never Gonna Fall in Love Again

Aug. 21, 1976

1:You'll Never Find Another Love Like Mine
2:If You Know What I Mean
3:Don't Go Breaking My Heart
4:Let 'Em In
5:I'd Really Love to See You Tonight
6:I'm Easy
7:Moonlight Feels Right
8:What I Did For Love *
9:I Need to Be in Love
10:Afternoon Delight

Aug. 28, 1976

1:You'll Never Find Another Love Like Mine
2:I'd Really Love to See You Tonight
3:If You Know What I Mean
4:Let 'Em In
5:Don't Go Breaking My Heart
6:What I Did For Love
7:I'm Easy
8:Moonlight Feels Right
9:Afternoon Delight
10:I Need to Be in Love

Sept. 4, 1976

1:You'll Never Find Another Love Like Mine
2:I'd Really Love to See You Tonight
3:Don't Go Breaking My Heart
4:Let 'Em In
5:What I Did For Love
6:If You Know What I Mean
7:Wham Bam Shang-a-Lang *
8:I Need to Be in Love
9:Afternoon Delight
10:I'm Easy

Sept. 11, 1976

1:I'd Really Love to See You Tonight
2:You'll Never Find Another Love Like Mine
3:Don't Go Breaking My Heart
4:Let 'Em In
5:What I Did For Love
6:Wham Bam Shang-a-Lang
7:If You Know What I Mean
8:I Need to Be in Love
9:I'm Easy
10:Afternoon Delight

Sept. 18, 1976

1:I'd Really Love to See You Tonight
2:Don't Go Breaking My Heart
3:You'll Never Find Another Love Like Mine
4:Wham Bam Shang-a-Lang
5:Let 'Em In
6:What I Did For Love
7:Don't Stop Believin' *
8:If You Know What I Mean
9:I Need to Be in Love
10:I'm Easy

Sept. 25, 1976

1:I'd Really Love to See You Tonight
2:Don't Go Breaking My Heart
3:Wham Bam Shang-a-Lang
4:Let 'Em In
5:You'll Never Find Another Love Like Mine
6:Don't Stop Believin'
7:What I Did For Love
8:If You Leave Me Now *
9:If You Know What I Mean
10:I'm Easy

Oct. 2, 1976

1:Don't Go Breaking My Heart
2:I'd Really Love to See You Tonight
3:Don't Stop Believin'
4:If You Leave Me Now
5:Wham Bam Shang-a-Lang
6:Let 'Em In
7:Nadia's Theme *
8:You'll Never Find Another Love Like Mine
9:What I Did For Love
10:If You Know What I Mean

Oct. 9, 1976

1:Don't Go Breaking My Heart
2:If You Leave Me Now
3:Don't Stop Believin'
4:I'd Really Love to See You Tonight
5:Nadia's Theme
6:You'll Never Find Another Love Like Mine
7:Wham Bam Shang-a-Lang
8:What I Did For Love
9:Let 'Em In
10:Like a Sad Song *

Oct. 16, 1976

1:Don't Go Breaking My Heart
2:If You Leave Me Now
3:Like a Sad Song
4:Don't Stop Believin'
5:Muskrat Love *
6:I'd Really Love to See You Tonight
7:Nadia's Theme
8:You'll Never Find Another Love Like Mine
9:Wham Bam Shang-a-Lang
10:What I Did For Love

Oct. 23, 1976

1:If You Leave Me Now
2:Don't Go Breaking My Heart
3:Muskrat Love
4:Nadia's Theme
5:After the Lovin' *
6:Like a Sad Song
7:Don't Stop Believin'
8:I'd Really Love to See You Tonight
9:You'll Never Find Another Love Like Mine
10:Wham Bam Shang-a-Lang

Oct. 30, 1976

1:Muskrat Love
2:If You Leave Me Now
3:After the Lovin'
4:Don't Go Breaking My Heart
5:Nadia's Theme
6:Don't Stop Believin'
7:Like a Sad Song
8:I'd Really Love to See You Tonight
9:You'll Never Find Another Love Like Mine
10:Wham Bam Shang-a-Lang

Nov. 6, 1976

1:Muskrat Love
2:After the Lovin'
3:If You Leave Me Now
4:Nadia's Theme
5:Don't Go Breaking My Heart
6:You Don't Have to Be a Star *
7:Don't Stop Believin'
8:Like a Sad Song
9:I'd Really Love to See You Tonight
10:You'll Never Find Another Love Like Mine

Nov. 13, 1976

1:Muskrat Love
2:After the Lovin'
3:You Don't Have to Be a Star
4:If You Leave Me Now
5:Nadia's Theme
6:Don't Go Breaking My Heart
7:Don't Stop Believin'
8:Stand Tall *
9:Like a Sad Song
10:I'd Really Love to See You Tonight

Nov. 20, 1976

1:Muskrat Love
2:After the Lovin'
3:You Don't Have to Be a Star
4:Stand Tall
5:If You Leave Me Now
6:Nadia's Theme
7:Sorry Seems to Be the Hardest Word *
8:Don't Go Breaking My Heart
9:Don't Stop Believin'
10:Like a Sad Song

Nov. 27, 1976

1:Muskrat Love
2:After the Lovin'
3:Stand Tall
4:Sorry Seems to Be the Hardest Word
5:Torn Between Two Lovers *
6:You Don't Have to Be a Star
7:If You Leave Me Now
8:Nadia's Theme
9:Like a Sad Song
10:Don't Stop Believin'

Dec. 4, 1976

1:After the Lovin'
2:Muskrat Love
3:Sorry Seems to Be the Hardest Word
4:Torn Between Two Lovers
5:You Don't Have to Be a Star
6:Stand Tall
7:Lost Without Your Love *
8:If You Leave Me Now
9:Nadia's Theme
10:Like a Sad Song

Dec. 11, 1976

1:After the Lovin'
2:Sorry Seems to Be the Hardest Word
3:Muskrat Love
4:Torn Between Two Lovers
5:You Don't Have to Be a Star
6:Lost Without Your Love
7:Stand Tall
8:Evergreen *
9:If You Leave Me Now
10:Nadia's Theme

Dec. 18, 1976

1:After the Lovin'
2:Torn Between Two Lovers
3:Sorry Seems to Be the Hardest Word
4:Muskrat Love
5:You Don't Have to Be a Star
6:Lost Without Your Love
7:Evergreen
8:New Kid in Town *
9:Stand Tall
10:If You Leave Me Now

Dec. 25, 1976

1:After the Lovin'
2:Torn Between Two Lovers
3:Sorry Seems to Be the Hardest Word
4:Evergreen
5:Lost Without Your Love
6:New Kid in Town
7:You Don't Have to Be a Star
8:Muskrat Love
9:If You Leave Me Now
10:Stand Tall

1977

It was the kind of year when the Egyptian president, Anwar Sadat, could make a first-ever step on Israeli soil to talk peace . . . when a mysterious slayer known as Son of Sam could terrorize New York before being captured . . . when the nation suffered its coldest January in history.

And yet, somehow, 1977 will always be remembered as the year Elvis Presley died unexpectedly at the age of forty-two, setting off mourning usually reserved for Presidents. No less stunning was the death weeks later of Bing Crosby.

There was never any question about the movie of the year: *Star Wars*, which set a new all-time box-office gross. The top song of the year was Leo Sayer's recording of "When I Need You," with seven weeks as Number One. The other records of the year were nonplaying: Seattle Slew became the first horse ever to win the Triple Crown of racing without suffering a defeat . . . Al Geiberger shocked the world by shooting an incredible 59 in the Danny Thomas-Memphis Golf Classic . . . A. J. Foyt became the first man ever to win four Indianapolis 500 races . . . Tokyo's Sadaharu Oh belted his 756th career home run, breaking Hank Aaron's baseball record . . . St. Louis Cardinal Lou Brock stole his 893rd base, breaking Ty Cobb's record . . . Texas State Senator Bill Meier filibustered in Austin for forty-three hours, setting a world record.

President Jimmy Carter set precedents during his first year in office, going informal to his inauguration, banning "Hail to the Chief," carrying his own baggage, spending the night with at-random American families, holding "Dial-a-President" call-in radio programs, and telling people to "Call me Jimmy." It was the year his budget director, Bert Lance, resigned under fire; the year of the prison escape and recapture of Martin Luther King's slayer, James Earl Ray; the year convicted killer Gary Gilmore was executed by a Utah firing squad, the first person to be executed in the United States in nearly ten years.

It was the year of "Roots" on TV, and tragedy in the headlines, when fire claimed 164 nightclub victims at the crowded Beverly Hills Supper Club in Southgate, Kentucky. Ironically, history's worst aviation disaster occurred on the ground when 581 died as Pan Am and KLM jumbo jets collided on the runway at Santa Cruz Airport in the Canary Islands. And Hanafi Moslem gunmen terrorized the nation's capital in March, seizing three Washington buildings and holding 149 hostages for thirty-eight hours, killing one and wounding several.

388

Jan. 1, 1977

1:Torn Between Two Lovers
2:Sorry Seems to Be the Hardest Word
3:After the Lovin'
4:Muskrat Love
5:You Don't Have to Be a Star
6:Lost Without Your Love
7:Evergreen
8:New Kid in Town
9:Stand Tall
10:If You Leave Me Now

Jan. 8, 1977

1:Torn Between Two Lovers
2:Sorry Seems to Be the Hardest Word
3:Lost Without Your Love
4:Evergreen
5:You Don't Have to Be a Star
6:After the Lovin'
7:Muskrat Love
8:New Kid in Town
9:Weekend in New England *
10:Stand Tall

Jan. 15, 1977

1:Torn Between Two Lovers
2:Evergreen
3:Sorry Seems to Be the Hardest Word
4:New Kid in Town
5:Weekend in New England
6:Lost Without Your Love
7:After the Lovin'
8:I Like Dreamin' *
9:You Don't Have to Be a Star
10:Muskrat Love

Jan. 22, 1977

1:Evergreen
2:New Kid in Town
3:Torn Between Two Lovers
4:Weekend in New England
5:I Like Dreamin'
6:Lost Without Your Love
7:After the Lovin'
8:Sorry Seems to Be the Hardest Word
9:Muskrat Love
10:You Don't Have to Be a Star

Jan. 29, 1977

1:Evergreen
2:New Kid in Town
3:Lost Without Your Love
4:I Like Dreamin'
5:Torn Between Two Lovers
6:You Make Me Feel Like Dancing *
7:Weekend in New England
8:After the Lovin'
9:Sorry Seems to Be the Hardest Word
10:You Don't Have to Be a Star

Feb. 5, 1977

1:Evergreen
2:New Kid in Town
3:Lost Without Your Love
4:I Like Dreamin'
5:Say You'll Stay Until Tomorrow *
6:Torn Between Two Lovers
7:You Make Me Feel Like Dancing
8:Weekend in New England
9:After the Lovin'
10:Sorry Seems to Be the Hardest Word

Feb. 12, 1977

1:Evergreen
2:Say You'll Stay Until Tomorrow
3:New Kid in Town
4:Lost Without Your Love
5:I Like Dreamin'
6:Dancing Queen *
7:Torn Between Two Lovers
8:After the Lovin'
9:Weekend in New England
10:You Make Me Feel Like Dancing

Feb. 19, 1977

1:Evergreen
2:Say You'll Stay Until Tomorrow
3:New Kid in Town
4:I Like Dreamin'
5:Lost Without Your Love
6:Dancing Queen
7:Southern Nights *
8:Weekend in New England
9:After the Lovin'
10:Torn Between Two Lovers

* Newcomer

Feb. 26, 1977

1:Evergreen
2:Southern Nights
3:Say You'll Stay Until Tomorrow
4:New Kid in Town
5:Sam *
6:I Like Dreamin'
7:Lost Without Your Love
8:Dancing Queen
9:After the Lovin'
10:Weekend in New England

Mar. 5, 1977

1:Southern Nights
2:Evergreen
3:Sam
4:Say You'll Stay Until Tomorrow
5:New Kid in Town
6:I Like Dreamin'
7:Don't Give Up On Us *
8:Year of the Cat *
9:After the Lovin'
10:Lost Without Your Love

Mar. 12, 1977

1:Southern Nights
2:Sam
3:Say You'll Stay Until Tomorrow
4:Don't Give Up On Us
5:Evergreen
6:New Kid in Town
7:Year of the Cat
8:I Like Dreamin'
9:Lost Without Your Love
10:After the Lovin'

Mar. 19, 1977

1:Southern Nights
2:Sam
3:Say You'll Stay Until Tomorrow
4:Don't Give Up On Us
5:Right Time of the Night *
6:Evergreen
7:After the Lovin'
8:Year of the Cat
9:New Kid in Town
10:I Like Dreamin'

Mar. 26, 1977

1:Southern Nights
2:Sam
3:Don't Give Up On Us
4:Say You'll Stay Until Tomorrow
5:Right Time of the Night
6:Evergreen
7:New Kid in Town
8:Year of the Cat
9:I Like Dreamin'
10:After the Lovin'

Apr. 2, 1977

1:Southern Nights
2:Don't Give Up On Us
3:Sam
4:Right Time of the Night
5:Say You'll Stay Until Tomorrow
6:Evergreen
7:When I Need You *
8:Year of the Cat
9:New Kid in Town
10:After the Lovin'

Apr. 9, 1977

1:Don't Give Up On Us
2:Right Time of the Night
3:Southern Nights
4:Sam
5:When I Need You
6:Say You'll Stay Until Tomorrow
7:Evergreen
8:Year of the Cat
9:After the Lovin'
10:New Kid in Town

Apr. 16, 1977

1:Don't Give Up On Us
2:Right Time of the Night
3:When I Need You
4:Southern Nights
5:Sam
6:Hello, Stranger *
7:Say You'll Stay Until Tomorrow
8:Evergreen
9:Year of the Cat
10:After the Lovin'

Apr. 23, 1977

1:When I Need You
2:Right Time of the Night
3:Don't Give Up On Us
4:Hello, Stranger
5:Southern Nights
6:Sam
7:Say You'll Stay Until Tomorrow
8:Evergreen
9:Hooked On You *
10:Year of the Cat

Apr. 30, 1977

1:When I Need You
2:Hello, Stranger
3:Hooked On You
4:Right Time of the Night
5:Don't Give Up On Us
6:Southern Nights
7:Sam
8:You're My World *
9:Evergreen
10:Say You'll Stay Until Tomorrow

May 7, 1977

1:When I Need You
2:Hello, Stranger
3:Hooked On You
4:Right Time of the Night
5:You're My World
6:Southern Nights
7:Don't Give Up On Us
8:Love's Grown Deep *
9:Sam
10:Evergreen

May 14, 1977

1:When I Need You
2:Hello, Stranger
3:Hooked On You
4:You're My World
5:Right Time of the Night
6:Southern Nights
7:Love's Grown Deep
8:Don't Give Up On Us
9:Evergreen
10:Sam

May 21, 1977

1:When I Need You
2:Hello, Stranger
3:Hooked On You
4:Looks Like We Made It *
5:Love's Grown Deep
6:You're My World
7:Angel in Your Arms *
8:Right Time of the Night
9:Southern Nights
10:Sam

May 28, 1977

1:When I Need You
2:Hello, Stranger
3:Looks Like We Made It
4:Love's Grown Deep
5:You're My World
6:It's Sad to Belong *
7:Hooked On You
8:Angel in Your Arms
9:Right Time of the Night
10:Southern Nights

June 4, 1977

1:When I Need You
2:Looks Like We Made It
3:Love's Grown Deep
4:It's Sad to Belong
5:Hello, Stranger
6:You're My World
7:Knowing Me, Knowing You *
8:Hooked On You
9:Angel in Your Arms
10:Right Time of the Night

June 11, 1977

1:Looks Like We Made It
2:It's Sad to Belong
3:Love's Grown Deep
4:When I Need You
5:My Heart Belongs to Me *
6:Knowing Me, Knowing You
7:Hello, Stranger
8:You're My World
9:Hooked On You
10:Angel in Your Arms

June 18, 1977

1:Looks Like We Made It
2:It's Sad to Belong
3:My Heart Belongs to Me
4:Knowing Me, Knowing You
5:Love's Grown Deep
6:You're My World
7:When I Need You
8:Angel in Your Arms
9:Hooked On You
10:I Just Want to Be Your Everything *

June 25, 1977

1:It's Sad to Belong
2:My Heart Belongs to Me
3:Looks Like We Made It
4:I Just Want to Be Your Everything
5:Love's Grown Deep
6:When I Need You
7:You're My World
8:Higher and Higher *
9:Knowing Me, Knowing You
10:Angel in Your Arms

July 2, 1977

1:It's Sad to Belong
2:My Heart Belongs to Me
3:Looks Like We Made It
4:Higher and Higher
5:Knowing Me, Knowing You
6:You're My World
7:Love's Grown Deep
8:I Just Want to Be Your Everything
9:When I Need You
10:Angel in Your Arms

July 9, 1977

1:It's Sad to Belong
2:My Heart Belongs to Me
3:Looks Like We Made It
4:You're My World
5:Higher and Higher
6:Knowing Me, Knowing You
7:Love's Grown Deep
8:I Just Want to Be Your Everything
9:Angel in Your Arms
10:When I Need You

July 16, 1977

1:It's Sad to Belong
2:My Heart Belongs to Me
3:I Just Want to Be Your Everything
4:Looks Like We Made It
5:You're My World
6:Higher and Higher
7:Knowing Me, Knowing You
8:Love's Grown Deep
9:On and On *
10:When I Need You

July 23, 1977

1:It's Sad to Belong
2:My Heart Belongs to Me
3:I Just Want to Be Your Everything
4:Looks Like We Made It
5:Higher and Higher
6:On and On
7:You're My World
8:Knowing Me, Knowing You
9:Love's Grown Deep
10:When I Need You

July 30, 1977

1:My Heart Belongs to Me
2:It's Sad to Belong
3:Looks Like We Made It
4:Higher and Higher
5:I Just Want to Be Your Everything
6:You're My World
7:Knowing Me, Knowing You
8:On and On
9:When I Need You
10:Love's Grown Deep

Aug. 6, 1977

1:My Heart Belongs to Me
2:It's Sad to Belong
3:Looks Like We Made It
4:I Just Want to Be Your Everything
5:Higher and Higher
6:You're My World
7:On and On
8:Knowing Me, Knowing You
9:Love's Grown Deep
10:Nobody Does It Better *

Aug. 13, 1977

1:My Heart Belongs to Me
2:It's Sad to Belong
3:I Just Want to Be Your Everything
4:Looks Like We Made It
5:Nobody Does It Better
6:On and On
7:Higher and Higher
8:You're My World
9:Knowing Me, Knowing You
10:Love's Grown Deep

Aug. 20, 1977

1:My Heart Belongs to Me
2:It's Sad to Belong
3:Nobody Does It Better
4:I Just Want to Be Your Everything
5:On and On
6:Looks Like We Made It
7:Higher and Higher
8:I Believe in Miracles *
9:You're My World
10:Love's Grown Deep

Aug. 27, 1977

1:I Just Want to Be Your Everything
2:My Heart Belongs to Me
3:Nobody Does It Better
4:On and On
5:Handy Man *
6:Looks Like We Made It
7:It's Sad to Belong
8:Higher and Higher
9:I Believe in Miracles
10:You're My World

Sept. 3, 1977

1:I Just Want to Be Your Everything
2:Nobody Does It Better
3:Handy Man
4:On and On
5:My Heart Belongs to Me
6:Swayin' to the Music *
7:Looks Like We Made It
8:I Believe in Miracles
9:It's Sad to Belong
10:You and Me *

Sept. 10, 1977

1:I Just Want to Be Your Everything
2:Nobody Does It Better
3:Handy Man
4:On and On
5:My Heart Belongs to Me
6:Swayin' to the Music
7:You and Me
8:I'm in You *
9:It's Sad to Belong
10:I Believe in Miracles

Sept. 17, 1977

1:Nobody Does It Better
2:On and On
3:Handy Man
4:I Just Want to Be Your Everything
5:Don't It Make My Brown Eyes Blue? *
6:My Heart Belongs to Me
7:I'm in You
8:You and Me
9:It's Sad to Belong
10:Swayin' to the Music

Sept. 24, 1977

1:Nobody Does It Better
2:On and On
3:Handy Man
4:I Just Want to Be Your Everything
5:Don't It Make My Brown Eyes Blue?
6:Just Remember I Love You *
7:Swayin' to the Music
8:You and Me
9:I'm in You
10:My Heart Belongs to Me

Oct. 1, 1977

1:Nobody Does It Better
2:On and On
3:Just Remember I Love You
4:Don't It Make My Brown Eyes Blue?
5:Handy Man
6:You Light Up My Life *
7:Swayin' to the Music
8:It Was Almost Like a Song *
9:I Just Want to Be Your Everything
10:You and Me

Oct. 8, 1977

1:Nobody Does It Better
2:Just Remember I Love You
3:On and On
4:Don't It Make My Brown Eyes Blue?
5:You Light Up My Life
6:Handy Man
7:Swayin' to the Music
8:It Was Almost Like a Song
9:You and Me
10:I Just Want to Be Your Everything

Oct. 15, 1977

1:Nobody Does It Better
2:Just Remember I Love You
3:You Light Up My Life
4:Don't It Make My Brown Eyes Blue?
5:We're All Alone *
6:On and On
7:It Was Almost Like a Song
8:Swayin' to the Music
9:I Just Want to Be Your Everything
10:Handy Man

Oct. 22, 1977

1:Nobody Does It Better
2:Just Remember I Love You
3:We're All Alone
4:How Deep is Your Love? *
5:Don't It Make My Brown Eyes Blue?
6:You Light Up My Life
7:On and On
8:Swayin' to the Music
9:It Was Almost Like a Song
10:I Just Want to Be Your Everything

Oct. 29, 1977

1:Just Remember I Love You
2:We're All Alone
3:How Deep is Your Love?
4:You Light Up My Life
5:Nobody Does It Better
6:Don't It Make My Brown Eyes Blue?
7:On and On
8:I Just Want to Be Your Everything
9:It Was Almost Like a Song
10:Swayin' to the Music

Nov. 5, 1977

1:Just Remember I Love You
2:We're All Alone
3:How Deep is Your Love?
4:You Light Up My Life
5:Don't It Make My Brown Eyes Blue?
6:Blue Bayou *
7:Nobody Does It Better
8:It Was Almost Like a Song
9:Swayin' to the Music
10:On and On

Nov. 12, 1977

1:We're All Alone
2:You Light Up My Life
3:How Deep is Your Love?
4:Blue Bayou
5:Just Remember I Love You
6:Don't It Make My Brown Eyes Blue?
7:Here You Come Again *
8:Nobody Does It Better
9:It Was Almost Like a Song
10:On and On

Nov. 19, 1977

1:You Light Up My Life
2:How Deep is Your Love?
3:We're All Alone
4:Blue Bayou
5:Slip Slidin' Away *
6:Here You Come Again
7:Your Smiling Face *
8:Just Remember I Love You
9:Don't It Make My Brown Eyes Blue?
10:Nobody Does It Better

Nov. 26, 1977

1:You Light Up My Life
2:How Deep is Your Love?
3:We're All Alone
4:Blue Bayou
5:Here You Come Again
6:Your Smiling Face
7:Slip Slidin' Away
8:Just Remember I Love You
9:Nobody Does It Better
10:Don't It Make My Brown Eyes Blue?

Dec. 3, 1977

1:How Deep is Your Love?
2:Here You Come Again
3:Blue Bayou
4:Slip Slidin' Away
5:We're All Alone
6:Your Smiling Face
7:How Can I Leave You Again? *
8:You Light Up My Life
9:Don't It Make My Brown Eyes Blue?
10:Nobody Does It Better

Dec. 10, 1977

1:How Deep is Your Love?
2:How Can I Leave You Again?
3:Here You Come Again
4:Slip Slidin' Away
5:We're All Alone
6:Your Smiling Face
7:Blue Bayou
8:Just the Way You Are *
9:You Light Up My Life
10:Don't It Make My Brown Eyes Blue?

Dec. 17, 1977

1:How Deep is Your Love?
2:Here You Come Again
3:How Can I Leave You Again?
4:Just the Way You Are
5:Blue Bayou
6:Slip Slidin' Away
7:Your Smiling Face
8:We're All Alone
9:You Light Up My Life
10:Desiree *

Dec. 24, 1977

1:How Deep is Your Love?
2:Just the Way You Are
3:How Can I Leave You Again?
4:Here You Come Again
5:Blue Bayou
6:Your Smiling Face
7:Slip Slidin' Away
8:Desiree
9:You Light Up My Life
10:We're All Alone

Dec. 31, 1977

1:How Deep is Your Love?
2:Just the Way You Are
3:Here You Come Again
4:How Can I Leave You Again?
5:Desiree
6:Blue Bayou
7:You Light Up My Life
8:We're All Alone
9:Slip Slidin' Away
10:Your Smiling Face

1978

It was a year of deadly numbers, and a ghastly recipe of cyanide and children's fruit punch . . . It left a staggering 914 dead in mass suicide-murders that wiped out the Jonestown commune of Americans in Guyana shortly after investigating newsmen and a U.S. congressman were killed trying to leave . . . The grim numbers hit home when 144 died in San Diego as a jet and a private plane collided in the United States' worst air disaster . . . In Des Plaines, Illinois, investigators turned up the bodies of thirty-three boys and young men, sexually molested and murdered by John Gacy, Jr., exceeding the twenty-seven in a similar 1973 Houston case . . . But the number that probably made the biggest impact in 1978 was thirteen, as Howard Jarvis began a taxpayer revolt with California's Proposition 13.

Other numbers in 1978 included three popes all in one year, with the world being stunned by the death of Pope John Paul I only thirty-four days after he had been elected . . . The number three kept cropping up: Muhammad Ali became the first to win the heavyweight title three times when he beat Leon Spinks . . . Affirmed became the eleventh horse in history to win racing's Triple Crown.

Ten weeks as Number One piled up for "Time Passages," making it the top song of the year . . .

Mickey Rooney got married for the eighth time . . . And we all felt our ages when both Mickey Mouse and Shirley Temple turned fifty.

If 1977 was the nation's coldest winter, 1978 was its snowiest as blizzards paralyzed the country . . . It was the year of the world's first test-tube baby, Louise Brown, born to Mrs. John Brown in England . . . There was palace upheaval in Iran; terrorism in Italy, where Aldo Moro, leader of the Christian Democratic Party, was slain; and "Holocaust" on TV as that series became 1978's viewing counterpart to 1977's "Roots" . . . The San Francisco mayor and a city supervisor were slain in City Hall by a disgruntled former city supervisor . . . And 1978 will be remembered as the year President Carter gathered Egypt's Anwar Sadat and Israel's Menachem Begin at Camp David to agree on a peace settlement.

But the numbers game prevailed: Three American men from Albuquerque made history's first Atlantic crossing in a balloon, from Maine to France in 137 hours, 18 minutes . . . Six masked gunmen got $5,000,000 in the United States' biggest heist, at New York's Kennedy Airport . . . And Ray Blazina and Bobbi Sherlock of Pittsburgh set a new single-kiss record, maintaining it 130 hours, two minutes and seventeen seconds.

Jan. 7, 1978

1:Just the Way You Are
2:How Can I Leave You Again?
3:Here You Come Again
4:Desiree
5:How Deep is Your Love?
6:Slip Slidin' Away
7:Blue Bayou
8:The Way You Do the Things You Do *
9:You Light Up My Life
10:We're All Alone

Jan. 14, 1978

1:Just the Way You Are
2:How Can I Leave You Again?
3:Desiree
4:Here You Come Again
5:How Deep is Your Love?
6:The Way You Do the Things You Do
7:Slip Slidin' Away
8:The Next Hundred Years *
9:Blue Bayou
10:You Light Up My Life

Jan. 21, 1978

1:Just the Way You Are
2:Desiree
3:How Can I Leave You Again?
4:Here You Come Again
5:How Deep is Your Love?
6:The Next Hundred Years
7:The Way You Do the Things You Do
8:Slip Slidin' Away
9:You Light Up My Life
10:Blue Bayou

Jan. 28, 1978

1:Just the Way You Are
2:Desiree
3:How Can I Leave You Again?
4:Here You Come Again
5:The Way You Do the Things You Do
6:The Next Hundred Years
7:How Deep is Your Love?
8:Lady Love *
9:Slip Slidin' Away
10:Blue Bayou

Feb. 4, 1978

1:Desiree
2:Just the Way You Are
3:The Way You Do the Things You Do
4:Lady Love
5:How Can I Leave You Again?
6:The Next Hundred Years
7:How Deep is Your Love?
8:Here You Come Again
9:Everybody Loves a Rain Song *
10:Slip Slidin' Away

Feb. 11, 1978

1:Desiree
2:Just the Way You Are
3:Everybody Loves a Rain Song
4:Lady Love
5:Ready For the Times to Get Better *
6:The Way You Do the Things You Do
7:How Can I Leave You Again?
8:How Deep is Your Love?
9:The Next Hundred Years
10:Here You Come Again

Feb. 18, 1978

1:Just the Way You Are
2:Desiree
3:Everybody Loves a Rain Song
4:Can't Smile Without You *
5:Lady Love
6:Before My Heart Finds Out *
7:The Way You Do the Things You Do
8:Ready For the Times to Get Better
9:How Deep is Your Love?
10:The Next Hundred Years

Feb. 25, 1978

1:Everybody Loves a Rain Song
2:Can't Smile Without You
3:Before My Heart Finds Out
4:Just the Way You Are
5:Lady Love
6:Ready For the Times to Get Better
7:The Way You Do the Things You Do
8:Desiree
9:How Deep is Your Love?
10:The Next Hundred Years

* Newcomer

Mar. 4, 1978

1:Can't Smile Without You
2:Before My Heart Finds Out
3:Everybody Loves a Rain Song
4:Just the Way You Are
5:Ready For the Times to Get Better
6:Lady Love
7:The Way You Do the Things You Do
8:Desiree
9:How Deep is Your Love?
10:The Next Hundred Years

Mar. 11, 1978

1:Can't Smile Without You
2:Before My Heart Finds Out
3:Everybody Loves a Rain Song
4:The Circle is Small *
5:We'll Never Have to Say Goodbye Again *
6:Just the Way You Are
7:The Way You Do the Things You Do
8:Lady Love
9:Ready For the Times to Get Better
10:Desiree

Mar. 18, 1978

1:Can't Smile Without You
2:We'll Never Have to Say Goodbye Again
3:Before My Heart Finds Out
4:The Circle is Small
5:Ready For the Times to Get Better
6:Sweet, Sweet Smile *
7:The Way You Do the Things You Do
8:Everybody Loves a Rain Song
9:Lady Love
10:Just the Way You Are

Mar. 25, 1978

1:We'll Never Have to Say Goodbye Again
2:Can't Smile Without You
3:Before My Heart Finds Out
4:The Circle is Small
5:Ready For the Times to Get Better
6:Sweet, Sweet Smile
7:Just the Way You Are
8:The Way You Do the Things You Do
9:Lady Love
10:Everybody Loves a Rain Song

Apr. 1, 1978

1:We'll Never Have to Say Goodbye Again
2:Can't Smile Without You
3:Before My Heart Finds Out
4:The Circle is Small
5:Sweet, Sweet Smile
6:Ready For the Times to Get Better
7:Everybody Loves a Rain Song
8:Lady Love
9:The Way You Do the Things You Do
10:Just the Way You Are

Apr. 8, 1978

1:We'll Never Have to Say Goodbye Again
2:Can't Smile Without You
3:Before My Heart Finds Out
4:Ready For the Times to Get Better
5:The Circle is Small
6:Dust in the Wind *
7:Sweet, Sweet Smile
8:The Way You Do the Things You Do
9:Lady Love
10:Everybody Loves a Rain Song

Apr. 15, 1978

1:We'll Never Have to Say Goodbye Again
2:Can't Smile Without You
3:The Circle is Small
4:Before My Heart Finds Out
5:Ready For the Times to Get Better
6:Dust in the Wind
7:If I Can't Have You *
8:The Closer I Get to You *
9:Sweet, Sweet Smile
10:The Way You Do the Things You Do

Apr. 22, 1978

1:We'll Never Have to Say Goodbye Again
2:Can't Smile Without You
3:Ready For the Times to Get Better
4:Before My Heart Finds Out
5:The Circle is Small
6:Dust in the Wind
7:The Closer I Get to You
8:If I Can't Have You
9:Too Much, Too Little, Too Late *
10:Sweet, Sweet Smile

Apr. 29, 1978

1:We'll Never Have to Say Goodbye Again
2:Can't Smile Without You
3:Ready For the Times to Get Better
4:Before My Heart Finds Out
5:Too Much, Too Little, Too Late
6:The Closer I Get to You
7:Dust in the Wind
8:The Circle is Small
9:If I Can't Have You
10:Sweet, Sweet Smile

May 6, 1978

1:Can't Smile Without You
2:We'll Never Have to Say Goodbye Again
3:Too Much, Too Little, Too Late
4:The Closer I Get to You
5:Ready For the Times to Get Better
6:Dust in the Wind
7:If I Can't Have You
8:Before My Heart Finds Out
9:The Circle is Small
10:Sweet, Sweet Smile

May 13, 1978

1:Can't Smile Without You
2:Too Much, Too Little, Too Late
3:The Closer I Get to You
4:We'll Never Have to Say Goodbye Again
5:You're the Love *
6:I'm On My Way *
7:Dust in the Wind
8:Ready For the Times to Get Better
9:If I Can't Have You
10:The Circle is Small

May 20, 1978

1:Too Much, Too Little, Too Late
2:You're the Love
3:Can't Smile Without You
4:Even Now *
5:I'm On My Way
6:The Closer I Get to You
7:Bluer Than Blue *
8:We'll Never Have to Say Goodbye Again
9:Dust in the Wind
10:Ready For the Times to Get Better

May 27, 1978

1:Too Much, Too Little, Too Late
2:Even Now
3:You're the Love
4:Bluer Than Blue
5:Can't Smile Without You
6:I'm On My Way
7:The Closer I Get to You
8:We'll Never Have to Say Goodbye Again
9:Ready For the Times to Get Better
10:Dust in the Wind

June 3, 1978

1:Even Now
2:Bluer Than Blue
3:You're the Love
4:Too Much, Too Little, Too Late
5:I'm On My Way
6:The Closer I Get to You
7:Can't Smile Without You
8:Ready For the Times to Get Better
9:We'll Never Have to Say Goodbye Again
10:Dust in the Wind

June 10, 1978

1:Even Now
2:Bluer Than Blue
3:You're the Love
4:I'm On My Way
5:Too Much, Too Little, Too Late
6:Can't Smile Without You
7:We'll Never Have to Say Goodbye Again
8:The Closer I Get to You
9:Baker Street *
10:Ready For the Times to Get Better

June 17, 1978

1:Even Now
2:You're the Love
3:Bluer Than Blue
4:Too Much, Too Little, Too Late
5:Baker Street
6:I'm On My Way
7:Can't Smile Without You
8:Ready For the Times to Get Better
9:We'll Never Have to Say Goodbye Again
10:The Closer I Get to You

June 24, 1978

1:Bluer Than Blue
2:Even Now
3:You're the One
4:Baker Street
5:Too Much, Too Little, Too Late
6:If Ever I See You Again *
7:Songbird *
8:I'm On My Way
9:Can't Smile Without You
10:We'll Never Have to Say Goodbye Again

July 1, 1978

1:Bluer Than Blue
2:If Ever I See You Again
3:Even Now
4:You're the Love
5:Songbird
6:Baker Street
7:Too Much, Too Little, Too Late
8:Can't Smile Without You
9:I'm On My Way
10:We'll Never Have to Say Goodbye Again

July 8, 1978

1:Bluer Than Blue
2:If Ever I See You Again
3:Songbird
4:You're the Love
5:Even Now
6:Copacabana *
7:Baker Street
8:Too Much, Too Little, Too Late
9:Can't Smile Without You
10:I'm On My Way

July 15, 1978

1:If Ever I See You Again
2:Bluer Than Blue
3:Songbird
4:You're the Love
5:Even Now
6:Copacabana
7:My Angel Baby *
8:Baker Street
9:You Needed Me *
10:Too Much, Too Little, Too Late

July 22, 1978

1:If Ever I See You Again
2:Songbird
3:Bluer Than Blue
4:My Angel Baby
5:Copacabana
6:You're the Love
7:Three Times a Lady *
8:You Needed Me
9:Even Now
10:Baker Street

July 29, 1978

1:Songbird
2:My Angel Baby
3:If Ever I See You Again
4:Bluer Than Blue
5:Three Times a Lady
6:Copacabana
7:You Needed Me
8:Even Now
9:Baker Street
10:You're the Love

Aug. 5, 1978

1:Songbird
2:My Angel Baby
3:Three Times a Lady
4:You Needed Me
5:Fool, If You Think It's Over *
6:Bluer Than Blue
7:Copacabana
8:Baker Street
9:If Ever I See You Again
10:Even Now

Aug. 12, 1978

1:My Angel Baby
2:Three Times a Lady
3:Fool, If You Think It's Over
4:You Needed Me
5:Songbird
6:Copacabana
7:Bluer Than Blue
8:You're a Part of Me *
9:Talking in Your Sleep *
10:Baker Street

Aug. 19, 1978

1:Three Times a Lady
2:Fool, If You Think It's Over
3:My Angel Baby
4:Talking in Your Sleep
5:You're a Part of Me
6:Hopelessly Devoted to You *
7:You Needed Me
8:Songbird
9:Copacabana
10:An Everlasting Love *

Aug. 26, 1978

1:Three Times a Lady
2:Fool, If You Think It's Over
3:Talking in Your Sleep
4:My Angel Baby
5:You're a Part of Me
6:Hopelessly Devoted to You
7:An Everlasting Love
8:You Needed Me
9:Songbird
10:Copacabana

Sept. 2, 1978

1:Three Times a Lady
2:Fool, If You Think It's Over
3:Talking in Your Sleep
4:My Angel Baby
5:You Needed Me
6:Hopelessly Devoted to You
7:An Everlasting Love
8:Love Is in the Air *
9:You're a Part of Me
10:Songbird

Sept. 9, 1978

1:Fool, If You Think It's Over
2:Three Times a Lady
3:Talking in Your Sleep
4:Love Is in the Air
5:You Needed Me
6:Right Down the Line *
7:Hopelessly Devoted to You
8:An Everlasting Love
9:My Angel Baby
10:You're a Part of Me

Sept. 16, 1978

1:Fool, If You Think It's Over
2:Love Is in the Air
3:Talking in Your Sleep
4:Three Times a Lady
5:You Needed Me
6:Right Down the Line
7:Hopelessly Devoted to You
8:Devoted to You *
9:An Everlasting Love
10:You're a Part of Me

Sept. 23, 1978

1:Fool, If You Think It's Over
2:Love Is in the Air
3:You Needed Me
4:Right Down the Line
5:Devoted to You
6:She's Always a Woman *
7:Talking in Your Sleep
8:Hopelessly Devoted to You
9:Three Times a Lady
10:An Everlasting Love

Sept. 30, 1978

1:Right Down the Line
2:Love Is in the Air
3:You Needed Me
4:Fool, If You Think It's Over
5:Devoted to You
6:She's Always a Woman
7:Hopelessly Devoted to You
8:Three Times a Lady
9:Ready to Take a Chance Again *
10:Talking in Your Sleep

Oct. 7, 1978

1:Love Is in the Air
2:Right Down the Line
3:Devoted to You
4:You Needed Me
5:She's Always a Woman
6:Fool, If You Think It's Over
7:Ready to Take a Chance Again
8:Talking in Your Sleep
9:Three Times a Lady
10:Hopelessly Devoted to You

Oct. 14, 1978

1:Love Is in the Air
2:Right Down the Line
3:You Needed Me
4:Devoted to You
5:She's Always a Woman
6:Fool, If You Think It's Over
7:Ready to Take a Chance Again
8:Hopelessly Devoted to You
9:Talking in Your Sleep
10:Three Times a Lady

Oct. 21, 1978

1:Right Down the Line
2:Devoted to You
3:She's Always a Woman
4:Love Is in the Air
5:You Needed Me
6:Ready to Take a Chance Again
7:Fool, If You Think It's Over
8:Talking in Your Sleep
9:Three Times a Lady
10:Hopelessly Devoted to You

Oct. 28, 1978

1:Right Down the Line
2:She's Always a Woman
3:Love Is in the Air
4:You Needed Me
5:Devoted to You
6:Ready to Take a Chance Again
7:Time Passages *
8:Fool, If You Think It's Over
9:Talking in Your Sleep
10:Hopelessly Devoted to You

Nov. 4, 1978

1:Right Down the Line
2:She's Always a Woman
3:Time Passages
4:Love Is in the Air
5:You Needed Me
6:Ready to Take a Chance Again
7:Devoted to You
8:Talking in Your Sleep
9:Fool, If You Think It's Over
10:Our Love, Don't Throw It All Away *

Nov. 11, 1978

1:Time Passages
2:Right Down the Line
3:Our Love, Don't Throw It All Away
4:You Don't Bring Me Flowers *
5:Ready to Take a Chance Again
6:Change of Heart *
7:She's Always a Woman
8:Love Is in the Air.
9:You Needed Me
10:Devoted to You

Nov. 18, 1978

1:Time Passages
2:Our Love, Don't Throw It All Away
3:You Don't Bring Me Flowers
4:Right Down the Line
5:Ready to Take a Chance Again
6:Change of Heart
7:You Needed Me
8:Love Is in the Air
9:She's Always a Woman
10:Devoted to You

Nov. 25, 1978

1:Time Passages
2:Our Love, Don't Throw It All Away
3:You Don't Bring Me Flowers
4:Ooh, Baby, Baby *
5:Change of Heart
6:My Life *
7:Ready to Take a Chance Again
8:Right Down the Line
9:You Needed Me
10:Love Is in the Air

Dec. 2, 1978

1:Time Passages
2:Ooh, Baby, Baby
3:Our Love, Don't Throw It All Away
4:You Don't Bring Me Flowers
5:Too Much Heaven *
6:My Life
7:Change of Heart
8:Ready to Take a Chance Again
9:You Needed Me
10:Right Down the Line

Dec. 9, 1978

1:Time Passages
2:Ooh, Baby, Baby
3:My Life
4:Too Much Heaven
5:Our Love, Don't Throw It All Away
6:You Don't Bring Me Flowers
7:Change of Heart
8:Can You, Fool? *
9:Ready to Take a Chance Again
10:You Needed Me

Dec. 16, 1978

1:Time Passages
2:My Life
3:Ooh, Baby, Baby
4:Too Much Heaven
5:Our Love, Don't Throw It All Away
6:Can You, Fool?
7:You Don't Bring Me Flowers
8:Change of Heart
9:Ready to Take a Chance Again
10:You Needed Me

Dec. 23, 1978

1:Time Passages
2:My Life
3:Ooh, Baby, Baby
4:Too Much Heaven
5:Our Love, Don't Throw It All Away
6:The Gambler *
7:Can You, Fool?
8:You Don't Bring Me Flowers
9:Change of Heart
10:Ready to Take a Chance Again

Dec. 30, 1978

1:Time Passages
2:My Life
3:Ooh, Baby, Baby
4:The Gambler
5:Our Love, Don't Throw It All Away
6:Too Much Heaven
7:You Don't Bring Me Flowers
8:Can You, Fool?
9:Ready to Take a Chance Again
10:Change of Heart

1979

If the top movie of 1979 was *Apocalypse Now,* the top crisis was OPECalypse Now, as the Organization of Petroleum Exporting Countries drove the price of American gasoline up to $1 a gallon, caused mile-long lines at service stations (when you could find one open), and finally caused odd-even days of gas rationing . . . Elsewhere, the villain of the year was Ayatollah Khomeini, who took over after the Shah of Iran fled to the United States. Iranian students held more than fifty Americans hostage in demand for the Shah's return . . . Flop of the year: The Susan B. Anthony dollar, the buck that never got passed. In a year of soaring inflation and orbiting gold prices, it was suggested the new coin should have been called the J. C. penny.

It was a year of records: The Pittsburgh Steelers beat the Dallas Cowboys to become the first team to win three Super Bowls . . . Britain's Sebastion Coe set a record for the mile run (3:48:95), and Maxine Nightingale recorded the best record when "Lead Me On" became the top song of the year with seven weeks as Number One . . . The grimmest record of the year: 275 killed in the worst air disaster in United States history as an American Airlines DC-10 jetliner crashed just after takeoff at Chicago's O'Hare Airport.

It was the year of *The China Syndrome* on the screen, a fictional tale of a leaking nuclear power plant that a few days later became a fact in Harrisburg, Pennsylvania, with thousands being evacuated around Three Mile Island . . . For those who thought Elvis Presley's death in 1977 would be the only time a show-business passing would grab nationwide front-page bannerlines, 1979 will be remembered as the year one morning's bannerlines proclaimed: "John Wayne, American, Dies" . . . It was finally the year for equal rights: Hurricanes were named for males (Bad Boys of the Year were Frederic and David—with the latter becoming Goliath), and Margaret Thatcher became Britain's first woman prime minister.

After nearly thirty-one years as hostile neighbors, Egypt and Israel signed a formal treaty at the White House with peacemaker Jimmy Carter signing as a witness . . . Pope John Paul II visited the United States, terrorists took the life of Britain's Lord Louis Mountbatten, Skylab finally fell and didn't hit anybody, and a feared Soviet Union troop buildup in Cuba turned out to be the Cuban fizzle crisis.

404

Jan. 6, 1979

1:Time Passages
2:My Life
3:Ooh, Baby, Baby
4:Too Much Heaven
5:Our Love, Don't Throw It All Away
6:The Gambler
7:Can You, Fool?
8:You Don't Bring Me Flowers
9:I Believe You *
10:Promises *

Jan. 13, 1979

1:Time Passages
2:Ooh, Baby, Baby
3:My Life
4:Too Much Heaven
5:Our Love, Don't Throw It All Away
6:Promises
7:The Gambler
8:This Moment in Time *
9:Can You, Fool?
10:I Believe You

Jan. 20, 1979

1:This Moment in Time
2:My Life
3:Ooh, Baby, Baby
4:Lotta Love *
5:Time Passages
6:The Gambler
7:Too Much Heaven
8:Promises
9:I Believe You
10:Our Love, Don't Throw It All Away

Jan. 27, 1979

1:This Moment in Time
2:Lotta Love
3:My Life
4:The Gambler
5:Ooh, Baby, Baby
6:Promises
7:A Little More Love *
8:Too Much Heaven
9:Time Passages
10:I Believe You

Feb. 3, 1979

1:This Moment in Time
2:Lotta Love
3:The Gambler
4:A Little More Love
5:I Just Fall in Love Again *
6:My Life
7:Too Much Heaven
8:Promises
9:Ooh, Baby, Baby
10:Time Passages

Feb. 10, 1979

1:I Just Fall in Love Again
2:Lotta Love
3:The Gambler
4:This Moment in Time
5:Forever in Blue Jeans *
6:A Little More Love
7:Too Much Heaven
8:Promises
9:Time Passages
10:My Life

Feb. 17, 1979

1:I Just Fall in Love Again
2:Forever in Blue Jeans
3:Lotta Love
4:The Gambler
5:A Little More Love
6:This Moment in Time
7:Promises
8:Crazy Love *
9:Time Passages
10:No-Tell Lover *

Feb. 24, 1979

1:I Just Fall in Love Again
2:Forever in Blue Jeans
3:Crazy Love
4:No-Tell Lover
5:Lotta Love
6:The Gambler
7:A Little More Love
8:This Moment in Time
9:Promises
10:Time Passages

* Newcomer

Mar. 3, 1979

1:I Just Fall in Love Again
2:Crazy Love
3:Forever in Blue Jeans
4:No-Tell Lover
5:Lotta Love
6:Dancin' Shoes *
7:A Little More Love
8:Music Box Dancer *
9:Promises
10:This Moment in Time

Mar. 10, 1979

1:Crazy Love
2:I Just Fall in Love Again
3:Forever in Blue Jeans
4:Lotta Love
5:Music Box Dancer
6:Dancin' Shoes
7:This Moment in Time
8:A Little More Love
9:No-Tell Lover
10:Promises

Mar. 17, 1979

1:Crazy Love
2:I Just Fall in Love Again
3:Forever in Blue Jeans
4:Music Box Dancer
5:Lotta Love
6:No-Tell Lover
7:Dancin' Shoes
8:Just One Look *
9:A Little More Love
10:Promises

Mar. 24, 1979

1:Crazy Love
2:I Just Fall in Love Again
3:Forever in Blue Jeans
4:Music Box Dancer
5:Just One Look
6:No-Tell Lover
7:Lotta Love
8:Dancin' Shoes
9:Stumblin' In *
10:A Little More Love

Mar. 31, 1979

1:Crazy Love
2:I Just Fall in Love Again
3:Forever in Blue Jeans
4:Music Box Dancer
5:Stumblin' In
6:Blow Away *
7:Can You Read My Mind? *
8:Just One Look
9:Dancin' Shoes
10:No-Tell Lover

Apr. 7, 1979

1:Crazy Love
2:Blow Away
3:Stumblin' In
4:Can You Read My Mind?
5:I Just Fall in Love Again
6:I Never Said I Love You *
7:Forever in Blue Jeans
8:Music Box Dancer
9:Just One Look
10:Dancin' Shoes

Apr. 14, 1979

1:Crazy Love
2:I Never Said I Love You
3:Blow Away
4:Can You Read My Mind?
5:Love Is the Answer *
6:I Just Fall in Love Again
7:Music Box Dancer
8:Forever in Blue Jeans
9:Just One Look
10:Stumblin' In

Apr. 21, 1979

1:I Never Said I Love You
2:Crazy Love
3:Blow Away
4:Love Is the Answer
5:Can You Read My Mind?
6:Stumblin' In
7:Just When I Needed You Most *
8:I Just Fall in Love Again
9:Music Box Dancer
10:Just One Look

Apr. 28, 1979

1:I Never Said I Love You
2:Love Is the Answer
3:Crazy Love
4:Just When I Needed You Most
5:Blow Away
6:Can You Read My Mind?
7:Stumblin' In
8:Reunited *
9:I Just Fall in Love Again
10:Music Box Dancer

May 5, 1979

1:Love Is the Answer
2:Just When I Needed You Most
3:I Never Said I Love You
4:Blow Away
5:Crazy Love
6:Can You Read My Mind?
7:Reunited
8:She Believes in Me *
9:Stumblin' In
10:I Just Fall in Love Again

May 12, 1979

1:Love Is the Answer
2:Just When I Needed You Most
3:She Believes in Me
4:I Never Said I Love You
5:Reunited
6:Crazy Love
7:Blow Away
8:Deeper Than the Night *
9:Stumblin' In
10:Can You Read My Mind?

May 19, 1979

1:Just When I Needed You Most
2:She Believes in Me
3:Love Is the Answer
4:Reunited
5:Deeper Than the Night
6:Blow Away
7:Stumblin' In
8:Can You Read My Mind?
9:I Never Said I Love You
10:Crazy Love

May 26, 1979

1:She Believes in Me
2:Just When I Needed You Most
3:Love Is the Answer
4:Deeper Than the Night
5:Reunited
6:Blow Away
7:Can You Read My Mind?
8:I Never Said I Love You
9:Stumblin' In
10:Crazy Love

June 2, 1979

1:She Believes in Me
2:Just When I Needed You Most
3:Love Is the Answer
4:Deeper Than the Night
5:Say Maybe *
6:Shadows in the Moonlight *
7:Reunited
8:Blow Away
9:Can You Read My Mind?
10:I Never Said I Love You

June 9, 1979

1:Just When I Needed You Most
2:She Believes in Me
3:Love Is the Answer
4:Say Maybe
5:Shadows in the Moonlight
6:When You're in Love With a Beautiful
7:Deeper Than the Night   Woman *
8:Reunited
9:Blow Away
10:Can You Read My Mind?

June 16, 1979

1:Shadows in the Moonlight
2:She Believes in Me
3:Say Maybe
4:Just When I Needed You Most
5:Love Is the Answer
6:When You're in Love With a Beautiful
7:Deeper Than the Night   Woman
8:Reunited
9:Lead Me On *
10:Morning Dance *

June 23, 1979

1:Shadows in the Moonlight
2:She Believes in Me
3:Say Maybe
4:Lead Me On
5:When You're in Love With a Beautiful Woman
6:Since I Don't Have You *
7:Up On the Roof *
8:Morning Dance
9:Just When I Needed You Most
10:Reunited

June 30, 1979

1:Shadows in the Moonlight
2:Lead Me On
3:Morning Dance
4:She Believes in Me
5:Say Maybe
6:Since I Don't Have You
7:Up On the Roof
8:When You're in Love With a Beautiful Woman
9:Just When I Needed You Most
10:Reunited

July 7, 1979

1:Lead Me On
2:Shadows in the Moonlight
3:She Believes in Me
4:Morning Dance
5:Since I Don't Have You
6:When You're in Love With a Beautiful Woman
7:Up On the Roof
8:Say Maybe
9:Mama Can't Buy You Love *
10:Heart of the Night *

July 14, 1979

1:Lead Me On
2:Shadows in the Moonlight
3:She Believes in Me
4:Morning Dance
5:Since I Don't Have You
6:Mama Can't Buy You Love
7:Up On the Roof
8:When You're in Love With a Beautiful Woman
9:Heart of the Night
10:Main Event *

July 21, 1979

1:Lead Me On
2:Shadows in the Moonlight
3:Morning Dance
4:Mama Can't Buy You Love
5:She Believes in Me
6:Heart of the Night
7:Main Event
8:When You're in Love With a Beautiful
9:Since I Don't Have You   Woman
10:I'll Never Love This Way Again *

July 28, 1979

1:Morning Dance
2:Lead Me On
3:Mama Can't Buy You Love
4:Shadows in the Moonlight
5:Heart of the Night
6:Main Event
7:I'll Never Love This Way Again
8:Different Worlds *
9:When You're in Love With a Beautiful
10:She Believes in Me   Woman

Aug. 4, 1979

1:Lead Me On
2:Morning Dance
3:Mama Can't Buy You Love
4:Shadows in the Moonlight
5:Main Event
6:I'll Never Love This Way Again
7:Different Worlds
8:Heart of the Night
9:When You're in Love With a Beautiful
10:She Believes in Me   Woman

Aug. 11, 1979

1:Lead Me On
2:Mama Can't Buy You Love
3:Morning Dance
4:Main Event
5:Shadows in the Moonlight
6:I'll Never Love This Way Again
7:Different Worlds
8:Heart of the Night
9:Rise *
10:When You're in Love With a Beautiful
            Woman

Aug. 18, 1979

1:Lead Me On
2:Mama Can't Buy You Love
3:Main Event
4:Morning Dance
5:I'll Never Love This Way Again
6:Different Worlds
7:Rise
8:Shadows in the Moonlight
9:Heart of the Night
10:When You're in Love With a Beautiful Woman

Aug. 25, 1979

1:Mama Can't Buy You Love
2:Lead Me On
3:Main Event
4:Different Worlds
5:I'll Never Love This Way Again
6:Rise
7:Morning Dance
8:Where Were You When I Was Falling in Love?
9:After the Love Has Gone *
10:Shadows in the Moonlight

Sept. 1, 1979

1:Lead Me On
2:Main Event
3:Rise
4:Different Worlds
5:Mama Can't Buy You Love
6:Where Were You When I Was Falling in Love?
7:After the Love Has Gone
8:If You Remember Me *
9:I'll Never Love This Way Again
10:Shadows in the Moonlight

Sept. 8, 1979

1:Different Worlds
2:Rise
3:Where Were You When I Was Falling in Love?
4:Lead Me On
5:After the Love Has Gone
6:Main Event
7:If You Remember Me
8:Shadows in the Moonlight
9:Mama Can't Buy You Love
10:I'll Never Love This Way Again

Sept. 15, 1979

1:Different Worlds
2:Rise
3:Where Were You When I Was Falling
4:Lead Me On   in Love?
5:Shadows in the Moonlight
6:I'll Never Love This Way Again
7:Main Event
8:If You Remember Me
9:After the Love Has Gone
10:This Night Won't Last Forever *

Sept. 22, 1979

1:Rise
2:Different Worlds
3:Where Were You When I Was Falling
4:After the Love Has Gone   in Love?
5:Lead Me On
6:You Decorated My Life *
7:If You Remember Me
8:I'll Never Love This Way Again
9:This Night Won't Last Forever
10:Main Event

Sept. 29, 1979

1:Where Were You When I Was Falling
2:Rise   in Love?
3:After the Love Has Gone
4:You Decorated My Life
5:Different Worlds
6:Broken Hearted Me *
7:This Night Won't Last Forever
8:I'll Never Love This Way Again
9:Lead Me On
10:If You Remember Me

Oct. 6, 1979

1:Where Were You When I Was Falling
2:Rise   in Love?
3:You Decorated My Life
4:After the Love Has Gone
5:Broken Hearted Me
6:You're Only Lonely *
7:Different Worlds
8:This Night Won't Last Forever
9:I'll Never Love This Way Again
10:Lead Me On

Oct. 13, 1979

1:Where Were You When I Was Falling in Love?
2:Broken Hearted Me
3:You Decorated My Life
4:Rise
5:After the Love Has Gone
6:This Night Won't Last Forever
7:You're Only Lonely
8:Different Worlds
9:Lead Me On
10:I'll Never Love This Way Again

Oct. 20, 1979

1:Broken Hearted Me
2:Where Were You When I Was Falling in Love?
3:You Decorated My Life
4:Rise
5:This Night Won't Last Forever
6:You're Only Lonely
7:After the Love Has Gone
8:I'll Never Love This Way Again
9:Lead Me On
10:Different Worlds

Oct. 27, 1979

1:Broken Hearted Me
2:You Decorated My Life
3:You're Only Lonely
4:Where Were You When I Was Falling in Love?
5:Rise
6:This Night Won't Last Forever
7:Ships *
8:Half the Way *
9:I'll Never Love This Way Again
10:After the Love Has Gone

Nov. 3, 1979

1:Broken Hearted Me
2:You're Only Lonely
3:You Decorated My Life
4:Where Were You When I Was Falling in Love?
5:Ships
6:Rise
7:This Night Won't Last Forever
8:Half the Way
9:After the Love Has Gone
10:I'll Never Love This Way Again

Nov. 10, 1979

1:Broken Hearted Me
2:You're Only Lonely
3:You Decorated My Life
4:Ships
5:This Night Won't Last Forever
6:Rise
7:Still *
8:Half the Way
9:Where Were You When I Was Falling
10:Better Love Next Time *   in Love?

Nov. 17, 1979

1:You're Only Lonely
2:Broken Hearted Me
3:You Decorated My Life
4:Ships
5:Still
6:Better Love Next Time
7:This Night Won't Last Forever
8:Rise
9:Half the Way
10:Where Were You When I Was Falling
                              in Love?

Nov. 24, 1979

1:You're Only Lonely
2:Broken Hearted Me
3:You Decorated My Life
4:Ships
5:Still
6:Peter Piper *
7:Better Love Next Time
8:Do That to Me One More Time *
9:This Night Won't Last Forever
10:Half the Way

Dec. 1, 1979

1:You're Only Lonely
2:Broken Hearted Me
3:You Decorated My Life
4:Ships
5:Better Love Next Time
6:Peter Piper
7:Do That to Me One More Time
8:Still
9:Half the Way
10:This Night Won't Last Forever

410

Dec. 8, 1979

1:You're Only Lonely
2:Broken Hearted Me
3:Better Love Next Time
4:Do That to Me One More Time
5:Send One Your Love *
6:Ships
7:Still
8:Deja Vu *
9:Peter Piper
10:You Decorated My Life

Dec. 15, 1979

1:You're Only Lonely
2:Send One Your Love
3:Deja Vu
4:Do That to Me One More Time
5:We Don't Talk Anymore *
6:Peter Piper
7:Better Love Next Time
8:Still
9:Broken Hearted Me
10:I'd Rather Leave While I'm in Love *

Dec. 22, 1979

1:Send One Your Love
2:You're Only Lonely
3:Deja Vu
4:I'd Rather Leave While I'm in Love
5:Do That to Me One More Time
6:We Don't Talk Anymore
7:Better Love Next Time
8:Peter Piper
9:Broken Hearted Me
10:Still

Dec. 29, 1979

1:Send One Your Love
2:Deja Vu
3:I'd Rather Leave While I'm in Love
4:We Don't Talk Anymore
5:You're Only Lonely
6:Do That to Me One More Time
7:Peter Piper
8:Better Love Next Time
9:Still
10:Broken Hearted Me

1980

And so we entered the Electrifying Eighties, with the most electrifying moment saved for the eleventh month when Ronald Reagan was elected President of the United States in an unpredicted landslide over incumbent Jimmy Carter.

It was the year the Gipper won one for himself, and also the year of the actors' strike. It was a time no one thought they'd ever see: When Ronald Reagan was the only actor working.

The whodunit of the year turned out to be a shedunit. The shots heard around the world were fired by Kristin, J. R. Ewing's mistress. And the night the world finally got that answer "Dallas" became the highest-rated TV show in history as 83 million watched.

We knew immediately who fired the other shots heard around the world. John Lennon signed his life away, giving an autograph to Beatle fan Mark David Chapman, twenty-five, who later that night murdered Lennon in New York.

On Broadway, *Grease* closed after 3,388 performances, passing *Fiddler on the Roof,* to become the longest-running show in Broadway history. Hits at the movies were *Ordinary People* and *The Empire Strikes Back.* Musically, the top song of the year was "Lost in Love," six weeks as Number One.

It was the year gold got so high, the country's motto became "Ingot We Trust," and inflation got so bad Bo Derek became a "12." Shirley Temple became a grandmother, and it was Bye Bye, Ber-tie when Bert Parks, sixty-five, was fired as Miss America Pageant emcee for being too old.

Tragedies of the year: An earthquake killed more than 3,000 people in Italy. A fire at the MGM Grand Hotel in Las Vegas claimed eighty-four lives. Atlanta was terrorized as eleven black children were found murdered and four remained missing. The last of the red-hot lavas was Mount St. Helens, which blew its top in Cougar, Washington, leaving thirty-four dead and thirty-two missing. An aborted rescue mission of the hostages in Iran left eight American military men dead in the desert as two aircraft collided on the ground. And at year's end, fifty-two American hostages taken in 1979 were still prisoners.

It was on your marks, get set, Stop! for American track stars at the Summer Olympics in Moscow as the U.S. led a sixty-two–nation boycott because the Soviets had invaded Afghanistan. Records of the year were Poland's Wladislaw Kozakiewicz pole-vaulting 18 feet, 11½ inches, and East Germany's Gerd Wessig high-jumping 7 feet, 8¾ inches. The Pittsburgh Steelers beat the Los Angeles Rams to become the first team in history to win four Super Bowls, Swedish tennis star Bjorn Borg won Wimbledon for the fifth consecutive time, the U.S.'s Eric Heiden won five gold medals in speed skating at the Winter Olympics. And it was Ladies First at the Kentucky Derby when Genuine Risk became the first filly to win that race in sixty-five years.

412

Jan. 5, 1980

1:Send One Your Love
2:Deja Vu
3:I'd Rather Leave While I'm in Love
4:Do That to Me One More Time
5:Looks Like Love Again *
6:We Don't Talk Anymore
7:You're Only Lonely
8:Better Love Next Time
9:Peter Piper
10:Still

Jan. 12, 1980

1:Send One Your Love
2:Deja Vu
3:I'd Rather Leave While I'm in Love
4:Do That to Me One More Time
5:Looks Like Love Again
6:You're Only Lonely
7:We Don't Talk Anymore
8:Yes, I'm Ready *
9:Better Love Next Time
10:Peter Piper

Jan. 19, 1980

1:Deja Vu
2:Send One Your Love
3:I'd Rather Leave While I'm in Love
4:Yes, I'm Ready
5:When I Wanted You *
6:Looks Like Love Again
7:Do That to Me One More Time
8:We Don't Talk Anymore
9:You're Only Lonely
10:September Morn' *

Jan. 26, 1980

1:Yes, I'm Ready
2:September Morn'
3:Deja Vu
4:I'd Rather Leave While I'm in Love
5:When I Wanted You
6:Longer *
7:Do That to Me One More Time
8:Send One Your Love
9:Looks Like Love Again
10:We Don't Talk Anymore

Feb. 2, 1980

1:Yes, I'm Ready
2:Longer
3:When I Wanted You
4:September Morn'
5:Deja Vu
6:Do That to Me One More Time
7:Send One Your Love
8:Looks Like Love Again
9:I'd Rather Leave While I'm in Love
10:We Don't Talk Anymore

Feb. 9, 1980

1:Longer
2:Yes, I'm Ready
3:September Morn'
4:Daydream Believer *
5:When I Wanted You
6:Deja Vu
7:Send One Your Love
8:Do That to Me One More Time
9:We Don't Talk Anymore
10:Looks Like Love Again

Feb. 16, 1980

1:When I Wanted You
2:Daydream Believer
3:Longer
4:September Morn'
5:Yes, I'm Ready
6:Give It All You Got *
7:Do That to Me One More Time
8:Send One Your Love
9:Deja Vu
10:Looks Like Love Again

Feb. 23, 1980

1:Give It All You Got
2:Daydream Believer
3:Longer
4:When I Wanted You
5:September Morn'
6:Yes, I'm Ready
7:Deja Vu
8:Send One Your Love
9:Looks Like Love Again
10:Him *

* Newcomer

Mar. 1, 1980

1:Daydream Believer
2:Give It All You Got
3:When I Wanted You
4:Three Times in Love *
5:Longer
6:Him
7:September Morn'
8:Yes, I'm Ready
9:Deja Vu
10:Looks Like Love Again

Mar. 8, 1980

1:Give It All You Got
2:Three Times in Love
3:Daydream Believer
4:Him
5:When I Wanted You
6:Longer
7:September Morn'
8:Yes, I'm Ready
9:Lost in Love *
10:With You I'm Born Again *

Mar. 15, 1980

1:Give It All You Got
2:Three Times in Love
3:Lost in Love
4:Him
5:With You I'm Born Again
6:When I Wanted You
7:Daydream Believer
8:Longer
9:September Morn'
10:Yes, I'm Ready

Mar. 22, 1980

1:Lost in Love
2:Three Times in Love
3:Give It All You Got
4:Him
5:With You I'm Born Again
6:Longer
7:Daydream Believer
8:When I Wanted You
9:I Can't Tell You Why *
10:September Morn'

Mar. 29, 1980

1:Three Times in Love
2:Lost in Love
3:Give It All You Got
4:With You I'm Born Again
5:I Can't Tell You Why
6:Him
7:Longer
8:Daydream Believer
9:When I Wanted You
10:September Morn'

Apr. 5, 1980

1:Lost in Love
2:Three Times in Love
3:With You I'm Born Again
4:Give It All You Got
5:I Can't Tell You Why
6:Him
7:Longer
8:When I Wanted You
9:Daydream Believer
10:September Morn'

Apr. 12, 1980

1:Lost in Love
2:With You I'm Born Again
3:I Can't Tell You Why
4:Three Times in Love
5:Him
6:Don't Fall in Love With a Dreamer *
7:Give It All You Got
8:Longer
9:When I Wanted You
10:Daydream Believer

Apr. 19, 1980

1:Lost in Love
2:I Can't Tell You Why
3:With You I'm Born Again
4:Three Times in Love
5:Don't Fall in Love With a Dreamer
6:Heart Hotels *
7:Him
8:Give It All You Got
9:When I Wanted You
10:Longer

Apr. 26, 1980

1:Lost in Love
2:Don't Fall in Love With a Dreamer
3:Heart Hotels
4:I Can't Tell You Why
5:With You I'm Born Again
6:The Rose *
7:Three Times in Love
8:Him
9:Give It All You Got
10:When I Wanted You

May 3, 1980

1:Lost in Love
2:Don't Fall in Love With a Dreamer
3:Heart Hotels
4:Gee Whiz *
5:The Rose
6:Biggest Part of Me *
7:I Can't Help It
8:With You I'm Born Again
9:Three Times in Love
10:Him

May 10, 1980

1:The Rose
2:Don't Fall in Love With a Dreamer
3:Gee Whiz
4:Lost in Love
5:Biggest Part of Me
6:Heart Hotels
7:I Can't Help It
8:With You I'm Born Again
9:Him
10:Three Times in Love

May 17, 1980

1:The Rose
2:Don't Fall in Love With a Dreamer
3:Biggest Part of Me
4:Gee Whiz
5:Lost in Love
6:Heart Hotels
7:I Can't Help It
8:With You I'm Born Again
9:Three Times in Love
10:Him

May 24, 1980

1:The Rose
2:Biggest Part of Me
3:Don't Fall in Love With a Dreamer
4:Gee Whiz
5:Heart Hotels
6:I Can't Help It
7:She's Out of My Life *
8:Lost in Love
9:With You I'm Born Again
10:Three Times in Love

May 31, 1980

1:The Rose
2:Biggest Part of Me
3:She's Out of My Life
4:Little Jeannie *
5:Should've Never Let You Go *
6:Heart Hotels
7:Don't Fall in Love With a Dreamer
8:Gee Whiz
9:I Can't Help It
10:Lost in Love

June 7, 1980

1:The Rose
2:Little Jeannie
3:She's Out of My Life
4:Should've Never Let You Go
5:Biggest Part of Me
6:Steal Away *
7:Gee Whiz
8:Heart Hotels
9:Don't Fall in Love With a Dreamer
10:Lost in Love

June 14, 1980

1:Little Jeannie
2:The Rose
3:Should've Never Let You Go
4:She's Out of My Life
5:Steal Away
6:Biggest Part of Me
7:Magic *
8:Don't Fall in Love With a Dreamer
9:Gee Whiz
10:Heart Hotels

June 21, 1980

1:Little Jeannie
2:Should've Never Let You Go
3:The Rose
4:She's Out of My Life
5:Magic
6:Steal Away
7:Biggest Part of Me
8:Don't Fall in Love With a Dreamer
9:Gee Whiz
10:Heart Hotels

June 28, 1980

1:Little Jeannie
2:The Rose
3:Should've Never Let You Go
4:Magic
5:She's Out of My Life
6:Steal Away
7:Biggest Part of Me
8:Against the Wind *
9:Don't Fall in Love With a Dreamer
10:Gee Whiz

July 5, 1980

1:Little Jeannie
2:The Rose
3:Magic
4:Steal Away
5:Biggest Part of Me
6:Should've Never Let You Go
7:She's Out of My Life
8:Don't Fall in Love With a Dreamer
9:Gee Whiz
10:Against the Wind

July 12, 1980

1:Little Jeannie
2:The Rose
3:Magic
4:Should've Never Let You Go
5:Steal Away
6:She's Out of My Life
7:Biggest Part of Me
8:Love the World Away *
9:Against the Wind
10:Gee Whiz

July 19, 1980

1:Magic
2:Little Jeannie
3:Steal Away
4:The Rose
5:Stand By Me *
6:She's Out of My Life
7:Love the World Away
8:Should've Never Let You Go
9:Against the Wind
10:Biggest Part of Me

July 26, 1980

1:Magic
2:Little Jeannie
3:Stand By Me
4:Steal Away
5:More Love *
6:Love the World Away
7:The Rose
8:She's Out of My Life
9:Against the Wind
10:Should've Never Let You Go

Aug. 2, 1980

1:Magic
2:Stand By Me
3:More Love
4:Why Not Me? *
5:Love the World Away
6:Little Jeannie
7:Steal Away
8:The Rose
9:She's Out of My Life
10:Against the Wind

Aug. 9, 1980

1:Magic
2:Stand By Me
3:Why Not Me?
4:More Love
5:Love the World Away
6:Little Jeannie
7:The Rose
8:Steal Away
9:Against the Wind
10:She's Out of My Life

Aug. 16, 1980

1:Magic
2:Why Not Me?
3:Stand By Me
4:More Love
5:The Rose
6:Love the World Away
7:Little Jeannie
8:Steal Away
9:She's Out of My Life
10:Against the Wind

Aug. 23, 1980

1:Why Not Me?
2:Magic
3:Stand By Me
4:Drivin' My Life Away *
5:More Love
6:Love the World Away
7:Little Jeannie
8:Steal Away
9:She's Out of My Life
10:The Rose

Aug. 30, 1980

1:Why Not Me?
2:Magic
3:Don't Ask Me Why *
4:Drivin' My Life Away
5:No Night So Long *
6:You're the Only Woman *
7:Stand By Me
8:More Love
9:Love the World Away
10:Little Jeannie

Sept. 6, 1980

1:Don't Ask Me Why
2:No Night So Long
3:Drivin' My Life Away
4:Why Not Me?
5:You're the Only Woman
6:Magic
7:Late in the Evening *
8:Stand By Me
9:Little Jeannie
10:More Love

Sept. 13, 1980

1:Don't Ask Me Why
2:No Night So Long
3:Drivin' My Life Away
4:You're the Only Woman
5:Xanadu *
6:Late in the Evening
7:Why Not Me?
8:Magic
9:Stand By Me
10:More Love

Sept. 20, 1980

1:No Night So Long
2:Don't Ask Me Why
3:Drivin' My Life Away
4:Xanadu
5:You're the Only Woman
6:More Love
7:Late in the Evening
8:Why Not Me?
9:Magic
10:Stand By Me

Sept. 27, 1980

1:No Night So Long
2:Don't Ask Me Why
3:Xanadu
4:More Love
5:Drivin' My Life Away
6:You're the Only Woman
7:Late in the Evening
8:Why Not Me?
9:Stand By Me
10:Magic

Oct. 4, 1980

1:No Night So Long
2:Xanadu
3:Don't Ask Me Why
4:Never Knew Love Like This Before *
5:Look What You've Done to Me *
6:Drivin' My Life Away
7:Late in the Evening
8:Why Not Me?
9:You're the Only Woman
10:Stand By Me

Oct. 11, 1980

1:No Night So Long
2:Xanadu
3:Look What You've Done to Me
4:Never Knew Love Like This Before
5:Don't Ask Me Why
6:Could I Have This Dance? *
7:Drivin' My Life Away
8:Late in the Evening
9:Why Not Me?
10:You're the Only Woman

Oct. 18, 1980

1:No Night So Long
2:Xanadu
3:Look What You've Done to Me
4:Could I Have This Dance?
5:Don't Ask Me Why
6:Never Knew Love Like This Before
7:Late in the Evening
8:Drivin' My Life Away
9:You're the Only Woman
10:Why Not Me?

Oct. 25, 1980

1:Xanadu
2:Could I Have This Dance?
3:Look What You've Done to Me
4:No Night So Long
5:Never Knew Love Like This Before
6:On the Road Again *
7:Don't Ask Me Why
8:Late in the Evening
9:Drivin' My Life Away
10:You're the Only Woman

Nov. 1, 1980

1:Could I Have This Dance?
2:Xanadu
3:Look What You've Done to Me
4:More Than I Can Say *
5:On the Road Again
6:Never Knew Love Like This Before
7:No Night So Long
8:Don't Ask Me Why
9:Late in the Evening
10:Drivin' My Life Away

Nov. 8, 1980

1:Xanadu
2:Could I Have This Dance?
3:More Than I Can Say
4:Never Be the Same *
5:On the Road Again
6:Never Knew Love Like This Before
7:Look What You've Done to Me
8:No Night So Long
9:Don't Ask Me Why
10:Late in the Evening

Nov. 15, 1980

1:Could I Have This Dance?
2:Never Be the Same
3:More Than I Can Say
4:On the Road Again
5:Suddenly *
6:Never Knew Love Like This Before
7:Look What You've Done to Me
8:Xanadu
9:No Night So Long
10:Don't Ask Me Why

Nov. 22, 1980

1:Never Be the Same
2:More Than I Can Say
3:Suddenly
4:Love On the Rocks *
5:On the Road Again
6:Could I Have This Dance?
7:Never Knew Love Like This Before
8:Look What You've Done to Me
9:Xanadu
10:No Night So Long

Nov. 29, 1980

1:Never Be the Same
2:More Than I Can Say
3:Suddenly
4:Every Woman in the World *
5:Love On the Rocks
6:On the Road Again
7:Never Knew Love Like This Before
8:Could I Have This Dance?
9:Look What You've Done to Me
10:Xanadu

Dec. 6, 1980

1:Never Be the Same
2:More Than I Can Say
3:Every Woman in the World
4:Suddenly
5:Love On the Rocks
6:On the Road Again
7:Could I Have This Dance?
8:Never Knew Love Like This Before
9:Xanadu
10:Look What You've Done to Me

Dec. 13, 1980

1:Never Be the Same
2:More Than I Can Say
3:Every Woman in the World
4:Suddenly
5:It's My Turn *
6:Love On the Rocks
7:On the Road Again
8:Never Knew Love Like This Before
9:Could I Have This Dance?
10:Xanadu

Dec. 20, 1980

1:More Than I Can Say
2:Never Be the Same
3:Every Woman in the World
4:Suddenly
5:Love On the Rocks
6:It's My Turn
7:Xanadu
8:Never Knew Love Like This Before
9:On the Road Again
10:Could I Have This Dance?

Dec. 27, 1980

1:More Than I Can Say
2:Every Woman in the World
3:Love On the Rocks
4:Never Be the Same
5:Suddenly
6:It's My Turn
7:Never Knew Love Like This Before
8:On the Road Again
9:Could I Have This Dance?
10:Xanadu

Index

Listed alphabetically are 2,583 different songs. Thirty were revived over the years, making a grand total of 2,613 entries. Included are how many weeks each song was on the listings (19), how many weeks, if any, that it was Number One (19-2), and the year, or years, where it may be found.

A

Aba Daba Honeymoon, (12), 1951
About a Quarter to Nine, (8), 1935
Accent On Youth, (4), 1935
Accentuate the Positive, (13-4), 1945
Across the Alley From the Alamo, (9), 1947
Afraid to Dream, (7), 1937
After Awhile, (2), 1945
Afterglow, (1), 1936
Afternoon Delight, (14), 1976
After the Love Has Gone, (11), 1979
After the Lovin,' (26-4), 1976-77
Again, (19-2), 1949
Against the Wind, (8), 1980
Ain't No Mountain High Enough, (10), 1970
Ain't No Way to Treat a Lady, (11-3), 1975
Ain't No Woman, (7), 1973
Ain't That a Shame?, (9), 1955
Air That I Breathe, The, (10), 1974
Al Di La, (15), 1962
Alexander's Ragtime Band, (8), 1938
Alfie, (8), 1966
Alice Blue Gown, (1), 1940
All, (7), 1967
All-American Boy, The, (4), 1959
All Ashore, (9), 1938-39
All By Myself, (12), 1976
Allegheny Moon, (15), 1956
Alley Cat, (12), 1962
Alley Oop, (15-1), 1960
All I Do Is Dream of You, (10), 1934
All I Ever Need Is You, (10-4), 1971-72
All I Have to Do Is Dream, (12-3), 1958
All I Know, (11-4), 1973
All I Remember Is You, (1), 1939
All I Want For Christmas Is My Two
    Front Teeth, (1), 1948
All My Life, (10), 1936
All My Love, (20-3), 1950
All of Me, (17-4), 1931-32
All of My Life, (12), 1945
All or Nothing At All, (16-1), 1943
All Shook Up, (14-3), 1957
All the Things You Are, (11-2), 1939-40
All the Way, (14-1), 1957-58
All This and Heaven Too, (7), 1940
All Through the Day, (21-2), 1946

All Through the Night, (7), 1934-35
Almost Like Being in Love, (14), 1947
Almost Persuaded, (4), 1966
Alone, (13-5), 1936
Alone Again (Naturally), (22-7), 1972
Alone At a Table For Two, (1), 1936
Alone Together, (14), 1932-33
Along the Navajo Trail, (12), 1945
Alvin's Harmonica, (5), 1959
Always, (12), 1944-45
Always and Always, (1), 1938
Always in My Heart, (4), 1942
Amapola, (19-6), 1941
American Pie, (14-4), 1972
Amor, (21-2), 1944
And I Love You So, (16-5), 1973
And It Still Goes, (1), 1949
And Mimi, (12), 1947-48
And So Do I, (1), 1940
And So to Sleep Again, (11), 1951-52
And the Angels Sing, (12-4), 1939
And the Grass Won't Pay No Mind, (8), 1970
And Then Some, (11-1), 1935
And Then You Kissed Me, (1), 1944
And There You Are, (1), 1945
And We Were Lovers, (14-1), 1966-67
And When I Die, (11), 1969-70
Angel in Your Arms, (8), 1977
Angie Baby, (13-3), 1974-75
Anna, (1), 1953
Annabelle, (1), 1939
Annie Doesn't Live Here Anymore, (16), 1933-34
Annie's Song, (13-3), 1974
Anniversary Song, The, (19-6), 1947
Another Somebody Done Somebody Wrong
    Song, (12-4), 1975
Answer Me, My Love, (17), 1954
Anyone Who Had a Heart, (9), 1964
Anything Goes, (10), 1934-35
Anytime, (20), 1952
Apple Blossoms and Chapel Bells, (1), 1940
Apple Blossom Wedding, An, (12), 1947
Apple For the Teacher, An, (1), 1939
April Fools, The, (7), 1969
April in Paris, (16-4), 1932-33
April in Portugal, (20-2), 1953

April Love, (13-7), 1957-58
Aquarius/Let the Sunshine In, (16-6), 1969
Aren't You Glad You're You?, (12), 1946
Are You Having Any Fun?, (7), 1939
Are You Lonesome Tonight?, (17-6), 1960-61
Are You Sincere?, (4), 1958
Around the World, (19-1), 1957
Ask Anyone Who Knows, (10), 1947
As Long As He Needs Me, (10), 1963
As Long As I'm Dreaming, (6), 1947
As Time Goes By, (21-4), 1943
At a Perfume Counter, (1), 1938
A-Tisket, A-Tasket, (11-6), 1938
At Last, (10), 1942
At Long Last Love, (6), 1938
At Seventeen, (17-4), 1975
At the Balalaika, (9), 1940
At the Hop, (11-3), 1958
Auf Wiederseh'n, Sweetheart, (16-3), 1952
Autumn Leaves, (22-3), 1955-56
Autumn of My Life, (12), 1968
Autumn Serenade, (1), 1945
"A" You're Adorable, (13), 1949

B

Baby, Don't Get Hooked On Me, (14-3), 1972
Baby Face, (14), 1948
Baby, I'm-a Want You, (13-3), 1971-72
Baby, It's Cold Outside, (8), 1949
Baby Love, (10), 1964
Baby, the Rain Must Fall, (17), 1965
Back Home Again, (12-2), 1974
Bad, Bad Leroy Brown, (9), 1973
Baia, (1), 1945
Baker Street, (10), 1978
Bali Hai, (17), 1949
Ballad of Davy Crockett, The, (19-9), 1955
Ballad of the Green Berets, The, (13-5), 1966
Ballerina, (19-5), 1947-48
Bambina, (1), 1938
Banana Boat Song, The, (15-1), 1957
Band of Gold, (12), 1956
Battle of New Orleans, The, (16-6), 1959
Be Anything, But Be Mine, (12), 1952
Beat o' My Heart, The, (15-3), 1934
Beautiful Brown Eyes, (1), 1951
Beautiful Lady in Blue, A, (9), 1936
Beautiful People, (10), 1971
Be Careful, It's My Heart, (15), 1942
Because of You, (27-11), 1951-52
Because You're Mine, (21), 1952-53
Been to Canaan, (8-1), 1972-73
Beep Beep, (8), 1958-59
Beer Barrel Polka, (12), 1939
Before My Heart Finds Out, (12), 1978

Beg Your Pardon, (11), 1948
Behind Closed Doors, (15), 1973
Bei Mir Bist Du Schon, (8-2), 1938
Bell Bottom Trousers, (15), 1945
Bells of San Raquel, The, (4), 1941-42
Be My Life's Companion, (11), 1952
Be My Love, (21), 1951
Besame Mucho, (17-3), 1944
Be Still, My Heart, (10), 1934
Best of Everything, The, (9), 1959-60
Best of My love, The, (13-2), 1975
Best Things in Life Are Free, The, (7), 1948
Better Love Next Time, (10), 1979-80
Betty Coed, (6), 1930
Bewildered, (1), 1938
Bewitched, (21-5), 1950
Beyond the Blue Horizon, (16-3), 1930
Bibbidi Bobbidi Boo, (8), 1950
Bible Tells Me So, The, (4), 1955
Bicyclettes De Belsize, Les, (13), 1968-69
Bidin' My Time, (10), 1930-31
Big Bad John, (13-5), 1961
Biggest Part of Me, (12), 1980
Big Girls Don't Cry, (15-5), 1962-63
Big Hunk o' Love, A, (17-2), 1959
Bird Dog, (6), 1958
Black and White, (11-2), 1972
Blacksmith Blues, (15), 1952
Blame It On the Bossa Nova, (12), 1963
Bless the Beasts and Children, (2), 1971
Blossom Fell, A, (10), 1955
Blossoms On Broadway, (9), 1937
Blow Away, (11), 1979
Blow, Gabriel, Blow, (5), 1934-35
Blowin' in the Wind, (22), 1963
Blue Again, (6), 1930-31
Blue Bayou, (13), 1977-78
Blueberry Hill, (14),1940
    Revival: (19), 1956-57
Bluebird, (3), 1975
Bluebird of Happiness, (5), 1948
Blue Evening, (1), 1939
Blue Hawaii, (6), 1937
Blue Lovebird, (2), 1940
Blue Moon, (18-1), 1934-35
    Revival: (13-4), 1961
Blue on Blue, (14), 1963
Blue Orchids, (11-1), 1939
Blue Prelude, (13), 1933
Bluer Than Blue, (13-3), 1978
Blues in the Night, (13-2), 1942
Blue Suede Shoes, (11), 1956
Blue Tango, (27-2), 1952
Blue Velvet, (19-4), 1963-64
Bobby's Girl, (14), 1962-63
Bob White, (3), 1938
Body and Soul, (17-3), 1930-31
Boll Weevil Song, The, (7), 1961
Bonaparte's Retreat, (3), 1950
Boogie Woogie Bugle Boy, (12-2), 1973
Boo Hoo, (11-6), 1937
Born Free, (12-5), 1966
Botch-A-Me, (6), 1952
Both Sides Now, (12), 1969
Boulevard of Broken Dreams, (9), 1934
Boy Named Sue, A, (11-2), 1969

Brand New Key, (13), 1971-72
Brandy, (16), 1972
Brazil, (18-3), 1943
Break Away, (12-1), 1976
Breaking Up Is Hard to Do, (15-3), 1962
Breeze and I, The, (13), 1940
Bridge Over Troubled Water, (11-6), 1970
Bristol Stomp, (10), 1961
Broadway Rhythm, (1), 1935
Broken Hearted Me, (14-4), 1979
Broken Record, The, (5), 1936
Brother, Can You Spare a Dime?, (13), 1932-33
Bushel and a Peck, A, (16-2), 1950-51
But Beautiful, (16), 1948
But For Love, (4), 1969
Butterfly, (12), 1957
Buttons and Bows, (18-10), 1948-49
By a Waterfall, (15-3), 1933-34
Bye Bye, Baby, (3), 1950
Bye Bye Blues, (16-2), 1930
Bye Bye Love, (10), 1957
By the River Sainte Marie, (5), 1931
By the Time I Get to Phoenix, (19-6), 1967-68

C

Cabaret, (10), 1966-67
Cab Driver, (7), 1968
Calcutta, (21-6), 1961
Call Me, (17), 1966
Call Me Darling, (8), 1931
Call Me Irresponsible, (14-3), 1963
Call of the Canyon, The, (1), 1940
Call, The, (11), 1976
Camelot, (8), 1961
Canadian Sunset, (17-7), 1956
Can Anyone Explain?, (6), 1950
Candy, (13-4), 1945
Candy and Cake, (3), 1950
Candy Man, The, (20-3), 1972
Can I Help It?, (1), 1939
Can't Buy Me Love, (13-5), 1964
Can't Get Used to Losing You, (12), 1963
Can't Help Falling in Love, (15), 1961-62
Can This Be Love?, (5), 1930
Can't Smile Without You, (21-5), 1978
Can't Take My Eyes Off You, (21-2), 1967
Can't You Read Between the Lines?, (1), 1945
Can You, Fool?, (6), 1978-79
Can You Read My Mind?, (11), 1979
Carefree Highway, (11), 1974
Careless, (14-5), 1940
Careless Hands, (7), 1949
Carelessly, (13-2), 1937
Carioca, (13), 1934
Carolina in the Pines, (8), 1975

Catch a Falling Star, (14-4), 1958
Cathedral in the Pines, (8), 1938
Cathy's Clown, (17-5), 1960
'Cause My Baby Says It's So, (1), 1937
C'est Magnifique, (1), 1953
C'est Si Bon, (1), 1953
Champagne Waltz, The, (9), 1934
Chances Are, (15-3), 1957-58
Change of Heart, (6), 1978
Change Partners, (9-2), 1938
Changing Partners, (17), 1953-54
Chanson D'Amour, (11-1), 1958
Chantilly Lace, (9), 1958
Chapel of Love, (10), 1964
Charade, (14), 1963-64
Charlie Brown, (8), 1959
Charmaine, (7), 1951-52
Chasing Shadows, (11-5), 1935
Chattanooga Choo Choo, (14-2), 1941-42
Chattanoogie Shoe Shine Boy, (12-6), 1950
Cheek to Cheek, (11-5), 1935
Cheerful Little Earful, (6-1), 1930
Cherish, (12), 1966
Cherry Pink and Apple Blossom
        White, (20-1), 1955
Chi-Baba, Chi-Baba, (13), 1947
Chickery Chick, (14), 1945-46
Children's Marching Song, The, (7), 1959
Chim Chim Cheree, (8), 1965
Chipmunk Song, The, (7-3), 1958-59
Christmas Dreaming, (6), 1947-48
Christmas Song, The, (2), 1946-47
Christopher Columbus, (1), 1936
Cinderella, Stay in My Arms, (4), 1939
Cindy, Oh Cindy, (8), 1956-57
Circle is Small, The, (10), 1978
Civilization, (15-1), 1947-48
Clair, (15-3), 1972-73
Classical Gas, (11-3), 1968
Climb Every Mountain, (6), 1959-60
Cling to Me, (5), 1936
Closer I Get to You, The, (10), 1978
Close to Me, (1), 1936
Close to You, (19-7), 1970
Cocktails For Two, (7), 1934
Coffee Song, The, (1), 1946
Cold, Cold Heart, (16), 1951-52
Come Back to Me, (8), 1965-66
Come Monday, (9), 1974
Come On-A My House, (12), 1951
Come On Over, (12-2), 1976
Come Rain or Come Shine, (3), 1946
Come Saturday Morning, (4), 1970
Come See About Me, (11), 1964-65
Comes Love, (7), 1939
Come Softly to Me, (13-5), 1959
Come to Baby Do, (1), 1946
Come What May, (1), 1952
Comin' In On a Wing and a Prayer, (21-3), 1943
Continental, The, (9-1), 1934
Copacabana, (8), 1978
Cottage For Sale, A, (9), 1930
Could Be, (8), 1939
Could I Have This Dance?, (12-2), 1980
Could It Be Magic?, (8), 1975
Count Every Star, (13), 1950

Country Boy, (9), 1975-76
Count Your Blessings, (16), 1954-55
Cowboy's Work Is Never Done, A, (11), 1972
Cracklin' Rosie, (10), 1970
Crazy Love, (15-6), 1979
Cross Over the Bridge, (12), 1954
Cross Patch, (1), 1936
Cruising Down the River, (19-8), 1949
Cry, (20-5), 1952
Cry, Baby, Cry, (9-1), 1938
Cryin' For the Carolines, (10), 1930
Crying, (13), 1961
Crying In the Chapel, (13), 1953
    Revival: (12-3), 1965
Cuanto Le Gusta, (9), 1948-49
Cuban Love Song, (9), 1931-32
Cycles, (15), 1968-69

D

Daddy, (15-6), 1941
Daddy, Don't You Walk So Fast, (10), 1972
Daddy's Little Girl, (11), 1950
Daisy a Day, (8), 1973
Dance With a Dolly, (15-1), 1944-45
Dance With Me, Henry, (11), 1955
Dancing in the Dark, (18-3), 1931
Dancing On the Ceiling, (4), 1930
Dancing Queen, (3), 1977
Dancing With Tears In My Eyes, (13-2), 1930
Dancin' Shoes, (6), 1979
Dang Me, (12), 1964
Daniel, (10), 1973
Danny's Song, (8-2), 1973
Dark Moon, (10), 1957
Darkness On the Delta, (11), 1932
Darn That Dream, (8-1), 1940
Dawn, (12), 1964
Day After Day, (1), 1938
Daybreak, (5), 1942
Day By Day, (13), 1946
Daydream Believer, (10-1), 1980
Day Dreaming, (1), 1942
Day In, Day Out, (10-1), 1939
Day in the Life of a Fool, A, (8), 1966-67
Days of Sand and Shovels, The, (9), 1969
Days of Wine and Roses, (17-3), 1963
Dear Heart, (18-1), 1965
Dear Hearts and Gentle People, (16-7), 1949-50
Dearie, (13), 1950
Dearly Beloved, (17), 1942-43
Dedicated to the One I Love, (13), 1961
Deeper Than the Night, (6), 1979
Deep in a Dream, (14), 1938-39
Deep in the Heart of Texas, (13-5), 1942

Deep Purple, (12-7), 1939
    Revival: (16), 1963-64
Deja Vu, (13-1), 1979-80
Delicado, (10), 1952
Delilah, (6), 1968
Delta Dawn, (14-2), 1973
Desiree, (13-2), 1977-78
Devil May Care, (5), 1940
Devoted to You, (10), 1978
Diamonds Are Forever, (12), 1972
Diana, (8), 1957
Dickey-Bird Song, The, (14), 1948
Did I Remember?, (13-6), 1936
Didn't We?, (5), 1969
Did You Ever Get That Feeling
    in the Moonlight?, (2), 1945
Did You Ever See a Dream
    Walking?, (16-5), 1933-34
Did You Mean It?, (5), 1936
Different Worlds, (13-2), 1979
Dinner For One, Please, James, (6), 1936
Dipsy Doodle, The, (10), 1938
Doctor, Lawyer, Indian Chief, (11), 1946
Does Anybody Really Know What Time
    It Is?, (6), 1971
Doggie in the Window, (14-1), 1953
Do I Love You?, (4), 1940
Doin' What Comes Naturally, (17), 1946
Do I Worry?, (14), 1941
Dominique, (14-5), 1963-64
Domino, (10), 1951-52
Dommage, Dommage, (7), 1966
Donna, (10), 1959
Do Nothing Till You Hear From Me, (1), 1944
Don't, (4), 1958
Don't Ask Me Why, (12-2), 1980
Don't Be Cruel, (13), 1956
Don't Be That Way, (9), 1938
Don't Blame Me, (19), 1933
Don't Break My Pretty Balloon, (7), 1968
Don't Break the Heart That Loves You, (12-1), 1962
Don't Cry, (1), 1943
Don't Cry, Joe, (14-3), 1949-50
Don't Ever Change, (1), 1945
Don't Expect Me to Be Your Friend, (11-1), 1973
Don't Fall in Love With a Dreamer, (13), 1980
Don't Fence Me In, (16-8), 1944-45
Don't Forbid Me, (11), 1957
Don't Get Around Much Anymore, (16-3), 1943
Don't Give Up On Us, (11-2), 1977
Don't Give Up the Ship, (2), 1935
Don't Go Breaking My Heart, (16-3), 1976
Don't It Make My Brown Eyes Blue?, (13), 1977
Don't Let the Stars Get in Your Eyes, (21-5), 1952-53
Don't Let the Sun Catch You Crying, (9), 1964
Don't Let the Sun Go Down On Me, (7), 1974
Don't Pull Your Love, (14), 1971
Don't Sit Under the Apple Tree, (13-5), 1942
Don't Sleep in the Subway, (13-3), 1967
Don't Stop Believin', (11), 1976
Don't Sweetheart Me, (2), 1944
Don't Worry 'Bout Me, (10), 1939
Don't You Know I Care?, (1), 1945
Do That to Me One More Time, (13), 1979-80
Double Trouble, (1), 1935
Do Wah Diddy Diddy, (10), 1964

Down Argentina Way, (7), 1940-41
Downtown, (18-4), 1965
Down Yonder, (18), 1951-52
Do You Care?, (16), 1941
Do You Know the Way to San Jose?, (7), 1968
Dragnet, (5), 1953
Dream, (19-5), 1945
Dream a Little Dream of Me, (11-2), 1931
Dream Awhile, (1), 1936
Dream Baby, (8), 1971
Dreamer's Holiday, A, (18-1), 1949-50
Dream Is a Wish Your Heart Makes, A, (2), 1950
Dream Lover, (12), 1959
Dreams of the Everyday Housewife, (10), 1968
Dream Valley, (2), 1940
Drivin' My Life Away, (11), 1980
Drums In My Heart, (9), 1932
Drum, The, (8), 1971
Dueling Banjos, (10-2), 1973
Duke of Earl, (8), 1962
Dungaree Doll, (8), 1956
Dust in the Wind, (9), 1978

Everybody Loves a Rain Song, (10-1), 1978
Everybody Loves Somebody, (15-6), 1964
Everybody's Out of Town, (11), 1970
Everybody's Somebody's Fool, (19-2), 1960
Everybody's Talkin', (18), 1969-70
Every Day, (5), 1935
Everyday I Love You, (8), 1948
Every Day of My Life, (15-2), 1972
Every Little Moment, (1), 1935
Every Now and Then, (1), 1935
Every Single Little Tingle of My Heart, (1), 1935
Everything a Man Could Ever Need, (8), 1970
Everything I Have Is Yours, (13), 1934
Everything I Love, (14), 1941-42
Everything Is Beautiful, (16-4), 1970
Everything's Been Done Before, (1), 1935
Everything's Coming Up Roses, (14), 1959
Everytime We Say Goodbye, (2), 1945
Everytime You Touch Me, (10), 1975
Everywhere You Go, (1), 1949
Every Woman in the World, (15), 1980-81
   (Totals include 1981 carry-over weeks)
Ev'ry Time, (1), 1945
Exactly Like You, (17-4), 1930
Exodus, (16), 1960-61

E

Early in the Morning, (11), 1970
Easier Said Than Done, (8-2), 1963
Easter Parade, (15), 1933-34
East of the Sun, (9-2), 1935
Easy Come, Easy Go, (16), 1970
Easy to Love, (5), 1937
Easy to Remember, (8), 1935
Ebb Tide, (19-5), 1953-54
Eeny Meeny Miney Mo, (4), 1935-36
Eh Cumpari, (8), 1953-54
Elmer's Tune, (14-3), 1941-42
El Paso, (23-2), 1959-60
El Rancho Grande, (3), 1939
Elusive Butterfly, (10), 1966
Embraceable You, (14-5), 1930-31
Emotion, (10), 1975
Empty Saddles, (1), 1936
End of the World, The, (12), 1963
End, The, (4), 1958
Engine, Engine Number Nine, (9), 1965
England Swings, (7), 1966
Enjoy Yourself, (7), 1950
Entertainer, The, (14-2), 1974
Eres Tu, (15), 1974
Eternity, (9), 1969
Evelina, (1), 1945
Even Now, (12-3), 1978
Eve of Destruction, (8), 1965
Evergreen, (23-6), 1976-77
Everlasting Love, An, (6), 1978
Everybody Has the Right to Be Wrong, (1), 1965

F

Faded Summer Love, A, (7), 1931
Faithful Forever, (9), 1940
Fallin' In Love, (9), 1975
Far Away Places, (20-3), 1949
Farewell, My Love, (3), 1937
Fascination, (15-1), 1957
Father of Girls, The, (4), 1968
F.D.R. Jones, (3), 1939
Feelin', (8), 1969
Feelings, (10), 1975
Feel Like Makin' Love, (12-3), 1974
Fellow On a Furlough, A, (2), 1944
Ferryboat Serenade, (11-1), 1940
Ferry Cross the Mersey, (11), 1965
Feudin' and Fightin', (14-1), 1947
Fever, (10), 1958
Fiddle-Dee-Dee, (6), 1949
Fifty Ways to Leave Your Lover, (16-2), 1976
Fine and Dandy, (7), 1930
Fine Romance, A, (7), 1936
Fire and Rain, (15), 1970-71
Firefly, (4), 1958
First Time Ever I Saw Your Face, The, (15-5), 1972
First Time I Saw You, The, (4), 1937
Five Minutes More, (16-4), 1946
Flat Foot Floogey, (6), 1938
Flowers For Madame, (1), 1935
Flowers On the Wall, (14), 1966

Fly Away, (12-4), 1975-76
Flying Down to Rio, (10), 1934
Fool, If You Think It's Over, (14-3), 1978
Fool On the Hill, (16-3), 1968
Fools Rush In, (11-1), 1940
Fool Such As I, A, (14), 1959
Fool That I Am, (4), 1948
Footloose and Fancy Free, (1), 1935
For All We Know, (10-2), 1971
Forever and Ever, (21), 1949
Forever in Blue Jeans, (10), 1979
Forget Him, (9), 1964
Forgive Me, (11), 1952
For Me and My Gal, (10), 1943
For Once in My Life, (15), 1967-68
For Sentimental Reasons, (20-7), 1946-47
For the First Time, (14), 1943-44
For the Love of Him, (14-2), 1970
Forty-Second Street, (11), 1933
For You, (16-2), 1930
For You, For Me, Forevermore, (2), 1946
Four Walls, (7), 1957
Four Winds and the Seven Seas, The, (1), 1949
Free Again, (12), 1966-67
Free Man in Paris, (6), 1974
Frenesi, (19-3), 1940-41
Friendly Persuasion, (6), 1956
Friend of Yours, A, (2), 1945
From Atlanta to Goodbye, (4), 1969
From the Top of Your Head, (3), 1935
From the Vine Came the Grape, (3), 1954
Frosty the Snowman, (4-1), 1950-51
Full Moon, (1), 1942
Full Moon and Empty Arms, (7), 1946
Funny Face, (8), 1972-73

G

Gal in Calico, A, (14-1), 1946-47
Galveston, (14-2), 1969
Galway Bay, (11), 1949
Gambler, The, (10), 1978-79
Games That Lovers Play, (15), 1966-67
Gaucho Serenade, (1), 1940
G'Bye Now, (3), 1941
Gee Whiz, (11), 1980
Gentleman Obviously Doesn't Believe, The, (1), 1935
Gentle On My Mind, (17-6), 1967-68
Georgia On My Mind, (2), 1941
Georgy Girl, (16), 1967
Get a Job, (9), 1958
Get Down, (14), 1973
Get Happy, (7), 1930
Get Off of My Cloud, (8), 1965
Get Out of Town, (3), 1939
Get Rhythm in Your Feet, (1), 1935

Get Up and Boogie, (3), 1976
Ghost of a Chance, A, (19), 1932
Gigi, (14), 1958
Girl, A Girl, A, (5), 1954
Girl From Ipanema, The, (14), 1964
Give It All You Got, (11-3), 1980
Give Me Love, (9), 1973
Glad All Over, (6), 1964
Glory of Love, The, (11-1), 1936
Glow Worm, (18-2), 1952-53
Go Away, Little Girl, (12-4), 1962-63
Gobs of Love, (1), 1942
Go Fly a Kite, (1), 1939
Goin' Out of My Head, (15), 1964-65
Golden Earrings, (14), 1948
Goldfinger, (17-3), 1965
Gone, (8), 1957
Gone Fishin', (1), 1950
Gone With the Wind, (3), 1937
Gonna Build a Mountain, (10), 1962-63
Goodbye, (8), 1969
Goodbye, Baby, (1), 1959
Goodbye to Love, (13), 1972
Good For Nothin' But Love, (1), 1939
Good Life, The, (9), 1963
Good Luck Charm, (12-2), 1962
Good Morning, (1), 1939
Goodnight, Angel, (3), 1938
Goodnight, Irene, (17-4), 1950
Goodnight, My Love, (12-4), 1937
Goodnight, Sweetheart, (17-9), 1931
Goodnight, Sweetheart, Goodnight, (4), 1954
Goodnight Wherever You Are, (15), 1944
Good, the Bad and the Ugly, The, (11), 1968
Good Timin', (13), 1960
Good Vibrations, (6), 1966-67
Goody Goodbye, (2), 1939
Goody Goody, (9-4), 1936
Got a Date With an Angel, (8), 1931-32
Gotta Be This Or That, (16), 1945
Gotta Get Some Shuteye, (4), 1939
Gotta Travel On, (6), 1959
Great Day, (9-4), 1930
Great Pretender, The, (13), 1956
Green Door, (15), 1956-57
Green Eyes, (11), 1941
Greenfields, (14), 1960
Green Grass Starts to Grow, The, (7), 1971
Green Leaves of Summer, The, (13), 1960-61
Guantanamera, (8), 1966
Guilty, (5), 1931
    Revival: (13), 1947
Guitar Boogie Shuffle, (5), 1959
Guy Is a Guy, A, (12), 1952
Gypsies, Tramps and Thieves, (13), 1971
Gypsy, The, (21-8), 1946

H

Hair of Gold, Eyes of Blue, (15), 1948
Half as Much, (18), 1952
Half-Breed, (7), 1973
Half the Way, (6), 1979
Hands Across the Table, (9), 1934
Handy Man, (7), 1960
    Revival: (8), 1977
Happening, The, (8), 1967
Happiness Is Me and You, (3), 1974
Happy Days Are Here Again, (13-6), 1930
Happy Heart, (13-2), 1969
Happy in Love, (2), 1942
Happy Organ, The, (13-1), 1959
Happy Wanderer, The, (12), 1954
Harbor Lights, (11), 1937
    Revival: (19-2), 1950-51
Hard Day's Night, A, (14-2), 1964
Hard to Get, (11), 1955
Harper Valley P.T.A., (9-2), 1968
Haunted Heart, (16), 1948
Have I Told You Lately That I Love You?, (1), 1950
Have You Ever Been Lonely?, (10), 1933
Have You Forgotten So Soon?, (4), 1938
Have You Got Any Castles, Baby?, (11), 1937
Have You Heard?, (8), 1953
Have You Never Been Mellow?, (13-2), 1975
Having My Baby, (6), 1974
Hawaiian Wedding Song, (8), 1959
He, (17), 1955-56
He Ain't Heavy, He's My Brother, (8), 1970-71
Heart, (13), 1955
Heartaches, (12), 1931
    Revival: (17-2), 1947
Heartaches By the Number, (15-2), 1959-60
Heart and Soul, (10), 1938
Heartbreak Hotel, (11-2), 1956
Heart Hotels, (10), 1980
Heart of My Heart, (15), 1954
Heart of the Night, (7), 1979
Hearts of Stone, (16), 1955
Heatwave, (12), 1933-1934
Heaven Can Wait, (11-2), 1939
He Don't Love You, (10-2), 1975
Heigh Ho, (11), 1938
He'll Have to Go, (18), 1960
Hello, Dolly, (19-6), 1964
Hello Mudduh, Hello Fadduh, (8), 1963
Hello, Stranger, (9), 1977
Hello, Young Lovers, (2), 1951
Help!, (14-2), 1965
Help Me, (11-1), 1974-75
Help Me, Rhonda, (6), 1965
Help Yourself, (8), 1968
Here, (5), 1954
Here Comes Cookie, (9-1), 1935
Here Comes That Rainy Day Feeling Again, (10), 1971

Here I'll Stay, (3), 1949
Here In My Heart, (13), 1952
Here Lies Love, (13), 1932
Here's Love in Your Eye, (1), 1936
Here's to Romance, (4), 1935
Here You Are, (3), 1942
Here You Come Again, (14), 1977-78
Hernando's Hideaway, (15-1), 1954
He's a Rebel, (14), 1962
He's Got the Whole World in His Hands, (10-3), 1958
He's Home For a Little While, (1), 1945
He's My Guy, (2), 1942
He's So Fine, (13-4), 1963
He Wears a Pair of Silver Wings, (13-4), 1942
Hey! Baby, (11-3), 1962
Hey, Jealous Lover, (8), 1956-57
Hey, Jude, (16-6), 1968
Hey, Look Me Over, (16), 1961
Hey! Paula, (11-3), 1963
Hey, There, (19-10), 1954
Hey There, Lonely Girl, (8), 1970
High and the Mighty, The, (17), 1954
Higher and Higher, (10), 1977
High Hopes, (18), 1959
High Noon, (3), 1952
High On a Windy Hill, (13), 1941
Him, (13), 1980
Hi, Neighbor, (1), 1941
Hit the Road, Jack, (11-2), 1961
Hold Me, (15), 1933
Hold Me, Thrill Me, Kiss Me, (10), 1953
Hold Me Tight, (6), 1969
Hold My Hand, (11), 1954-55
Hold Tight, (3), 1939
Home, (12), 1931
Homesick, That's All, (1), 1945
Honey, (20-7), 1968
Honey-Babe, (10), 1955
Honeycomb, (10), 1957
Honey, Come Back, (12), 1970
Hooked On You, (9), 1977
Hoop-Dee-Doo, (13), 1950
Hopelessly Devoted to You, (11), 1978
Hop Scotch Polka, (2), 1949
Horse With No Name, A, (6), 1972
Hot Canary, (1), 1951
Hot Diggity, (15), 1956
Hound Dog, (9), 1956
House of the Rising Sun, The, (14), 1964
Houston, (15), 1965
How About You?, (5), 1942
How Are Things in Glocca Morra?, (14), 1947
How Blue the Night, (2), 1944
How Can I Be Sure?, (9), 1972
How Can I Leave You Again?, (11), 1977-78
How Can You Mend a Broken Heart?, (15-4), 1971
How Could You?, (1), 1937
How Deep Is the Ocean?, (16-2), 1932
How Deep Is Your Love?, (20-5), 1977-78
How'dja Like to Love Me?, (6), 1938
How Do I Know It's Real?, (1), 1942
How Do You Speak to An Angel?, (1), 1953
How High the Moon, (3), 1940
    Revival: (11), 1951
How Important Can It Be?, (11), 1955
How It Lies, How It Lies, How It Lies, (1), 1949

How Many Hearts Have You Broken?, (10), 1944
How Soon?, (14-3), 1947-48
How Sweet It Is, (10), 1975
How Sweet You Are, (3), 1943
Hucklebuck, The, (1), 1949
Hummingbird, (6), 1955
Humpty Dumpty Heart, (1), 1942
Hundred Pounds of Clay, A, (19), 1961
Hurry Home, (2), 1939
Hurting Each Other, (6), 1972
Hush, Hush, Sweet Charlotte, (12-2), 1965
Hut Sut Song, The, (11-3), 1941

I

I Almost Called Your Name, (5), 1967-68
I Almost Lost My Mind, (13), 1956
I Am . . . I Said, (9-3), 1971
I Am Woman, (15-1), 1972-73
I Apologize, (10), 1951
I Believe, (23-3), 1953
I Believe I'm Gonna Love You, (10), 1975
I Believe in Miracles, (4), 1977
I Believe in You, (10), 1961-62
I Believe There's Nothing Stronger
        Than Our Love, (10), 1975
I Believe You, (4), 1979
I Came Here to Talk For Joe, (2), 1942
I Can Dream, Can't I?, (3), 1938
        Revival: (17-2), 1949
I Can Help, (14), 1974
I Can See Clearly Now, (9-2), 1972
I Can't Begin to Tell You, (18-1), 1945-46
I Can't Believe I'm Losing You, (8), 1968
I Can't Escape From You, (3), 1936
I Can't Love You Any More, (3), 1940
I Can't Stop Loving You, (17-5), 1962
I Can't Tell You Why, (6), 1980
I Could Have Danced All Night, (16), 1956
I Couldn't Believe My Eyes, (3), 1935
I Couldn't Sleep a Wink Last Night, (13-1), 1944
I Cover the Waterfront, (6), 1933
I Cried For You, (2), 1939
Idaho, (11), 1942
I'd Do It All Over Again, (1), 1945
I Didn't Get to Sleep At All, (15-1), 1972
I Didn't Know About You, (1), 1945
I Didn't Know What Time It Was, (7), 1939-40
I Didn't Slip, I Wasn't Pushed, I Fell, (1), 1950
I'd Like to Teach the World to Sing, (13), 1971-72
I'd Love to Take Orders From You, (1), 1935
I'd Love You to Want Me, (9), 1972
I Do, I Do, I Do, I Do, I Do, (7), 1976
I Don't Care If the Sun Don't Shine, (9), 1950
I Don't Care Who Knows It, (2), 1945
I Don't Know Enough About You, (17), 1946

I Don't Know How to Love Him, (9), 1971
I Don't Know What He Told You, (9), 1974
I Don't Know Why, (3), 1931
I Don't See Me in Your Eyes Anymore, (10), 1949
I Don't Want to Love You, (2), 1944
I Don't Want to Make History, (1), 1936
I Don't Want to Set the World On Fire, (14-4), 1941
I Don't Want to Walk Without You, (13-1), 1942
I Double Dare You, (13-1), 1938
I'd Rather Leave While I'm in Love, (8), 1979-80
I'd Rather Listen to Your Eyes, (1), 1935
I'd Really Love to See You Tonight, (18-3), 1976
I Dream of You, (15), 1944-45
I'd've Baked a Cake, (13-3), 1950
If, (20-10), 1951
I Fall in Love With You Every Day, (3), 1938
I Feel Fine, (12-3), 1964-65
I Feel Like a Feather in the Breeze, (6), 1936
If Ever I See You Again, (7-2), 1978
If Ever I Would Leave You, (16), 1961
If He Walked Into My Life, (16), 1966
If I Can't Have You, (5), 1978
If I Could Reach You, (13-4), 1972
If I Didn't Care, (7), 1939
If I Give My Heart to You, (15-2), 1954-55
If I Had a Talking Picture of You, (3), 1930
If I Love Again, (15-3), 1933-34
If I Loved You, (19-3), 1945
If I Should Lose You, (1), 1936
If It's the Last Thing I Do, (7), 1937-38
If I Were a Bell, (1), 1951
If Not For You, (17-1), 1971
I Found a Dream, (5), 1935
I Found a Million Dollar Baby, (11-3), 1931
If the Moon Turns Green, (1), 1935
If There Is Someone Lovelier Than You, (4), 1935
If You Could Read My Mind, (11-1), 1971
If You Go Away, (17), 1967
If You Know What I Mean, (13), 1976
If You Leave Me Now, (15-1), 1976-77
If You Love Me, (12), 1974
If You Love Me, Really Love Me, (12), 1954
If You Please, (5), 1943
If You Remember Me, (5), 1979
If You Wanna Be Happy, (11-2), 1963
I Get a Kick Out of You, (14-2), 1934-35
I Get Along Without You Very Well, (8), 1939
I Get Around, (8), 1964
I Get Ideas, (17), 1951
I Get So Lonely, (17), 1954
I Give You My Word, (13), 1940-41
I Got a Name, (8), 1973
I Got It Bad and That Ain't Good, (1), 1942
I Got Rhythm, (13), 1930-31
I Got Stung, (5), 1958
I Got the Sun in the Morning, (15), 1946
I Got You, Babe, (14-3), 1965
I Guess I'll Have to Dream the Rest, (13), 1941
I Guess the Lord Must Be in New York City, (3), 1969
I Hadn't Anyone Till You, (8), 1938
I Had the Craziest Dream, (15), 1942-43
I Have Eyes, (7), 1939
I Hear a Rhapsody, (16-10), 1941
I Heard You Cried Last Night, (14), 1943
I Hear You Knocking, (4), 1955
I Honestly Love You, (10-5), 1974

I Just Can't Help Believing, (15), 1970
I Just Fall in Love Again, (14-4), 1979
I Just Want to Be Your Everything, (20-3), 1977
I Know Now, (8), 1937
I Left My Heart at the Stage Door Canteen, (12), 1942
I Left My Heart in San Francisco, (19-5), 1962
I Let a Song Go Out of My Heart, (14-1), 1938
I Like Dreamin', (11), 1977
I'll Be Home For Christmas, (4), 1943-44
I'll Be Seeing You, (24-10), 1944
I'll Buy That Dream, (13-2), 1945
I'll Catch the Sun, (9), 1969
I'll Close My Eyes, (18), 1947
I'll Dance At Your Wedding, (11), 1948
I'll Follow My Secret Heart, (6), 1934
I'll Get By, (25), 1944
I'll Have to Say I Love You in a Song, (11-1), 1974
I'll Keep the Lovelight Burning, (2), 1942
I'll Never Love This Way Again, (16), 1979
I'll Never Say "Never Again" Again, (8), 1935
I'll Never Smile Again, (16-7), 1940
I'll Play For You, (8), 1975
I'll Pray For You, (1), 1942
I'll See You Again, (7-2), 1930
I'll Sing You a Thousand Love Songs, (13-1), 1936-37
I'll String Along With You, (8), 1934
I'll Take an Option On You, (10), 1933
I'll Walk Alone, (21-8), 1944
I Love, (8), 1974
I Love a Parade, (8), 1931
I Love Louisa, (8), 1931
I Love My Friend, (6), 1974
I Love Paris, (9), 1953
I Love the Guy, (2), 1950
I Love to Whistle, (2), 1938
I Love You, (20-3), 1944
I'm a Fool to Care, (2), 1954
Imagination, (13-3), 1940
I'm Alone Because I Love You, (4), 1930
I'm Always Chasing Rainbows, (13), 1946
I'm an Old Cowhand, (4), 1936
I Married an Angel, (7), 1938
I'm Beginning to See the Light, (11-2), 1945
I'm Building a Sailboat of Dreams, (3), 1939
I'm Building Up to an Awful Letdown, (3), 1936
I'm Confessin', (7), 1930
    Revival: (7), 1944-45
I'm Easy, (13-2), 1976
I'm Getting Tired So I Can Sleep, (1), 1942
I'm Gonna Lock My Heart, (7), 1938
I'm Gonna Love That Guy, (10), 1945
I'm Gonna Sit Right Down and Write Myself
    a Letter, (5), 1936
    Revival: (10), 1957
I'm Henry VIII, I Am, (4), 1965
I'm In a Dancing Mood, (7), 1936-37
I'm In the Mood For Love, (12-2), 1935
I'm In You, (3), 1977
I'm Leaving It Up to You, (14-2), 1963-64
    Revival: (9-2), 1974
I'm Living In a Great Big Way, (1), 1935
I'm Looking Over a Four Leaf Clover, (15-2), 1948
I'm Making Believe, (16), 1944-45
Immigrant, The, (6), 1975
I'm Nobody's Baby, (11), 1940
I'm On a Seesaw, (8), 1935

I'm On My Way, (9), 1978
Impossible Dream, The, (15-2), 1966
I'm Putting All My Eggs In One Basket, (9), 1936
I'm Shooting High, (6), 1936
I'm Sittin' High On a Hilltop, (7), 1935-36
I'm Sorry, (17-3), 1960
I'm Stepping Out With a Memory Tonight, (2), 1940
I'm Telling You Now, (12-3), 1965
I'm Through With Love, (11), 1931
I Must See Annie Tonight, (3), 1939
I'm Walkin', (11), 1957
I'm Walking Behind You, (21-3), 1953
I'm Yours, (17-3), 1952
In a Little Gypsy Tea Room, (16-2), 1935
In an Old Dutch Garden, (12), 1940
In an 18th Century Drawing Room, (1), 1939
Indian Summer, (13-1), 1940
I Need to Be in Love, (13-2), 1976
I Need Your Love Tonight, (8), 1959
I Need You Now, (18-1), 1954-55
I Never Knew Heaven Could Speak, (5), 1939
I Never Mention Your Name, (1), 1943
I Never Said I Love You, (9-2), 1979
In Love in Vain, (13), 1946
In My Arms, (10), 1943
Intermezzo, (19-2), 1941
In the Arms of Love, (18-5), 1966
In the Blue of Evening, (21), 1943
In the Chapel in the Moonlight, (15-3), 1936-37
    Revival: (10), 1954
In the Cool, Cool, Cool of the Evening, (15), 1951
In the Middle of a Dream, (4), 1939
In the Middle of a Kiss, (12-1), 1935
In the Middle of an Island, (8), 1957
In the Misty Moonlight, (12), 1968
In the Mood, (1), 1940
In the Still of the Night, (1), 1938
In the Summertime, (6), 1970
In the Valley of the Moon, (14-3), 1933
In the Year 2525, (11-2), 1969
I Only Have Eyes For You, (18-4), 1934
I Poured My Heart Into a Song, (8), 1939
I Promise You, (1), 1939
I Remember You, (4), 1942
I Said My Pajamas, (9), 1950
I Saw Mommy Kissing Santa Claus, (4-1), 1952-53
I Saw Stars, (8), 1934
I Say a Little Prayer, (14), 1967-68
I See a Million People, (1), 1941
I See the Moon, (3), 1953
I See Your Face Before Me, (1), 1938
I Shall Sing, (6), 1974
I Should Care, (7), 1945
Is It True What They Say About Dixie?, (12-5), 1936
Isle of Capri, (13-4), 1935
Isn't This a Lovely Day?, (8), 1935
Is That All There Is?, (11-3), 1969
I Still Get a Thrill, (8), 1930
I Still Love to Kiss You Goodnight, (3), 1937
I Surrender, Dear, (15-3), 1931
Is You Is Or Is You Ain't My Baby?, (13), 1944
It All Comes Back to Me Now, (16), 1941
It Can't Be Wrong, (19), 1943
It Could Happen to You, (13), 1944
It Doesn't Matter Anymore, (10), 1959
It Don't Matter to Me, (7), 1970

It Had to Be You, (13), 1944
It Happened in Monterey, (11), 1930
I Think I Love You, (13), 1970-71
I Think of You, (10), 1971
It Is No Secret, (6), 1951
It Isn't Fair, (14), 1933
    Revival: (13), 1950
It Looks Like Rain in Cherry Blossom Lane, (13-6), 1937
It Might As Well Be Spring, (17-3), 1945-46
It Must Be Him, (18-6), 1967
It Never Dawned On Me, (1), 1935
It Never Rains in Southern California, (10), 1972-73
It Only Happens When I Dance With You, (4), 1948
It's a Blue World, (9), 1940
It's a Good Day, (11), 1947
It's a Great Feeling, (2), 1949
It's a Hundred to One I'm in Love, (1), 1939
It's All in the Game, (17-8), 1958
It's Almost Tomorrow, (9), 1956
It's Always You, (12), 1943
It's an Old Southern Custom, (2), 1935
It's a Sin to Tell a Lie, (12), 1936
It's a Wonderful World, (1), 1940
It's Been a Long, Long Time, (16-5), 1945-46
It's Been So Long, (10), 1936
It's Dangerous to Love Like This, (1), 1935
It's De-Lovely, (12-1), 1936-37
It's Going to Take Some Time, (11), 1972
It's Impossible, (20-5), 1970-71
It's Just a Matter of Time, (7), 1959
It's Late, (1), 1959
It's Love, Love, Love, (13-3), 1944
It's Magic, (17-2), 1948
It's My Party, (9), 1963
It's My Turn, (10), 1980-81
    (Totals include 1981 carry-over weeks)
It's Never Too Late, (1), 1939
It's Not For Me to Say, (12), 1957
It's Now Or Never, (13-5), 1960
It's One of Those Nights, (17-1), 1972
It's Only a Paper Moon, (14), 1933
It's Only Make Believe, (11), 1958-59
It's Over, (7), 1964
It's Sad to Belong, (17-5), 1977
It's So Peaceful in the Country, (1), 1941
It's the Same Old Dream, (3), 1947
It's the Talk of the Town, (18-1), 1933
It's Too Late, (13-2), 1971
It's Too Soon to Know, (4), 1958
It's Wonderful, (2), 1938
Itsy Bitsy Bikini, (14-1), 1960
It Was Almost Like a Song, (7), 1977
It Was a Very Good Year, (7), 1966
It Was So Beautiful, (12), 1932
I Understand Just How You Feel, (7), 1954
I've Been This Way Before, (8), 1975
I've Got a Date With a Dream, (3), 1938
I've Got a Feeling You're Fooling, (6), 1935
I've Got a Gal in Kalamazoo, (11-1), 1942
I've Got a Lovely Bunch of Cocoanuts, (6), 1950
I've Got a Pocketful of Dreams, (15-4), 1938
I've Got My Eyes On You, (5), 1940
I've Got My Love to Keep Me
    Warm, (7), 1937
    Revival: (11), 1949-50
I've Gotta Be Me, (7), 1968

I've Got You Under My Skin, (12), 1936-37
I've Had It, (4), 1959
i've Heard That Song Before, (15-4), 1943
I've Told Every Little Star, (15-3), 1932-33
Ivory Tower, (10), 1956
Ivy, (3), 1947
I Wanna Be Around, (14), 1963
I Wanna Be Loved, (16), 1950
I Want My Share of Love, (1), 1939
I Want to Be Wanted, (12-2), 1960
I Want to Hold Your Hand, (15-7), 1964
I Want You, I Need You, I Love You, (3), 1956
I Was Lucky, (3), 1935
I Went Out of My Way, (1), 1941
I Went to Your Wedding, (19), 1952-53
I Will Follow Him, (11-2), 1963
I Will Wait For You, (14), 1965-66
I Wished On the Moon, (2), 1935
I Wish I Didn't Love You So, (16-3), 1947
I Wish I Knew, (14), 1945
I Wish I Were Aladdin, (1), 1935
I Wonder, I Wonder, I Wonder, (16-1), 1947
I Wonder Who's Kissing Her Now?, (15-1), 1947
I Won't Dance, (13-2), 1935
I Won't Last a Day Without You, (12-2), 1974
I Won't Mention It Again, (9), 1971
I Won't Tell a Soul, (1), 1938
I Would Be in Love (Anyway), (7), 1970
I Write the Songs, (12-3), 1975-76

J

Jailhouse Rock, (10), 1957
Jambalaya, (17), 1952-53
Java, (14), 1964
Jealous Heart, (10), 1949
Jean, (19-5), 1969
Jeepers Creepers, (12-5), 1938-39
Jersey Bounce, (14), 1942
Jesse, (7), 1973
Jezebel, (4), 1951
Jim, (12), 1941
Jingle, Jangle, Jingle, (14-5), 1942
Johnny Angel, (11-2), 1962
Johnny Doughboy, (14), 1942
Johnny One Time, (9), 1969
Johnny Zero, (7), 1943
Johnson Rag, The, (6), 1950
Julie, Do Ya Love Me?, (8), 1970
June in January, (10-2), 1935
Just a Little Bit South of North Carolina, (9), 1941
Just a Little Fond Affection, (11), 1945-46
Just an Echo in the Valley, (19-3), 1932
Just Another Polka, (3), 1953
Just a Prayer Away, (7), 1945
Just Friends, (13-2), 1932
Just in Time, (7), 1956-57

Just One Look, (6), 1979
Just One More Chance, (14), 1931
Just One Way to Say I Love You, (11), 1949
Just Remember I Love You, (10-2), 1977
Just the Way You Are, (17-5), 1977-78
Just Too Many People, (9), 1975
Just Walking in the Rain, (20-1), 1956-57
Just When I Needed You Most, (11-2), 1979

K

Kansas City, (11-1), 1959
Kansas City Star, (8), 1965
Keep an Eye on Your Heart, (1), 1941
Keep It a Secret, (14), 1953
Keep On Singing, (10-2), 1974
Kentucky Rain, (10), 1970
Kewpie Doll, (10), 1958
Killing Me Softly With His Song, (11-1), 1973
King of the Road, (16-3), 1965
Kiss Me Goodbye, (9), 1968
Kiss Me Goodnight, (1), 1935
Kiss Me Sweet, (2), 1949
Kiss of Fire, (15-7), 1952
Kisses Sweeter Than Wine, (8), 1957-58
Knockin' On Heaven's Door, (12), 1973
Knock, Knock, Who's There?, (1), 1936
Knock Three Times, (12), 1970-71
Knowing Me, Knowing You, (11), 1977
Ko Ko Mo, (13), 1955

L

L.A., Break Down, (10), 1968-69
Lady, (15-2), 1967
Lady From 29 Palms, The, (10), 1947
Lady in Red, The, (8), 1935
Lady Love, (11), 1978
Lady of Spain, (15), 1952-53
Lady, Play Your Mandolin, (6), 1930
Lady's in Love With You, The, (12), 1939
Lambeth Walk, (11), 1938
Lamp Is Low, The, (7), 1939
La Roo, La Roo, Lilli Bolero, (9), 1948
Last Date, (16), 1960-61
Last Farewell, The, (10), 1975
Last Kiss, (11), 1964

Last Mile Home, The, (1), 1949
Last Night, (8), 1939
Last Roundup, The, (16-3), 1933
Last Song, (8-1), 1973
Last Time I Saw Her, The, (15), 1971
Last Time I Saw Him, (12-4), 1974
Last Waltz, The, (17), 1967-68
Last Word in Lonesome Is Me, The, (7), 1966
Late in the Evening, (10), 1980
Laughing On the Outside, (12-1), 1946
Laughter in the Rain, (16-3), 1974-75
Laura, (14-1), 1945
Lavender Blue, (14), 1948-49
La Vie En Rose, (17-1), 1950
Lay Some Happiness On Me, (5), 1967
Lazy Bones, (15-5), 1933
Leader of the Pack, (11), 1964-65
Lead Me On, (19-7), 1979
Leanin' On the Old Top Rail, (2), 1940
Learnin' the Blues, (16-1), 1955
Learn to Croon, (9), 1933
Leave Me Alone, (12-3), 1973-74
Leaving On a Jet Plane, (14-4), 1969-70
Lesson, The, (8), 1968
Let 'Em In, (11), 1976
Let It Be, (10-4), 1970
Let It Snow! Let It Snow! Let It Snow!, (13-2), 1946
Let Me Be There, (11), 1973-74
Let Me Go, Lover, (15-2), 1954-55
Let Me Go to Him, (9), 1970
Let Me Love You Tonight, (6), 1944
Let Me Whisper, (2), 1938
Let's All Sing Like the Birdies Sing, (5), 1932
Let's Call the Whole Thing Off, (1), 1937
Let's Dream This One Out, (1), 1941
Let's Face the Music and Dance, (7), 1936
Let's Fall in Love, (12-2), 1934
Let's Get Away From It All, (2), 1941
Let's Get Lost, (12-1), 1943
Let's Have Another Cup of Coffee, (14-2), 1932
Let's Put Out the Lights, (14), 1932
Let's Sail to Dreamland, (1), 1938
Let's Sing Again, (1), 1936
Let's Swing It, (1), 1935
Let's Take an Old-Fashioned Walk, (10), 1949
Let's Take the Long Way Home, (2), 1945
Letter, The, (6), 1967
Let There Be Love, (6), 1940
Let Your Love Flow, (13), 1976
Let Yourself Go, (7), 1936
Liechtensteiner Polka, (1), 1958
Life Can Be Beautiful, (1), 1947
Life Is a Song, (10-2), 1935
Life Is Just a Bowl of Cherries, (9), 1931
Life Is So Peculiar, (1), 1950
Light My Fire, (8), 1967
Lights Out, (12-2), 1936
Like a Sad Song, (9), 1976
Lilacs in the Rain, (12), 1939-40
Linda, (19-4), 1947
Linger in My Arms a Little Longer, Baby, (3), 1946
Lion Sleeps Tonight, The, (14), 1961-62
Lisbon Antigua, (19-4), 1956
Little Bird Told Me, A, (16-3), 1948-49
Little Bit Independent, A, (7-2), 1935-36
Little Bitty Tear, A, (13), 1962

M

Main Event, (11), 1979
Mairzy Doats, (13-1), 1944
Make Believe Island, (13-2), 1940
Make It With You, (14-1), 1970
Make Love to Me, (19), 1954
Make Someone Happy, (16), 1961
Make the World Go Away, (15), 1965-66
Make Yourself Comfortable, (8), 1955
Mama Can't Buy You Love, (10-1), 1979
Mama Inez, (7), 1931
Mama, That Moon Is Here Again, (1), 1938
Mame, (16), 1966
Mam'selle, (19-3), 1947
Managua, Nicaragua, (14), 1947
Manana, (14-1), 1948
Man and a Woman, A, (15-2), 1967
Man and His Dream, A, (5), 1939
Mandy, (13-2), 1974-75
Manhattan Serenade, (13), 1942
Man Who Shot Liberty Valance, The, (8), 1962
Man Without Love, A, (14), 1968
Man With the Banjo, (6), 1954
Man With the Mandolin, (8), 1939
Many Times, (11), 1953-54
Marching Along Together, (9), 1933
Maria Elena, (22-2), 1941
        Revival: (15), 1963-64
Marianne, (14-3), 1957
Marshmallow World, A, (11), 1950-51
Masquerade, (14), 1932
Masquerade Is Over, The, (8), 1939
Matchmaker, Matchmaker, (7), 1964-65
Maybe, (12-3), 1940
Maybe It's Because, (9), 1949
Maybe You'll Be There, (21), 1948-49
May I Never Love Again, (3), 1941
Me and Julio Down By the Schoolyard, (9), 1972
Me and Mrs. Jones, (11-2), 1973
Me and My Arrow, (11), 1971
Me and My Melinda, (1), 1942
Me and the Moon, (9), 1936
Me and You and a Dog Named Boo, (11), 1971
Meet Mr. Callaghan, (4), 1952
Melancholy Mood, (2), 1939
Melodie D'Amour, (6), 1957
Melody From the Sky, A, (9-1), 1936
Melody of Love, (23-6), 1955
Memories, (5), 1969
Memories Are Made of This, (19-4), 1955-56
Men in My Little Girl's Life, The, (18-2), 1966
Merry-Go-Round Broke Down, The, (10), 1937
Mexico, (5), 1961
Michael, (14-2), 1961
Michelle, (16), 1966
Mickey Mouse's Birthday Party, (1), 1936
Midnight At the Oasis, (11), 1974
Midnight Blue, (11-3), 1975
Midnight Cowboy, (13), 1969-70
Midnight in Moscow, (6), 1962
Midnight Masquerade, (3), 1947
Milkman, Keep Those Bottles Quiet, (7), 1944
Million Dreams Ago, A, (1), 1940
Mimi, (7), 1932
Miss You, (11), 1942
Mister and Mississippi, (12), 1951
Mister Blue, (14-1), 1959-60

Mister Custer, (6-1), 1960
Mister Five by Five, (10), 1942-43
Mister Lonely, (10-3), 1964-65
Mister Sandman, (23-8), 1954-55
Mister Tambourine Man, (13), 1965
Mister Wonderful, (6), 1956
Misty, (26), 1959-60
Mockin'bird Hill, (19-3), 1951
Mockingbird, (17), 1963
Moments to Remember, (14), 1955-56
Moment to Moment, (12), 1966
Mona Lisa, (20-8), 1950
Monday, Monday, (10-3), 1966
Monster Mash, (7), 1962
Moonglow, (12), 1934
        Revival: (16-3), 1956
Moon Got in My Eyes, The, (7), 1937
Moon Is a Silver Dollar, The, (3), 1939
Moonlight and Shadows, (10), 1937
Moonlight Becomes You, (14-2), 1943
Moonlight Cocktail, (13), 1942
Moonlight Feels Right, (13), 1976
Moonlight Gambler, (8), 1957
Moonlight Mood, (6), 1943
Moonlight On the Colorado, (9), 1930
Moonlight Serenade, (3), 1939
Moon Love, (12-4), 1939
Moon Over Miami, (10-1), 1936
Moon River, (24-9), 1961-62
Moon Was Yellow, The, (7), 1934
More, (25-8), 1963
More and More, (15), 1945
More I See You, The, (23-1), 1945
More Love, (10), 1980
More, More, More, (4), 1976
More Than I Can Say, (15-4), 1980-81
        (Totals include 1981 carry-over weeks)
More Than You Know, (5), 1930
Moritat, (11), 1956
Mornin', Beautiful, (6), 1975
Morning Dance, (11-1), 1979
Morning Has Broken, (10), 1972
Morning Side of the Mountain, (5), 1951
Most Beautiful Girl, The, (15-3), 1973-74
Most of All, (11), 1970-71
Mother-in-Law, (6), 1961
Mountain's High, The, (10), 1961
Mrs. Brown, You've Got a Lovely Daughter, (8-1), 1965
Mrs. Robinson, (8), 1968
Mule Train, (10-1), 1949-50
Music Box Dancer, (9), 1979
Music From Across the Way, (11), 1972
Music Goes Round and Round, The, (6-3), 1936
Music, Maestro, Please, (12-4), 1938
Music, Music, Music, (12), 1950
Music to Watch Girls By, (14), 1967
Muskrat Love, (15-5), 1976-77
My Adobe Hacienda, (13), 1947
My Angel Baby, (9-1), 1978
My Baby Just Cares For Me, (2), 1930
My Boy, (7), 1975
My Boyfriend's Back, (12), 1963
My Cabin of Dreams, (11), 1937
My Cup Runneth Over, (17-4), 1967
My Darling, My Darling, (13), 1948-49

My Devotion, (15-4), 1942
My Dreams Are Getting Better All
    the Time, (17-3), 1945
My Elusive Dreams, (5), 1970
My Eyes Adored You, (12), 1974-75
My Favorite Things, (18), 1959-60
My Foolish Heart, (21-9), 1950
My Future Just Passed, (8), 1930
My Girl, (11), 1965
My Girl Bill, (6), 1974
My Guy, (10), 1964
My Happiness, (20), 1948
    Revival: (9), 1959
My Heart Belongs to Me, (16-4), 1977
My Heart Belongs to Only You, (6), 1964
My Heart Cries For You, (16-1), 1951
My Heart Has a Mind of Its Own, (11-3), 1960
My Heart Is An Open Book, (7), 1959
My Heart Tells Me, (19-9), 1943-44
My Ideal, (16), 1930-31
    Revival: (7), 1944
My Life, (12), 1978-79
My Little Town, (10-1), 1975-76
My Love, (11), 1973
My Margarita, (1), 1938
My Maria, (12-2), 1973
My Melody of Love, (12-2), 1974-75
My Moonlight Madonna, (16), 1933
My Old Flame, (5), 1934
My One and Only Highland Fling, (1), 1949
My Own, (3), 1938
My Prayer, (14), 1939-40
    Revival: (14-1), 1956
My Reverie, (13-8), 1938-39
My Shining Hour, (2), 1944
My Shy Violet, (6), 1968
My Silent Love, (16-5), 1932
My Sister and I, (14-2), 1941
My Song, (7), 1931
My Special Angel, (7), 1957-58
    Revival: (15), 1968
My Truly, Truly Fair, (14), 1951
My Way, (13), 1969
My Way of Life, (9), 1968

Never Gonna Fall in Love Again, (13-4), 1976
Never in a Million Years, (13), 1937
Never Knew Love Like This Before, (14), 1980-81
    (Totals include 1981 carry-over weeks)
Never My Love, (16), 1967
Never On Sunday, (14), 1960
Nevertheless, (20-1), 1950-51
New Kid in Town, (17), 1976-77
New Moon and An Old Serenade, A, (5), 1939
New Sun in the Sky, (6), 1931
New World Coming, (8), 1970
Next Hundred Years, The, (8), 1978
Nice 'n' Easy, (11), 1960
Nice Work If You Can Get It, (10), 1937-38
Nickel Song, The, (4), 1972
Night and Day, (18-5), 1932-33
Night Before Christmas, The, (1), 1938
Nightingale, (11-2), 1975
Nightingale Sang in Berkeley
    Square, A, (7), 1940-41
Night Is Young and You're So
    Beautiful, The, (13), 1936-37
Night the Lights Went Out in Georgia, The, (10), 1973
Night They Drove Old Dixie Down, The, (17-5), 1971
Night Was Made For Love, The, (4), 1931
Ninety-Nine Miles From L.A., (10-1), 1975
Ninety-Six Tears, (4), 1966
Nobody Does It Better, (18-6), 1977
No Can Do, (1), 1945
No Love At All, (8), 1971
No Love, No Nothin', (12), 1944
No Night So Long, (13-5), 1980
No, No, a Thousand Times No, (3), 1934
No, Not Much, (9), 1956
No Other Love, (21-3), 1953
No Other One, (3), 1935
No Regrets, (4), 1936
North to Alaska, (9), 1960
No Strings, (1), 1935
No-Tell Lover, (7), 1979
No Two People, (1), 1953
Now I Lay Me Down to Dream, (1), 1940
Now Is the Hour, (22-10), 1948
Now It Can Be Told, (9), 1938
Now's the Time to Fall in Love, (9), 1931-32
Now That I Need You, (1), 1949
Number 10 Lullaby Lane, (7), 1941

N

Nadia's Theme, (11), 1976
Nature Boy, (14-6), 1948
Naughty Lady of Shady Lane, The, (14), 1954-55
Nearness of You, The, (5), 1940
Near You, (19-6), 1947-48
Neither One of Us, (8), 1973
Never Be Anyone Else But You, (8), 1959
Never Be the Same, (13-4), 1980-81
    (Totals include 1981 carry-over weeks)
Never Ending Song of Love, (16), 1971

O

Object of My Affection, The, (17-3), 1934-35
Ode to Billy Joe, (17-4), 1967
Off Shore, (3), 1954
Of Thee I Sing, (16), 1932
Oh!, (16), 1953
Oh, Babe, What Would You Say?, (7), 1973
Oh, But I Do!, (11), 1947

Oh Happy Day, (8), 1953
Oh, Johnny, Oh, (11), 1939-40
Oh, Look At Me Now, (8), 1941
Oh, Ma, Ma, (3), 1938
Oh, My Papa, (17), 1954
Oh, Pretty Woman, (12-4), 1964
Oh, What a Beautiful Mornin', (15), 1943-44
Oh! What It Seemed to Be, (17-8), 1946
Oh, You Crazy Moon, (8), 1939
Old Cape Cod, (10), 1957
Old-Fashioned Love Song, An, (12-2), 1971-72
Old Lamplighter, The, (14), 1946-47
Old Master Painter, The, (14), 1949-50
Old Piano Roll Blues, The, (11), 1950
Old Spinning Wheel, The, (5), 1933
Ole Buttermilk Sky, (19-6), 1946-47
Ole Faithful, (14-1), 1933
On a Clear Day You Can See Forever, (15-5), 1965-66
On and On, (14), 1977
On a Slow Boat to China, (17-2), 1948-49
Once in a Lifetime, (6), 1962
Once in Awhile, (11-7), 1937-38
Once Upon a Midnight, (1), 1935
Once Upon a Time, (17), 1962
One Day of Your Life, (11), 1970
One Dozen Roses, (15-2), 1942
One Less Bell to Answer, (15-2), 1970-71
One Mint Julep, (10), 1961
One Night, (8), 1958-59
One Night in Monte Carlo, (1), 1935
One Night of Love, (15-3), 1934
One Rose, The, (6), 1937
One-Two-Three, (14), 1965-66
One-zy, Two-zy, (7), 1946
Only Forever, (13-3), 1940
Only Love Is Real, (15), 1976
Only Yesterday, (11-2), 1975
Only You, (8), 1955-56
On the Atchison, Topeka and Santa Fe, (14), 1945
On the Beach at Bali Bali, (9), 1936
On the Good Ship Lollipop, (6), 1935
On the Isle of May, (9), 1940
On the Road Again, (13), 1980-81
    (Totals include 1981 carry-over weeks)
On the Sentimental Side, (5), 1938
On the Street Where You Live, (22-1), 1956
On the Sunny Side of the Street, (12), 1930
On Top of Old Smoky, (13-2), 1951
On Treasure Island, (14-1), 1935-36
Ooh, Baby, Baby, (11), 1978-79
Open the Door, Richard, (1), 1947
Open Up Your Heart, (4), 1955
Orange Blossom Lane, (1), 1941
Orange-Colored Sky, (9), 1950
Orchids in the Moonlight, (7), 1934
Organ Grinder's Swing, (8), 1936-37
Other Man's Grass Is Always Greener, The, (2), 1968
Our Day Will Come, (15-2), 1963
Our Lady of Fatima, (2), 1950
Our Love, (10-2), 1939
Our Love Affair, (11), 1940
Our Love, Don't Throw It All Away, (12), 1978-79
Out in the Cold Again, (9), 1934
Out of Nowhere, (13-4), 1931
Out of the Question, (10), 1973
Out of This World, (1), 1945

Outside of Heaven, (7), 1952-53
Over the Rainbow, (15-7), 1939

P

Page Miss Glory, (4), 1935
Painting the Clouds With Sunshine, (12), 1930
Paloma Blanca, (12-2), 1976
Papa Loves Mambo, (15), 1954-55
Paper Doll, (23-3), 1943-44
Paper Mache, (10), 1970
Paradise, (21-7), 1931-32
Pardon My Southern Accent, (2), 1934
Paris in the Spring, (8-1), 1935
Party Doll, (11), 1957
Party's Over, The, (6), 1956-57
Pass Me By, (10), 1965
Patricia, (15-2), 1958
Peanut Vendor, The, (19), 1930-31
Peggy Sue, (7), 1957-58
Peg O' My Heart, (23-10), 1947
Pennies From Heaven, (14-4), 1936-37
Penny a Kiss, A, (7), 1951
Penny Serenade, (10), 1939
People, (23-5), 1964
People Will Say We're in Love, (30-3), 1943-44
Peppermint Twist, (14-1), 1961-62
Perfidia, (17), 1941
Personality, (10), 1946
Peter Cottontail, (2), 1950
Peter Piper, (8), 1979-80
Petite Fleur, (4), 1959
Photograph, (9), 1973-74
Piccolino, (1), 1935
Picnic, (16-3), 1956
Pieces of April, (8), 1973
Pink Shoelaces, (12), 1959
Pistol-Packin' Mama, (15), 1943-44
Pittsburgh, Pennsylvania, (8), 1952
Play a Simple Melody, (12), 1950
Play, Fiddle, Play, (6), 1932
Playground in My Mind, (6), 1973
Playmates, (11), 1940
Please, (16-5), 1932-33
Please Be Kind, (14-1), 1938
Please Believe Me, (4), 1936
Please Don't Talk About Me, (9), 1931
Please, Mister, Please, (11-5), 1975
Please, Mr. Postman, (13), 1961-62
    Revival: (9-2), 1975
Please, Mr. Sun, (14), 1952
Please Please Me, (10), 1964
Poetry Man, (11), 1975
Poinciana, (14), 1944
Pony Time, (8), 1961
Poor Little Fool, (9-1), 1958

Poor People of Paris, (15-6), 1956
Powder Your Face With Sunshine, (15-2), 1949
Practice Makes Perfect, (15-2), 1940
Praise the Lord and Pass the
    Ammunition, (12), 1942-43
Pretend, (17-3), 1953
Pretty Kitty Blue Eyes, (2), 1944
Prisoner of Love, (20), 1946
Problems, (7), 1958-59
Promises, (11), 1979
Promises, Promises, (12), 1968-69
Proud Mary, (10), 1969
Proud One, The, (7), 1975
P.S. I Love You, (12), 1953
P.T. 109, (11), 1962
Puff, the Magic Dragon, (16), 1963
Purple People Eater, The, (11-6), 1958
Put On a Happy Face, (18), 1960
Put That Ring On My Finger, (4), 1945-46
Put Your Arms Around Me, Honey, (15), 1943

Q

Quarter to Three, (12), 1961
Quentin's Theme, (11), 1969
Quicker Than You Can Say Jack Robinson, (1), 1935
Quiet Village, (10), 1959

R

Rag Doll, (9), 1964
Rag Mop, (6), 1950
Rags to Riches, (15-2), 1953-54
Rainbow, (5), 1957
Raindrops Keep Fallin' On My Head, (15-5), 1969-70
Raining in My Heart, (6), 1959
Rain in My Heart, (14-3), 1969
Rainy Day People, (10-1), 1975
Rainy Days and Monday, (12-6), 1971
Rainy Night in Georgia, (12), 1970
Ramblin' Rose, (18-2), 1962
Raunchy, (9), 1957-58
Reach Out, I'll Be There, (12), 1966
Ready For the Times to Get Better, (19), 1978
Ready to Take a Chance Again, (14), 1978
Red Roses For a Blue Lady, (12), 1949

Red Sails in the Sunset, (15-4), 1935-36
Release Me, (13), 1967
Remember Me?, (11-1), 1937
Remember Pearl Harbor, (4), 1942
Remember When, (2), 1945
Rendezvous With a Dream, A, (4), 1936
Restless, (1), 1935
Return to Me, (8), 1958
Return to Sender, (14), 1962-63
Reunited, (10), 1979
Rhinestone Cowboy, (16), 1975
Rhythm and Romance, (1), 1935
Rhythm in My Nursery Rhymes, (1), 1936
Rhythm of the Rain, (13), 1963
Ricochet, (16-1), 1953-54
Riders in the Sky, (14-3), 1949
Right Down the Line, (13-4), 1978
Right Time of the Night, (12), 1977
Ringo, (13-4), 1964
Rise, (15-1), 1979
Rise 'n' Shine, (9), 1932-33
River Stay 'Way From My Door, (3), 1931
Robins and Roses, (9), 1936
Rock and Roll Waltz, (14-3), 1956
Rock Around the Clock, (16-2), 1955
Rockin' Robin, (7), 1958
Rocky Mountain High, (11), 1973
Roll Along Prairie Moon, (2), 1935
Room Full of Roses, (16-2), 1949
Rosalie, (12-2), 1937-38
Rose Ann of Charing Cross, (4), 1943
Rose in Her Hair, The, (1), 1935
Rose O'Day, (10), 1942
Rose, Rose, I Love You, (2), 1951
Roses Are Red, (16-4), 1962
Roses in December, (10), 1937
Roses in the Rain, (2), 1947
Rose, The, (18-5), 1980
Round and Round, (15-5), 1957
Roving Kind, The, (2), 1951
Ruby, (16), 1953
Rudolph, the Red-Nosed Reindeer, (7), 1949-50
Rum and Coca-Cola, (11), 1945
Rumors Are Flying, (15-2), 1946-47
Runaround Sue, (12-2), 1961
Runaway, (18-5), 1961
Running Bear, (18-3), 1960
Running Scared, (8), 1961
Run to Him, (10), 1961-62
Run to Me, (9), 1972

S

Sabre Dance, (12), 1948
Sad Movies, (13), 1961
Sail Along Silvery Moon, (13), 1958
Sailboat in the Moonlight, A, (14-3), 1937
Sam, (13), 1977
Same Old Story, The, (2), 1940
Sam's Song, (13), 1950
San Fernando Valley, (13), 1944
Santa Claus Is Coming to Town, (8-1), 1934-35
Satan Takes a Holiday, (1), 1937
Satisfaction, (14), 1965
Saturday Night, (11), 1945
Saturday Night at the World, (11), 1968-69
Save the Last Dance For Me, (11-3), 1960
Save Your Kisses For Me, (6), 1976
Say, Has Anybody Seen My Sweet
    Gypsy Rose?, (15-4), 1973
Say It, (7), 1940
Say It Isn't So, (18-6), 1932
Say Maybe, (6), 1979
Says My Heart, (12-4), 1938
Say Something Sweet to Your
    Sweetheart, (1), 1948
Say You'll Stay Until Tomorrow, (13), 1977
Say You're Mine Again, (12), 1953
Scarborough Fair, (6), 1968
Scatterbrain, (13-6), 1939-40
School Day, (3), 1957
Sea of Love, (18), 1959
Seasons in the Sun, (9), 1974
Seattle, (10), 1969
Second Avenue, (5), 1974
Second-Hand Rose, (7), 1966
Second Time Around, The, (13), 1960
Secret Love, (18-7), 1954
Secretly, (14), 1958
Seein' Is Believin', (1), 1935
Seems Like Old Times, (2), 1946
Send a Little Love My Way, (11), 1973
Send One Your Love, (12-4), 1979-80
Sentimental Journey, (16-5), 1945
Sentimental Me, (10), 1950
Separate Ways, (5), 1973
September in the Rain, (14-5), 1937
September Morn', (12), 1980
Serenade in Blue, (10), 1942
Serenade in the Night, (1), 1937
Serenade of the Bells, (18), 1947-48
Seven Lonely Days, (5), 1953
Seventeen, (14), 1955
Shadow of Your Smile, The, (17-6), 1965-66
Shadows in the Moonlight, (16-3), 1979
Shadow Waltz, (13), 1933

Shake Down the Stars, (3), 1940
Shanghai, (16), 1951
Shanty in Old Shanty Town, A, (21-7), 1932
Sh-Boom, (14), 1954
She Believes in Me, (14-2), 1979
She Didn't Say Yes, (7), 1931
Sheila, (19), 1962
She'll Always Remember, (2), 1942
She Loves You, (15-2), 1964
Shepherd Serenade, (13), 1941-42
Sherry, (18-5), 1962
She's a Lady, (8), 1971
She's a Latin From Manhattan, (6), 1935
She's Always a Woman, (9), 1978
She Shall Have Music, (6), 1936
She's Out of My Life, (14), 1980
Shifting, Whispering Sands, (4), 1955
Ships, (7), 1979
Shoo Fly Pie, (8), 1946
Shoo Shoo Baby, (18-2), 1943-44
Shop Around, (8), 1976
Short Shorts, (2), 1958
Should I?, (12), 1930
Should've Never Let You Go, (9), 1980
Shrimp Boats, (16), 1951-52
Shrine of St. Cecilia, The, (9), 1942
Shuffle Off to Buffalo, (11-4), 1933
Side by Side, (12), 1953
Sierra Sue, (12-1), 1940
Silhouettes, (10), 1957-58
Silly Love Songs, (10), 1976
Sin, (23-7), 1951-52
Since I Don't Have You, (5), 1979
Sincerely, (16), 1955
Sing, (11-2), 1973
Sing an Old-Fashioned Song to a Young
    Sophisticated Lady, (1), 1936
Sing, Baby, Sing, (8), 1936
Singing Hills, The, (8), 1940
Singing the Blues, (18-7), 1956-57
Sing Something Simple, (13), 1930
Sink the Bismarck, (12), 1960
Sinner Kissed an Angel, A, (1), 1941
Sioux City Sue, (14), 1946
Sitting By the Window, (2), 1950
Sittin' On the Dock of the Bay, (13-2), 1968
Six Lessons From Madame LaZonga, (1), 1940
Sixteen Candles, (8), 1959
Sixteen Tons, (19-7), 1955-56
Sixty Seconds Got Together, (3), 1938
Skokiaan, (9), 1954
Skybird, (8), 1975-76
Sky High, (5), 1975-76
Skylark, (12), 1942
Sleep Walk, (16-2), 1959
Sleepy Lagoon, (18-3), 1942
Sleighride in July, (2), 1945
Slipping Around, (13), 1949-50
Slip Slidin' Away, (12), 1977-78
Slow Poke, (21-7), 1951-52
Slumming On Park Avenue, (1), 1937
Small Fry, (2), 1938
Small World, (15), 1959
Smile, Darn Ya, Smile, (6), 1931
Smoke Gets in Your Eyes, (16-5), 1933-34
    Revival: (12-4), 1958-59

Snowbird, (15-5), 1970
So Beats My Heart For You, (13-2), 1930
So Far, (12), 1947-48
So Far, So Good, (1), 1940
Soft Lights and Sweet Music, (16-4), 1932
So Help Me, (11), 1938
So In Love, (12), 1949
Soldier Boy, (11-2), 1962
Solitaire, (14-3), 1975
Solitude, (9), 1935
So Long, (3), 1951
So Madly in Love, (2), 1952
So Many Memories, (1), 1937
Somebody Else Is Taking My Place, (12-3), 1942
Someday, (12), 1949
Someday I'll Find You, (12-4), 1931
Someday I'll Meet You Again, (3), 1944
Some Enchanted Evening, (23-10), 1949
Someone Like You, (8), 1949
Some Sunday Morning, (1), 1946
Something, (11), 1970
Something Better to Do, (9-3), 1975
Something's Gotta Give, (11-1), 1955
Something to Remember You By, (19-5), 1930-31
Somethin' Stupid, (12-5), 1967
Sometime, (2), 1950
Sometimes, (1), 1942
Somewhere Along the Way, (17), 1952
Somewhere in the Night, (1), 1946
Somewhere My Love, (17-6), 1966
So Much in Love, (14), 1963
Songbird, (11-2), 1978
Song From Moulin Rouge, (25-8), 1953
Song Is You, The, (16-2), 1932-33
Song Sung Blue, (18-6), 1972
Soon, (10-1), 1935
Sooner or Later, (5), 1947
Sophisticated Lady, (13-2), 1933
So Rare, (11-1), 1937
     Revival: (14), 1957
Sorry Seems to Be the Hardest Word, (12), 1976-77
Soul and Inspiration, (17-3), 1966
Sound of Music, The, (20), 1959-60
Sounds of Silence, The, (5), 1965-66
South America, Take It Away, (13), 1946
Southern Nights, (15-5), 1977
South of the Border, (15-5), 1939-40
South Sea Island Magic, (5), 1936
So You're the One, (16), 1940-41
Spanish Eyes, (13), 1966
Spanish Flea, (5), 1966
Sparrow in the Treetop, (7), 1951
Speaking of Heaven, (2), 1939
Speak Low, (4), 1943
Speak To Me of Love, (12), 1932
Spinning Wheel, (9-2), 1969
Spoonful of Sugar, A, (7), 1965
Stagger Lee, (9-3), 1959
Stairway to the Stars, (12-4), 1939
Stand By Me, (12), 1980
Stand By Your Man, (12), 1969
Standing On the Corner, (10), 1956
Stand Tall, (9), 1976-77
Stardust, (15), 1931-32
Stardust On the Moon, (2), 1937
Star Eyes, (2), 1944

Star Fell Out of Heaven, A, (10), 1936
Star Gazing, (1), 1935
Starlit Hour, (9), 1940
Stars Fell On Alabama, (11-3), 1934
Stars Will Remember, The, (4), 1947
Stay, (12-1), 1960-61
Stay As Sweet As You Are, (9-4), 1934-35
Stay Awhile, (10), 1971
Steal Away, (12), 1980
Stein Song, The, (10), 1930
Steppin' Out, (9), 1974
Step to the Rear, (11), 1968
Still, (9), 1979-80
Stompin' at the Savoy, (1), 1936
Stones, (12), 1971-72
Stoney End, (15), 1970-71
Stop and Smell the Roses, (10-1), 1974
Stop Beating Round the Mulberry Bush, (10), 1938
Stop! In the Name of Love, (16-2), 1965
Stop! It's Wonderful, (2), 1939-40
Stop! You're Breaking My Heart, (1), 1937
Stormy Weather, (13-6), 1933
Straight Life, The, (12), 1968-69
Strange Enchantment, (5), 1939
Strange Interlude, (3), 1932
Strange Music, (3), 1944
Stranger in Paradise, (19-6), 1953-54
Stranger in Town, A, (1), 1945
Stranger On the Shore, (16-2), 1962
Strangers in the Night, (17-7), 1966
Street of Dreams, (10), 1933
Strike Up the Band, (5), 1930
Stripper, The, (18-1), 1962
Stroll, The, (5), 1958
Stuck in the Middle With You, (4), 1973
Stuck On You, (13-4), 1960
Stumblin' In, (10), 1979
Suddenly, (14), 1980-81
    (Totals include 1981 carry-over weeks)
Suddenly There's a Valley, (11), 1955-56
Sugar Shack, (12-5), 1963
Sugartime, (13-2), 1958
Sugar Town, (14-2), 1967
Sukiyaki, (13-3), 1963
Summer Breeze, (6), 1972
Summer Souvenirs, (2), 1938
Summer Wind, (13), 1965
Sunday in the Park, (1), 1938
Sunday, Monday or Always, (18-6), 1943
Sundown, (10-1), 1974
Sunflower, (13), 1949
Sunny, (14), 1966
Sunny Side Up, (2), 1930
Sunrise Serenade, (15), 1939
Sunrise, Sunset, (10), 1964-65
Sunshine Cake, (2), 1950
Sunshine On My Shoulders, (12-2), 1974
Superstar, (18-5), 1971-72
Surf City, (13), 1963
Surrender, (16), 1946
Susie Darlin', (2), 1958
Swayin' to the Music, (10), 1977
Sweet and Gentle, (4), 1955
Sweet and Lovely, (19-3), 1931
Sweet and Slow, (1), 1935
Sweet As a Song, (4), 1938

Sweet Caroline, (12), 1969
Sweet Dreams, Sweetheart, (14), 1945
Sweetest Sounds, The, (19), 1962
Sweethearts Forever, (11), 1932
Sweetheart Tree, The, (4), 1965
Sweet Is the Word For You, (1), 1937
Sweet Leilani, (12), 1937
Sweet Little Sixteen, (3), 1958
Sweet Lorraine, (3), 1944
Sweet Maria, (4), 1967
Sweet Memories, (12), 1968
Sweet Someone, (2), 1938
Sweet Surrender, (7-2), 1972-73
Sweet, Sweet Smile, (8), 1978
Sweet Violets, (10), 1951
Swinging On a Star, (20), 1944
Symphony, (20-7), 1945-46
Syncopated Clock, (1), 1951

T

Take a Letter, Maria, (12), 1969-70
Take Good Care of My Baby, (13-4), 1961
Take It to the Limit, (11), 1976
Take Me, (6), 1942
Take Me Back to My Boots and Saddle, (8), 1935-36
Take Me Home, Country Roads, (16), 1971
Take My Heart, (12-2), 1936
Takes Two to Tango, (1), 1952
Taking a Chance On Love, (17), 1943
Talking in Your Sleep, (13), 1978
Talk It Over in the Morning, (8), 1971
Talk to the Animals, (14), 1967-68
Talk Until Daylight, (6), 1969
Tallahassee, (6), 1947
Tammy, (15-10), 1957
Tangerine, (14), 1942
Taste of Honey, A, (12-2), 1965
Teach Me Tonight, (13-1), 1954-55
Tea For Two Cha-Cha, (13), 1958
Tears From My Inkwell, (1), 1939
Tears On My Pillow, (6), 1958
Teddy Bear, (10), 1957
Teen-Age Crush, (5), 1957
Teen Angel, (17-2), 1960
Tell Laura I Love Her, (8), 1960
Tell Me a Story, (2), 1953
Tell Me That You Love Me, (6), 1935
Tell Me Why, (13), 1952
Tell Me You're Mine, (5), 1953
Telstar, (7), 1962-63
Temptation, (19-3), 1934
Ten Cents a Dance, (7), 1930
Tender Is the Night, (8), 1962
Tennessee Birdwalk, (9), 1970
Tennessee Waltz, (20-6), 1950-51
Tequila, (13-3), 1958

Terry's Theme From Limelight, (4), 1953
Thanks a Million, (6), 1935-36
Thanks For Everything, (7), 1939
Thanks For the Memory, (10-3), 1938
Thank You For a Lovely Evening, (11), 1934
That'll Be the Day, (5), 1957
That Lucky Old Sun, (15-3), 1949-50
That Old Black Magic, (15), 1943
That Old Feeling, (12-4), 1937
That's All I Want From You, (12), 1955
That's Amore, (16), 1953-54
That's For Me, (16), 1945-46
That's Life, (15-4), 1966-67
That's My Desire, (16-2), 1947
That's the Way I've Always Heard
   It Should Be, (14), 1971
That Sunday, That Summer, (12), 1963
That's What You Think, (1), 1935
That's Why Darkies Were Born, (4), 1931
Theme From Mahogany, (12-2), 1975-76
Theme From A Summer Place, (19-9), 1960
Theme From Summer of '42, (17), 1971-72
Theme From The Apartment, (14), 1960
Theme From Valley of the Dolls, (13), 1968
Them There Eyes, (10), 1931
Then Came You, (7), 1974
Then You Can Tell Me Goodbye, (9), 1968
There Are Such Things, (18-6), 1942-43
There Goes That Song Again, (13), 1944-45
There I Go, (19-4), 1940-41
There, I've Said It Again, (11), 1945
   Revival: (19-3), 1963-64
There'll Be Some Changes Made, (16), 1941
There Must Be a Way, (6), 1945
There's a Gold Mine in the Sky, (14), 1937-38
There's a Harbor of Dreamboats, (2), 1943
There's a Kind of Hush, (14), 1967
There's a Lull in My Life, (8), 1937
There's Always a Happy Ending, (1), 1936
There's a Small Hotel, (6), 1936
There's a Star-Spangled Banner Waving
   Somewhere, (1), 1942
There's Honey On the Moon Tonight, (1), 1938
There's No Tomorrow, (10), 1950
There's No You, (3), 1945
There's Something in the Air, (4), 1937
There's Yes, Yes in Your Eyes, (11), 1949
There Will Never Be Another You, (3), 1942
These Boots Are Made For Walkin', (11-2), 1966
These Foolish Things, (12-2), 1936
They Can't Take That Away From Me, (7), 1937
They're Either Too Young Or Too Old, (14), 1943-44
They Say, (4), 1939
They Say It's Wonderful, (25-4), 1946
They Were Doin' the Mambo, (5), 1954
Things I Love, The, (18), 1941
Things We Did Last Summer, The, (10), 1946-47
Thing, The, (11), 1950-51
Thinking of You, (14), 1950-51
Third Man Theme, The, (20), 1950
This Can't Be Love, (11), 1938-39
This Changing World, (2), 1940
This Diamond Ring, (9), 1965
This Guy's in Love With You, (17-9), 1968
This Is Always, (8), 1946
This Is It, (1), 1939

This Is My Song, (20-5), 1967
This Is No Dream, (2), 1939
This Is No Laughing Matter, (4), 1942
This Is Worth Fighting For, (2), 1942
This Love of Mine, (12), 1941-42
This Moment in Time, (9-3), 1979
This Night Won't Last Forever, (12), 1979
This Ole House, (17), 1954-55
This Time It's Real, (1), 1938
This Year's Kisses, (9-3), 1937
Thoroughly Modern Millie, (14), 1967
Those Lazy-Hazy-Crazy Days of Summer, (14), 1963
Those Were the Days, (13-4), 1968-69
Thousand Stars, A, (13), 1960-61
Three Bells, The, (18-4), 1959
Three Coins in the Fountain, (15-4), 1954
Three Little Fishes, (9), 1939
Three Little Sisters, (8), 1942
Three Little Words, (8-3), 1930
Three On a Match, (6), 1932
Three's a Crowd, (4), 1932
Three Times a Lady, (14-3), 1978
Three Times in Love, (13-1), 1980
Thrilled, (5), 1935
Thrill Is Gone, The, (4), 1931
Thunderball, (8), 1966
Ticket to Ride, (9-2), 1965
Tie a Yellow Ribbon Round the Ole
        Oak Tree, (15-3), 1973
Tie Me Kangaroo Down, Sport, (13), 1963
Till, (7), 1957
Till I Waltz Again With You, (18-4), 1953
Till Reveille, (15), 1941
Till the End of Time, (20-7), 1945
Till There Was You, (8), 1958
Time After Time, (9), 1947
Time For Love, A, (4), 1966
Time For Us, A, (21-6), 1969
Time in a Bottle, (11-2), 1973-74
Time On My Hands, (18-4), 1930
Time Passages, (18-10), 1978-79
Times of Your Life, (10), 1975-76
Time, Time, (12), 1967
Time Waits For No One, (17), 1944
Time Was, (9), 1941
Tina Marie, (4), 1955
Tiny Bubbles, (4), 1967
Ti Pi Tin, (12-6), 1938
Tiptoe Through the Tulips, (14-3), 1930
Today's the Day, (7), 1976
To Each His Own, (19-8), 1946
Together, (16), 1944-45
Together, Wherever We Go, (13), 1959
To Know Him Is to Love Him, (12-1), 1958-59
To Mary, With Love, (1), 1936
Tom Dooley, (20-5), 1958-59
Tomorrow Is Another Day, (1), 1937
Tonight, (8), 1957
Tonight We Love, (15-4), 1941-42
Tonight You Belong to Me, (11), 1956
Too Fat Polka, (3), 1948
Too Late to Turn Back Now, (11), 1972
Toolie, Oolie, Doolie, (12), 1948
Too Marvelous For Words, (6), 1937
Too Much, (7), 1957
Too Much Heaven, (11), 1978-79

Too Much, Too Little, Too Late, (13-2), 1978
Too-ra-loo-ra-loo-ral, (1), 1945
Too Romantic, (7), 1940
Too Young, (25-12), 1951
Top Hat, White Tie and Tails, (5), 1935
Top of the World, (12-1), 1973-74
Topsy II, (8), 1958
Tormented, (1), 1936
Torn Between Two Lovers, (13-3), 1976-77
To Sir, With Love, (15-1), 1967-68
Tossin' and Turnin', (14-7), 1961
To the Door of the Sun, (8), 1975
Touch Me in the Morning, (14), 1973
Touch of Your Hand, The, (11), 1933-34
Touch of Your Lips, The, (7), 1936
To Wait For Love, (7), 1968
To You, (6), 1939
To You, Sweetheart, Aloha, (1), 1940
Traces, (14-4), 1969
Tracks of My Tears, (11), 1976
Trade Winds, (15-1), 1940
Tragedy, (5), 1959
Travelin' Man, (12-2), 1961
Tree in the Meadow, A, (21-10), 1948
Trolley Song, The, (15-5), 1944-45
Truckin', (1), 1935
True, (2), 1934
True Confession, (9), 1937-38
True Grit, (15), 1969
True Love, (22), 1956-57
Trust in Me, (10), 1937
Try a Little Kindness, (15), 1969-70
Try a Little Tenderness, (9), 1933
Trying, (5), 1952
Tryin' to Get the Feeling Again, (14-6), 1976
Try to Remember, (11), 1960
Tu-Li-Tulip-Time, (1), 1938
Turn Back the Hands of Time, (4), 1951
Turn! Turn! Turn!, (9), 1965-66
Turn Your Radio On, (2), 1971
Tweedle Dee, (16-1), 1955
Twenty-Four Hours a Day, (1), 1935
Twenty-Four Hours of Sunshine, (2), 1949
Twenty-Six Miles, (5), 1958
Twilight Time, (16-1), 1958
Twist, The, (11), 1961-62
Two Cigarettes in the Dark, (12-3), 1934
Two Dreams Met, (1), 1940
Two Hearts in Three Quarter Time, (7), 1930
Two Hearts That Pass in the Night, (5), 1941
Two in Love, (3), 1941
Two Sleepy People, (12), 1938-39
Tzena, Tzena, Tzena, (9), 1950

When I Grow Too Old to Dream, (16), 1935
When I'm With You, (10-2), 1936
When I Need You, (18-7), 1977
When It's Lamplighting Time in the Valley, (8), 1933
When I Wanted You, (15-1), 1980
When Mother Nature Sings Her Lullaby, (6), 1938
When My Dream Boat Comes Home, (17), 1936-37
When the Lights Go On Again, (17), 1942-43
When the Moon Comes Over the
    Mountain, (14-6), 1931
When the Poppies Bloom Again, (2), 1937
When the Swallows Come Back to
    Capistrano, (13), 1940
When They Ask About You, (15), 1944
When They Played the Polka, (1), 1938
When Will I Be Loved?, (9), 1975
When Will I See You Again?, (8), 1974-75
When You're Hot, You're Hot, (6), 1971
When You're in Love With a Beautiful
    Woman, (11), 1979
When Your Hair Has Turned to Silver, (12-3), 1930
When Your Lover Has Gone, (12-1), 1931
When You Say Love, (13), 1972
When You Wish Upon a Star, (13-5), 1940
When Yuba Plays the Rumba On the Tuba, (3), 1931
Where Am I?, (3), 1935
Where Are You?, (9), 1937
Where Did Our Love Go?, (12), 1964
Where Do I Begin?, (20-9), 1971
Where in the World?, (1), 1938
Where Is the Love?, (10-1), 1972
Where Love Has Gone, (10), 1964
Where Or When, (8), 1937
Where the Blue of the Night Meets the Gold
    of the Day, (9), 1931-32
Where the Boys Are, (21), 1961
Where Was I?, (10), 1940
Where Were You When I Was Falling
    in Love?, (13-3), 1979
While a Cigarette Was Burning, (9), 1938
While You're Away, (1), 1945
Whispers in the Dark, (12-4), 1937
Whistle While You Work, (12), 1938
White Christmas, (15-10), 1942-43
White Cliffs of Dover, The, (18-6), 1941-42
White Sails, (9), 1939
White Silver Sands, (4), 1957
White Sport Coat, A, (10), 1957
Who Blew Out the Flame?, (1), 1938
Who Cares?, (6), 1932
Whole Lotta Loving, (4), 1959
Whole World Is Singing My Song, The, (14), 1946-47
Who Loves You?, (5), 1936
Who Put the Bomp?, (10), 1961
Who's Afraid of the Big Bad Wolf?, (15-1), 1933
Whose Honey Are You?, (1), 1935
Who's in the Strawberry Patch With Sally?, (8), 1973-74
Who's Sorry Now?, (10), 1958
Who Will Answer?, (2), 1968
Who Wouldn't Love You?, (12), 1942
Why, (12-1), 1959-60
Why, Baby, Why?, (4), 1957
Why Do Fools Fall in Love?, (6), 1956
Why Don't You Believe Me?, (18-5), 1952-53
Why Don't You Fall in Love With Me?, (14), 1942-43
Why Not Me?, (12-2), 1980

Why Shouldn't I?, (1), 1935
Why Was I Born?, (4), 1930
Wichita Lineman, (15-7), 1968
Wildfire, (13-1), 1975
Wild Horses, (3), 1953
Willow Weep For Me, (10), 1932-33
Will You Love Me Tomorrow?, (11-2), 1960-61
Winchester Cathedral, (17-6), 1966-67
Windy, (16-4), 1967
Winter Wonderland, (13), 1934-35
Winter World of Love, (8), 1970
Wise Old Owl, The, (9-1), 1941
Wishing, (13-4), 1939
Wishing You Were Here, (8), 1974-75
Wish Me a Rainbow, (2), 1967
Wish That I Wish Tonight, The, (1), 1945
Wish You Were Here, (17-3), 1952
Witchcraft, (5), 1958
Witch Doctor, (10), 1958
With All My Heart, (6), 1936
With My Eyes Wide Open I'm Dreaming, (12-2), 1934
Without a Song, (8), 1930
Without a Word of Warning, (6), 1935
Without Love, (11-4), 1970
Without You, (14-5), 1972
With Pen in Hand, (10), 1968
With Plenty of Money and You, (11-1), 1937
With These Hands, (7), 1953
With the Wind and the Rain in Your Hair, (12), 1940
With You I'm Born Again, (12), 1980
Wives and Lovers, (15), 1963-64
Wolverton Mountain, (9), 1962
Woman in Love, A, (2), 1956
Woman's Way, A, (6), 1969-70
Woman, Woman, (6), 1968
Wonderful Baby, (9), 1975
Wonderful Guy, A, (8), 1949
Wonderful World, (17), 1960
Wonderland By Night, (16-3), 1960
Wonder of You, The, (13), 1970
Wonder When My Baby's Coming Home?, (2), 1942
Wonder Why, (3), 1951
Wooden Heart, (10), 1961
Woodpecker Song, The, (16-7), 1940
Woody Woodpecker, (12-2), 1948
World Is Waiting For the Sunrise, The, (8), 1951
World of Our Own, A, (4), 1965
World We Knew, The, (16-2), 1967
World Without Love, A, (20-1), 1964
Would I Love You?, (13), 1951
Would There Be Love?, (1), 1935
Would You?, (10), 1936
Would You Like to Take a Walk?, (15), 1930-31
Wrap Your Troubles in Dreams, (7), 1931

X

Xanadu, (16-2), 1980

Y

Ya Got Me, (1), 1938
Yakety Yak, (10-1), 1958
Year of the Cat, (8), 1977
Yellow Bird, (13), 1961
Yellow Days, (14-2), 1967
Yellow Rose of Texas, The, (16-9), 1955
Yes, I'm Ready (10-2), 1980
Yes Indeed!, (1), 1941
Yesterday, (14-5), 1965
Yesterday Once More, (15-4), 1973
Yesterdays, (13), 1933-34
Yesterday When I Was Young, (12), 1969
You, (8-1), 1936
You and I, (19-5), 1941
You and I Know, (1), 1937
You and Me, (6), 1977
You and Me Against the World, (13-2), 1974
You and Me That Used to Be, The, (6), 1937
You and the Night and the Music, (7), 1935
You and Your Beautiful Eyes, (1), 1951
You Are My Lucky Star, (8-3), 1935
You Are the Sunshine of My Life, (11-2), 1973
You Belong to Me, (22-9), 1952-53
You Belong to My Heart, (7), 1945
You Brought a New Kind of Love to Me, (13), 1930
You Call Everybody Darling, (18-1), 1948
You Call It Madness, (7), 1931
You Can't Be True, Dear, (18-3), 1948
You Can't Pull the Wool Over My Eyes, (10), 1936
You Can't See the Sun When You're Crying, (3), 1947
You Can't Stop Me From Dreaming, (12-1), 1937-38
You Couldn't Be Cuter, (2), 1938
You'd Be So Nice to Come Home To, (18), 1943
You Decorated My Life, (12), 1979
You Do, (14-1), 1947-48
You Don't Bring Me Flowers, (9), 1978-79
You Don't Have to Be a Star, (13), 1976
You Don't Have to Say You Love Me, (14), 1966
You Do Something to Me, (8), 1930

You Gave Me a Mountain, (13-2), 1969
You Go to My Head, (7), 1938
You Hit the Spot, (5), 1936
You Keep Coming Back Like a Song, (14), 1946-47
You Leave Me Breathless, (7), 1938
You Light Up My Life, (17-2), 1977
You'll Always Be the One I Love, (1), 1947
You'll Know, (1), 1951
You'll Never Find Another Love Like Mine, (18-5), 1976
You'll Never Know, (25-9), 1943
You Make Me Feel Brand New, (10), 1974
You Make Me Feel Like Dancing, (3), 1977
You Must Have Been a Beautiful Baby, (9-3), 1938-39
You Needed Me, (23), 1978
Young at Heart, (23-2), 1954
Younger Than Springtime, (1), 1949
Young Love, (17-5), 1957
You Only Live Twice, (9), 1967
You Oughta Be in Pictures, (8), 1934
Your Cheatin' Heart, (13), 1953
You're a Builder-Upper, (6), 1934
You're a Heavenly Thing, (1), 1935
You're All I Need, (9-1), 1935
You're an Education, (8), 1938
You're an Old Smoothie, (11), 1932-33
You're a Part of Me, (6), 1978
You're a Sweetheart, (11-2), 1938
You're a Sweet Little Headache, (3), 1939
You're Breaking My Heart, (20-6), 1949
You're Driving Me Crazy, (9), 1930-31
You're Getting to Be a Habit With Me, (11), 1933
You're Gonna Hear From Me, (10), 1966
You're Just in Love, (16), 1951
You're Laughing At Me, (1), 1937
You're Lonely and I'm Lonely, (2), 1940
You're My Everything, (15), 1931-32
You're My World, (18), 1977
You're Not the Kind, (1), 1936
You're Only Lonely, (16-5), 1979-80
You're Sixteen, (6), 1960-61
    Revival: (8), 1974
You're So Darn Charming, (1), 1935
You're So Vain, (9-1), 1973
You're the Best Thing That Ever
    Happened to Me, (6), 1974
You're the Love, (12), 1978
You're the Only Woman, (9), 1980
You're the Top, (8), 1934-35
You Rhyme With Everything That's
    Beautiful, (2), 1943
Yours, (17), 1941
Yours and Mine, (2), 1937
Your Smiling Face, (7), 1977
Yours Truly Is Truly Yours, (1), 1936
You Send Me, (10), 1957
You Started Me Dreaming, (7), 1936
You Think of Everything, (1), 1940
You Took the Words Right Out of My Heart, (2), 1938
You Try Somebody Else, (11), 1931
You Turned My World Around, (5), 1974
You Turned the Tables On Me, (6), 1936
You've Lost That Lovin' Feelin', (16-2), 1965
You Walk By, (16), 1941
You Was, (1), 1949
You Were Only Fooling, (13), 1948-49
You Won't Be Satisfied, (10), 1946

You Won't See Me, (10-2), 1974
You, You Darlin', (1), 1940
You, You, You, (27-4), 1953-54

Z

Zing a Little Zong, (2), 1952
Zing, Zing, Zoom, Zoom, (6), 1951
Zip-A-Dee-Doo-Dah, (18), 1946-47